KOSOVO
IN THE HEART OF THE POWDER KEG

Compiled and Edited
BY ROBERT ELSIE

EAST EUROPEAN MONOGRAPHS, BOULDER
DISTRIBUTED BY COLUMBIA UNIVERSITY PRESS, NEW YORK

1997

EAST EUROPEAN MONOGRAPHS, NO. CDLXXVIII

Copyright © 1997 by Robert Elsie
ISBN 0–88033–375–8
Library of Congress Catalog Card Number 97–60361

Printed in the United States of America

"There is a joy that never palls - the first glimpse into the unknown land. On the other side of the pass, a magnificent valley lay below us, thickly wooded with beech, and beyond were the lands which two rival races each claim as their birthright - one of the least-known corners of Europe."

Edith Durham 'High Albania' (1909)

TABLE OF CONTENTS

Introduction

The breakup of Yugoslavia and the ensuing Balkan conflict have their roots in the heart of the Balkans, in Kosovo. Yet the question of Kosovo, where East meets West, where Europe meets the Third World, where the east-west axis of Islam meets the north-south axis of Eastern Orthodoxy, and where Slav meets non-Slav, remains largely ignored or at least misunderstood by the international community. The present book endeavours to rectify this situation, however modestly, by providing the Western reader with a multifarious introduction to Kosovo, its people and its fate. It is only when the Kosovo issue has been solved, not without painful compromise from all sides, that the Balkan conflagration can be contained and brought to an end.

Originally conceived of as a political and historical essay, this work soon took on the form of a reader, a collection of texts by various authors from various periods, in order to approach Kosovo and attending problems from a variety of perspectives - historical, political, literary and documentary.

The reader begins in section 1 with *Political and literary perspectives* on the region. *Kosovo, the Gordian knot of the Balkans* is a lucid and penetrating study by Christine von Kohl and Wolfgang Libal of the International Helsinki Federation. It provides an excellent historical and cultural introduction to Kosovo, including an in-depth review of the major political developments of the last two decades which have led to the present stalemate.

Also of exceptional interest for an understanding of Kosovo is *The wedding procession turned to ice* by Albanian writer Ismail Kadare, a short novel which evokes the explosive events of the Albanian uprising in Kosovo in March and April 1981, as experienced by a surgeon at a Prishtina clinic. Though a work of fiction, it conveys the political realities of Kosovo in the eighties as well as any work of non-fiction could.

Section 2, *Approaches to the present dilemma*, comprises a number of political writings and analyses of the current situation: *The right to self-determination* by Kosovo scholar Rexhep Ismajli; *The Albanian question and its solution*, an extract from the latest monograph on the issue by the eminent Rexhep Qosja; *The question of Kosovo*, an essay again by Ismail Kadare; and a recent report on the appalling human rights situation in Kosovo by Amnesty International.

Section 3, *Historical documents and observations*, provides background material from 1908 to 1944 which offers much insight into the historical development of the Kosovo conflict and will, I trust, facilitate an understanding of the gravity of the present situation. It begins with a rare and delightful description of a forbidden journey through the mountains of Albania into Kosovo, *In the debatable lands*, by Edith Durham (1863-1944), that remarkable English traveller and perspicacious expert on the Albanians, Serbs and Montenegrins. Miss Durham, as she is still known in Balkans, travelled widely in the most dangerous and isolated reaches of the peninsula in the early years of the twentieth century, in particular in the northern Albanian mountains. Her love of the wild Albanian tribes and her efforts on their behalf bestowed upon her the title of *kraljica e maltsorëvet*, queen of the mountain people. *Albania's Golgotha* by Leo Freundlich is a compilation of news reports which seeped out of Kosovo around the time of the first Balkan War. The Memorandum addressed to the League of Nations in 1930 by three Catholic priests shows that the situation in Kosovo had not much improved a generation later. The ideology of ethnic cleansing is documented in the following texts, including works by noted Serbian intellectuals such as academician Vasa Čubrilović and Nobel Prize winner Ivo Andrić.

Section 4, *Conversations with contemporaries*, endeavours to address the issues on a more personal level. It involves a series of interviews and conversations with leading figures of Albanian public life who give their views on the origins of the crisis, their personal experience in the eye of the storm, and what possibilities they feel can be found to contain it.

Appendixed to this reader is an extensive bibliography on Kosovo which, by bringing together publications representating all political views and persuasions, endeavours to be comprehensive. It should be pointed out that the bibliography includes a good number of monographs of subtle racism and others of open hatred and propaganda which have, alas, laid the intellectual and spiritual foundations for the crimes of our age. While the present author wishes to distance himself categorically from such works, he believes it is up to each individual to read and judge for him or herself.

A remark must be made at this juncture on the use of Balkan place names. The texts presented in this reader were taken or translated from a variety of sources and periods, and offered a variety of designations for the same place names. Some authors use the Serbian-language terms for towns in Kosovo, names which are still often found in English-language atlases and guidebooks. Other authors use the Albanian-language terms which will be less familiar to the Western reader. For the sake of standardization and of neutrality, I have endeavoured here, where no clear-cut English term was available, to give both the Albanian and the Serbo-Croatian forms, i.e. *Gjakova / Djakovica*. I am well aware that this is cumbersome and that there are inconsistencies, but I hope that readers will be patient. It is a rather thorny issue. No particular political interpretation should be made of the use of individual place names in this work.

For the term *Kosovo*, Albanian authors now prefer to use the Albanian form *Kosova* in their works, even in English and other foreign languages, e.g. *Republic of Kosova*. English usage of eastern European toponyms is in flux at the moment. Now that Byelorussia has become Belarus, and Moldavia has become Moldova, there is no particular reason why the traditional term Kosovo should not be replaced by Kosova. I have nonetheless preferred to stick to the commoner form Kosovo for the moment, simply because it still constitutes standard usage in the English-language media.

Albanian-language place names themselves can be written with or without the postpostive definite article, for example in the feminine form: Prishtina vs. Prishtinë, Tirana vs. Tiranë, Kosova vs. Kosovë; and in the masculine form: Prizreni vs. Prizren, Shkodra vs. Shkodër, Shkupi vs. Shkup (Skopje). There has been an increasing tendency in foreign-language works on Albania in recent years to use the feminine place names with the definite article, i.e. Tirana, and the masculine place names without the definite article, i.e. Prizren, a policy which I have adopted for this work.

In conclusion, I would like to stress that this book is not conceived or intended as an indictment of the Serbian people as a whole. At the most, it is an attempt to elucidate some of the factors which have allowed many of them to be manipulated so tragically in recent years.

If freedom and democracy, human rights and equal opportunity can be introduced and maintained, I have faith that peaceful co-existence will once again prevail between the Albanians and Serbs in Kosovo. At the moment, one can only hope.

Robert Elsie
Eifel mountains, Germany
Autumn 1995

1. Political and literary perspectives

Kosovo
The Gordian knot of the Balkans

Christine von Kohl & Wolfgang Libal

Preface

Kosovo is a region in the south of Serbia no larger than the US state of Connecticut. The population is presently more than 80% Albanian, making it a major area of compact non-Slavic settlement within the former state of the southern Slavs. With the fall of Yugoslavia and the new political situation which has arisen there, this province has taken on a significance far exceeding that which it possessed as part of the former Yugoslav federation.

If Serbia, irrespective of whatever legal form it takes on as a state, insists on continuing its occupation of Kosovo and its use of police state tactics there, the present Yugoslav crisis will soon take on the perilous proportions of a Balkan crisis. To put it in other terms: following the separation of Slovenia, Croatia, Bosnia-Hercegovina and Macedonia, rump

Yugoslavia will only survive in the long run if some sort of settlement can be reached between the Serbs and the Albanians.

Kosovo is an extremely critical area in the Balkans. Whatever happens here will, as a matter of course, affect Albania, the 'motherland' of the Kosovo Albanians, as well as Macedonia, with its substantial Albanian minority. Greece and Bulgaria will not remain untouched either.

This books deals with the past and present of Kosovo, its emotional significance for the Serbs and the Albanians, and the relations between these two peoples over the centuries, as well as with prospects for peace in this region of the Balkans.

The Serbs and Albanians, left to their own devices, do not seem able to unravel the Gordian knot of Kosovo. If the catastrophe is to be averted, the nations of Europe and the international community will have to assume at least some responsibility for a new order in this part of former Yugoslavia.

Vienna, Austria
May 1992

The land and its people

Before delving into the history of this part of former Yugoslavia, its significance for Serbs and Albanians, and the complex relations between these two peoples, we shall begin with some facts about the land and its people.

Kosovo covers an area of about 11,000 square km. In 1981, it had a population of almost 1,600,000. It is difficult to tell how many inhabitants Kosovo has today since the Albanian population boycotted the 1991 census. The Yugoslav Bureau of Statistics made a rough estimate in March 1991 of 1,800,000 inhabitants, of whom 1,680,000, or 82.2% of the total population, were Albanian. The 1981 census had indicated a total population in Kosovo of 1,588,000, of whom 1,226,736, or 77.4%, were Albanians.

Different terms are used to refer to Kosovo. The Albanians call the region *Kosova*. Until 1968 the autonomous province was officially designated as *Kosovo-Metohija*. The Albanians then requested that the name of the province be changed simply to *Kosovo* as they did not see any particular historical justification for the term *Metohija*.

The Serbs refer to the fertile land between Peja / Peć and Prizren in the west of the province, on the border to Albania, as *Metohija*, which derives its name from the Greek term *metoh*, meaning church lands. Most of the churches and monasteries in this part of the province were founded by the kings of Serbia in the thirteenth and fourteenth centuries.

Now that the autonomy of the province has been radically curtailed under the present Serbian constitution of 1989, it has once again been named *Kosovo-Metohija*. The Albanians refuse to recognize this name, just as they refuse to recognize the designation *Old Serbia*, which is often encountered in writings on Serbian history.

There are also various terms for the Albanian population of Kosovo. In conversation, the Serbs often refer to the Albanians as *Shiptars*, which has a slightly derogatory tone to it, although it comes from the Albanian word *Shqiptar*. This term was originally used in Kosovo only to refer to the mountain clans of northern Albania. The Turks called the Albanians *Arnauts*, a term to be found in earlier Western literature. The Serbs in the past also used the term *Arbanasi*.

Topographically speaking, Kosovo is a basin ringed on almost all sides by mountains. To the south and west, the mountain ranges reach a height of 2,600 meters. In the Kosovo basin itself are fertile valleys, some of which, like *Kosovo Polje* near Prishtina, extend to form wide plains.

There is relatively little land for agriculture in relation to the number of inhabitants. With 147 people per square kilometer, Kosovo is particularly densely populated. The Yugoslav average is only 88. Farms are accordingly small and property values are much higher than in other parts of Yugoslavia. Families in Kosovo are large - an average of 6.9 people to a family unit. The male head of the family is the one who makes the decisions. The women play secondary roles. In the countryside, it is still the fathers who decide whom their children will marry. Women have recently had access to higher education in Kosovo and there are now some socially and politically active women's groups. A women's magazine in Prishtina provides information, commentaries and discussion on current affairs and problems of the day.

About 70% of the population is Moslem, 20% (mostly the Serbs and Montenegrins) is Orthodox, and 10% (mainly Albanians) is Catholic. Traditionally, there has been a good deal of tolerance among the religious communities and even co-operation in times of crisis. Important religious festivities have always been attended by members of other faiths. Up to the eighties, the town of Gjakova / Djakovica was the centre of the Bektash, an important Islamic sect which is rejected by fundamentalist Moslems.

Religion did not play a very important role in the lives of Kosovo Albanians until recently. History offers us many examples of leading Albanian figures who changed their religion for military or political advantage. Opposition to communist atheism has however strengthened ties to religion somewhat.

The Albanian language uses the Latin alphabet and is a member of the Indo-European family, within which, like Greek and Armenian, it forms a group of its own. The theory of the Illyrian origin of the Albanian language remains controversial at the international level. At the Orthography Congress held in Tirana in 1972, an attempt was made to unite the two main dialects, Gheg and Tosk, into a literary standard. Up to the end of the sixties, the Kosovo Albanians had used a northeastern Gheg dialect, but they decided to accede to the 1972 agreement.

Tourists in Kosovo will appreciate the monasteries dating from the golden age of the mediaeval Serbian Empire, which had its political and religious foundations here. Travellers interested in Byzantine frescos and icons and in church architecture bearing eastern and western influences will find much to delight their eyes, as will those interested in the religious and secular architecture of the Ottoman Empire. In Prishtina, Prizren and Peja / Peć, one finds fifteenth and sixteenth century mosques and bathhouses that are among the most beautiful in all of southern Yugoslavia. Of particular fascination is the Imperial Mosque of Prishtina which was built by Mehmet II the Conqueror in 1461, a mere eight years after he conquered Constantinople, putting an end to the thousand-year-old Byzantine Empire, and changed the name of the metropolis on the Bosphorus to Istanbul, making it the capital of his own empire. Of interest in Prizren are the Mosque of Sinan Pasha and the Bathhouse of Gazi Mehmet Pasha. In some towns, including Peja / Peć, one can still see *kullas*, formidable stone towers inhabited by wealthier Albanian families. Only the upper floors have windows. The ground floors of these defensive structures have narrow embrasures for shooting.

Visitors interested in history will not fail to visit *Gazimestan*, the site of the famed Battle of Kosovo Polje. In May, the rolling landscape is covered in *bozhur*, the red poppies of Kosovo, which according to Serbian tradition sprout in soil drenched with the blood of Serbian warriors. If a west wind should prevail, a visit to the battle site can be less appealing, however. On such occasions, heavy clouds of smoke waft over the hills from the nearby power station of the industrial complex. The open pit mine for the extraction of the substantial lignite reserves in the region is surrounded by a complex of seven power stations as well as by factories for the production of nitrates and chemical fertilizers, which are less than environmentally sound.

Kosovo is rich in natural resources. The one-time gold and silver mines of Novobërda / Novo Brdo in the mountains southeast of Prishtina, which is estimated itself to have had a population of 40,000 in the Middle Ages, have now been abandoned, but silver, lead, nickel, zinc and magnesite are still being mined in the Mitrovica area. The Trepça / Trepča mining complex, once owned by an English company, is one of the largest producers of refined lead on earth.

The moment one enters Kosovo from Serbia, one is struck by the differences between Serbian and Albanian houses. The one-storey whitewashed homes of the Serbs with their fenced gardens and orchards are scattered throughout the countryside. The homes of the Albanians, with their barns and stables, are surrounded by high unplastered walls protecting them from the sight of potential enemies and of envious neighbours. In the old days, when bloodfeuding was common, such walls actually did offer protection for those whose lives were in danger.

The smaller towns, such as Peja / Peć, Prizren, Gjakova / Djakovica, Ferizaj / Uroševac and Podujeva / Podujevo, have historical centres with one-storey houses whose slanting tiled roofs look as if they might collapse at any moment. The main streets are lined with stores, workshops, cafés and eating-houses offering dishes of meat grilled on charcoal fires. There are also countless jewellery shops, many of which sell intricate filigree work in silver. Many goods are sold out on the street, notably colourfully ornamented harnesses for horses and donkeys and richly embroidered tableclothes. In Prizren, you can still see the Hasi women from the mountains in their colourful costumes, complete with wooden crinolines at the hips. The white, red and black headpieces worn by the men indicate their religion and nationality.

The people are mostly small in build and look as though they had been working hard all their lives. Their faces are gaunt and haggard, and many have blue eyes. Some stare inquisitively, others risk a hesitant glance while still others look cold and haughty.

The inhabitants of Kosovo live at close quarters with one another, not only in the cramped accommodations of the poor, but also in the wealthier homes to be found in the cities. Not only do they have many children, but several generations live together under the same roof, a colourful conglomeration of brothers and sisters, cousins, uncles and in-laws. When entering a house, it is customary to take off one's shoes and place them in the row at the door.

Kosovo is still very much the Orient, much more so than many areas of the Middle East.

The Battle of Kosovo Polje
History, myth and political significance

On 28 June 1989, Kosovo Polje, the plain of the blackbirds north of Prishtina, was filled with people. A million, perhaps even two million people assembled at the foot of the square stone tower marking the site of the battle that was fought there six hundred years earlier. It was a Serbian demonstration in the heart of the autonomous province of Kosovo, now believed to be inhabited by almost 90% Albanians.

They came from all parts of Serbia in chartered buses and trains. Many came by car, while others living in the north or abroad flew in by plane. The young people wore jeans and corduroys; elderly villagers arrived in their traditional costumes, the men with *opanki* sandals on their feet and the traditional three-cornered *čajkača* on their heads. In the midst of the multitude stood German, the aged Patriarch of the Serbian Orthodox Church, in his splendid robes, accompanied by an impressive retinue of bearded metropolitans and bishops.

The celebrations marking this St Vitus Day, *Vidov dan* in Serbian, were orchestrated with superlative precision to render them a powerful display of Serbian nationalism. This was a historical commemoration, but one with an explosive political dimension.

The main speaker at the event was the Serbian leader, President Slobodan Milošević. After a brief reference to the past, he turned his attention to the present, calling the lost battle 600 years earlier a consequence of disunity and treachery among the Serbs, and adding that "today, six hundred years later, we are fighting once again. New battles lie before us. They are not military battles, although we cannot exclude such a possibility."

His message was soon to become bloody reality, not in Kosovo, but first of all in Slovenia and Croatia, and then in Bosnia-Hercegovina.

The rally at the battle site was significant for Milošević and the Serbs for another reason. Over the months leading up to the demonstration, the Serbian government had systematically curtailed the political rights of the autonomous province and had put down Albanian resistance with open police brutality. The official toll at the Albanian demonstrations of March and April 1989 was twenty-four dead and hundreds of injuries and arrests.

These demonstrations occurred after the provincial parliament in Prishtina had been coerced, under enormous pressure from Belgrade, into passing an amendment to the constitution abolishing the autonomy of the province. In a festive session, the Serbian Parliament in Belgrade proclaimed triumphantly that "Serbia has recovered its state and constitutional sovereignty," at the same time as people were being killed in political demonstrations in Kosovo.

The celebrations on the historical battlefield on 28 June were thus seen as a triumph of the Serbs in their fight to recover the full state sovereignty which, so they believed, they had been deprived of in Tito's Yugoslavia. The euphoria of the masses was echoed in the refrain of the

Song of the Serbian Trumpeter, "Blow stronger, blow louder, oh brother and hero, for the Plain of the Blackbirds is Serbian once more." Both the melody and the words come from the Balkan Wars of 1912 and 1913 when the Serbs drove the Turks out of southern Serbia and Macedonia and seized control of the historic battlefield after more than five hundred years of Turkish rule. In 1989, the song regained popularity as part of the new political battle waged by the Serbs.

In order to compehend the historical and political significance of the Battle of Kosovo Polje for the Serbs and for their identity, it is imperative to understand history.

On the fateful day of 28 June 1389, a mere thirty-four years after the Turks had crossed the Dardanelles and begun their conquest of Europe, Serbian Prince Lazar and Sultan Murad I stood face to face on the battlefield in the heart of the Balkans. The mediaeval Serbian state was already on the decline, but Lazar managed to assemble an impressive army, as did Murad, who had recently won a decisive victory in Bulgaria. The figure of 100,000 warriors on each side is probably exaggerated. Modern historians believe that each army disposed of about 30,000 fighters, a considerable force at the time.

Little is known about the battle itself. Christian and Turkish sources are of a later date and generally unreliable. It is not even known whether Sultan Murad was stabbed to death by a false turncoat, the Serbian knight Miloš Obilić, the day before the battle or at the start of fighting. The Turkish reaction was swift at any rate. They proclaimed Murad's eldest son Bayazid as sultan and slew the second son Yakub in order to ensure that there would be no rivalry among the army commanders in such a critical situation. One Turkish source spoke of Yakub having been 'put at Allah's disposal'.

The Christian army was defeated and Prince Lazar was taken alive by the Turks. Bayazid then had him decapitated on the battlefield in revenge for the murder of his father.

The mediaeval Serbian Empire collapsed and the road to the north and to the west lay open to the Turks. The latter did not continue their advance further into the Balkans because their empire in Anatolia was being threatened by the Mongol warrior Tamerlane. Instead, Bayazid contented himself with creating a number of Serbian vassal states.

Europe's reaction to the events in the middle of the Balkans was decidedly strange. The courts of the West believed initially that the Christian army had been victorious. In August 1389, Bosnian King Tvrtko reported to Florence that his forces had beaten the Turks. The Venetian Signoria, whose agents were usually well informed, knew only that a battle between Serbs and Turks had taken place and that Murad had been killed, but did not know who had won or who the new sultan was. To be on the safe side, at the end of July it gave its ambassador to Adrianopolis two letters, one addressed to Bayazid and the other addressed to Yakub. It is therefore no wonder that Western Europe was long unaware of the significance and repercussions of the Battle of Kosovo Polje.

No less surprising was the reaction of the Serbs to the defeat they had suffered at the hands of the Turks. It was not the historical events of the battle and the political consequences of their defeat that caught their imagination, but rather the myths and legends that were woven around the battle in the following decades. The Serbs became obsessed with the parade of Serbian heroes out of the 'white citadel' of Kruševac, with the two black ravens who bore the ill tidings of the battle to the queen, with the 'maid of Kosovo' who tended to the heroes wounded on the battlefield, giving them 'cool water and red-golden wine', with the two-meter-high candle at the Monastery of Dechani which Queen Militsa had ordered, specifying that it be lit only when Kosovo was avenged, and with Kraljević Marko, the king's son, the doer of heroic deeds. Marko did actually exist as a historical figure, but he was really only a minor vassal to the Turks in Prilep in Macedonia and died in 1394 in a battle in southern Walachia while fighting for the Turkish side.

Although these myths and legends have little to do with the historical realities, they were of supreme significance for the Serbs. The radiance and splendour they conferred upon the past enabled them as a nation to survive the dark centuries of foreign rule and created the emotional foundations for the freedom they would one day achieve.

Kosovo, the heartland of the Serbs

The significance of Kosovo in the national conscience of the Serbs does not rest exclusively on the Battle of Kosovo Polje and the myths attached to it. This fertile land in the south of Serbia was the heartland of the feudal Serbian state in the Middle Ages, which arose out of the principality of Rascia (Raška), comprising territory around the modern city of Novi Pazar.

Kosovo, with its capital Prishtina, was the northern frontier of the Byzantine Empire at the time. In the twelfth and thirteenth centuries, it gradually came under the control of the Serbian Nemania dynasty which had its power base here. Kosovo was thus to become the heart of the Serbian Empire which, at its zenith under Emperor Stephan Dushan (1331-1355), stretched from the Danube to the Aegean and Ionian Seas.

Kosovo was also the breadbasket and economic heart of the Serbian Empire in the Middle Ages. It produced fine wines and silken textiles. Wool from Peja / Peć was famous, known to merchants from Dubrovnik (Ragusa) as *fina lana de Albania*. The Trepcha mines north of Prishtina produced silver, lead and iron ore. The mines at Novobërda / Novo Brdo south of the capital yielded not only silver but also precious gold.

From the early thirteenth century on, Kosovo was also the religious centre of Serbia. The Patriarch of the autocephalic Serbian Orthodox Church has his headquarters in Peja / Peć, where the three grand patriarchal churches of the period can still be seen today. Peja / Peć remained the centre of the religious and ecclesiastical administration of the Serbian Orthodox Church long after the great Serbian Empire had collapsed and, like the rest of the Balkans right up to Hungary, fallen under the sway of the Ottoman crescent. In 1557, when the Sublime Porte deemed it politically appropriate to reestablish the Patriarchate, abolished after the fall of the Serbian state, the authority of the latter over Orthodox Christians reached from northern Macedonia to Eger, northeast of Budapest.

The magnificent monasteries of the region are proof of the important role played by the Serbian Orthodox Church in Kosovo, not only in the Middle Ages, but also later under Turkish rule. Most of them were donated by the kings of Serbia. Their exquisite architecture and rich sculptures, mosaics, frescos and icons reflect Kosovo's position at the crossroads of many cultures. Artistic influences from Greek Orthodox Byzantium entwine with elements from Roman Catholic Dalmatia and Italy. Every cultured Serb takes pride in the monasteries of Dechani (Dečani) and Grachanitsa (Gračanica) and in the churches such as the resplendant Bogoroditsa Ljevishka (Bogorodica Ljeviška) in Prizren, not to mention Peja / Peć itself.

Whenever Serbs look upon Kosovo as their 'Holy Land', they do so for the three above-mentioned reasons: the fatal Battle of Kosovo Polje, the memory of the heartland of their mediaeval empire, and the pride they take in their cultural heritage here. There is no room in this reverie for the Albanians who now make up about ninety percent of the roughly two million inhabitants of Kosovo. Accordingly, Slobodan Milošević did not even mention them in his speech of 28 June 1989.

Natives or immigrants?

The debate on the origins of the Albanian population in Kosovo has consumed tonnes of paper on both the Serbian and the Albanian sides. Usually, the aim of the debate has been to provide scientific evidence to support political theses. To put it briefly, the question is whether the Albanians, as descendants of the Illyrians and thus ancient inhabitants of the Balkans, were present in Kosovo in the sixth and seventh centuries when Slavic tribes conquered and settled the land, or whether the Albanian tribes descended onto the plains of Kosovo and settled them after the Turkish conquest and after the departure of most of the Serbs at the end of the seventeenth century.

Even though the Albanians, as an historical element in Kosovo, were not prominent during the mediaeval Serbian Empire, they were nonetheless present. They were living as simple shepherds and stockbreeders in their *katundi*, settlements up in the mountains, or working as manual labourers in the mines. This is how they are referred to in Serbian and, later, Turkish chronicles and in documents from Dubrovnik. In the fifteenth and sixteenth centuries there then seems to have been a mass migration of these mountainous Albanian tribes down into the villages on the plains.

Without delving into details of this Serbian-Albanian controversy, let us content ourselves with what the Serbian historian Sima M. Ćirković noted in his book 'Kosovo and Metohija in Serbian History': "Careful and unbiased research proves that the thesis previously held among historians that there were no Albanians on the territory of what is presently Kosovo can no longer be upheld. Nor can one accept the assertion made by some Albanian historians and publishers that Kosovo has been inhabited by Albanians without interruption since ancient times. Modern Kosovo was far from regions where Albanians seem to have settled in the early Middle Ages" (a rectangular-shaped area from Shkodër and Durrës, to Prizren and Ohrid, corresponding broadly to modern-day northern and central Albania).

The great migrations

It can be safely assumed that, despite the constant trickle of Albanians down onto the fertile plains of Kosovo, there was no substantial change in the basically Christian structure of the population of the region up to the end of the seventeenth century. This is confirmed in a report by a Catholic missionary from the year 1683 that "the Agha of Gjakova / Djakovica knew how to keep the wild Albanians under control who were coming down to the fair plains of Metohija."

We have noted in passing that the Albanians prefer the term 'Kosovo' or 'Kosova' used by the Turkish administration at the time. The area of the Balkans inhabited by the Albanians was, at that time, divided into four *vilayets* or government districts: Janina (Ioannina, now in northern Greece), Monastir (Bitola, now in the former Yugoslav Republic of Macedonia), Prishtina and Shkodër (Scutari). Metohija, as previously mentioned, refers to the fertile lands along the Albanian border between Peja / Peć and Prizren. From the thirteenth century on, the kings of Serbia donated most of the land there to the church for monasteries. For such reasons, Metohija is a land very dear to the hearts of the Serbs.

Towards the end of the seventeenth and in the eighteenth centuries, there occurred an event in the Balkans which decisively altered the ethnic and religious structure of the population in Kosovo to the disadvantage of the Serbs.

In 1683, the Turks were defeated at the gates of Vienna. In 1686, Austrian troops took Budapest and in 1689 they recaptured Belgrade. The European part of the Ottoman Empire seemed to be disintegrating. A small portion of the Habsburg army under the command of General Eneas Silvio Piccolomini advanced down to Skopje and laid waste to the city. Emperor Leopold I called upon the Christian population of the Balkans to rise in revolt and throw off the Turkish yoke. Reaction to this appeal was particularly strong in Kosovo, most of all among the Orthodox Serbs, but also among the Catholic Albanians. The dawn of freedom appeared to be at hand.

But fortune was not to smile upon the Austrian Empire or upon the *rayah*, as the Turks called the Christian population, regardless of ethnic background. Piccolomini died in Prizren of the plague and his successor, the Duke of Holstein, found himself faced with a dilemma. The Habsburg Empire was now being threatened on its western border on the Rhine by Louis XIV, the Sun King, and Emperor Leopold I was accordingly forced to withdraw his troops from the Balkans and even to abandon Belgrade. The Serbs and Albanians who, placing their faith in the Emperor in Vienna, had risen in revolt against their oppressors, were now helpless to protect themselves against the retaliation of the Turks who had in the meantime consolidated their military and political position under a new leadership in Istanbul.

What followed in Kosovo has become the object of a controversy between Serbian and Albanian historians. There is consensus only on the fact that Albanian tribes also took part in the revolt against the Turks. The Serbs for their part accuse the Albanians of having changed sides at the decisive moment and thus betraying the Christian cause. The Albanians retort in their own defence that the Duke of Holstein never confirmed the agreements reached with the rebels and that it was the Emperor in Vienna who withdrew his troops, leaving the Albanian tribes to the mercy of the Turkish soldiers and their Tatar auxiliaries. The Turks had, in addition, taken hostages among several Albanian tribes in order to ensure the submission of the latter.

The matter is of little consequence for us today. Much more decisive for Kosovo was the ensuing emigration in 1690 of a good part of the Serbian population under the leadership of Partriarch Arsenije III Crnojević. The Patriarch, whom the Turks had not succeeded in capturing in Peja / Peć, fled northwards, accompanied by a small group of faithful monks. He was joined en route by thousands of Serbian families, fearful of Turkish reprisals. This mass migration was furthered even more by promises made to the Orthodox Serbs by Emperor Leopold to give them land regained from the Turks north of the Sava and Danube, to respect their religious freedom and to guarantee them a certain degree of political autonomy.

It has never been ascertained how many Serbs abandoned their homes in southern and central Serbia and took refuge in the areas then occupied by the Habsburg monarchy. The numbers vary from 30,000 to 100,000, according to whether individuals or families are counted. These emigrants found refuge not only in the present-day Vojvodina but also further north as far as Budapest.

But not all the Serbs left Kosovo. After three months of plundering, murder and enslavement, the Sublime Porte came to the conclusion that Kosovo would become a wasteland if its troops continued their campaign of repression. An amnesty was thus decreed by which the Serbs were guaranteed impunity as well as the restoration of and respect for their property if they returned to their villages, which in some areas they did. What Ćirković notes in the aforementioned book 'Kosovo and Metohija in Serbian History' is nonetheless true: "The great migration of the Serbs in

1690 constitutes one of the gravest and most decisive events in Serbian history."

The migration of the Serbs at the end of the seventeenth century resulted in a gradual shift of the Serbian political power base northwards, to the region of the Šumadija forests south of Belgrade. Of prime significance for the cultural rebirth of Serbia was the present-day Vojvodina, which remained part of the Habsburg Empire until 1918. It was in the Šumadija forests that the movement for Serbian independence from the Ottoman Empire took its course and it was the Vojvodina which fostered the intellectual rebirth of the Serbian nation.

Another wave of Serbian emigration from Kosovo, the Morava Valley and the region around Nish took place later as a result of the war that Russia and the Austrian Emperor waged against the Turks in 1735-1739. As his predecessor Leopold I had done, Charles VI called upon the Christian population south of the Danube to rise in arms against Turkish rule. And as twenty years earlier, the revolt was put down because Austria and Russia lost the war and the Turks retook northern Serbia including Belgrade, which had been an Austrian province for twenty years.

It is not known how many Serbs abandoned their land during this second migration under Partriarch Arsenije IV Jovanović and found refuge in the Habsburg Empire. Their numbers were not as large as in the first exodus. Smaller groups continued to migrate northwards in the nineteenth century.

Such population movements had a long-term effect on Kosovo. The ethnic composition of the population changed because Albanians settled in the abandoned villages on the plains and, for the first time, in the towns. Most of these settlers were Catholics to start with, but by the end of the seventeenth century, the population had converted increasingly to Islam. Not only the Albanians converted, but also Serbian families who had stayed behind or returned to Kosovo. The religious composition of the population changed accordingly. Both peoples wanted to secure property rights and to be exempted of the taxes imposed upon the Christians. The large-scale immigration of Albanians had economic consequences for Kosovo, too. In many parts of the province, the one-time inhabitants of the mountains transformed the farmland into grazing land.

How these developments in southern Serbia are viewed depends upon whether one hears them from the Albanian or the Serbian side. Albanian historians, for instance, dispute that the ethnic composition of the population only changed after the emigration of the Serbs in 1690 and the immigration of the Albanian mountain tribes. They allege that Kosovo was inhabited by an Albanian majority much earlier. There is, however, little evidence in support of this theory, either in Turkish taxation lists or in ecclesiastical reports. The classification of ethnic groups was a dubious affair at the time. Serbs were often classified as Albanians and vice versa.

The first Russian consul in Prizren, Evgeniy Timayev, at any rate came to the conclusion in the second half of the nineteenth century that the Albanians had colonized Old Serbia. "The Albanians are taking over more and more land and settling it. It may soon happen that they will begin to play a role in the destiny of Europe, irrespective of the fact that the vast majority of them are uneducated and quite savage... The Turkish government seems to take great satisfaction in the fact that there are no more Christians in the province, and the Christian population puts up no resistance to the massive influx of Albanians since they are too few in number and dreadfully divided among themselves."

Timayev gives no precise figures concerning the ethnic and religious composition of the population of Kosovo and Metohija. He perhaps regarded the statistics published by the Turkish side as too unreliable. It was only at the start of the twentieth century that statistics for the European regions of the Ottoman Empire became more precise. They were checked for the European regions by the Austro-Hungarian consulates and amended where necessary. Accordingly, in 1903, there were 111,350 Orthodox, 69,250 Moslem and 6,600 Catholic Serbs in what is now Kosovo and Metohija, a total of 187,200 Serbs. Of the total of 230,000 Albanians, 215,050 were Moslems, 14,350 Catholics and 900 Orthodox.

The League of Prizren:
A belated national awakening

The Albanian 'national awakening' took place relatively late, compared to that of the Serbs, Greeks and Bulgarians. This is true both for the awakening of their cultural and intellectual identity and for their struggle for political independence.

The reasons for this were twofold. Most of the Albanians lived in isolated mountain valleys, cut off from the outside world. In addition, the Albanians were subjected primarily to the culture of the empire they lived in, i. e. Islam, and there were indeed many Albanians who took advantage of career opportunities in the Ottoman administration and in the army. The Albanians, or 'sons of the eagle' as they call themselves, were among the most faithful subjects of the Ottoman Empire. The number of Albanian pashas, and viziers, and indeed of grand viziers (prime ministers) and commanders was extraordinarily high in proportion to their numbers. Even today, Albanians can be heard to complain of the five hundred years they suffered under the Turkish yoke and, at the same time, list with great pride the number of grand viziers which their small nation gave to the Sublime Porte.

In the second half of the nineteenth century, a process of intellectual and political renewal began to take root among the Albanians, too. This movement began initially among the Catholic Albanians of the diaspora in southern Italy, descendants of emigrants who fled Albania after the Turkish conquest, and among the exiguous number of Albanian intellectuals in Istanbul. Clubs were formed to encourage the use of the Albanian language and to promote books and literature in Albanian. These were as yet illegal in the Ottoman Empire and had to be smuggled into the Albanian-speaking districts.

The movement first acquired a political character during the Russo-Turkish war of 1877-1878. Since Serbia and Montenegro had both been involved in the final phase of this conflict, the European Powers came to the conclusion at the Congress of Berlin in June 1878 that it was time to restructure relations among the Balkan states. This galvanized the Albanians into action, who feared that their country would fall prey to the Slavic kingdoms under the protection of Russia that were expanding at Turkey's expense. Indeed, the Treaty of San Stefano concluded between Russia and Turkey did forsee the annexation of extensive regions of Albanian territory by the newly created state of Bulgaria and by Serbia.

On 10 June 1878, a mere three days before the start of the Congress of Berlin, the Albanians in Prizren, the second largest town in Kosovo, formed the League for the Defence of the Rights of the Albanian People, later to be known as the League of Prizren. It was the first political organization created by the Albanians since the time of Scanderbeg, the hero of Albanian independence of the mid-fifteenth century.

Accordingly, about 300 delegates from the four Albanian *vilayets* of Janina, Monastir, Prishtina and Shkodër gathered in Prizren on the banks of the Bistrica River to voice the demands of their people. Most of the delegates were from the upper strata of Albanian society: wealthy merchants and artisans from various towns, landowners of mostly Moslem faith, pashas and beys from the lowlands, and tribal leaders from the northern Albanian mountains, most of whom were Catholic.

It was in a small, one-storey yellow house, which is now among the main tourist attractions of Prizren, that leaders of the League formulated the catalogue of demands which they transmitted to the Great Powers in Berlin. Among their demands was not national independence for Albania, but simply territorial integrity within the Ottoman Empire. The delegates knew full well that their people were not yet in a position to counter the expansionist designs of the Bulgarians, Serbs, Montenegrins and Greeks. The Ottoman Empire still constituted for them protection against the territorial appetite of the other, mostly Orthodox Christian peoples of the Balkans who had already gained their independence.

The League demanded that the four Ottoman *vilayets* in which the majority of the population was Albanian be united into one. This part of the Ottoman Empire, with about two and a half million inhabitants, would then be given autonomy, with an Albanian administration, an Albanian court system, Albanian schools and a local Albanian militia. There would also be a national assembly as a legislative body. The Moslem pashas and beys regarded the League as a means of defending their privileges and social position against possible reforms by the Sublime Porte.

Though the Sublime Porte did not agree to the demand for autonomy, it co-operated initially with the League for political reasons. When it no longer needed the League to defend the Empire against the territorial demands of Serbia, Montenegro and Bulgaria, and when it saw that the League had acquired a substantial political weight and was organizing open rebellion in Kosovo, it expedited troops to Kosovo and Metohija and put an end to the first national organization of the Albanians. The leaders of the League were arrested and banned to Asia Minor.

The League of Prizren was the first occasion on which representatives of the Albanian people had demanded that all Albanians be able to live in one territorial unit, even though they did not go so far as to demand an independent state. The first step was thus taken towards the creation of a Greater Albania, comprising not only the people of modern-day Albania, but also the Albanians of Greece, Macedonia and Kosovo. The Albanian nationalist movement began in a town in Kosovo.

The Albanians caught up between Turkey, the new Balkan states and the Great Powers

The Albanian-inhabited regions of the Ottoman Empire were to find no peace even though the League of Prizren had been broken up. Over the next three decades, from 1880 to the Balkan Wars of 1912-1913, there occurred one uprising after the other in Kosovo and in the motherland. The rebels were not concerned primarily with political independence for Albania, but rather with the defence of the social and economic privileges enjoyed by the feudal Moslem landowners of the region who felt threatened by centralist reforms in Istanbul. Administrative autonomy was just as important to the townspeople, be they Moslem, Orthodox or Catholic, as the promotion of an Albanian national culture, i. e. the setting up of schools and printing presses, and the creation of literary clubs and societies. The mostly Catholic tribes of the northern mountains endeavoured again and again to protect and expand their de facto autonomy from the Turkish authorities.

The rebirth of the Albanian people within the Ottoman Empire took place in an age of agony for Turkey in Europe. It was an era of expansion for those Balkan nations who had already gained their freedom and one of diplomatic manoeuvring among the Great Powers in their endeavours to solve the so-called Eastern Question in their own interests. It was not easy for the Albanians to find their way in the tangled web of overlapping political interests after having lived for so long in a quiet backwater of the Empire and rarely having been confronted with contemporary European politics. For the Christian peoples of the Balkans, the Albanians were indistinguishable from the Turks, since about 70% of the Albanians had by then converted to Islam. These peoples were competing to seize for themselves the biggest chunk of Albanian land from the Turkish collapse. Many Albanian leaders, for their part, viewed the Ottoman Empire at the end of the nineteenth and the beginning of the twentieth centuries as their only guarantee of protection from the expansionist designs of the Serbs, Montenegrins, Bulgarians and Greeks. Even when they rose in revolt against the Turks, they were concerned only with the amalgamation of all Albanian vilayets into one and with a certain degree of autonomy under the protection of the Sublime Porte.

This was also the goal of the political movement of 1897-1899, the so-called League of Peja / Peć, which, as the name implies, was concentrated in Kosovo, as was the League of Prizren twenty years earlier. Even in the uprisings of 1910-1912, in which the Kosovo Albanians played an important role, it was still only a question of Albanian autonomy within the Ottoman Empire. The government in Istanbul only gave in to Albanian demands for economic, political, administrative and cultural rights after tens of thousands of Albanian rebels occupied Skopje, the capital of modern-day Macedonia, in August 1912. These rights were tantamount to autonomy for the Albanian vilayets, although the term was not used at the time.

The unrest in this part of the Ottoman Empire also led to a deterioration of relations between the Albanians and Serbs in Kosovo. The Serbian side claims that about 400,000 Serbs were forced out or expelled from Kosovo in the three decades between 1880 and the Balkan Wars.

The Balkan Wars
The return of the Holy Land

A mere two months had passed since the Albanian uprising and the occupation of Skopje when Montenegro, Serbia, Greece and Bulgaria attacked Turkey with the declared intention of driving it out of the European continent. The swift advance of the Serbs into Macedonia, of the Bulgarians down to the Aegean, of the Montenegrins into northern Albania and of the Greeks towards Salonika and into southern Albania created a totally new situation for the Albanians. Autonomy within the Ottoman Empire was now a dream of the past. The only solution to prevent the carving up of Albanian territory among the victors was to declare Albania independent with the backing of those Great Powers, such as Austria-Hungary and Italy, that were interested in preventing a Serbian and thus Russian encroachment into the Adriatic. As the Serbs were marching towards Durrës (Durazzo), the Montenegrins besieging Shkodër (Scutari) and the Greeks approaching Vlora (Valona), Albanian politician Ismail Qemali succeeded in convoking a national assembly in Vlora and on 28 November 1912 in declaring Albania a free, sovereign and independent nation. The red flag of Scanderbeg, bearing the black, double-headed eagle, was ceremoniously hoisted on the balcony of the assembly building.

The existence of the new Balkan state only became a reality, however, when the Conference of the Ambassadors of the six Great Powers of Europe met at the end of July 1913, at which time they recognized its independence and fixed its borders.

The territory of the new Albanian state, reborn after five hundred years of foreign occupation, did not by any means include all the territories inhabited by the Albanian people. Only about 800,000 Albanians were to become citizens of the new state. Almost as many Albanians remained outside its borders under the control of Serbia and Greece, which emerged as victors in the first Balkan War. Kosovo and Metohija and their economically viable towns of long-standing tradition such as Prishtina, Prizren and Peja / Peć fell to Serbia, as did the territories in western Macedonia around the towns of Tetova / Tetovo, Gostivar and Dibër / Debar.

The third Serbian army celebrated its victory over the Turks with a commemorative church service in Grachanitsa monastery not far from Prishtina, the last endowment of the great King Milutin, which was constructed between the years 1313 and 1321. Grachanitsa was a worthy venue for traditionalist Serbs since it ranks among the greatest creations of Byzantine-Macedonian-Serbian art of the first half of the fourteenth century. The church service also served as an occasion to revive the memory of the Battle of Kosovo Polje 524 years earlier. It was at Grachanitsa that Prince Lazar and his knights dined on the eve of the battle. In 1924, the two huge candles donated to the Monastery of Dechani by Queen Militsa, wife of Prince Lazar who was vanquished and decapitated at the Battle of Kosovo Polje, were lit by King Alexander. The second Balkan War and the First World War had prevented this ceremony from taking place earlier.

The first Balkan War which resulted in the subjection of hundreds of thousands of Albanians to Serbian rule is at the root of all nationalist tension between the two peoples in this century. For the Serbs, the Albanians were nothing but Turks and enemies because most of them had converted to Islam. Nor were the Serbs ready to forget the role the Albanians had played in the Turkish army in quelling Christian uprisings. They also accused the Albanians of refusing to take part in the fight against the Turks and of supporting the Ottoman Empire until the very end.

The Serbs' treatment of the non-Slavic population under their control was in blatant contrast with the grandure of their mediaeval history. The relatively liberal constitution of the Kingdom of Serbia in the nineteenth and twentieth centuries was not valid for Kosovo. Here, government orders were carried out by decree and in an extremely oppressive manner. The government in Belgrade held the view that the Albanians were "not a people, but rather a collection of tribes divided and fighting among themselves, who had no common language, writing or religion."

Estimates as to the number of Albanian civilians of Moslem faith who died in the fighting and in subsequent pogroms range from 12,000 to 30,000. Not only many Turks, but also a good number of Albanians preferred to abandon Kosovo and seek refuge in Turkey or in newly independent Albania.

The actions of Serbian troops in the conquered territories were severely criticized by Dimitrije Tucović, head of the Social Democratic Party, in his 1914 booklet 'Serbia and Albania'. The Serbian soldiers, he wrote, were obsessed with vengeance. Even their clergy called upon them to take revenge for Kosovo, that is, for the Battle of Kosovo Polje. When the Turks conquered the region in the Middle Ages, he continued, they had no intention of wiping out the peoples they had conquered, as the governments of the Balkan bourgeoisie were now endeavouring to do. Tucović regarded the subjugation of Kosovo as an act of colonialism and advocated the unification of Kosovo with the Albanian state and the setting up of a Balkan federation of equal states.

The Serbian government did not oppose the creation of an 'autonomous Albania' after the first Balkan War, but adamantly refused to draw its borders along ethnic lines. Regions with a "mixed Serbian-Albanian population, which have been forcefully converted to Islam and made Albanian and in which for centuries the Serbian population has been under pressure to leave" were not to fall to Albania. In a memorandum to the Conference of the Ambassadors, it reiterated that Serbia and Montenegro would never agree to anyone else taking possession of Kosovo and Metohija, including Peja / Peć, Dechani and Gjakova / Djakovica, as this was "the Holy Land of the Serbian nation since time immemorial."

The struggle for Kosovo during the First World War

Just as it has been shown in the previous chapters that the fate of Kosovo was determined in good part by the relations between the Habsburg monarchy and the Ottoman Empire in peace and war, one must pay particular attention in the coming passages to developments in the now independent Albanian state. The internal order or rather disorder and the position of this country in the diplomatic and military conflict waged among the European powers for influence and supremacy in the Balkans cast their shadow upon developments in Kosovo.

When the First World War broke out in the summer of 1914, triggered by the assassination in Sarajevo of Archduke Ferdinand, the heir to the Austrian throne, the one-and-a-half-year-old Kingdom of Albania was still in a state of chaos. The provisional government of Ismail Qemali in Vlora had not managed to take control of the country any more than had the opposition government of pro-Serbian Esad Pasha, which was formed in Durrës in the autumn of 1913. Equally powerless was Prince Wilhelm zu Wied, whom the Great Powers had selected to become King of Albania and who had arrived in March 1914 to take the throne of 'his' country. On the contrary, the Moslem population of central Albania rose in revolt against him in May 1914; in northern Albania, the *bajtaktars* or tribal leaders remained virtually independent; and in southern Albania an Autonomous Republic of Northern Epirus was set up under Greek influence. The reign of the German prince, protected by the naval vessels of the Great Powers in Durrës harbour, was confined for all practical purposes to the town of Durrës and the surrounding area. When the war finally broke out, the ships were withdrawn and the prince was abandoned to his fate. He left Albania on 3 September 1914, without abdicating, and never returned to the country again.

Chaos also reigned in the Serbian-Albanian border region. Thousands of Albanians fled to Albania following the Serbian annexation of Kosovo. There, they set up armed units which returned to Kosovo, attacking

Serbian border posts, police stations and army barracks, and calling upon the native population to rise in arms against the new rulers. After the outbreak of the First World War and the start of Austria's military campaign against Serbia, some of these units were equipped by Austria-Hungary in order to keep the Serbs occupied in the south. These Albanian 'irregular' troops, attacking Kosovo with forces at times numbering several thousand men, posed a serious threat to the Serbian administration and to Serbian troops. This was particularly true after Turkey entered the war on the side of the Axis, an act which further motivated the majority of Albanian Moslems in their struggle against the Serbs.

The elderly Prime Minister of Serbia, Nikola Pašić, endeavoured to counter the threat posed by the Albanians by backing Esad Pasha. Not only did he support Esad financially, but he also allowed him to recruit Albanian troops in southern Serbia to return to Albania and seize power there. Esad Pasha succeeded, too, but was soon to encounter difficulties in an uprising which the Turks had fomented. Pašić asked the Entente for permission to send Serbian troops to Albania to support Esad, but Great Britain and France refused because they were already negotiating with Italy about the latter's entry into the war on the side of the Entente. Italy had strong interests of its own in Albania. When the Serbian government ignored the refusal of Great Britain and France and actually did send troops to intervene in Albania, the Entente forced Pašić to withdraw them.

The collaboration which Pašić envisioned with Esad Pasha was the first attempt to create a Serbian-Albanian union, but it was not to be the last, as the history of relations between Belgrade and Tirana after the First and Second World Wars shows. Each occasion was linked to the border question, to the fate of Kosovo and its people.

By the autumn of 1915, Bulgaria and Austria-Hungary had begun to vie for Kosovo when the Serbian army, together with the king and government, was forced to retreat through Albania to Corfu. This followed Bulgaria's declaration of war on the side of the Axis and the new German-Austrian offensive against Serbia. Most of Kosovo and Metohija, including the towns of Prishtina and Prizren, fell to Bulgaria during the seizure of Serbian territory in the autumn and winter of 1915-1916. Austria-Hungary found itself forced to make do with Mitrovica and Peja / Peć. When at the end of the war the Bulgarians began setting up a civilian administration in Kosovo as part of the new political order in the Balkans, they encountered resistance on the part of Vienna, which sent troops into the area of conflict. The two sides then dispatched ultimatums to one another. The situation escalated to such an extent that the high military command of the German Empire intervened and divided Kosovo anew, a division which Bulgaria and Austria-Hungary were finally force to accept. It was stipulated in this connection, however, that the division was only for the duration of the war and was to have no prejudicial effect on any post-war settlement which might be reached.

This was important because the Bulgarians, should they win the war, intended to extend their territory right to Elbasan in central Albania. Austria-Hungary, for its part, wanted Kosovo to be part of a Greater Albania, under Austro-Hungarian influence.

The defeat of the Axis powers in 1918 made all these plans superfluous. What now began with the victory of the Entente was a tug-of-war for Albania, and thus for Kosovo, between the newly-created Kingdom of the Serbs, Croats and Slovenes (SHS), later to be known as Yugoslavia, and Italy, which was endeavouring to expand its influence to the other side of the Straits of Otranto. Whenever the 'peace-makers' of 1919 considered reducing Albania to an Italian protectorate, Belgrade would lay claim to northern Albania including Shkodër (Scutari) and Durrës (Durrazzo). It took almost three years for the Conference of the Ambassadors in London to agree, with a few exceptions, to leaving the borders of Albania as they had been before the war. Italy received the island of Sazani (Saseno) near the Bay of Vlora (Valona) as a military base, and Kosovo and the Albanian territory in what is now Macedonia went to the Serbs. In neither case was the population in the territories concerned consulted.

No minority rights for the Albanians in the Kingdom of Yugoslavia

In the 1920s, an adventurous young lady - the child of a Serbian father and a Scottish mother - set out on a journey through Yugoslavia and ventured into the godforsaken reaches of Kosovo, or Old Serbia as it was called at the time. Her name was Lena A. Yovitchitch. She sketched her impressions and adventures in a small book published in 1926 entitled *Pages from here and there in Serbia*. In it she describes the journey from Mitrovica to Peja / Peć in the following terms:

> "From here the road rises in zig-zags and goes through a lonely pass which is still the happy hunting ground of Albanian brigands. Many a traveller has been attacked on this bit of the road, which explains the armed policemen, with their guns and belts full of cartridges, stationed at every few yards. Albanians, in national dress, also stand on guard; they are obliged to take their share in protecting the road, and should they not give warning of the approach of their marauding kinsmen, they pay the penalty with their lives. Since this method has been adopted, we were told that the raids have been few and far between..."

The insecurity on the roads of Kosovo which Lena Yovitchitch described was in part due to highway robbers, but equally to politically motivated guerrillas and underground fighters attacking both Serbian soldiers and police and Serbian colonists who had been given land in Kosovo. They often received their orders from Albania where, at the end of First World War, a committee of Kosovo refugees had been founded in Shkodër (Scutari) that openly supported a Greater Albania. It encouraged the Albanians of southern Serbia, Montenegro and Macedonia to rise in revolt.

The situation in those parts of the new state of the southern Slavs inhabited by an Albanian majority was confusing enough because of continual differences of opinion in the governments and among the public of the new kingdom under Serbian leadership on whether the protection of ethnic minorities, to which the Kingdom of the Serbs, Croats and Slovenes had been obliged to subscribe in the Treaty of St Germain and in the special agreement of 1920, also applied to the Albanians. One side held the view that minority rights only applied to the ethnic minorities that had joined the new state under the peace treaties which followed the First World War, in other words the Germans, Hungarians, Romanians, and so on, but not to the Albanian minority which, like the Bulgarians and Turks, had been part of the Kingdom of Serbia before the First World War.

This controversy was of purely academic significance, however. The reality of the situation is well described in the Kosovo book of Dimitrije Bogdanović: "In practice, the Albanians do not benefit from the minority rights enjoyed by the Germans, Italians and Hungarians. There is sufficient evidence to lead us to the conclusion that the Albanians are systematically discriminated against, in particular in the field of culture and education."

Jens Reuter notes in his book 'The Albanians in Yugoslavia' (*Die Albaner in Jugoslawien*): "The Albanians had no right to develop their national culture, whereas the recognized minorities had a right to schooling in their mother tongue and to financial support in the field of education and the exercise of their religion. School education in Albanian was just as illegal as the publication of books and literature in that language."

The consequence of this policy was that over three-quarters of the Albanians in Kosovo remained illiterate between the two world wars since they refused to send their children to Serbian schools. According to official statistics in 1940, only 12,000 Albanian children attended Serbian elementary schools, a very small number for a population of 700,000.

Nonetheless, the Serbian authorities did not pursue any consistent course of assimilation. For the Serbs, the Albanians, or Shiptars, as they called them, were simply foreigners to be kept in check and suppressed. The Serbian attitude to the Albanians in the south of the country was expressed in its most radical form by Vasa Čubrilović, member of the Serbian Academy of Sciences and Arts. Čubrilović, who as a student had been a member of the group of assassins responsible for the death of Archduke Ferdinand, the heir to the Austrian throne, openly advocated the expulsion of the Albanians from Yugoslavia. In his memorandum on 'The Expulsion of the Albanians', presented in March of 1937, he complains that the Serbian authorities are trying to solve the major ethnic problems of the Balkans by Western methods. Gradual colonization, however, Čubrilović claimed, had failed. There was no possibility of assimilating the Albanians as a people.

> "The only way and the only means to cope with them is the brute force of an organized state in which we have always been superior to them... if we do not settle accounts with them in time, within 20 to 30 years we shall have to cope with a terrible irredentism, the signs of which are already apparent and which will inevitably put all our southern territories in jeopardy...
>
> The mass evacuation of the Albanians is the only effective course we can take... The first prerequisite is the creation of a suitable psychosis... with coercion by the state apparatus. The law must be enforced to the letter so as to make staying intolerable for the Albanians: fines, imprisonment, the ruthless application of all police dispositions... compulsory labour and any other measure that an experienced police force can contrive... Private initiative, too, can assist greatly in this direction. We should distribute weapons to our colonists, as need be. The old form of *chetnik* action should be organized and secretly assisted... Finally, local riots can be incited. These will be bloodily suppressed with the most effective means, though by colonists from the Montenegrin clans and the *chetniks*, rather than by means of the army."

The result of this strategy was that about 45,000 people left Kosovo between the two world wars. Albanians and Turks emigrated either to Turkey, which accepted many Moslem Albanians, or to Albania. According to Albanian sources, over 50,000 Albanians were imprisoned in Serbian jails in this period.

The political course of the Serbian authorities drove the Albanians underground, forcing them to set up guerrilla bands to defend their political interests and human rights. The attacks carried out by such bands were condemned by the Serbs as terrorism and put down with extreme brutality.

In the above-mentioned book 'Kosovo and Metohija in Serbian History', such repression is euphemistically referred to as the "confiscation of the property of guerrillas, the internment of their families, the destruction of their homes and the occasional use of the army, the police and the artillery against villages offering armed resistance."

An agrarian reform was also carried out in Kosovo between the wars, but with the primary intent of changing the ethnic rather than the social structure of the population. Property which had belonged to the Turkish state and municipalities was redistributed, as was the property of big Turkish landowners. Those benefitting from the redistribution were primarily new colonists from Serbia, Montenegro and the Serbian areas of Bosnia, Hercegovina and Dalmatia. A total of 60,000 new colonists of Slavic origin came to settle in Kosovo before the Second World War.

The Albanians had no real representation in government between the two world wars. Up to the mid-twenties, there existed a *Dzemijet* society for the defence of the Moslems, which managed to take part in elections and demanded autonomy for the Kosovo Albanians. In the 1925 elections, this party was subjected to such extreme pressure by the Serbian authorities that it did not win a single seat. Its president was tried and sentenced to life in prison. After the elections, the *Djemijet* was banned completely for subversive activity.

At the start of the Second World War, Kosovo and Metohija were the picture of a country under a hostile colonial administration. The Albanian majority was politically oppressed and, in economical and cultural terms, was left behind in the dust.

Greater Albania
A brief dream during the Second World War

Albania had ceased to exist as an independent state two years before Germany invaded Yugoslavia on 6 April 1941. On 7 April, Good Friday

1939, Mussolini occupied Albania with his troops, forcing King Zog to flee abroad. The Italians did not speak of the annexation of Albania, but rather of the 'union' of the two kingdoms under the crown of Victor Emmanuel III. For all intents and purposes, however, Albania had become an Italian protectorate.

Kosovo was initially unaffected by the Axis defeat of Yugoslavia. Not only was Kosovo occupied for the most part by the Italian army (the German *Wehrmacht* occupied only Mitrovica with its lead and zinc mines, and the Bulgarian army got a few areas in the east and south), but the Italians reunified Kosovo politically and administratively with the 'motherland', thus, by the grace of Mussolini, creating a Greater Albania.

Germany allowed this Greater Albania to continue to exist even after the capitulation of Italy in September 1943 when it marched into the Italian occupation zones in the Balkans and disbanded the Italian forces there. Germany went even further. Albania was to be an "Albania that is independent of its own initiative," according to directives from Berlin transmitted to Hermann Neubacher, the 'special envoy of the German Foreign Office for southeast European affairs'.

There was, of course, no question of genuine independence for the country, at least not as long as the war lasted. Though there was no more Italian *luogotenente*, no governor-general exercising legislative and executive power on behalf of the King of Italy, German troops were present throughout Greater Albania, as were the SS Skanderbeg Divisions formed of Albanians to fight Enver Hoxha's Communist Party. There was a constituent assembly in Tirana, the capital of this 'independent' Albania, as well as a government and regency council. The national assembly went so far as to terminate the country's alliance with the Axis and to declare Albania neutral. But in view of the wartime situation, this step was just as illusory as the country's 'sovereignty'. The two governments agreed to add the word 'relative' to their description of the country's sovereignty, a rather curious denomination in international law.

The creation of Greater Albania meant not only the fulfilment of an age-old dream for the Kosovo Albanians, but also liberation from Serbian oppression. They acquired their own administration, police, courts, schools and cultural institutions.

But for the Serbs in Kosovo, this period constituted an age of persecution, beginning from the fall of Yugoslavia in the spring of 1941 and the reunification of Kosovo with the Italian-occupied motherland. Hermann Neubacher noted in his memoirs, 'Special Assignment Southeast' (*Sonderauftrag Südost*):

> "The Albanians did not delay in expelling as many Serbs as they could from the country. Those being expelled were often forced to pay local authorities for the exit permit. Obviously, the Emigration Tax of the Third Reich had served as a good example. I urgently recommended to the Albanian government that they put an end to the expulsion of the Serbs, when General Nedić (the Serbian head of government under the German occupation) approached me to voice his complaint. When I realized that my protest had fallen on deaf ears, I threatened to resign from my duties in Albania, saying I would have to leave the matter of protecting Albania from the territorial designs of the Bulgarians to someone else. Xhefar Devar (the Albanian Minister of the Interior), who had influence in Kosovo, promised to intervene, which he did with success. Despite this, much damage was done after 1941."

How many Serbs were driven out of Kosovo between the spring of 1941 and the autumn of 1944 is just as difficult to ascertain as the number of Albanian immigrants who moved into the homes left behind by the Serbs. Serbian sources often refer to 80,000-100,000 people, a figure which would seem to be exaggerated. On the other side of the coin, in a report in the Belgrade newspaper *Politika* on 24 February 1989, the Yugoslav Minister of the Interior referred to 15,000 settlers having moved into Kosovo from Albania in the period in question.

Playing the nationalist card resulted initially in German troops not being attacked by the partisans of the *Balli Kombëtar*, National Front, who had opposed the Italians. In Kosovo, this policy also meant that the movement of Albanian communist partisans was very slow to develop. Also impeding the growth of this movement was the constantly vacillating course of the Yugoslav Communist Party in the nationality question, which we shall look at further on.

In 1941, at any rate, the Communist Party of Yugoslavia (CPY) had a mere 270 members in Kosovo, of whom 20 were Albanians. Up to September 1942, no contacts existed between this group and the Yugoslav partisan leadership under Tito. The Headquarters of the National Liberation Struggle for Kosovo and Metohija only came into existence in April 1943. Its military operations were insignificant, in particular after the Italian capitulation when the Germans set up an Albanian Kosovo Regiment. This regiment, together with the above-mentioned SS Skanderbeg Division, kept firm control over the region.

Just how difficult the situation of the CPY was can be inferred from a resolution passed by its provincial committee in November 1943. It noted that the Albanian masses were aware that the defeat of Germany was now inevitable but were afraid of "retaliation and the return of the old order," i. e. the restoration of Serbian rule.

In a report to the Central Committee of the CPY dating from the final days of January 1944, the communists in Kosovo explained even more candidly that the Albanian masses regarded the fascist occupants, and the Germans in particular, as their friends and liberators. It was the Germans who had allowed them to have schools in their own language, a civil service and an administration which returned to them the property which had been taken away from them, had given them a flag and the right to bear arms, and had thus made it possible for them to kill and drive out all the non-Albanians. The communist partisans, Serbs and Albanians, could not operate in Kosovo since 'reactionary forces' were still in a position to mobilize the people against them.

Communist vacillation on the nationality question

The activities of the communist partisans in Kosovo were handicapped all the more by the vacillation of the CPY on the nationality question and the resulting contradictions within the party. The nationality policy of the CPY had by no means been consistent between the two world wars. In the years immediately following World War I, the communists attached no particular importance to the nationality problem in Yugoslavia, believing that a social revolution was imminent. By the mid-twenties, in accord with Comintern policies, the communists viewed the right of all peoples to self-determination as a means of breaking apart the multi-ethnic state of Yugoslavia created by the post-war treaties, and of liberating the various peoples from the "yoke of the Serbian bourgeoisie." In 1936, however, and again in line with the policies of the Comintern, they altered their position in favour of maintaining the unity of Yugoslavia. The national rights of the Albanians, they said, should be defended just as much as those of other peoples. But there was no more discussion about Kosovo leaving Yugoslavia and joining the motherland.

The Kosovo communists were not present in the Bosnian town of Jajce at the end of November 1943 when Tito's partisans laid the foundations for post-war Yugoslavia as a federal state under their control. They did, however, hold a conference from 31 December 1943 to 2 January 1944 in Bujan / Bujane, a village on present-day Albanian territory just across the border from Prizren, and passed a resolution asserting among other things that:

"Kosovo and Metohija is a territory inhabited primarily by Albanians whose desire it has always been to be united with Albania. We therefore regard it as our duty to show the Albanian population the way they must go in order to fulfil this desire. The only way for the Albanians in Kosovo and Metohija to be united with Albania is by joining in the common struggle with the other peoples of Yugoslavia against the invaders and their running-dogs.

The only way to obtain freedom is for all peoples, including the Albanians, to hold their fate in their own hands, including the right to self-determination and to secession."

Tito regarded this resolution as an "anti-Yugoslav act" that contravened the directives of Jajce. The Politburo of the CPY thus declared the resolution invalid. In the spring of 1944, it forced the regional leaders in Kosovo to delete the passage in the resolution referring to the unification of Kosovo and Metohija with Albania. In January 1945, the governments of Yugoslavia and Albania signed a treaty stipulating that Kosovo and Metohija was to remain in Yugoslavia, and in July 1945, the regional parliament of Kosovo spoke out in favour of the inclusion of the region within the Yugoslav Republic of Serbia.

The wing of the Albanian CP favouring a Greater Albania was also forced to submit to the will of the Yugoslav CP. In August 1943, the Albanian communists organized in the National Liberation Struggle signed a pact with the nationalist and anti-communist *Balli Kombëtar* (National Front) and co-founded a Committee for the Salvation of Albania. The objective of this committee was not only the fight against the occupiers, but also the creation of a Greater Albania. The Yugoslav CP intervened at once and the Central Committee of the Albanian CP was forced to rescind its resolution and distance itself from the Committee for the Salvation of Albania. In a subsequent letter to their Albanian comrades, the Central Committee of the CPY warned that bringing up the question of the unification of Kosovo and Metohija with Albania would only impede the struggle against the occupiers. New Yugoslavia would be a land of free peoples in which there would be no room for the oppression of the Albanian minority.

Although the Resolution of Bujan / Bujane was formally rescinded, it was not erased from the memory of the Albanians. For one thing, a number of people who subsequently became leading party functionaries had been involved in drafting it, among them Fadil Hoxha, who rose to become Tito's representative in the Yugoslav state presidium. It was also the Resolution of Bujan / Bujane which the provisional government of the Republic of Kosovo used at the end of December 1991 in support of its application for recognition by the European Community as an independent state.

Back to the vicious circle of hatred and violence after 1945

In the autumn of 1944, the German *Wehrmacht* was forced to withdraw from southeast Europe and by the end of November, Kosovo was liberated. It was not Tito's partisans who took power, though, but rather the Albanian nationalists of the *Balli Kombëtar* who had gained the upper hand militarily. They fought on to preserve Greater Albania after the retreat of the *Wehrmacht* and Germany's capitulation, and were widely supported by the population. At the beginning of December 1944, Fadil Hoxha, who directed the operations of Tito's partisans in Kosovo, noted in an order of the day that the enemy, that is, the *Balli Kombëtar* fighters, had succeeded in some areas of Kosovo in "allying themselves with the masses to organize resistance to us in the countryside."

In order to overcome the anti-communist nationalists among the Kosovo Albanians, the high command of Tito's partisans was obliged to call upon the support of two division of Enver Hoxha's communist partisans from Albania and to place Kosovo and Metohija under military rule in February 1945. It was only after months of intense and extremely brutal fighting that Tito's forces succeeded in overcoming the resistance of the majority of Kosovo Albanians to reunification with Yugoslavia. Military rule, which was a virtual state of siege, was only lifted in July 1945.

This was obviously not an auspicious prelude to relations between the 'new' communist-ruled Yugoslavia and the Albanians within its borders, nor for relations with Albania itself, even though the communists had taken over power in that country, too. A treatment of the various phases in the relations between Tito and Enver Hoxha and their respective parties during the war and in the years immediately following would go beyond the scope of this work, in particular since the back and forth, the sudden changes of course and the often perplexing manoeuvring of the two sides make the topic extraordinarily complex. We may note with certainty, however, that the Communist Party of Albania (CPA) was founded in 1941 with the active support of the Yugoslav CP. Representatives of the CPY were also at Enver Hoxha's headquarters throughout the war, even though maintaining contact with Tito and the Yugoslav party leadership often proved very difficult. The attempt to establish a common front between the Albanian communists and nationalists was one of the indications that the emissaries of the CPY had a decisive influence on the political course of the CPA.

More obscure is the attitude of the two parties to the problem of Kosovo and Metohija. Both within the CPY and the CPA, views diverged as to whether this part of southern Serbia inhabited by an Albanian majority should be united with Albania or remain within Yugoslavia. Vladimir Dedijer, Tito's biographer, speculates in his book 'Yugoslav-Albanian relations' that some groups within the Albanian party welcomed the occupation of Yugoslavia and Greece in the hope that Hitler and Mussolini would create for them an 'ethnic' or Greater Albania including Kosovo and Metohija. Dedijer's book was, however, published in 1949 at the height of the conflict between Stalin and Tito, and consequently of that between Tito and Enver Hoxha. It was convenient for propaganda purposes to expose links between the Albanian communists and the fascists.

The situation was more complicated than one might imagine, especially when one considers that Miladin Popović, a Serb who served as the CPY's permanent representative with the Albanian CP, was in favour of Kosovo and Metohija one day joining Albania. He had even proposed that the operations of the communist groups against the occupying powers and against the Albanian nationalists in Kosovo and Metohija be placed under the command of the Albanians.

Tito wanted no part of it, though, and by the autumn of 1943, informed his emissaries assigned to the Albanian CP, the CPA itself and the communists in Kosovo that "the new Yugoslavia which is arising will be a country of free nations and there will be no room in it for the repression of least from a social and economic point of view. At the beginning of March 1945, it banned Serbian and Montenegrin colonists who had been settled in Kosovo between the two world wars and had been expelled during the occupation, from returning to Kosmet. An exception was made only for those who had joined Tito's partisans.

Figures vary substantially, as always, as to the number of Serbs and Montenegrins whose return to Kosovo was made impossible by the revision of the land reforms carried out between the two wars. It is said on the one hand that 1,683 families were not able to return to Kosovo, and on the other hand that over 2,000 Serbian and Montenegrin families from Kosovo were given (formerly German) property in the Vojvodina after the war. It can be safely assumed that of the 15,000 families who were settled in Kosovo up to the outbreak of the war under the so-called land reforms, very few were denied permission to return. Nonetheless, in the second half of the eighties, when Tito's policies towards the Albanians were being severely criticized in Serbia, one of the main points of contention was the ban on the return of colonists to Kosovo.

The conflict between Stalin and Tito broke out in June 1948, a mere three years after the end of the war, and was to mean more hardship for the Albanian population of Kosovo. Of all the leaders of the communist countries of Eastern Europe, Enver Hoxha was the most extreme in his denunciation of the 'fascist bands of Tito' and in his appeals to the peoples of Yugoslavia, including the Kosovo Albanians, to overthrow the Tito regime. Accusing the Yugoslav leadership of wanting to make a Yugoslav colony out of Albania, he broke off party relations with Belgrade a few days after Stalin's anathema on Tito.

On the obvious assumption that the Tito regime would not be able to withstand the pressure from Moscow and its satellites, the Albanians smuggled agents and armed groups into Kosovo to carry out acts of sabotage. This convinced the Yugoslav leadership to further strengthen the already oppressive police regime in the 'most dangerous part of the country' and create an atmosphere of open terror. Recruits and members of the secret police consisted almost exclusively of Serbs. Their supreme commander was also a Serb: Aleksandar Ranković, a figure from within the highest party circles, minister of the interior and top man responsible for security throughout Yugoslavia.

This new wave of political repression of the Kosovo Albanians reached its peak in the mid-fifties with the disarmament campaign. The police systematically search all Albanian homes for weapons and physically mistreated the male members of the families, in particular when they found no weapons. This resulted in Albanians having to buy weapons to deliver to the police so as to be left in peace and quiet. Considering the significance of the rifle for an Albanian, "which is not a mere instrument but a part of his body," as Hermann Neubacher once noted, one can understand that the Albanian population interpreted this police campaign as a conscious move to humiliate them. In the aforementioned 'Book on Kosovo' by Dimitrije Bogdanović, which is by no means kind to the Albanians, its author notes that the action was carried out with a rigour "going beyond all measure and turning into terror against the population."

It was only at the beginning of the sixties that police pressure in Kosmet let up somewhat. In the federal constitution of 1963, Kosmet acquired the status of an 'autonomous province', and was thus, from a legal point of view, put on equal footing with the Vojvodina. Replacing the people's committee as the supreme governing authority was now a provincial assembly. The two autonomous provinces also obtained representation of five votes each in the chamber of nationalities of the federal parliament, in which the republics were all represented equally. Aside from these changes, however, Kosovo and Metohija and the Vojvodina remained firmly in Serbia's grip. Some legal experts hold the view that Serbia's control of the autonomous provinces now became even stronger since the new constitution strengthened the centralist character of the individual republics.

The turning point came three years later, in July 1966, at the Brioni Plenum which saw the fall of the dreaded Aleksandar Ranković.

The Brioni Plenum and its consequences

Kosovo and the Albanians were by no means at the top of the agenda at Tito's residence on the Adriatic island of Brioni at the fourth session of the Central Committee of the League of Communists of

Yugoslavia (LCY), as the Yugoslav Communist Party was officially called in 1952. The central issue was a conflict between reformist and conservative forces within the party. The conservatives were condemned for high-handedness and for the excessive power of the secret police which, as was noted, had escaped the control of the party. Their most important representatives, including Ranković, were thus either forced into retirement or relieved of their functions in the police and the party.

The Kosovo Albanians were to benefit politically from the decisions taken at Brioni, in particular since the Central Committee expressly condemned the activities of the UDBA (Secret police) in the province and condemned the discrimination of the Albanians as a violation of the political course of the party.

Not all the 'files' have been opened on this meeting which was of extraordinary significance for Yugoslavia at the time. Over a quarter of a century after the events at Brioni, it can only be said with any degree of certainty that the main charge against Ranković, that he had been secretly monitoring the conversations of Tito and his wife Jovanka, was unfounded, and that this accusation was simply used against him to remove him from his functions in the party and government. It can also be said for certain that the hopes for reform and democratization within the party attached to that session of the Central Committee proved illusory, as became clear in the late sixties and early seventies when Tito clamped down on all attempts at reform in Slovenia, Croatia and Serbia. One can only agree with what Koča Popović, longtime foreign minister, later said about the session, which he had attended personally: "The bureaucratic, demagogical, and indeed military and political struggle against Ranković (military information service KOS versus the secret police UDBA) was in actual fact exploited as a means of consolidating the very same political order of bureaucratic dogmatism and personality cult." Stripping away the communist party jargon, this means simply that Tito sacrificed Ranković to the democratic currents and reform movements in the party in order to prevent his own position from being questioned later on. The historic fourth plenum of the Central Committee on Brioni was thus nothing but a trick, and that is what Koča Popović called it.

All the same, Brioni left its mark on Yugoslav politics. It stimulated the country's evolution towards a federal structure, encouraged liberalization, brought about a change of course in the nationality question, and furthered the democratization of public life, despite the setbacks that occurred from time to time. Most of all, state centralism was brought to a definitive end. It was the decisions taken at Brioni that brought about the changes in the 1974 constitution leading the way to a very high degree of federalism.

Brioni was of extraordinary significance for the Albanians in Kosovo. Freed of the yoke which had weighed heavily upon them and upon party functionaries for twenty years, they now endeavoured to realize their national demands and expand the scope of their autonomy. With the help of the media, the Kosovo issue became more and more the focus of public attention after 1966. Tito played his part, too, by stressing again and again during his trip to Kosovo in March 1967 that it was necessary to overcome the deep-rooted contradictions of the past with patience.

A new future dawned for the Kosovo Albanians. But the heritage of oppression was daunting indeed, as was the resistance of many Serbs and the impatience of many Albanians.

The autonomous provinces acquire a new status

After 1966, following the defeat of the 'centralists' in the LCY leadership, a movement arose within the party for the further federalization of government structures and for corresponding changes in the constitution. After a number of steps taken in the late sixties and early seventies, the new constitution of 1974 redefined the position of the Autonomous Province of Kosovo within the federation.

This redefinition of the position of Kosovo constituted a major element in the struggle to come between the Serbs and Albanians. The Serbs insisted on the fact that the province was part of the Republic of Serbia, whereas the Albanians, for their part, stressed the position of the province as a constituent element of the Yugoslav federation. Article 1 of the new constitution stipulates at any rate that the Socialist Federal Republic of Yugoslavia is a "federal state of freely united peoples and of their socialist republics as well as of the autonomous provinces of Kosovo and the Vojvodina, which are parts of the Republic of Serbia..."

The two autonomous provinces are also specifically referred to in Article 2, which lists the republics and provinces of the Yugoslav federation. Article 4 makes reference to the equality of the founding peoples and national minorities, and a 'socialist province' is defined as a social community in which the workers and citizens can realize the sovereign rights of their peoples and national minorities. Article 5 specifies that neither the territory of the republics and autonomous provinces nor the borders of the Yugoslav federation may be altered without the consent of the provinces and autonomous provinces. Article 321, in conclusion, stipulates that the state presidency, as the collective executive organ of state, consists of one representative for each of the republics and autonomous provinces.

As we can see, the position of the autonomous provinces was substantially strengthened in the new constitution. It was the party leadership in Kosovo which had led criticism of the 1963 constitution for embedding the autonomous provinces too deeply within the Republic of Serbia, for making the rights and duties of the provinces dependent not upon their own constitutions but upon the laws of the Republic of Serbia and for limiting the fiscal autonomy of the provinces. The Kosovo leadership demanded that the autonomous provinces be placed on a virtually equal footing with the republics, arguing that they would then be in a better position to solve the economic and social problems they were facing and contribute to equality among the ethnic groups of the Yugoslav federation.

These arguments were brought up at just the right time when, in the late sixties, the idea began to take root throughout Yugoslavia that the country's federal structure needed to be revamped.

The constitutional amendments introduced between 1968 and 1971 and the new constitution of 1974 brought about a radical change of the constitutional position of the autonomous provinces. Although they remained within the Republic of Serbia, the autonomous provinces now also enjoyed direct relations with the federation, equivalent to those of the republics. These autonomous entities became just as responsible as the republics for certain affairs once attributed to the federal government. On the one hand, they continued to be responsible for their own social development, but on the other hand they now also played a direct role in federal politics.

Instead of statutes, Kosovo and the Vojvodina acquired constitutions of their own, of course in conformity with the constitutions of the federation and of the Republic of Serbia. Not only could the provincial parliaments pass laws, but the provinces were given their own supreme courts and could organize government administration on their own, as the republics already could. The provinces were represented by their own delegations to the Council of Republics and Provinces, as the chamber of nationalities of the federal parliament was now known, and were free to act independently of Serbia. The most important element in the constitutional change was that the rights and duties of the autonomous provinces were now of an original, direct nature and were derived from the federal constitution, not from the Republic of Serbia. The provinces thus acquired a status virtually equal to that of the republics.

The extensive independence enjoyed by the provinces caused a split within Serbia, which was now regarded as an 'asymmetric federation' within the Yugoslav federation as a whole. The government of Serbia could only rule over certain parts of the republic, i. e. Serbia proper. Even in the fields of defence, state security, economic planning and justice, Belgrade did not have clear responsibilities for the whole of the republic.

A strong opposition thus began to arise within Serbia in the early sixties when the new constitution was being prepared. This movement voiced its objections, in particular to equal treatment at the federal level for the Autonomous Province of Kosovo. Fears were expressed that the state sovereignty of Serbia was being curtailed. The movement was kept under control as long as Tito was alive, but following his death in May 1980 and the unrest in Kosovo in 1981, it broke out all the more ferociously and reached its peak in the second half of the eighties, serving as a platform for the rise to power of Slobodan Milošević.

An emotional debate had taken place in 1968 in the Central Committee of the Serbian CP about the rise of an 'Albanian peril', incited by Dobrica Ćosić, one of the most popular writers of Serbia. He regarded Serbian culture in Kosovo as being jeopardized by rabid Albanian nationalism and decried the fact that many Serbs had been forced to leave Kosovo as a result of Albanian pressure. The issue of Serbian and Montenegrin 'emigration' from the province was thus put on the agenda of the party leadership and, twenty years later, would be used as a pretext to defend the measures taken by the Serbian government to curtail the autonomy of Kosovo.

Ćosić lost out in 1968 when the majority of members of the Serbian Central Committee rejected the allegation that political reasons were at the heart of Serbian and Montenegrin emigration from Kosovo. It was noted, in contradiction to Ćosić's allegations, that of the approximately 10,000 inhabitants of Kosovo who left the province annually, 9,000 were Albanians and only 1,000 were Serbs and Montenegrins. The weak economy was the cause of emigration. Ćosić was accordingly expelled from the party as a 'nationalist'.

In expressing his apprehensions about the consequences of further autonomy for Kosovo, this writer and veteran of the partisan war, who was also a member of the Serbian Academy of Sciences and Arts, was merely giving a voice to the emotions which would overflow throughout Serbia in the eighties.

Irritation among the Serbs, impatience among the Albanians

The Albanians celebrated the end of police oppression under Aleksandar Ranković as a national liberation. But there was also impatience, in particular among the young people of the province.

In his book 'The Kosovo Question' (*Kosovsko pitanje*), the Croatian economist Branko Horvat wrote:

"The social unrest among students in Belgrade during the first half of 1968 was echoed a few months later by students in Kosovo, with nationalist and irredentist tones. The Albanian flag had been illegal, and up to 1966, people were still being sent to prison for raising it. The official language of the administration was primarily Serbian. An irrational Albanization of everything now took its course... The gradual rise of nationalist euphoria was, however, accompanied by an increase in unemployment in the economically backward province. The underdevelopment of the region and the rise in unemployment there were the result of mistakes made in development and economic policies both in Kosovo and throughout the country. In the emotionally charged atmosphere reigning at the time, the isolation and underdevelopment of Kosovo were interpreted as discrimination caused by Slavic encirclement, in particular in view of the breakdown of normal cultural links with the province, transforming it into an economic and cultural ghetto. This, in turn, created a situation favourable to irredentist propaganda from Albania and from secret separatist groups within Kosovo. Any move could set off an avalanche..."

In November 1968, during the first demonstrations in Kosovo to result in fatal casualties, social, economic and political demands were accompanied by extremist, nationalist slogans. Among the slogans to be seen and heard were: "We want a university! Down with colonialism in Kosovo!" and even "Long live Albania, long live Enver Hoxha!" It is uncertain to what extent *agents provocateurs* and separatist groups had mingled with the crowds of demonstrating students. It was on this occasion that a demand first arose which was to play a major role in Kosovo politics for the next twenty years: "We want a republic!" What the protesters meant was that they wanted Kosovo to have the same status as the republics within the Yugoslav federation.

The constitutional amendments which were to give the autonomous provinces virtually the same status as the republics had not yet entered into force at the time. But even after the amendments and the new constitution came into effect by 1974, demands were still heard for a seventh republic within the Yugoslav federation, one with an Albanian majority. Such demands were not officially voiced by any leading Albanian politicians, but could, nonetheless, be read on leaflets, on walls and on protest banners. Whether it was articulated or not, the argument behind the demand was that the 1,200,000 Albanians in Kosovo (according to the 1971 census) should not be denied what the 1,100,000 Macedonians and 500,000 Montenegrins had both been accorded.

As far as Belgrade was concerned, the demand for a Republic of Kosovo was 'counter-revolutionary'. Branko Horvat noted that he could find "no good reason for this definition," but it was used anyway and was supported by the following arguments:

1.   Only the six founding nations of Yugoslavia (the Serbs, Croats, Slovenes, Moslems, Montenegrins and Macedonians) had the right to a republic of their own because they were sovereign. The Albanians as a people already enjoyed this right in their own country, i. e. in Albania. The Albanians in Yugoslavia were a national minority with no right to a republic of their own.

2.   In view of the right to self-determination, which includes the right to secession, an Albanian republic in Yugoslavia would, in the long run, lead to separation from Yugoslavia and to unification with the 'motherland'.

3.   If the Kosovo Albanians were to get a republic of their own, they would immediately want to include in their republic the 380,000 Albanians living in Macedonia, which would call into question the borders between the republics.

4.   The 1974 constitution gave Kosovo an autonomy status which, de facto, placed the province on an equal footing with the republics.

Stepchild of the Yugoslav economy

In economic terms, Kosovo was the most backward part of Yugoslavia at the end of the war. In 1948, 80.9% of the population made their living in agriculture. One hundred hectares of land were cultivated by an average of 183 farmers, an incredible overpopulation by European standards. There was hardly any industry, with the exception of the Trepcha lead and zinc complex which had belonged to a British firm before the war.

The ratio of the per capita gross national product in 1952 between Kosovo and Slovenia, the most prosperous part of the country, was 1 to 4.1. Between 1947 and 1952, the gross national product grew by 0.7% annually.

The economy of Kosovo was first given direct support in the second half of the fifties. Construction was begun on the Kosovo Polje thermal power station, more investments were made to exploit the substantial lignite reserves in the region, several factories and agricultural complexes were set up, and new roads were built. Nonetheless, per capita investment lagged well behind the national average for Yugoslavia. Up to the first half of the sixties, such investment was less than 39% of the national average. Industrial growth did increase following the establishment of a federal fund for the underdeveloped regions, but when compared to Yugoslavia as a whole, the economy of the autonomous province was still far behind. In 1965, per capita GNP in Kosovo was still less than one quarter (1 to 4.6) what it was in Slovenia.

The Brioni Plenum and the fall of Ranković marked an economic turning point for Kosovo. Substantial funds flowed into the province from the federal development fund. By 1970, per capita investment had reached about 80% of the national average. New sectors of the economy were created, but energy and mining continued to benefit most from such investments. Heavy industry, requiring much capital but creating comparatively few new jobs, remained in the lead with a volume of 61.4%. Manufacturing represented only 38.6% of total industrial production.

By the late seventies, the economy of Kosovo was developing at a more rapid pace. Annual growth reached 11%, employment in the state sector rose by an annual 7.2%, the per capita GNP was three times higher than it had been immediately after the war and rose to 800 dollars a year. Between 1948 and 1981, the proportion of the population working in agriculture sank from 80.9% to 54.6%. Agricultural production rose by about 4.4% in approximately the same period.

Despite this, the discrepancy between the economic development of Kosovo and that of the rest of Yugoslavia was still growing. By 1981, the ratio of the per capita GNP between Kosovo and Slovenia was 1 to 5.4, and by 1984 1 to 6.1.

The gap widened not only compared to the more affluent parts of the country, but even when compared to the other underdeveloped regions, such as Macedonia, Bosnia-Hercegovina and Montenegro. In 1979, per capita GNP was only 28% of the Yugoslav average, while it was 67% of that of Macedonia, 65% of that of Bosnia, and 69% of that of Montenegro.

According to economists, the continued underdevelopment of Kosovo was fostered by too little investment and investment in the wrong sectors. In the last planned period before the economic crisis of 1976-1980, not even half the proposed investments were actually carried out. Almost 60% of funds were allocated to the energy sector and to non-ferrous metallurgy.

Jens Reuter of the *Südost-Institut* in Munich described Kosovo's economic development as follows:

"The structure of investments made in Kosovo is one of the reasons for the conspicuous lack of jobs. Unemployment should have been fought by investments in labour-intensive industry rather than in capital-intensive sectors such as heavy industry and energy. In 1985, unemployment in Kosovo was 3.33 times the Yugoslav average."

One reason for the lack of investment in Kosovo is the belief that work ethics were particularly weak there. The mistaken belief that Albanian workers are lazy is still widespread in Serbia. On top of this, a visit to Prishtina suffices for one to realize that a good deal of investment funds were squandered on prestige projects catering to the communist oligarchy. With its pompous highrises, banks and sixteen-floor Grand Hotel plunked into a virtually destitute region, and with a population which has grown from 14,000 to 140,000 since the end of the war, Prishtina looks like a ridiculous imitation of Manhattan.

The poorhouse of Europe:
huge families and mass unemployment

The population explosion is one of the reasons and, at the same time, one of the consequences of poverty in Kosovo. Families need children to support them, a system which has proven its worth in times of crisis. Children mean security in old age in a society which has no confidence in the possible benefits of the welfare state. The Serbs, for their part, regard the population explosion among the Kosovo Albanians, who have the highest birth rates in Europe, as an anti-Serbian plot, lamenting: "They are giving birth to soldiers to fight against us!" and "With all the children they have, they are trying to make Kosovo ethnically pure!" Nor are the Serbs to be persuaded of the contrary by the fact that the Albanians have an equally high birth rate in regions where there are no Serbs at all and that everywhere on earth, it is the poor who have the most children.

Family planning is impossible in Kosovo at the moment, due in good part to a lack of sex education in the population, but also, and perhaps more importantly, because all Albanians, both men and women, are convinced that any attempt by the government to introduce birth control is nothing but a Serbian plot to 'exterminate' them.

The extremely rapid growth in population has had a disastrous effect on the economy. No society, and certainly not that of an underdeveloped region like Kosovo, can support such a trend. In 1921, there were 410,000 Albanians in Yugoslavia. Today there are about 2,500,000. As Croatian sociologist Stipe Šuvar calculated in 1981, there would be about 1,000,000 Albanians in Kosovo today if birth rates had conformed to the average for the rest of Yugoslavia. Seen from the opposite perspective, if all of Yugoslavia had Albanian birth rates, the country would now have 50,000,000 inhabitants instead of 23,500,000. The annual population increase in Kosovo is 25.1%, compared to 3.8% in Croatia. It is no wonder, therefore, that economic development could not keep pace.

When Tito opened the borders in the mid-sixties so that Yugoslav citizens could travel and work abroad freely, he gave impetus to two phenomena which helped camouflage the weaknesses of the system and of the economy for a number of years. Firstly, there was a substantial flow into the country of foreign currency from Yugoslav *gastarbeiters* working in the developed countries. The corresponding increase in purchasing power by their families at home did much to stimulate local business. The new homes constructed in the countryside and in the suburbs of major cities created the impression of a dynamically developing society. Secondly, emigration was an excellent means, politically speaking, of preventing or at least postponing political unrest arising from discontent with social and economic developments. This was especially true of Kosovo where discontent was greatest and the protest loudest.

The economic underdevelopment of Kosovo is particularly evident from the following figures. In 1979, in other words before the outbreak of the Serbian-Albanian conflict, Kosovo contributed a mere 2.1% to the GNP of Yugoslavia although it constituted 7.8% of the population of the country. In comparison, in the same year Croatia contributed 26.1% to the GNP with a population representing 19.6% of the total. Unemployment in Kosovo was the highest in all of Yugoslavia, with a rate of 43.4% in 1983. According to a study carried out in 1988 by the Belgrade Centre for Demographic Research, the unemployment figure for all of Yugoslavia was 25.9%.

There are no absolute figures available for unemployment in Kosovo, or at least no reliable figures, since very few Albanians are registered as unemployed. No one with a roof over his head and supported by his family is officially considered unemployed. The authorities have no compelling reason to publish the actual level of employment because a lower figure is to their political advantage. Western observers estimate that there were about 250,000 persons out of work in Kosovo in the early eighties. The official figure was 72,000. The situation becomes even more dramatic when we consider that over 52% of the people of Kosovo are under the age of nineteen. Of the 72,000 individuals officially unemployed at the time, 73% were under the age of thirty.

A statistic from 1985 serves to illustrate the strong ethnic imbalance in unemployment figures. Of 600 persons holding jobs in Kosovo, 109 were Albanians, 228 were Serbs and 258 were Montenegrins. By way of contrast, it must be remembered that the

Albanians represented 77.5% of the population and the Serbs and Montenegrins a mere 15%.

It comes as no surprise, therefore, that members of the new academic generation who have enjoyed a better education than their parents and who understand the significance of developments in society, are the ones to take to the barricades to voice their social and economic grievances.

The beginning of the end. Who was pulling the strings?

March 11, 1981 will be remembered in the history of Kosovo as the beginning of the end, the beginning of the end of the upward-looking developments in the province which had begun with the fall of the brutal Serbian police chief Aleksandar Ranković, Tito's right-hand man, and which reached their zenith with the Constitution of 1974 and the opening of the Serbian offensive against this very constitution.

Things all began one afternoon with a rather innocent protest at the university in Prishtina. The students protested against the quality of food served at the university cafeteria, against mismanagement in the kitchen, against the long line-ups at mealtimes, against the depressing lighting in the cafeteria and, in general, against their poor living and study conditions in over-crowded dormitories and lecture halls.

It was a relatively small group of protesters that gathered within the university initially, but then several hundred of the students took to the streets and marched downtown along Marshall Tito boulevard. The usual evening promenade along the boulevard was exceptionally lively on that mild spring evening. A lot of people had just come back from the stadium after watching a game between the 'Partizan' team from Belgrade and the local Prishtina team, which had ended peacefully in a victory for the Serbian side.

The demonstrators called for improvements in university facilities and moved on towards the party headquarters. Both university professors and party officials endeavoured to calm the students down and talked to them for about an hour. Their presence seemed to have done the trick initially, for the protesters began to return towards the student dormitories. But then, suddenly, a group of about 200 students arrived from another direction, shouting, "We demand the release of our fellow students!" The news that protesters had been arrested spread like wildfire. Other slogans were shouted against the party leadership in Kosovo. Using tear gas, the police set upon the crowd which had been joined by many curious passers-by and had now swollen to several thousands. Fighting broke out and the students began throwing stones. A total of 18 people were injured, including two policemen who were seriously wounded.

"I was afraid a revolution would break out," admitted party chief Mahmut Bakalli in a conversation in December 1991 to explain why he had called out the province's security forces. The brutality of the police was to have disastrous consequences. Bakalli spend hours with the students on the evening after the demonstration to persuade them that things would improve at the university and promised that no one would be prosecuted. In return, he insisted that the students pledge not to take to the streets anymore.

The Yugoslav public first learned of the demonstration two weeks after it had taken place, that is, after the events of 26 March which were to shake the whole country profoundly.

According to Bakalli, there was much hectic activity behind the scenes in the days between 11 and 26 March. Obscure political groups and factions geared up for action, and all sides tried to use the situation to their own advantage.

Had Enver Hoxha found an opportunity to weaken the Yugoslavia of his ex-rival, the 'revisionist' Tito, by promoting oppositional Kosovo Albanians? Tirana must have known that its dreams of a greater Albania and political unrest in Kosovo were not to the strategical advantage of Enver Hoxha's rule. As far as can be determined today, only tiny groups of dogmatic communists in Kosovo, devoid of political influence, regarded Hoxha's Albania as their native land.

The extensive autonomy which had been granted to Kosovo was, on the other hand, a thorn in the flesh of the Serbian nationalists and extremists in the province and in Serbia proper. That the troubles in Kosovo escalated to such an extent one year after Tito's death leads us to suspect that it was these groups who recognized the time had come for action.

There has also been speculation that both sides, the Yugoslav/Serbian UDBA (secret police) and the secret service of the Serbian-dominated Yugoslav People's Army KOS on the one hand, and the Sigurimi (the Albanian secret police) on the other, were interested in destabilizing Kosovo, though for very different reasons.

Although there has been no concrete evidence to support such speculation, there can be no doubt, as subsequent events have shown, that it was the Serbian nationalists who profited most.

The violence escalates

Though hectic political manoeuvring was under way behind the scenes between 11 and 26 March, everything remained calm on the surface, as if the events had been forgotten. Students in Prishtina kept faithfully to the campus and waited for the promised improvements to come about. Therefore, the news broadcast on the afternoon of 25 March announcing that a demonstration had taken place in Prizren, a tranquil town some 75 km south of the capital, struck like a bolt of lightning.

The demonstration began at noon with about thirty students invading the joint courtyard of the Pedagogical Institute and the Teacher Training College and shouting protests in Albanian about their miserable teaching and living conditions. According to Serbian newspaper reports, not many other students from the two institutions took part in the demonstration. A few window panes were broken before the protesters set off for the School of Medicine and its dormitory. On their way, some shop windows were smashed and a police vehicle was overturned. Most passers-by avoided the demonstrators. Some indeed harangued them. No one else joined in.

When the security forces blocked the road, the demonstrators threw stones at them. One policeman was injured. The whole event lasted no more than an hour. The protesters included students from various schools, some of them from near-by Suhareka / Suva Reka.

The fact that, in contrast to the events of 11 March in Prishtina, no other students and passers-by joined in on the demonstration leads to the supposition that the whole thing had been a provocation, and a badly organized one at that. But who could have been behind it, and for what reasons?

An analysis of the events of 26 March 1981 can perhaps help clarify things. March 26 was a day to remember in Prishtina for two reasons. Firstly, an outdoor reception was to be held in the city centre to welcome the Youth Relay Teams who were expected to arrive at 5 p.m. The annual Youth Relay, passing through all parts of Yugoslavia, culminated on Tito's birthday, 25 May, in a Youth Festival at the Army Stadium in Belgrade. Lampposts and houses throughout Prishtina were decked out in flags. Groups of students and workers, organized by the Socialist Alliance, were to be bussed in from other parts of the province to line the streets of the capital.

Quite independently of the festivities, a group of university students had gathered in the early hours of the morning on the lawn in front of the university building. Heated discussions were already under way with party officials and professors about the unsatisfactory conditions at the university. Much mention was made of the promised improvements which had still not been carried out. A demand was also made, in a more aggressive tone, for the release of the students taken into custody on 11 March and still in detention.

The students eventually lost patience and took to the streets. There were now several hundred of them bearing banners expressing their demands. But there were also nationalist slogans to be seen, "Kosovo for the Kosovars", "We are Albanians, not Yugoslavs" and "Republic status for Kosovo". According to Serbian news reports, no passers-by joined the demonstration this time either.

Suddenly, special units of the Serbian police appeared on the scene. Blocking off the streets through the centre of town which were to be used by the Rally Teams, they advanced on the demonstrators who retreated to the university dormitories. The police stormed the dorms and with extreme brutality began beating up students, regardless of whether they had taken part in the demonstration or not. The screams of the students could be heard out on the streets and the news of the beatings spread quickly. This time it was not Bakalli, head of the CP of Kosovo, who called in the security forces. It was Rrahman Morina, minister of the interior in the province, who turned to his federal counterpart Franjo Herljević for 'assistance'. Bakalli later demanded that a commission be set up to investigate the 'abuse of force' on the part of the federal police. "The commission never did anything at all," says Bakalli today.

According to the official toll, twenty-three demonstrators and fourteen policemen were injured. Twenty-one people, among them the 'ringleaders of the riot', were arrested.

Neither that day nor the days following did the Yugoslav public learn what had happened in Prishtina. Belgrade television broadcast the news of the arrival of the Youth Rally with video footage - taken from a previous year's newscast.

"Hostile forces" - a useful term

On 28 March, the 'Demonstrations of 11 and 26 March at the student dormitories in Prishtina' were first officially mentioned during an extraordinary session of the Socialist Alliance in Prishtina. The events were described as "hostile, and organized by hostile forces as part of a hostile plot to destabilize Yugoslavia and destroy its unity as a state, using economic and social problems as a pretext".

Such wording alleging unspecified 'hostile forces', common throughout the Stalinist period, was to be used more and more in the days, weeks and months that followed. This typical party terminology was designed on the one hand to snuff out criticism of the miserable state of affairs in the province which had triggered the demonstration, and on the other hand to make it clear that, 'to protect Yugoslavia', a resolute and unequivocal response would be forthcoming. Accusations were also made, in the traditional manner, against the 'foreign press' for reporting on 'people allegedly arrested and injured' during the riot of 11 March, although it was 'well known' that no such cases existed.

The situation was to become even more explosive. Between 31 March and 2 April, hefty and bloody confrontations took place between demonstrators and the security forces in Prishtina and in a number of smaller towns in Kosovo. This time it was not only the students who took to the barricades. Workers in industry also left their jobs to join the angry demonstrators protesting against the brutal force which had been exercised by members of the security forces from all over Yugoslavia. (One must not forget in this respect that family bonds are particularly close among Albanians. If one Albanian student is beaten up or arrested by the police, at least a hundred people ranging from close family members to distant relatives are emotionally affected.)

"It is a nightmare that won't go away," said a Prishtina girl to a reporter from the Belgrade daily newspaper *Politika* to describe what she had experienced. Witnesses spoke of "incredible brutality".

On 2 April, a state of siege was imposed over the whole region. Using tanks, the army sealed off Prishtina. Aircraft circled around the capital day and night. The military was also deployed in Podujeva / Podujevo and Ferizaj / Uroševac. In contrast to earlier demonstrations, the media now provided prompt and detailed coverage of the events. The numer of casualties, however, was first announced on 6 April at a press conference in Belgrade for Yugoslav and foreign journalists: 11 dead (including 2 policemen) and 57 injured.

The official figures were regarded with a good deal of suspicion. Both Serbs and Albanians spoke of a much larger number of casualties. Even today, there are still no reliable statistics. One can assume that about one hundred Albanians died in the riots. It is certain that many of the injured were not treated in hospital because their families were fearful of reprisals.

Yugoslavia was shocked. This was not the first serious show of opposition in the country. There had been earlier signs of discontent, in particular in 1968 in Kosovo and later on in Croatia. It was, however, the first occurrence of massive, repeated and bloody confrontations between the population and the security forces. It was also the first time the army had been deployed.

The state of siege was lifted gradually in Kosovo so that primary schools could reopen by 13 April and secondary schools a few days later. At the university and at the colleges in various towns the situation was officially normalized a few weeks later, but in actual fact remained extremely tense. The state of siege was only completely rescinded at the start of the following winter.

'Purges' in Kosovo
- consternation in Yugoslavia

The trials conducted against the demonstrators and so-called 'ringleaders' went on for years. Proceedings took place behind closed doors. Access was technically authorized, but only a chosen few were actually allowed to attend the trials.

The party underwent a so-called process of 'differentiation', sanctioned by the Serbian Central Committee in its 'Resolution on Events in Kosovo.'

A number of leading party officials and hundreds of rank and file members were purged. The first spectacular step was the resignation of party head Mahmut Bakalli on 5 May 1981. All that seeped out of the endless party meetings and discussions at all levels were the same old phrases and the same old accusations. What surprised many people, however, was the repeated statement that only a 'small group' of individuals was involved. Why then had the police, the security forces and the legal system reacted with such vehemence and severity?

The key word in all discussions, public statements and commentaries was 'counter-revolution', a notion with often lethal consequences for the victims. The use of this term was allegedly based on the fact that the call for 'republic status for Kosovo' was aimed at detaching a part of Yugoslavia from the rest of the federation and uniting it with Albania to create a Greater Albania. With this tactic, Serbian politicians endeavoured to disguise the fact that the crisis was a problem between Serbia and the Albanian majority in Kosovo and present it in terms of a Yugoslav problem.

This interpretation also ignored the fact that the vast majority of Albanians did not regard the demand for a republic of their own as anti-Yugoslav. On the contrary, the Albanians in Kosovo had every reason to be grateful to Tito for the status he had given the province after 1966. And they were indeed grateful.

The demand for equality with the other 'state-forming' peoples of the multi-ethnic federation would have required a change in the constitution, but not the 'destruction' of Yugoslavia. Croats, Slovenes, Bosnians and other Yugoslavs were not disturbed by the thought, but for Serbia, a Republic of Kosovo would have meant a major loss of land and economic resources, not to mention of prestige within the country as a whole. The Macedonians were also against a Republic of Kosovo because the demand was linked to a change in Kosovo's borders with Macedonia, Montenegro and southern Serbia. The Albanians of Macedonia, who constitute 30 to 35% of the population there, demanded that the areas of Macedonia with an Albanian majority be incorporated into a Republic of Kosovo. This demand was - and still is - subject to debate, but was not a major element in the movement of 1981. It was simply in the interests of Serbian policy to interpret the demand for a Republic of Kosovo in this light. The gravest consequence of the events of the spring of 1981, however, was the immediate start of a ruthless campaign against the Albanian population of Kosovo in all Serbian media.

There were of course protests in the non-Serbian media against false, inaccurate and late reporting, and a Yugoslavia-wide debate about the legal system which condemned the mostly very young 'counter-revolutionaries' to extremely long prison sentences. Horror and dismay were felt throughout the country at Serbia's unbound ambitions over the autonomous province. Slovenian politicians in particular were the first to recognize that it was Serbian policies that were jeopardizing the existence of the federation as a whole. The Slovenian communists decided at that time to go their 'own way' so as not to be caught up in the tide of Serbian expansionism.

The dilemma of the Albanian communists and that of the security forces

The term 'counter-revolutionary' did not appear in a joint declaration issued by the Central Committees of Serbia and Kosovo right after the riots of April 1981. The president of the province, Xhavid Nimani, had however spoken of 'counter-revolution' in his appeal to the people of Kosovo on 2 April. The strongest condemnation of events was made on 5 April by the Albanian member of the Yugoslav state presidium, Fadil Hoxha. There was much talk of the 'socialism of self-administration' which was said to be a thorn in the flesh of 'counter-revolutionary' circles in Kosovo. According to Fadil Hoxha at the time, the full realization of this system would solve all the problems in Kosovo. He also announced that Yugoslavia would offer even more generous economic assistance to Kosovo to help it out of its economic woes. In view of the disastrous economic situation throughout Yugoslavia, this announcement was treated with scorn.

At a press conference for foreign journalists on 17 April, Mahmut Bakalli made a radical change in his usual strategy of playing down criticism, discontent and open opposition among the Albanians. His attitude was now one of total surrender to the position of the Serbian leadership. He did not, however, use the term 'counter-revolution'. The speech of 4 May in which Bakalli offered his resignation caused a good deal of dismay among the Albanians. His change of heart was evident from the very start of the speech: "I agree with the judgement that the demonstrations were hostile and counter-revolutionary..." He also accused the leadership in Albania of being responsible for an "abuse of the co-operation between our two countries."

Bakalli had enjoyed the confidence of his compatriots. Even non-communist Albanians had regarded him as an official who supported the interests of Kosovo at the federal level. The fact that he and his fellow colleagues from other parts of Yugoslavia were also looking after their own personal interests was not grounds for open criticism at the time. There is no doubt that he played a part in improving university and school education in Kosovo, but he also bore responsibility for the economic stagnation of the province. Huge sums were poured into grandiose projects, international loans were badly used, and the bank accounts of development agencies, into which all the republics had transferred considerable funds, were plundered. He paid next to no attention to the steadily rising unemployment figures.

One very delicate issue in the analysis of the demonstrations and their causes is the role played by the security forces. Mahmut Bakalli had called in the Albanian police to quell the student riot of 11 March. On 2 March, it was the provincial minister of the interior who had appealed to Belgrade for 'fraternal assistance'. Special units of the federal police were called into Kosovo. At the same time, both the 'territorial defence force' and the reserves were mobilized. The 'territorial defence force' is part of the Yugoslav defence system and is financed and organized by all the republics and provinces. Its main objective is to defend strategic sites and installations. The weapons of the 'territorial defence force' are stored in special depots and its units are subordinate to the high command of the Yugoslav People's Army.

At the above-mentioned press conference at the beginning of April, Stane Dolanc, Slovenian member of the presidium of the CPY, noted typically that, "the Yugoslav People's Army was not involved in the confrontation at all. Its duty is simply to guard specific objects... The security forces were expressly ordered not to use fire arms. The first two victims were among the demonstrators. It was the demonstrators themselves who opened fire on the crowd and killed two of their people... It is absolutely certain that the bullets did not stem from the security forces because they had not yet used their weapons..."

According to Albanians who witnessed the events, both the Albanian police and the Yugoslav, i.e. Serbian security forces were responsible for the bloodbath. The Serbs alleged that the Albanian demonstrators had pushed women and children into the front row to make it difficult for the security forces to 'defend themselves'. Only gradually did they succeed in pushing the women and children aside and getting them out of the danger zone.

The fact that two policemen and eleven demonstrators were killed is evidence enough that the security forces were not simply defending themselves passively. Albanian doctors who treated Albanian protesters spoke of numerous bullet wounds. It is highly unlikely that these wounds were inflicted by people on their own side.

In the autumn of 1981, a group of doctors was invited to take part in a meeting in Prishtina with the Serbian minister of health and social affairs. "We felt as if we were on trial," reported one of the participants. Facing them was not only the minister, but also representatives of the army who wanted more specific information about whom the doctors had treated, what sort of treatment they had provided, what types of injuries they had encountered and who had donated blood for the patients. According to the Albanian doctors, the meeting was held because the military did not trust the official statistics (11 dead and 121 injured). The army believed that the real figure of those injured must have been much higher. Albanian doctors also reported with considerable bitterness that, during the demonstrations at the beginning of April, their Serbian colleagues had refused to treat wounded Albanians.

During a visit to the town of Podujeva / Podujevo on the afternoon of 2 April 1981, we (three foreign journalists) witnessed a unit of the local Albanian territorial defence force returning from their deployment. The stench of tear gas still lingered in the air. The young men in their blue uniforms had just removed their helmets and gas masks, and we could see how shaken and exhausted they were. And no wonder. Aside from the fact that this was probably their first 'real' mission, they had found themselves in the moral dilemma. The Albanian security forces had been used to put down a number of riots even before 1981, in particular those involving young students in Kosovo, and had been none too gentle about doing so either. At the time, they could still identify their actions with the interests of their country, especially since they had been drilled to stamp out all unrest from the very start in order to maintain public order in Kosovo. Now the Albanian security forces were wondering whether they had not been taken over by the Serbian command. They were being used in a bloody conflict which was no longer a purely Kosovo affair, but one which had taken on a Yugoslav dimension.

The Albanian police and the officers of the territorial defence force had been recruited from the ranks of reliable communist party members. For Kosovo Albanians, party membership not only provided particular advantages but was often a necessity of life. No Albanian could get a good job or an apartment without being a party member. The 90,000 or so individuals who had joined the party enjoyed obvious privileges which contrasted sharply with the general economic misery in the province.

The worsening of the political situation as a consequence of the events of spring 1981 placed all Albanian communists, not just high party officials, in a moral dilemma. They were forced to choose between their loyalty to their people, which automatically meant that their privileges and material existence were at stake, and their loyalty to the Yugoslav state and its leadership which had conferred substantial autonomy on Kosovo, an autonomy that was now being jeopardized.

Deep-rooted Serbian fears: emigration, expulsion, genocide

The fact that more and more Serbian families have been leaving Kosovo, including families who have lived there for generations, has been portrayed in the Serbian media since 1981 as a national tragedy. Such reporting has often included the term 'genocide'. Whether or not this term was consciously employed by the political leadership or simply occurred spontaneously, it does reflect deep-rooted Serbian fears.

Both in Serbian politics and in Serbian literature, the same argument is encountered time and again: the Serbs have been misunderstood and humiliated, their very survival is at stake. Serbian identity is a combination of dreams of Serbian heroism and grief over lost Serbian grandeur. Out of these dreams and grief, coupled with pain and anger at unfulfilled ambitions and a feeling of being isolated and misunderstood, has arisen an ideology that is out of touch with reality. Thus the Serbs can be manipulated by their politicians, who take advantage of their nationalist feelings, as the Serbian communists have done since 1981. The Serbs naively believe what they dread the most - that the existence of the Serbian people in Kosovo is jeopardized by the rights Tito conferred on the Albanians. These fears became all the more real when they came to realize that, in the period from 1961 to 1981, the Slavic population in Kosovo fell from 27.5% to 14.9% of the total.

Ever since 1968, after the first serious riots in Kosovo involving loss of life, there has been much talk in Serbian circles of mass emigration and indeed of the expulsion of Serbian and Montenegrin families from Kosovo. The Serbs in Kosovo were convinced that their security was in jeopardy.

This topic was taboo in public for a long time because it would have caused "friction between the peoples and national minorities." In 1981, the Slovene politician Stane Dolanc typically declared, "It is not true that the Serbs [in Kosovo] have emigrated and settled in Serbia since 1968. The few of those who did emigrate departed before 1968..." Economic reasons were at the heart of Serbian emigration since their position in Kosovo changed radically after the fall of Aleksandar Ranković. Up to that time, they had enjoyed extensive privileges and were disproportionately represented in the administration, in business and in the police. After 1966, they were confronted with the fact that the Albanians were taking full advantage of their new status.

Jobs in Kosovo now required a knowledge of the Albanian language. Albanian employees in companies where managers spoke only Serbian refused to follow orders, even though they understood the language, which they had learned in school. The police, the legal system and other sectors of public life were quickly 'Albanicized'.

Independent observers note that, while some pressure was exerted by the Albanians, it was primarily economic reasons which prompted Serbian families to leave Kosovo. It should also be noted that Serbs and Montenegrins also emigrated from regions in which they formed an absolute majority. There are no reliable statistics on the total number of Serbian emigrants from Kosovo from 1966 to 1991. The Serbian side refers to figures of between 200,000 and 400,000 and has repeatedly alleged in this connection that the security of Serbs in Kosovo is in jeopardy. This may be true for those Serbian party officials and police officers who were obliged at the local level to enforce regulations and guidelines set up by Aleksandar Ranković. Nor is it unthinkable that some Albanians whose relatives had been mistreated during the Ranković era, believed after 1966 that the time had come to take vengeance. What is certain is that a hard core of former Ranković collaborators is still active in Kosovo. They are members of the fanatically anti-Albanian Bozhur League which is busy implementing

Belgrade's policies in Kosovo and is responsible for many acts of brutality committed against Albanians.

What the future Patriarch had to report on emigration

It was extremely difficult during this period, not only for foreign observers but also for Yugoslavs themselves, to ascertain what was true in the muddle of false allegations, mutual accusations and panic. The closest we can come to reliable figures on the emigration or 'expulsion' of the Serbian inhabitants of Kosovo can be seen in the reports of the Orthodox bishop of the diocese of Rashka-Prizren, which more or less coincides with the territory of Kosovo.

Bishop Pavle, now Patriarch of the Serbian Orthodox Church, reported the following on 12 May 1959 to the Holy Synod:

> "There is also pressure on us in this region, the repercussions of which could become disastrous. I am referring to the continuous emigration of our people. When I was in Devići last winter, my host offered to sell me the last three houses in the neighbouring village of Ludovice for the monastery, otherwise he would sell them to the Shiptars. In the Turkish era before the First World War, there were 17 (Serbian) homes in this village and just as many Albanian houses. The people left their homes after that war. There are only six left. Now the last three families are leaving. It is the same everywhere in the region. In Vitomirica near Peć, which was settled after the First World War, there was not a single Shiptar house. Now there are 100. In Dobruša there were no Albanian houses either. Now there are 160, etc., etc."

Two years later, on 27 April 1961, the bishop reported:

> "We remained concerned about the unchecked emigration of our people, which is taking place more or less throughout the eparchy. Some say it is due to a fear of reprisals by the Shiptars and Turks, should political turmoil take root in the region. We have all felt their aggression at one time or another recently. Others allege that those in power give preference to the many Shiptars in the administration who support one another and who give legal preference to their own people. Where the Serbs are

concerned, they enforce the full extent of all regulations, though always in a perfectly legal manner. Serbian party members are involved in this, too, so that no one can accuse the Shiptars of chauvinism and the like. Our people cannot survive economically and, as a consequence, they emigrate. There are other reasons, too: jobs in industry, better education for the children, etc., grounds which are both understandable and justifiable. But the most important factors are the first two, which, in my estimation, are the major causes for the disturbing level of emigration."

Six years later, in April 1967, Bishop Pavle pointed to new reasons for emigration:

"The rate of emigration seems to have declined somewhat last year though the general trend and the reasons remain the same, indeed they have perhaps become more acute. Since the Fourth Plenary Session and the reorganization of the Secret Service in particular, the emigration of Serbs from Kosovo and Metohija has been explained here in the following manner: Ranković and his clique are the ones behind Serbian emigration, which provides them with arguments against the Shiptars. We do not know to what extent emigration is attributable to this or to other reasons. We do know that after the Fourth Plenary Session, the Serbs in general were made responsible for the mistakes said to have been made in this region by Ranković and other members of the Secret Service, something which has made our position here even more difficult."

Ten years later, on 1 April 1977, the bishop noted:

"Emigration of our people continues unabated. When I first arrived in the eparchy twenty years ago, there were two parishes and two priests in Podujevo with over a thousand households. Five years ago, when the current priest arrived, there were still 610 households. Now there are only 350... In my talks with government officials, I have been told that our people are emigrating for economic reasons, to enjoy the advantages which a big city has to offer, better education for the children, better jobs, etc. These reasons do exist and certainly play a role. We have never denied this. But worst of all is the organized pressure coming from a number of citizens of Albanian nationality. People are harassed and attacked in order to create an atmosphere of insecurity which makes emigration look inevitable. In many places people are told outright: 'Get out. This is not Serbian land!'"

The bishop's reports refer to attacks carried out against priests, monks and nuns, to arbitrary rulings against institutions of the church, and to the unauthorized take-over or utilization of property belonging to the church and monasteries. But such things also happened before the Albanians had any say in Kosovo, when the Serbian communists were in power.

Bishop Pavle's predecessor in the Rashka-Prizren diocese, Bishop Vladimir reported in March 1954 for instance:

"It must be noted that arbitary acts are committed by the authorities against church property. There are many cases in which heavy taxes have been imposed or in which church land or buildings have been confiscated. A building belonging to the church was taken over in the village of Dechani (Dečani); church-goers in Peć were forbidden access to the chapel, the pulpit and the rectory even though the entrance was on church property. In the village of Ljubista, the municipal council is using church property for its offices and refuses to pay rent. When the church demanded that rent be paid, the municipal council simply declared that the building was not church property. Since there are no documents available and no one has the courage to confirm the church's universally recognized ownership of the property, nothing can be done... Property rights are being questioned at the Monastery of Visoke Dečani, too. When land was confiscated, the monastery lost fertile fields right beside the complex. In compensation, it received 15 hectares of barren land 15 kilometers away..."

One can conclude from these reports that much of the harassment and persecution which the Serbs suffered in Kosovo after 1966 when the position of the Albanians in their autonomous province improved, was not the result solely of Albanian nationalism, but derived rather from a tradition which the Serbian communists exploited, using it against the Albanians for nationalist reasons and against the Orthodox

Church for ideological reasons. Nonetheless, the Serbian Orthodox Church was not the only religious denomination which suffered under the communist regime in Yugoslavia.

Scapegoats and prejudice

After 1981, the Serbian media began waging an open campaign against the Albanians in connection with the emigration or 'expulsion' of the Serbs and Montenegrins from Kosovo. It was alleged, for instance, that the Albanians were raping Serbian women and girls, that they were beating up Serbian men, burning their fields, rustling their cattle, destroying their churches and cemeteries.

Reports that Serbian nuns in Kosovo had been raped by Albanians caused an uproar in Serbia. The victims were identified as nuns of the convent of Peja / Peć. These allegations were repeated for years on end and it is unlikely that any Serbs doubted the truth of the reports. And yet, the mother superior of the convent declared in the spring of 1991 that she knew of no such cases.

In the autumn of 1990, a group of respectable and politically independent legal experts and sociologists published a study in Belgrade which dealt critically with the image of the Albanians created by political circles in Serbia and with the situation of the Serbs in Kosovo. They paid particular attention to the alleged 'rapes' and 'expulsions'. The study showed that over twice as many charges were laid for rape in Serbia proper as in Kosovo, where the figure was about half the average for Yugoslavia and far below the rate in the Vojvodina. Between 1979 and 1987, of the 323 cases of rape or attempted rape reported in Kosovo, only 9.6% were committed by Albanians against Serbian and Montenegrin women. (From 1982, the annual figure decreased and between 1987 and 1989 no cases were registered at all).

It was also alleged that the Albanian offenders were not being apprehended and that, for nationalist reasons, the local police and justice system were not interested in prosecuting such cases.

One of the examples of allegations that Albanians were desecrating Serbian sanctuaries involved a fire which broke out in part of the Patriarchate in Peja / Peć on 16 March 1981. The building in question, the residence of the Patriarch from Belgrade, was uninhabited at the time of the fire and was severely damaged. Parts of the precious library were saved by the priests and nuns.

Rumour immediately spread among the Serbs that the Albanians had set the fire. The late arrival of the fire brigade and the technical difficulties in combating the fire were also attributed to Albanian 'sabotage'. The Serbian Orthodox Church in Belgrade fanned the flames of hatred too, although none of the commissions set up managed to identify the arsonists.

Interestingly enough, until 1981, the Monastery of Peja / Peć had been guarded for generations by a family of Albanian Moslems. Seasonal workers from the region were regularly employed by the monastery up to 1990 and were regarded as reliable. Whether they decided of their own accord no longer to seek employment at the monastery or whether they were prevented by fanatical relatives from doing so is not known. In any case, the Albanians have always treated the many Serbian monasteries built in Kosovo over the centuries with great respect.

The fact that the Serbs regard the emigration of their compatriots from the province as an 'expulsion' by aggressive and nationalistic Albanians seeking an 'ethnically pure' Kosovo and that they attribute all sorts of wicked deeds to the Albanians, is not solely a result of the contemporary political situation. It stems also from profound differences between the two peoples, differences of a historical, religious, social and cultural nature.

For many Serbs in Belgrade, the Shiptars, as they call the Albanians, are nothing more than seasonal workers who shovel coal into the cellars, repair furnaces in the winter, sweep the streets, take any type of occasional work in the vegetable markets and live in incredibly primitive cramped quarters. That their work is usually appreciated by their Serbian employers and that they are regarded as particularly reliable does nothing to alter this one-sided view. Nor are these Serbs impressed by the fact that Albanians also live and work away from home in other parts of Yugoslavia where they carry on trades as confectioners, silversmiths, artisans and merchants just the same as workers of other nationalities.

In Kosovo itself, Orthodox Serbs nurture feelings of superiority and distrust towards the Albanians, most of whom are Moslems, in particular because of the differences in the ways of life of the two peoples. The urban Serbs are, to put it briefly, more modern. The Albanians live in a more traditional clan culture and are more isolated than the Serbs from western influence. In the course of history, they have had little opportunity to manifest their culture abroad. The Serbs are generally uninformed about Albanian literature, painters or composers. They know of the Albanians at most through their handicrafts, their folk music and their impressive folk dances.

Although the Serbs themselves, as inhabitants of the Balkans, are none too fastidious when it comes to government laws and regulations, the Albanians are much more suspicious of authority and more likely to ignore laws. Only for short periods of time in the course of their history have they ever been confronted with a government authority which they could regard as their own. Authority for the Albanians has almost always been that of the foreign occupier and oppressor. As a result, they tend to ignore written laws and to avoid confrontation with the legislative authorities whenever they can.

Many people in Kosovo drive without a licence. Many simply do not pay their rent or their taxes. Of course, a good number of Serbs do the same. The Balkan mentality here has been compounded by the after-effects of the communist system which was tolerant of the 'privileged'. But even 'normal' citizens are none too quick at fulfilling their 'duties'. For various reasons, no community spirit has ever taken root. The municipal administration in Prishtina did not function well before 1989. Garbage was strewn across sidewalks and down staircases, and heaped in parks and courtyards behind apartment buildings. Now the situation is even worse. The Serbs have taken over the municipal administration and the Albanian population refuses to co-operate.

It is in this context that one must understand surveys which point to a rejection, dislike and mistrust of the Albanians by the Serbs in general, and in particular by students. They consider the Albanians 'backward', 'hostile to other peoples', 'withdrawn', 'uncouth', 'irascible', 'lazy' and 'selfish'. The majority of those surveyed would refuse to share the same republic with them, the same neighbourhood, the same group or indeed the same room, or to accept an Albanian as a spouse, a colleague or employer.

In a study published in 1987 in Belgrade, Dragan Pantić showed that for young Serbs, the Albanians came last on a list of twenty nationalities to be considered for the choice of a spouse. They were preceded by the Turks, the Arabs, the Gypsies, the Africans and the Bulgarians.

In letters to the much-read daily newspaper *Politika* and to the weekly *NIN* in Serbia, Kosovo Albanians are usually described as 'beastly', 'monstrous', and 'disgusting'. Albanian protests against Serbian policies in Kosovo are always dismissed as anti-Serbian, irredentist and counter-revolutionary. Anyone defending the Kosovo Albanians in Yugoslavia or abroad will find himself accused of participation in an anti-Serbian plot and will be denounced for collusion with the Vatican, for spreading Bolshevist-Catholic-Moslem propaganda and for supporting Ustashi emigrés. Letters to the editor constantly refer to the Serbs' 'sacred right' to absolute rule in Kosovo and insist that there can be no dialogue with the Albanians on this question.

The criminalization of the Albanians: Heavy punishment for 'planned' crimes

In 1983, the proportion of Albanians among those convicted in Yugoslavia for political reasons was 41.8% (followed by 25.7% Croatians and 14.1% Serbs). At the beginning of 1991, there were officially 91 Albanian 'political' prisoners (Albanian sources give a much higher figure), of whom eight had been sentenced between 1981 and 1985 to 15 years in prison, four to 14 years, four to 12 years and the rest to two to seven years. Most of these individuals were under the age of twenty-five at the time of conviction.

As to the offences and the light in which they were seen, it is not without interest to refer to the report of the federal prosecutor which was published in excerpts on 24 May 1981. It reads in part as follows:

"A group calling itself '*Albanikos*' was uncovered. It consisted of 14 members and carried out its hostile activities in Kamenica e Kosovës / Kosovska Kamenica where it was the author of numerous slogans and where it gathered and distributed hostile literature, e.g. a conspiracy manual. The group was stopped before it could damage telephone lines and set fire to grain supplies. It possessed one rifle and three pistols... and was ready to commit extremely serious offences... It planned to liquidate certain members of the security forces. The group is characterized by close family ties between the organizers and its members. For every activity, it used a code name, which is proof of a high level of organization and of its conspiratory nature...

A group consisting of 13 individuals was active from March 1981 to February 1983 in Gjakova / Djakovica, where its members were arrested. They were the authors of the 1200 pamphlets they distributed. They also set fire to the platform which was to be used to welcome the Tito Rally Teams to Gjakova / Djakovica on 19 May 1982 and attempted to set fire to a military vehicle... The group had its own articles of association and met under the national flag of the Kosovo Albanians...

A group of ten individuals, mostly students, was active in Peja / Peć from October 1980. It organized the Peja / Peć demonstration of 3 April 1981 and endeavoured to organize other such demonstrations on 4 and 11 April...

A group of seven individuals was active in Prishtina beginning in 1981. In addition to procuring and distributing hostile literature, the group sent anonymous letters to various persons and organizations in February 1983. In March 1983, it endeavoured to organize a demonstration and distributed a pamphlet... 20 copies of this pamphlet were handed out in Mitrovica e Titos / Titovo Mitrovica."

The report goes on and on. The list of the federal prosecutor also referred to the destruction of portraits of Tito, graffiti on the wall of a Serbian Orthodox church, tape recordings of broadcasts by Radio Tirana, participation in the 1981 demonstrations, and contacts with

Albanian workers and emigré circles in Europe and America. According to official sources, from 1981 to 1983, "8,567 hostile slogans were written, 2,358 pamphlets distributed, and 688 authors unmasked" in Kosovo.

None of the 'hostile groups' had actually committed an act of violence. At the most, they had simply planned actions. No stores of weapons were ever discovered. Despite this, there was talk of 'plots threatening the security of Yugoslavia'. The Serbian authorities themselves committed a grave offence against a basic principle of justice by punishing 'planned' offences in Kosovo, i.e. offences which had not actually been committed.

The criminalization of Albanians was exemplified by an incident which caused a scandal in the mid-eighties. In an army barracks at Paračin, a small Serbian town between Belgrade and Niš, a young recruit running amok shot and killed four of his fellow soldiers and wounded five others. The man then committed suicide. Before there was any evidence to indicate whether the crime was politically motivated or simply the work of a deranged individual, the Belgrade newspaper *Politika* published the headline "Kelmendi [the recruit's name] shoots at Yugoslavia... The murderer not only pulled the trigger... he attacked one of the main pillars of Yugoslav unity and stability, the Yugoslav People's Army... and the most sensitive element of its being, its young men, who have always taken pride in their uniforms... Yesterday's massacre in Paračin is tragic proof once again that counter-revolution in Kosovo is a Yugoslav problem... The tragedy of Paračin is a Yugoslav tragedy..."

Of the four victims, two were Moslems, one Croat and one Serb. In an extremely questionable trial, eleven soldiers of Albanian nationality were convicted as accessories to the crime. They were sentenced to up to twenty years in prison. No convincing evidence was ever offered that the action itself had had a political background.

Milošević came, spoke and conquered
- with the support of the masses

In September 1986, the Belgrade tabloid *Večernji novosti* caused an uproar throughout Yugoslavia by publishing excerpts from a memorandum by the Serbian Academy of Arts and Sciences. The newspaper later declared that the text had only been taken from a draft which was still in preparation and had not been destined for publication.

A final version of the memorandum never appeared, though neither the Academy nor the authors of the text ever really distanced themselves from the unequivocally nationalist theses and demands set out in the memorandum. The Serbian party leadership at the time, in particular Ivan Stambolić, president of the republic, who was to be ousted a year later by Milošević, did hasten to condemn the text as an excess of Serbian nationalism, but it was too late. The theses contained in the memorandum certainly did not fall on deaf ears among the Serbs, including the intellectuals. All that remained was for them to be implemented politically.

In their analysis of the structure of the Yugoslav federation as mirrored in the 1974 constitution, the authors came to the conclusion that the republics of Yugoslavia and their peoples did not have equal rights since the Serbs had been deprived of a state of their own. Serbia was the only one of the six Yugoslav republics to have two autonomous provinces within its borders which were almost on an equal footing with the republics. Serbian state sovereignty was thus curtailed.

In addition, the authors noted, a considerable number of Serbs were forced to live in other republics such as Croatia and Bosnia-Hercegovina, and were in danger of being assimilated. In Kosovo, they claimed, the Serbs were being massacred by the Albanian majority. Since 1981, an open and total war was being waged against Serbs and Montenegrins. Every means ought to be used to counter the expulsion of the Serbs from their heartland since the fate of Kosovo was a matter of existential significance to the whole Serbian nation.

The authors of the memorandum argued that an anti-Serbian coalition of Slovenes and Croats was endeavouring to keep Serbia down according to the maxim "a weak Serbia means a strong Yugoslavia."

In the Vojvodina, the memorandum went on, the national identity of the Serbs and their Orthodox church was only preserved under Austro-Hungarian rule. Nowadays there were efforts under way to separate the Serbian population in the Vojvodina from Serbia.

The ideology of the Comintern and of the CPY had presented the Serbs as the 'jailkeeper' of other peoples in the first Yugoslavia. No other Yugoslav people had been held back so systematically in the affirmation of their intellectual and cultural identity. The 1974 constitution must, they argued, be revised in order to protect Serbia's legitimate interests and to solve the problem of its existence as one state.

These theses constituted the basis for the politics of Slobodan Milošević after 1987 although he never specifically referred to the memorandum in this respect. Milošević, forty-six years old at the time and firmly entrenched in the party hierarchy, succeeded in having himself elected as head of the party in September 1987. He had already given his views on the 'Kosovo problem' in the spring of 1987 while he was still party chief in Belgrade, convinced that these views would facilitate his rise to the national leadership. It was at a huge organized rally of Serbs and Montenegrins in May 1987 in Kosovo Polje, a Serbian-inhabited village not far from Prishtina, during which protests were voiced against the 'expulsion by force' of the Serbs from Kosovo, that Milošević pronounced the words which were to make him a popular hero: "Let no one trample upon this people."

Milošević is considered the founder of the *mitinsi* (meetings) which, to the outside observer would seem to be an eruption of spontaneous emotions on the part of the Serb masses, but which, in actual fact, were all well orchestrated in advance. It was the leaders of the Serbs and Montenegrins in Kosovo who had shown him just how effective such methods could be for carrying out his political objectives, in particular when they arrived en masse in the Yugoslav capital in the spring of 1986 in two convoys of about one thousand people each, to voice their complaints. Many of the protesters were villagers clad in traditional dress: with a peakless brown *čajkača* on their heads, riding breeches and puttees in earthen hues, and primitive sandals on their feet.

The women were mostly dressed in black. They accused the Albanians of wanting to expel them from their villages and charged the security forces and the party leadership in Kosovo with being on the side of the 'irredentists' and of abandoning them to their fate.

Milošević refined the methods and, with the support of party organizations, the police and army transformed them into an effective weapon to reach his objectives. First, he brought the Kosovo problem 'into focus', and then, in the summer and autumn of 1988, got rid of his political opponents in the Vojvodina. In January 1989, he mobilized the masses, overthrew the government and party leadership in Montenegro and replaced them with his own people.

When he endeavoured to do the same thing in Slovenia, he encountered stiff and open opposition on the part of Slovenian president Janez Stanovnik, who sealed off the borders to the Serbs who were en route to Slovenia to 'confront' the Slovenian leadership. The peoples of the rest of Yugoslavia had read the writing on the wall.

Kosovo remained open to attack and pressure from the Serbian leadership, which was now trying to overthrow the Albanian officials of the CLY in Kosovo who opposed the abolition of the province's autonomy status. He exerted pressure on these Albanian officials, using marches and the above-mentioned mass meetings in Belgrade and other towns in Serbia and Kosovo, where he was not above transporting participants in by chartered buses and trains from all over Serbia. Among his targets were Fadil Hoxha, the 'grand old man' of Kosovo, who according to the banners of protesters was destined for the gallows, and Azem Vllasi, once considered 'Tito's pet' as head of the party's youth organizations for all of Yugoslavia. The Serbian masses clamoured for his execution. In the spring of 1989, Milošević announced at a mass meeting in front of the parliament building in Belgrade that Vllasi would be arrested. A few days later he was indeed taken off to prison.

The Albanians also took to the streets. Mass protests were held once again in November 1988 when the young Kaqusha Jashari, who in the spring had taken over party leadership from Azem Vllasi, was forced to tender her resignation.

The drama is played out. *Mitinsi* in Albanian

About 3,000 miners from Stari Trg, a section of the Trepcha mine, protested against the resignation of party leaders Jashari and Vllasi. In a 'march in anger', they set out in the early hours of 17 November 1988 on the 52-kilometer march to Prishtina. With them they carried portraits of Tito and banners with pro-Yugoslav and pro-Tito slogans. This time it was not a question of nationalist demands, but simply of outrage about the massive Serbian interference in the leadership of the Albanian CP. Students and workers in Prishtina joined the protest that afternoon. The demonstrators gathered in the late evening at the Boro i Ramiz Stadium (named after two Kosovo partisans of the Second World War) in the city centre. Kaqusha Jashari and Azem Vllasi arrived at the stadium, both "as pale as wax with expressions of astonishment on their faces at the sheer numbers of Albanian protesters," and spoke to the angry crowd. Somehow, they did not find the right words or the right tone, for the atmosphere grew tenser and tenser by the hour.

Though the situation on the first day did not surpass that of the usual mass meetings, it became clear by 18 November that the protest was developing into the largest Albanian demonstration ever to take place in Yugoslavia. Protesters converged on Prishtina from all parts of Kosovo to express their discontent and air their political views. The police held back, though helicopters and other military aircraft circled over the demonstrations. By two in the afternoon, 70,000 people had flooded the stands of the stadium voicing their outrage at the anti-Albanian meetings which the Serbs had organized, "We swear to die for Kosovo!", "Comrade Tito, we are with you!" "We demand the return of our elected leaders, Vllasi and Jashari!" By 19 November, there were 200,000 people demonstrating in Prishtina. Leading politicians tried over and over to calm the masses and persuade them to return home. It was only when Remzi Kolgeci, acting on behalf of Kaqusha Jashari, announced that another session of the central committee of the Communist Party of Kosovo would be held to review the dismissal of the two political leaders, that the demonstrators calmed down and began slowly to leave the stadium. There was no violence and thus no involvement of the security forces. This protest by outraged Albanians proved just as much a signal for local Serbs as the Serbian *mitinsi* had proven for the Albanians.

As one might expect, the mass protests were regarded in Belgrade as 'organized counter-revolutionary manifestations' and had no impact on further Serbian intentions to 'intervene' in the political rule of Kosovo. People in the province now began to realize that Belgrade was indeed preparing to rescind the province's autonomy. Groups of students went on strike, shop owners closed their doors as a sign of solidarity. Daily life was soon paralyzed.

The masses were outraged once again when the former Albanian minister of the interior, Rrahman Morina, regarded by the Albanians as a stooge of Belgrade, was chosen as new head of the party. On 20 February 1989, about 1,300 miners resolved not to leave their pit 800 metres underground. Refusing from the outset to accept any kind of compromise, they formulated a number of political demands and threatened to continue their strike to the very end unless these demands were met. Their demands centered on the future of Kosovo: the 1974 constitution must not be altered in any way, the new party leaders must resign and the political attitude towards the Albanians in Kosovo since 1981 must change profoundly throughout Yugoslavia. The chairman of the Yugoslav presidium, Stipe Šuvar, the Serbian party leader Slobodan Milošević and the Albanian president of the province, Ali Shukrija, must come to the Stari Trg pit at once to discuss other impending issues with the miners.

Almost all the miners took part in this suicidal endeavour. The result was a wave of solidarity strikes throughout Kosovo. On 23 February, an unofficial general strike was held. The students locked themselves in the 25 May Sports Palace, raising their hands in a two-fingered V sign, which had become a symbol of the movement.

The streets of the city were emptied. Public transport had been brought to a standstill. Food shortages began to occur in some rural areas. By the fifth day of the strike, several hundred miners required medical attention. Divisions within the Albanian Communist Party became more apparent. More and more regional party and administrative institutions began openly to support the demands of the miners. The party leadership was paralysed by the chaos, but the security forces continued to show restraint.

In an open letter dated 20 February 1989, 250 Albanian intellectuals reiterated the demands of the miners that the status of the autonomous province not be altered and that the hostile attitude towards Albanians prevalent in political circles in Serbia and Macedonia be changed.

Ralf Dizdarević, chairman of the Yugoslav state presidium, Peter Gračanin, the president of the Republic of Serbia, Milošević and Šuvar arrived in Kosovo and talked to a delegation of the miners, but neither side gave an inch. On 23 February, the state presidium threatened to impose a 'state of siege'.

Finally, Azem Vllasi visited the striking miners at the pit. The health of many of them had deteriorated substantially and dramatic photos were distributed to the media. Vllasi endeavoured to persuade the miners to end their strike. Kosovo TV and Rilindja (the only Albanian-language daily newspaper in Kosovo) reported that for 'humanitarian' reasons, Rrahman Morina had decided to give in to the miners' demand and resign. The miners then brought their strike to an end.

A few days later, however, the miners realized that they had been deceived. Morina remained in office. Nothing had changed.

Even as the general strike against Serbian policies went on, the Serbian parliament in Belgrade passed the amendment changing the constitution, virtually doing away with the autonomy of the province. Only the approval of the provincial parliament in Kosovo was needed for the change in the constitution to enter into force.

Force against force. Snipers and dumdum bullets

On 23 March, the provincial parliament passed the constitutional amendment by 126 Albanian votes out of a total of 190. The members of parliament had been subjected to massive pressure. As they later reported, there were a large number of 'guests' present in the chamber at the time, members of the state police who prevented any free discussion on the amendment from taking place. Some members had voted openly against the constitutional amendment, but the votes were not counted properly in any case.

On 28 March, the Serbian parliament in a festive session officially proclaimed the amendment to the constitution. The speaker of the parliament declared that Serbia had recovered its state and constitutional sovereignty.

In Kosovo, though, there was nothing to celebrate.

In his book *Kosovo krv i suze* (Kosovo, blood and tears), which appeared in Ljubljana in 1990, Albanian journalist Blerim Shala published details of the confrontation between the forces of 'public order' of the federal police and army and the protesting public in the spring of 1989. According to Shala, about 110,000 Albanians came out to protest in the days following the passing of the constitutional amendment which, for all intents and purposes, abolished the autonomy status of the province.

The heaviest fighting was in Podujeva / Podujevo and the surrounding region. Here, fire arms were also used by the Albanian side. The local police chief was killed by Albanians, and the police made use of dumdum bullets. Shala also notes that snipers had been seen in action in Podujeva / Podujevo and had shot at a police helicopter from the minaret of a local mosque. It was primarily the older people who rose up in arms. They 'ruled the city for three hours'. Shala does not deny that here and in other incidents, the demonstrators used fire arms, threw stones and provoked the security forces.

A wave of arrests began in the final days of March and the first days of April 1989. Thousands of people were summarily sentenced to prison for 20 to 60 days. In Ferizaj / Uroševac alone, 1,032 workers were taken to court because they had not appeared on the job following the introduction of the 'special powers'. 841 workers were fired from their jobs or expelled from the party and fined.

The Albanian population reacted to the seizure of power by the Serbian police with inimity, outrage and threats. Albanian officials who had collaborated with the Serbs were also made to feel the brunt of popular disapproval. An empty coffin, for example, was delivered to the home of Rrahman Morina.

On 23 March, the police began to pick up Albanian intellectuals. About 240 well-known factory managers, economists, scholars, artists and officials, among them the nephew of Azem Vllasi who had had nothing to do with the politics of his uncle, were arrested in their homes in the early hours of the morning or on their way to work, and taken away in handcuffs in waiting vehicles to police stations or straight to prison in Kosovo or Serbia. No warrents of arrest were issued and no trials were conducted.

The worst fate was reserved for those imprisoned in Leskovac, a small Serbian town, where prisoners were subjected to 'special treatment'. On a trip to Prishtina in the late summer of 1991, I had an opportunity to hear what had taken place. It was the first time the family father had talked in front of his wife and children of the details of what he had suffered. He survived, but not without serious and long-term health complications which were untreatable, in particular, because of the abominable situation of medical services in Kosovo.

The declaration of the prisoner was also included in the report to the International Helsinki Federation for Human Rights and read as follows: "Two police officers took me by the arms and dragged me out into the prison courtyard. At the entrance stood twenty to thirty guards lined up in two rows. They were armed with canes and clubs and forced us to run the gauntlet. They beat us so savagely that some of the prisoners fell to the ground and were beaten even further. All of the guards were Serbs. The beatings went on for 25 to 30 minutes. We were then dragged back to our cells. But this was not the end of it. The next day, 29 March, at about 10 o'clock, the prisoners were taken to the prison office and told they would be kept in solitary confinement until further notice. Guards then entered the room and began beating with prisoners with clubs again. This treatment lasted for two days."

The solitary confinement without trial lasted for three to four months. Not only foreign organizations, but Serbian organizations too, including the Writers' Union in Belgrade, protested against this action which constituted a flagrant violation of all principles of international law and human rights.

Some of the Serbian guards who were responsible for and took part in the torture were tried several months later by a Serbian court where the victims testified. Foreign observers held the view, however, that the sentences imposed were in no relation to the crimes committed.

The use of 'solitary confinement', even for prisoners who were apolitical and had not taken part in the demonstrations, was designed to intimidate the whole Albanian population. A number of trials against young Albanian farmers, who had been driven into local towns to take part in the demonstrations, served the same purpose. The defence lawyers at these trials, which were closed to foreign observers, reported that the state prosecutors and courts were carrying out political orders, and blatantly ignoring the facts of the cases and relevant legal norms.

Reference must also be made in this connection to the trial of Azem Vllasi, the most prominent Albanian official of the younger generation at the federal level. His trial began on 28 August 1989, after he had been in custody for six months, during which he said he was not maltreated. He was accused of the most serious crime in the Yugoslav penal code which, under certain conditions, was subject to the death penalty: counter-revolutionary activity, destroying the fraternity and unity of the peoples and national minorities of Yugoslavia, and sabotaging the country's economic potential. Vllasi was also held responsible for the deaths of 24 demonstrators who had been slain by the security forces at the end of March. He was considered the instigator of the resistance although he was already in prison at the time. The trial had to be postponed several times following massive protests and ended in the charges against Vllasi and his co-defendants being dropped.

Two opposing sovereignties

The uprising of spring 1989 lasted two days. The official toll: 24 dead, including two policemen, and hundreds of people wounded and arrested. Albanian sources give a much higher casualty figure; they refer to 200 deaths. Many of the slain were not reported in order to protect their families from reprisals.

June 28, 1989, the six-hundredth anniversary of the Battle of Kosovo Polje, was used by Slobodan Milošević as an occasion to organize a gigantic rally for the 'return of the Serbs' to Kosovo. The media in Belgrade acclaimed the rally as an even of historic significance. The Albanians, in whose region the event took place, looked on in grief and anger.

At the end of January and beginning of February 1990, the Albanians attempted again to protest before the whole world against oppression and the tyrannical behaviour of the police and to demand human rights, freedom and democracy. The protest ended in fighting. The official toll this time was 34 deaths.

The terror exercised by the federal police, which after the withdrawal of the Slovenian and Croatian contingents consisted entirely of Serbian units, increased dramatically. In July 1990, the Belgrade government went one step further by depriving the provincial authorities of their power. It prevented the provincial parliament from meeting by simply expelling the members of parliament from the building.

The Albanian MPs then assembled on the steps outside the parliament building on 2 July 1990 and proclaimed the sovereign Republic of Kosovo within the Yugoslav federation and its secession from Serbia. The Serbian authorities reacted by dissolving the provincial parliament. The provincial government was also deposed. Under emergency legislation, executive power in the province was taken over by a sort of board of Serbian government officials under the chairmanship of the vice-president of the Serbian parliament, Momčilo Trailović. Kosovo was now ruled by a government of occupation.

Nothing changed in this situation after the promulgation of the constitution of the Republic of Serbia on 28 September 1990 because this new constitution contained the provisions of the constitutional amendment of the spring of 1989. Little reference was now made to the extensive autonomy rights granted to the province under the federal constitution of 1974. Like the Vojvodina, Kosovo, which was now officially called 'Kosovo-Metohija', continued to enjoy a formal autonomous status, but its autonomy now derived entirely from the sovereignty of the Republic of Serbia. The autonomous provinces are thus no longer constitutive elements of the Yugoslav federation.

The new Serbian constitution, one is told in Belgrade, guarantees the Albanian minority within the republic all internationally recognized rights. This is the approach taken by Serbian politicians at international conferences on the Yugoslav crisis.

By 1992, two years after the promulgation of the new Serbian constitution, none of the provisions on the autonomy of Kosovo and the Vojvodina had yet been realized. Neither of the provinces have statutes and articles setting out their responsibilities, nor does Kosovo have a provincial assembly (parliament), a government or an administration of its own.

The political representatives of the Albanians who take part in the co-ordinating council of political parties in Kosovo reject this type of 'autonomy'. Even before the constitution of the Republic of Serbia was proclaimed, the Albanian members of the dissolved provincial parliament assembled in Kaçanik / Kačanik, a town near the Macedonian border. There, on 7 September 1990, they proclaimed a constitution of their own for Kosovo. Article 1 of this constitution reads as follows: "The Republic of Kosovo is a democratic state of the Albanian nation and of the following nationalities, minorities and citizens: Serbs, Moslems, Montenegrins, Croatians, Turks, Roma and others living in Kosovo." Article 2 reads: "The Republic of Kosovo is a sovereign and independent state."

The era which began with the fall of Aleksandar Ranković in 1966 had come to an end. The era in which the Albanians in Kosovo felt at home in their own house and behaved accordingly was a thing of the past. For twenty-five years, a particular form of government held sway under a party which called itself communist and 'socialist self-administrative'. The federal party did not exercise less control over the party organizations in the autonomous province after 1966, but the Serbs had loosened the reins somewhat and the Albanians in the Communist Party felt protected by Tito. Kosovo was ruled no differently than other parts of Yugoslavia, i.e. it was subject to economic policies carried out by more or less competent party officials, to a politicized justice system and to a politicized police. Though most of the adminstrative jobs were taken away from the Serbs and Montenegrins and given to the Albanians, they were given primarily to members of the Communist Party and apparatchiks, including the rank and file members of the provincial parliament.

One need not be particularly clever or excessively pro-Serbian to imagine that the Slavs in Kosovo were not treated with tender loving care during those years. The statements of both sides are unreliable when it comes to analyzing the situation at the time. Only in the future, if ever, will we be able to make an objective evaluation of this era. Two things are clear, however, with regard to political developments since 1981. Firstly, it is evident that relations between the Albanians and Serbs are much more complex than either side could imagine. There is no doubt that in some regions and in some spheres of life, the two peoples maintained normal and even friendly relations with one another. At the same time, defensive and hostile reactions were common in other spheres of life. Secondly, it is evident that the Albanian party leadership failed miserably in its policies which, by endeavouring to sweep national conflicts and social discontent under the rug, indirectly gave impetus to nationalism. Political leaders sought the support of 'their' people, but had no other goals in life than looking after their own interests and security. It can be assumed that some Serbian criticism was justified, in particular Serbian accusations that the police and justice system in Kosovo maintained a double standard and dealt more harshly with the Serbs than with the Albanians.

The above-mentioned report of the Helsinki Federation noted in retrospect two main mistakes on the part of the political authorities in Kosovo. The government did not succeed in protecting minorities from attack, nor did it endeavour to create a system of justice providing protection for all inhabitants of the province. It attempted rather to dismiss all discontent as separatism. "That the authorities acted in this manner in order to maintain good relations with the federal party and with the federal government is no excuse. Serious violations of human rights were committed. Any permanent solution to the Kosovo conflict must guarantee full rights to the minorities, in particular to the Serbian minority. Nonetheless, it cannot be said that the military occupation of Kosovo is serving this objective in any way..."

Police in the hospitals, armed doctors

It gradually became clear that the Serbian administration was endeavouring to seize power in all sectors of life in Kosovo. Following the 'special treatment' reserved for intellectuals, the Serbian rulers now focussed on the field of health care. In the summer of 1990, Albanian doctors who had made themselves unpopular in 1981 by treating the demonstrators were dismissed from their jobs in the hospitals. Their dismissals were accompanied by dramatic scenes. Police units forced their way into the university clinic, the largest and most modern hospital in Prishtina, and arrested doctors while they were on duty. Witnesses also reported that Serbian doctors were carrying revolvers at work under their white coats. In the general confusion, one of them had indeed shot himself in the foot. Previous to July 1990, 70 Albanian and 50 Serbian doctors had worked at the university clinic.

Serbian health officials justified this action to foreign observers by alleging that the doctors in question "did not possess the professional qualifications required for the job, were negligent in their duties to the patients and, instead of being at work, attended political gatherings." Some of the doctors whose qualifications were in question had been trained in western Europe.

Albanian nurses were also dismissed from various hospitals in the province. About 240 doctors and 1,000 other employees were affected by this action which continued over the several years with further dismissals from hospitals and health care centres.

Albanian patients were the ones most affected by these measures. They were now being treated by Serbian doctors and nurses who did not speak Albanian. Hospital reports and the register of patients had to be written in Serbian and in the Cyrillic alphabet, and Albanian names, even those of newly born babies, were given Serbian endings. As a result, Albanian patients stopped going to the hospitals. In a report to the International Helsinki Federation in August 1991, an Austrian doctor, Werner Vogt, noted that "the consequence of these measures is an increase in the already high rates of infectious diseases. Since the dismissal of a highly qualified epidemologist of the Institute of Public Health in Prishtina, fluctuations of such diseases can no longer be monitored... The prevalence of epidemic diseases is also fostered by poverty. 45% of the population of Kosovo do not have access to clean water and 30% have no sewage facilities at all..." Vaccinations now cover only 50% of the population, as opposed to 95% before July 1990. People do not trust Serbian doctors, and Albanian doctors do not have access to the requisite vaccines. In a number of incidents, the police have confiscated drugs from hospital pharmacies.

Pregnant women go without medical attention. They have their babies at home under disastrous sanitary conditions. The distrust of Serbian doctors is fomented by rumours that Albanian women have been sterilized without being consulted and that their babies have been stolen.

Albanian doctors do their best to help, despite severe harassment by the police. A number of private clinics and medical offices have opened, but they are subject to the arbitrary whims of the local Serbian administration, even though private practices have been lawful throughout Yugoslavia for years now.

Relations between the Albanian population and the Serbian administration deteriorated substantially as a result of the poisoning scandal which affected over 3,000 school children prior to the firing of the Albanian doctors. The Albanian side claimed that the poisoning resulted from nerve gas which entered the bodies of the children through the respiratory tract. The Serbian authorities spoke of 'organized mass hysteria'. Investigations by international humanitarian organizations have come up with no definitive conclusions as to the type of toxic material involved, nor were they able to establish unequivocally how such toxic material could have been spread. The behaviour of the Serbian police during the affair was particularly distressing. They did their utmost, using armed police units, to prevent the children from reaching hospital and from being treated.

The power of the media and the decline of education

The Serbian authorities did not delay in taking control of the media through their 'emergency legislation' for Kosovo. The police occupied the radio and television building in Prishtina on 5 April 1990. 1,300 journalists and technicians lost their jobs. Six broadcasting stations and five other local stations were taken over by Belgrade. The Albanian population still gets daily news and other programmes, but these are either programmes translated from Serbian into Albanian or programmes broadcast directly in Serbian. The population thus receives only information which has passed through the hands of the Serbian censors.

A few months after the occupation of the radio and television building, the offices of the only Albanian-language daily newspaper *Rilindja* were taken over and 250 journalists were dismissed from their jobs. This measure was the start of a universal campaign against Albanian journalists, including those employed as local correspondents for Serbian newspapers or working free-lance. Croatian newspapers, especially the Zagreb daily *Vjesnik*, became important sources of information for readers in Kosovo since they carried many news articles and reports on the situation in the province. Slovenia provided assistance. Publishing companies there took over the printing of books and magazines from Kosovo which would never have been authorized by the Serbian authorities.

Journalists were arrested, beaten up and sentenced summarily to up to 60 days in prison. Some of them were to suffer such treatment several times over. Many did not give up, however, and did their best to ensure that at least some weekly and monthly magazines continued to appear, even though not on a regular basis. The editor in chief of the women's weekly *Kosovarja* was sentenced to 60 days in prison because she called for 'an end to police terror' on the front page of the magazine.

Typical of Serbian 'cultural policies' is the case of the National Theatre in Prishtina. For decades up to mid 1991, Albanian, Serbian and Turkish actors had offered a mixed repertoire of performances in the various languages, which were well received by the public. Despite harassment from the Serbian side, everyone involved was dedicated to continuing the work. But to no avail. The Serbian administration fired all the Albanian employees down to the last stage-hand and gave the theatre a new name, the 'Serbian National Theatre'.

The situation at schools in Kosovo has been even more dramatic.

Conflicts inevitably arise in the field of education wherever a national minority lives together with a majority population. Rightly or wrongly, the minority always feels that the majority is intent on undermining or destroying its ethnic identity by assimiliation. Schools can be misused for this purpose.

The tense relations between Albanians and Serbs in Kosovo are more than apparent in this field. With the exception of a few isolated villages, there have only been Albanian-language schools since the Italian and German occupation of the Second World War. After 1945, at least three-quarters of the Albanian population was still illiterate. Only a small minority of Albanians had graduated from secondary schools or universities. 27,000 pupils attended the 278 elementary schools, more than half of whom were children from Serbian families, even though the Albanians constituted the vast majority of the population. In 1970-1971, there were still no more than 372 elementary schools. The first eight-grade schools were introduced in 1958-1959 and in the following decades their number rose to 334. In many villages there are still no elementary schools and in others, pupils must walk a long way to get to these eight-grade schools, and even farther to secondary schools.

If the number of Albanian children was small, the number of Albanian teachers was proportionally even smaller. It was only in 1958-1959 that the first college was founded in Kosovo, the Teacher Training College of Prishtina. By 1973-1974, over 70% of all instructors were Albanian. One by one, new faculties were established and by 1970, Kosovo had a university of its own with 13 faculties, including a school of medicine. Up to that time, Albanians seeking higher education had been forced to go to Belgrade, Zagreb, Sarajevo or Skopje. This did, however, have the advantage of fostering contacts with the outside world. Many of these Albanian students made friends with students of Serbian, Croatian and other Yugoslav nationalities, an important experience for their return to Kosovo.

In 1990, the University of Prishtina published a monograph marking the twentieth anniversary of its existence. The book begins with a portrait of Tito, a whole ten years after his death. It is hard to imagine such a publication appearing elsewhere in Yugoslavia at the time with such an introductory dedication. The choice of the Albanian publishers is easy to understand, and has nothing to do with a love of communism or of the Titoist socialism of self-administration. Their choice had a political significance of a different nature. First of all, the Albanians are grateful to Tito for releasing them from the yoke of Aleksandar Ranković and his reign of terror and for paving the way for the 'Albanization' of the education sector in Kosovo. Secondly, the portrait of Tito symbolized opposition to Serbian criticism of Tito's policies in Kosovo. Visitors to Serbian schools and government offices may now be startled to see portraits of Slobodan Milošević, the father of Greater Serbian politics since 1986, hanging from the walls and in windows, but throughout the rest of Kosovo, it is Tito who still hangs in place. It often happens that Serbian policemen, carrying out the orders of the occupying authorities in Belgrade and using the offices of the Albanian colleagues they expelled, sit under a portrait of Tito, the very man whose 'anti-Serbian' policies stirred such fervent Serbian emotions, even after his death in 1980.

Children, the victims of politics

With the Serbification of the school system in Kosovo, the Serbian administration demanded in August 1990 that Albanian schools teach according to Serbian rather than Albanian curricula.

This measure caused a wave of protest, culminating in the refusal of Albanian teachers and educational authorities to comply with the decree and with a general boycott of the schools. Those who suffered most from the boycott were of course the hundreds of thousands of Albanian children, whose education was interrupted and whose future was decisively jeopardized. Also affected were most of the teachers who had not received their salaries since the end of 1990, and Albanian school principals who were dismissed and replaced by Serbian officials.

The resistance of Albanian parents and teachers was not directed primarily against the Serbian curricula as such, but more against what they regarded as the real aim of the decree: the annihilation of the culture and education of the Albanian people in Kosovo. This apprehension was not unfounded. One high-level Serbian official is said to have described the measure as being aimed at casting the Albanians back to the status they had had in the fifties when the Albanian language and Albanian schools were outlawed.

Officially, the reason for the introduction of Serbian curricula and for the decree reducing the number of Albanian schools by about half is that schools and the university in Kosovo are bastions of counter-revolutionary resistance and that Albanian students are being politically indoctrinated and misused by their teachers. All Albanian pupils, so the Serbs say, should be able to attend school and all Albanian teachers should receive their salary - on the condition that they accept Serbian curricula and sign an oath of allegiance to Serbia. As few Albanians are willing to take such a step, school buildings remain surrounded by tanks and armed police to prevent the pupils and teachers from entering them.

In the late autumn of 1991, a delegation of the Helsinki Federation arrived in Prishtina to inspect the situation in the field of education. During a visit to one of the largest schools in the capital (which now taught only Serbian children - five in all), in the company of the well-informed Albanian principal, the newly appointed Serbian principal called the police, who arrived on the spot within minutes. It was only after long and tedious negotiations that the delegation was allowed to talk to the two principals.

In the spring of 1990, before the conflict about the curricula broke out, the Serbian side had introduced segregation. Up to that time, Serbian and Albanian children had been taught separately in their native languages, but shared recesses in the same school yard. With the introduction of segregation, the Serbian children began attending school in the morning and the Albanian children in the afternoon. For Albanian pupils, this has meant a reduction of the length of classes from 45 to 35 minutes. The new regulation resulted of course in the physical separation of the two groups. The authorities defend the measure saying that Serbian parents were afraid their children would be mistreated by the Albanian children. The Albanians regarded the separation as apartheid.

Albanian teachers and parents made repeated attempts to improvize a school system in private homes and, in the winter of 1991, some progress appeared to have been made between Albanians and Serbs on the subject of school education, but no real solution of any kind has been found to date. The provisional coalition government in exile issued repeated instructions in the autumn of 1991 that children should return to school as usual at the start of the school year. The Serbian administration did not officially react. The actual decision-making process was thus transferred to the local level. This has led to a situation where in some areas, children now attend elementary and secondary schools and are taught according to the Albanian curriculum, whereas in other areas principals and teachers have been arrested, parents harassed and teaching suspended.

For the 1991-1992 school year, the Serbian authorities announced that there was room for 10,250 pupils at secondary schools in Kosovo, meaning room for 28.8% of all Albanian pupils wishing to attend. On the other side of the coin, 5,735 Serbian pupils were allowed to apply for secondary schools even though only 4,900 of them had finished elementary school.

The situation at the University of Prishtina is no different. Here an equal number of Serbian and Albanian students are allowed to register, even though the number of Albanian graduates is nine times higher than that of Serbian graduates. Up to November 1991, for instance, 16 of the 19 teachers in the Albanian Department of the Faculty of Arts in Prishtina had been fired, as well as eight of the 18 teachers in the English Department. Out of six teachers in the Department of Oriental Studies (Arabic and Turkish), only one assistant is left. Some Albanian teachers were instructed by the authorities to hold their lectures in Serbian because no professors from Serbia could be found to replace them.

The University of Prishtina was a focal point of Serbian criticism because it had worked in close co-operation with the University of Tirana ever since its founding. This co-operation was in full accord with the conditions set forth in an international cultural agreement. Since there was a lack of qualified university instructors and of teaching material in Albanian, a few professors were brought in from Tirana to hold guest lectures. Textbooks which had been written and published in Tirana became compulsory reading at the university in Kosovo. Albanian

Communist Party officials in Kosovo were thus accused by the Serbian side of permitting the political indoctrination of students by Albania.

University professors and members of the Academy of Sciences of Kosovo have appealed time and again to national and international organizations and institutions to send delegations to Kosovo to investigate the situation of their Albanian colleagues and students at first hand. Up to now, they have received no reply.

A 'nationalized' economy: starving them out

'Emergency measures' were instituted in the economic sector just as rigorously as they were in the educational and social sectors. The first intervention occurred in 1989. Companies, whether profitable or not, were closed down. The employees, a majority of whom were always Albanians, were fired. In other companies which were to continue production, only Albanian specialists were replaced by Serbs initially, but subsequently unskilled workers were fired as well. Anyone who was prepared to recognize the Republic of Serbia as his homeland and verify this with his signature was, however, allowed to keep his job. Forms were handed out for this purpose.

Up to the middle of March 1992, according to Albanian sources, 'emergency measures' were applied to 223 industrial enterprises, and a total of 85,000 Albanians lost their jobs. In the same period, a number of new companies were founded to ensure jobs for the Serbs and Montenegrins. About 900 new apartments were also built for Serbian and Montenegrin immigrants.

About 30,000 Albanian shopkeepers were fined the equivalent of approximately 340 US dollars and had their stores and businesses closed down (i.e. locked up by the authorities) for six to twelve months for having taken part in strikes and demonstrations. Participation in the general strike of 3 September 1990, which was widely and peacefully observed throughout the province, was subject to particularly hefty reprisals. Fines and other punishment were still being imposed for the 1990 general strike in the spring of 1992.

Many people who lost their jobs also lost their homes. In Kosovo, as throughout Yugoslavia, it was usual for companies to provide accommodation for their employees in the form of apartments and houses which could be rented or purchased. Nowadays, dismissed employees and their families are often expelled from their homes without any warning and thrown out onto the street, from where they watch Serbian or Montenegrin families move in.

The economic situation has become more and more dramatic for most Kosovo Albanians in recent years. Their situation would be much more acute were it not for the financial and material support provided by family members working abroad or in other parts of former Yugoslavia, and for the assistance provided by associations of emigré workers and international aid organizations.

Throughout 1991 there was a steady stream of young Kosovo Albanians on their way to Macedonia, Croatia, Slovenia and even to Serbia in search of work and money to support their families. About 80,000 Albanians have fled abroad since the beginning of the war between Serbia and Croatia in order to avoid conscription.

Daily life for the Albanian population in Kosovo is characterized on the one hand by police terror and on the other by a lack of any legal protection or recourse from government and court measures. If someone is slain, his relatives cannot go to the police because the police are Serbian. If someone is robbed, there is no Albanian court for him to go to because all the Albanian judges have been dismissed. Old age pensions and children's allowances (which are no longer paid for school children anyway) must be applied for on forms in Serbian accompanied by an oath of allegiance to the Republic of Serbia. Funds earmarked for cultural and social affairs are utilized by the Serbian administration for other purposes. For instance, money collected by public donation for a new radio and television building in Prishtina and deposited in an account at the Kosovo Bank, was simply transferred to Belgrade together with all the other assets of the bank.

These extremely difficult, dramatic and tragic years for the people of Kosovo have had at least two positive effects. Firstly, there has been a good deal of solidarity among relatives, colleagues, neighbours and religious groups. (A Catholic priest succeeded in reconciling family members who had been involved in a blood feud for years. The reconciliation agreed upon was valid not only for the present emergency situation, as Albanian tradition would have it, but in perpetuity.)

Secondly, a new political leadership has grown up within the Democratic League, a movement of several hundred thousand members, which has managed to unite all political currents into one common opposition to the Serbian policies of Slobodan Milošević. The eleven different political parties in the region are still abiding by their agreement. Extremist groups calling for an armed uprising play no major role in political life. The people still have faith in the Kosovo government in exile.

The Democratic League, with its Gandhian strategy of passive resistance, has succeeded in persuading the population that an armed uprising would be fatal. Together with the Forum for Freedom and Human Rights, it has managed to maintain an astounding unity among the people, the intellectuals and the politicians. The Forum has at its disposal a large number of highly qualified experts - unemployed professors, legal experts, doctors, and so on. As soon as reports of any incident reach the Forum, a team of staff members sets out at once to calm down the participants, record the events in question and provide information.

Daily life in Kosovo

The weekly bulletins issued by the Forum for readers at home and abroad provide a realistic picture of daily life in Kosovo. Here is an example.

Bulletin No. 82

concerning repression on the part of the Ministry of the Interior
and other Serbian government authorities in Kosovo
from 2 to 8 March 1992.

Another death in Kosovo. At about 10 a.m. on 4 March, a patrol
of the Yugoslav People's Army shot and killed Dalipe Fanaja
(28) about 1,000 meters from the Albanian border near Prizren.
The newpaper *Bujku* reported that soldiers had initially followed
Dalipe and threatened her with their rifles. It is therefore
possible that she fell into their hands alive. The commander
knew the woman and had beaten her savagely a few months
earlier.

March 2. A police patrol in Peja / Peć beat up Blerim Krasniqi
in his workshop because he refused to divulge the address of
Naim Goge, who was being sought by the police. Also beaten
up was Luan Sipa who happened to be in Blerim's workshop at
the time.

The police ransacked the home of teacher Din Shabaja in
Poçesta / Počesta in search of his son who was to be
conscripted. As they could not find him, they arrested the father
instead, who was brutally assaulted at the police station and
ordered to return later. Din has also fled for fear of his life.

The police confiscated DM 250 and 8,000 dinars from Samedin
Krasniqi of Bilusha / Biluša (near Prizren) while he was on his
way between Suhareka / Suva Reka and Prizren.

Miner Beqir Gashi from Hajvalia / Ajvalija near Prishtina was
arrested today for his participation in the strike of November
1989.

About 30 police officers surrounded the house of Bajram
Krasniqi in Vllashnja / Vlasnje near Prizren in the early hours of
the morning. Five officers armed with clubs entered the house
and beat up the inhabitants, sparing neither the women nor the
children. They found no weapons, but confiscated portraits of
Albanian historical and cultural figures and took with them

twenty-year-old Safet Krasniqi who had not yet done his military service.

March 3. A group of 15 young men of Serbian nationality attacked three Albanian youths and beat up a fourteen-year-old high school student named Artan Bajrami because he had refused to give a Serb a cigarette. Artan suffered severe injuries to his face, head and ribs.

The municipal offices in the villages of Llash. Drenoc / Vlasko Grenovac and Carralluka / Caraluka, District of Malisheva / Maleševo were closed down and the furnishings and equipment taken away by truck. Muhamet Krasniqi, Ajet Thaçi and Hysen Noti were fired.

The police arrested and beat up Ramadan Duraku and his son (from Peja / Peć). Weapons were sought at their home but none were found. Bajram Murtezaj was also arrested and beaten up at the police station in Peja / Peć. He was ordered to bring in his son to be conscripted.

In Mitrovica e Titos / Titovo Mitrovica, the police arrested Qerkin Ismajli. The reasons for the arrest are unknown.

The large crane (50-60 m) belonging to the Trajko Grković Construction Company in Ferizaj / Uroševac has been dismantled and transported to Serbia.

Sejdi Sejdiu, former political prisoner and member of the Forum for Human Rights in Nerodimja / Nerodimlje, District of Ferizaj / Uroševac, was invited to the police station for 'informatory talks' for the seventh time to give information on his activities on behalf of this branch of the Forum.

Nexhmedin Emini and his son Bekim, a pupil at the local secondary school, were invited for 'informatory talks' with the police in Dragash / Dragaš because the son was caught with Albanian school books on his way to his Albanian lessons.

Sabit Sahiti (32) from Gjilan / Gnjilane, father of two children, committed suicide. He hanged himself in a garage.

March 4. The vegetable market supervisors and some police inspectors in Peja / Peć organized a raid on a local jewellery shop. They searched the shop and confiscated all property belonging to the workshop.

The house of Ramiz Daka, chairman of the Democratic Forum in the village of Korisha / Koriš near Prizren, was searched for weapons and for its owner. The house was then demolished, but no one was arrested.

After house to house searches, the police arrested former political prisoners Salihu from Deçan / Dečan and Avdulla Hasanmetaj. Grounds: search for weapons and for material on their activities in political parties.

41 Albanian employees were fired from the Kosovatrans Company in accord with the 'emergency measures act'. Ten buses and two cars are out of service as a result.

The government of Serbia has announced that the provincial administration in Kosovo, in which very few Albanians are employed, is to be curtailed. According to the decree, only the secretariats for economy and finance, for agriculture, and for education, culture and science will remain. The number of employees has been cut back from 1,174 to 349.

Twelve Albanian employees were fired from the child care centre in Peja / Peć on the grounds that they were 'technologically redundant'.

It was reported today that police carried out a raid on Albanian jewellery stores in Gjilan / Gnjilane and confiscated 50 kilos of gold and jewels.

In Prishtina, the police robbed ten jewellery stores. Six kilos of gold and jewels were confiscated from the workshop of the Vezdek brothers alone. In Gjakova / Djakovica, the police stole gold amounting to about DM 500,000.

In Prishtina, the police broke into the J. B. Tito Elementary School during a meeting of the parents of Albanian pupils and took the school principal, Bajram Hajrullahu, to the police station for 'informatory talks', where they demanded that he provide them with a list of those who had attended the meeting. Present at the interrogation were Milan Novaković, director of educational funding in Prishtina, and Vitomir Šipić, principal of the Serbian part of the school.

In Gjakova / Djakovica, the police searched the house of Naim Kepuska for weapons. Selajdin Doli, Shukri Xerxa, Gajim Efendi and Salih Caka were arrested on the street on their way to work.

In Gjilan / Gnjilane, the police arrested Selam Zhariani who is to be conscripted. They also searched the home of Enver Cerkini. As he was not at home at the time, they also search the home of his father, Bajram. Finding no weapons, the police officers began shooting in the vicinity of the house.

March 6. Since the implementation of the 'emergency measures' in the Ereniku agricultural enterprise in Gjakova / Djakovica, the industrial equipment belonging to this enterprise has been transferred to the Bambi Company of Požarevac (Serbia). The general manager of the enterprise in Gjakova / Djakovica, a Moslem named Numan Tahirović, was replaced against his will by a new manager, Petar Tutovac.

About 500 employees of Albanian, Turkish and Moslem nationality were fired from their jobs at the Progress plastic factory in Prizren. The newly installed director, Miki Vučković, has hired Serbs and Montenegrins instead.

...

Postscript: Are we on the verge of a third Balkan War?

The destruction by the Serbian regime of Slobodan Milošević of the provincial autonomy of Kosovo and consequently the forced submission to Serbian rule of about 1,700,000 Albanians marked the beginning of the disintegration of the Socialist Federal Republic of Yugoslavia. The other non-Serbian peoples of the federation realized that their turn would be next, and since no agreement could be reached with the Serbs on a new basis for a joint democratic Yugoslavia in the post-Tito era, they chose the road of national independence for their republics instead, an independence which was subsequently recognized by the international community.

The problem of the Kosovo Albanians has remained unsolved, though they constitute 17% of the population of the new 'Federal Republic of Yugoslavia', consisting of Serbia and Montenegro. The Montenegrins, the second nation in this new state, with their 616,000 people, constitute little more than 6% of the total population of the 'new Yugoslavia', which is in no way worthy of its name.

Up to the present, the tragedy of former Yugoslavia has been played out between the Slavic nations of that multi-ethnic state and has been kept within Yugoslavia's international borders. Should the conflict between Serbs and Albanians in southern Serbia develop into an open war, it would take on a new dimension and, like a brush fire, spread beyond the borders of former Yugoslavia to affect all of the Balkans. Neither the people of the Republic of Albania nor the Albanian population of independent Macedonia, who constitute between 25 and 30% of the total population of that republic, could possibly remain indifferent to the fate of their brothers in Kosovo. They would become involved as a matter of course, which would make a third Balkan War inevitable, in particular since Greece and Bulgaria would see their interests in the region jeopardized. The inner-Yugoslav war would thus take on a European dimension.

If Kosovo, the Gordian Knot, can be unravelled peacefully instead of being cut in twain, it will only be through dialogue. It will be of absolutely no consequence whether the Serbs or the Albanians settled in this region of the Balkan Peninsula first, or whether others were there before them. It will be equally unimportant whether the Serbs have treated the Albanian worse than the Albanians have treated the Serbs. Not the past, but the present and future will be decisive for this dialogue, which will require an international framework, since both sides are still too tightly wedged into the corners into which they have forced one another.

Two aspects will be of supreme importance. Firstly, Europe cannot allow a CSCE Member State to use all the power at its disposal to rob a people within its borders of its economic, social, cultural and legal existence to the point of threatening its very physical existence. Secondly, the Albanians and Serbs must come to realize that their future depends on genuine co-existence between peoples with different traditions, cultures and religions. Every individual in the region must be allowed equal opportunities, without linguistic, economic, social, cultural or religious distinctions being made.

For the Serbs, Kosovo is the 'holy land' of their history. For the Albanians, Kosovo is the quintessence of their future. We cannot allow one side to be deprived of its history, nor the other side to be deprived of its future. The problem cannot, at the end of the twentieth century, be solved by force, as was often attempted in the past. The Yugoslav crisis has taken on an international dimension and this dimension cannot continue to ignore the south of Serbia, even though the political and diplomatic framework established by the Brussels documents is inadequate. The politicians of Europe and of the international community, with all their diplomatic and legal experts, will, as a matter of course, have to go new ways to facilitate permanent co-existence between the Serbs and Albanians in one form of state or another. A regulated 'minority status' for the Albanians within a united Serbia and Montenegro will never be enough. Now more than ever, the political representatives of the Kosovo Albanians are demanding equality with the other nations in the region.

If we look back upon the disintegration of Yugoslavia, we cannot deny that many lives could have been saved and much material and psychological damage could have been avoided if Western governments and their diplomatic representatives in Belgrade had been in a position to evaluate developments in that country accurately, to draw the right conclusions and to take appropriate political and diplomatic action.

Let us hope that such mistakes will not be repeated in the case of Kosovo. Otherwise, it could happen that the Albanians and their political leaders, who up to now have endeavoured to avoid armed confrontation with an overpowering Serbia, bloodshed and senseless sacrifice, see no other alternative than a suicidal uprising. Kosovo would become a time bomb ticking away in the southeast corner of Europe. If nothing is done to unravel the Gordian Knot now, the bomb may explode tomorrow.

[Taken from *Kosovo. Gordischer Knoten des Balkan.* (Europaverlag, Vienna & Zürich 1992). Translated from the German by Robert Elsie]

The wedding procession turned to ice

A novel by Ismail Kadare

I

Morning of the first day

She sensed that an ominous day had dawned as soon as she was out on the street. The weather had been dull and cloudy the day before too and, like today, only the shards of broken glass in front of smashed windows had seemed to gather some of the light. Still, perhaps because of the fog or for some other reason, the sombreness of that day had held a touch of luxury. The greyness of this morning, on the other hand, seemed only miserable and depressing by comparison, as if all the light had been sucked into the heaviness of the surroundings. It is probably because the fog has lifted, she thought. Perhaps like a veil that makes a woman's face more enticing, the fog had worked its magic on the day itself.

The slivers of glass covering the sidewalks seemed to have hardened in the cold. The morning light that had been caught in them had already expired. She quickened her steps, refusing to so much as glance at the military patrols stationed between the Grand Hotel and the bank building. A bit farther down the road, a couple of municipal workers, perched on a wooden ladder with brushes and whitewash, were busy painting over a huge slogan which covered the wall of a building: 'KOSOVA REPUBLIKË'. They had already effaced the syllable 'KO' as well as the beginning and end of the word 'REPUBLIKË', so that only the letters 'SOVA PUBL' remained. She turned away from it immediately as if from the horror of a mangled body before her, but it did not stop the phrase 'sova publ, sova publ' from going through her mind over and over. She squinted, a habit she had when she wanted to ban an unpleasant thought, but even though this one was still only vague and half-formed, she could not rid herself of the vision that the word *sova*, which in most of the Slavic languages means 'owl', conjured up in her mind.

The curb of the sidewalk on the right side of the street leading to the hospital had been smashed by tanks and had not yet been repaired. This was the spot where the armoured police vehicles had first plowed into the crowd of demonstrators. You could still see the tracks on the asphalt. She hurried on. A round column displayed posters for movies and theatre events, half torn away by the wind. 'Concert,' she noted mechanically and turned away so to avoid reading any further. All that now seemed like mouldy leaves fallen from another age. There were no more evening concerts, films, birthday parties or Sundays. There was only the state of siege. The state of siege and 'SOVA PUBL'. Ravens circling the plain strewn with corpses, as in folk ballads of old.

Farther down the road, among the rain-shredded posters on the side of a closed kiosk, she caught sight of a portrait of Tito of which only the bottom half remained. The lips and chin without the rest of the face conveyed a menacing air of discontent. What would the old man have done if he were still alive, she wondered. She knew that thousands, indeed tens of thousands of people all over Yugoslavia were asking themselves the same question and coming up with vastly different answers.

Behind the glass at the gate to the hospital grounds she recognized the silhouettes of the policemen who had been keeping watch day and night ever since the events. She showed her pass without turning to look and proceeded down the fine gravel walk that slowed her pace. As usual, she entered the surgery ward with its familiar odour of chloroform and iodine with a sigh of relief. But this feeling was interrupted suddenly by the unexpected presence of a stranger in the corridor. It was not the fact that a stranger had entered the ward before visiting hours that bothered her nor the fact that he was not wearing the obligatory white gown, a flaw she could never forgive anyone for, but something else which annoyed her - something about his attitude. She sensed immediately that he was neither a patient nor an anxious relative awaiting news of the outcome of an operation. She knew that he had no connection with the hospital. What is more, and this upset her more than anything, it was obvious from the way he leaned against the wall that he was trying to blend in. He showed no sign of uneasiness, on the contrary he conveyed a surreptitious air of self-assurance. The surgeon hesitated. Even though she was director of the clinic and set great store in discipline, she did not succeed for some reason in showing her displeasure at the presence of the stranger. The incipient anger she felt collapsed into a mixture of fear and disgust. She was sure she had seen him somewhere before, but could not remember where. It was the sort of memory that seemed slightly unreal, perhaps belonging more to the realm of dreams or imagination than to a person one had actually met.

He looked away as she passed, as if he had taken no notice of her. For a moment she was tempted to stop and ask, "Who are you? What are you doing here at this hour of the day? Have you got a pass?" But the sensation which had stemmed her anger at the stranger a few seconds earlier cooled her desire to check up on him, and she walked by, pretending not to see him.

At the end of the corridor behind a ceramic vase containing a huge cactus, she thought for a moment that she recognized another individual of a similar stature, but her attention was soon diverted by a notice on the board for job advancements: 'General assembly of the hospital collective at 11 o'clock. Full attendance required. Secretary of the Local Section of the Communist League of Yugoslavia.'

From the reflection of the wet ink, it was obvious that the notice had just been written. She frowned. An assembly without her authorization? But she was in no mood to protest.

She put on her white blouse in the changing-room, greeted her staff and held the regular morning briefing, a routine which helped her dispel the sense of uneasiness which had been following her ever since she left the house. There were two operations set for that morning. Then the assembly... What if they started harping again on the wounded demonstrators? She sighed, trying to rid herself of the image of the stranger in the corridor. He was probably there for the assembly. To hell with him.

The operating room was clean and warm. The clatter of surgical instruments and the sparkle of nickel created a familiar harmony. The first operation, a routine hernia, would be followed by a prostate. Every operation now reminded her of the ones she had carried out on 'that day'. She would never forget them as long as she lived. The patients were dripping blood before she had even set the scalpel to them. It was all horrible, like living in another age. Only the surgical instruments looked modern. The wounds of the demonstrators seemed right out of the Middle Ages: bodies mutilated by tanks, appalling wounds... She tried to think of something else. The scalpel cut through the patient's skin with ease, revealing a layer of white fat. Oh God, she sighed to herself, have the days of peace and calm with their routine operations returned, or is this all a dream? There were rumours that horrifying tortures were still taking place in the prisons.

"Doctor," whispered the head nurse who was assisting her, "did you hear about the eleven o'clock meeting?"

"Yes, I did, I saw the notice," she replied without turning.

The surgical scissors which the head nurse was holding seemed to reflect her unease, though the doctor could not see her eyes to make sure.

The doctor turned and smiled for a moment, as if to say: "Don't worry, this too will pass."

The first operation was short. The second took longer. At one point, when she was about to make a very delicate incision, her eyes met those of the head nurse, eyes which looked even bigger and brighter above the white face mask. Those eyes were speaking to her, "Be careful, doctor!"

She understood their message at once. In any other circumstances she would have felt insulted, but not now. Since the 'events', whenever she had to operate on the genital organs of any Serb, male or female, the head nurse was always at hand to remind her of the risks. There were rumours that Albanian female students taken into custody by the police during the demonstrations had been sterilized. All of Kosovo had quivered at the thought. No one could believe that that symbolic crime of former days had been revived. To counteract the rumours, the other side had alleged that it was Albanian doctors, and not the Serbian police, who had brought back that quintessential act of warfare between the races.

How disgusting, she thought as she signalled to the assistant to suture the wound. She had never been wont to inquire about the nationality of her patients and did not intend to start now! Nonetheless, she could not ignore the problem. All sorts of incredible provocations were possible. Nothing was beyond belief in these times.

It was almost eleven o'clock. One could sense in the behaviour of the team no sign of the relief which usually follows an operation, the weary gestures, the heavy sighs, an occasional tired smile. The atmosphere was different, as if they were about to begin a new and more difficult operation.

The wound was sutured and the patient was being cleaned, but everyone's thoughts seemed to be elsewhere. Two or three heads lifted, one after the other, to look at the clock on the wall. It was four minutes to eleven. The doctor's eyes involuntarily crossed those of the anaesthetist at the very moment the two were removing their masks. Are we really taking our masks off? the doctor wondered. The antipathy between the two was more clearly revealed on their unmasked faces. There are two of them, she reflected, as she glanced from the anaesthetist to the assistant. Two Serbs against four Albanians. Her thoughts froze. "My God, how dreadful," she said to herself. It would never have occurred to her before to start counting.

The orderlies removed the patient who now seemed quite superfluous in the operating room. It was two minutes to eleven and someone shouted, "Hurry up!" They removed their rubber gloves and dropped the scalpels and scissors into the sterilizer. The atmosphere was so tense that the doctor would not have been surprised to find herself attending the meeting with the instruments still in her hands.

They left the operating room and joined the flow of people heading towards the auditorium.

"Have they called the assembly for the same reasons as last time?" asked someone beside her.

"I think so," an indifferent voice replied.

"What's the point? This is the fourth time that we have to listen to the same old tune. Haven't they had enough already?"

The voices moved away ahead of her and she could no longer make out their murmuring. There was no doubt in her mind that the meeting would concentrate once again on the medical care given to the demonstrators. She would be the centre of attention once more. Even in the corridor, as the mass of people headed for the auditorium, she could feel the eyes on her.

On entering the auditorium, she caught a glimpse of the Tanjug reporter. What is he doing here, she wondered. He had been to the hospital a number of times, but always on ceremonial occasions such as the inauguration of the surgical wing of the building, the first kidney transplant and of course Tito's visit. He had interviewed her once and they had had a cup of coffee together afterwards, but this time he looked away the moment he saw her, pretending not to recognize her.

II

Denunciation day

The auditorium was almost full when she entered. The late-comers were trying to find seats by squeezing into the back rows. In a reflex of self-defence, she too looked towards the back, but at that moment a voice cried out, "Doctor!", causing her to turn. To the right of the entrance stood a small group of men.

"Your place is up on the platform," said the assistant director of the hospital with a smile which his sallow countenance rendered all the more icy. Beside him were the secretary of the local section of the Communist League, the secretary of the trade union and two other people from outside the hospital, one of whom, the director of the provincial public health council, she knew well.

"Kostić," said the other new arrival, "from the presidium of the Communist League."

"All right, it is time to begin," announced the assistant director waving his hand from the presidium table, "will you all take your seats please."

The knot she had felt tightening in her stomach all morning spread through her body as she sat down facing the auditorium. She had the impression of weighing twice as much as normal, of being crushed under a paralyzing weight, as though she were slipping into a deep sleep. But in spreading, the knot had now relieved the tension just under her diaphragm where it had been lodged.

She had been head of surgery for some time now and was used to seeing the audience from the platform, but in the last couple of weeks, ever since the meetings about the wounded demonstrators had begun, it looked different. The space occupied by the eyes and teeth on the faces of some members of the audience had shrunk, while on others it had grown. But it was not just that. The silence which reigned in the auditorium was different now. It was an all-absorbing silence which threatened to sweep you away.

She again noted the Tanjug reporter sitting in the front row. His face, which always seemed to have a certain festive air in the light of the flashbulbs, was now cold, frozen in an unnatural expression. The big, heavy camera he had with him this time was different from the one he usually carried. What was it for? It looked like anything but a camera.

She noted that the assistant director had risen to his feet with the apparent intention of starting the meeting.

"Comrades," he began once the audience had settled down, "we are meeting here today at the request of the presidium of the provincial Communist League to reexamine a number of questions raised at previous meetings, questions which have not been fully answered."

A murmuring swept through the auditorium and the speaker paused for a moment. He coughed a couple of times and then looked to the left and right as if expecting the murmuring to continue. But silence was soon restored, leaving him stranded like a man abandoned to misfortune.

"It is true that we, I mean, all of us here including those of us on the executive board of the institution," continued the speaker, "were of the opinion, or rather believed that we had dealt with the problem sufficiently, but the presidium of the Communist League," he added, pointing towards the delegate beside him, "does not share this view. It believes that we have dealt with the problem in a superficial manner, that we have not delved sufficiently into details and what is more, have not yet discovered those among us who bear responsibility." He spread his arms while his face took on a lemony colour. "This is the view of the presidium and we are gathered here once again to do what we have neglected up to now. Let us therefore begin. Who wishes to speak first?"

The assistant director fell back into his chair. From the corner of her eye, the doctor could see the delegate purse his lips in a dissatisfied manner.

"Who wishes to speak first?" the assistant director repeated.

In the ensuing silence, the chair of the delegate grated on the floor as he prepared to rise to his feet.

Turning to the assistant director, he began, "You noted that the presidium of the Communist League does not believe that you have dealt with the question sufficiently and repeated several times 'The presidium does not share our view'. I would therefore like to ask you: "What precisely is your view?"

"I have already expressed my views," the assistant director replied without turning his head.

"And you persist in this attitude?"

"Yes, until I hear of any new facts. Like you, like all of us here, I am waiting for some clarification."

"I was hoping for my part that you would be willing to help us clarify things," said the delegate and paused. "To be quite frank with you, Comrade Arian, I did not like the way you opened the meeting."

"Is that so?" said the assistant director, offended. "It is your right, Comrade Kostić, to dislike the opening or the closing of a meeting. It is your perfect right. There is no doubt about that, especially since you are an experienced leader of the League from whom we all have something to learn. Under the circumstances, I would propose that you chair the meeting."

He sat back stiffly in his chair, as if to show that he had retired from his function as chairman of the meeting.

"That is exactly what I intend to do," replied the delegate and rose from his chair, "I shall chair the meeting myself."

The assistant director, obviously surprised by this turn of events, glanced left and right.

The delegate considered the audience for a moment, cleared his throat and then began to speak.

From the start, it was evident that the tone of his voice, the clearing of his throat and all the other gestures were the product of long experience in meetings at which he had spoken, demanded explanations, expressed criticism or praise and meted out rewards or punishment.

He noted that because of the demonstrations in Kosovo, the Socialist Federal Republic of Yugoslavia was experiencing a difficult moment in its history, that its attainments were at stake as were its unity, independence and international reputation. One's attitude towards the demonstrators, he continued, and the fight against Albanian irredentism, had become the touchstone for every Communist, for every Yugoslav citizen regardless of nationality. The demand for a Republic of Kosovo was reactionary, counter-revolutionary and would be a disaster for

Yugoslavia. Anyone demanding this was tolling Yugoslavia's death knell.

He went on to say that the slogan 'Kosovo - Republic' meant nothing less than the secession of Kosovo from the Yugoslav federation and its union with Albania. "The Albanian irredentists have taken advantage of the death of our beloved President Tito to stab Yugoslavia in the back," he continued.

The doctor's eyes turned automatically to the huge portrait of Tito hanging on the side wall. She was reminded of the poster she had seen in the street, half torn away by the wind. The lips and the chin had the same resolute air, though less authoritarian, no doubt because the upper half of the face was now visible. Out on the street, his eyes were missing - a good excuse, she thought. "Half my face was missing. I didn't see the massacre." But you cannot say you do not see what is going on here, can you, old man?

The delegate continued to talk about the significance of the meeting. "In a way, I can understand the position of Comrade Arian. Solidarity with his colleagues, a romantic view of friendship, the old Albanian *besa*[1] etc., etc. I am aware of all that and we all know Comrade Arian as a man of honour and fairness, and if I interrupted him a bit abruptly I should like to beg his pardon. But I would like to go back to one other point which I just mentioned. Let me stress that the romantic ideas associated with the *besa*, solidarity among colleagues, all these virtues are quite understandable and indeed desirable under normal circumstances, but... (here his long experience at meetings came into play as his words became slower and louder)... but you must realize, comrades, that the circumstances in which we live are not, if you will, normal. I am speaking thus because we are dealing with a matter of inestimable importance. The interests of Yugoslavia are at stake. We must be prepared for any sacrifice, however painful it may be, to protect these interests."

---

[1] Alb. *besa* - Word of honour which among the Albanian tribes is rigidly respected. No crime was worse in traditional Albanian society than breaking the *besa*. - Translator's note.

The doctor glanced sideways at the assistant director who had turned an even brighter shade of yellow at the compliments paid to him by the delegate. Then her eyes suddenly met those of the stranger she had seen earlier that morning in the corridor. An old agent of the Secretariat of the Interior, she thought. A retired spy who would be called back to work on a volunteer basis from time to time when circumstances warranted. The old-fashioned Borsalino hat and the puffy cheeks of the well-nourished individual in enforced retirement betrayed him from the start. She had seen dozens of his kind during Tito's visit to Kosovo. She took a deep breath. It looked as though the secret police had begun their investigation within the hospital while she was in the operating room.

"Comrades, as a veteran Communist, let me speak candidly to you," continued the delegate. "Let us leave the generalities and get on with three questions, the answers to which I would like to hear from you."

With a gesture of self-confidence he had learned from his years on the podium, he placed the palms of his hands on the table and, balancing his weight on them, looked around at the auditorium and then at the members of the presidium sitting to his left and right. At the very moment their eyes met, the doctor felt a bolt of lightning pass through her body. A great emptiness welled up within her, mixed with the vision of the shredded concert posters she had seen that morning. Had it been Mozart or Bach? It did not matter. That time had passed. There was no more music, only this Requiem for Denunciation Day, a mediaeval fugue for inquisition and orchestra. How horrible!

"These questions are as follows: firstly, why were twelve extra beds set up in the surgery ward on the day of the events, i.e. on the first of April? Secondly, why were ambulances racing back and forth all day between Prishtina and Ferizaj and what were they doing? Thirdly, and most importantly, how and why did the hospital register containing the names of patients treated on the first of April disappear?" The delegate bent forward, balancing his weight on the table once again as if to prevent something from slipping out of his hands. "I expect answers from all of you, and in particular from you, Dr. Shkreli," he continued, turning towards the doctor, "You are head of the surgery unit, are you not?"

"Yes," she replied without looking at him, "I am the head of surgery."

"Well?"

"Well, I will answer your questions."

She rose and stared at the audience for a few seconds, trying to catch the eye of the head of administration.

"As far as the ambulances are concerned," the doctor began, "we discussed this question at several meetings and everything that was said has been noted in the minutes. As you must be aware, two of the drivers were laid off for irresponsibility. In none of the previous meetings was it ever proven that the ambulances had transported to or from the hospital any injured persons other than those operated on here. On the contrary, all that was proven was a simple neglect of duty on the part of the drivers, who as I have mentioned, were found guilty and punished. I have nothing more to add to this matter than what I stated at other meetings. Perhaps the head of administration can tell us something more?"

"Hum," said the delegate. "So you know nothing about the ambulances." He paused for a second. "And what about the beds that were set up? You are not going to tell us, I hope, that some drunk came up with the idea of setting up beds in the surgery ward? Or was this another instance of simple neglect of duty, or whatever?"

"No, I would not say that. The extra beds, as was made clear at previous meetings, had been planned for some time. I believe there are documents proving this, and even newspaper reports." She tried to catch the eye of the Tanjug reporter. "The newspapers on several occasions raised the issue of the need to increase the number of beds at this hospital, a measure which would demonstrate the great concern for public health in the province of Kosovo."

"There is no need for irony, Dr. Shkreli," the delegate broke in.

She turned towards him.

"A doctor is never ironic about such things," she replied.

"Carry on, carry on."

"Why the beds were set up on March 31, the very day before the bloody demonstrations, I really do not know."

The delegate's eyes remained fixed on her. He gave a cunning smile.

"Were you not surprised to see them?"

"No. I am accustomed to things like that. In an epidemic it is quite normal."

"But there was no epidemic, doctor."

"I know, but I still took no notice of them. Even though there was no epidemic, an increase in the number of beds is nothing unusual. You might have been surprised, but you must remember that we live our lives here in the constant presence of beds."

The delegate shook his head as if to say, 'I don't believe you.'

"Comrade Shkreli," he stated, "why such sophistry? You admitted yourself that on the first of April you treated wounded demonstrators."

"That is not true," she retorted, "I never stated anything of the kind. I said that I treated wounded patients, not wounded demonstrators."

"Is that not the same thing?"

"Not at all."

"Well, who were these wounded patients in your opinion? Did you not have the curiosity to inquire what all those wounded people were doing there that day?"

"No, I did not. A surgeon at the operating table has other worries than satisfying his curiosity."

"Is that so?"

"Exactly."

"You mean, you saw the beds that had been set up hurriedly overnight, the suspicious movements of the ambulances, the arrival of wounded patients one after the other, and yet you did not notice that something unusual was going on? That is quite a surprise, doctor. I appeal to you once again to tell me the truth. Did it never occur to you to wonder who all the wounded patients were?"

"We are quite used to wounded people coming here in various numbers. Come and have a look at our emergency ward. There are accidents all the time."

"You thought they were accident victims, did you?"

"I didn't think anything at all. I was busy trying to save them."

"Which must mean you thought they were accident victims."

"Perhaps I did."

"And the bullets? Did you not see any bullets?"

A deathly silence reigned in the auditorium.

"Bullets?" she said in the stifling atmosphere which hung over the audience, "of course I saw bullets."

The last words were spoken in a different voice, as she tried to conceal her unease.

The delegate turned sharply towards the audience, not as if surprised by the unexpected silence, but as if someone had let out a cry.

"Well," he asked in a voice which for the first time had lost its self-confidence, "what can you tell us about them?"

The doctor allowed the silence to persist for a few moments, allowing time for everyone in the room to become aware of the full reality of death - or perhaps simply waiting for the spasm which had stifled her voice to pass.

"Bullets are nothing special for a surgeon. Bullets occur in many suicides and other crimes."

"But a hail of bullets?"

"Yes, even a hail of bullets."

"Dr. Shkreli," continued the delegate, raising his voice, "before proceeding to the third question which I cannot spare you, before you tell us who caused the disappearance of the patient register containing the names of those treated on April 1, that is the register containing a list of the enemies of socialist Yugoslavia, before we proceed to this question, I would like to appeal to you once more to tell us the truth and answer whether, when you saw the wounded arriving one after the other covered with blood, you thought they were victims of suicide, accidents and acts of jealousy etc., or whether you knew the truth and, even though the list of their names may have disappeared, were consciously giving illegal, I repeat, illegal treatment to the enemies of Yugoslavia in a government-owned public health institution?"

"Before I answer, I too have a question to ask you," she replied. "Comrade Kostić, you are speaking here in front of hundreds of individuals about a multitude of people killed and wounded, about torrents of blood and hails of bullets. Do you not think that in so doing you are spreading anti-Yugoslav propaganda? The official communiqué stated that only nine people died and a few dozen were wounded. You would have us think that in our hospital alone, which is one of dozens of hospitals in the province, masses of demonstrators had been treated. You would have us believe that a real bloodbath took place. I would advise you to consider carefully what you are saying."

"You," the delegate cried, "how dare you to talk to me about the defence of Yugoslavia?"

His voice was piercing, as if a knife were at his throat.

"Yugoslavia, as you said yourself, belongs to us all," she retorted.

Suddenly the delegate appeared to lose his nerve. He looked as though he wanted to cry out, but from the movement of his lips it was obvious that he could not decide what to say.

"Where is the hospital register containing the names of patients treated on April 1?" he shouted.

"I don't know," replied the doctor coldly. "Ask the police to find it."

At these words, pandemonium broke out in the auditorium. For the second time her eyes met those of the now dumbfounded stranger she had seen in the corridor that morning.

The uproar continued as the voice of the assistant director cried out, "Settle down, please, we cannot carry on like this!"

III

Noon. At the Old Serbia Grill

Dobrila Djubrović was the last to leave the auditorium. The hospital corridors emptied quickly. He took a look at his watch as he stepped out onto the street. It was one thirty. Time for lunch, he thought.

The meeting had been set to continue at five o'clock. He had wondered several times, why so late? These assemblies should be held all at once with no interruptions to give the accused time to come up for breath. He knew the effect of this method well from his professional experience with the security forces. Interrogations used to carry on for days and nights on end without a break. The investigators would take turns whereas the victim stayed put. But nowadays...

Times had changed and everyone was getting soft. Luxury, democracy. Well, now they could see where that led. Even the doves had realized that things could not go on like this. Now they were all turning to the retired officers of the UDB, to the old hawks who had been forced out long ago and treated with general disdain.

The anger that had been pent up in him for years, suffocating him to the point where he had developed a kind of asthma, seized him again. He fleetingly recalled various moments of the day he had been pensioned off. A monotonous speech rattled off by some second-rate official, "Comrade, your merits... certainly... etc., etc." And then abandonment, total oblivion. He was invited to no more meetings or banquets. It was said that Ranković, too, their former boss, had been expelled like that in Belgrade, and was now in isolation in a villa with guards who were there more to keep watch over him than to protect him.

His old friend Vladan, with whom he went drinking from time to time, always said to him, "Just be happy, Dobrila, that they leave us alone and don't go snooping around in our past, the good old days when no one used to ask any questions."

Jovica, on the other hand, the third man of the 'indivisible trio' as they were called, shared his views. The three of them met occasionally at the Old Serbia Grill and let off steam together. They felt at home there and had nothing to fear. Most of the customers were in the same boat, retired or laid off from the Secretariat of the Interior after the plenary session at Brioni. Some people said that even the owner of the grill had worked as a cook at the camp on Goli Otok for a number of years, a fact which gave rise to some ironic grins and occasional bursts of laughter, interrupted by the coughing of the others.

The old resentments usually began to surface after the second glass. "They've forgotten us. They don't need us anymore. When there was work to be done that meant getting your hands bloody up to the elbows we were the first ones they would call, but now they've come up with new slogans: unity and fraternity among the peoples, human rights and other such nonsense." And as if that weren't enough, some historians had turned up to prove that this did not used to be Serbian land at all, but Albanian or Illyrian territory and that the Serbs arrived much later. It was enough to make you sick, really.

But no one really took any notice of them. They were remembered on rare occasions, like Tito's visit when they were all called back to work for a few days. But far from giving them any satisfaction, this only exacerbated the emptiness they felt. The festivities ended and the lights were turned out one after the other in the banquet halls whose entrances they had guarded. The tables were cleared of the expensive china and silverware and with it they too were cast back into oblivion. "No one wants us anymore. We've been thrown away like an old pair of galoshes," they lamented. "Just you wait and see. Don't give up hope," Vladan would retort, "our day will come."

And indeed, in mid-March, after the first demonstrations by Albanian students, there was a knock at Dobrila's door late one night. It was a different knock this time. It lacked the joyful resonance of a coming banquet, the lightheartedness of a gala dinner. Dobrila had decided several months earlier that he would not go back to that work for the few rotten dinars they paid. He could no longer stand the thought of those late-night festivities, of perfumed women in fur coats giggling in the company of their important husbands done up in dinner jackets and ties. No one ever thought of saying a word of thanks to Dobrila and the others or even noticed them on duty outside in the cold and dark of night. No, he would never go back.

But this time he realized that the situation was different. Here and there on the deserted pavement one could hear the steps of those who, like himself, were headed towards the Secretariat of the Interior. They were familiar faces, some of which he had not seen for years. Indeed some of them belonged to people he thought had died years ago. "They buried him without any ceremony at all, not even an obituary in the newspaper," he had said to himself. And here they were, alive after all, with eyes still swollen from sleep or from oblivion. Vladan and Jovica were already there. And Rajko in person, who had been forced into retirement like the rest of them, though not quietly with a pension but after vile accusations of sadism at the prison where he worked.

The chief spoke as they had expected, slowly and concisely: "Comrades, Yugoslavia needs you. This is why we have called you."

It was obviously a serious matter. It was just as he had imagined on the way here, though he had not wanted to believe it entirely so as not to be disappointed again. The chief continued to speak in the same grave tone. The Albanians had risen. But it was not simply a matter of demonstrations, as the press had reported in order to calm the situation. In his opinion, this was an uprising - the only term which could properly be applied to the present movement. It must therefore be treated as such and put down mercilessly. Dobrila would long remember the fervent exaltation he experienced that night. The word 'uprising' had a strange ring to it, something exceptional, even though it was used among hundreds of other words in TV news broadcasts every day. The reports spoke of tension in various regions of the globe, local warfare, a possible invasion of Poland, even nuclear blackmail, but one got used to them. But an uprising here in the middle of Europe had something archaic and terrifying about it. The sound of the word seemed to waken long dormant feelings in Dobrila which came back to him now as if he had been roused from a long sleep.

He took another look at his watch. He still had lots of time for lunch or for an afternoon nap before five o'clock, but he had no desire to return home. After a moment's hesitation, he set off for the Old Serbia Grill. Perhaps he would find his friends there and have a couple of drinks with them. They gathered more and more often there recently. They would exchange the news of the day and comment on affairs. The uprising had now been drowned in blood but the horror it inspired lingered on. One had to pay attention and be on one's guard more than ever. They had thought that after the massacre the Albanians would not dare to lift their heads, but this did not seem to be the case. More than anything Dobrila was frightened by the temerity of these people. That doctor at the meeting, for instance. How did she dare to speak out that way and put Comrade Kostić on the defensive, after all the tanks and bullets?

Every time he thought about it he had a sick feeling in the pit of his stomach. Such temerity was not normal. It was eery. As long as their spirit was not broken, things would continue as they were.

Dobrila noticed that he had hastened his step. He had to admit to himself that he was not rushing to the Old Serbia Grill simply for a drink with his friends or to hear the latest news, but above all to shore up his courage. As always, it was the only place he could really feel at home. But if up to then an atmosphere of wounded pride had reigned, there was now a new element: fear. There were no more protests against anyone. They just tried to keep up one another's courage, to boost one another's flagging spirits. They were impatient for the rebellion to be put down ruthlessly. "Don't listen to those Croatian and Slovenian sissies whose blood has been luke-warm for centuries", they would say. "Let's beat the Albanians to a pulp the way we used to... in the good old days."

Some people, nonetheless, still insisted on observing lofty principles and etiquette, as the meeting had shown. Dobrila did not like the tone of the meeting. He had felt ill at ease and had been seized by a blind fear. A couple of times he had wondered, "What are we doing here anyway? You'd think we still had to pussyfoot around with these people."

He had been sent there as an informer, to listen to any whispering in the corridor, especially during the break, and to help the other secret agents if necessary, although he did not even know who they were. Just an assistant again, he grumbled to himself, a volunteer. But he soon forgot his dissatisfaction.

In the distance he could see the steamy windows of the grill. He made out several vague silhouettes inside: Vladan and Jovica, his two fellow stool pigeons, seated in their usual corner. The aroma of grilled meat wafted into the street.

"Well, how did it go?" they asked him. "You were at the hospital, weren't you?"

He replied with a gesture of dissatisfaction as he pulled forward a chair.

"Nothing to report for the moment. We can't get that bitch yet. She's as slippery as an eel."

"Is that right?"

"And I think Comrade Kostić ventured too far into unknown territory. He made a mistake and the damned bitch of course took advantage of it."

Dobrila noticed that they were only half listening. They filled their glasses with slivovitz and offered him a drink.

"Don't worry. We've got good news."

"What?"

They bent towards him. Their eyes gleamed more from what they were about to say than from the alcohol itself. There was something in their expressions that Dobrila had never seen before.

"They're going to reopen the files," whispered Jovica.

"What?" stammered Dobrila, "*Majko Bože*, I don't believe it."

"Cheers, down the hatch!"

"My God, are you sure?" said Dobrila, "What if it's only a rumour, like in 1968? Do you remember the rumours they spread?"

"It's as real as this bottle in front of us," replied Jovan.

"Holy Mother of God," stammered Dobrila, "our day has come."

"Yes, Dobrila, it has finally come."

"I've thought about it so often without daring to believe that, that... I don't know what to say."

"It's too good to be true," said Vladan.

"And not just some of them, but all of them," cried Jovica, "all one hundred thirty-eight thousand, can you believe it?"

Dobrila was dumbfounded.

"Are you sure you're not kidding me, Jovica?"

"No, not at all! How many did you think they would open, twenty or thirty thousand? If there were so few, you wouldn't see me smiling. That's the number of cases that were open all the time. No state can survive without records. The tragedy is that after the plenary session at Brioni, they did away with a lot of them. There weren't enough left, and look what happened."

"Good Lord, the day has come," said Dobrila again, slapping his hand to his forehead. He could still not fathom the news and pleaded with his friends, "Play all the jokes you want on me, but not this one."

The reopening of the files had been one of his wildest dreams, always accompanied by an uneasy nostalgia. He had seen them in his sleep many times, in white rows, thousands of them, like cold tombstones, each with a name on it that was no longer of any use because the bodies had disappeared.

"We'll get that doctor of yours now! Clack, like a mouse in a trap," said Jovan closing the palm of his hand.

"We'll get them all now," added Vladan, "not just clack like a mousetrap, but clack like a file, ha, ha!"

The three of them laughed for a while and then ordered another round of slivovitz. From time to time, Dobrila raised his head and murmured something. The unbelievable had happened. The magic power which had been so brutally taken from them was restored, as in a fairy tale. Their life would be different from now on. The heroes of supernatural tales were no match for them.

Dobrila was seized by another moment of doubt.

"Are you sure you're not kidding?" he said, looking straight into their eyes. "I think I'd die if you were."

At that moment the owner of the grill brought them another bottle of slivovitz. Jovica raised his head.

"*Bože*, explain to the man that they are going to reopen the files. He doesn't believe it."

"The files?" said the owner. "They're already open."

A wave of enthusiasm fortified by the alcohol penetrated them all. There was no longer any doubt about it. A miracle had taken place.

"Come on, drink up," he said. "To the files!"

"To Serbia!"

"We've made it."

"Watch out," cautioned Vladan, "you've got to be back at five o'clock."

"To hell with it, give me another shot."

Dobrila's mind was becoming foggier and foggier. They talked about this and that, but the subject of the conversation always returned to the files. Empty tombs there might be, but they would soon fill up again. Those who had pried open the tombstones and escaped from their tombs would return. One by one they would climb back in and lie down stiffly in rows, thousands of them, waiting. And Dobrila and his friends would go and lift the tombstones one by one: oh, you're back, my little dove, you have returned! Let's take a look at what you've got in that head of yours, what you're whispering here and there. It wasn't enough for you to have an autonomous Kosovo. You had to have a republic, your own little republic, did you?

The conversation became more and more incoherent. They interrupted one another constantly, but it did not really matter. Our side has won, and who knows how happy old Ranković must be. He knew how to treat the Albanians. Shh! Pipe down a bit. We still don't know anything about his reaction. What do you mean? He must be delighted. He sacrificed his whole life for this fight, and he's still suffering for it, pent up like a bird in a cage up there in Belgrade.

Jovica began to sob. "The poor guy, all alone in his cage," he repeated until Vladan said, "Don't worry. Things will turn out alright. We just have to be patient." But Jovica could hold back no longer, "They set fire to the Patriarchate in Peć. They're sterilizing our Serbian girls. How are we supposed to be patient?"

"Well, we've given them tit for tat," replied Vladan. "On the first of April tanks rolled over human bodies. You can still see the bloodstains in front of Grmija department store, isn't that enough?"

"That's not very much," replied Jovica, "not much at all. Let them give us back the freedom we had under Karadjordjević to wipe them off the face of the earth, with their language, their damned alphabet that they claim is older than ours. Their superior language, their superior alphabet, it makes me sick!" he groaned.

"Wait a minute Jovica," Vladan insisted, "you can't do things that way anymore. You talk about the time of Karadjordjević, but we are living in a different time. You need strategy."

"Your blood has grown cold, Vladko," said Jovica shaking his head with a mixture of pity and disgust. "I'm sorry to have to tell you because you are my friend, but it looks like your blood has definitely grown cold."

Vladan smiled placidly. "Things can be done better with a cool head. A cool-headed attack succeeds, whereas your method is useless. And there is a lot at stake. There are supposed to be over two million Albanians. That's quite a few, Jovica. It gives you the shivers just to think about it." Jovica shook his head in objection, "The Serbs and Montenegrins are leaving Kosovo," he exclaimed. "They are abandoning our land, do you understand? We are getting to be like the Palestinians." He grabbed Vladan by the sweater. "And you talk about patience and other such nonsense. They are throwing us out of Old Serbia, our own country, they are kicking us out, do you understand?"

"Calm down, Jovica, you're right about that, but they won't get away with it. That's why the tanks are still here. Did you see the tracks they make?"

"I have more faith in the files than the tanks," replied Jovica, forgetting his rage temporarily. "The tracks that files leave are even harder to escape from." "You're right about that, brother, let's have another drink."

The tanks or the files, Dobrila thought to himself. Let's wait and see which is more effective. He sensed that someone was watching them from the next table and turned his head. Someone was indeed following their conversation attentively, a smirking face flushed with alcohol.

"So what are you staring at," said Dobrila, "Is something wrong?"

The stranger's smile broadened even further, seeming to extend right down to his neck, as if the lips were not large enough.

"I've been listening to what you were saying. By God, it's enough to make you die laughing." He struck the table with the palm of his hand and shook his head as if to shake off the tears. "God, it's hysterical. The cradle of Serbia. The cradle of Albania. What is this Kosovo that everyone calls their cradle? It's like Galilee, or Judea, more biblical than the Bible itself with all its crosses, forbidden prophets and apocalypses."

"What are you, a Serb, or born of another race?" Dobrila growled.

"I'm a Serb alright, just like you, brother, but you've gone over the brink!"

"What's going on?" asked Jovica, intrigued by Dobrila's conversation with the stranger.

"Nothing," replied Dobrila to avoid trouble. He turned his back on the stranger and murmured, "It's no wonder that Serbia is going nowhere with idiots like this. Jovica's right saying he can't stand them."

"That's the way I am and I am not changing," Jovica continued. "If we decide to wipe them out, let's wipe them out for good. All this discussing and philosophizing is not for me. Leave that to the Croatians. Thank God we Serbs have our own traditions. Look at Dobrila getting ready for his meeting. What a farce. Permit me if you will, Albanian comrade, to express a hint of criticism and to see what stance you take? If old Jovica had his way, it would be the machine gun, period. I'd drive the tanks right into the meeting and wipe out the podium, the agenda and everything else. But I know who's responsible for all this. The old man in Belgrade, it's all his fault."

"Shut up, Jovica. Don't use his name. What's wrong with you? Do you want them to get us? Leave the old man alone. He did what he could in the past, but times have changed. He couldn't do any more, do you understand?"

"Times have changed, have they?" Jovica hissed. "No, Vladko, times never change. Just like Jovica." He beat his chest so hard with his fists that his voice, shaking with emotion, seemed to have broken, "Twelve thousand Serbian tombs at the Luma Tower with their wooden crosses rotting in the rain. How can anyone forget them?"

Dobrila in turn was overwhelmed by the tragedy of it all.

IV

Afternoon. In the study

As soon as she entered the dark hallway, she heard the door to his study creak. He appeared to have been waiting for her.

"Well?" he asked from the doorway, his body silhouetted against the light from inside, "How did it go?"

"It was frightening," she replied, turning her head to the side as if to shake off something.

He waited until she had removed her coat and entered the study.

"The meeting was adjourned until this afternoon," she said, sinking into one of the armchairs.

His face darkened.

"You cannot imagine the barbarity of it all," she said.

He remained standing with his eyes fixed on her.

"We are living in cruel times," she added, "My God, what cruel times."

"The moment you phoned me, during the break, I knew something bad was happening."

"You just cannot imagine how barbarous the whole thing is," she sighed. "I don't think there has ever been such an insane inquiry anywhere on earth."

"Of course," he noted, "inquiries are usually held for the opposite reason, to find out who failed to provide assistance to the injured, whereas at your hospital everything is upside down."

"Exactly," she replied, "and that is what makes the whole thing so unbearable. It makes you want to scream."

She covered her face with her hands and burst into tears.

"Calm down," he said, placing his hand on her shoulder. "Calm down, Teuta."

For a while, the only sound in the study was that of her crying. Then she spoke. "I want to rest for a while. Could you have lunch by yourself?"

"Of course."

She went out and he stood alone in the middle of the room, turned away from the doorway as if transfixed by the idea that the person he had waited for all day had left the room so soon, the same way she had entered it. Cruel times, he repeated to himself. Barbarity.

He began pacing back and forth. For several years now, his whole life had consisted of this back and forth from one end of his study to the other. The gold-lettered titles on the backs of the books seemed to follow his movements with a dusty, bitter smile. He had written some of them himself, thick brown volumes all of them, with his name embossed on the cover: Professor Martin Shkreli, *Onomastics in Albanian heroic songs*; Martin Shkreli, *Albanian myths*; Martin Shkreli, *Aeschylus and the laws of the Albanian Kanun²*; Martin Shkreli, *The toponomy of Kosovo in the light of ecclesiastical records*; Martin Shkreli, *The theme of absence and imprisonment in Albanian ballads*; Martin Shkreli, *Anguish in....*

The postscript of each one of these books was the anguish he carried within him. Waiting to be arrested when, in the silence of the night, even the sudden squeal of breaks on the street outside could mean the loss of everything. It was the time of Ranković when you could lose your head for nothing. "It's easy to work now," he once told a group of friends, "but in those days things were different." The flame of Albanian culture in Kosovo had been on the verge of extinction. He and a few others had tended it and kept it alive in that time of darkness. But as the years passed, the drama of his existence, the compromises he was forced to make from time to time - a declaration on the occasion of Tito's birthday, a speech for some ceremony in Belgrade, the silence he had maintained about other things - were less and less understood.

The Serbs had always been unhappy with him, which did not mean on the other hand that the Albanians were always completely satisfied. He lived tortured by the thought that more was always expected of him than he was capable of giving. Occasionally, when he was all alone, he would give free rein to his anger: What more do they want, what more can I do to satisfy them? Should I provoke a scandal, should I ask to be thrown into prison? Then they'd be satisfied, but they'd be sorry too for having pushed me too far: "We judged him too harshly. He proved to us, once and for all, who he was. Maybe we should not have pushed him into making such a senseless sacrifice." But their belated regrets would solve nothing.

Each time his thoughts returned to the subject, he felt all his strength drain out of him. Overcome by emotion, by his wounded pride and by the frustration of seeing that none of his work was appreciated as it should have been, he would take refuge in a euphoric melancholy which provided some relief.

---

² The Kanun of Lekë Dukagjin was the traditional legal code of the northern Albanian tribesmen. - Translator's note.

In fact, what they called his compromises in most cases had not been dictated by the need to survive. From time to time he had hoped vaguely that something would change in the relations between the Serbs and Albanians. His hope was rekindled every time he opened a book by Šufflay or Tucović and would manage to persuade himself that the deadly hatred that reigned between the two peoples would fade one day. But then there were other moments when he lost all hope and believed in nothing at all. It seemed to him that the relationship between these two peoples would never be governed by anything but darkness, rancour and a bloody moon, and that they would never come to love one another, however many books, songs, Christs, Romeos and Juliets might try to bring them together.

Two peoples hating one another... It was something quite inconceivable for normal minds. Of all the ugliness on earth, this was perhaps the most unbearable. Every time he thought about it, he had visions of the globe with its continents, countries and peoples hurtling off into space, a tiny and eminently absurd planet. The two sides were there somewhere in the cosmos, he thought, surrounded by stars, galaxies, terrifying black holes, and yet the hatred would not die.

He had told this to a number of his colleagues and most of them, including the Serbs, had agreed with him. With sadness in their eyes, they listened to the discussion which in one way or another was going on in every Yugoslav family.

Hating one another... and as if the trials and tribulations of day-to-day existence were not enough, the two peoples met on the battlefield of dreams, in the delirious universe of their ancient epics. And like a dream, everything took on awesome and frightening proportions: open wounds, rainbows, darkness.

This horror must end, he would reflect wearily. In spite of all the disillusionments, he still wanted to believe that the day would come when, after such profound and exhausting hatred, they would begin to love one another.

There were people for whom the word 'love' had a strange sound, as if it were from another planet. But not for him.

And finally, after the fall of Ranković, it seemed as if the miracle were finally happening. At the first signs of a thaw - the right to fly the Albanian flag and the authorization for cultural contacts with Albania - he spent whole nights on end in delirium. History had confirmed his dreams. The ice had not yet been broken, mistrust and scepticism persisted among those unwilling to believe that a new age had begun. Others preferred to spend hours discussing whether Tito was trying to make amends for his harsh treatment of the Albanians or whether he had been forced to make concessions. But it did not really matter. Time would tell, he thought. That was what was important.

More than ever he now believed in what earlier had seemed the most unlikely thing on earth: an end to the hatred between Serbs and Albanians. It would obviously be no easy matter. A thousand years of bloodshed, terror and nightmares lingered in the collective memory. And yet, he believed that the furies of vengeance were beginning to mellow. Indeed he was even thinking of calling a proposed new book of essays 'The Twilight of the Furies'.

It was a time with a climate all its own, a time of ceremonies. Joint delegations, symbols of fraternity among the peoples of Yugoslavia, were sent abroad. The newspapers and television reported the events incessantly. Declarations and poetry were published, films were broadcast. And yet, all of these changes seemed to affect only official, academic and literary circles. Among the people, the same age-old hostility continued to prevail. On the main street of Prishtina in the evening, the Albanians walked down one side and the Serbs down the other. There were hardly any mixed marriages, or even love affairs between the two peoples. It will pass, he thought. The thaw will reach the people just as the warmth of spring gradually penetrates the deep layers of frozen soil. It would not be easy after a winter that had lasted eleven centuries. No, it would not be easy at all.

He broached the subject with some of his colleagues in the cafés of Prishtina during their long conversations in which burning idealism and dreams mingled with scepticism for hours on end. He was of the opinion that if one of the two peoples would take the first step towards the other, this act - or rather this honour, he corrected himself - would be a sign of superiority.

He said this with a smile, aware of the difficult position in which he was putting his adversaries, who on the one hand appreciated a man of unfailing objectivity using terms which had long been banished from speech in Yugoslavia, but on the other hand, refused to consider their own people taking the first step, however superior they might be considered as a result. "The Serbs owe us a debt for the rivers of blood they have spilled," they would reply. "They must ask our forgiveness." "No," he insisted. "The more civilized side is always the first to forgive. Though forgiving does not mean forgetting." And when they refused to listen and demanded an eye for an eye, he resisted, maintaining that one atrocity must never be countered by another, but by other means. "All the laws, codes and philosophy which go to form the Albanian mentality exclude collective murder," he continued. "Look at our thousand-year-old Kanun, it allowed only for the murder of individuals, and that only after a cooling-off period of between twenty-four hours and thirty days. That meant an obligatory period of peace between murders. If you murdered, you had to wait. It was someone else's turn, and during this interval there were rituals to be respected to avoid any possibility of a massacre. No, a massacre must never be answered with a massacre, genocide never with genocide." At this point he liked to recall the Aeschylian maxim that 'if you abuse justice, right is on the side of your opponent'. No, he had though about it a long time, and it was his unshakeable conviction that fighting chauvinism with chauvinism was like combatting the plague by infecting yourself with it. What would we have to gain, he would ask. The plague itself, above all else.

His confused friends lost the thread of their arguments and the conversation took another turn. In a calm, almost soothing voice, he liked to talk about the smaller peoples of the globe who were linked by similarities in their customs, clothing and even their languages - the Celts, the Albanians, the Basques, the Scots and other small nations which he liked to classify as subalpine. Let us take the first step in their direction, he repeated. The honour will then go to us subalpines.

As usual, his words were met with either incomprehension or open scepticism. This same discussion was going on everywhere in one form or another. In the Gadimja Cave a stalactite and a stalagmite were growing towards one another along a single axis. Geologists had calculated that it would take one and a half million years for these formations, which the press and television had dubbed the Romeo and Juliet of Kosovo, to meet. Although nothing more specific was said, it was generally understood that the Romeo was Albanian and the Juliet Serbian and the time span of one and a half million years was proof of how unlikely it was that the hostility between the two peoples would disappear in the foreseeable future.

Martin Shkreli knew this and more. And yet, as dark and bloody as the old Albanian epic songs had been, they were occasionally illuminated by the white veils of young brides, by marriages and wedding processions which were to unite the Serbs and the Albanians. But such weddings were always accompanied by uncertainty, for the attendants of the groom never reached the bride's home. The Oras, the furies of the Albanians and Slavs, turned the wedding procession to ice before it reached its destination. The ancient epics could well have been subtitled: 'The impossible wedding procession' or 'The wedding procession turned to ice'. He himself thought that, more vividly than any other image, this transformation of the wedding procession symbolized the disparity between the desire for the marriage and the actual situation, in short between dreams and reality. Still, for Martin Shkreli, the main thing was that the desire existed at all. He believed that the time had come for the curse to be lifted. After being frozen in the ice for one thousand years, the wedding procession would finally come back to life and continue its journey towards the interrupted wedding.

One day, in one of the courses on early Albanian literature he gave at the Faculty of Arts once a week, he had suddenly been seized by a whim to decipher some words which had been written on the blackboard and then hastily erased. He was surprised by his own curiosity. Between classes, the students often amused themselves by scrawling funny sayings on the blackboard and then wiping them off just before the professor entered the room. He was aware of this, and yet something enticed him that day to try to read the faint and ephemeral traces of chalk which remained on the blackboard. 'Shpend Brezftohti + Mladenka Marković = ?' "Love?" he wondered. He had a tremendous urge to rush up to the blackboard and wipe out the callous question mark and write in its place ten times, a hundred, a thousand times over the Albanian and Serbian words for love: *dashuri* and *ljubav*.

What he had hoped for for years was finally happening. The day will soon come, he whispered to himself. It is certain to come. Let the sceptics believe in the one and a half million years in the cave. The miracle is taking place before our very eyes.

He knew Shpend Brezftohti. He was one of his best students. Mladenka must be the Serbian girl with the hazel-coloured hair who often sat beside him. He had never taken an interest in the personal relationships of his students before, but after that, whenever they came to class, he would watch them attentively and try to discover what had taken place between them in the past week. Sometimes he thought it was all his imagination and that there was nothing between them, but on other days he believed the impossible had indeed occurred.

And indeed, every passing day brought something to strengthen this belief. There were evenings when the Grand Hotel was full of Albanians from Tirana. He was almost certain that a new, long-awaited era had dawned. And then suddenly like a bolt of lightning out of the blue, the month of March arrived and with it, the student demonstrations. But even when he saw the crowds fill the streets, waving flags and banners reading 'Kosovo - Republic', and other slogans, he did not give up hope. He was sure the problem would soon be resolved. After all, none of the demands were new, not even the main one for republic status. In 1968, when demands had been made for the right to fly the Albanian flag and for republic status for Kosovo, they had feared the worst, but nothing happened. On the contrary, one of the demands had been granted. It would be no different this time.

They were tense, feverish days. The atmosphere was explosive, as if a nerve had been touched. He had not yet had a chance to discuss all this with his colleagues when the first of April dawned.

'Kosovo's day has come...'

He had had that line from a poem by De Rada[3] on his mind since early morning, replacing the word Arbëria with Kosovo. Or perhaps this sacred line had pushed its way up from the bottom of his memory like a curious bystander, shoving people out of the way to get a better view of the disaster.

When the first shots rang out in the distance, he froze and covered his face with his hands. The whole world shuddered and

---

[3] Girolamo De Rada (1814-1903), Italo-Albanian poet, publisher and nationalist figure from Calabria. - Translator's note.

exploded. He was on the point of getting down on his knees to pick up the fragments of broken glass from the windowpanes and lamps, the books, the torn manuscripts, but when he uncovered his eyes he realized numbly that everything was in place: the walls of his study, the windowpanes, the books and furniture. The destruction had been within him. The muffled sound of firing continued in the distance. He opened the door to the balcony and went out into the cold. The shots were more distinct now and between them he could hear a rumbling noise with an awesome rhythmic echo. Tanks, he thought. He did not remember how long he stood there. From time to time amidst the firing and rumbling of tanks, he heard the piercing wail of fire trucks and ambulances. The sky itself, ashamed of its tranquillity, began to shudder. He saw low-flying aircraft approach trailing black smoke, and then helicopters hovering in the air, motionless and terrifying, above the screaming and groaning crowds who were scattering in all directions.

"How can this happen?" he cried, "such horror in the middle of Europe, in the nineteen eighties?" He thought once or twice of his wife at the hospital, but the explosions and shooting distracted him and made it difficult for him to think clearly. Blood is flowing down there, he said to himself, still not wanting to believe it. Perhaps the shots were only to disperse the crowds. But his heart knew it was not true. The wail of the ambulances pierced him to the marrow.

When the shooting died down he put on his coat, not knowing quite what he intended to do, and went out. He wanted to go downtown, but an army patrol stopped him at the first corner. The soldiers were in their winter uniforms, with helmets and machine guns. Paratroopers, he thought, the Nish Army Corps.

He spent the rest of the day pacing back and forth in his study, waiting for his wife to return. He still did not know what had happened. The telephone was dead. Everything seemed dead.

When she returned well after dark he knew the instant he saw her face that something had happened which could never be undone. Another hundred years of hatred, he thought with a kind of indifference. Perhaps two hundred. Perhaps another thousand.

"Well?" he asked in a hushed voice.

She shook her head, her face streaming with tears.

"It was horrible, Martin. A bloodbath."

She fell back onto the sofa and wept. He stroked one shoulder and then the other, but there was no way of soothing her convulsions. It would have been easier to calm an earthquake with his hands.

"You would never believe it," she moaned, "you would never ever believe it."

"I heard the shooting and the tanks."

"It was worse, much worse."

A bloodstain under her arm caught his attention and he stared at it in horror.

"You were wounded and you didn't tell me?"

"What are you talking about?"

"You're wounded. Your blouse is covered with blood."

"Where? Oh that."

She gave a twisted smile, her face a mixture of bitterness, pain and horror.

"Look."

She wearily removed her jacket, then her blouse and skirt, and he was shocked to see that even her underwear was stained with blood.

"Don't worry," she said, "I'm not wounded. It's other people's blood."

"Other people's blood," he repeated faintly.

"I operated on demonstrators all day."

"I heard the ambulances."

"Your student, that Romeo."

"Shpend Brezftohti?"

"I hardly recognized him. His ribcage was shattered."

A disaster, he thought. A disaster for us all. "Go and wash. I can't bear to look at you like that."

"What do you mean, wash?" she asked. "How can I wash?"

He stared at her. The words were devoid of meaning, or so it seemed to him. Perhaps other words were needed, a different syntax, a different kind of logic, to express what was happening.

"How can I wash?" she had said. She could never wash off the blood. Perhaps this was the meaning of the words she had spoken almost unthinkingly. But his mind had conjured up another more savage association. It was thus that Lady Macbeth had spoken of her crime. But his wife had played the opposite, the completely opposite role. It was they who were trying to turn what she had done into a crime. From the very start of that incredible inquiry at the hospital, every word they used had become twisted. What they called justice was a crime, and treating the victims became a criminal act.

The clock struck three. Let her rest, he said to himself. There was still time until five o'clock. He himself had no appetite, but he put a few things on the table anyway to make her think he had eaten.

The afternoon light filtered through the drapes, oblivious of its intrusion. He continued to pace back and forth across the room, which was gradually cooling off. The golden lettering of the book titles on the shelves of his library gave him a sense of being watched. On a couple of tightly packed shelves he had a whole history of hatred. Dozens of books on genocide, massacres, a real 'library of atrocities' as he used to say to himself, books full of denunciations and poison. You would think they had been printed not on earth but on a planet of serpents. The doctrine of academician Čubrilović on the extermination of the Albanians published a year ago by the Croatians, the old Albanian frontier epics, the Slav epics... Everything that could stir up the two peoples against one another was to be found on those shelves. Crimes from ancient times, anguish, visions of horror, calamity - not books, in short, but nests of scorpions issued from the printing press.

"We are not the ones who developed a doctrine for the extermination of the Serbs," he said to himself, turning abruptly towards the bookcase as if in response to a call. He moved forward a couple of steps and made a movement as if to stroke the many volumes of Albanian epic verse. "You are awakening, ancient titan," he thought. "It is for you that all this is happening."

For a long time his eyes remained fixed on the thick volumes. The chilly reflection of their blue covers seemed to contradict him. "He will not be awakened now," the professor thought to himself. "His limbs have been frozen for too long. It is we who are called upon to bear witness."

The epic of the impossible wedding procession, he murmured to himself, while trying to imagine the shattered ribcage of Shpend Brezftohti. If he were still alive, he would probably be delirious now, and in the midst of his delirium he would perhaps have a vision of his impossible marriage with Mladenka. The total upheaval of everything.

He took a look at his watch. "I wonder how Teuta is doing," he thought, wondering whether or not to wake her.

V

Afternoon. The book of the dead

In the other room, Teuta had not closed her eyes for a second. She had simply lain on her back and stared at one corner of the ceiling and then another. As if from some unseen loudspeaker above her, the questions asked at the meeting continued to rain down on her one after another. Have there ever been cases of suicide with six or more bullets in the corpse? Who gave the supplies officer the order to remove more beds from the storeroom? And what happened to the list of patients?

The worst questions came from the middle of the ceiling. She answered them slowly, promising herself after each one that she would not respond to any more. They are a filthy bunch and don't deserve an answer. And yet in her brain she continued to go over each response. The order for the beds was certainly at least a month old. It was no doubt simply a coincidence that it was carried out just before that fatal day. As for the suicides by gunshot, they were of course extremely rare, but not to be excluded. From her military training at the university, she remembered the description of machine guns, particularly malfunctions such as blockages, or accidental triggering of the firing mechanism. As for the patient register... Every time she pronounced these words, her subconscious mind associated the register of the wounded with the book of the dead. The Book of the Dead of ancient Egypt. The book of Job. It all came back to her in a muddle from her studies.

I refuse to speak to you anymore, you pack of barbarians, she said to herself. She closed her eyes so as not to see the ceiling anymore, and yet she felt a need to reply. I shall only answer to myself, she decided.

And indeed, she had already asked herself most of these questions. Who had given the order to increase the number of beds on the night of March 31? She really didn't know. In the previous meetings she had impressed everyone with the calm composure with which she had replied, "I never gave any order of the kind." Afterwards, everyone waited for the truth to come out, most of them anxiously, some regretfully, and other with savage delight: the thread must eventually lead to her and to no one else, since she was, after all, the head of the surgery department. Nonetheless, the more complicated the matter got, the more suspicion pointed in other directions, away from her. The supplies officer cited an observation by the head of administration supporting his claim that he had been behind schedule in setting up the beds that had been called for in the hospital's equipment plan. The head of administration, in turn, with minutes of the meeting in question in hand, stated that he had been the object of a similar observation on the part of the hospital management concerning the delay a month earlier, following publication of an article in the press demonstrating that the figures in the hospital's plan did not correspond to reality. The nursing aides upon whom the delegates focussed last in their relentless determination to find out why the beds had been set up on that night in particular and not the night before or the one after, were for the most part poor, uneducated women whose ignorance and tears stripped the situation of all drama, forcing the members of the presidium to abandon this line of questioning and say, "It's alright now, it's alright, that's enough, no one is holding a knife to your throat. We were simply asking for an explanation."

"Then who did give the order?" she had asked herself time and time again. Was it indeed purely by chance that the twelve beds had been set up the very night of March 31? It seemed a highly unlikely coincidence. Who then had given the order? She had suspected all of them, one after the other: the supplies officer, the head of administration, the secretary of the local section of the Communist League, his assistant, the three deputy directors and even the director-general himself. She had considered each of them, and had developed two different hypotheses: either the order had been given for humanitarian reasons as a sign of solidarity (in which case she was distressed at having been excluded from the secret), or it had been given as a provocation and there was a Judas in their ranks.

But the days passed and neither hypothesis had been proven. "Why twelve beds?" she had once asked herself during a meeting while the supplies officer and the head of administration referred for the hundredth time, as if in a recurring nightmare, to the discrepancy between the projected statistics and the actual number of beds, a discrepancy which both had been criticized for, the former by his immediate superior, the latter by hospital management which, as everyone knew, had been alerted by an article in the press. Why twelve, she wondered, until it suddenly dawned on her: the numbers nine and twelve occurred constantly in early Albanian ballads about the dead. Obsessed with this thought, she now believed she was beginning to solve the enigma. Twelve beds as in the old ballads. That would mean that no one had given the order for the number of beds to be increased. There was no need to do so. It had arisen of itself, from the depths of the collective unconscience. There had been unrest in Kosovo throughout the month of March, but it was not until the last night that one could sense that blood was about to flow. You could smell it in the air. Just as beds used to be set up so often in the mountain *kullas*[4] before a battle or an impending catastrophe for those who might be wounded (a precaution as natural as the preparations taken by hotels at the start of the tourist season), they had been set up in the surgery ward as soon as there was a smell of blood in the air, just as in ancient times.

She was sure that not even those implicated in the affair would have been able to explain why it had been done on that particular night. They were neither lying nor looking for loopholes when they submitted minutes of meetings at which they had been criticized for the delay. It was all true. But even if they had wanted to, none of them would have been in a position to explain the origin of the order which they had confusedly carried out as if in a state of hypnosis. For the same reason, the replies of the poor nursing aides - half words, half tears - were destined to remain only partially clear, like objects half submerged in water.

The same probably applied to the patient register, she thought. Let them search all they want with their secret police, dogs, laboratories and damned equipment, they'll never find anything.

Her gaze remained fixed for a long time on the smooth white surface of the ceiling. A sense of calm finally seemed to have returned to her. What more do you want to know, she asked, mentally addressing Kostić. She expected him to question her about the wounds from automatic rifles, and more. She thought he would mention the tanks, but he was careful not to fall into the trap.

"And bullets? Did you not see any bullets?"

She had seen them and had of course understood that something had happened. She realized that the wounded had been transported straight from the scene of the massacre and every time she clanked an extracted bullet into the metal bowl, a shiver went up her spine. She heard the voices of the old women she had known as a child, relating in the solemn tone appropriate to such tragic events, "Then they shot Azem.

---

[4] Alb. *kulla* - Fortified towers, in particular in the northern Albanian Alps. - Translator's note.

They got him in the lower ribs..." The voices blended with the routine monologue of the operating room: "Scalpel! Lancet! Pulse!"

She had not asked any questions herself so as not to put anyone in a difficult position. On several occasions her eyes met those of the assistant. On the other hand, she avoided the eyes of the anaesthetist, without quite knowing why. They were both Serbs and certainly realized what was going on. The assistant stared in a troubled, confused manner, as if the structure of his eyeballs had been altered, so that he was now looking inward instead of outward. She had difficulty imagining the reaction of this Serbian assistant of hers. A feeling of guilt for his compatriots who had committed such an atrocity? Blunt fear or a feeling of uneasiness at the sight of blood which suddenly ceased being 'operating room blood', if one could used such a term, but had become something else: blood spilt in a crime inherited from ancient times, enough to nauseate even a surgeon? Whether it was for this reason or for all three that he was unusually silent she could not tell. Later, recalling his silence, she thought to herself, it was better that way.

For he had maintained this silence even when they discovered an unusual trauma on one of the bodies, a section of a leg which had been completely crushed. Tank tracks, she cried to herself, restraining the shout which almost escaped her lips. Her eyes met those of the assistant for the last time. "What is this?" the expression in her eyes inquired and his expression, though already vague, endeavoured to reply, "Tank tracks, ma'am, what else could it be?"

The clock in her husband's study chimed. Ding, ding, ding, ding. The doorhandle turned silently.

"I'm up," she said when he appeared in the doorway.

"Don't you want anything to eat?" he asked.

She attempted to smile, thinking that even if her attempt did not succeed, it would at least wipe away some of the distress on her face.

"I'll try. Have you eaten?"

He made a gesture as if to say, "Don't worry about me."

She sat for a few minutes at the dining room table, more to convince herself and her husband at the same time that she had eaten something. Then they had a cup of coffee and he accompanied her to the door, without saying 'take care' or 'keep a cool head' or anything of the sort one usually says on such occasions. He simply gave her an affectionate smile, and she wondered as she left whether he did not think her stronger than she was. She was thankful at any rate for the quiet affection in his look and for the confidence he had in her, even if it were exaggerated.

Several times on her way, and again one last time as she was about to enter the hospital, she thought about that look, and suddenly it seemed to her that she understood the cause of the profound serenity in her husband's face. His confidence seemed to come from something that transcended the meeting, transcended even her, the women who had shared his life for almost twenty years.

VI

Afternoon of denunciation day

The meeting had been under way for an hour. The head of administration had spoken again, as had the supplies officer and the two elderly nursing aides, who ended up as always breaking into tears. Most of what was said was virtually identical to what had been said that morning, and at times Teuta felt as if it was not yet noon. The head of the maintenance service began with a lengthy explanation of how the ambulance drivers had used the hoses to wash the vehicles, which they had done several times on the first of April.

"Did you see blood with your own eyes?" Kostić interrupted.

"What do you mean?" the other replied somewhat perplexed.

"I am asking you whether or not you saw blood with your own eyes."

The head of the maintenance service shook his head.

"It never occurred to me, comrade Kostić. It was only today that I found out it was blood."

"Did you not wonder why the vehicles were being washed so often?"

"Well, how can I explain it? I did wonder in a way, but I didn't attach any importance to it. I thought the drivers were up to their old shenanigans, some minor infraction of the rules, like transporting butter or chickens or something and that they had been washing the cars to get rid of the evidence. That's what I thought."

"And then you and your men hurriedly fired the drivers to get rid of all the evidence yourselves," said Kostić.

"I am not authorized to fire the drivers," he replied.

"It doesn't matter who was authorized, you or someone else," snapped Kostić. "Have you got anything else of importance to say? If so, make it short."

The head of the maintenance service began once again to describe the washing of the vehicles, but his explanations were so roundabout and laborious, getting more and more complicated with every sentence, that the audience felt that they were becoming entangled in the same hose the drivers had used to wash the ambulances and which he would not cease to talk about.

The members of the presidium heard Kostić mumble 'idiot!' to himself, before raising his weary voice to cry, "Enough. We've already heard all that!"

Teuta Shkreli felt her stomach contract again. During the entire discussion about the drivers, attention had been drawn away from her. Now it seemed that the inquiry would soon get back to her. The extra beds, the ambulances, the disappearance of the register, - it was all gradually turning into a kind of delirium.

"And you? What can you tell us? You took part in the operations, didn't you?"

A heavy silence fell on the auditorium once again.

This was the first time that Kostić had addressed the two Serbs: the assistant and the anaesthetist. "When he is finished with them he will be back at me," the doctor thought.

The assistant rose first. He looked as troubled as he had at the beginning of April. His words were dry and seemed all the more so since it was evident at once that they were being uttered from a mouth devoid of saliva. He had no doubt that the patients operated on had been wounded during the demonstrations, he explained. There were not only bullet wounds from automatic rifles, which had been spoken of several times, but also traces of tear gas in the victims' faces and signs of other traumas caused by equipment which only the security forces disposed of.

"Did you not feel it was your duty to ask your superior who the people were that you were treating?"

"Who the people were was so evident that there was no need for such a question."

"Nevertheless, you should have asked, comrade doctor," Kostić continued. "If you had asked this question, Dr. Shkreli would not be able to hide behind her moral alibi. Or was it that continuous pressure was being exerted against you, as a doctor of Serbian nationality, to the extent that you felt intimidated?"

The assistant gave no reply.

"Well?" continued Kostić, "you mean you knowingly aided and abetted in the treatment of the enemies of Yugoslavia?"

"That is not the question," the assistant replied. "Enemies, even prisoners have a right to treatment."

"But they were not prisoners," Kostić cried out, "on the contrary, not a single pair of handcuffs has been found, not even a list of names. It is absolutely incredible!"

"That never occurred to me," said the assistant, "nor the fact that they might have been released, or indeed..."

"Indeed what?" asked Kostić when he noticed the assistant hesitate.

"Nothing," replied the assistant.

The testimony of the anaesthetist was almost the same. There was no doubt that the wounded were demonstrators. The fact was obvious whether one wanted to believe it or not. Everyone had known about the demonstrations and even from the hospital they could hear the sounds of gunfire. It would have been ridiculous to look for any other explanation of these injuries.

In reply to Kostić's question as to why she had taken part in treatment of criminals, the anaesthetist replied calmly that there was nothing unusual about it. Indeed...

Kostić was about to ask the same question he had asked of the assistant, "Indeed what?", but the anaesthetist continued, not allowing herself to be interrupted.

"Indeed in such cases, it is quite normal to keep criminals alive, for obvious reasons."

A vague murmur passed through the auditorium. Glancing left and right, the speaker was about to add something, but then seemed to change her mind and sat down.

The wave of murmuring in the auditorium continued. Teuta Shkreli's eyes met those of the man in the Borsalino hat she had seen that morning in the corridor. His face was flushed to the extreme and he moved his lips and neck constantly, like a drunkard trying to interrupt a conversation. Farther off, she saw the Tanjug reporter with the camera in his hands, which looked even more outdated with its black case.

Kostić began to speak once again.

"I appeal to you to treat these matters more seriously," he said. "Now, I was about to propose that we return to the question of the extra beds set up on the night of March 31, though some of you will no doubt think I am beating the same old drum again. I am quite certain that is what some members of the audience will be thinking. But let them think whatever they want. We shall return to this question not two or three times, but fifty times if need be. We will beat this drum time and time again until the truth becomes crystal clear because, as I said to you this morning, comrades, it is no small matter. The survival of Yugoslavia itself is at stake," he continued with a short pause for emphasis, "and it is up to each of us to ensure that the bell does not toll for our country."

Apparently satisfied with his metaphor (and the ensuing silence in the auditorium proved that it had been appreciated by those present), he looked around the room for a few moments.

"Why indeed, comrades, do I attach such significance to the question of the beds? Is it simply out of a desire to condemn someone or other? I have no such desire or aim. Dr. Shkreli would seem to have misunderstood me this morning. I have the greatest respect for her and her husband, who is known to be one of the most distinguished citizens of Kosovo. If I was impatient with her this morning or spoke discourteously, I would like to beg her pardon. I am not in any way ashamed of doing so, since, as I mentioned to you, comrades, greater interests are at stake."

He paused once again, reached for the glass beside the water jug and filled it half full. What happened during the lunchbreak? the doctor wondered. Even before he had begun this last speech, she had sensed that Kostić had lost the self-confidence he had had that morning. Was it something to do with her and her husband - perhaps they were preparing to force him to make a statement condemning the demonstrators - or was it a temporary easing in the general tension? She had no idea.

The man with the Borsalino hat whose eyes never left her for an instant seemed equally surprised at the tone of Kostić's last words. The Tanjug reporter gave a nasty look like someone refusing to hear what he was being told.

It could be something else, she said to herself. It was possible that in order to give a semblance of legality and fairness to the proceedings, to create the impression of a fight against all forms of chauvinism, that they had come up with the idea of condemning some overly zealous Great Serbian chauvinist, and that Kostić, well known as such, had got wind of the plan. Perhaps during the lunchbreak someone had made an allusion or his friends had warned him of the danger he was in.

"Before returning once again to our point of departure, to the beds," Kostić continued, "I would like to note that, seen from the outside, this matter might appear quite harmless and indeed I am certain that there are many here in the auditorium thinking to themselves 'Why does he attach such importance to such a small detail?' To be honest with you, comrades, it seems to me that the explanation which was given and which continues to be used, namely that the hospital plan had called for an increase in the number of beds for some time, etc., etc. does not hold up. Everyone knows that the real reason for the increase in the number of beds has to do with the demonstration." Kostić paused again, reached for the glass, but did not touch it. "To tell you the truth, comrades, the fact that extra beds were added because of the demonstration is not, in my eyes, a reprehensible act. I repeat, I do not regard this as a reprehensible act. I regard all the misunderstandings which arose at the beginning of the troubles as an understandable sign of sympathy and pity for the wounded students at a time when it was still not clear who they were and under what circumstances the events had occurred. A sentimental reaction is quite understandable under such circumstances, a desire to help the wounded, whoever they may be. Thus, as I have stated, I do not regard this as a crime. Of course I am disappointed that you are not willing to tell the truth, but to be absolutely sincere with you, I do not regard this as a crime either. Just as the motives I referred to are understandable, one can also comprehend the reticence to admit having willingly - or rather unwillingly - taken part in activities which may have seemed quite natural at the time, but which later turned out to be reprehensible. I am not sure if I am making myself clear, comrades."

"The sly fox," Teuta Shkreli thought to herself, as Kostić eyed the audience, his gaze rendered almost gentle by the very slightest of smiles.

"Comrade Kostić," she said calmly, "though the tone of your voice is rather different from that of this morning, I would nonetheless like to ask the question which you yourself posed rhetorically a moment ago: why such an emphasis on the beds? I mean, if both the motives of those who gave assistance to the injured and the motives causing them to deny having done so are evident to you, then we are entitled to ask: why prolong this prosecution?"

"This is not a prosecution, doctor," said Kostić with a chill in his voice, "I do not think I look like a prosecutor, do I? Or sound like one either."

"Excuse my inappropriate wording," she countered. "But the question remains: if everything is clear, why such emphasis on the beds?"

Kostić seemed to be having difficulty suppressing the savage gleam in his eyes. Then his face took on his expression of earlier - chilly and grey.

"There is still something unclear about the matter," he said in a restrained voice betraying a certain cautious hesitancy, "and it has to do with the date on which the new beds were added. They were set up the night of March 31, were they not, doctor?"

She nodded.

"This would appear to be of significance," he continued with the same hesitancy, "of primary significance."

"What do you mean?" she inquired, fearing that he would not reveal his thoughts further.

Indeed, the hesitancy Kostić felt about speaking his mind could almost be read on his face. He observed the audience, which was waiting like a suction-pump for him to release the words he was holding back.

"If the beds were set up on March 31, it meant that someone knew that the demonstration would take place the next day," he replied slowly, "and consequently, that someone was receiving orders from somewhere."

"Comrade Kostić," Dr. Shkreli broke in vigorously, "excuse my interrupting, but you spoke a few minutes ago about honesty and I do not think you are being entirely honest with us now."

"How dare you?" he said in a low voice.

"You said just now that treating the injured, setting up extra beds etc. was no great crime, nor was the reticence of those involved to own up. Now it turns out that you believe nothing of the sort. On the contrary, you allege that the beds were set up by secret order, illegally and so on. I would like to know which of these opinions is true."

A great commotion broke out in the auditorium. Kostić shook his head and waved his hand several times as if to say 'no', but it was unclear whether the gesture was meant to silence the audience or to contradict the doctor, or both.

"Dr. Shkreli," he protested, "you misunderstand me. I was simply stating a hypothesis."

"It was an accusation you made," she countered, "and it is an insult to us all."

"How dare you?"

To the doctor's amazement, it was not Kostić who shouted this but the man in the Borsalino hat who had leapt to his feet. The veins in his neck throbbed so violently that his crimson face seemed about to burst.

"Who are you?" demanded the doctor.

"How dare you insult the chief!" he bellowed, slurring his words. "You think we are back in the days when you could do whatever you wanted?"

"You are drunk," said the doctor, "Who let you in here?"

"Throw him out," ordered a voice from the podium which she recognized as belonging to the assistant director.

As two men approached to seize the drunken man, his stupefied gaze seemed to appeal to Kostić who, however, like everyone else, confirmed the order to have him thrown out with a wave of his hand. The drunk tried to resist but the two who had seized him by the arms managed to drag him out. As he passed through the doorway, he turned and shouted a torrent of abuse, but all they could make out of his ravings was, "sterilization of Serbian girls!"

"Quiet please, comrades," Kostić repeated several times. "I was only stating a hypothesis," he continued, once calm had been restored. "Perhaps it was an error on my part, but I simply wanted to show how one can be led astray by treating a matter like that of the beds too lightly. That is all I wanted to say. There is no need to dramatize the situation."

"Comrade Kostić," said the doctor, rising to her feet, "I am not the one who is dramatizing. Things are sufficiently dramatic in themselves. To insinuate that someone here in this auditorium has secret contacts with a conspiratorial group or is receiving orders from them is dramatic enough, isn't it? How can we accept such an insult?"

Kostić again shook his head in a gesture of denial, but his expression betrayed a certain weariness.

"Comrade Shkreli, it is your right to stick to your obsessive ideas if you want to. I can only repeat that it was not my intention to insult anyone. I simply stated, and I continue to maintain, that what happened here at this hospital on April 1, and at other hospitals in Kosovo, was no coincidence. It can be no coincidence, comrades, that extra beds were added just before the events began, that the ambulances were on the go in town all day long and in particular that the patient register has disappeared without a trace. Its disappearance means that we have lost the names of the very people who headed the rebellion, who shot at the police and battled with them. Do you realize the significance of this loss, doctor?"

"You are right on that point," she replied, "but that does not give you the right to make serious accusations concerning these other matters. As far as the patient register is concerned, as head of the surgery department, I can only tell you this: if the authorities who are investigating the matter discover the slightest shred of evidence that I had any connection whatsoever with its disappearance, I am willing to go straight to prison of my own accord, to be convicted without a word of defence. What more can I say?"

A stir ran through the auditorium once again. Amidst the dozens of faces turned towards her, Teuta became aware of one pair of eyes that were fixed on her hungrily. They were those of Dr. Rexha. At the morning session, too, when the disappearance of the register was mentioned, she had felt the intensity of his gaze, but had soon forgotten about it. It was impossible to take Dr. Rexha's face seriously. Even when he was seated, it was indissociable from his absurdly thin, elongated, puppet-like body. It was due not least to his appearance that the doctor had acquired a reputation as something of an oddity, not only in the surgery department, but in the whole hospital.

This time, however, despite the ridiculous proportions of his body, his disquieting stare made the doctor shiver. Those eyes which she was used to noticing quite casually, now had something electrifying about them. They seemed on the verge of exploding, as if they could no longer contain the emotion within them. What could it be, she wondered. And almost immediately it came to her: he knew something.

Shaken by the idea, she quickly looked away, as if to avoid a danger, but out of the corner of her eyes she noticed that his gaze was still fixed on her. He knows something, she thought once again with alarm. Something about the Book of the Dead.

Silence had returned to the auditorium. The assistant director was speaking. Slowly, like someone who wishes to avoid atracting attention, she directed her gaze once more towards Dr. Rexha. She gasped inwardly on seeing that his eyes were still fixed on her. He knows something, that's for sure, she thought. But why is he staring at me like that? She did not know whether it was better to disarm his stare with a smile or to pretend to ignore him. Either tactic might aggravate the situation.

She tried not to think about him. It was probably just her imagination and Dr. Rexha's expression meant nothing. The meeting had once more taken a monotonous turn, giving the impression more than ever that things were starting up all over again. The anaesthetist, replying to the assistant director's question, was explaining again that a number of the wounded did not need anaesthesia because they were already unconscious. "That is not what I asked you," said the assistant director, but the anaesthetist carried on undeterred. Perhaps because they were discussing anaesthetics and loss of consciousness, or because of the monotony of the discussion, the audience seemed to drift off into a state of general slumber. The dark circles under the eyes of many of those present betrayed their fatigue and impatience to have the meeting drawn to a speedy conclusion. The same apathy could be felt on the podium. Even Kostić's mind seemed to be wandering from time to time.

The assistant director looked at his watch and whispered something to Kostić. "Finally," she thought. Curfew hour was approaching and they would not be able to continue this torture indefinitely. Kostić nodded his approval. Even he seemed to want to extricate himself from this hopeless situation. It was obvious that something had happened during the afternoon break. A suggestion from above, a change of tactics or something else which no one could have imagined. Certainly there must have been some settling of scores among the Serbian officials too, even bitter power struggles. Who knew? Kostić's change of attitude was no coincidence.

"Be a bit more concise, comrade," said the assistant director to the person he was questioning.

The general impatience to end the meeting was now obvious. Some of the officials on the podium were engaged in private conversations, and this loss of attention communicated itself to the auditorium. Teuta felt a weight lift off her chest. This meeting too has passed, she thought, just like the others.

After consulting Kostić, the assistant director rose with the obvious intention of bringing the meeting to a close. He spoke briefly about the recent events which had shaken not only Kosovo and Yugoslavia, but all this region of Europe.

"All of us have something to learn from these events," he continued, "I believe that, despite some minor misunderstandings which, frankly, are inevitable on such occasions, our meeting here today has been very useful. Very useful indeed. It has at least taught us one thing: not to waiver in our vigilance. I am sure that Comrade Kostić agrees with me on this point. As far as I understand, this was his primary objective: to remind us to be vigilant."

Kostić nodded in agreement. His desire for peace and conciliation was obvious now.

After the meeting had ended, Kostić shook hands with everyone in turn, the last person he encountered being the doctor.

"Good-bye, doctor," he said, "let us let bygones be bygones."

He laughed and so did she. There was no longer the least sign of animosity in his expression. They were still surrounded by a group of people who smiled in approval at this conciliatory conclusion. Suddenly, as if to complete the scene, a camera flash went off to the right. The doctor turned, her smile dissipating at once. The expression of the Tanjug reporter was more that of a man who had just fired a weapon than that of a photographer pleased with his shot. It was fierce and tense, and betrayed a mixture of irony and hatred. She would not have been surprised at all if a puff of smoke had emerged from his camera.

The image of the reporter's face haunted her on her way home. That shot was no coincidence, she thought. Neither was Kostić's about-face. It was obvious that something was going on between them.

Her thoughts were interrupted by the sound of steps behind her. Before she could be sure that someone was trying to catch up with her, she saw a long shadow stretching out under her feet and heard someone gasp:

"Doctor!"

"Oh, it's you, Rexha," she said faintly, feeling a chill creep up her spine. With the reporter still on her mind, she had forgotten all about Rexha's tormented stare.

"Doctor," he stammered in a choked voice, "I wanted... I wanted..."

"What?" she broke in, refusing to look at him. "Can't it wait until tomorrow, at the hospital?"

"No," he replied, "I must speak to you now. Every time they mentioned the register, at the meeting..."

"Dr. Rexha," she interrupted once again, "These are not things to be discussed on the street. Come to my office tomorrow."

"No," he repeated obstinately.

She turned towards him.

"How dare you force me to listen to you?" she exclaimed in an authoritative tone.

He attempted to reply, and suddenly his thin, elongated body awoke in her a sentiment of pity rather than fear.

"I am not trying to prov... provoke you," he stammered. "You know, I was the doctor on duty the night of April 1."

Now he is going to tell me that he stole the register, she thought to herself. Why on earth does he have to confide his secret in someone, and why me in particular? All of the self-assurance she had shown at the meeting rested upon her not knowing the secret.

"Rexha," she said to him gently, "it's late now and the curfew is approaching. Let's leave it until tomorrow."

He swayed back and forth on his two long, puppet-like legs.

"I don't want to talk," he said, "I just want to give you this cassette."

Before she had time to wonder what the cassette might contain - music, a radio programme or statements by Radio Tirana about the events in Kosovo - she felt the cold plastic case in her hand. Her first instinct was to hand it back and tell him that such behaviour was not proper for a man of his age, or even, at the risk of insulting him, warn him that his act looked very much like a provocation? But then she decided that the most dangerous thing to do would be to stand there listening to him or discussing the situation at this late hour. At least, it had nothing to do with the patient register. That indeed would have been reason for alarm, but simply giving someone a cassette was nothing out of the ordinary, after all.

She stuffed the cassette into her purse and without giving him time for the slightest explanation, wished him good night. Then she hurried off, feeling safe only when she knew she was far enough away to be out of hearing distance, should he try to call her back.

She gave a sigh of relief. The fool, she murmured several times to herself. As if the events of the day had not been enough, now this idiot had scared her half to death for no reason at all. And what if the cassette contained only music? Anything was possible with an imbecile like that. Stupid, she thought to herself, but without any real anger towards him. I was the doctor on duty the night of April 1, she said, repeating his words, and shuddered. Was the cassette really innocent? Simply the whim of an eccentric perhaps?

That must be it, she thought to herself. What else could one expect from someone as strange as Dr. Rexha. After all, she knew nothing about the contents of the cassette. She could just as easily throw it into the gutter and be rid of all the worry.

What foolishness, she said to herself. Why should she have to put up with nonsense like this? In the distance she could see the light shining in the window of Martin's study. He will be waiting for me, she thought and hurried on. She could not wait to tell him everything that had happened.

VII

Twilight. Night

She turned towards her coffee which had grown cold in the meanwhile.

"There, I think I've told you everything," she said, putting her cup on the table. "What happened here?"

"I got a call from the Academy," he replied. "A meeting has been called for tomorrow."

"Oh?"

"Yes. It seems they are going to organize assemblies for writers and journalists, too."

"Now I see," she said. "That's why Kostić suddenly became so conciliatory."

"Precisely. That was my thought too when you mentioned him, but I didn't want to interrupt you."

"The standard manoeuvre," she said, "first the stick, then the carrot."

"If they ask me to make a public statement, I'm going to refuse," he stated, staring for some reason at the section of the bookshelves near the window. She tried to recall which books were in that section, but was too exhausted to think much about such details.

"Did you hear anything on the radio?" she asked.

He nodded.

"There is talk of repression. The truth is slowly coming out."

"When everything that happened here and is still happening comes to light, the whole world will shudder."

"That's true," he said, although she was not sure whether he was agreeing that the truth would come to light or that the world would shudder. "That's true. There are only a few objective newspapers left."

"It's mind-boggling," she uttered.

"It's barbaric, and worse." He cracked his knuckles nervously, as he often did when he was searching for a word or expression. "A demonstration takes place with people demanding... what are they demanding after all? Something that has been held in esteem for two thousand years, ever since the time of Caesar and Brutus, a noble aim, a 'republic'. And at the end of the twentieth century right in the middle of Europe they send in tanks against these people. Under the circumstances it shouldn't be difficult to choose sides."

"Unimaginable," she murmured for some reason.

"You can be against Albania," he continued, "or even against the Albanians in general, but in such a situation, with demonstrators on one side and tanks on the other, how could anyone side with the tanks?"

He rose and paced back and forth in the study.

"What else is new?" she inquired after a moment, "What did you do this afternoon?"

A faint and timid gleam shone in his eyes.

"I wrote a few lines of poetry."

"Poetry?" she said, "really?"

He rarely wrote poetry. In all his life he had only published a dozen poems, half of which written in his youth.

"Only four lines," he said, "maybe I'll add more later."
"Will you read them to me?"

"Sure. All the more willingly since they will have to be committed to memory. I'll have to burn the paper."

"Is it about...?"

She couldn't find the appropriate word. What would future generations call the as yet unnamed age which they were living in now? The time of terror? The season of revolt? The year of the republic? The age of denunciation?

"Yes," he said, and taking a slip of paper from his desk, began to recite:

Intrepid giants, you rose
With decency and majesty,
For a Republic you chose
And were put down by a monarchy.

"I don't like the word 'decency' but I haven't found anything better to replace it with."

"That doesn't matter," she interrupted, "Read it to me again, will you?"

When he looked up, he saw that she was shaking her head, as if to efface the pain from her expression.

"I can't stand it," she said, "I can't stand it anymore." Her shoulders trembled under the onslaught of sobs.

It took some time for her to regain her composure.

"Shall we have another cup of coffee?" he asked.

The clinking of the cups and the aroma of coffee calmed the atmosphere. She told him something she had forgotten, about the drunken spy who had been thrown out, and they tried to laugh a bit. But in the midst of their laughter, as if stabbed by the point of a knife, she was transfixed by the premonition that their levity was perhaps premature.

"It can't be that easy for them," he stated, "not that easy at all."

"The whole machinery has been put into motion," she said. "I didn't even know that Yugoslavia had so many party, government and state organizations, so many different socialist councils and communist leagues. God only knows how many provincial, inter-provincial and federal committees and assemblies there are. Who would believe it? I wonder if anyone takes it all seriously?"

"What did you say?" he interjected. "Say that again, will you?"

"I said I wonder if anyone takes it all seriously."

"Wonderful," he said, "you've hit the nail on the head, Teuta. That's the key to the enigma... I mean, that's the explanation: Does anyone take it all seriously? Therein lies the secret of Kosovo at this very moment. It's like the scene in 'Alice in Wonderland' where Alice says to the officials who wants to condemn her to death: 'You're nothing but a pack of cards.' Remember that scene? It's the same here in Kosovo. It's like Alice in Wonderland and the playing cards trying to chop off her head."

"But these playing cards have tanks and prisons," she observed.

"I know, but that doesn't change a thing."

"They're still arresting people."

"They're insane," he said. "How many more are they going to arrest?"

"I've heard they're planning to replace all the top leaders of the province of Kosovo. The young wolves are hungry, eager to make careers for themselves."

"Of course they are," he replied. "There will always be false prophets and new Judases ready to betray for thirty pieces of silver. There will be the crucified and the crucifiers, Pilates who will wash their hands of the matter, Fausts who will sell their souls and Mephistopheleses who will buy them. There will be tyrants and Prometheuses. Within a few months, Kosovo will have lived through the whole tragedy of mankind."

In the silence which ensued, she tried to suppress a sigh.

"Kosovo is strong," he added, as if she had been about to voice an objection. "It will survive."

As they talked, he became aware that she was staring at her hands. The blood of Kosovo had flown between her fingers. No waters of the ocean could 'wash this blood clean'. There she was, his wife, this very antithesis of a Lady Macbeth, sitting pensively on the sofa.

"None of us will ever be the same, after what has happened," he said quietly. "This afternoon, a young writer came to see me to pick up a manuscript he had given me to read before the events. It was an unusual book, interesting though rather superfluous. 'Hairstyles Around the World' it was called. It contained all sorts of facts and reflections on hairstyles over the centuries, curious information, medicinal and philosophical aspects, changes in fashion. Peoples' methods of combing their hair, their significance, legends about the connection between hair and strength, the theme of hair colour in literature, stress caused by balding, capillomania, capillophobia, racism and hair, haircutting rites, the use of wigs by the aristocracy etc., even shampoo ads and the profits made by the various cosmetic trusts. It was not an uninteresting book to leaf through, but the author blushed from ear to ear when he heard I had read it. 'I wish you hadn't,' he told me. 'I'm ashamed of it.' And he added, 'If there is anything of interest to be said on this subject, it can only be about the shaven heads of the prisoners in the jails of Kosovo. But my book doesn't have anything to say about that.' That's what he told me."

"You are right," she said, "none of us will ever be the same."

Only the ticking of the clock broke the ensuing silence.

"For a Republic you chose and were put down by a monarchy," she repeated to herself.

"You've had a hard day," he said, "wouldn't you like to lie down?"

"No, not yet. Oh, what is the matter with me," she exclaimed a moment later, "we have to think about supper. Is there anything in the fridge?"

"I think so. But you're tired. Let me make supper."

She smiled.

"If the book you were telling me about had been about cooking around the world, maybe..."

He started to laugh.

She got up and he followed her into the kitchen. The familiar clatter of pots and pans was a relief to their ears. As she beat the eggs for an omelette, they continued talking about the meeting to be held the next day at the Academy, about Kostić's change of attitude, connected no doubt with the struggle for power between two mighty clans, the Serbs on the one hand and the Croats and Slovenes on the other. Of course, things were going on outside the borders of Kosovo, too. The federalists could not just sit back with their arms crossed before the fury of the Serbs. The latest statements by Bakarić and Dolanc... Up there too, at the heart of things, the fuse was burning.

"The heart of things is right here," he said suddenly, pointing out the window where the dark of night had already fallen. "They say that one-third of the Yugoslav army is stationed here."

After supper, she washed the dishes and returned to the study to join her husband who was fiddling with the television antenna to try to overcome the interference caused recently by the jamming of Radio Tirana.

The last news broadcast had begun, but the interference was so strong that it was impossible to watch it.

"Stay where you are," she said, "I think they're talking about us."

"You can't see anything."

"But you can hear the sound a bit. Stay where you are."

"You're right. They are talking about us."

The speaker was presenting commentaries by the foreign press on the events in Kosovo.

"It's a miracle," she uttered, "a miracle, Martin."

"Too bad we didn't turn it on earlier."

As they listened, he suddenly recalled something which had happened that afternoon. After the news he would tell her. Mark Rugova, his greatest adversary in the debates between Martin and his friends, had paid him an unexpected visit. He was in a bad state. Not only his eyes but his hair, too, had a glassy sheen.

"Have you seen what they have done to us?" he cried out before he had even entered the room. "We baptised the word 'republic' in blood. What other country on earth has produced so many Brutuses in this century? Thousands of them. What do you have to say now?"

He waited for a few seconds for Martin to contradict him, then lept from the sofa and began pacing around the study.

"Well, what do you have to say now?" he shouted again. "Civilized behaviour, the advancement of justice, Aeschylus' Oresteia... Come on! If that's the way it is, I'd rather not be among the civilized. To hell with Aeschylus and his justice. I want my own justice in the name of the blood that has been spilt and demands retribution."

Martin was about to interrupt when Mark took a piece of paper out of his pocket and brandished it in front of him.

"Look what a Serbian colleague of mine wrote: 'I am ashamed, ashamed of what has happened. This shame I share with all those who lay claim to the true Serbian culture, in the name of which I fall to my knees and beg forgiveness of you, my colleague, my brother, my fellow human being.' That's what he wrote. And I couldn't care less. No forgiveness will bring the dead back to life. Or do you still believe in such nonsense?"

Martin hesitated for a second. Was this the right day to argue the point? But Mark had already forgotten his question and continued.

"And they have the audacity to blame us! Good God, there is a limit to everything. Soon they will start accusing the victims of tiring out the executioners, of costing the murderers too much ammunition, of disrupting the movement of tanks with their mangled bodies... Do you hear what I am saying? Tell me the truth, Martin, I would sincerely like to know, do you still believe in that nonsense about Aeschylian justice, about the renunciation of vengeance..."

"Yes, I do," Martin broke in.

Martin had replied without hesitation, but his assurance waivered as Mark slammed the door behind him, muttering 'deluded soul'. For a long time, he stayed frozen to the spot, wondering if Mark was not right after all.

They sat listening to the television commentary, but all the while his thoughts were fixed on his meeting with Mark Rugova. No, Mark, he said to himself, you are wrong.

The black lines of the jammed transmission continued to dance madly across the screen, but the news on Kosovo was over and they turned their backs on the television. They were in a jubilant mood. Their hope for an easing of tensions had not been premature at all. Kostić's sudden affability and the rumours about a power struggle between the two rival clans were no coincidence. Although it was late in coming, world opinion was making itself felt. The Serbs were on the defensive and the federalists were finally taking action. There were rumours that things were stirring in the Vojvodina too, not to mention the mass meetings and demonstrations that had taken place all over Europe. No, Kostić's retreat was no coincidence. There were signs of change everywhere. It had to come. The madness could not continue much longer.

He took a bottle of cognac out of the cupboard and poured himself half a glass.

"Would you like some?"

"All right," she said, "but only a drop."

"Cheers," he said, "to the Republic!"

"For a Republic you chose," she said to herself.

"Cheers, Martin."

"Don't you want to go to bed," he inquired. "You should get some rest."

"I'm not the least bit sleepy. And anyway, I want to listen to the last news broadcast."

He changed the channel for Belgrade and looked at his watch.

"What an exhausting day," she said. She felt relaxed now, almost happy.

The familiar theme for the national news from Belgrade roused her from her drowsiness. As usual, the first item was about a state visit by an African prime minister. Statements on non-alignment, on the Third World followed - the same old platitudes. There were reports on Poland and on the economy. Nothing about Kosovo at all, she said to herself and got up. She said good night to her husband and left the study.

What was it that made her come back in a second later? Had she sensed the sudden movement of Martin's head towards the bedroom door she had just closed? In fact, he had looked around not so much to call her back but to ensure that she had closed the door behind her. He had even had time to breathe a sigh of relief that she was gone and could no longer hear the broadcaster's voice. Although he was not yet sure what the report was about, as soon as he heard the reference to the hospital where his wife worked, it would have been the most normal thing in the world for him to call her: "Teuta, come back, they're talking about your meeting at the hospital today." But he did nothing of the kind, and even thought to himself, "Thank goodness she's gone." Neither at that moment nor later could he explain what ominous foreboding kept him from calling her back.

Intrigued by the look in his eye, she regarded him quizzically from the doorway of the bedroom for a moment or two, as if to say, "What are you doing there behind my back, plotting with the TV?" His impression of having been caught in the act was so strong that he almost jumped up to turn off the television. But of course he could do nothing of the kind, nor could he tell her to go to bed as one does a child who is too young to watch a certain television programme. There was nothing he could do. It was too late.

Too late indeed. His wife was no longer looking at him. She was staring at the television as if mesmerized by the images unfolding before her. It was no longer a premonition: something ominous was indeed happening on the screen. She immediately recalled the fierce expression of the Tanjug reporter and the final flash of his camera, like the crack of a gun. The report was on the meeting of that morning, which the correspondent described as liberal, "No answers were given at the meeting to the questions raised both there and by public opinion throughout Yugoslavia. On the contrary, there has been an obvious desire right from the beginning to terminate the affair as quickly as possible. But the issues cannot be evaded that easily. The questions which have aroused the interest of the public remain unanswered. Who requisitioned the hospital's ambulances at three in the afternoon, at the very height of the demonstration? Why has the register of admissions for April 1 still not been found and, finally, who ordered extra beds to be set up the night before the events, thus pointing to a preconceived plan and not, as has been falsely claimed at previous meetings, a decision taken spontaneously in the early afternoon of April 1, when the urgent need for them became apparent? These and other questions require precise answers and not the evasive responses and alibis which were offered at the hospital in Prishtina today... We continue with other stories in the national news."

Their eyes met at this point.

"The bastards," she murmured. "Who would believe that Tanjug is run by such bastards."

His face was even paler than hers. Their happiness had been premature. Kostić's change of heart and their supposition that something had happened during the afternoon break, the apparent shift in the balance of power, the counter-attack by the federalists, had all been nothing but a big lie.

"They really are bastards," he agreed. "Going around spying on everybody... it's disgusting."

"I never thought they would sink so low," she mumbled. "And they call themselves a news agency..."

"Nothing but fucking spies," he exclaimed, turning off the television.

She looked up. It was the first time she had heard her husband use such language.

"That means it was useless for us to..."

"No," he interrupted, "no, it's not the way you think, Teuta. I haven't changed my mind from what we were discussing earlier. You mustn't forget that at Tanjug, just as in the Ministry of the Interior and parts of the army, the supporters of Great Serbian chauvinism are still in control."

"That's what I've heard," she sighed.

"It's no use upsetting yourself over it," he continued. "Such a ridiculous news agency. Come on. You found the perfect word for them: bastards." He tried to laugh. "It's late, Teuta, let's go to bed."

As she prepared to follow him into the bedroom, a thought pulled her up short. She had just remembered the order issued three days earlier requiring the front doors to be left unlocked at night.

"The door," she whispered, "did you unlock the door?"

"Oh, I forgot!" he exclaimed, "Good God, everywhere else on earth, before going to bed, people ask, 'Did you lock the door?' Here it's just the opposite. They ask whether you've left it open."

"I wonder how far back they had to go for that one," she said. "Some mediaeval custom, no doubt."

"I've never heard of such a rule being enforced anywhere, not even in curfews during the Nazi occupation."

"Maybe this is something they thought up on their own."

"That's quite possible."

"Wait a second," she added, as he headed towards the door. "The poem. If you leave the door unlocked, you'll have to burn it."

"You're right," he said and went over to his desk. "I'll read it one last time to commit it to memory."

"Don't worry. I'll remember it. All the time we were talking, the lines kept going through my mind."

She listened to the sound of his steps down the hallway and the click of the key turning in the lock. How dreadful, she thought and shivered with a mixture of disgust and cold.

She had heard that many people, despite the police order, could not get used to sleeping with their doors unlocked and preferred to lock them and run the risk of prosecution rather than spend a sleepless night. There were nights on which they themselves took a sleeping pill. I'll need a Valium tonight, she thought as Martin got into bed. She searched through her purse to find the little vial and suddenly froze. Her fingers had touched something smooth and cold. The cassette, she thought, horror-stricken. How could I have forgotten it?

"Good night," said Martin, slipping under the covers.

"Good night," she replied and turned off the lamp.

VIII

Night of the open doors

"Good night," she repeated in the darkness of the bedroom. She still had her hand in her purse. How could she even think of sleep under such circumstances. The cold plastic case of the cassette froze in her hand. Not only the unlocked doors, but now the cassette, too, to ruin her sleep. A stick of dynamite would not have been any worse.

She slowly released the cassette and withdrew her hand. What should she do? Should she get up quietly and hide the cassette somewhere, or... But hide it where? It would be no less dangerous anywhere in the house. She had no other choice but to... No, she said to herself abruptly. She could never do that. To destroy the cassette would be an act of cowardice. The man who had given it to her, had run a terrible risk. Who knows what risks had been taken with it until it reached her, only for her to destroy it? Never, she thought. All the safe hiding places in the house crossed her mind: the floorboards, the garden, the garage, the cushions of the sofa. It should not be difficult to find a place for such a small object.

And what if all this worry were in vain, she thought. She felt a wave of anger against Dr. Rexha rising within her. "The fool," she murmured to herself, "the fool." It was idiots like him who could drive you mad. But the anger did not last long. She knew she was being unfair to the doctor, for the simple reason that she still did not know what was on the cassette. She was accusing him without having listened to it. But what if...

That would be unfair of me, she thought all of a sudden. How could I... (words like 'judge', 'accuse', 'fear' all mingled in her brain to form a sort of extra-linguistic mush). She had to listen to the cassette before she could... judge (etc., etc.) the doctor. Not to listen to it would be like refusing to answer a call for help. Perhaps it was a desperate appeal?

On the other side of the bed, Martin turned over again. It would be better not to disturb him. After all, she still had no idea of what the tape was about. It could be something serious, as she suspected, but it could also be nothing at all.

At this point she was not even sure what she would have preferred: a dangerous cassette, but one whose contents at least had to be taken seriously, or something completely harmless but grotesque. All in all, she would probably prefer the former. Despite the risks involved, despite everything...

She had made her decision: she would listen to the cassette. She waited a few more minutes to be sure her husband was asleep, and then got up. She was perfectly calm. She closed the door carefully behind her and stood for a while in the middle of the dark living room, unable to decide on the best place to sit. She needed a spot far enough from the bedroom, but at the same time far enough from the main door. If the police were to make an unexpected entry, she would have to have enough time to... The unlocked door, she thought. What a disgrace!

She stood in the living room for several minutes, trembling in the cold. She knew she should move, do something. First of all, find the tape recorder.

She finally managed to overcome her paralysis. She remembered that the tape recorder was in Martin's study. She would go and get it and then find an appropriate place to listen to the tape. The bathroom occurred to her several times because of the possibility of locking the door, but she decided against it. By locking herself in the bathroom, she would have the impression that someone else was forcing her to listen to the tape.

She quickly located the tape recorder, turned off the light and stood in the dark again, not knowing quite where to go. Her daughter's room, she thought. She entered the hall, careful not to bump into anything, and opened the door. Since her daughter had left for Zagreb to study, they rarely entered that room. Teuta shivered slightly at its emptiness. The radiators hardly worked anymore. She approached the window. There was no sign of life outside. They could not break in that quickly, she thought, unless there was a special unit like those used for freeing hostages.

Her fingers searched in the dark for the eject button on the tape recorder to put the cassette in. Turning on the light was out of the question. The sound of the tape turning told her that she had found the right button. Her heart was pounding. I have to listen to it, she repeated to herself several times, as if in response to a voice deep inside urging her to give up. And what if... Suddenly the blank cassette came to life. But what was it? You could not really call it a noise or a voice. It was a... nothing. The only thing she knew for sure was that she had pressed the right button. She bent over to get closer to the speaker. Music of sorts, but very vague. Hardly audible. Echoes as if from another world. What could it be? Voices from the hereafter, melodies of dreams, if dreams had melodies... Nonsense, she thought to herself. It was simply a cassette with remnants here and there of music which had been erased. Why would he have handed her an empty cassette? The joke of a madman, unless... No, she should not decide too hastily - there might be something on the other side. She listened for a while to the vague noise, inaudible music from another world, and was just about to change sides when something like a gust of wind came out of the speaker. It sounded like someone gasping for breath or groaning, both at the same time perhaps. "They're shooting from behind," a stifled voice uttered, as if emanating from the porous body of the wind. "Watch out! They're shooting from the windows, damn them!" The words were spoken by the same voice which had groaned. "The whole Nish Army Corps is on the attack. Watch out, they're shooting from the windows. God help us if the tanks show up..."

She was bent over the tape recorder, her ear to the speaker, in a position she assumed many times a day at the hospital when following the agony of a dying patient. Indeed she was so absorbed in listening to the sounds of pain that she almost spread her arms out in the darkness to feel if the patient was still alive, to take his pulse, his temperature. At that moment she remembered that it was only a tape recorder and that the injured victim was far away, etherialized, so to speak. It was only his delirious ravings, registered under who knows what circumstances that Dr. Rexha had wanted her to hear.

"They're shooting from behind... Enough... The republic, come what may... That's it, that's it..." The voice dissolved into a groan from time to time, then the words became distinct again. The groaning receded like a wave, only to rise up once more, blocking out everything else.

As she listened, immobile, she felt her hands ought to have been holding syringes, giving penicillin, or morphine to dull the patient's pain.

In fact, she herself had not heard any suffering of the kind that day. Most of the wounded were unconscious, and none of them was delirious. Perhaps Dr. Rexha had given her the cassette for this reason, as a sort of soundtrack to the day's mute activities, the way the sounds and voices are dubbed into a film.

The cassette came to a sudden halt and in the ensuing silence it was as if half of humanity had perished. She knew that she would not be able to pull herself away easily. And so it was. She played the cassette again and again, each time recalling the faces of the patients whom she had treated on the first of April.

When she returned to the bedroom, making every effort to be quiet, her husband awoke.

"What's wrong?" he asked. "Where have you been?"

"It's nothing," she replied, realizing at the same time that it was unfair to hide the truth from him. "I want you to listen to something."

Without saying another word, he got up and followed his wife into their daughter's bedroom. As soon as he heard the voice of the wounded man, he whispered, as if in a dream:

"It sounds like the voice of Shpend Brezftohti."

"Really?"

They listened to the recording several times and each time Martin was sure that he recognized the voice as Shpend.

The day dawned. A grey gloom invaded the room through the window panes.

"Daybreak," he said, "we can lock the door."

She went down the hallway to turn the key in the lock, returning to the study to find him with the cassette in his hand.

"You can hide it among the books," she said, nodding towards the libary.

Once he had found a spot for it, he returned to her side, noticing how pale she was from the sleepless night she had spent.

"You should get at least an hour of sleep," he suggested gently, "You may have another difficult day before you."

She turned towards the picture window to see what kind of day it would be. The cold, grey weather continued to assail the window panes. A day of denunciation, she thought. What else could such a day bring?

IX

Day

It was one of those rare days on which she arrived at the hospital late. Her head was still sluggish, the result of her sleepless night. Nonetheless, walking down the hallway to her office, she felt a certain satisfaction at the relief her presence caused in the eyes of those she met. "Why are you late?" they seemed to say. "You can imagine how worried we were on a day like today." If only they knew what a night she had been through!

Once in her office, she took off her coat and sat down at her desk where she remained motionless for a moment with her eyes fixed on the calendar. Wednesday, April 15. Sunrise 5:02 a.m. Sunset 6:20 p.m.

"Well, here we are," she said to herself in a sort of stupour. Her thoughts were still a bit unclear, foggy. She mused upon the infinite series of days brought forth by the universe, days according to a precise grid of hours, minutes and seconds. It was a superb creation, worthy of the immensity of the cosmos, bathed in freedom and light, but progressively debased by the inhabitants of this planet called Earth.

She surprised herself by this unusual flight of fantasy. Her eyes remained fixed on the calendar as if to prolong the daydream. The days, like everything else recently, were out of touch with nature. Whereas in the past one spoke of cold days or hot days, cloudy or sunny days, now they were divided differently: days of denunciation and others which were simply days. The seasons, the air, the birds, the rain, the falling leaves formed no part of the former. The same was true of the nights which, though no worse than the days, were also cut off from the rhythms of nature. Nights, spring nights, autumn nights, starry nights... None of them existed any longer. There were nights of open doors, leaving one sluggish and inert as she was today. That was all. How barbaric, she thought to herself.

She finally rose from her desk and took her white coat off the hanger. On her agenda were two operations, her rounds, and the usual briefing at noon.

What would this new day have to offer? The question arose in her mind once again as she was leaving her office. There was no hint of upset in the hallway. The eyes of the head nurse betrayed no particular sign of tension. Had they listened to the national news? The faces of her Serbian assistant and the anaesthetist showed nothing. Nevertheless, a couple of times during the operation she sensed a certain hostility in the reflection of the surgical knife. She could hardly wait for the coffee-break between the two operations to probe more deeply the attitudes of her colleagues. Fortunately, the coffee room was full so they could speak quietly to one another without drawing attention to themselves. "Did you watch the news last night? It was incredible. I could hardly believe my eyes, though we are accustomed to a lot of things nowadays."

She spoke alone with the head nurse and a cardiologist. As they talked, they held their coffee cups close to their mouths so that no one could read their lips. "I don't understand why the global news services don't revolt and break off ties with them. They should cut off their teletypes." "That's easier said than done. Do you think the major news services really care so much about people's problems? They're used to things like that." "I don't think that Tanjug can make things any worse. The wound has to be treated as quickly as possible, not irritated further. I even heard that they are preparing to present us with a formal apology. Anyway, it's in the interests of Yugoslavia to put an end to all this hatred. Tanjug can do all the mudraking it wants. Passions will calm. Didn't Kostić arrive like a hawk the day before, and turn into a dove? That is what will happen: tension, appeasement, tension, appeasement - until everything is back to normal." "You're right. Let Tanjug howl all it wants. No one listens to them anyway. But what were you saying about an apology?" "It is apparently being discussed, though I can't really believe it. If it is true, it would be amazing, considering the circumstances."

They continued discussing the subject on their way back to the operating room. Rumour had it that the whole Serbian people were preparing to ask forgiveness for the massacre of the Albanians. Women, children and old people were to march forth in a long procession bearing old Slavic icons, candles, portraits of Tito... Such were the rumours, though they were probably no more than a figment of someone's imagination, and a rather morbid one at that.

They entered the operating room with a real feeling of relief. The assistant and the anaesthetist were already there, their faces calm. They were all tired of the hostility and needed rest. The patient to be operated on, as if especially chosen, was not an Albanian or a Serb, but a Gypsy. All that was missing to complete the picture of the ideal operating room was some background music and a solemn declaration of unity and brotherhood between the peoples.

The Gypsy smiled nervously as they laid him out on the operating table.

"Now count to ten."

The numbers emerged, enunciated one by one from the Gypsy's mouth, weakly and each one more remote than the last, as if they were trying to escape the unhealthy body on the point of losing consciousness.

The operation took longer than they expected. They were surprised to see it was almost two o'clock by the time they had finished. They had to have lunch before doing their rounds.

As the team left in a group for the lunchroom, the doctor thought to herself that in spite of everything, they could still work together in peace, that if they could spend whole days devoid of hatred, one hundred such days would suffice, or one thousand at the most, for the wound to heal. The scar would be covered over with new skin, strong enough not to be infected again so easily by the slightest scratch. Her thoughts returned to the rumour of an apology which, though it was no doubt pure fantasy, nevertheless corresponded to the secret desire of both sides.

"You look happy," the head nurse whispered at her side.

"Why shouldn't I be? The operation was a success, wasn't it?"

"Of course. And Boro told me you were wonderful today."

"Really?"

She had in fact noticed a gleam of admiration in the eyes of her assistant at the most difficult moment of the operation. Oh, she sighed to herself, we can live without hatred. And again, against her will, the image of a long procession of old Slavic icons, candles and portraits of Tito came into her mind.

Lost in these thoughts, she entered the lunchroom only to encounter sombre faces. The expressions were the same ones she had seen on the worst days of all.

"What has happened?" her eyes seemed to inquire, though they received no answer. Something dreadful had taken place. Something extraordinary, it seemed, since no one, by so much as a look or a gesture, would betray the slightest hint of what was going on. The event was of such gravity that the means of expressing it had not yet been created.

"Has something happened?" she finally asked impatiently of a young doctor seated at the table on which she had placed her tray.

The doctor stared at her for a few seconds.

"Yes, of course something has happened."

Her fork remained poised in mid-air. How was it that not one day passed without something going wrong? What a bother, she thought.

"Well, what is it?" she inquired quietly.

"Someone threw a bomb at the Yugoslav Embassy in Tirana."

"A bomb? In Tirana?"

He nodded.

She did not know what to do with her fork. The object in her hand had suddenly lost all meaning. The words she had just heard the doctor speak seemed devoid of meaning, too. A bomb... in Tirana.

Slowly, as if in a dream, she envisaged the trajectory of the bomb before it hit the Embassy building. Suddenly, more rapidly than she had expected, it picked up speed and struck. She grasped the full implications of the tragedy. A bomb. There was someone who could not stand to see a day pass without anger and hatred.

"It's true," the doctor added without looking up.

"But who could have done it?" she whispered.

He shrugged. They did not know one another well enough to pursue the conversation any further. And anyway, there was no need to say more. It was well known who was inciting hatred. Last night Tanjug, today the bomb. Someone could not stand to live without poisoning their existence. And what if... (she tried to repress the thought, but it was too late), what if there were dark forces at work in Tirana too, spreading poison. She refused to believe it, and yet, it was there that the bomb had been thrown.

She was about to ask whether the Albanian government had made an official statement when the doctor got up and said good-bye.

"It looks like the heat is going to be on again," said the head nurse as they were returning to the ward.

"Of course. That's why the bomb was thrown in the first place."

At three o'clock, as they were getting ready to make their rounds, the victim of a traffic accident was brought in and the doctor, along with her team, found herself back in the operating room. She sensed right away that her assistant and the anaesthetist had heard the news about the bombing. As if the bomb had exploded right in their midst, fragments of it struck their cheeks, the corners of their mouths and all the other parts of the face needed to make a smile among friends.

This is what our days will be like from now on, the doctor thought to herself as she stretched out her hand for the scalpel. She was so absorbed by the thought of the bomb that she forgot for a moment that the bloodstained body in front of her was the victim of a traffic accident and bent over the mutilated body, searching for splinters from the explosion.

It was late in the afternoon when she finally prepared to leave the hospital, exhausted from a hard day's work. The hallway was so dimly lit that she had to look at her watch several times, and as she was leaving, Sanija, the elderly cleaning lady of the ward, called out to her:

"It's hard to believe how fast time flies, doctor. God must be shortening our days."

The old woman's words came into her mind several times on her way back home.

X

Night of the open files

With the exception of a few isolated lights in the Grand Hotel, the downtown buildings were all pitch dark. Dobrila stared at the hotel for a moment and then shook his head mysteriously. The silence and the emptiness in all directions were broken only by his steps on the sidewalk, and those of Vladan beside him. On either side of the street they saw silhouettes of soldiers in their raincapes standing in the dark. They could not make out the faces but were well aware that their every move was being followed. They had not been stopped by anyone, perhaps because of the confident sound of their steps on the pavement or their nonchalant air. It was a thrill for Dobrila to be out like this, long after the curfew, when everyone else had to stay indoors.

"Halt. Your permits!"

This sudden cry caught both of them unawares. They nonetheless relished someone checking their papers, knowing full well that everything was in order.

The soldier took a close look at their permits and gave Dobrila a long stare before returning the documents to them. Dobrila smiled.

"Where are you from?"

The solder gave no reply.

"A Slovene," said Dobrila when they were a few steps out of hearing distance. "Why do they send us material like that?"

"They've replaced part of the Serbian forces," said Vladan, "so that no one can say..."

"That's stupid," Dobrila broke in, "It's Serbs we need here and not sissies who don't even know how to wipe their noses."

"There's nothing you can do about it. It's politics," Vladan replied.

Dobrila drew a flask from his coat pocket, took a slug of slivovitz and offered it to his companion who shook his head.

"Let's get out of here," said Vladan, "It's better up in the residential neighbourhoods."

He was right, and the word 'better' was hardly strong enough to describe the magical attraction of the residential neighbourhoods with their row upon row of front doors, shrouded in shadow, heavy masses of wood and iron complete with bronze fittings - not one of which was locked or bolted. One had only to turn the handle and step inside. It was like women with nothing on under their skirts, Jovica had said on the first of their nocturnal rounds. All you had to do was reach out your hand... But neither that night nor any of the nights that followed did they have the courage to enter anywhere. Something stopped them at the last moment every time they tried. But the idea alone that they could force their way into any of the houses, demand to see the inhabitants' papers, pull the women from their beds, interrupt their love making and prevent the fertilization of an embryo, was a source of untold pleasure for them.

"Let's check this one out," Dobrila said in a low, muffled voice.

Vladan looked towards a doorway on their right, only to realize that Dobrila had not been referring to any one door in particular.

"We've got time," he replied, "we'll decide later."

The same story every night, Dobrila thought. When would they finally do it? What if the special order were withdrawn before they had gotten around to trying out their magical powers. If only Jovica were here.

"Where is Jovica, by the way?" he grumbled.

"We'll probably meet up with him."

The neighbourhood was plunged in darkness, except for a very few yellowish lights which shone from windows here and there.

"Look, there's the house of that damn doctor woman," uttered Dobrila, stopping for a moment. "Last night and the night before that window was lit up until midnight. I kept watch here for quite a while. What I would give to know what was going on in there so late at night! I was on the point of going in once, but I don't know what it was that stopped me. And on top of that, the guy I was with was a complete twit."

Vladan gave a cough. Both of them were breathing heavily.

"You know what?" said Vladan, nodding towards the window. "I wouldn't mind showing that bitch my teeth. And we might discover something too."

"What do you think you would find there?" Vladan asked. "Books, that's probably all they've got."

"Give me the flask, will you?" said Dobrila who was first to move on. They both had a drink. Then Dobrila stopped again. "Look over there," he said, pointing to the sign at the entrance of one of the buildings. "That's the office for the Serbs and Montenegrins wanting to emigrate from Kosovo. Do you see what I mean? That is where Serbia is wasting away."

He glared at the sign, as if it were indeed a black hole sucking up the strength of Serbia.

Valdan shrugged and returned to the flask. Dobrila too had another drink. His head was beginning to spin. He stopped a second time to have another look at the doctor's house, but was unable to find it. Stifled rage mixed with anguish marked his expression.

"Have you got the little transistor?" Vladan inquired. "It's almost time for the news. Turn it on. Let's hear what happened about the bomb."

Dobrila removed the radio from his pocket. His fingers twisted the dial back and forth, picking up noise from a whole series of unknown stations.

"That's the one," ordered Vladan suddenly, seizing him by the elbow. "They're talking about it now."

They stopped, to be able to hear the broadcast more clearly. The announcer was indeed talking about the bomb. "The Albanian government declared that the explosion on the balcony of the kitchen of the Yugoslav Embassy in Tirana was caused by the Yugoslavs themselves with the sole aim of exacerbating relations between the two countries and justifying their reign of terror in Kosovo. 'We have already explained to you what happened in the kitchen of your embassy,' declared the Deputy Minister of Foreign Affairs of Albania to the Yugoslav Ambassador in Tirana in a markedly sarcastic tone...."

"What kind of language is that?" said Dobrila, not believing his own ears.

"It's not Belgrade," said Vladan, "you've got the wrong station."

Dobrila swore.

"What happened in the kitchen of your embassy," repeated Vladan. "Good God, even if our ambassador were a Gypsy no one would dare speak to him like that!"

"It's an insult to us all," said Dobrila on the verge of tears. They're treating us like a nation of Gypsies. Gimme the flask."

"How dare they!" murmured Vladan.

They continued their walk in silent despair, emitting the occasional sigh. Dobrila had stopped to removed the flask from his pocket again when they heard the steps of someone in a hurry. A shadow was approaching from the end of the deserted street. When it got closer they could hardly believe their eyes.

"Jovica!"

"Where have you been?" he said, breathing heavily. "I've been looking for you for an hour."

"Well," uttered Dobrila, "it would have been better if you hadn't found us."

"Why? Has something happened to you?"

"To us? Nothing... Except that we're being insulted. Did you hear the news? They called us Gypsies. Here, have a drink."

"What news? What Gypsies?" inquired Jovica, taking the flask.

They tried to explain to him what they had heard, but he was not really paying attention. There was a glimmer of delight in his eyes.

"What is this nonsense you're giving me about news on the radio?" he interrupted. "I'm the one who's got the news." The two of them gaped at him inquiringly and Jovica nodded. "I'm the one who's got the news," he repeated. "Do you know what? Those... files I was telling you about the other day, well, they're going to open them this very night."

"What?"

"The files, I'm telling you. Tonight. A friend of mine who works there told me. That's why I've been trying to find you."

"Tonight? Really?"

"Exactly. Let's get going."

"Where to?"

"Back there. A friend of mine will let us in."

"My God!" exclaimed Dobrila.

"We start tonight, whether you believe me or not."

"I believe you, Jovica, I believe you. Everything you say always turns out to be true."

Dobrila was soon out of breath, not from the speed of their return but from pure emotion. His chest had turned to dough. He wanted to stop, lie down at Jovica's feet and beg him, "Kick me, kick me with your muddy boots. I'll put up with any humiliation you give me for the glad tidings you've brought us."

They were checked again in front of the Secretariat of the Interior. The lower floors of the building were lit up. Jovica went in, telling them to wait out on the street.

"What if..." Vladan began, after they had waited for a few minutes.

"Shut up," Dobrila interrupted him, "don't ask for bad luck."

In his own mind, Dobrila was already fearing the worst. Jovica was taking his time. Lord, he mumbled to himself, take away anything you want, take away all my pleasures, but please, please don't take this away from me.

He was sure he could not bear such a disappointment. He would age fifty years and crumble to dust on the spot. There was no sign of movement in the courtyard. Everything seemed dead, and perhaps Jovica had forgotten them completely. He had probably opened one of the files and was so enthralled by his reading, like a character in a Thousand and One Nights, that he had forgotten everything. Jovica, you can't do this to us.

But Jovica reappeared when they had almost given up, arriving, surprisingly enough, from the direction of the street.

"How did you get over there?" Dobrila muttered on seeing him approach. "Did you take a plane, or what?"

"Follow me," Jovica interrupted. "We'll go in the back door."

They followed him in silence down the alley which led around the back.

"We thought you had forgotten us."

Jovica made no reply. He stopped in front of a low door neither of them had ever noticed before and tapped gently.

It seemed like a dream as they passed through the small doorway, descended the stairs and found themselves in a basement. It consisted of a long room with a vaulted ceiling under which stretched endless rows of shelves like those in the stacks of a library. They could make out a few vague forms moving back and forth in the shadows. Jovica gestured towards the shelves. That was where they were stored, thousands, tens of thousands of them, like orderly rows of coffins, with the names of the deceased written on the covers. 'Oh thou traveller who passeth by, bide but for a moment...' The air was full of the smell of dust, of candles, of ancient cemeteries. Dobrila was overwhelmed by a poignant feeling of sorrow. How could the files have been abandoned all those years, deprived of the love and devotion that was rightfully theirs? They had been stolen like the hair of some mighty magician in which lay the source of his supernatural power, they had been stripped of the supreme joy that gave meaning to their existence, ruthlessly savaged, mutilated and abandoned.

'Oh thou traveller...' Suddenly his eyes rested on one of the files above him bearing the name of Dr. Shkreli. Ah, my dove, there you are.

He had an uncontrolled desire to throw himself upon it, to tear off the cover in a fury as if he were ripping off her clothes, her underclothes, to see her naked before him... A hand seized him by the elbow.

"Don't show so much curiosity," Jovica whispered.

Oh, if Jovica only knew what thoughts had crossed his mind!

"I thought I recognized one of the names."

"Whatever you do, don't show too much curiosity. There is a time for everything."

"Time for everything," Dobrila repeated to himself. It was true, after all. The victims were locked up forever, with no hope of escape. You could escape from prison. You could even steal a body from the grave, but no one ever escaped from the files.

Dobrila heaved a great sigh. They sauntered pensively along the rows of file-laden shelves. Dobrila was once again taken by a wave of sorrow. They had been deprived of the files for so many years and now their beloved files were being returned. But what was the use? It was too late. Others would taste the delights they promised.

Peering up out of the corner of his eye, he noticed how new and white the files looked on the sturdy shelves, whereas they themselves had grown grey and wrinkled with age.

Suddenly a silvery moth, still quivering, fell out of one of the files, like a teardrop falling from his eyes.

Dobrila could hardly keep himself from bursting into tears.

XI

Denunciation day

The situation worsened again, as had been expected. The news that one hundred forty thousand files were to be reopened spread in a matter of hours, creating the same climate of fear as the order about the unlocked doors, if not worse. Doubly exposed now, the people prepared themselves for more repression.

At the hospital, as elsewhere, the meetings began again. They were chaired by the same presidium, with the same opening speeches by the assistant director, followed by statements from the delegate and the introductory discussion which repeated almost word for word what had been said before: 'On the night of March 31, I was on duty at the hospital,' or: 'On the morning of April 1, when I began my shift...'.

Dr. Shkreli wanted to throw up. They were the very same statements, the same breaks between sessions, even the same monotonous repetition of 'nevertheless' and 'I cannot say for certain', etc., etc., phrases which were so alike as to turn one's stomach.

How long would this disgraceful process continue, she wondered and inwardly began preparing the statement she was sure she would have to give at one of these meetings. Yes, it is true that we treated the wounded and were aware that they came straight from the demonstration. It was our duty as doctors to do so and we would do it again if another massacre took place. Yes, yes, yes, let them all hear it. We did what in every time and in every corner of the globe has been considered moral and humane, whereas your aim at this meeting is both immoral and inhumane, and would always have been considered so in every time, even in the Middle Ages, and in every country from here to the North Pole. Put an end to this disgrace immediately.

The voices of the speakers droned on in the auditorium like a record stuck in the groove. Who gave the order for the extra beds to be set up on the evening of March 31? What happened to the patient register... The voice of the anaesthetist seemed to be lulling the audience to sleep. Count to ten... one... two... three... followed by more numbers in the strange language of the gypsies. The distant voice of the delegate penetrated their slumber: Where are the dead?

What an absurd question, she thought to herself. The dead always know where they are: in Hades.

Twilight fell. The light of day was rapidly fading in the large windows. Another day shortened by God, as old Sanija would say.

XII

Night. Day. Then twilight

Another night of unlocked doors passed and then, as it had for millions of years, day dawned. Just like all the other days which had passed, this too would be a day of denunciation. The sun rose at 4:53 a.m. and would set at 6:26 p.m. As usual, they entered the auditorium, the members of the presidium, ancient figures risen from the stone age, took their seats and amidst the smell of ether which seemed to emanate from the anaesthetist, the questioning resumed: Who ordered the extra beds to be set up on the night of March 31? What happened to the dead?

At more or less the same time, Professor Martin Shkreli, taking his afternoon walk along the streets near his house, was preoccupied with the same questions. Twilight was falling. A hospital-white moon was poised on the horizon. I'll go a little further, he thought. There is still plenty of time before the curfew.

His thoughts were with his wife. How would she answer the questions asked of her in that hellish auditorium? Who had ordered the extra beds to be set up on the night of March 31? What had happened to the patient register, and to the patients themselves?

One of them is in my study, he thought. His tortured voice at least, if not his body.

Every time he listened to the cassette he was more and more certain that the delirious ravings and moans were those of Shpend Brezftohti.

Perhaps he would meet him one day, on a future 'day of the republic' for instance, and say to him, "Come on over to my place, Shpend. I've kept something for you."

It had been dark for some time now but he still had no desire to return home. He was reminded suddenly of the files which had just been opened. I wonder what mine contains? He had an almost physical sensation that part of his past was being touched by the strange hands of some ignorant brute. A shiver of disgust traversed his whole body. A repulsive age, he thought to himself.

The street was deserted. This meant that the curfew hour had arrived. Nevertheless, he did not hurry. The moon wrapped the façades of the two-story villas looming behind their walled enclosures in a ribbon of pale light, broken here and there by dark masses of clematis.

Suddenly he stopped. Among the trees behind the wrought iron fence of one of the villas half lit by the moonlight, he made out a silhouette. It was that of a couple: a girl and a boy, nothing unusual on that street before the troubles began. But it was not the re-appearance of a custom temporarily abandoned which startled him. Not at all... The boy's dark hair contrasted with the mask of his face, glowing with an unearthly whiteness in the moonlight. The girl's hair shone like a misty halo. Yes, it was them, Shpend Brezftohti and Mladenka Marković!

His eyes remained fixed on them for a moment as if he were afraid that he had been mistaken. Then he hurried on without even wondering any longer whether it had really been them, as new and more pressing questions began to preoccupy him. How had they managed to meet in the climate of general hatred? Perhaps she had hidden him and secretly nursed him back to health, and now they were saying farewell? Or was Mladenka perhaps embracing him to ask his forgiveness, and he, by the simple act of stroking her hair, was granting it? Or were they simply a man and a woman embracing, beyond the reach of time and the events of the world?

Could it be possible, he asked himself as he hastened homeward. Could it be possible that after being frozen in ice for a thousand years, the wedding procession had chosen our time for the first signs of its revival?

He was still engrossed in these thoughts when he arrived home. Upon entering, ignoring his wife's air of alarm and without giving any explanation for his late return or even asking how her day had been, he blurted out, "I think I saw Shpend Brezftohti... alive... in front of one of the villas."

XIII

Neither day nor night. Another time

Shpend Brezftohti was not in front of one of the villas. He was far from the spot where Martin Shkreli believed he had seen him, far beyond the outskirts of the city. His face and body were covered with mud and gravel, and it would have been difficult to recognize him even by bending to look closely with a flashlight. Not even the white light of the moon could reach him for the simple reason that he was under the ground.

Those who buried him will never be known. The place they chose was the muddy bed of an underground stream, and only the water gently caressed his hair, as if combing it over and over.

He slept peacefully under the earth, and from his chest, its ribs mangled by iron bars, came only silence. Above the earth, born perhaps from the last moan to come from his chest, a gentle breeze rose to bear his lamentations over the plain of Kosovo, becoming a whirlwind on the outskirts of towns and villages, and traversing the highways until it reached the foot of the Sharr mountains, where the cliffs, under their light cover of snow, did indeed resemble a wedding procession turned to ice.

1981-1983

[*Krushqit janë të ngrirë,* taken from *Koha e shkrimeve* (Naim Frashëri, Tirana 1986). Translated from the Albanian by Robert Elsie]

2. Approaches to the present dilemma

The right to self-determination

Rexhep Ismajli

The Albanians in former Yugoslavia, of whom there are about three million according to an estimate from the year 1991, live in a region bordering on Albania, an area of compact settlement in the southern part of Montenegro, throughout Kosovo, in three districts of southern Serbia and in western Macedonia. The Albanians, direct descendants of the Illyrians, have inhabited this region, in which they constitute a majority of 90%, without interruption since ancient times and form the autochthonous population of the region. As a result of invasions and migration during the Middle Ages and under Turkish rule, Slavs, Turks and Roma settled in this region as minorities. After various waves of migration and subsequent colonization, the Slavic population grew substantially and now constitutes about 10% of the total population of the region. The Albanians in this region, who make up almost half of the total Albanian population in the Balkans, can look upon a history going back over two thousand years. They have created their own culture, infrastructure, social network, pattern of urban settlements and communications network. They also look back upon their own wars of liberation and upon long and varied relations with the neighbouring peoples. The town of Prizren situated in this zone was the centre of the nineteenth-century Albanian national movement for liberation from the Ottoman Empire, a movement with a clear western,

European orientation. Its slogan was: "The faith of the Albanian is Albanianism!" (*Feja e shqyptarit asht shqyptarija!*). This movement was and remains a source of inspiration for political activity. The Albanians in Yugoslavia speak the same dialects and use the same literary language as the Albanians in Albania. After 1878, the Serbian government deported the inhabitants of about 700 Albanian villages in the region west of Nish / Niš. In the Sanjak of Novi Pazar and in Montenegro, the Albanians were assimilated in good part by Serbo-Croatian-speaking Moslems.

After the Balkan Wars (1912-1913), half of ethnic Albanian territory and half of the Albanian population found itself in the 'Kingdom of the Serbs, Croats and Slovenes' as a result of the Serbian occupation of Kosovo and of the subsequent drawing, at the Conference of London, of an arbitrary border at the expense of the Albanians and without consultation with them. This border was subsequently confirmed at the Paris Peace Conference. By this time, the Albanians had managed to liberate their lands from the Turks (1908-1912), but were nonetheless weakened and did not have the power to resist Serbian troops who were supported by the Allies.

The Albanians have never accepted the situation created in 1912-1918 since it was created against their will. This fact has been demonstrated by countless uprisings. Yugoslavia practised a policy of rigorous persecution and suppression in the period between the two World Wars. The land was colonized by the Slavs, and the native Albanian peasants were accordingly dispossessed of their property. Over 300,000 Albanians were expelled to Turkey and Albania and all signs of Albanian culture were suppressed. Yugoslav policies towards the Albanians between the two World Wars may be regarded without exaggeration as genocide.

During the Second World War, a good part of this Albanian territory was united with the new Albanian state which had been created at the time. Albanian-language schools were opened for the first time in this region. At the Conference of Bujan, which was attended by Kosovo participants equivalent in rank to the leadership of the Yugoslav AVNOJ organization, a resolution was passed for the return of this territory to Albania after the war. Martial law and a state of siege were nonetheless imposed in Kosovo when the war did come to an end. Under these conditions, Kosovo was simply declared an autonomous region within a federal Serbia, as part of the Yugoslav federation.

The Albanians themselves were divided among four federal entities: Kosovo, Macedonia, Serbia and Montenegro. Up to 1966, they suffered harsh persecution by the police. Approximately 400,000 people were forced to resettle in Turkey, over 100 were slain and a further 60,000 were tortured by the police.

Between 1963 and 1974, Kosovo expanded its autonomy as an entity of the Yugoslav federation and attained virtually the same status as that enjoyed by the republics. This resulted in a level of emancipation which by 1981 enabled the Albanians to express their wishes once more. But again, a state of siege was imposed and all the attributes of a brutal police state introduced, resulting in the complete abolition of the autonomy of Kosovo. All institutions were forced to suspend their activities, the mass media in Albanian were abolished, and human rights were violated more than anywhere else in Europe. Over 100 Albanians were killed and thousands of others were imprisoned for long periods of time. Over 100,000 Albanians were fired from their jobs. All Albanian-language elementary and secondary schools were closed down as was the University of Prishtina. The Academy of Sciences and Arts of Kosovo was declared abolished. The Albanians were marginalized from public and social life, expelled from economic activities, and even banned from the provision of health services.

During its eighty years of existence, the Yugoslav state did its utmost to divide up ethnic Albanian territory and deprive it of its Albanian character.

The Albanians in Yugoslavia are not a minority, neither in relation to the Albanians of Albania nor in relation to the other peoples of former Yugoslavia. They constitute the third largest group in Yugoslavia, after the Serbs and Croats: in numbers, in culture, in the range of their ethnic settlements, in language, in tradition, in homogeneity and in their natural and human potential.

They are just as compactly settled on their ethnic territory as the Slovenes in Slovenia and the Serbs in Serbia proper.

In this ethnic Albanian territory live almost half of all Albanians, but less than 2% of all Serbs.

The border between Albania and the territories in Yugoslavia inhabited by Albanians is completely arbitrary. It is based neither on ethnic nor on geographical considerations. As a result of this division, important economic and cultural centres such as Dibër / Debar, Tetova / Tetovo, Prizren, Gjakova / Djakovica and Peja / Peć have been deprived of their natural economic and geographical regions, and most of northern Albania, for its part, has been deprived of its urban centres and markets. As such, economic and cultural links and lines of communication built up over centuries were suddenly destroyed.

The Albanians in Yugoslavia were, as mentioned above, divided among four federal entities. This was done in order to weaken and destroy their national identity.

Within the borders of post-1918 Yugoslavia, the Macedonians and the Bosnian Moslems acquired the status of nations after the Second World War. The Albanians were deprived of this right for the sole reason that they were part of a divided nation, there being an Albanian state outside Yugoslavia. Onto the Albanians was thus forced the status of a minority within the context of a large multinational state, i. e. former Yugoslavia. But no matter how much territory Serbia takes, it cannot confine the position of the Albanians to that of a minority.

With the introduction of democratic reforms throughout Eastern Europe, the Albanians in former Yugoslavia, who played a major role in this process, are resolved to use peaceful means to solve their problems and to ensure the maintenance of democracy. Both Serbia and Yugoslavia, the term now given to Greater Serbia, are equally resolved to combat these endeavours with unabated force, repression and state-organized terror.

In the period 1912-1918, Serbian claims to Albanian territory were justified by the need for an access to the sea. Now they are being justified by the presence in Kosovo of the patriarchate of the Serbian church and by Serbian history, which, by the way, completely ignores the history and culture of the Albanians. The Serbian church and the Serbian past in Kosovo can best be compared, as to their present significance, with the Arab mosques of Spain or with the Greek partriarchate in Istanbul. Serbian claims to the Vojvodina, from which the Germans were expelled in 1945, and to the Krajina are justified on ethnic grounds, even though the ethnic composition of these regions came about by subsequent colonization. In Kosovo, for its part, Serbian claims are justified by mythology. Serbian imperialism is the main cause of all the present-day troubles in the Balkans.

Even for legal reasons, Kosovo and the Albanians cannot be said to form part of Serbia:

- in 1878, at the time of the Congress of Berlin, Kosovo was not part of Serbia,

- at the second conference of AVNOJ in November 1943, Kosovo was not part of Serbia,

- when Serbia was constituted as a federal entity in November 1944 (during the great constitutional parliamentary assembly for the liberation of Serbia), Kosovo was not within Serbia,

- at the Yugoslav constitutional assembly, during which the Federal Republic of Yugoslavia was called into existence (1945), Kosovo was not part of Serbia,

- in 1946 under martial law, Kosovo became part of a "federal Serbia within the Yugoslav federation", but even in this capacity, Kosovo still has the legal right today to demand its secession from Serbia,

- from 1968 to 1989, Kosovo achieved virtually the same level of sovereignty as that enjoyed by the republics of Yugoslavia.

The sovereignty and independence of Kosovo have been defined in the following documents:

1.   the Declaration of Independence (2 July 1990),

2.   the Constitution of the Republic of Kosovo (7 September 1990),

3.   the Referendum on the Independence and Sovereignty of Kosovo (26-30 September 1991),

4.   the Resolution on the Independence and Sovereignty of Kosovo
        (18 October 1991), and

5.   the free elections held in Kosovo to elect a Parliament and the
        President of the Republic (24 May 1992).

        Kosovo and the Albanians in other parts of former Yugoslavia
refused to take part in the creation of a third Yugoslavia, which was
constituted on 27 April 1992 and made up of Montenegro and Serbia.

        Since Yugoslavia no longer exists as a state, and since Kosovo
and the Albanians have the same rights as other successors to the no
longer existent Yugoslav federation, there is no legal basis for
transferring their rights to Serbia. European support for Serbian rule in
Kosovo is tantamount to forcing a perpetual colonial status upon the
Albanians, one of the oldest peoples of Europe.

        Such support would also do nothing to secure peace in the
region and could force the Albanians to look for other means to free
themselves.

Important dates for the status of Kosovo and the Albanians

1878
Kosovo, a portion of the Sanjak of Novi Pazar and Macedonia were part of the *vilayets* of Kosovo and Monastir in European Turkey. The Serbian government expelled to Turkey the inhabitants of about 700 Albanian villages from a region north of Kosovo, situated approximately between Kruševac and Nish / Niš.

1878-1881
The League of Prizren was founded in Prizren as the focus of the national movement of all Albanians. The aim of the League of Prizren was the liberation of all Albanians from Turkish rule. It was banned by the Turkish government in 1881, but continued to function illegally.

1912
Kosovo and the Albanians drove out the Turkish army. The Serbian army, supported by its allies (Russia and France), conquered Kosovo and Macedonia.

1919
Kosovo and Macedonia were joined to the subsequent Kingdom of Yugoslavia by the Treaty of Versailles, without the Albanian and Macedonian population ever being consulted. Their territory was divided into *banovinas*.

1919-1940
The Albanians were severely persecuted. They were robbed of their land, and over 300,000 persons were resettled in Turkey, a treaty having been signed to this end by Yugoslavia and Turkey. Projects were devised aiming at the extinction of the Albanians, e.g. the draft of Ivo Andrić (1939), and memorandums of Vaso Čubrilović (1937, 1944).

Serbian and Montenegrin colonists from Lika, Herzegovina and Montenegro were brought into the Albanian region as colonists.

1940-1945   Kosovo and a part of western Maccedonia were united with Albania under an Italian protectorate. Schools in Albanian were opened.

1943   A conference, equivalent to the second Yugoslav AVNOJ conference, was held in Bujan. It passed a resolution calling for the unification of Kosovo with Albania after the war.

1945   The Albanians were conscripted and sent to the Syrmian front. About 6,000 mobilized but unarmed Albanians were massacred in Bar. The Drenica revolt was bloodily quelled. Martial law was imposed in Kosovo. Kosovo was kept under military rule as part of Yugoslavia even though Tito had promised the Albanians unification.

1946-1966   Brutal oppression by the police: Over 100 dead, and tens of thousands of people tortured. The Albanological Institute was closed down in 1955, well-known intellectuals were deported, and about 400,000 Albanians were resettled to Turkey.

1963   The new Yugoslav constitution gave Kosovo the same autonomy status as the Vojvodina.

1966-1968   The fall of Ranković. The Albanian school system expands. Teaching in higher education begins in Albanian. The Albanological Institute is re-established.

1968   Republic status is demanded for Kosovo in discussions on the constitution. A language conference is held and determines that the Albanian literary language for use in Yugoslavia is to be identical to that for use in Albania. Student demonstrations demanding a 'Republic of Kosovo' are suppressed by the army and by the police. Many young people are imprisoned.

Numerous amendments to the constitution are made which result in an improvement of the status of Kosovo.

1970   Founding of the University of Prishtina.

1972   Orthography Congress in Tirana attended by delegates from all Albanian territories in Yugoslavia. A resolution is passed that one literary language be adopted for all Albanians.

1974   The new Yugoslav constitution is promulgated. Kosovo is recognized as one of the eight founding entities of Yugoslavia and acquires its own constitution, government, courts, planning authorities, education system and institutions for general development. These are under the direct auspices of the federal government and not dependent upon the government of Serbia.

1981   Student demonstrations. Demands are made for a Republic of Kosovo. At least eleven dead. The demonstrations, which threaten to turn into a general uprising, are put down by the army and police. A state of siege is declared. The demonstrations and the demands of the students are condemned as counter-revolutionary. Draconian punishment for many young people. Intellectuals are 'differentiated' and fired from their jobs. Teaching curricula are 'cleansed' of national content.

1987-1989 The autonomy of Kosovo is gradually undermined and done away with. Milošević comes to power. The miners in Trepça / Trepča go on strike. Demonstrators from all over Kosovo march on Prishtina in support of autonomy. A state of siege is declared once again.

1989   A new Serbian constitution is promulgated, doing away with the autonomy of Kosovo for all practical purposes. Appeal by 215 Albanian intellectuals for the defence and consolidation of autonomy status.

Persecution of the signitories. Incarceration in Serbian prisons of political leaders from Kosovo, of 250 intellectuals and of countless young people.

1989   The League of Communists is dissolved. The first groups of opposition parties are formed. In December, the Democratic League of Kosovo is formed which soon receives wide support among the Albanians. Other parties are founded, too. Peaceful passive resistance on the part of the Albanians becomes stronger and more evident in public.

1990   On 2 July, the Parliament of Kosovo constitutionally declares the Republic of Kosovo. On 5 July, the Parliament of Serbia unconstitutionally declares the Parliament of Kosovo to be illegal. In Kaçanik / Kačanik on 7 September, the Parliament of Kosovo promulgates the Constitution of the Republic of Kosovo. Serbia closes down Albanian-language radio and television stations in Prishtina. The only Albanian-language daily newspaper, *Rilindja*, is banned. Albanian-language schools are closed down. Thousands of Albanian doctors and health-care workers are fired from hospitals.

1991   A referendum is held from 26-30 September during which 87.5% of the population vote for Kosovo as an independent and sovereign state.

1992   The provisional multiparty government of Kosovo, some members of which are in exile, continues its work. On 24 May, free multiparty parliamentary elections are held in which 24 political parties and groups take part. The Democratic League of Kosovo wins a majority in the new four-party parliament. Political parties representing the Serbo-Croatian-speaking Moslems and the Turks in Kosovo also take part in these elections. Dr Ibrahim Rugova is elected by 97% of the votes as President of the Republic of Kosovo.

Table 1

Number of Albanians according to the census of 1981 and to estimates
from 1991:

Kosovo	Southern Serbia	Macedonia	Montenegro
1981			
1,226,736	72,748	377,726	37,735
77.4%	1.3%	19.8%	6,5%
1991			
1,730,000	90,000	800,000	40,000
to 1,830,000	100,000	900,000	
90%	1.4%	40%	7.5%

Table 2

The languages of Yugoslavia by percentage of speakers:

	1981	1991
Serbo-Croatian	72.9%	73.1%
Albanian	7.8%	9.1%
Slovenian	7.9%	7.7%
Macedonian	6.1%	6.1%
Hungarian	1.8%	1.7%
Other languages	3.5%	2.3%

Table 3

Number of Albanians employed as compared to the total number of
persons employed and to the total population figure in % for 1981:

	Albanians employed	% of Albanians
Yugoslavia	2.9%	7.7%
Serbia	0.4%	1.3%
Kosovo	63.3%	77.4%
Macedonia	6.7%	19.8%
Montenegro	3.1%	6.5%

Table 4

Books, brochures and newspapers published in Yugoslavia in 1986
according to language:

Albanian	404	2.6%
Serbo-Croatian	10,380	68.8%
Slovenian	2,384	15.7%
Macedonian	840	5.5%
Total	15,103	100%

Table 5

Number of Albanian pupils in Yugoslavia during the 1984/1985 school
year:

Elementary schools	384,914
Secondary schools	77,692
Total	462,606

[Translated from the German by Robert Elsie]

The Albanian question and its solution

Rexhep Qosja

The Albanian question - the problem of a divided people

The proposals which have been made up to now for a solution to the Albanian question and, within this framework, for an international solution to the Kosovo problem, show that not all the historical, political, social, economic, geopolitical and humanitarian factors involved have been understood, or at least not clearly and properly understood. The basic argument in support of this assertion is that it is essentially wrong to treat the Albanian question as the question of an ethnic minority.

Although it is commonly used by political and government organizations, the term 'ethnic minority' is one of those terms whose meaning should depend on a specific definition and not simply on the vagaries of common usage. According to common usage, the term 'ethnic minority' has come to mean the members of an ethnic group living in an ethnically identical territory outside the country they belong to ethnically. As the word 'minority' is an intregal part of the term 'ethnic minority', the ethnic group in question must consequently be a real minority, firstly in comparison with the nation it is related to, even though these people live in another country, and secondly, in comparison with the other people and peoples with whom it shares territory.

The Albanians were not an ethnic minority in former Yugoslavia, i.e. communist Yugoslavia, nor are they an ethnic minority in the countries created or being created out of former Yugoslavia.

How can this be true?

The Albanians were not an ethnic minority in former Yugoslavia because they were about eight times as numerous as the Montenegrins, who had their own republic within the Yugoslav federation. They were also about two and a half times as numerous as the Macedonians, who had their own republic, too. They were more numerous than the Slovenes, who had their own republic, and more numerous than the Moslems, who also had their own republic within the framework of the former Yugoslav federation. Thus, they were not a minority in communist Yugoslavia for the simple reason that they were a majority in comparison with a good number of the 'state-forming' peoples of the federation.

The Albanians are not an ethnic minority in rump Yugoslavia, the present state of Yugoslavia as it is called by the Serbs and Montenegrins alone, because they are still more numerous than the Montenegrins who have their own republic within this Yugoslavia. Nor are the Albanians a minority within Serbia, because you cannot call one-third of the population of a multinational state such as Serbia an ethnic minority.

The Albanians are not an ethnic minority in the Former Yugoslav Republic of Macedonia, now an independent and internationally recognized country, because they account for over one-third of the total population of this multinational republic, too.

And even if they were an ethnic minority in rump Yugoslavia (Serbia and Montenegro) or in the Former Yugoslav Republic of Macedonia, there is one other reason why the Albanians in former

Yugoslavia can no longer be regarded as an ethnic minority - they constitute half the population of the Albanian nation. Living on their own ethnic and historical territory along the border that separates Macedonia, Serbia and Montenegro from Albania, a territory which is ethnically and geographically continuous with Albania, these Albanians are just as numerous as the inhabitants of the Republic of Albania itself, i.e. about three million individuals. Half of a nation cannot be called an ethnic minority of any country, irrespective of the number of inhabitants that country may have. The half of the nation living under foreign jurisdiction should not enjoy any fewer privileges than the other 'state-forming peoples' there or than the other half living under its own jurisdiction.

What conclusions can be drawn from the above?

If there are just as many Albanians in former Yugoslavia as in Albania itself, people living on their own ethnic and historical territory which forms a geographical continuity with the Republic of Albania, it is then logical that these Albanians in former Yugoslavia, i.e. in contemporary Yugoslavia (Serbia and Montenegro) and in the Former Yugoslav Republic of Macedonia, cannot be considered an 'ethnic minority' but rather as part of a *divided nation.* Consequently, the Albanian question must not be seen or dealt with in terms of a minority problem, but rather as the question of a *divided nation.*

The Albanian question has not evolved from the problem of an ethnic minority to the problem of a divided nation simply because the Albanian population in former Yugoslavia has grown. It was a question of a divided nation from the very start. During the Conference of Ambassadors in London, at a time when there were about 748,000 Albanians in Albania itself, there were also about 1,200,000 Albanians abroad, in lands occupied by Serbia, Montenegro and Greece. Albania cannot really be called a national state in the broadest sense of the term since half of the Albanian nation lives beyond the country's national borders. The Republic of Albania is the homeland of only half of the Albanian people, the national state of a *divided Albanian nation.*

There are other nations in Europe with a good portion of their population living in foreign countries. When the Austro-Hungarian Empire collapsed in 1918, for instance, it left countless Hungarians outside the borders of Hungary. There are still about three million of them at the present. When the Soviet empire broke apart in 1991, about twenty million Russians found themselves outside the borders of Russia. But neither the Hungarians nor the Russians consider themselves divided nations. The three million Hungarians living in countries outside the borders of Hungary constitute less than one-third of the Hungarian nation and the twenty million Russians living in countries outside the borders of Russia constitute less than one-seventh of the Russian nation. In other words, neither the Hungarians nor the Russians, although many of their people live in other countries, are divided nations. There is only one *divided nation* in Europe, and that is Albania.

The Albanian question - a colonial question

The Albanian question is not simply a human rights question. To put it another way, if the Albanian question is simply one of human rights, then all colonial problems must be treated as such, i.e. in terms of human rights.

The question of Kosovo is a colonial question because Kosovo has the status of a colony. It is no coincidence that French writer Paul Garde described the status of Kosovo in the following terms: "A Moslem majority with a high birth rate versus a Christian minority clinging to political and economic power and with a low birth rate: i. e. a colonial situation."[5]

There can be no doubt that the human rights of the Albanians in former Yugoslavia, and in Kosovo and Macedonia in particular, have been severely violated and that their basic freedoms have been radically curtailed. These human rights violations and the curtailment of the basic freedoms of the Albanians in former Yugoslavia, as well as in present-day rump Yugoslavia (Serbia and Montenegro) and in the Former Yugoslav Republic of Macedonia, are by no means a contemporary phenomenon, nor even a phenomenon of the last 12 to 13 years during which the problem has become better known to the outside world. On

---

[5] cf. Garde 1992, p. 228.

the contrary, these violations have been a permanent feature and consequence of the colonial status of the Albanians. It is indeed this status, that of an ethnic community in a colonial situation under the rule of a foreign people, that has made the violations in former Yugoslavia not only possible, but also systematic, i. e. a permanent feature of life there! The Albanians were discriminated against in the past in Yugoslavia and are being discriminated against in present-day Yugoslavia (Serbia and Montenegro) and in Macedonia as well, primarily because they are Albanians, an unwanted ethnic group within the federation of the southern Slavs. They are not allowed to have their own homeland within the framework of Yugoslavia even though they are more numerous than many other peoples who have their own republics, not because there exists a sovereign state of Albania on the other side of the border, encompassing half the Albanian population, but because Kosovo and Albanian territories in general (including all natural resources above and under ground) are considered to be the exclusive property of those who conquered them in 1878, and in 1912-1913, and yet again in 1945, i.e. the Serbs, Montenegrins, and Macedonians.

Greater Serbian propagandists have devised slogans for the promotion of Serbian ideals in Kosovo, such as, "Kosovo is the cradle of the Serbian state," "Kosovo is the cradle of Serbian civilization," "Kosovo is the cradle of the Serbian soul," "Kosovo is the Serbian Jerusalem," etc., etc. It is with such slogans that Serbian politicians, statesmen and intellectuals have always endeavoured to justify their occupation of Kosovo. It is naive of them to believe that Serbia has a right to possess Kosovo, with its 90% Albanian inhabitants, on the basis of ancient mythology and for other, primarily religious reasons. Serbia possesses Kosovo because of its natural resources. Kosovo is small in territory, a total of 10,885 km², but it has extensive natural resources. It has excellent farmland and enough water for irrigation, as well as forests and alpine pastures. Kosovo also has substantial mineral resources, including both common and rare minerals: lead, copper, zinc, nickel, chromium, silver, gold, bismuth, indium, germanium, selenium, mercury, and especially coal deposits which, according to Serbian specialists, may amount to thirteen billion tons. These riches in Kosovo have been a source of woe for the Albanians because they have condemned the population to a colonial situation. The mineral resources of Kosovo, some of which are of strategic importance, are never processed in Kosovo itself, but rather by industries in Serbia, Croatia and Slovenia, or are exported as raw materials of strategic importance to countries with which Yugoslavia has had commercial relations. The price of these natural resources was never fixed by their producer, Kosovo, but rather by the Republic of Serbia or by the Yugoslav federation.

Aside from being exploited as a source of cheap raw materials for Serbian and Yugoslav factories, Kosovo has also been exploited as a source of cheap labour: miners for Kosovo and manual labourers for other regions of former Yugoslavia. Albanians from Kosovo and Macedonia carry out 80% of heavy manual labour in the urban centres of Slovenia, Croatia and Serbia, and to some extent in those of Bosnia and Herzegovina, and at low wages, too. In Maribor, Ljubljana, Rijeka, Zagreb, Belgrade, Novi Sad and Sarajevo there were and are many Albanians who do the jobs that no Slovene, Croat, Serb or even Bosnian would volunteer to do. Even today, there are about 60,000 Albanians in Belgrade, most of whom offer their services at a lower price than Serbian workers do.

Serbia keeps Kosovo as a colony as did many colonial powers in the past, not only to exploit its natural resources, but also for demographic reasons. Since the time it took over Kosovo in the Balkan Wars of 1912-1913, Serbia has undertaken numerous campaigns to depopulate Kosovo of as many Albanians as possible and replace them with Serbs and Montenegrins. There have been four major campaigns of Serbian and Montengrin colonization in Kosovo up to the present. Before World War II, Serbia colonized Kosovo with Serb and Montenegrin immigrants from the poorest regions of Montenegro and Hercegovina, thus resolving its own social problems and the social problems of Montenegro. After World War II, Serbia sent to Kosovo its surfeit of workers, including a good number of experts who had not managed to find employment in the other regions of Yugoslavia. There were two reasons for this: on the one hand, this served to solve the problem of unemployment, and on the other it served to alter the ethnic structure of Kosovo.

Despite the fact that international organizations have constantly criticised Serbia for its crude behaviour in Kosovo, it continues to carry out colonialist demographic policies by importing Serbs who do not find work in Serbia, refugees from Bosnia and even from Croatia - managers, civil servants, technicians, health care workers, security officers, policemen and soldiers, most of whom become permanent residents of Kosovo with a role of their own, that of dominating the political and economic life of the country.

The colonialist economic and demographic policies of Serbia in Kosovo are also based on a Serbian colonial theory about the origins of the Kosovo Albanians. According to this theory, which we have had pushed down our throats for years, before and after 1981, the Albanians as a people ought to be thankful to be under the rule of the superior Serbs. As the present generation of Serbian racists would have it, we ought to be grateful for the civilizing effects their work has had on the rough and rugged nature of the Albanians who would otherwise have been left behind in the dust of the Balkan Wars. They explain away the reaction of the Albanians who insist they would not only be happier outside of Serbia's iron embrace, but also more advanced, as being due to lack of information. The natives are never grateful to their civilizing 'well-meaning' rulers.

Although Kosovo has often come up in Montenegrin politics since the Eastern Crisis, it is not an issue of central importance to the Montenegrins. And how could it be? Kosovo was only part of Montenegro for a short period in the twelfth century when King Baldwin occupied the Serbian principality of Rascia (Raška) and again from 1912 to 1916 when Prince Nikolla occupied Dukagjin. In view of the brevity of Kosovo's links with Montenegro and of the fact that it was only after the First World War that a modest number of Montenegrin colonists ever settled in Kosovo, we cannot consider Kosovo as an issue of historic significance to Montenegro, either from an ethnic or from a territorial point of view.

Kosovo is not an issue of essential significance to Serbia either, despite the fact that it has been raised to the level of mythology in Serbian national politics.

Kosovo was Serbian for somewhat longer than it was Montenegrin but, compared to its long history, this period was relatively brief. It found itself within the extensive mediaeval Serbian Empire from the twelfth to the fourteenth centuries and again after 1912 when Serbia occupied Kosovo during the Balkan Wars. On the other hand, Kosovo has been Albanian for long periods of its history. In fact, even when it was incorporated into the mediaeval state of Montenegro and into the mediaeval Serbian Empire, and later into Serbia and Yugoslavia, Kosovo was never really theirs from an ethnic point of view. From the time of the Roman Empire, through the Byzantine age, the mediaeval Serbian Empire, the centuries of the Ottoman Empire and the years of royalist Yugoslavia, Kosovo was inhabited by Albanians and by their predecessors, the Illyrians. In other words, the Illyrians and their Albanian successors formed the majority of the population of Kosovo throughout history. They were the native population of the country. All the other peoples, the Romans, the Byzantines, the Serbs, the Turks, and again the Serbs, came as invaders and colonists. They entered the country or passed through, returning to where they had originally come from, and left Kosovo with a number of colonies of varying sizes. If this is the case, and history shows us that it cannot be otherwise, then Serbian interests and Albanian interests in Kosovo cannot be identical. Serbian interests in Kosovo were to a great extent and still are the interests of a colonial power, of exploiters. Albanian interests in Kosovo were and are the vital interests of the native population. From an ethnic and territorial point of view, therefore, Kosovo is an issue intrinsically linked to the destiny of the Albanian people. For this reason, the political struggle of the Albanian people to free themselves of Serbia and Yugoslavia and to gain independence is an anti-colonialist struggle, a legitimate struggle for freedom and independence.

The consequences of the colonial status of Kosovo and of the other territories inhabited by Albanians in Yugoslavia (Serbia and Montenegro) and Macedonia, i. e. the countries which have arisen out of the second Yugoslavia, have been multifarious and dire. There are ramifications of social, economic, political and nationalist factors, and factors related to culture and civilization, among others. These consequences are felt not only by the Albanian population of rump Yugoslavia (Serbia and Montenegro) and Macedonia, but also by the Albanians living in Albania.

The geopolitical and strategic aspects of the Albanian question

The Albanian question is a matter of substantial geopolitical and strategic interest with regard to territory. For some parties, Kosovo was of greater interest in the past than it is in the present, whereas for others it will be of greater interest in the future than it was in the past.

Looking at ethnic maps which have been published in various books and periodicals in Europe and the United States over the past few years, serving to elucidate the ethnic structure of the Balkans, one gets a feeling for the geopolitical and strategic significance of the peninsula in the years to come, and for the role which the Albanian question will play in any possible geopolitical constellation.

The Albanians have always been strongly influenced by their geopolitical position. The lands they have inhabited since ancient times have been crossroads for the Great Powers - the Great Powers of the West as well as the Great Powers of the Orient. It is also here that the great cultures of the Middle Ages met and intertwined: Roman Catholicism, Byzantine Orthodoxy and Sunni Islam. Nolens volens, the Albanians found themselves in the eye of many a storm created by the Great Powers and, more often then not, misfortune was their lot.

Because of their geostrategic position at various moments of history, the Albanians have been regarded by the Great Powers as a people capable of playing various geopolitical roles. Up to the end of the Middle Ages, for instance, the Albanians were regarded as a barrier to the penetration of Islam. And because over the centuries, over half of them converted to Islam, they were regarded by the East as a barrier to the penetration of Christian interests in the Balkans. Since there are Albanians of all three faiths, however, they were never willing or able to play one of these essentially religious roles exclusively. Subsequently, in the modern age, because they inhabited territories of geopolitical and geostrategic importance to the three great geopolitical powers of the age - the Ottoman Empire, the Austro-Hungarian monarchy and the Russian Empire - the Albanians (and other Balkan peoples) were assigned other historical functions by the Great Powers of Europe: sometimes religious, sometimes ethnic and sometimes ideological. Austria-

Hungary, Italy and Germany hoped that the Albanians would create a barrier to the spread of the southern Slavs, who seemed uncontainable, in particular in view of support from another of the Great Powers, Russia. But the Albanians did not play the role they were assigned, and Serbia and Montenegro were able to penetrate deep into the southeast Balkans. On the one hand, no Albanian national elite could be found to play the game for the Great Powers in the Eastern Crisis, but more importantly, these same powers sacrificed Albanian interests to what they regarded as the loftier interests of their own states.

Later, from the First World War onwards, England and the United States hoped that the Albanians would play the role of a barrier to the spread of communism. But once again, the Albanians did not play the role they were supposed to. Not only did they not form a barrier to the spread of communism, they used all their energy to fling open the gates and windows of their lonely stone mansions to the aggressive and impoverishing designs of communism.

Why?

During the First World War, the Albanians had hoped for assistance from the Western powers for a just solution to their national question. But in vain. None of the Powers showed any such willingness. Italy, for instance, had territorial ambitions of its own on the Albanian coast, ambitions that would soon spread to all Albanian territory. In 1939, Mussolini's Italy occupied Albania and the Western Powers did not even consider it necessary to react to this aggression as they did to the other aggressive moves of the Fascists and Nazis at the time.

During the course of the Second World War, the Western Powers, England and the United States, made no promises to nationalist forces in Albania that they would help them solve the greatest of their problems, i.e. the national question. On the contrary, from the memoirs of British officer Reginald Hibbert who was in Albania from 1943 to 1944, memoirs published in a book with a telling title: *Albania's national liberation struggle, The bitter victory,* it is clear that England gave its wholehearted support to the territorial integrity of the Kingdom of Yugoslavia, i.e. to maintaining the status quo in the Balkans. This meant that Kosovo and other Albanian territory were to remain under Slav rule. In short, for British foreign policy the Albanian question did not exist.

Ignored by the West, many Albanians turned their attention in another direction. The fact that half of the Albanian people and almost half of their territory were under Serbian and Montenegrin domination created an illusion for many Albanians strongly influenced by communist ideology and politics, that this ideology could bring about a solution to the national question which, after the inevitable defeat of Italy and Germany, had become just as acute as it had been before the war. It was indeed this illusion, created at a time of desperation for the West, which facilitated Albania's inclusion in the communist alliance between Yugoslavia and the Soviet Union, an event which was to have tragic consequences for the nation and for the political, economic and intellectual life of the Albanian people. The consequences of this ideological alliance, from which the Albanians would only free themselves half a century later when communism finally faded into the annals of European history, are evident to anyone visiting Albanian territory. The ruins of communism are obvious, as are the systematic impoverishment of a people divided into several countries and the brutal and systematic violations of human rights and basic freedoms.

In their history up to the present day, the Albanians can thus be seen in various geopolitical roles, as part of international political alliances cut out for them and as part of international political alliances not cut out for them. They acquiesced willingly to some of these alliances whereas others were imposed upon them against their will. Politics in the Balkans have always been like this. They have often made use of the Albanians, and of other Balkan peoples. But what of the present situation? A new world order is presently being created and, if this can be accomplished without war as in the past, but rather with peaceful democratic means, one could hope that the age of unwanted geopolitical alliances is over. And yet, such geopolitical constellations still exist in the Balkans. And quite logically so, because Balkan issues have never been dealt with or resolved without the assistance of powers from outside the Balkans. The small nations of the Balkan peninsula and small nations elsewhere on earth are well aware that their interests cannot be realized and will never be able to be realized without the help of an alliance with some European or global power.

Western analysts have suggested that three political alliances may arise in southeastern Europe now that Yugoslavia has collapsed. The first of these would be a sort of re-creation of Austria-Hungary, i.e. Austria, Hungary, the Czech Republic, Slovakia, Slovenia and Croatia.

The second would be Greece, rump Yugoslavia (Serbia and Montenegro), Romania and Bulgaria, and the third would be Turkey, Albania, Moslem Bosnia (following the division of the Republic of Bosnia and Herzegovina into three parts), and the Islamic communities of Macedonia, Bulgaria, Montenegro and Serbia. Aside from historical and cultural traditions and economic links, the uniting factor, indeed the decisive factor in these alliances is religion.

Serbia has shown the most interest in such a religious alliance recently. Even though no open political alliance has been created as yet, a cultural alliance already exists, uniting Russia, Georgia, Armenia, Belarus, Greece, Bulgaria, Romania and Montenegro. This is not the only indication in our era, in which cold war and the division of the globe into ideological blocs has been overcome, that there exist political forces and indeed countries which long to return to the logic of blocs and divisions along religious lines. During his visit to Italy, the leader of the Russian Liberal Democratic Party, Vladimir Zhirinovsky, declared that one of his greatest political ambitions was to create a federation of Slavic peoples of one blood. Their capitals would be Moscow, Warsaw, Sofia and Belgrade.

Although Albania has joined the conference of Islamic states, the Albanians cannot seriously take part in any alliance based on religion. They are themselves divided into three religous groups and any such alliance would only cause friction within the country.

The Albanian people have their roots in Western civilization. Considering the harm that has been done to them by the alliances which have been formed in the Balkans and in Europe over the last two centuries, it is understandable that they now prefer a world without alliances and blocs. Such alliances can only serve to hinder contemporary achievements, such as the process of European integration.

A united Europe of free and equal European peoples is the only alliance in which the legitimate rights of the divided Albanian people can be realized.

Regardless of what the future may bring to Balkan politics and regardless of whether this future will be compatible with a new and just world order or a new world disorder dominated by force, the Albanian coastline will continue to be of strategic interest. As in the past, whoever controls this coastline can easily control the Adriatic. And it is obvious that whoever controls the Adriatic will find it easier to control the Mediterranean. This was Albania's misfortune in the past. Whether things have changed remains to be seen.

The social and economic aspects of the Albanian question

The Albanians remain the poorest people in Europe, both the half of them living in rump Yugoslavia (Serbia and Montenegro) and Macedonia and the other half living in Albania itself. This is apparent from their towns and settlements with their antiquated infrastructures which are not really fit for human habitation, but also from the pale faces of the inhabitants, malnourished children in elementary schools, malnourished students in secondary schools and universities, malnourished peasants working in the fields, malnourished workers toiling in the factories - pale and sallow faces at all levels of Albanian society. There are other peoples in southeastern Europe whom one could call more or less poor, but poverty among the Albanians is something quite different. It is systematic, permanent and universal poverty. Under the monstrous communist system, this poverty became a threat to the very survival of the nation. As the great Albanian writer Ismail Kadare aptly put it, "it threatened the very essence of our race."[6] If Albanians in rump Yugoslavia (Serbia and Montenegro) and Macedonia are not dying of hunger, it is only because they are living off the remittances of other Albanians who have managed to find work in the West, i.e. in the United States, Canada, Australia and especially in Western Europe. The inhabitants of Albania, for their part, manage to survive only with the help of aid from the international community and from the remittances of the increasingly large number of emigrants working in Western Europe and in the United States.

Why are the Albanians so incredibly poor? Because they don't know how to work? Because they don't want to work? No.

---

[6] Ismail Kadare, *Nga një dhjetor në tjetrin*, Paris 1991, p. 35.

One of the reasons for the economic backwardness and poverty of the Albanians was the communist system which held them in power for almost half a century. But this is not the only reason, and certainly not the earliest historical reason for this state of things. The Albanians were late to develop economically. As a people they were poor long before communism and, as anyone can guess from their present state, they will remain poor for some time after the fall of communism, at least for as long as they are divided into several countries. The division of Albanian territory into several states and consequently, the disintegration of the Albanians as a people has, as a matter of course, impoverished them even further and jeopardized their economic survival. As a result, opportunities for their development, progress and well-being have been cramped, confined and restricted. How could it be otherwise? This ethnic, cultural and geographical entity, i.e. a natural entity, has been unnaturally and forcibly chopped into pieces and is now struggling to return to its unity of old, for which the political, economic, commercial, intellectual and cultural prerequisites no longer exist.

Our Balkan neighbours, the Serbs and Montenegrins, and subsequently the Macedonians, who took possession of Albanian territory either because they feared the understandable and inevitable irredentist demands of the Albanians or because they were simply power-hungry, will do their utmost to ensure that any agreements reached between the Albanians on the two sides of the border will be blocked - not only political agreements, but also any cultural, economic and commercial ties. The Albanian people are therefore in a political and economic situation unknown to them in the past. In Kosovo and in other parts of former Yugoslavia they find themselves in a colonial situation which has become more intolerable than it was under the Turks. Their language and culture are proof of their common identity as one people but so is poverty, which has become the common denominator of their economic and social situation. With this in mind, it is clear that their dreams of freedom and independence, cherished for five hundred years under the Turkish yoke, have ended in a national catastrophe, i.e. in the division of a nation. One half of this nation ended up under foreign rule no better than the one before it and the other half, after years of trials and tribulations to maintain its independence, ended up in an unspeakable communist dictatorship, from which it will take much longer to recover than might be expected at the moment.

The border which runs through the middle of Albanian territory, as if right through the heart of the nation, has been the major cause of the systematic and seemingly never-ending poverty of the Albanians on both sides of the border. This poverty in turn, not to mention persecution and political terror in Yugoslavia, has been the major factor in the uninterrupted emigration of Albanians abroad from the time of the Balkan Wars to the present day: to Turkey, to the United States, Australia, Canada and subsequently to Western Europe. This flow of emigrants, which has been much more rapid and dramatic in recent years, has brought the Albanian question to the fore of international politics. This mass migration, the consequences of which the Western world is only beginning to comprehend, is caused more than anything by the division of Albanian territory and the division of the Albanian people. It is the result of a political and historical error now working at the expense of those who committed it in the first place: the Great Powers of Western Europe. Indeed, this political injustice is returning to haunt them, and they will, alas, have to pay dearly for it.

The political aspects of the Albanian question

The Albanians in former Yugoslavia, i.e. in rump Yugoslavia (Serbia and Montenegro) and in Macedonia, constitute a major political problem in the Balkans, a problem which must be resolved in the interests of the Albanians, but also in the interests of their Balkan neighbours. The European Community, now the European Union, and the United States of America have become convinced over the last few years that the strikes, protest marches and demonstrations of the Albanians which have helped draw the world's attention to this people's plight since 1981, are understandable and inevitable. The European Union and the United States have managed to gain a more or less true impression of the situation faced by the non-Serbian population of Yugoslavia, and in particular, by the non-Slavic population there, and have come to realize that for the Albanians, Yugoslavia means nothing more than an expanded Serbia.

The Serbs are a small people, no more numerous in fact than the Greeks, Bulgarians or Albanians. And yet, after their expansion and the recognition of this expansion at the Congress of Berlin in 1878, and after an extraordinary expansion during the Balkan Wars and the recognition of their conquests by the Great Powers at the Conference of Ambassadors in London in 1912-1913, the Serbs became a power to be reckoned with, not only within Yugoslavia which was created as a state in 1918, but also throughout the Balkans. The unconditional support they received from Russia as well as help from England and France enabled Serbia to more than triple its territory within the space of eighty years before 1918 and to transform itself into an aggressive state, whose expansion was felt not only in Yugoslavia but in the Balkans as a whole. With the army, the police and the diplomatic corps at its disposal throughout Yugoslavia's seventy-three years of existence, Serbia was able most of the time to determine the political, economic and social fate of the other peoples, in particular of the Albanians who were the most defenceless of the ethnic groups within the Yugoslav federation.

An anti-Albanian attitude has always been a fundamental feature of nationalist ideology among the Serbs, and this has done much to determine national and government policies towards the Albanians in Yugoslavia. The Albanians were seen by Serbia and by Yugoslavia as an ethnic group to be harassed at all costs and forced into emigration. The reasons for this chauvinist attitude towards the Albanians are ethnic, political, religious and strategic. Since 1912, there has never been a single day in the existence of Serbia, Macedonia and Montenegro when their jails have not been teeming with Albanian political prisoners. These people were imprisoned because they refused to accept their people's situation or because there were doubts as to their loyalty towards the Yugoslav state. Even in the years 1966 to 1981, in which a relatively liberal atmosphere towards the Albanians is considered to have reigned in Serbia, Montenegro and Macedonia, Yugoslav prisons were teeming with Albanian political prisoners. Whether the number of Albanian political prisoners in Yugoslavia rose or fell depended on factors over which the Albanians themselves had no control. It depended on internal relations within Yugoslavia, on the level of tension reigning between Serbian, Croatian, Slovenian and Macedonian nationalists, on Yugoslavia's international status and, last but not least, on relations between Yugoslavia and Albania. The number of Albanian political prisoners in the prisons of Serbia, Montenegro and Macedonia usually rose whenever relations among the republics within Yugoslavia worsened, i.e. whenever the Serbs, Croats and Slovenes were preoccupied with one another over economic, social and political issues, over the country's federal structure or over relations with the other states of the Balkans.

The number of Albanian political prisoners in Serbian, Macedonian and Montenegrin jails also rose or fell whenever Yugoslavia changed its political course with regard to the European or global powers, e.g. to Germany or Italy, or to any of the political and military alliances, to the Soviet Union or to the United States.

The number of Albanian political prisoners in Serbian, Macedonian and Montenegrin prisons was particularly affected by any deterioration of relations between Yugoslavia and Albania. Whenever Albania allied itself with a European or global power with whom Yugoslavia had bad relations or of whom Yugoslavia was apprehensive, the number of Albanian political prisoners in Yugoslav prisons rose sharply. Whenever Albanian propaganda against Yugoslavia or Yugoslav propaganda against Albania increased, which happened often from 1912 onwards, Kosovo and other Albanian territories in Serbia, Macedonia and Montenegro were transformed into one huge concentration camp in which the Albanians realized that night had fallen, but did not know if another day would ever dawn. On such occasions, there was not enough room for all the Albanians in Serbian, Macedonian and Montenegrin prisons, so new prisons had to be built, and when these overflowed, Albanian political prisoners were dispatched to Croatia, Slovenia and Bosnia and Herzegovina. Without sovereignty of their own, without a government of their own, without their own diplomats, police and army, i.e. without a country of their own, the Albanians were and have been left to the mercy of the Yugoslav state, the country of the Serbs, Macedonians and Montenegrins, who were free to do as they pleased with them: to persecute the Albanians, to imprison them, to murder them or to free them.

In view of political and state terror against them, but not only for this reason, the Albanians have never been willing to accept Serbo-Montenegrin or Macedonian power over them, nor will they accept it today.

The year 1981 saw the beginning of the open political expulsion of the Albanians from public life in Yugoslavia. At the same time began the de-Yugoslavization of Albanian political opinion in the media and, subsequently, in political practice. The Albanians as a people made it known to Yugoslavia that they were not willing to accept the situation they had been forced into and also made it known that they had the right to decide their future themselves. This is politically understandable. The Albanians demand no more rights than the other peoples already have. Self-determination for the Albanian people in Kosovo and in other Albanian regions of former Yugoslavia means an end to the colonial situation they are stuck in. It also means an end to a life of suffering in which they have been dispensed political democracy, freedom and civil rights bit by bit, as if on a druggist's scales, or deprived of such freedoms completely. It means an end to persecution, oppression, incarceration and murder, an end to universal and systematic destitution and an end to their extremely poor quality of life. It also means an end to anguish and to the psychological, emotional and physical stress which have weighed heavily upon the present generation and which will weigh upon the coming generation, too. In the final analysis, self-determination for the Albanian people means preservation of their ethnic identity from new calvaries of persecution and expulsion as well as from biological, physical, emotional and cultural annihilation.

Anyone informed about the past and the present of the Balkans will understand that the Albanians are not demanding anything more than what has been granted to and enjoyed by the other peoples of former Yugoslavia. In other words, they want no more than to be treated equally with the other peoples of the Balkans and not to be treated as if they were at the bottom of the barrel. With the collapse of Yugoslavia, all the traditional peoples of the Balkans, with the exception of the Albanians, have come to fulfil their national aspirations. The Greeks, Bulgarians and Romanians managed to realize their national aspirations in the nineteenth century and now, the Slovenes, Macedonians and Montenegrins are in the process of realizing theirs, as are the Serbs, Croats and Moslems. But what of the approximately seven million Albanians in the Balkans who are in jeopardy? Their neighbours, in this case the Serbs and Macedonians, are realizing their own interests at the expense of the Albanians.

This makes resolving the Albanian question all the more complex.

At a time when the aspirations of the Serbs, Croats and Moslems of Bosnia and Herzegovina are close to being fulfilled by the division of that country into historical ethnic states, no one has the right to demand of the Albanians that they fulfil their aspirations any differently. Is it proper for the Serbs, Croats and Moslems of Bosnia and Herzegovina to enjoy the right to self-determination, and for the Albanians in Yugoslavia (Serbia and Montenegro) and Macedonia to be denied this right? It is unjust to apply certain political criteria to the Serbs and Croats and to apply other criteria to the Albanians. How is it that the 1,000,000 to 1,200,000 Bosnian Serbs enjoy the right to self-determination when the 2,000,000 Albanians in Kosovo are deprived of this right? How are the 600,000 to 700,000 Croats in Bosnia and Herzegovina to enjoy the right to self-determination when the 700,000 to 800,000 Albanians in Macedonia are being denied this right? How is it that the 1,300,000 Montenegrins enjoy the right to self-determination, but not the 3,000,000 Albanians in former Yugoslavia? The principle of equal treatment must apply. One cannot play around with political principles without severe political and historical consequences for the region.

The Great Powers are perhaps unable to understand the situation of smaller peoples because they have not been confronted with such problems and do not have the same way of looking at the world. But if the Great Powers can make an effort to understand the Serbs, Croats and Moslems in Bosnia and Herzegovina, why can they not make an equal effort to understand the Albanians in Yugoslavia (Serbia and Montenegro) and Macedonia?

There can be no doubt that the Albanian question is not merely a problem for the Albanians. It is a matter for other Balkan peoples, too: for the Serbs, the Macedonians, the Montenegrins and the Greeks. Indeed it is a matter for the Balkans and for Europe as a whole. A solution to the Albanian question, a just solution to the Albanian question, also means a solution to the problems in the relations between the Albanians and the Serbs, between the Albanians and the Macedonians, between the Albanians and the Montenegrins, and between the Albanians and the Greeks. A just solution to the Albanian question would, in the final analysis, also mean a solution to the Balkan question as a whole because, now that the Serbian, Croatian, Moslem and Macedonian questions have found an initial solution, only the Albanian question remains to be solved to attain basic order in the

Balkan. Without a just solution to the Albanian question, there can be no legal order, humanity or peace in the Balkans. What is more, without a solution to the Albanian question, i. e. the last remaining national question in the Balkan peninsula, there can be no democracy there. The well-known Yugoslav dissident Milovan Djilas once called Kosovo a millstone around the neck of Serbian democracy, a weight which cannot be removed until the Kosovo question is resolved. "In Serbia, we must first of all solve the Kosovo question so that we can begin to consolidate our democracy. There will be no modern Western-type democracy in Serbia until the Kosovo question is solved."

And this is not true of Serbia alone.

The Albanian question is also a millstone around the neck of Macedonian democracy, because Macedonia cannot take its place in the modern democratic world either without solving the problem of the Albanians there, who constitute over one-third of the population.

It may seem paradoxical, but the unresolved Albanian question is a millstone around the neck of Albanian democracy, too. It is an illusion to believe that Albania, the state of one half of the Albanian nation, can consolidate liberal and democratic institutions and maintain a stable democratic society while the other half of the Albanian nation across the border lives in a state of oppression and exploitation under foreign rule. In other words, Albania, as the state of one half of the Albanian nation, will never find peace or stability as long as the problem of the other half of the Albanian nation is not resolved, a problem which constitutes the greatest national challenge facing the Albanian people as a whole. The unresolved Albanian question will inevitably interfere with relations between Albania and the Albanian people and their neighbours. In Albania, in Kosovo and in Macedonia, there can easily be found servile and mediocre Albanian politicians willing to present the Albanian question as non-existent and to create the illusion for our Balkan neighbours and for the international community that the case should be regarded as closed. But such an illusion fades quickly and its initiators are inevitably regarded by the Albanians as compromised.

If it remains unsolved, the Albanian question will continue to be a source of irritation and indeed of political conflict catapulting the Balkans from one crisis to the next. The dissatisfaction of the Albanians will only grow and become more evident, and will continue to burden the Balkans and countries elsewhere. This is obvious to anyone who has an eye for Albanian and Balkan realities. If they are not given equal rights with the other peoples of the Balkans, the Albanians will continue to be severely frustrated and agitated by regimes which are not their own, i.e. which they cannot identify with, and will continue to be obsessed by the fact that they are the only people in the Balkans to be severely discriminated against, to be damned by history. With all this in mind, one cannot exclude the possibility that they will give vent to their frustration beyond their ethnic borders and indeed outside the Balkans. A culture of vengeance could arise among the Albanians forced into emigration as well as among those in their Balkan homeland, and this could turn into wide-spread protests and movements which would know no end. In short, a peace created in the Balkans to the detriment of any one of the Balkan peoples, in this case of the Albanian people, cannot last long.

National self-determination - a just solution to the Albanian question

What is the just and permanent solution to the Albanian question? What solution can be found that will make the Albanian people equal to the other peoples in the Balkans? What solution can we come up with to resolve not only the Albanian question, but as a consequence, the Balkan question, too.

As can be seen from the observations above, various responses have been given to the Albanian question in the course of the last eighty years, during which time the issue has grown into what it is today. Various theoretical and practical solutions have been proposed by various parties. But all 'solutions' proposed for the Albanian question up to the present are outdated. Even the much-lauded solution to the question of Kosovo in the 1974 Yugoslav Constitution did not resolve the Albanian question and was thus rejected by the Albanian people in 1981. This solution is outdated for two reasons: firstly, because there no longer exists the Yugoslavia upon which that solution was based and, secondly, because it was outdated at the time and was historically unacceptable for the Albanian people since it did not foresee national self-determination for them. At present, any similar solution to the question of Kosovo within the framework of rump Yugoslavia (Serbia and Montenegro) or within the framework of a possible Yugoslavia to come, which might be composed of Serbia, Montenegro, and the Serbian Republic in Bosnia and Herzegovina, would not be considered satisfactory by the Albanians because it is an inner-Yugoslav solution or, better said, one within the framework of Greater Serbia. Yugoslavia fell apart because it did not provide an adequate solution to the national question of the peoples living within it. How could Yugoslavia, reduced to the scale of a Greater Serbia, now possibly constitute a solution to the question of Kosovo or to the Albanian question as a whole?

Now that Yugoslavia has disintegrated, now that other countries have been created on the basis of their right to self-determination, i.e. the independent country of Slovenia, the independent country of Croatia, the independent country of Macedonia, the independent country of Serbia and Montenegro, and now that the independent Moslem state, the second Serbian state and the second Croatian state being created in Bosnia and Herzegovina are free to join rump Yugoslavia (Serbia and Montenegro) or Croatia if they so wish, the proper and permanent solution for the Albanians can only be national unification, based on the right to self-determination. This is a right which belongs to the divided Albanian people on their territory in former Yugoslavia, land which is geographically continuous with the Republic of Albania and on which the Albanians are either the only inhabitants or the majority inhabitants.

This will mean a change of borders. Borders, after all, are not sacrosanct, for they were not created by God. The history of the human race is a history of the fixing and changing of borders, mostly, alas, in time of war. Fortunately, borders have more recently begun to be fixed and changed in peacetime. Borders are changed and must be changed wherever it is in the interests of the peoples living in the region in question. After the reunification of the two Germanies as an important factor for European stability, after agreement within the international community on the division of Bosnia and Herzegovina along ethnic lines, and after the separation of the Serbs and Croats in Croatia with the help of UN forces, there can be no legal or humanitarian argument against such a change for the Albanians. An British expert in strategic affairs, convinced that a just and lasting solution to the question of

Kosovo could be achieved by altering the border between Serbia and Albania, noted recently that in most cases, it was cheaper, less bloody and, in general, more humane to alter unjust borders peacefully than to defend existing borders in never-ending wars. If we have learned one lesson from European history, it is this: the more a border expresses a demographic division, the more secure and stable it will be.

All those who sincerely desire that Serbian-Albanian and Albanian-Serbian relations be placed on a footing of goodwill, i.e. that good neighbourly relations be maintained, should consider the following question. Which is better: for about 2,000,000 Albanians to be within the borders of Serbia for the sake of about 200,000 Serbs and Montenegrins, or for about 200,000 Serbs and Montenegrins to be within the borders of Albania for the sake of about 2,000,000 Albanians? Which is more appropriate from the point of view of long-term security, justice and humanity: that Kosovo with its roughly 2,000,000 Albanians be left in Serbia or that it be united with Albania?

Political, moral and historical logic offer only one response to this question: Albanian demands are justified.

Those who still hold that the ethnic problems of the Balkans must be resolved at the expense of the Albanians will counter that the Albanian unification is tantamount to the creation of a Greater Albania. But what kind of argument is this? Russia, with its more than 17,075,400 km² and 150,000,000 inhabitants is not called Greater Russia. United Germany with its 357,000 km² and 80,000,000 inhabitants is not called Greater Germany. Nor is China with 9,511,000 km² and 1,200,000,000 inhabitants called Greater China. In contrast to this, some people still insist on using the term Greater Albania for a united Albania, made up of the present-day Republic of Albania and Albanian territory in former Yugoslavia, a geographical entity in which the Albanians are either the only inhabitants or the majority inhabitants and which would extend over a total surface of about 50,000 - 55,000 km² and have approximately 7,000,000 inhabitants.

No, a united Albania, made up of the two halves of the divided Albanian nation, cannot be called a Greater Albania, but rather a natural Albania. And even in this case, there would still be many Albanians 'left over' in Serbia, Macedonia and Montenegro, i.e. Albanian minorities living in those countries. Albania, consisting of Albanian territory on both sides of the present border, is not a Greater anything. An Albania reunited with Kosovo, being a geographical entity in which the Albanians are either the only inhabitants or the majority inhabitants, can certainly not be called Greater Albania.

On the other hand, a Serbia including Kosovo with a 90% Albanian population is a Greater Serbia. Macedonia, including its western territories in which the Albanians are either the only inhabitants or by far the majority inhabitants, is a Greater Macedonia.

Albanian unification is therefore not tantamount to the creation of a Greater Albania, but rather tantamount to the realization of the right to national self-determination, a right which some peoples in the Balkans were early to realize and which other peoples are now realizing - all with the exception of the Albanians, who have been and continue to be denied this right.

There is no doubt that a just and permanent solution to the Albanian question would be of historical significance not only to the Albanians, but also to the Balkans as a whole, but of course only if it is brought about as it should be brought about, by peaceful and democratic means. As long as the Albanian question continues to exist in its present form and content, the Albanians will remain the condemned prisoners of the Balkans, and Yugoslavia (Serbia and Montenegro) and Macedonia will remain the sick men of the peninsula.

Our Balkan neighbours and the international community must come to comprehend the injustice done to the Albanians and be convinced of their unequal status compared to other peoples in the Balkans. Endless statistics could be added to the information given above. At the time of the Eastern Crisis, for instance, the number of Albanians in the Balkans was approximately equal to that of the Greeks, Serbs and Bulgarians, and the territory they inhabited was of approximately the same size as that which these peoples (Greeks, Serbs and Bulgarians) disposed of. At the present, however, the seven million Albanians in the Balkans, inhabiting as a majority a territory of about 55,000 to 60,000 km^2, hold sovereignty over only 28,565 km^2 of this land, whereas in the other part of this Albanian territory, sovereignty is held by their neighbours, i.e. the Serbs, Macedonians and Montenegrins. About 7,500,000 Serbs hold sovereignty over about 140,000 km^2. About 500,000 Montenegrins hold sovereignty over about 13,812 km^2.

About 1,300,000 Macedonians hold sovereignty over about 25,713 km², and about 9,500,000 Greeks hold sovereignty over about 130,938 km².

It is more than obvious that the interests of our Balkan neighbours have been realized to the detriment of the vital interests of the Albanian people.

It is also more than obvious that the injustice under which the Albanians are forced to live, compared to their neighbours, is so great and with such ramifications that it must, of necessity, disturb their Balkan neighbours too.

The Albanians now believe that their national interests must be realized, and that the interests of their neighbours must be maintained at the same time. The neighbouring peoples must come to this conclusion, too, i.e. that their national interests must be maintained and that the interests of the Albanians must be recognized and realized. The Albanians are not demanding, nor should they ever demand, anything more or anything less than what the other peoples of the Balkans already have. They demand of the others a promise of equality and good will in the Balkans, and demand for themselves the right to be equal with the others.

The Albanians, I repeat, have been put at a dreadful disadvantage in comparison with other peoples of the Balkans. It is not in the overall long-term interests of the Balkan peninsula to keep the Albanian nation divided into various states, and consequently to keep it worn down, poor and frustrated, to keep it in a position in which the Albanians are acutely aware of the injustice done to them and constantly infuriated that this injustice has not been corrected. It is in the interests of the Balkans that the Albanians be given an equal chance with their neighbours to become an advanced and developed nation which, as a consequence, will feel at home in the community of Balkan and European states. It is in the interests of the Balkans that the Albanians be united in their own country just as the other peoples of the peninsula are united in theirs, so that the Albanians can make a positive contribution to Balkan and European co-existence, so that they can meet the demands which will be made of them in the future.

There is no doubt that Albanian unification is the legitimate and democratic right of the Albanian people, a right which has come to the surface after much delay and which is still being thwarted, but which, as it is becoming clearer to everyone, is both politically and morally justifiable and historically inevitable.

Unification of the divided Albanian nation can still be hindered by the Great Powers, but not by the course of justice.

In their endeavours to realize this right, the Albanians must not forget that there is only one Balkan peninsula despite the myriad of peoples living in it, and that they must come to terms with their neighbours and live with them on a permanent basis.

Our Balkan neighbours, for their part, must not forget that there is one thing which has proven stronger than any weapon: the will of nations for freedom and independence.

[Taken from *Çështja shqiptare, Historia dhe politika* (Instituti Albanologjik, Prishtina 1994), p. 287-316. Translated from the Albanian by Robert Elsie]

The question of Kosovo

Ismail Kadare

Kosovo is a word one hears more and more often, but unlike names such as Bosnia or Sarajevo, regions of the Balkans in the grips of open conflict and war, "Kosovo" is always spoken with a certain reserve, almost in a whisper. One would almost think one were living among the peoples of the ancient world, for whom certain words always had to be spoken in a hush, especially when they were felt to be associated with evil spirits. This is the way people refer to Kosovo. It is as if they were apprehensive about it, as if there were some inherent force of evil there which could be awakened by too much noise. This is how it is referred to at international conferences, at the end of news broadcasts or at the conclusion of interviews: always as a short "by the way" item.

Some European politicians have warned quite openly, "Careful with Kosovo! We must take care not to encourage the Albanians to rise in revolt and not to incite the Serbs to carry out a bloodbath!" What they really mean is, "Let us don the veil so that our view of Kosovo is blurred! Let us plug our ears so that we can hear nothing but a muffled voice! Otherwise, the tragedy will cause us anguish and keep us awake at night...!"

And yet, the tragedy will not go away. The spectre of a living hell hovers over two million Albanians. Refusing to look at the truth and trying to assuage our conscience by trying to stop the evil from spreading is like shutting a wild beast up in the same cage with its victim, content in the knowledge that the cage is locked and the beast cannot escape. But what of the victim? The tragedy of Kosovo is becoming apparent throughout the continent. Two million Albanians are not the only ones who will have to come to terms with it. Their backs are bent, their souls weighed down under the burden. Taken hostage, their hands tied, they search the horizon for salvation...

Any truth about a people, or indeed about a human being, is part of the truth about mankind. In this respect, the truth about Kosovo transcends the misfortune of a single people. What it describes can happen to any one of us. Kosovo is a test of the conscience of mankind at the end of the millenium.

Kosovo has been the scene of crimes for decades now. During the years of the Second World War, time verily stood still there. Kosovo was under a continuous state of siege, with raids, shootings and summary executions. Schools were closed, the regional parliament dissolved, broadcasting and newspapers shut down, and mass expulsions carried out by force, with everything from police dogs to the burning down of homes.

It all now seems incredible, too much to believe. You have to be there to understand what is really happening. But let one statistic suffice. Over the last three years, according to Albanian sources, 800,000 people have been interrogated by the police, 584,373 according to the Serbian police itself. Take the average of the two figures, if you will. And let us add one more detail to complete the picture. Until December 1993, Arkan (Željko Ražnjatović), wanted by the police in a number of European countries for various offences including murder, represented Kosovo as an elected member of the Serbian parliament.

On his forays through the country with his followers, Arkan loves to meet Albanians. On such occasions, he is fond of asking, "What's keeping you from leaving? Where is the pluck you once had?" Then he brandishes his revolver.

Such is Kosovo.

When people hear about the trauma Kosovo is going through, many of them wonder, "How can such things take place in twentieth-century Europe?"

Everything is possible once evil is unleashed, and it has been given free rein in the Balkans for quite some time now. The drama of Kosovo in this century is a tragedy in several acts. The first act was played out when this part of Albania was cut off from its motherland and given to the newly-created state of Yugoslavia, an artificial entity which was to be at the origin of many a crisis in the Balkans. Serbia had many allies at the time, among them Russia. Albania, for its part, was alone and isolated. The Austro-Hungarian Empire, the fledgling Balkan nation's only support, had collapsed just before the outbreak of the First World War. The spirit of good will, nourished by American President Wilson, was not enough to curb a wave of anti-Albanian sentiment. The age-old Balkan country, one of the most ancient on the European continent, was sliced up and torn to pieces. Kosovo and other regions comprising almost half the nation found themselves beyond the borders of the new state.

Kosovo has been an integral part of Albanian territory for at least eighteen centuries of the last two millenia. Only for two centuries, the twelfth and thirteenth, was it occupied by the southern Slavs. In 1918, the southern Slavs, that is the Serbs, found themselves amongst the victors. They demanded a reward for the assassination they had carried out in Sarajevo. And they were given it in the form of Kosovo and other territories in Montenegro and Macedonia. Dismissing as irrelevant the other eighteen centuries, they made sure that only the two centuries of Slav occupation counted. Most grievous of all, no account was taken of the wishes of the inhabitants of Kosovo. To the cynical politicians of the time it did not matter who lived on the land. The population was of no more importance to them than were the cattle and the forests. Perhaps even less so.

During the Second World War, the Italians, and subsequently the Germans, looking out of course for their own interests, but also not unaware of what German tradition had to say about the Balkans and about the Albanians in particular, rectified the mistake that had been made by the Great Powers. They reunited Kosovo with Albania, adding five years to the eighteen centuries. But what rectification could there be if it was brought about by the Nazis? Once the war was over, it gave just one more reason for being against the Albanians. No one dared to raise his voice in protest that, despite who the Nazis were and what crimes they had committed, they had been right about Kosovo and the victors were wrong. There exists an attitude, not unlike the one seen in 'socialist realism', manifesting itself not only in the East as one might have expected, but throughout the world, which prevents us from taking a cold and lucid glance at certain consequences of the Second World War, in particular at the price which Europe and the world paid to defeat the Nazis. Half of Europe was reduced to slavery in the process. Tens of millions of people were murdered and basic human values distorted, indeed the fate of entire nations was cast to the wind. It will take centuries to pull these countries back out of the mire, if we are ever able to do so. The vile spectre of Russian communism sprouted in the very camp of the victors. Its fruits were not long in ripening. It almost seems as though the Nazis, in their downfall, had succeeded in countering the verdict of history and in laying the serpent's eggs.

One of the first fruits, the bitterest of all, was the communist state of Yugoslavia. It was more ferocious than the rest, and more hypocritical too. It donned the robes of a dissident and liberal country, a land of country fairs and festivals, and became the cynosure of the Third World, a place for international conferences on peace, on the arts, on cinema. The West thought it had the country on its side. The East pretended to have it as its enemy. But over the years, the naked and simple truth came out. Yugoslavia was the most successful diversion of the East-West conflict. It is no coincidence that real communism evolved initially among the north-eastern Slavs, i.e. the Russians, and took root subsequently among the southern Slavs, i.e. the Serbs.

Let us return to the year 1945 which saw the rise of this communist state. Its foundations were bathed in the blood of tens of thousands of Albanians. All the young communist countries waded in blood at the start, but primarily in their own blood. Yugoslavia, for its part, was an exception. It spilt the blood of another nation. The first act of its government was to proclaim a state of siege in Kosovo. Denounced as nationalists for simply refusing to accept the union of Kosovo and Serbia, and as pro-German simply because the German goals happened to coincide with their own aspirations, tens of thousands of Albanians were massacred in the most barbaric manner. Throughout the Second World War, the Slavic communists, the Russians and Serbs, did much to exploit the alleged pro-German sentiments of the smaller peoples of the continent - the Tatars, the Croats, the Kosovo Albanians, the Balts etc. It is, nonetheless, difficult to hold a grudge against these peoples for believing in German propaganda in their struggle to free themselves of Slav oppression and for regarding Germany as their only hope to escape the evils which had plagued them for centuries.

They were wrong, of course. They fled from the serpent, only to throw themselves into the clutches of the wolf, so to speak. The intentions which were wrongly attributed to them and the vengeance which followed constituted the first major crime committed by the victors.

It was the Kosovo Albanians who were to pay the highest price. The bodies of hundreds, often thousands of dead were hurled into common graves, over which History has remained silent up to now. These innocent victims were spared but one accusation, that they were striving for unification with Albania. This could not be, because, far from attempting to prevent the massacre, communist Albania joined in, putting the whole nation to shame. One cynical slogan of the period, 'Communists have no homeland,' was to be outdone by another equally crude saying, 'The real homeland of all communists is the Soviet Union'.

Such was the second act in the tragedy of Kosovo. Caught up between the two communist cohorts, Serbia and Albania, Kosovo abandoned all hope of resistance.

The West, not wishing to disturb the idyllic tryst with the immoral state of Yugoslavia or jeopardize relations with the Russians, took the massacres in its stride. There may also have been other reasons of which we are still unaware. At any rate, it was in Kosovo that communist Yugoslavia rediscovered its taste for blood, as had the savage monarchy which preceded it. The blood of a foreign, non-Slavic people posed no moral dilemma for the country. On the contrary, shedding such blood afforded pleasure and brought career advancement and honours. In 1937, a Serbian academician called Vasa Čubrilović published a memorandum on ways and means of getting rid of the Albanians, such as mass extermination and terror. Čubrilović was never taken to task for his proposals. In the communist period he was even elected head of the Serbian National Academy of Sciences, after having been honoured by the Soviet Academy!

It is no secret that Russian influence makes itself felt from time to time in the Balkans. Declarations from figures such as Zhirinovsky should therefore come as no surprise to Westerners. They are often quite in line with official policy. The trip Zhirinovsky made to Serbia to spur on Serbian crimes heralded the arrival of Russian troops under the banner of the United Nations. That same evening, in true Zhirinovsky style, the speaker on Russian television declared that Russia had now returned to the Balkans for good.

There is an indelible link between the crimes committed by the communists on the steppes of Russia and those perpetrated in the mountains of the Balkans. If Russia is to rid itself of the evils of communism, which would ensure its survival and enable the world to breathe freely, it must not be allowed to project or maintain such evils in another region, especially not in the Balkans. We must not forget that, contrary to what is commonly thought, only twenty-five of the seventy million inhabitants of the Balkan peninsula, i.e. about one-third, are Slavs. The others are Romanians, Greeks, Albanians, and Turks who have nothing to do with Russia.

Other scholars from the Academy of Sciences, too, were subsequently honoured for their zeal in the Albanian question. One of them, writer Dobrica Ćosić, has recently acceded to the presidential council of rump Yugoslavia (Serbia and Montenegro) for his well-known outpourings of hatred and for his doctrine of ethnic cleansing.

The career of Ćosić is telling. As one of the architects of Greater Serbian strategies and as a member of the Central Committee of the Communist Party, this Yugoslav ex-Zhdanovite was expelled by Tito in 1966 when his anti-Albanian zeal became all too evident. Having lost power because of the Albanians, Dobrica Ćosić was celebrated as a dissident. And what a dissident he is! When things resumed their 'natural course', the once-persecuted Ćosić was doubly recompensed. He was made president himself.

There were other Serbian and Yugoslav writers and intellectuals - to whom their county will one day pay hommage - such as Danilo Kiš, Predrag Matvejevitch, Bogdanović, Mirko Kovač, Berković, etc., who suffered genuine persecution, in particular for their refusal to be involved in the anti-Albanian hysteria. Unfortunately, their voices have been silenced in the deafening campaigns against the Albanians.

The third act in the drama of Kosovo began in 1981. The Albanians rose up to demand the creation of a republic within the Yugoslav federation. A republic like the others - like Slovenia, which has fewer people than Kosovo, like Macedonia, which has fewer still, or like Montenegro, which has only a quarter of Kosovo's population. Each people had its own republic, but the wish of the Albanians, the third largest ethnic group in Yugoslavia after the Serbs and the Croats, was considered a crime. After all, they were not Slavs, and a country called Yugoslavia, the country of the southern Slavs, could only belong to the Slavs!

Albanian demonstrations were quelled with exemplary savagery. A bloodbath took place, complete with tanks, aircraft, torture and a wave of unprecedented terror. Kosovo was encircled by the army, locked in and, once taken prisoner in the absence of witnesses, savagely raped. In 1984, Danilo Kiš told the author of the present lines that he had had an opportunity to hear a tape recording (a film was impossible to obtain) of the sounds of the massacre. This, he noted, was enough for him to comprehend that hell had been created on earth. And yet, still suffering from the side-effects of the drug of Yugoslav 'liberalism', the world took little note of the massacre in Kosovo and understood even less that this reaction was the harbinger of crimes to come. A fatal attack had been made against Balkan civilization. Inhumanity was allowed to flourish. The path now lay open.

One of the most successful tricks of our age was produced in Kosovo before everyone's eyes. The country was proclaimed the cradle of Serbian civilization when in fact it had been settled much earlier by other peoples. It was here that the Serbs began playing their bloody game for the first time. They declared that they were being pushed out by the Albanians and at the very same time began preparations for the expulsion of the Albanians, Bosnians and Croats. With a great show of concern, they spread the word that the Albanians were conducting a campaign of ethnic cleansing against them in Kosovo, against the very people who were preparing the crime. Finally, they clamoured that the Kosovo Albanians were raping their women as they themselves were preparing the foul deed themselves.

The 1981 Albanian uprising against the Serbs, like the Hungarian uprising of 1956, constituted a double revolt, directed as it was both against Slavic oppression and against communism. The Albanians were the first to quit the Yugoslav Communist Party en masse because it had become a symbol of ethnic oppression. Just as in earlier centuries they had renounced their Christian faith so as not so share it with the Serbs, they now refused to share the ranks of the same Communist Party with them.

Unfortunately, the Albanian uprising of 1981 was misunderstood or was criticized as inopportune. Its main fault was that it stood in the way of the on-going love affair between the Western world and a depraved Yugoslavia. The Albanians were thus abandoned to the mercy of the Serbs. To compound the misfortune, the other peoples of Yugoslavia, the Croats, Slovenes, and Bosnians, who were soon to suffer the same fate themselves, refused to lend their support to the 'foreign' people.

Encouraged by the world's silence, the Serbs doubled and tripled the terror in Kosovo. In 1989, they put an end to the autonomous status of the province, proclaimed a state of siege and carried out a new massacre against the innocent population. As Kosovo was burying its dead, Yugoslav television broadcast cynical scenes of banqueting in Belgrade where the victory, i.e. the forced abolition of autonomy in Kosovo, was celebrated to the flow of champagne.

Albania's voluntary isolation from the rest of the world proved, without a doubt, to be to the detriment of the Kosovo Albanians and to the advantage of the Serbs. If Europe had reason to abide in silence on Albania, which had walled itself in, there was no justification for its remaining silent on Kosovo. As part of a country judged to be a friend of the West, this half of the Albanian nation should have been treated more kindly instead of being forced to pay for the folly of others.

Contempt for Albania and the Albanians is a similar injustice, a double standard. Many a moral lecture has been given to intellectuals in Albania since the collapse of communism there, yet no account has been taken of the complete isolation that was imposed on them. In the years 1966-1969, virtually all Albanian writers and a good number of other prominent intellectuals were sent off to the countryside for 'spiritual regeneration' on collective farms. There was an unprecedented wave of deportations. The Western press did not publish a single line about this crime, which went on for several years and which cannot be said to have been entirely hidden from view. In Kosovo, Albanian writer Adem Demaçi spend twenty-seven years in prison and was only released in 1990 after serving all of his sentence. His case was well-known, and yet no one intervened at the international level to come to his assistance. But there is no need to dwell on the past. As recently as March 1994, the Serbian authorities prohibited Rexhep Qosja, member of the Academy of Sciences and one of the most prominent writers of Kosovo, from travelling to Paris to participate in the promotion of his novel 'Death comes with such eyes', which had just been published by Gallimard in a French translation. And so forth.

It has often been said that too little is known about Albania and the Albanians. I do not raise this aspect of the problem merely to complain about the conspicuous lack of information or to appeal to European intellectuals to do something about such an anti-European attitude, unfortunately still wide-spread in the Balkans, nor, on the other hand, to attribute to others the faults of the Albanians themselves. It is simply that this indifference is at the very heart of the matter. Whenever the Albanian question is brought up, one encounters a hesitancy, a sense of unwillingness, and an embarrassed silence, not to mention a rather unpleasantly condescending attitude towards the country. The fact remains, however, that Albania is the only country in Europe over the last two thousand years to have lost half of its territory and more than half of its population - millions of people who now live across the border. A narrow-minded attitude towards this tiny country or attempts to justify such a barbarious amputation become totally absurd when we compare Albania to a gigantic country like China, keeping a jealous hold over its two million Tibetans who represent no more than a thousandth of its population, or to Russia, covering one-sixth of the face of the earth, which covets every inch of its territory, or to Serbia, which proclaims that everywhere Serbs hang their hats is Serbia.

Yet, the hesitancy, the indifference and the embarrassed silence persist. Few people would venture to claim that the Albanians are at fault, but equally few people venture to assert the contrary with any sense of resolve or sympathy. What is it that is distorting people's view of this issue, one of the most distressing in the Balkan peninsula?

For forty years, Tito's Yugoslavia did its utmost to muddy the waters, hypocritically playing on its friendships, using banks, and even drawing on its secret files to commit blackmail (the famous picture of Kurt Waldheim, former Secretary General of the United Nations, is one example).

Every time a criminal act was criticized, 'mitigating circumstances' were cited. For crimes committed in Kosovo, the mitigating circumstance was a 'historical argument'. Looking back over what has been written about Kosovo, we see that most authors refer in their introductions to the same old legend, the myth that Kosovo belongs historically to Serbia. Kosovo as the cradle of Serbia. Kosovo as Serbia's Jerusalem. Kosovo as an ancient Serbian land on which the Albanians are newly arrived intruders. This is the myth, or rather the fallacy and the key to the aforementioned enigma. This is what weakens resolve, blinds reason and makes people hesitate.

This is why, instead of seeing the hell being created before their very eyes and listening to the victim, certain politicians prefer to listen to the henchman. They weep over the henchman's hard lot and appeal for compassion with his sufferings. The henchman, too, has his problems, after all. Let us not be unkind. We must not scoff at his version of history.

To get to the truth of the matter, we must nonetheless rid ourselves of this blinding fallacy. It is a thankless task to study historical archives and chronicles in order to comprehend the present. It is even more thankless to try to ascertain which people are autochthonous to a country and which are not. But from time to time, this becomes necessary. Crime has been committed in the Balkans by means of falsification of history, and it is only with the help of history that this crime can be understood. To plead with the Albanians not to dwell on the past (at a time when everyone else is invoking history for their own ends), to ask them to stop constantly referring to their roots, their stock, their Illyrian origins, and their habitation, over the last two thousand years, of territory they still inhabit today, is like asking the protagonist in a duel to throw away his shield at the very moment the attacker brandishes his sword.

Let us take a look at how history is presented. The anti-Albanian propaganda spread by the Serbs is based on the following version of history. Although the Serbs are but a minority in Kosovo (about 8%), Kosovo, according to the Serbs, is the cradle of Serbian civilization, and for this reason they have a strong historical attachment to the country. In 1389, the Serbs fought a great battle against the Turks on the Plain of Kosovo and much Serbian blood was spilt. According to this version, the Serbs were the original inhabitants of Kosovo and the Albanians did not arrive until later. Consequently, the Albanians are foreigners who should either keep their mouths shut or leave the country.

This is a blatant lie. No serious historian or reliable historical source has ever been able to provide evidence that the Serbs were the original inhabitants of Kosovo and that the Albanians were later immigrants. On the contrary, the Albanians were there from the very start. It is the Slavs who arrived later - indeed quite a bit later.

However, in this age of mediocrity, amateur scholarship and vulgar propaganda, misinformation has a tendency to acquire force of law, and myths of the type I have just referred to, if backed by sufficient money, are eventually accepted as fact. It is now our television screens which often serve to stifle historical truths.

All serious historians have for centuries now accepted that the Albanians and the Ancient Greeks are the oldest inhabitants of the Balkan peninsula. The Albanians are considered the direct descendants of the Illyrians. In the second century A.D., Ptolemy the Greek first mentioned the name of a people known as the *Albanoi* as inhabitants of what is now Central Albania. In 1695, the German philosopher Gottfried Wilhelm Leibnitz, one of the greatest thinkers in the history of mankind, defended his thesis about the Illyrian origins of the Albanian language in a speech before a German Academy. These two early examples suffice to show that the thesis of the autochthonous character of the Albanians is not a recent one and was not even brought forth originally by Albanians. It has existed for centuries and derives from neutral sources.

All historians, whether serious or not, even Slav and Serbian historians, admit unanimously that the Slavs arrived in the Balkans in the seventh and eighth centuries and settled the peninsula from the tenth to the twelfth centuries. This Slavic migration led to an open conflict with the ancient Illyro-Albanian inhabitants of the peninsula. Under

Serbian pressure, the latter withdrew into regions they have inhabited to this very day, i.e. the Republic of Albania and north-eastern Albania, the land which is now called Kosovo and is under Serbian rule.

Kosovo is adjacent to Albania and has always been inhabited by Albanians (by Albanians alone up until the 7th-9th centuries and subsequently by an Albanian majority and a Serbian minority). Kosovo was certainly not uninhabited before the arrival of the Serbs. It is one of the most fertile parts of the Balkan peninsula and consequently would have been settled early on. The Greeks did not lay claim to it. The question is therefore very simple. Who was living in Kosovo before the arrival of the Serbs? Setting aside as unlikely suggestions of ghosts and spirits, it is quite obvious to the casual observer that the inhabitants of Kosovo were the same people who inhabit the region today, the Albanians.

The thesis of Kosovo as the cradle of Serbian civilization rests on a temporary Serbian occupation of Kosovo for a period of two centuries (11th-12th). It was during this period that the Orthodox churches were constructed, after earlier Roman Catholic sites of worship were demolished (the Albanians were all Christians at the time, some Catholic, some Orthodox).

To make the great lie more attractive to a larger public, including a bevy of amateurs in the press and in politics, another dramatic element was added to the story: the Battle of Kosovo. It is well known that many peoples, especially smaller nations, have a tendency to scrounge around in their history for some national catastrophe or disaster, which they repeat to themselves over and over, making it the focus of national revival. They also delude themselves into thinking that once reparations are made for their sufferings, they will attain the paradise they dream of.

There is nothing wrong with this in itself. Indeed, dreams and illusions often have positive consequences. But if such an illusion serves to justify a subsequent crime, a war of destruction or worse, if it permits a small group of individuals to hold onto power, it then becomes a national calamity for the country in question, and for its neighbours, too.

The Battle of Kosovo took place in June 1389 (it was on the six hundredth anniversary of the battle that Milošević launched his policy of vengeance against the Albanians, aimed at their definitive annihilation, and declared that it was not the Ottoman Turks whom the Serbs had fought on the Plains of Kosovo, but the Albanians).

In current Serbian propaganda, the Battle of Kosovo has become something of a jewel, the diamond at the heart of an anti-Albanian myth. According to the propaganda, the Battle of Kosovo was a struggle between the Christian Serbs and the Moslems of the Ottoman Empire. The very salvation of Europe was at stake as Serbian resistance stood in the way of the Turkish invasion of the continent. So heroic was the struggle that both of its leaders, the Serbian Prince Lazar and Sultan Murad I, perished on the battlefield.

Though this version is easy to sell in the tabloid press, it is a gross travesty of the truth. The Battle of Kosovo had nothing to do with the struggle between the Serbs and the Ottoman Turks and did nothing for the 'salvation of Europe'. On the contrary, it poured oil onto the flames. It must also be noted in passing that the deaths of the two adversaries were less than heroic.

Let us examine the details one by one. The propaganda does not tell us who actually took part in the battle. The historical documents do. On the one side were the Balkan princes with their allies: the Serbs, Albanians, Romanians, Bosnians (some say the Croats, too). Facing them was the army of the Ottoman Empire. The Serbs are silent about the participation of all the other peoples in order to keep the glory all to themselves ('glory' which should normally go to the victors, that is, the Turks). Historians tell us not only of the participants in the battle, but also the names of the five commanders-in-chief of the Balkan alliance: Serbian Prince Lazar, Bosnian King Tvrtko, Romanian Prince Mircea, and the Albanian Counts Balsha and Jonima. It is true that Prince Lazar was chosen to take over the general command. The Serbs seem to have had more troops than the rest, but the others were also present in force.

The second lie is the romantic fable about the Battle of Kosovo saving Europe from Islam. (Evident is the analogy to the war in Bosnia which current Serbian propaganda is endeavouring to draw. The Serbs wish to present themselves as the defenders of Christianity against Islam). This assertion is just as childish as the first when we recall that the Battle of Kosovo resulted in a total victory for the Turkish army. History offers no instance of a victory by an aggressive state standing in the way of the victor's advance. Quite the contrary. Not only did the Battle of Kosovo do nothing to impede the advance of the Ottoman Empire, it assisted it. It was in Kosovo that the Ottoman Turks came to realize that Christian Europe with all its princes and counts, with all its banners and aristocratic titles, was no match for the mighty Ottoman army composed of thousands of anonymous soldiers who offered blind obedience to their commanders. Theirs was a modern army the likes of which Europe had never seen before. The fact that the Ottoman superpower postponed its invasion of Europe had nothing to do with the Battle of Kosovo (which delayed the conquest only for the time it took to fight the battle, i.e. ten hours), but was in fact the work of Tamerlane the Terrible, who had set upon the Ottoman Empire like a frenzied beast with an even more anonymous, more frightening force: the Mongol hordes.

Let us, in conclusion, take a look at the death of the two military leaders, an element which affords an opportunity to add a few poignant colours and gives the scene an apocalyptic touch. In fact, neither the Balkan leader Lazar nor the Turkish Sultan Murad were killed in circumstances of romantic heroism. They died after the battle wass over under much more prosaic conditions. The Serbian prince was captured and executed, and the Turkish sultan was killed, after the battle too, under mysterious circumstances. The fact that the council of viziers had arranged for the legitimate heir to the throne, Yakup Çelebi, to be executed in the mayhem, and had proclaimed the young Bayazid as the next sultan, suggests that a premeditated palace coup was involved.

These are the truths about the Battle of Kosovo which history has transmitted to us, truths which, alas, have been drowned out by a pack of lies and amateur interpretations.

All this can be understood much more easily if we see events in their Balkan context. Here are the dates: 1389: the Battle of Kosovo. A disastrous defeat for all the Balkan countries. The Ottoman Empire prepares to invade Europe. 1404: the fatal battle against Tamerlane during which the Empire is almost annihilated. At the beginning of the fifteenth century, the Ottoman Empire recovers and invades the Balkans once again. 1444: George Castriota, called Scanderbeg by the Turks, an Albanian count decorated by the pope as a champion of Christ and defender of Christianity, liberates Albania. Sultan Murad II sets out to force him into submission. Having suffered heavy losses, the sultan is murdered during his retreat (Albanian romantics, who are not bad at glorifying their own national history, have alleged that he died of despair at having failed to conquer Albania. At least they have stopped short of inventing an Albanian hero or heroine to slay the sultan in his tent!). 1453: an ominous year for Christianity - the fall of Constantinople, the second Rome. Its conqueror, Mehmet II Fatih, sets out to subjugate Albania once and for all. In 1478, Shkodër, the last Albanian fortress, capitulates (almost ninety years after the Battle of Kosovo!), while the Venetian-Albanian stronghold of Durrës holds out until 1499. During the siege of Shkodër, the Turkish conquerors led the assault to cries of "Rome! Rome!", revealing that their immediate plan was the invasion of Western Europe. By 1500, the beginning of the sixteenth century, the Ottoman Empire was nearer than ever to fulfilling its age-old dream of conquering Europe and defeating the Christian world.

It is more than obvious that the true course of history is vastly different from that presented by the people trying to manipulate it today. It is equally obvious that the defence of Christianity was never a Serbian monopoly - not in the past and even less so in the present. Indeed, the acts committed by the Serbs today in the name of Christianity threaten to defile the conscience of the human race, and in particular, the conscience of Europe.

The Battle of Kosovo should serve as the symbol for the brotherhood of the peoples of the Balkans, as in fact it was. Unfortunately, the memory of that battle has been transformed into a phantasm thirsting for the blood of those who fought side by side in 1389.

The truth about Kosovo has implications that go far beyond the field of history and are linked to the moral values of our age.

In order to explain the 'madness' which has seized the Balkans today, one must keep in mind what happened to the peoples who were defeated and forced to submit to the awesome mechanisms of the Ottoman Empire. The complexity of their relations with this superpower gave rise to many a paradox that cannot be satisfactorily accounted for by the explanations often given by historians from both sides - official

Ottoman chroniclers and the romantic bards of the Balkans. For the former, the work of the Ottomans was the triumph of emancipation, while the latter see only that the peoples of the Balkans stood between Europe and the monster. The scoreboard is not as unequivocal as one might think. It is true that, up to the fifteenth century, the peoples of the Balkans did their utmost to impede and delay Ottoman expansion, but it is equally true that, thereafter, by an irony of fate, they assisted the Ottoman Empire in reaching its zenith. The Empire was early to realize that exploiting the vigour and intelligence of these impetuous peoples was to its advantage. Without them, it could not force Europe into submission. The Ottoman army, the most modern on earth at the time, was renowned for its basic unit, the anonymous and highly disciplined Turkish soldier. What it lacked was a spirit of adventure and something of the madness of the Balkans. High-ranking officers, generals and admirals from the Balkans, Albanians in particular, began with time to distinguish themselves in the service of the Empire, a rather curious form of revenge by a conquered people! As with the army, officials from the Balkans began to rise to prominence in other fields, too: government, administration, diplomacy and commerce. The Albanians, together with the Jews and the Greeks, advanced to high positions under the envious eye of other peoples who preferred to keep their distance.

The more its dream of conquering Europe took shape, the more the Ottoman Empire implemented its new political strategy with regard to the Balkans. In 1656 there occurred an event of some significance. Mehmet Qyprilli (Köprülü), who originated from central Albania, was appointed Prime Minister of the Ottoman Empire. This appointment was not designed to appeal to the masses. It was more the type of nomination practised by multinational states today, i.e. the selection of members of a national minority for honorific posts. Qyprilli thus found himself at the helm of that multinational giant. The first condition he set for his acceptance of the post was that the sultan not oppose any of his decrees. And so it was. Not only did Qyprilli finish his days as Prime Minister, but his son inherited the job. It was the incredible story of a dynasty which survived, parallel to that of the sultans, for three centuries. For about a hundred years, this family furnished the Ottoman Empire with prime ministers, dozens of ministers, generals and governors. (As late as 1956, the Turkish minister of foreign affairs was still a Qyprilli). The Qyprilli waged military campaigns against Hungary and Poland, conquered Crete, part of the Ukraine, and on and on.

The Qyprilli were at the epicentre of power. Throughout the huge empire there were, in addition, dozens of high-level Albanian officials who reigned over vast regions with an iron fist. As an indication of the extent to which Albanians reached high offices, mention may be made of one figure: Ali of Tepelena, popularized in France by Victor Hugo and Alexandre Dumas. He reigned as a tyrant over half of Albania and Greece and was a truer incarnation of the 'Turkish Yoke' than were the sultans themselves. This is true of many other Albanians who assumed positions of power. Being as tyrannical as most other high officials of the age, they created a climate of terror and dismay for other peoples. Not only were they closely identified with their Ottoman masters - and rightly so, since they had become an integral part of the mechanisms of oppression - but their reknown gradually caused the whole Albanian nation to acquire the same reputation. The Albanians came to be considered privileged and domineering. The other peoples who, not enjoying such status, saw themselves as the butt of contempt and oppression, developed a feeling of resentment against this nation and a desire to take revenge on it. This was the case, in particular, of the southern Slavs, close neighbours of the Albanians.

Thoughtful observers in the Balkans have countered that it is wrong to confuse such tyrannic pashas with the Albanian nation as a whole, and certainly wrong to make the Albanians pay for the cruelty, ambition and whims of such figures. After all, the Albanians suffered as much as anyone from the iron fist and crazed folly of these leaders. The Albanian poets of the age told this to the world even before the crimes had been committed.

Nonetheless, the damage was done and its effects lingered on even after the collapse of the Ottoman Empire at the beginning of the twentieth century. The time was ripe to take revenge on the Albanians. Misunderstandings, jealousy and resentment spread. In 1912, the Balkan states, urged on by Russia, set upon Albania to tear it to pieces. The fate of the half of the Albanian nation that fell under Serbian domination was particularly tragic. The Serbs, who had been oppressed and badly treated as *rayah* by the Ottomans, finally had the 'masters of the Balkans' at their mercy.

Vengeance is one of the most savage feelings in human beings. Even in one individual it can do much damage, but when awakened in an entire nation, it takes on the proportions of a real catastrophe.

It is the desire for revenge that now, almost a century later, continues to nourish anti-Albanian sentiment among the Serbs. This is the key to the enigma. This is why blind Serbian hatred will not subside. This explains the crimes, the massacres committed against the Albanians, but also the day to day insults, why men are beaten up and kicked around in front of their wives and children. It is also the key to understanding Arkan's challenge, "What's keeping you from leaving? Where is the pluck you once had?"

Insulting a people whose hands are tied, exacting vengeance by telling someone who is already on his knees that his hour has come and that he is going to have to pay, is one of the greatest pleasures a criminal can have. It is at such times that the veneer of humanity in mankind is at its thinnest.

March 1994

[Taken from *Ibrahim Rugova. La question du Kosovo. Entretiens avec Marie-Françoise Allain et Xavier Galmiche* (Fayard, Paris 1994), p. 7-29. Translated from the French by Robert Elsie]

Police violence in Kosovo province
The victims

Amnesty International

Amnesty International's concern

Over the past year, human rights abuses perpetrated by police against ethnic Albanians in the predominantly Albanian-populated province of Kosovo in the Republic of Serbia have dangerously escalated. Thousands of ethnic Albanians have witnessed police violence or experienced it at first hand. In late July and early August, within a period of two weeks, three ethnic Albanians were shot dead by police officers and another wounded. Two other ethnic Albanians were shot dead near the border with Albania by officers of the Yugoslav Army. In several of these cases, the authorities claimed that police or military had resorted to firearms in self-defence. However, in at least two cases, one of them involving the death of a six-year-old boy, the police officers in question do not appear to have been under attack.

Amnesty International fears that ethnic tensions which are potentially explosive have risen as officers of the largely Serbian police force have increasingly resorted to the routine use of violence. These developments have taken place in the context of a continued confrontation between the Serbian authorities and ethnic Albanians, the majority of whom refuse to recognize Serbian authority in the province and support the demand of the Democratic League of Kosovo (LDK), Kosovo's main party representing ethnic Albanians, for the secession, by peaceful means, of the province from the Federal Republic of Yugoslavia (FRY).

Amnesty International has no position on the status of Kosovo province; the organization is concerned solely with the protection of the human rights of individuals. One of these rights is the right not to be subjected to torture or cruel, inhuman or degrading treatment or punishment. This right is provided for under Article 7 of the International Covenant on Civil and Political Rights and under the United Nations Convention against Torture and Other Cruel, Inhuman or Degrading Treatment or Punishment, both treaties which are legally binding on the FRY. Amnesty International considers that the level of abuses perpetrated by police in Kosovo province can only be explained as part of an official policy to retain control of the province by extreme intimidation. The organization also notes the very high degree of impunity enjoyed by police officers.

Ethnic Albanian human rights activists, members of the Council for the Defence of Human Rights and Freedoms in Prishtina, now report many incidents of police abuses every day. Brutal beatings with truncheons, punching and kicking are the most common forms of violence, but electric shocks have also sometimes been used by police officers. Police officers commonly express ethnic hatred towards their victims, who are verbally abused for being Albanian. A particularly savage and pathological instance of ethnic hatred is shown on the cover of this report: a police officer slashed a Serbian symbol on the chest of an 18-year-old ethnic Albanian student. Many victims have been so badly injured they have needed medical treatment or hospitalization; several have died, apparently as a result of injuries they received from beatings.

Police repression in the FRY is not confined to Kosovo province however. Amnesty International believes that while the routine use of violence by police is at its most extreme in Kosovo province, there is a similar pattern of abuses against Slav Muslims in the Sanjak (Raška) region of Serbia and Montenegro, as has been documented by the Humanitarian Law Fund, an independent Yugoslav human rights organization based in Belgrade. Local communities in Serbia have also protested on several occasions this year about police brutality against Serbian fellow citizens; these incidents, together with the rapid rise in the crime rate and allegations of major corruption amongst senior officers, have provoked debate on police abuses amongst the Serbian public.

Amnesty International documented its concerns in Kosovo province in two reports earlier this year. *Yugoslavia: Ethnic Albanians - Trial by Truncheon* (AI Index: EUR 70/01/94), issued in February, highlighted its concern about the use of torture and other ill-treatment to obtain self-incriminating statements from ethnic Albanian defendants charged with political offences, which are later used to convict them in court.

Yugoslavia: Police violence against ethnic Albanians in Kosovo province (AI Index: EUR 70/06/94), issued in April, focused on the use of violence by police in the course of the arms raids which have become a major feature of policing in Kosovo since the outbreak of armed conflict in former Yugoslavia in 1991.

The present report focuses on a small number of individual victims, whose cases are illustrative. It shows the extreme injuries inflicted on them by police officers. It cannot, however, describe the humiliation, pain and anger experienced by these victims, their families and many others like them.

Amnesty International calls on the Yugoslav and Serbian authorities to enforce adequate controls and monitoring of police discipline, to insist that police officers at all levels respect international standards for law enforcement, to institute independent and impartial investigations into allegations of torture and ill-treatment and to bring those responsible for such abuses to justice.

Background

Kosovo province (officially called the Autonomous Province of Kosovo and Metohija) lies in the south of the Republic of Serbia, bordering on Albania. It has a population of some two million; the great majority (about 85 per cent) are ethnic Albanians. Inhabited for centuries by a mixed population, Kosovo occupies a major place in the national consciousness of both Serbs and ethnic Albanians. For the Serbs, it is the heartland of the mediaeval Serbian kingdom where many of the greatest monuments of the (Christian) Serbian Orthodox Church are located. The ethnic Albanian population (predominantly Muslim) recalls that it was in Kosovo that the Albanian national revival began, with the founding of the League of Prizren in 1878. Since 1981, this ethnic rivalry has become increasingly and dangerously embittered, as ethnic Albanian demands, whether for republic status within Yugoslavia, secession, or unification with Albania, have been countered by repression.

Under the 1974 Constitution of the Socialist Federal Republic of Yugoslavia (SFRY), Kosovo province was granted considerable autonomy, including its own government and parliament, constitutional court, supreme court and representatives in all federal institutions. It had earlier gained its own university where the Albanian language was the language of instruction for ethnic Albanian students.

Kosovo province is economically backward and suffers from high unemployment, although it is rich in natural resources. The rapid demographic growth of the ethnic Albanian population has been accompanied by the emigration of many Serbs and Montenegrins, due both to economic factors and to fears of domination by the ethnic Albanian majority.

Economic problems exacerbated nationalist unrest among ethnic Albanians which resurfaced dramatically in 1981 when there were wide-spread demonstrations in support of the demand that Kosovo cease to be part of Serbia and be granted republic status within the Yugoslav federation. The demonstrations were halted in bloodshed. Mass arrests followed. According to official figures, from 1981 to 1988, over 1,750 ethnic Albanians were sentenced by courts to up to 15 years' imprisonment for nationalist activities; another 7,000 were sentenced to up to 60 days' imprisonment for minor political offences.

In 1987, the League of Communists of Serbia under the leadership of Slobodan Milošević, appealing to Serbian national sentiment, committed itself to regaining Serbian control over Kosovo by means of changes to the province's constitution designed to limit Kosovo's autonomy.

In March 1989 the Kosovo parliament, under pressure from Serbia (tanks were stationed outside the parliament building at the time), approved the constitutional changes. There followed six days of violent clashes between ethnic Albanian demonstrators and security forces, in which - according to official figures - 24 people, two of them police officers, were killed and several hundreds wounded (unofficial sources cited far higher figures). Over 900 demonstrators, among them school pupils, were jailed for up to 60 days or fined, sacked or disciplined for taking industrial action in solidarity with ethnic Albanian strikers. Purges of local members of the League of Communists of Kosovo, of journalists, teachers and others followed.

In 1990, ethnic conflict intensified in Kosovo province. Between 24 January and 3 February 1990 there were further violent clashes in many parts of Kosovo between security forces and ethnic Albanian demonstrators, in which at least 30 ethnic Albanians died and several hundred others were injured. Over 1,000 ethnic Albanians who went on strike in support of the demonstrations or in other ways peacefully expressed nationalist dissent were imprisoned for up to 60 days. In July, the Serbian parliament suspended the Kosovo Government and parliament after ethnic Albanian members of the Kosovo parliament declared Kosovo independent of the Republic of Serbia. Thousands of ethnic Albanians who refused to declare their approval for the Serbian measures lost their jobs, generally to be replaced by Serbs and Montenegrins.

At the end of September 1990, Serbia adopted a new constitution which deprived Kosovo province of most of its remaining autonomy. In December, ethnic Albanians responded by boycotting Serbian elections, in which the communist party (renamed the Socialist Party) retained power. (In the course of 1990 numerous opposition parties were legally established throughout the SFRY and by the end of the year multi-party elections had taken place in all six republics.) Since then, most ethnic Albanians in Kosovo province regard Serbian authority and measures in Kosovo as illegitimate and prefer to recognize as their representatives ethnic Albanians elected in elections which are not recognized by the Serbian authorities. At the same time, ethnic Albanians have organized 'parallel' institutions outside official state structures, particularly in education, welfare and, to a lesser extent, in health.

In April 1992, following the break-up of the SFRY, a new state, the Federal Republic of Yugoslavia (FRY), comprising the Republics of Serbia and Montenegro, was proclaimed in Belgrade. Leaders of Kosovo's main ethnic Albanian political party, the Democratic League of Kosovo (LDK), now demanded Kosovo's full independence from Yugoslavia, a goal which they pledged to obtain by peaceful means. As tension in the province mounted, and with armed conflict raging in Bosnia-Herzegovina, the Conference on Security and Cooperation in Europe (CSCE) established in October 1992 a long-term mission in Kosovo to monitor the human rights situation. However, since July 1993, both the CSCE and the United Nations Special Rapporteur on Yugoslavia have been refused permission by the Yugoslav Government to base monitoring missions of long duration in the FRY. The authorities have also refused visas to several human rights organizations, including Amnesty International. A wave of arrests of ethnic Albanians on political charges followed the departure of the CSCE mission from Kosovo in July 1993. Continued international concern has led to attempts to initiate a dialogue between the Serbian authorities and ethnic Albanian leaders: however, each side has so far insisted on conditions unacceptable to the other, and as yet no significant steps appear to have been taken, despite some tentative and informal contacts.

The police force in Kosovo province

Policing is divided between the force responsible for public order (the militia) and the state security service. According to ethnic Albanian sources, some 4,000 ethnic Albanian police officers have been dismissed from their posts since 1990 after refusing to accept and recognize the measures introduced in Kosovo province by the Serbian Government. The province is now policed by a force that is very largely Serbian and Montenegrin, recruited partly locally, but also from Serbia and Montenegro and Serbian-populated areas of Croatia and Bosnia-Hercegovina. It is reported that Serbs anxious to avoid war service in the Yugoslav National Army during the conflict with Croatia sometimes chose employment instead in the police forces in Kosovo. However, there have also been reports that service in Kosovo is unpopular with police from Serbia, in particular from the capital Belgrade, and is regarded by some as the equivalent of demotion. In July 1994, a former state security officer, Dragan Mladenović, reportedly alleged in an interview with the German radio station *Deutsche Welle* that after protesting about corruption amongst his colleagues, he had been sent to Kosovo as a punishment. He accused the Deputy Minister of Internal Affairs of involvement in drug and arms smuggling and of deliberately staging an incident in Gllogovc / Glogovac (Kosovo) in May 1993 in which two police officers were killed, with the aim of provoking armed conflict in the province.

The human rights situation in 1994

Political trials

The wave of arrests and trials of ethnic Albanians on political charges which began in July 1993 has continued. By the end of July 1994, over 85 ethnic Albanians had been convicted and sentenced to prison sentences of up to 10 years. Further trials were under way. A significant proportion of the accused are political activists, usually (but not exclusively) members of the LDK. Most have been charged with planning to achieve the secession of Kosovo from the FRY by force of arms and its independence or unification with Albania. In a few cases, the defendants possessed weapons or appear to have engaged in procuring weapons, but this has been the exception rather than the rule. To Amnesty International's knowledge, none of the accused has been charged with using violence. There have also been several trials of young men accused of having undergone military training in neighbouring Albania.

These trials have been characterized by frequent flagrant breaches of procedure, particularly in the stages immediately following arrest and during investigation proceedings, which have undermined the defendants' right to defence. In almost all cases, the defendants at the trial rejected the charges against them. They alleged that false self-incriminating statements were extorted from them by beating and threats following arrest and said they had not withdrawn these statements when brought before an investigating judge for fear of renewed ill-treatment. Medical evidence was in some cases available to support these allegations. Convictions have to a great extent been based on these contested statements, often with little supporting evidence. Amnesty International considers that, on the basis of the information so far available to the organization, at least some of those convicted are prisoners of conscience and that charges against them of seeking to change Kosovo's status by force were not convincingly substantiated in court. (Amnesty International has documented these concerns in greater detail in its report, *Yugoslavia: Ethnic Albanians - Trial by truncheon* [AI Index: EUR 70/01/94.])

At the beginning of August 1994, seven young men - Fehmi Lestrani, Shkëlzen Bajrami, Nexhmedin Sadriu, Luan Heta, Beqir Muleci, Hysni Franca and Bajram Gallopeni were on trial before the district court of Prishtina accused of having received military training in Albania. Other ethnic Albanians under arrest and due to go on trial included Ukshin Hoti, chairman of UNIKOMB (an ethnic Albanian political party), three LDK activists from Malisheva / Mališevo (Osman Krasniqi, Mustafa Morina and Rrahim Paçarizi) and Mustafa Ibrahimi, Ismail Kastrati and Sylejman Ahmeti, officials of the local Chamber of Commerce (not recognized by the Serbian authorities).

In addition to these trials, since the beginning of 1994 over 20 ethnic Albanians have been sentenced to up to 60 days' imprisonment for 'minor' political offences, such as holding political or sports meetings without official permission.

Arms searches and police violence

The most widely experienced form of police violence in Kosovo province is that undergone by families during police searches for arms. These have become a prominent feature of policing in Kosovo since the outbreak of armed conflict in former Yugoslavia in 1991. Over the past year, arms searches have increased dramatically, and are now conducted on a daily basis, most intensively in border villages and rural areas, but also more generally throughout the province.

Legal and illegal possession of arms is widespread in Kosovo province, as elsewhere in the FRY. Many reports state that during these raids, police have confiscated not only illegal weapons (generally revolvers and hunting rifles), but also arms for which the owner possesses a licence. There have also been reports of police ordering a family to go out and purchase a gun to be handed over. In other cases, families have been forced to hand over money or valuables to police, or police have confiscated individual passports.

Because of the traditional pattern of settlement in rural areas of Kosovo, in which large extended families tend to live together, police raids are normally witnessed and personally experienced by many relatives. The sense of insecurity they provoke is further exacerbated by the pervasive presence in the province of the Yugoslav Army, and by the belief, strongly held by ethnic Albanians, that local Serbian communities have not only been spared these searches, but have actually been given arms by the authorities.

Accounts of arms searches repeatedly refer to the deliberately intimidating and destructive way in which they are conducted: furniture is broken up, the inmates of the house are threatened, shouted and sworn at, and the men of the house are frequently arrested and beaten in local police stations or, even more humiliatingly, in their homes in front of their families. These beating are often severe, causing injuries: reports of the victim losing consciousness as a result of beating, or of suffering bruising, broken teeth or ribs, are not uncommon. It is not only those found to possess unlicensed arms who are at risk of being beaten: those who do not possess weapons may also find themselves bearing the brunt of police frustration. The principle of 'guilty by association' seems often to apply: police officers unable to find a specific man they are looking for are frequently reported to have instead arrested or beaten a member of his family. While most police violence is directed against adult males, in some instances the elderly, women or children who are members of the family have not been spared beatings. There have also been cases in which police have explicitly arrested a family member as a hostage in order to force a relative to give himself up to police. Some families have been repeatedly searched by police officers who have shouted at them, "Get out of here" or "Go to Albania".

Police violence, together with economic hardship and the fear of military call-up to the Yugoslav Army, have led several hundred thousands of ethnic Albanians, the majority young men, to leave the country, primarily for western Europe. The authorities' unstated policy appears to be to actively encourage their departure, while promoting (with no marked success) the settlement of Serbs in Kosovo, both those who left Kosovo in recent years and new settlers, including refugees from Croatia and Bosnia-Herzegovina and from Albania (Montenegrins), with the aim of changing the demographic balance. Ethnic Albanians frequently describe the combined effect of these policies as a covert form of "ethnic cleansing".

The cases of Ali Murati (aged 90), Fevzi Musliu, Marjan Kita, Ilaz Rexhepi, Bahri Shyti, Fatmir Çitaku, Milazim Binaku and Ymer Dajaku (see appendix) are illustrative of the extreme brutality to which police frequently resort in searching for arms.

Typical targets of police violence

Among the most frequent targets of police violence or harassment are ethnic Albanians who, by their political or other activity, are prominent in the organization of the 'parallel' society which ethnic Albanians have created outside the official state structures. They include political activists, in particular members of the LDK, but also members of other ethnic Albanian political parties; teachers and academics, former political prisoners, human rights activists, trade unionists, those involved in the organization of humanitarian aid to families in need, even local sports leaders. Journalists, former police officers and former military, also appear to be targeted.

The account of Ramiz Osmani, an LDK activist from Bare near Mitrovica e Kosovës / Kosovska Mitrovica, is similar to many other reports involving the arrest, beating, interrogation and other forms of harassment of political activists.

"On 3 February 1994, I and other members of the Mitrovica branch of the LDK were invited by the president of the LDK in Bajgora / Bajgore village to attend a local LDK meeting there called on account of a massive increase in police activity in the area. The meeting began at about 11:30 AM in the village primary school. [During the meeting] the commander [named] of Stari Tërg / Stari Trg police station and a Serb civilian carrying a gun came into the classroom and ordered me to come with them. After we left the room, the police commander turned back and also took out Zejnel Istrefi, the president of the local branch of the LDK... When we reached the tarmacked road, the [named] police officer was waiting in a 'Niva' jeep, who began to beat us. Although there was room in the car, they put me in the boot and began to beat me... On arrival in Stari Tërg / Stari Trg [police station] they beat and swore at us in the most brutal way. Three police officers and the civilian who 'accompanied' us from Bajgora / Bajgore beat me. This went on until 3:30 PM, when they sent me to police headquarters in Mitrovica where they held me until 7:30 PM, and Zejnel until 10 PM. In Mitrovica they did not beat me much but they questioned me about the meeting... and the status of Kosovo. They hoped to find evidence of the organization of defence units and to intimidate us into stopping our [political] activities. After I was released, I had to seek medical care."

Kadri Avdiu, another LDK local activist (see appendix), describes a similar experience.

The issue of education has become one of the key points of confrontation in Kosovo. In 1990 and 1991, the Serbian authorities introduced a uniform curriculum throughout the whole of the Republic of Serbia and abolished the province's educational authority. The total number of enrolments in Albanian-language secondary schools was drastically reduced and a considerable number of educational institutions were closed. Many subjects at Prishtina University were no longer taught in the Albanian language but only in Serbian. More than 18,000 ethnic Albanian teachers and other staff in Albanian-language schools and the university who refused to recognize these changes and follow the new curriculum were dismissed. Instead, they created a parallel educational system, using the old curricula, and lessons began to be held in private homes. The Serbian authorities have systematically harassed those involved in education, including members of the teachers' trade union, teachers, university lecturers, private citizens who have made their homes available for teaching and even pupils themselves. Schools have been broken into and raided, teachers arrested, interrogated or beaten and lessons repeatedly interrupted. In March, the Serbian authorities closed and sequestrated the Academy of Sciences and Arts of Kosovo and the Institute of Albanian Studies (see the case of Sadri Fetiu in the appendix).

Nebih Zogaj and Bajram Samadraxha, headmasters of primary schools near Malisheva / Mališevo, are examples of teachers who have been subjected to severe and repeated police violence. In June 1994, Nebih Zogaj was arrested on nine occasions and repeatedly severely beaten by police in Suhareka / Suva Reka police station. On the first occasion, on 1 June, police reportedly also searched his offices at the school. Following his second beating by police on 9 June, he was admitted to hospital in Gjakova / Djakovica for treatment for injuries. He was discharged on 13 June and the very same day was again summoned to the police station in Suhareka / Suva Reka, where he was again beaten, allegedly losing consciousness. On release he was readmitted to hospital.

Bajram Samadraxha was arrested at his school on 3 June; he was again arrested on 9 and 13 June, when he was also reportedly beaten in Suhareka / Suva Reka police station.

Other instances of police brutality against ethnic Albanians

There are also frequent reports of police violence against people suspected of illegal activity, such as black market dealing in cigarettes or foreign currency. A particularly tragic case is that of Hajdin Bislimi (see appendix), who appears to have been arrested by police because they suspected his young sons of buying stolen goods. Severely beaten at a police station in Mitrovica e Kosovës / Kosovska Mitrovica on three consecutive days in May 1994, he died in hospital in July.

Incidents in which police violence appears to be quite random or to be motivated by momentary irritation or drunkenness are also not uncommon. For example, there appears to have been no specific reason for the arrest of 18-year-old Arian Curri (see appendix).

Cases of police violence in which the victims have not been ethnic Albanians

While the overwhelming majority of victims of police violence in Kosovo province are ethnic Albanians, there have also been other cases, as when 12 (Slav) Muslim students from Montenegro were beaten by police in Mitrovica e Kosovës / Kosovska Mitrovica in April 1994 (see appendix).

Moreover, in at least one recent case known to Amnesty International, the victims of police violence in Kosovo province were almost certainly Serbs (or Montenegrins). On 26 May 1994, the Belgrade newspaper *Borba* reported that the Municipal Assembly of Podujeva / Podujevo had decided to sue five police officers who on 14 May, for no apparent reason, had stopped and beaten Tomislav Dragičević and Žika Milosavljević (their names suggest they are Serbs or Montenegrins) while they were driving children back from school. The two men had to be admitted to hospital in Prishtina for three days as a result of the beatings. At a press conference held in Prishtina on 25 May, the president of the Municipal Assembly of Podujeva / Podujevo reportedly announced that it had been decided at an emergency meeting of the assembly to inform all public prosecutors, from the district to the Republic and Federal levels, as well as the police of all ranks, that the Municipal Assembly of Podujeva / Podujevo demanded that proceedings be started against the five police officers and they be brought to justice. The prompt action taken by municipal authorities in this case appears to be in striking contrast with the lack of official reaction in cases where the victims of beatings are ethnic Albanians. However, Amnesty International has not yet learned of any outcome to this case.

The law and police impunity

Article 191 of the Criminal Code of the FRY punishes with up to three years' imprisonment officials who in the performance of their duties physically ill-treat, intimidate or insult another person. Article 65 of the Serbian Criminal Code provides for a sentence of up to five years' imprisonment if the ill-treatment is intended to extract a confession (or up to 15 years if the ill-treatment is very serious). Torture or cruel, inhuman or degrading treatment or punishment are also prohibited under Article 7 of the International Covenant on Civil and Political Rights and under the United Nations Convention against Torture and Other Cruel, Inhuman or Degrading Treatment or Punishment, both treaties which are legally binding on the FRY.

In practice, police officers in Kosovo province daily violate these provisions and in only the most extreme cases, involving the death of the victim (but not always even then) are those responsible brought to justice.

In December 1993, the District Court of Prizren sentenced two police officers to three years' imprisonment each for causing physical injuries to an ethnic Albanian, Arif Krasniqi, whom they had beaten at a police station, which resulted in his death. The officers were released pending appeal.

On 6 March 1994, a police officer shot and killed an ethnic Albanian, Faik Maloku, and seriously wounded Xhevat Bejzaku (who tried to intervene) in a restaurant in Fushë Kosova / Kosovo Polje. It appears that the officer had asked Faik Maloku to show his identity card and when he failed to do so, explaining that he did not have it with hin, an argument started. The officer was detained for investigation.

On 27 July 1994, a police officer fired at a car near Rahovica / Rahovica (Ferizaj / Uroševac municipality), killing Fidan Brestovci, a six-year-old ethnic Albanian boy and wounding his mother Makfira. On the following day, the District Public Prosecutor's office in Prishtina issued a statement that the officer, Boban Krstić, had been arrested and criminal proceedings had been started against him. According to the statement, the incident was the result of an error: the officer had been waiting in ambush for "the perpetrator of a number of criminal acts" (not named) who was reported to be driving the same make of car as that in which the Brestovci family was travelling. When their car failed to respond to the police officer's sign to stop, he had fired at it. Bajrush Brestovci, the father of Fidan, who was driving the car, later publicly denied that he had been signalled to stop.

These are the only recent cases known to Amnesty International in which the authorities have taken legal action against police officers responsible for deaths or injuries of ethnic Albanians, despite the ample evidence available of severe abuses.

In October 1991, Mikel Marku, an elderly ethnic Albanian lawyer, was beaten unconscious by police at police headquarters in Peja / Peć. Despite the pleadings of his two nephews who were with him, he was refused medical aid until the next morning when he was taken to hospital in a coma caused by head injuries. He remained in a coma until his death 10 days later. Hospital records showed that he died after being admitted with head injuries which had caused paralysis of the right side of the body and bruising to other parts of the body. The autopsy report of 11 November 1991 (of which the family was denied a copy until 8 April 1992) noted multiple post-traumatic injuries to the head, trunk and extremities (see Amnesty International's report *Yugoslavia: Ethnic Albanians - Victims of torture and ill-treatment by police* [AI Index: EUR 48/18/92], issued in June 1992).

In January 1992, in the absence of any action by the authorities against those responsible for his death, his family initiated criminal proceedings against two named police officers and other unknown police officers on charges of homicide under Article 47, paragraph 1, of the Serbian Criminal Code. According to a press report, in October 1993 the District Public Prosecutor in Peja / Peć refused Mikel Marku's family's request to start criminal proceedings against the police officers on the grounds that Mikel Marku had died from natural causes - a heart attack due to arteriosclerosis. In January 1994 it was reported that the district court of Peja / Peć had issued a decision approving the prosecutor's refusal on the grounds that even if the police officers had injured Mikel Marku, his death was due to a different cause, arteriosclerosis. In February 1994, the press reported that Mikel Marku's family had appealed against this decision to the Supreme Court of Serbia. Amnesty International has not yet learned of any ruling by this court.

Appendix - Illustrative cases

Ethnic Albanians beaten in connection with arms searches

Ali Murat MURATI, aged 90, from Llapashtica e Poshtme / Donja Lapaštica village near Podujeva / Podujevo

Ali Murati was beaten by police who carried out an arms search at his home on 11 February 1994. According to his statement: *"At about 3 PM, 15 or 16 police officers and two state security officers from Prishtina suddenly arrived in three police NIVA jeeps and an official car. A number of them surrounded our locality, carrying their arms and ready to fire into my courtyard. At [the family's] old house, four or five police officers and two state security officers began to carry out a search and to ill-treat members of the family... They took hold of me as I was standing on the staircase of the old house with members of my family and led me some 50 to 60 metres away into the new house. As soon as they brought me inside, they began to threaten me in the most brutal way, demanding that I hand over weapons, pistols, guns, automatic rifles. I told them repeatedly that I did not possess any arms and they could carry out a detailed search. They began to beat me in the most violent way, one after another, five or six of them, without stopping, until 4:30 PM... I lost consciousness. The medical examination, certificate and photographs... are proof that they caused me severe bodily injuries and endangered my life."*

Fevzi MUSLIU, from Stanovci i Poshtëm / Donje Stanovce village near Vuçitërna / Vučitrn.

Fevzi Musliu was severely beaten and injured by police in Prilluzha / Priluzje police station on 2 December 1993. Police are alleged to have threatened him: "If you don't have a gun, go and buy one, or we'll beat you to death". His father, Bislim, was also beaten by police the same day. After his release, Fevzi Musliu began to urinate blood and was obliged to seek medical treatment. His health worsened in the days that followed and by 12 December he was reportedly critically ill. In February 1994 he left the country to receive medical care abroad.

Marjan Frrok KITA, from Krusheva e Madhe / Veliko Kruševo, near Klina / Klina.

On 26 January 1994, Marjan Kita was summoned to the police station in Klina to be questioned about arms which he denied possessing. He was beaten at the police station and allegedly again the following day and on 1 February 1994.

Ilaz REXHEPI, from Kaçubeg / Kačubeg near Podujeva / Podujevo.

According to a statement by his son: "*Today, on 12 April 1994, Ilaz Rexhepi was arrested at home [in the village of Kaçubeg / Kačubeg] and taken to the police station in Lluzhan / Lužane where he was brutally beaten for three hours and then driven back to a spot near the village and left in a ditch beside the road. [Ilaz Rexhepi] was beaten on the pretext that he possessed arms, but [the police] had already confiscated them two months earlier. On that occasion they also beat him.*"

Bahri SHYTI, from Oshlan / Ošljane village near Vuçitërna / Vučitrn.

On 19 April 1994 police carried out arms searches at the homes of the brothers Abdullah, Mustafa, Hamdi and Haki Shyti in Oshlan / Ošljane. During the search they demolished doors and furniture and beat Patriot and Bahri, the sons of Abdullah. Bahri Shyti was so badly injured he was admitted to Mitrovica e Kosovës / Kosovska Mitrovica hospital for treatment, where he remained until 29 April 1994. A medical certificate issued by the hospital on that date states that he was treated for *contusion with subconjunctival haemorrhage of the right eye; laceration under the right eye; bruising on back and upper part of both arms; bruising on both buttocks; bruising of toes of left foot.* The certificate concludes that these injuries were caused by *"heavy blows with a blunt instrument"*.

Fatmir ÇITAKU, from Baj / Baje village near Mitrovica e Kosovës / Kosovska Mitrovica.

Fatmir Çitaku was beaten in Rudnik / Rudnik police station on 6 May 1994. On that day about 20 armed police searched the home of his father Bekë Çitaku in Baj / Baje for arms. After the search they arrested Fatmir Çitaku and took him to Rudnik police station where they beat him and injured him. The police allegedly returned the following day and beat his 70-year-old father, Bekë, in front of the family.

Milazim BINAKU, aged 61, from the 'Tavnik' district of Mitrovica e Kosovës / Kosovska Mitrovica town.

Police arrested Milazim Binaku on 5 May at his home in the 'Tavnik' district of Mitrovica e Kosovës / Kosovska Mitrovica. They held him at the police station until 1:30 PM, demanding that he hand over a gun. When he denied possessing one, the police officers drove him back to his house, where they carried out a search. When they found nothing, they took him back to the police station and beat him. They then released him after ordering him to report again to the police the following day.

Ymer DAJAKU, aged 47, from Rakinica / Rakinice near Sërbica / Srbica.

On 2 June 1994 Ymer Dajaku received a summons to report to the police station in Rudnik for questioning about arms; when he reported to the police station the next day, he was detained for two hours and beaten.

Ethnic Albanian women beaten

Shukrije HAXHA from Brajina village near Podujeva / Podujevo.

On 31 July 1994 police carried out an arms search at the home of Faik Haxha in Brajina. His wife, Shukrije, was at home at the time, but her husband and sons were out. According to the statement she gave to a local human rights activist on 1 August, three police officers came to her home and began to search for arms, turning everything upside down. *"When they didn't find a gun, they said to me, 'Give us the gun or we'll kill you'. They didn't kill me, but they left my back, thighs and arms covered in bruises. They also put a rifle-butt between my legs but they didn't injure me... It's better that they beat me than my sons... It didn't last for more than 20-35 minutes; two or three times I felt dizzy from their blows, but I didn't lose consciousness, nor did I swear at them. I wasn't frightened, but I kept telling them that we didn't have a gun. We've hardly enough money for bread, much less a gun! They, however, swore at me and insulted me and when they left, they said they would be back 'for the gun'!"*

Ethnic Albanian political activist beaten

Kadri AVDIU, aged 33, from Bellopoja / Belopoje village, president of an LDK local branch in Tërnava / Trnava near Podujeva / Podujevo. He was arrested on 27 June. According to his account.

"Three police officers arrested me. They came to my home at 12:30 PM and arrested me and my brother Ali, ordering us to had over weapons. They demanded]that we hand over] weapons for personal use and weapons which the LDK was allegedly distributing to the population of Tërnava / Trnava. They took me to the police station [in Lluzhan / Lužane], where they questioned me about 20 to 80 automatic rifles which the LDK had allegedly distributed to poor families. According to them, wealthier families were ordered by the LDK to buy their own weapons. At the police station in Lluzhan / Lužane, commander X [named] and a police officer Y [named] told me that we

would have done better to hand over weapons at home rather than to be taken to the police station. The officer who beat me later, Y, was a member of the Radical Party, known for its brutality... At the police station, commander X and officer Y interrogated me. They asked me for an automatic rifle, which they said I had for my personal protection, supposedly given to me by the LDK. They claimed that six people had reported me to the police. After a long conversation in which I denied I had weapons, they told me at last to hand over a revolver. They told me they were ready to register the revolver in my mother's name so that I wouldn't suffer any consequences for it. Then they changed the subject... and accused me of being head of [ethnic Albanian] police. They asked me how many police officers I had under my orders... When I denied everything, they said that my brother who was outside had confessed to everything they accused me of. Since the window was open and he had heard what we were saying, my brother said loudly: "Don't lie! It's not true I admitted everything. We've nothing to admit!" They shut the window and said to my brother, "We'll show you, when your turn comes!"

Then commander X asked me provocative questions: "Do you believe in God?" he asked. "Yes!" I said. "Do you have a Koran at home?" I said I had. "Can you swear on the Koran that you haven't received arms from the LDK and that you haven't any personal weapons?" they asked. "Yes, I can swear it a hundred times!" I said. "You can swear it, but you're lying!" they said...

X began to punch me on the sides of my head and on the left side of my jaw. He hit me seven or eight times. The blows were very hard. I thought he had broken my jaw. After these blows, he told me it was my last chance to confess I had arms. He said that if I refused, they would torture me and then I would confess to everything. I told them they were abusing me in vain, I had nothing to confess. They ordered me to take off my shoes and lie on the floor. I did. Two police officers tied my legs with a belt above the ankles and lifted me up. They placed a chair under me... Y picked up a stick over a metre long, and holding it with both hand, hit the soles of my feet. He hit me repeatedly without stopping. I saw the stick break. Then I lost consciousness for the first time. After they poured cold water over my head and slapped my face I came to. They began to hit me again. They told me I should confess everything, to save my life. "We'll kill you, we won't release you till you confess!" They repeatedly hit me. I think the stick broke four times.

They found another stick and hit me. I lost consciousness four times. Then commander X came into the room. He threw water over me, and then punched me on the back, to check whether I was faking or had really lost consciousness. When he saw my state, he ordered them to stop the torture. "This one isn't stubborn, he's a fool!" he told the officers. Y told him I had admitted everything. When he asked if this was true, I interrupted him and said I had confessed to nothing and had nothing to confess. "Do you want to be beaten again?" they asked me. "I've nothing to confess even if you kill me!" I said. They told me to stand up, but I couldn't for the pain. I fainted again and they threw water over me to revive me. Then they gave me a little water to wet my lips, but did not allow me to wash my feet which burned with pain. They ordered me to walk about the room... While I was walking - it was terrible because of the pain in my feet - they demanded that I resign from my position as president of a local LDK branch. While telling me to resign as soon as possible, they struck me four blows on the back with a stick as thick as the handle of a spade. They ordered me to report to the police station the following day at 1 PM. "How can I, in the state I'm in, and what for?" I asked. They hit me on the back a few more times after this question and released me. It was 1:40 PM."

Kadri Avdiu subsequently sought medical care in Prishtina. He has since not returned home. The police have again come to his house looking for him and his brother. They have demanded that his brothers report to the police in his place. *"The third time they came for me, the police shut my brother's workshop in Bellopoja / Belopoje... They are asking my brothers to make me report to the police. They come looking for my four brothers."*

[On 5 July] police threatened his brother Shefki that they would kill him if Kadri did not report to the police within three days. [On 6 July] the police searched the home in Bellopoja / Belopoje. After the search had finished, they ordered the five brothers to report to the police.

Ethnic Albanian academic beaten

Sadri FETIU, director of the Institute of Albanian Studies, Prishtina.

On 8 March 1994, the authorities closed by force the Institute of Albanian Studies in Prishtina, after orders to evacuate it were ignored by ethnic Albanians working at the Institute. On this occasion, groups of Serbian civilians (possibly plainclothes police), and armed police entered the building and beat those who had remained inside. In a statement published on 14 March, the Committee for the Defence of Human Rights and Freedoms in Prishtina said that among those beaten and injured were the following academics: "*The director, Sadri Fetiu (who received injuries to his head, face, nose, jaw and had three teeth broken); Ragip Mulaku (injuries to his head, left hand and spine); Mehmet Halimi (injuries to a leg, a rib, and his head and face); Professor Anton Çetta (injuries to his head, left hand and spine); the archivist Hajdin Hajdini (injuries to the face, head and both legs); Xheladin Shala (injuries to his body and head)*". The statement continued that armed Serbian civilians, together with police officers, subsequently beat a number of people in the street outside. One of the victims was Abdyl Kadolli, a journalist and Secretary of the Forum of Intellectuals of Kosovo, who was reportedly forced into a car by two men dressed as civilians, beaten and driven to a spot five kilometres outside the town where he was released late in the evening.

Ethnic Albanian student beaten

Arian CURRI, aged 18, a secondary school student from the village of Strellci i Epërm / Gornji Streoci near Peja / Peć. He was on his way home by bus after school on 6 April 1994, when, on the outskirts of Peja / Peć, police boarded the bus and arrested him.

According to his statement: "*Two police officers entered the bus and began to check the identity cards of the passengers. I was at the back of the bus. I saw them take out two young men through the front door. When they reached me, they asked me for my identity card. I gave it to them, and then one of the officers suddenly grabbed me by the hair and pulled me out of the bus. They handcuffed me and put me in their car. They took all three of us to the police station. They led us inside and separated us. They took me into a room and then the beating and torture began. Next they tied me to a radiator and three police officers sat on me; one of them pulled out a knife and after he had pulled up my shirt he cut a cross [on my chest] with a Cyrillic "S". After two hours they put me in a car and brought me back to the bus stop in Peja / Peć."* (The cross and four Cyrillic Ss stand for the Serbian motto: "Only unity saves the Serb".)

Hajdin Istref BISLIMI, from 'Bair' district of Mitrovica e Kosovës / Kosovska Mitrovica. He was arrested, beaten and released on three consecutive days in May 1994. He died in hospital on 6 July 1994.

On 9 May 1994, police arrested Hajdin Bislimi, aged 53, at his home and took him to police headquarters in Mitrovica e Kosovës / Kosovska Mitrovica. The police apparently suspected his two sons, aged 15 and 10, of having stolen goods from a Rom (Gypsy). At the police station, Hajdin Bislimi was beaten. He was released the same day, but the following two days he was again arrested, beaten and released. On 11 May, his brother found him lying unconscious outside the police station and took him to the town hospital, where he was put in an intensive care ward. Several days later, he was transferred to hospital in Prishtina, where he was twice operated on for a stomach ulcer. He remained in hospital until his death on 6 July 1994. It appears that his death was caused by a perforated ulcer, which may have been induced by the beatings inflicted on him. No autopsy was carried out. When his family requested a certificate, they were reportedly given one which was neither stamped nor signed, and which they therefore refused to accept.

Muslim students from Montenegro beaten

According to an article in the Montenegrin weekly *Monitor* of 6 May 1994, on the night of 20/21 April, five police officers and two state security officers (inspectors) arrested 12 (Slav) Muslim students (all but two of them from Rožaj and Bijelo Polje in Montenegro) at a student hostel in Mitrovica e Kosovës / Kosovska Mitrovica. The author of the article stated that the students had withheld their names out of fear of reprisals against them.

According to their account, at about 15 minutes after midnight, just as they were going to bed, police came to their rooms, checked their identity cards, while swearing at them and accusing them of singing nationalist songs and celebrating the bombing of Serb positions in Goražde (Bosnia Herzegovina). The police ordered the students to dress and then took them down to waiting police cars. As they got into the cars, police officers began to beat them. Instead of going directly to the police station 200 metres away, they were driven through the streets for some time before drawing up in front of the police station, where two lines of police awaited them and beat them with truncheons, punched them and kicked them as they walked into the police station. Inside, the beating continued; a police officer threatened them: "After 25 April we don't want to see you here in Mitrovica e Kosovës / Kosovska Mitrovica - or you'll be dead." They were then, one by one, taken down to the basement where they received a further beating. According to one student: "*After that... they took me to another room, ordered me to remove my shoes, and to lie on my front. They beat the soles of my feet with truncheons. They hit as hard as they could. It was indescribably painful. They lifted me up... I was struck with a truncheon blow in the stomach... I doubled up with pain, but he went on beating me about the head and back. When I began to lose consciousness they threw water over me...*"

Afterwards, according to the article, they were made to give statements and to sign them without reading them first. In the morning they were released after being charged with disturbing public order. They left for home the same day, and sought medical care. A medical certificate issued by the hospital in Berane (Montenegro), which one of the students showed to *Monitor*'s reporter, noted bruising on the head and body, including bruising under both eyes, on the back and collar bone and on the soles of the feet.

An emergency meeting of the municipal assembly in Rožaj was set to discuss the incident, but was postponed after the deputy police chief for the Kosovo Metohija district promised that a police representative would attend the meeting after investigating the incident. By 6 May this meeting had not yet taken place.

[Taken from *Amnesty International Report. September 1994. EUR 70/16/94*]

3. Historical documents and observations

In the Debatable Lands

Edith Durham

A universal *besa*[7] had been sworn till St. Dimitri (Nov. 6). I leapt at the chance of being the first foreigner to enter the 'closed' districts under the new state of affairs, and applied properly, through the Consulate, for a *teskereh*[8] to travel to Prizren. Djakova[9] was my object. The Young Turk authorities, pleased to find a British female willing to test the new régime in her own person, gave permission at once. Personally, I put all my faith on the inviolability of the *besa*.

We were going to a Moslem land, so Marko arranged that we should travel with two Moslem *kirijees* bound for Prizren with a caravan. Leaving Scutari[10] at 3 P. M. with one *kirijee*, Ren, a Djakova man, we crossed the plain by a fair road to the Drin, followed its right

---

[7] Sworn pledge [editor's note].

[8] Authorization [editor's note].

[9] Gjakova / Djakovica [editor's note].

[10] Shkodër [editor's note].

bank as far as Vaudys, and ferried over in the *trappa*. Vaudys is the frontier of Mirdita and the legendary capital of Paul Dukaghin, who, it is said, ruled from Vaudys to Djakova. But these tales are vague.

We rode up the valley of the Drin, fertile, rich in maize and grass, wood and water, caught up the caravan of ten packhorses heavily laden with bales of stinking goats' hides, and halted at dusk at Gomshiche, on a tributary of the Drin, Ljumi Gomshichet. The caravan camped in a field; Marko and I were put up at the church-house. Pack-saddling next morning was not done till 7 A. M.

We were on the old Prizren-Scutari trade-route - a right-of-way when nobody sees fit to close it - so were without local escort. It was therefore thought fit that, for safety, I should ride last of all the caravans. It was a hot day, and such air as there was bore the concentrated reek of all the ten packs of goat-hide straight to me. I objected. "It is very healthy," said Marko. "It stinks," said I. "With respect," said Marko, "it is not a stink. It is the smell caused by the way they are prepared."

I infinitely preferred to take the risk - which was *nil* - of being shot at by Mirdites, but my guardian angels insisted on at least two horses being ahead of me. We followed up the right bank of the Gomshiche River to the church of Dushaj, near which a tributary enters the main stream, and rode up the right bank of this tributary high on the hillside above the water, making many detours to head the streams that flowed to join it.

The wretched packbeasts were overladen. One hundred *okas* (over two hundred pounds) is a packload, without counting the heavy wooden saddle. They staggered downhill, had to be shoved and pulled up the worst places, and if they stumbled could with difficulty recover. Descending a stony track, one fell and would have turned a complete somersault downhill had not the pack jammed between the rocks of the narrow track. Tightly fixed, with its head twisted under it between its forelegs, it was in danger of strangulation, and was extricated with great difficulty. The men were stupid at the job nor did they see, till I pointed it out, that the luckless brute could not possibly rise till a rock that jammed one hindleg was moved. It was badly cut on head and knee, but was reloaded, and we started again.

The track was rough. I walked, and was well ahead at the bottom of one of the narrow valleys, when a second packhorse, forced by the size of its pack to go on the very edge, crashed over, rolling over and over with its legs tucked tightly under it, and fell some thirty feet into the stream below, the heavy pack and saddle saving it from many blows. There it lay helpless and terrified, wedged in a pool among rocks. It was a three-quarters of an hour job to raise and reload it. The dry hides absorbed a lot of water, and were so heavy that loads had to be redistributed.

We crawled slowly on - a wearisome drag. Every pack shifted, and had to be readjusted after every descent. About 4.30 we arrived at a *han*[11] not far from Puka, men and beasts all tired out, and camped for the night in a field. There was plenty of water. The horses, freed from their packs, were turned out to graze at twopence a head.

Two time-expired soldiers had joined our caravan, one a Moslem Serb from Plevlje, and the other an Albanian from Mitrovitza, both homeward bound. The Serb, a civil fellow, spoke little Albanian and kept quite apart from the others. He was deathly tired, groaned at the thought of the week's tramp yet before him, and rolled over fast asleep upon the ground as soon as we halted.

The *hanjee*[12] provided hay for my bed and a stewed fowl for my supper. The hides were piled high, the horses picketed in line. We sat round a fire on the ground - the two beaky-nosed, grey-eyed Djakova men and the two soldiers. The Serb - though a Turkish subject and a Moslem - appeared to be considered as much a foreigner as myself. There was a red glow of firelight and a crackling shower of sparks as dry brushwood was piled on. The picketed horses munched steadily at a feed of maize. Over all was the intense blue depth of the cloudless night sky, ablaze with a myriad of stars. I wondered why people ever lived in houses as I rolled up in my rug on the hay bed.

Two faithful dogs guarded us all night, and had they not chosen my hay as the most comfortable place to sleep in, and barked loudly

---

[11] Inn [editor's note].

[12] Innkeeper [editor's note].

close to my ear whenever an imaginary danger threatened, I should have slept very well. But to lie awake under the stars is not the misery of sleeplessness in a room - rather it is pure joy. I saw them fade slowly as the dawn crept up - the crescent moon hung low - there came a dash of brilliant yellow over the hills - another day had begun. We rose and shook ourselves, and those who wished went and dipped their hands and face in the stream.

The weary task of pack-saddling began again. I walked with Marko to the brow of one hill and saw over to the land of Berisha.

Puka is a very large tribe of seven bariaks - Puka, Komani, Dushaj, Cheriti, Chiri, Berisha and Merturi-Gurit, and Kabashi. It is partly Moslem and partly Christian. Puka is the gathering-place for all. Three days before, they had celebrated 'Constitution,' and enjoyed themselves immensely, said the *hanjee*. Now they would like to know what Constitution was.

By six the caravan started; we swallowed the usual dose of black coffee by way of breakfast, and rode up the hill to Puka proper - a mere bunch of hovels, the Kaimmakam's little better than the rest. A few Nizams hung about it, but let us pass unquestioned.

We entered into a desolate wilderness of sandhills - or rather hills of earth so friable that it disintegrates at every shower, and no blade nor leaf can find a hold upon it. Nor was there any living creature - nothing but round bare hills, fantastically water-hewn, and dead as the mountains in the moon. Part of the track had to be taken very carefully - a narrow, friable ledge high along the mountain-side.

We got down into Arshi - a fertile valley, an arm of Mirdite land, the bariak of Spachi, that runs into Puka - and pulled up at midday at Han Arshit.

Han Arshit provided nothing - not even coffee. Marko and I ate the remains of last night's fowl which we had saved. The wretched horse that had fallen over the cliff the day before was dead lame, and had to be left at the *han*.

Trade, said the *hanjee*, was not what it was in the old days. Then a hundred horses at a time were often put up at the *han*. The railway to Salonika had ruined Albania by diverting all the traffic that used to go to Scutari and Durazzo. They were all being starved out; nothing but the long-talked-of railway to the Adriatic could save the land - let the Constitution hurry up with it.

Arshi lies on a river - Ljumi Gojanit. We followed it up a stony valley, steeper and steeper, to its source at the top of the pass, Chafa Malit.

There is a joy that never palls - the first glimpse into the unknown land. On the other side of the pass, a magnificent valley lay below us, thickly wooded with beech, and beyond were the lands which two rival races each claim as their birthright - one of the least-known corners of Europe.

I hurried eagerly down the steep descent on foot, by a rough track to Flet. Flet is Moslem, save for six families, all large; one, consisting of fifty members, showed quite an imposing group of stone houses. A church, but three years old, served occasionally by the priest of Dartha, showed trim and white.

We pushed on to Han Zaa. The *han* was shut up. The *hanjee*, on being summoned, said he could supply nothing - nothing at all, and that there were neither fowls nor eggs in the neighbourhood. He gave us leave, however, to pick as many beans as we liked from his field for twopence. The two soldiers started bean-picking, and I shucked industriously. Marko sent a child foraging for a fowl, and went to borrow a caldron. An ancient hen was produced, and Marko, who is a perfect camp cook, had it simmering in a huge pot of beans within half-an-hour. The *hanjee* volunteered two wooden ladles and a large bowl, and in due time we fed the entire company off beans stewed with hen. As they would otherwise have had nothing but the remains of the day before yesterday's maize bread, this put all in high good humour. I declined a kind offer that I should sleep in the lee of the pile of odoriferous hides, lay down on a heap of hay about 10 P. M., and slept right through till half-past five next morning, when I was surprised to find I had rolled into a dry ditch, and had slept on top of Marko's thick walking stick and a large stone.

We were bound for Djakova, and the rest of the party for Prizren, so started at once with one *kirijee*. Free of the pack train, we pushed on quickly down the valley of the Goska, past Han Sakati, and by a steep descent to the Drin, which we successfully forded, led by a native who stripped and carried my saddlebags on his head. It was a ticklish job, and can only be crossed thus in very dry weather.

Following the Drin down a short way to its junction with the Kruma, we struck up the valley of the Kruma, and were in the land of the Hashi. A great wall-like cliff, rising on the stream's left bank, is known as the fortress of Lek Dukagjin.

Hashi is a large tribe, variously reckoned at 600 to 1000 houses, the large majority of which are Moslem. It is separated by the White Drin from the Moslem tribe of Ljuma on the one side, and on the other marches with the Moslem Krasnich. Hashi land includes the Pestriku Mountains, which the Mirdites state to be their own ancestral home. They migrated to their present home, and the land was subsequently occupied by Hashi, which is no relation to Mirdita.

We left the Kruma, and rode on to a high undulating plateau of loose, friable soil, covered with stunted oak-scrub, parched and sun-scorched. There was neither shade nor spring. A Moslem friend of the *kirijee*'s hailed him, and invited us all to take our midday rest at his place. The nearest spring on the track, he said, was two hours' distant, but he had plenty of water. We accepted gratefully, and followed him uphill. He had two houses side by side - ramshackle shanties made entirely of wood, save for the large chimney and fireplace of clay built up at the side.

He did not ask us in, but spread mats under a tree. His women - not veiled - stared at us from the doorstep of the farther house, and fetched a large jar of fresh water, but sent it to us by a boy. Several men joined us, and were very civil.

Our hosts had never seen a foreign woman dressed *alla franga* before in their land, and thought my coming rather a joke; for a Giaour[13] to be riding openly through Hashi to Djakova unarmed was unusual, to say the least of it - only the *besa* made it possible. They had heard of

---

[13] Non-Moslem [editor's note].

'Constitution,' but did not know what it was, only that there was a *besa* about it.

They were all of the same type as the Gusinje men - very tall, thin, and narrow-built, with large beaky nose and almost no chin, an odd bird-like pattern that seems to be wholly Moslem. They told us the land had once been all Christian, and that under the ruins of a church not far off was a vast treasure, but that it was impossible to find it - it was *amanet*.

They owned plenty of land, but it lay high, and lacked water. This year was a drought, and the pasture was all burnt up. The place they said was called Puka Zarisha. It is not marked in the Austrian staff map, which for all this neighbourhood is very faulty.

Returning to our track, we rode for over an hour through dull, dusty oak-scrub, then into a wood, where we watered the horses at the two-hour spring, and pushed on, as it was absolutely necessary to arrive before nightfall - passed a few wooden houses at Helshani, and met scarce a soul upon the road. It was a deserted wilderness. A long ascent brought us to the top of the pass, Chafa Prushit, and there lay Djakova on the plain below, with a long descent of rolling hill between us and it - red roofs glowing among the green trees, slim white minarets twinkling delicate like lilies. Djakova - as are all Turkish towns - is beautiful from a distance. And when it is civilised and black factory-chimneys arise in place of white minarets, it will be lovely neither within nor without. You cannot have everything.

I beheld it as a dream city - thought of the aching days of toil I had gone through vainly five years before, only to be turned back. The pleasing sensation of attainment wiped out temporarily the fatigue of a long, hot day in the saddle, and two scrappy nights' rest, and I hurried down the stony track - too steep for riding - on foot, a painful job enough, as I had started in new *opanke*[14], and had foolishly neglected to soak them in oil. The heat of the sun had shrunk the raw hide tight on to my feet and made it hard as iron. But it is only when you fail to reach the goal you set out for that raws really count.

---

[14] Native sandals [editor's note].

Finally, we came down to the banks of the Erenik and a great seven-arched stone bridge, the usual parapetless, steep, narrow Turkish bridge, whose bold elegance of design makes one pardon the fact that it can be used only by foot passengers, and is very inconvenient even for them. The majestic height of the middle arch raises it high above the wild floods of winter.

On the farther bank lay Djakova, golden in the evening glow. We rode up to the priest's house, where Marko, an old friend, was greeted heartily. Marko's cousin, the schoolmaster, turned up at once.

After twelve hours' almost continuous travel and very little food, I accepted gladly the orthodox cognac and black coffee, and contemplated a rest till supper-time. But there is no coping with Albanian hospitality; the schoolmaster had flown home as soon as he had greeted us, and I was told he was ready to receive us at once. I was plastered with dust and sweat - had not washed for three days, let alone had my clothes or even my footgear off - and begged to be excused. Marko insisted that I was perfectly clean and looked beautiful. The priest humanely gave me a bowl of water and a towel, and they allowed me five minutes.

I crawled wearily over the *kaldrmi* to the schoolhouse. *Kaldrmi* is large irregular stones jammed together to make a roadway. You cannot call it pavement. There is no word in any other European language to express it. It is *kaldrmi*. When a stone is missing - I do not know how it gets out, but it does - a hole is left deep enough to break the leg of man or beast that trips into it. *Kaldrmi* is a cheap way of making a road, it never wears out, for no one ever thinks of driving or walking on it if there is any way of dodging it, but when it wanders beyond a town it is apt to be removed by folk, who build houses with it.

Luckily the schoolhouse was near. A large company was assembled, very smartly dressed, all most kindly eager to welcome me. A daughter of the house, married in Prizren, was making her first visit home since marriage, and was in full Prizren bridal dress - quite wonderful.

Her hair was parted across the back of her head, and plaited into two plaits, one upward and one downward. The lower hung down as a pigtail and was ornamented with a few coins. The upper was made into a solid block on the top of her head, standing in a point over the forehead (This is probably the origin of the pointed headdress of the Scutarene Catholic women.) On this foundation was a mass of sham gold coins - three bands of them and a big central gold medal. The side hair was cut short in two different lengths, and greased into two solid slabs, that hung on either side of the face. Over all were seven rows of pearl beads and coins that hung in loops to the shoulders.

A zouave, a solid mass of gold embroidery, an embroidered fine white silk shirt, yards and yards of a thick silk sash, striped green and orange, wound round her till she was a huge unwieldy lump, and big white bloomers with gold ankle-pieces, made up her costume. The other ladies, in Scutari dress, laughed at her. And the schoolmaster's wife - who was *alla franga* and looked quite out of place in the picture - was held up to her as a shining example. But the Prizren bride outshone them all. Bizarre and glittering, her many dingle-dangles forced her to sit stiff and still like a Byzantine ikon, and her pallid face and dead black hair gave decorative effect to the blaze of gold and colour.

It was not till I saw her next day that I realised her costume. Then I was too tired. The hospitable *sofra* was spread with the usual chopped hard eggs, sliced melon, cheese, grapes, sweetmeats, all their best, with true Albanian liberality. And the usual spirit-drinking and snack-nibbling began, a process most painful when one is tired and wants real food. I struggled to speak Italian with the bride and the schoolmaster, and to air my weak Albanian on every one, with aching limbs and a splitting head and an empty stomach, into which politeness demanded that I should pour *rakia*. The room was suffocating. *Meze* (tidbits) and *rakia* were Marko's great delight. Many Albanians indeed prefer this part of an entertainment to the meal that it precedes. And all were happy. We returned at last to the priest's house, supped, and slept.

Djakova, like most Turkish towns that are not in a stone district, is built of mud. Two or three of the lowest courses of a wall only are of stone, then follows a beam, then eight or ten courses of sun-dried bricks (*chepchi*) and another beam - all quite haphazard. If the beam be crooked, mud is bunged into the hole and the bricks are humped over all irregularities, regardless of the fact that the wall bulges. If it be too crooked to stand alone, extra supports are shoved against it. All houses are surrounded by walls, the tops of which are tiled to prevent the rain from melting them, and the eaves of all the houses project widely for a similar reason. The streets, *kaldrmi* in the middle, and a sea of mud or a bed of dust on either side, according to weather, are incomparably filthy and stinking. All the muck from the privies, and every sort of refuse, are thrown out on to any open spot - street corners and cross roads, and the river bank - and left to fester. The carcase of a dead horse rotted in the sun, while the hooded crows - the only scavengers - tore at its gaunt ribs. No windows look upon the streets, which are flanked with blank mud walls, the doors in whose gateways are often plated with iron and dinted with bullets.

Djakova was founded about four hundred years ago by two stocks from Bitush Merturi - Vula and Merturi. Of these two the Vula stock still flourishes; our *kirijee* belonged to it. Merturi is reputed one of the oldest Albanian tribes, known in Roman times as Merituri. It is fair in type, and fair men seemed not uncommon in Djakova.

Djakova was all Christian at first, but the Vula stock perverted early. The Merturi remained Christian, but have now no representatives left in the town. Many of the neighbouring villages perverted in a block one Easter, when an Italian priest foolishly celebrated mass so early that when the villagers arrived at the town it was over. As he could not comply with their angry demand to repeat it for them, they went over to the nearest mosque.

In the town the number of Catholics has been steadily diminishing. Twenty years ago there were still a hundred Catholic families in Djakova. Little more than twenty now remain, and of these many are not of old town stock, but recent refugees from neighbouring villages. Sixty villages still remain Catholic in the district, but have few churches and no priests. Three priests and one Franciscan, resident in Djakova, ride - often at very great personal risk - from one village to another, doing their best to aid their scattered flock. These villages are offshoots of various Christian tribes that came at different dates - from Berisha, Shala, Mirdita, etc. As the Serbs weakened in power, the Albanians surged back again over the plains from which tradition tells that they had originally come.

As I was the first traveller that had come to Djakova with Government permission for a long while, I decided to report myself and Marko, in person, at the Konak at once.

There was no Kaimmakam. The late one had belonged to the Young Turk party, but the cheery Moslems of Djakova - hearing that other towns were deposing their governors - promptly chivied him, Constitution having, in their minds, done away with the necessity of any Turkish representative. The Kaimmakam was temporarily replaced by a Bimbashi (Colonel).

The small Catholic population keeps mainly to its own quarters, and my wish to go through the town to the Konak caused much nervousness. The day after the Constitution had proclaimed a general amnesty, and it was announced that Christians were henceforth to be justly treated, a Christian had been shot dead in the bazar by a Moslem zaptieh (policeman) for no offence. His relatives had not obtained redress, and the zaptieh was unpunished. It was dreaded that Constitution was a trick for allaying the fears of the Christians and then massacring them.

A Catholic consented to guide Marko and me to the Konak, but he put on a loaded revolver before he ventured out. A crown of Moslem boys gathered at once, and followed shouting and howling at us. Nor was it surprising, if it be true that (as I was afterwards told) I was the first quite unveiled woman that had walked through the town within any one's recollection, if ever. Marko and our guide were both horribly nervous. The latter kept his hand on the butt of his revolver all the time - to my annoyance, for under such circumstances fear should never be shown, whatever happens. I explained that lots of little London boys would jeer just as much at an Albanian woman in full dress. But this they would not believe, and hurried me along through narrow back streets, avoiding the bazar.

The Konak, a ramshackle, wood and mud building, stood in a big yard, through one of the walls of which an extra gateway had been made by simply smashing a hole. We passed through a ragged crowd of zaptiehs, suvarris, and their horses, and a general rag-tag and bobtail, and were shown up into a dingy room, where the Bimbashi, in uniform, sat *alla franga* on a chair, and the rest of the company, in native dress, squatted cross-legged on a wide seat that went all round the room. The most important - the head of the Moslem faith in Djakova - an old man in a white turban, with a long, white beard and immense white penthouse eyebrows, sat at the Bimbashi's right hand, and eyed me with marked displeasure.

The Bimbashi was very civil, but spoke no language I know. My remarks had, therefore, to be translated by Marko for the benefit of the whole company. They were all ears at once.

I showed my *teskereh*, and answered the usual questions. The Bimbashi who, as is the wont of Turkish officials, continued signing documents and giving instructions aside to various persons all the time he was conversing - (I have often wondered whether this is why Turkish affairs are always in a muddle) - expressed himself as delighted to see an English visitor. Of Djakova and neighbourhood he knew little. He reckoned that there were between two and three thousand houses in the town, but the number of inhabitants was quite unknown - a census must be taken under the new law. He was anxious to know how the conversion of England to Islam was proceeding, and regretted that press of business prevented his entertaining me at his house to discuss this question, but the laying of blood feuds, under the new *besa*, occupied him from dawn to dark. He hoped, however, to establish peace shortly.

Meaning to be polite, I wished all success to this beneficent work, and that the Constitution might spread peace and prosperity through the land.

At this the old white-beard, his eyes glaring stonily from their deep caverns, shouted something in a hoarse, deep voice. There was a general murmur. Marko looked uneasy and interpreted: "Tell that Giaour woman it is no affair of hers. She is not to interfere in the Sultan's business. It is the Sultan's business alone. We want no Giaours."

Marko replied we had no wish to interfere; we had but agreed with what the Bimbashi said. Some one coming in on business, I rose and said good-bye to the Bimbashi, who very politely called up a zaptieh and told him to escort me back.

We passed through a crowd at the gate, who growled angrily, "We have only had this Constitution a month, and the Giaours have already begun to come."

The zaptieh hurried us back, this time through the bazar. I noticed that the numerous gunshops were heaped with Mauser cartridges. My escort was too nervous to allow me to stay - unnecessarily, I believe, for I doubt if any one would have really molested me - and we arrived back safely. The native Catholic took off his revolver with a sigh of relief, and swore that not for five pounds would he again cross the town with me.

For the past ten months things had been going from bad to worse, and the worst was now feared to be imminent.

In the previous October (1907) an Albanian Franciscan, Frate Luigi, resident in Djakova, started to ride from Djakova to Ipek[15], with a Moslem *kirijee*. He was captured when not far from Djakova by a large party of armed Moslems, taken to Smolitza, a Moslem village, and there imprisoned in the room of a house. No ransom was asked, but he was held as hostage for the release of a brother of one of his captors, who had been imprisoned by the Turkish Government.

The Turkish Government was at once informed, but took no step whatever. The Catholic Church in Albania is under the protection of Austria, and the Austrian Consulate in Prizren was applied to also, without result. The Frate was several times threatened with death if he would not turn Turk, to which he replied, they might kill him as soon as they liked. He was not otherwise molested, and was given enough to eat. The Catholics in the neighbourhood, exasperated, called on the Catholic mountain tribes to come to their help. A dead pig was then found in the mosque in Smolitza (this is the usual Christian way of declaring war on the Moslems), and Fra Luigi was suddenly released, after ten weeks' detention, though the man for whom he was hostage was not. No explanation of the affair has ever been forthcoming.

There was more in the affair than meets the eye, but by whom engineered we shall never know. The report, widely current in the Sanjak and Slavonic borderlands, that so soon as Austria was ready to move she would cause to be got up a massacre of Christians of sufficient magnitude to compel her to go to the rescue, and make Europe give her another mandate to 'civilize' Balkan lands, occurred to my mind; more especially as in 1906 many Austrians in Bosnia had boasted to me that they meant to be in Saloniki, under the Austrian flag, by November 1909.

---

[15] Peja / Peć [editor's note].

The pig in the mosque aroused at once an attack on the Christians. The village of Ramotzi was accused of the deed; but to this day the doer of it is not known. Nevertheless, Ramotzi was attacked and thirty-one houses burned, with all their goods. One house was forced to surrender after forty-eight hours' siege. The defenders were promised safe-conduct, but were fired on when coming out - four killed, five wounded. In all, fourteen villages were attacked, and eighty-six houses burnt and plundered. Each contained from twenty to fifty inhabitants. When I was there, all were destitute and houseless. This went on through the spring of 1908. The Catholics were given till Ramazan (September) to turn Turk or be killed.

In Prizren also it was reported that a pig had been found in a mosque. This is believed to have been false. Even Hilmi Pasha said he did not believe it. The two men who said they had found it, declared they had at once thrown it in the river. On account of this alleged pig, a severe boycott was then started against all Catholics, who were almost reduced to starvation, and very many had to leave the town.

The worst case of persecution was that of the Bibez family of Bretkotzi. They had a group of very large houses, and great store of food and cattle. The head, though he had no quarrel with the Moslems, was told it was not seemly for a Christian to have such a large house, and that he must pull down a storey or it should be burnt. He asked the Kaimmakam for protection, and was given a hundred soldiers and some zaptiehs. He also appealed to the Austrian Consulate in Prizren.

After an anxious month, he received an ultimatum from the Moslems. He must turn Turk, or they would burn him out.

He hurried to Djakova, where the Kadi (the Kaimmakam being absent) swore to him that the soldiers should not be withdrawn, and that his goods were safe. He therefore did not remove any of them. A few days later the soldiers were suddenly all withdrawn by order of Shemsi Pasha (afterwards shot dead at Monastir), and a crowd of armed Moslems at once attacked. No lives were taken, but the entire group of houses, with the possessions of the whole family, were utterly destroyed. I made a vain attempt to draw the attention of a charitable in England to the piteous plight of these Catholic villages. The papers that had always space for the sufferings of the Orthodox in Macedonia had no corner to spare.

The people themselves thought their plight due to the European intervention in Macedonia, which had incensed the Moslems against Christians in other parts.

The aforesaid intervention did no good at all in Macedonia, and seems to have made matters worse elsewhere. It is possible that the Powers most interested intended that it should. At any rate, the English officers were carefully shoved into a corner where they could do least harm to other people's plans.

Djakova is in Kosovo vilayet. Kosovo vilayet was a most important part of the great Servian Empire of the Middle Ages. The Serb of to-day looks at it as part of his birthright, and of its recapture the young men see visions and the old men dream dreams.

Djakova, having been founded by Albanians after the fall of the Servian Empire, is naturally an Albanian town. Of its two thousand and odd houses, but one hundred are Serb Orthodox. These are segregated on the opposite side of the town from the Catholics, and have little or no communication with them. A Catholic actually told me he had never been in the Serb quarter. The two Churches distrust one another more than they do the Moslems.

There are no Serb villages near Djakova. But I heard that the feast of the Assumption would be celebrated by a great concourse of people at the Serb monastery of Devich, some twelve hours away, and arranged to go on pilgrimage with a Serb family of Djakova, and travel as they did, without escort, in a native cart - a *strema*. At 3.30 A. M. it clattered into the yard. I was asleep. It was pitch-dark. They could not wait, I was told. "Be quick, be quick!" I scrambled into my clothes, gulped a cup of black coffee, threw myself unwashen and uncombed into the cart, and we were off.

It was pouring rain. The dawn had not yet broken as we plunged through Djakova in the dark. I braced my feet hard against one side of the cart, and my back against the other. Save a little hay, it was uncushioned, and rocked, reeled, and rebounded over boulders of *kaldrmi*, into yawning holes, almost falling over on one side, only to recover and stagger on to one wheel or the other.

Marko and I bumped together like dried peas in a pod. We drew
rein at the door of the Servian school. Two *stremas*, full of men,
women, and children awaited us, well wedged and padded in with
cushions, *dusheks*, and *yorgans*, and heaps of coloured bundles - their
best clothes and provisions.

The chill, grey dawn broke as we drove through the iron-plated,
bullet-marked gate of the town, past stinking heaps of refuse,
unutterable filth - horses' bones - black mud - a forlorn graveyard - the
dismal barracks, with the great wall of a dismantled building alongside
melting into mud - where half-clad Nizams wandered drenched and
miserable, like damnèd souls forlorn in a circle of the Inferno.

The rain cleared as we came out on to the plain - the road, as
usual in these lands, bad, but considered good - boulders, mudholes,
gullies, which were taken at a canter and 'switchbacked.' Our driver was
a Serb of the heavily-built, fair, very broad-headed type, that one finds
in Bosnia but never in the mountains of High Albania. He, as indeed did
my travelling companions, spoke a mixture of Serb and Albanian, even
to each other, and when I questioned him in Serb replied sometimes
wholly in Albanian. I noticed that they never inflected their adjectives,
but said, "Dobro, po dobro, mnogo dobro," i.e. good, more good, much
good, for 'good,' 'better,' 'best,' as do the Slavs of Macedonia.

At first the plain was mostly covered with oak-scrub. Farther on
were a few houses and maize-fields. It is very sparsely inhabited. It was
impossible to follow our route in the Austrian staff map, it being very
faulty, which is not surprising if it be true, as I was assured, that no
European had been before by this track. Roughly speaking, we followed
up the right bank of the White Drin to its junction with the Dechanski
Bistritza, which we crossed, crossing also the Drin rather higher up. We
then followed up the Drin's left bank on a narrow road some ten feet
above the river. Here we pulled up to ask the way of some men, and one
of the *stremas* at once fell over the bank. The driver left it at the very
edge; the horses backed, and the whole thing capsized and rolled clean
over, the horses and the front wheels remaining on the road above. The
women screamed loudly, but as the tilt was very strong and they were
well wedged in with cushions they were luckily not thrown out. Half-an-
hour's repairing put all right. We left the river and struck uphill.

On the plateau on the top we found typical Servian *zadrugas*, family groups of houses enclosed in huge palisades (*palanka*). Thick stakes, some nine or ten feet high, cut into spikes at the top, are driven into the ground about eighteen inches apart. These are wattled together, not with simple withies but with twisted ropes of branches, very thick and solid. Outside, this dense wall is buttressed at short intervals with small tree trunks. The top is roofed with thick masses of blackthorn, which project so widely as to make it quite impossible for any one to climb the fence from without. Above the blackthorn project the spiked stakes. The whole mighty wooden wall is one of the most primitive types of fortification. So, in all probability, did the ancient inhabitants of Britain defend their hill encampments - as do the Serbs now - against both men and wolves.

We saw but one church and no mosque, but were told there were many Moslem families. The ruins of one old church were pointed out. Money enough had been collected to rebuild it, but the Sultan had refused permission. The families in this part mostly owned and worked the land they lived on. Further on were, for the most part, Moslem *chiftliks*. The track in many places was really good, and a proper road could easily be made.

After six hours' travel, we halted for an hour and a half at Han Zaimit, a wretched clay-built shanty which I did not enter. A scattered village not far off was called Zaimit Pes. A crowd of gypsies made their lair near the *han*. The real wild Balkan gypsies rarely bother about a tent, but crouch in the lee of any bush or bank that is near a water or fuel supply. Swarthy, scarlet-lipped, with black brilliant eyes, long heavy elf-locks of dead black hair, and unspeakably filthy, they are scorned alike by Serb and Albanian. The scorn they return tenfold, for they hold that they are the chosen of all races, and that none other knows how to enjoy the gift of life. One came up and boasted that he was the father of thirty-two children. The Serbs, not to be outdone, told of a Serb near Ipek who is father to twenty-four sons all by one mother, and that all are grown up and *pod oruzhja* (bearing arms). To cap this we were told of a Moslem with forty-two children, but by how many wives was unknown. After these cheerful proofs that the country was not depopulating, we proceeded, and lost the way several times and were much delayed. Passing through a village, Kopilich, we crossed a stream, Reka Devichit, and got up into a plateau, all scrub-oak, and topped one hummock after another without ever seeming to get any farther. On slopes below were many palisaded *zadrugas,* some with very large houses within them. Many were said to be Moslem. Others had crosses on them.

The descent was awful; the driver lashed up his horses, and, once off, we had either to smash or come to the bottom whole, plunging at a break-neck pace down a narrow gully over loose boulders. The terrified horses kept their legs somehow, and landed trembling and drenched with sweat at the bottom. As for me, I was pitched violently across and across the *strema.* Giddy with concussion I alighted, joined the streams of pilgrims, and ascended on foot to the monastery in the oak forest above - a mass of irregular white buildings that scrambled at different heights haphazard round three yards.

We passed through the lower yard with a seething mass of pilgrims, and went straight into the church on one side of it. It was about 5 P. M. The tiny church was dark, and crammed with people. My appearance created the greatest excitement. As I passed the side where all flocked to light tapers, the glare fell on me, and I was at once surrounded, seized upon, and fingered all over by an eager crowd. My hat, my kodak, my bag all were examined. How much money was in it? From what vilayet was I? Who was I? My name? - all regardless of the service which was in full swing. A man in European dress - a monastery secretary - hurried to the centre of hubbub, learnt that I was English, and dashed off to inform the officiating priests.

The heat was suffocating, and the fingering and pulling about more than I wanted after the twelve hours' jolting drive.

I left the church. Opposite it stood the house of the Archimandrite, or Hagi as they called him here. A steep flight of wooden steps led to a perfect rabbit-warren of pilgrims' rooms which were reached through a narrow door about four feet high. Beyond, a huge, white-washed, three-storeyed hospitium - with the usual big wooden balcony to each floor - surrounded two sides of a large yard. Below, on one side, was a smaller yard surrounded by stables. The whole was an indescribable confusion - a seething mass of pilgrims, babies, bundles, sacks, and rugs filled the entire space of the two yards, and each balcony and staircase, some seeking rooms, others camping where they were, all in search of some one or something - a deafening babel of voices. The third yard was a struggling tangle of packhorses, carts, draught-oxen, and buffaloes, and their owners. And no matter what any one was doing, they left off to come and examine me. The monastery servants, who preserved their wits wonderfully in the confusion, allotted a tiny room to our party, and I crowded into it with my Serb fellow-travellers, who proceeded to furnish it with their cushions and coverlets.

The Hagi himself visited me, so soon as he had concluded service in the church.

He was a tall, fair, handsome man, very friendly, and much relieved to find I understood Serb. Marko, who knows but little, asked him if he understood Albanian.

He laughed heartily and replied, "I am Albanian." Born of Albanian parents, he explained he had spoken Albanian only as a child. But having joined the Orthodox Church, he was now a Servian, and Servian was more familiar to him than his mother tongue.

So is it in the Debatable Lands. The Serbs have a converted Albanian as head of their monastery, and conversely, one of the most patriotic Albanian priests in Djakova was a Serb by birth - had spoken Serb only as a child, and now had almost forgotten it.

The Hagi at once said I was to be his guest. The Metropolitan of Prizren was there with some Servian schoolmistresses from Prishtina, and we should all be a party together. No foreigner, so far as he knew, had ever been to Devich with the exception of one Russian Consul - the good man was almost as excited over me as were the pilgrims. I came forth from the very temporary rest in the little room, and was introduced. To my amazement I found I was celebrated. Some one recognized me as having been in Dechani five years ago. "Ah, it is the Balkan Englishwoman, the friend of the Montenegrins!" The Metropolitan knew all about me - a schoolmistress lately from Saloniki, retailed my Macedonian career. We had supper on the terrace under a pergola. Fast day - but an excellent meal of river-trout, tomato salad, balls of rice and herbs rolled in vine leaves (*japrak*), and green paprikas stuffed with rice and frightfully hot. Plenty of *kaimak* (clotted cream), sheep-cheese, and fruit. It was the merriest party. You reached out and helped yourself to whatever was handy, and made the same plate do. And above, around, and beneath us was one vast picnic.

Rations were served out all hot from the kitchen, the air was heavy with the fumes of roast and baked, all food was gratis, and each had as much as he liked. People ran hither and thither with steaming bowls and trays. Save ourselves at the high table, every one fed off vessels of solid copper, tinned, of which the monastery had enough for two thousand and more pilgrims.

It is characteristic of the Balkan man, be he Slav or Albanian, that he can enjoy himself thoroughly and whole-heartedly, without ever becoming rowdy or losing his self-respect. There was no one to keep order among this vast concourse of happy people, nor was any one required. It is to be hoped that what is called civilisation may never reduce them to the barbarous level of 'Arry and 'Arriet on Bank holiday. I was towed off to sleep with the schoolmistresses, and we retired at 10.30, for which - having been on a pretty constant strain since 3 A. M., and having finished up with talking Servian all the evening, having had no practice for over a year - I was not sorry.

It was a small room, the floor entirely covered with mattresses. There were a great many of us. They kindly gave me the only bedstead. Unfortunately, however, one of the ladies was married, and her son and husband shared our room. So though I had a bedstead, it was impossible to go to bed in it properly. Fortunately, the only window was just above me, and I opened it surreptitiously.

The schoolmarms, declaring sleep was impossible, began to dance the *kolo*, but I was asleep from sheer exhaustion before they had done.

It was but a short sleep, for, suddenly, in plunged the *djakon*, telling us to get up and come to church. I wearily looked at my watch. It was 1 A. M. Only three ladies went. I slept again. In came the *djakon* again, this time to get medicine out of a drawer near my head. The floor being covered with sleepers, this made no end of commotion. At five, again the *djakon*, this time to do his hair! And then the Hagi for something or other. Further sleep was impossible.

My stable companions used a common comb. I was the proud possessor of a private one. I went out dirty, sticky, and staggering with sleep, and asked if it were possible to wash. When the Metropolitan was up, I could have his basin. Not before.

The great man having emerged, I was conducted to his washstand, and a serving-man poured two tablespoonfuls of water over my hands, which I rubbed on my face in the approved style - and my toilet was complete.

Outside, coffee was being served at the kitchen door (no food, of course). It waked me at once. I turned to the marvellous scene.

And it was truly marvellous - such costumes as I had never seen before and may never see again - many of them indeed museum pieces, all the best of every district.

The finest of all were from Ipek Caza. Ipek itself is almost entirely Moslem Albanian, the Serbs and Catholics form but a small minority; the villages around, however, are very largely Serb, and form a Serb island in an otherwise Albanian land.

The women's shirts are a mass of the very finest cross-stitch embroidery in dull red, blue and green, the colours all native dyes. Cross-stitch (very common in Russia) is Slavonic and does not occur on Albanian costume. It makes, of necessity, angular patterns. Albanian patterns are all of flowing lines adapted for braiding and gold thread. The flowing line is similarly found on old Albanian carved chests and ceilings.

Over the richly-embroidered shirt is a very short petticoat - a mere waist-frill some 12 inches deep - of striped material, the stripes being almost always all hand-work in the finest stitches. A very broad binder is bound round the lower part of the body like an abdominal support. Over this is a heavy, leathern belt, with brass plaques on it studded with red and green 'jewels' of glass, the workmanship poor. On the shoulders is a zouave of various colours, usually dark, with scarlet or yellow braid. The breast is quite covered with a mass of large silver coins - like Maria Theresas - and numbers of glass bead and coral necklaces and crosses, and hearts of glass like those popular in Bosnia. Some wore triangular leather amulet-cases on a string slung over one shoulder.

The married women wear a peaked head-dress, simliar to that of mediaeval ladies, but smaller. It is of white linen, with a finely embroidered edge in various colours, the ends hang down to the shoulders; over the top of the head, and hanging either side to the ear, is a broad band of turquoise-blue beads ending in a triangular dingle-dangle.

The hair is parted in the middle, and again lower down. The top section is twisted round a solid foundation to make a huge curl, a great sausage of hair stiff with grease, which curves forward on each side of the face, framing it completely. The end of the curl is sewn with coins - it is a head-dress that is made to last - sometimes as many as five Maria Theresas on each, and to make all firm both curls are sewn down to the leather band which goes under the chin, and is thickly covered with blue beads. Such of the hair as is not used for the curl is plaited and used as a support behind the curl to which it is fastened. The whole makes a solid block of hair - grotesque and extraordinary; at least so I thought till I came back to England and found every one's head swollen to double its size with stuffings, frizettes, and 'transformations.'

I had just started drawing, and was getting on well, when one of the schoolmarms espied me. With the best of intentions in the world she summoned everybody to see what I was doing, and all my chances were over. I was the centre of a mob all striving to see me do it again, and attention being turned on me, I was hunted all day. Every peasant wanted to speak to me, and most of them did; I was questioned till I was on the point of exhaustion, and all the time I had a ridiculous feeling that it was a case of the biter bit. For months I had been incessantly questioning about manners and customs, now I was myself the victim. I was asked about all that I did, and then "why?" The thing that bothered everybody was my straw hat; they had never seen one before; "Why do you wear wheat on your head?" Every one broke a little bit off the brim to make sure it really was "wheat."

"Do you wear it in the house?" "Do you sleep in it?" "Do you wear it to show you are married?" "To show you are not married?" "Did you make it?" "Are all the women in your vilayet (province) obliged to wear wheat on their heads?" "Is there a law about it?" "Or do you wear it *per chef* (for pleasure)?"

"I wear it because of the sun," said I desperately. "Why because of the sun?" "It is hot," said I. "No, it isn't," said they. They did not wear wheat because of the sun. Would I tell them the real reason? It occurred to me that if there was a Devich Anthropological Society it might report that it had found traces of sun-worship in the English, and mysterious rites connected with it that no questioning could elicit. I fell back on the answer that has so often tried me in others: "I wear it because I do. It is *nash obichaj* (our custom)."

This satisfied them wholly, for there is a proverb which says: "It is better that a village should fall than a custom." The brim of my hat looked as though it had been gnawed by rats all round, and I felt justified in pulling every one about mercilessly in return, and examining all their ornaments; but it was very fatiguing - on an empty stomach.

Two gypsy bands played incessantly, both at once. One instrument was a cylinder of earthenware with a piece of hide strained on the top, and slapped with the hand; another was a big drum. The sun was nearly at full strength, the air was thick with the dust of many dancing feet; the perpetual pom-pom-pom, rhythmical, insistent, throbbed like a fever pulse in the sizzling heat. Only for one half-hour, when a service was held in the yard outside the church (it was far too small to hold the congregation), did the band stop, and then there was singing.

Midday brought the much-needed dinner in the Metropolitan's room. I sat next to him, and was excellently well fed. But even the meal was a long and stiff *viva voce* examination in Servian. His Grace was pleased to express his admiration for the physical strength of the English. He himself, for example, though he had not had such a long and exhausting journey as I had, and accustomed to the country, was quite tired out!

After dinner all went to rest. I had two hours' heavy sleep in the crowded room of the night before. Then we were all poked up. Tumblers of water were passed round; Serbs are always water-thirsty. I amused every one highly by pouring mine over my head and neck.

Thus roused I went out again, and, as the first excitement about me had somewhat subsided, managed to get some photographs and drawings made.

Then a long strip of mats and carpets was laid right across the yard. The Hagi, his secretary, and some monks sat on cushions at one end, and I was invited to join them. A number of heads of families then sat in a long row, cross-legged, on either side the carpet. *Rakia* and the usual snacks were served all round. Each man in turn came up, kissed the Hagi's hand, and made an offering to the church - from a few piastres to a pound Turk, and the secretary inscribed each in a book. They were nearly all townsfolk from Prizren, Prishtina, Ipek, and Mitrovitza. The peasants had already left or were leaving. It was a very long job; about a hundred and fifty napoleons were collected.

Then came gifts in kind, brought for the most part by women - shirts, drawers, towels, and sheets, and handkerchiefs, many finely embroidered in colours and gold.

Almost all these town women were dressed *alla Turka*, had their hair dyed black, and their eyebrows joined by paint in the middle. One in particular wore a magnificent white satin overcoat (*koret*) brocaded with silver and stiff with raised silver embroidery - another, an equally fine one, of crimson velvet and gold. The apron, usually worn over the large bloomers, was of wonderfully fine silk tissue, embroidered in colour and gold. Native eye for colour, when let alone, rarely goes wrong, but alas, 'civilisation' is working sad havoc, and hideous parrots and bunches of flowers in Berlin wool-work (as taught in the schools) were among the most admired of the offerings to the Church. The curse of 'made in Germany' is already withering the land. The bad beginning, may be, of a bad end.

Supper was late. I was dog-tired, nor was there any corner where I could sit at peace. By this time two women from Andrijevitza, in Montenegro, two from Berani, a man from Ipek, and a young monk from the monastery of Miloshevo, in the *sanjak* of Novi-bazar, had all recognised and claimed acquaintance with me, and I sent greetings to all friends in each place.

It was strange, in the heart of the wilderness, to find so many that knew me.

The *djakon* took me to see the monastery library of old Slavonic church-books, both in print, from early presses, and in manuscript. They had been shockingly neglected, and, unluckily, no perfect copies remained of books that, even in their battered state, are of considerable value. It is possible that among the litter missing pages might be found. I begged that all that remained should be carefully preserved.

When it got dark, I sat on a stone by the wall, and got a rest for a few minutes. Then I was poked up to drink cognac with the Metropolitan. I would, by that time, gladly have drunk a quart. It kept me up till supper. Then we turned out again to see the *kolo* danced round bonfires, and sing national songs. We turned in at 11.30, I with orders to be ready to start at 3.30 A. M.

I seemed scarcely to have fallen asleep when the head of the Serb party I had come with knocked at the door. The carts were ready.

I collected my coat, belt, and boots, and crawled out over the sleeping schoolmarms into the chilly night air, reeling with sleep.

We swallowed our ration of coffee, and were soon off. The Serbs kindly lent us two sacks, which we stuffed full of hay, so that we were not so badly shaken on the return journey. The women of the Serb party reproached me with not having come to sit with them in their room in the monastery. I was sorry, for I felt that I had not been polite to them, and they meant most kindly. But all spare time - and it was not much - I had used in getting the opinion of as many different people as possible on the Constitution.

We arrived safely in Djakova about 6 A. M., said good-bye to our Serb friends at the entrance, and drove through the town, followed by a hooting, howling mob of Moslem boys, who hung on to the cart and poked up the cover with sticks - Marko and the driver very vexed and nervous, but bad words break no bones.

We found the priests as tired as we were. They had been out in the villages all the time we had been away. Typhoid had broken out in them. Water, on account of the drought, was scarce and bad, and all provisions short as a result of the recent persecutions. I could only prescribe complete rest, cleanliness, and a slop diet, and vainly strove to prevent the administering of the filthy local remedy - dogs' dung that has been dropped on a stone in the sun, powdered and given in water. Marko and one of the priests had absolute faith in it. They each knew cases which had survived it, and were reckoned as cures.

And I learnt that the only emetic known to the Albanian pharmacopoeia is human excrement and water - given in all cases of supposed poisoning; and that the remedy for dipsomania is the same, mixed with rakia.

So ended a weary day.

The Moslems of Djakova did not seem pleased with the Constitution, did not desire Turkish interference, and certainly objected to the visit of a Giaour. Subsequently I heard that there had been much talk about me, and that the Catholics were told that it was a good thing they had not harboured me a day longer.

The Christians, both Orthodox and Catholic, had not the smallest hope or faith in the Constitution.

Devich Monastery was founded after the great defeat of the Serb nation at Kosovo, and dates from the time of George of Smederevo (ob. 1457), who ruled a restricted Servia under Turkish suzerainty.

At that time the great emigration of Serbs to Hungary had not taken place, and the population must have been mainly Serb. The gathering at the monastery was unusually large, owing to the temporary peace. The very large majority were from Ipek caza, more than half of the whole gathering. And there, I was assured, was the largest Serb population. Near Djakova there was none. Those I questioned were much disappointed that the Government was to remain Turkish - had hoped for foreign intervention. They did not want a Turkish Government, because then the land would never be theirs. They wanted to own the land themselves, and not work on chiftliks. All Turkish Governments had been bad, and this would be also.

The Moslems of Ipek had not accepted the Constitution, and vowed they would accept no law that would interfere with their rights. The Serbs round Berana (part of the Vasojevich tribe) were very much disappointed about the Constitution. They did not want to be any more under any Turkish Government.

The report that in future they were all to be called Ottomans enraged Serb and Albanian alike. It was all another trick to keep them under the Turks. The Christian Powers ought not to permit it. At present all agreed it "was like a dream," but they expected a rude awakening, and the Serbs, regardless of the fact that in most places they are much in the minority, still have visions of the expulsion of all Moslems, and the reconstruction of the great Servian Empire.

I passed the rest of my time in the Catholic quarter. Djakova has always been renowned for its silver-workers. It is an interesting fact that throughout North Albania almost all silver-work is by Christians, and the trade is hereditary in families. The designs are therefore in all probability genuine Albanian, deriving from pre-Turkish times. In Djakova, Prizren, Prishtina and Mitrovitza, I found all silver-workers Christians.

As might be expected, Djakova revels in the supernatural, and miraculous happenings are frequent. In a mountain-side hard by, on the left of the road to Prizren, is a magic cavern. For miles does it go underground; none knows how far, some say even beneath the Drin. In it is a large and ancient city where no man now lives; but the bazar, to this very day, is stocked with all that is finest and best - fruit, flesh, fish, jewels, and fair raiments. But should any man venture to touch one single thing, his torch at once goes out, serpents spring up and devour him in the darkness. And these are no serpents; they are *oras* (spirits) that guard the cavern. No man has ventured in for many years.

I said I would, and asked to be guided to the spot, but none dared take me. Nor is this the sole spot that is miraculously guarded.

Not far from Djakova, on a hill, are the ruins of a chapel. A Moslem tried to dig there for treasure, but was at once struck dead by lightning out of a cloudless sky. Not sufficiently warned, some men went to remove stones for building purposes, but a crowd of serpents at once leapt from the ground, and the intruders only just escaped. For *oras* can take what form they please - birds, beasts, women, or serpents.

Quite recently a man was driving past with an ox-cart, when both of the oxen fell on their knees before the ruins; and the holiness of the spot being now proved beyond all doubt, none dare meddle with it in future. ...

The first *strema* we had engaged to take us to Prizren was requisitioned by a Moslem Bey at the last moment. We got off, finally, one morning at 8.30 A. M.

The road, quite a decent one, followed up the left bank of the Erenik as far as Ura Terzijit (the Tailors' Bridge) - a grand stone bridge of eleven arches - said to have been built three hundred years ago by the tailors of Djakova and Prizren.

Fording the river, we drove up the right bank, and struck across the White Drin. The Erenik joins the Drin through a narrow gully, where a hill arises from the plain, and is spanned by a lofty bridge of one large arch, Ura Fshait. Our driver suddenly loaded his Martini, and rushed off to shoot at two wild-geese on the river. It proved a wild-goose chase.

We drove along the plain, on the Drin's right bank, passing on our left a Moslem village, Djurtha, and on our right another, Ragova, both with mosques. Fording the Drin, we halted at midday at Han Krusha, a newly-built inn of mud bricks, whose Moslem owners were most civil. Then on over land that was fairly cultivated and looked fertile - maize, corn, and tobacco - and through Pirona, a large Moslem village, up over rising ground, and there lay Prizren in the valley below, with the ruins of an old castle and the white walls of modern barracks on the height beyond.

Fortune was favouring me beyond my deserts. Prizren was another of my dream cities, and I beheld it with my waking eyes.

Prince Nicholas' song - the song that enshrines in a few verses the Great Servian Idea - the song that every Serb school-child knows, "Onward, onward, let me see Prizren," rang in my memory. I had seen the tribesmen of Montenegro sing it with tears in their eyes. I had heard it secretly sung in Bosnia, where it is forbidden by the Austrian Government.

After the Russian-Turkish war, when the beaten Turk had to yield to Europe's demands, the dearest hope of the Serb people was that Prizren, the heart of the old Servian Empire, the capital of Tsar Dushan, would shortly again be theirs.

Pondering all these things, we clattered into the town.

Prizren is a large town, and highly picturesque. It lies both sides of the Prizrenski Bistritza (a tributary of the Drin), and spawls up the mountain-side, from which spirt and gush numberless streams of clear, cold water. The water supply is quite amazing, and the river would be a considerable size were it not diverted into three channels at different levels, which supply the town and work mills.

The streets are very fairly clean, and the town full of life and activity.

But even the best friend of the Serbs must admit that it is a Moslem Albanian town. The Servian Metropolitan had already lamented to me that the Serbs were in a considerable minority, but I had not expected to find them such a mere drop in the ocean.

The census just made under the Constitution gives:

Moslem houses..3500
Servian houses (with 4320 inhabitants)...........950
Catholic Albanian houses...............................180
Vlah houses..180

In the case of the Christians, I believe these figures to be fairly correct. The Prizren Moslems, already alarmed at the rumour that Constitution meant loss of privilege to them, and determined not to be compelled to give military service, were said to have understated the number of their houses and to have refused to give the number of inhabitants. It could be reckoned, I was told, at ten to a house.

Of the Moslems, some are genuine Ottoman Turks, settled since early days, but the bulk are Albanian.

Each nation that designs to pick up the pieces, when Turkey in Europe bursts up, keeps a Consul on the spot. A Russian represents Slav interests, to claim the land as Old Servia. An acute Austrian is posted there to forward his country's plan of 'Advance, Austria,' and Italy has had to plant a man to see what he is doing. The Moslem Albanian objects to the presence of all of them, and the Turkish Government impartially gives them all armed escort. There is something truly pathetic about the way Turkey, everywhere, carefully protects the gentlemen whose only *raison d'être* is to hasten the dismemberment of the land.

Servia sent a Consul some years ago; but he was almost immediately forced to withdraw by the populace.

Of one thing the populace is determined: that is, that never again shall the land be Serb.

The Moslem Albanian's game, here as elsewhere, had been to support the Turkish Government in order to keep out others, and he was already growling sullenly at the Constitution, as offering equality to Christian Slavs, and therefore threatening Albanian power.

The leading Serbs of the town kindly invited me to stay at a private house, but, as I did not wish to be attached to any political party, and meant to see life in general, I stayed at an inn, where folk of all sorts came to drink.

September 1st saw all the streets gay with flags, tissue-paper chains and fans, for the Sultan's accession day. I called, at the correct hour, at the Seralio. Over the entrance gate is a great wooden star, the rays of varying length, with tiny crescent moons on their tips (is it really the sun and moon?). The yard was full of Nizams, gendarmes, and officials in their best. Upstairs, the Vali-Pasha, gorgeous with medals and decorations, was receiving in state.

The Consuls were present in uniform. The police officer, who showed dirty ragged me in, said that the Vali-Pasha spoke Serb. He turned out to be a Herzegovinian from Trebinje. We got on beautifully. He had expected me before. Scutari had warned him of my approach. Had heard of me from Djakova, and sent suvarris to meet me, but I had disappeared. I explained I had been to Devich in a cart, without escort. I relied on the *besa*, and wanted no escorts. He hastened to say that peace and prosperity were established for evermore. I congratulated the Sultan, and was given a glass of pink syrup.

The Vali-Pasha was amazed at the route I had chosen. I could have come in comfort, he said, by steamer from Scutari to Saloniki, thence by rail, quite *alla franga*, to Ferizovich[16], and driven in a carriage to Prizren. For himself, he never went up country unless obliged - I never found a Turkish governor that did. The wild-cat methods of the English were beyond him. I might go where I pleased, but "sooner you than I" was his attitude.

Having thus advertised to authority the confidence which the British Empire put in the new order of things, I did not expound my private opinion, which was then, that the Turkish Empire was playing possibly the first scene of the last act of its tragic existence, but withdrew. And unluckily just missed a farcical interlude, for the chief accountant, accused of embezzling public funds, was attacked and chivied from the town with a petroleum can on his head.

It was a general holiday, bands pom-pommed all night. The heat was intense, and sleep impossible. I did not get to the bazar till 7.30 A. M. next morning, a scandalously late hour in these lands.

It was a grand bazar. Worth all the journey, for as yet it is but little spoiled with *alla franga*. The gold embroidery is not to be surpassed anywhere; the tailors' shops are a blaze of gorgeous colour and design. Had it not been for the difficulties of transport, I should have ruined myself. As for the carved walnut-wood frames inlaid with silver, they are the finest work of the kind I have seen anywhere. It was in Prizren in the olden days that the finest artists in gold and silver inlay flourished, and turned out yataghans and gunbarrels fit for fairy princes, and from thence they spread into Bosnia. The so-called Bosnian inlay is mainly of Albanian origin, and much of it actually Albanian handicraft.

The demand for very fine work is now slight - *alla franga* will maybe soon kill it - but there are still in Prizren workmen who can execute it.

The main trade is in rough and cheap ornaments for the peasants. The silver-workers are all Christians.

I wandered up and down and in and out the long wooden tunnels of the bazar streets, dark with hot, rich shadows, glowing with goods.

---

[16] Ferizaj / Uroševac [editor's note].

Gentian root and iris root are heaped at the herbalists', black nut for the black hair-dye of the Christians and logwood for the red of the Moslems, henna for the palms and finger-nails. Three-cornered amulets sewn up in velvet, strings of dried bamias for stewing, *jeleks* and *djemadans* richly embroidered with thick orange silk cord, horse-trappings with scarlet tassels, and gay saddle-bags.

Out in the big open spaces, in the glory of golden light, were piled tons of grapes, peaches, melons, pumpkins, gourds, glowing heaps of scarlet and orange tomatoes, shiny paprikas, yellow, green, and red, black purple patajans (aubergines), long green bamias, cabbage, lettuces, beans, in Arabian Nights profusion. Then I heard the East a-calling, and cried in my heart, as I thought of the Powers that crouched like beasts of prey upon the frontier ready to spring and shatter this world: -

"Confound their politics,
Frustrate their knavish tricks."

I remembered the words of an old Albanian, spoken long before Constitution days: "The Turkish Empire is an old house, decayed and crumbling. It is propped within and without, and will stand for who knows how long. But if any one tries to repair it, and moves but one prop - but one brick even - it will fall about his ears. It is too late to repair it." And the peace that reigned in the bazar seemed the hush before the storm.

"Constitution justice" was much discussed. On one of the festival days to celebrate the Constitution, a Moslem zaptieh had made an attempt on a Christian maiden for which he had been condemned to be flogged so severely that he died the next day. Encouraged by this, a Serb zaptieh had then arrested a Moslem for theft, and had been expelled from the town and the service. Serb zaptiehs were only to arrest Christians. A Moslem who had shot a man in Mitrovitza had been hanged at once without trial. This afforded satisfaction to the Christians, until it transpired that the shooting was really a pure accident, then the Moslems were enraged. The Young Turks were suffering from *trop de zèle*.

Next day I was to dine at the Servian Bogoslovia (Theological School) at noon. At 10.30 in rushed Marko, "You will not be able to dine with the Serbs. There is a revolution!" I rushed out to see. The alarm had already been given. In ten minutes every shop was shut and barred, and all the Moslems fully armed were rushing down the street to the Seralio, led by Sherrif Effendi, a very popular Hodja, acclaimed as their head by the Moslems of Prizren and Ljuma.

The armed crowd swung down the street in a pack, like wolves on the trail - a far finer show than the few ragged Nizams that followed. The air was full of rumours. Sherrif was said to be responsible for the expulsion of the Serb zaptieh. He and his were prepared to defend the Sheriat (Turkish law) at any price, and would tolerate no privileges for the Christians. They returned shortly, satisfied that no immediate attempt would be made on it.

The fact that the whole population can turn out under arms within ten minutes gives an idea of the possibilities of the town. Like a couchant tiger, brilliant, bizarre, and beautiful, it is ever ready to spring. Unlike the tiger, it is industrious. Having decided not to revolute further, for the time being, the whole crowd was at work again at the various primitive manufactures of the place, shops reopened, and eating-houses in full swing in another hour's time.

I went off to the Servian Bogoslovia. The Director, his wife, and three children were recently arrived from Belgrade. They received me with the greatest hospitality; were afraid the revolution would prevent my coming. The poor lady, terrified of the Albanians, was amazed to hear that I had been out to see it.

The school, a fine building, recently enlarged and repaired, holds a hundred students. Many come from Montenegro even. I went over it sadly. It seemed sheer folly to make a large and costly Serb theological school in a Moslem Albanian town, and to import masters and students, when funds are so urgently needed to develop free Serb lands.

The white castle of Tsar Lazar was but a dream in the night of the past. Around us in the daylight was the Albanian population, waiting, under arms, to defend the land that had been theirs in the beginning of time.

An old Bariaktar, eighty years of age, in the mountains, had, but a few weeks before, told me how Prince Nikola, flushed with victory, at the close of the war in 1877, had said to him: "You and I will live to see my flag float over Prizren!" "And neither he nor I will ever live to see it," said the old man.

We sat down to a regular Serb dinner, the first I had eaten for more than a year - *kiselo chorba* (sour soup), fried chicken paprika, *kiselo mleko* (sour milk), all excellent of its kind. The Director knew all about me, and regarded me as the champion of the Serbs in England. I accepted his hospitality unhappily, for I felt that, so far as Prizren and its neighbourhood were concerned, the cause was lost, dead and gone - as lost as is Calais to England, and the English claim to Normandy. And the mere terror of his wife showed how completely she felt herself a stranger in an unknown land. Yet I could not but admire the imaginative nature of the Serb, who will lead a forlorn hope and face death for an idea.

And - for I do not know the how manyeth time - I cursed the Berlin Treaty, which did not award to this people the truly Serb lands of Bosnia and Herzegovina, where they could have gathered their scattered forces and developed, but gave them to be crushed under Austria.

I left the poor little Serb quarter - the houses clustered on the hillside around the two churches (for there is an old and a new one), and the school - and found Marko waiting me without. He is the worthiest and kindliest of souls, but race instinct, that strongest of all human passions, prevails - he does not like the Shkia (Slav).

The real policy of Serb and Albanian should be to unite, and keep the foreign intruders from the Balkan Peninsula. But this will never be.

Poor Marko would never admit to me that there were any Serbs in Prizren. "What is that man?" I would ask.

"A native."

"What do you mean by a native?"

"He was born here."

"Yes, but is he a Serb or Albanian?"

"Lady, there are no Serbs here. This is an Albanian town."

Further pressed, he would admit: "Perhaps he belongs to that schismatic Church. I know nothing about his religion." And this, though Serb costume and speech were unmistakable.

Of early Servian days, naught now remains but the ruins said to be those of Tsar Dushan's white tower. I went in search of them up the valley of the Prizrenski Bistritza (called also Kara Potok), along the foot of the hill on which the fortress stands, and through a suburb (Kirch Bonar). We left the town behind us, and followed the lonely valley. Below us, men were collecting stones for building - poking them out of the half-dried bed of the stream with crowbars, and loading them on packhorses, which filed off to the town. The stones, I was told, were thus obtained "ready made," and all trouble of blasting and hewing saved. But the time spent in levering up one stone, and the impossibility of loading up more than about a dozen large ones on a pack-saddle, made the labour and loss of time quite appalling.

About half-an-hour up the valley, it turns suddenly, and the rocky crag on which stand the remains of Dushan's castle comes into view, rising isolated in a ring of mountains, the great Shar Planina rising up behind. Lonely and ruined, only a wall or two and some fragments remain of the white tower of the ballads - as wrecked as his Empire. Here he sat, and drank red wine with his Voyvodas. Hence he rode with a great army to sway the fortunes of the Balkans.

I turned from the desolate 'sic transit' spot, and, returning down the valley, found the women of Prizren on the river bank, bleaching hand-woven linen in the sun, and sprinkling it with fresh spring water, as they have done doubtless since the days of Dushan.

I decided that the best way of seeing Kosovo plain would be to drive over it with a Serb driver, the man that drove us to Devich. Leaving most of my scanty possessions with the *hanjee* till I returned, we left Prizren at 4.20 A. M., in a cold dawn - a lemon-yellow gash above the horizon marking where the sleepy sun would arise, as we drove through a large Moslem graveyard that lay desolate on either hand.

The first village of any size was Korisha, all Christian, consisting partly of Serbs and partly of Roman Catholic Albanians from Fandi. Above it, up a valley on the right, is a large Serb church, Sveti Marko.

On, past scattered groups of houses within stockades, land cultivated with maize and tobacco, across the little river Sofina, and over a low range of hills, we went, and descended to Suha Reka (lit. dry river), a large village which, in spite of its Serb name, is now, according to the Serb driver, all Moslem Albanian. A black and white mass of magpies was feasting on the stinking carcase of a horse at the entrance, and rose screaming as we passed. We crossed the stream (by no means a dry river) on a wooden bridge. Then we ascended again, and drove over a great plateau of scrub-oak. On the left, we passed Pechanj, a Moslem village, and Dulje, consisting of stockaded groups on either side of the road. The road was actually being re-made; men were working on it in three places, and new stone bridges were being built. What was done was really very good; of the rest, the less said the better. We passed over Chafa Duljash, and descended into the beautiful wooded valley of the Crnoleva, and halted for midday at Han Crnoleva, an Albanian house. The place-names, it will be noted, are all Serb. The driver, himself a Serb, said regretfully that everywhere the majority of the population is Albanian.

We descended the valley, rich with beech forests on either side, to Stimlje, a very large village, whence the main road leads to Ferizovich and the railway. There spread out, burnt, and parched before us for miles and miles, was Kosovo Polje, the fatal field on which the Turks gained the victory that established them, even to this day, in Europe - the Armageddon of the Servian people.

"Kosovo Polje," said the Serb briefly. It summed up all the fate of his race. In the spring every year, he added, all the unploughed land is covered with blood-red flowers that grow in memory of the fight; they are sent by God.

We struck across the great plain, uncultivated, desolate, and undulating; the parched turf was split into yawning cracks by the drought, the scrub hawthorn burnt brown, the track dusty, and we reached the Sitnitza, crawling shrivelled between banks of cracked mud - the river that once ran red with the blood of heroes.

"Thy Milosh, O lady, fell by the cold waters of the Sitnitza, where many Turks perished. He left a name to the Servian people that will be sung so long as there are men and Kosovo field," runs the ballad. Over this dreary plain spread the Turkish army, "steed by steed, warrior by warrior; the spears were like unto a black forest; the banners like the clouds, their tents like the snows, had rain fallen from the heavens it would have dropped, not upon the earth, but upon goodly steeds and warriors."

After Sitnitza we passed several stockaded villages - all Moslem - and the earth looked black and fat, but the plain as a whole lacks water. We plodded ceaselessly on through heat and dust, seeming to get no farther. Suddenly there was the iron track of the railway - an impossible anachronism - stretching as far as the eye could see on either hand across our path. "The railway!" I cried. "There is no railway here, lady," said the dozing Marko solemnly. Our *strema* bumped over the rails; he gazed at them: "Dear God!" he cried, and could scarce believe his eyes. We reached Lipanj[17], the station, which was crowded with buffalo-carts loaded with sacks of maize, waiting for the next train to Saloniki. Three trains run up and three run down every week, and none on Sundays. Marko mourned the days when all goods came down on packbeast to Scutari. This rail had killed Scutari, and indeed all the transport trade of North Albania. We left it and all sign of the twentieth century, and reached the borders of the plain - up over low, parched, dusty hills, and at last saw the cupolas of the Monastery of Grachanitza rising from the valley below. We arrived there at 5 P. M.

The imposing red and white church towered above us as we drove through a ramshackle wooden gateway into the monastery grounds, round which stood two old buildings, and one new and unfinished.

The old Stareshina, a jeromonah, and a young djakon, surprised and hospitable, came out to greet me, and we were soon sitting in the monastery balcony opposite the church, whose mellow tones glowed in the afternoon light. My companions had had one foreign visitor before. They thought he was French, but "he could not talk." I could, and their joy was great. They asked of the great world beyond the Turkish

---

[17] Lipjan / Lipljan [editor's note].

frontier; if it were true that there was a railway that went underground, and another that was on the roofs of houses - of electricity and motor cars. And we talked of Great Servia and Kosovo Polje. For from the Monastery of Grachanitza came forth the monks who gave the Communion to all the army of Tsar Lazar before the fatal fight, and the great church is a monument of pre-Turkish days.

It was founded by King Milutin (1275-1321), who planted his victorious standard even on Mount Athos - father of Stefan Dechanski, and grandfather of the great Stefan Dushan, said the Stareshina. Built of large stone blocks, with two courses of narrow red-tile bricks between each horizontal course and one between each upright, the red and white effect is original and beautiful; the wide mouldings are all of brick in patterns; the narrow, round-headed windows have herring-boned brickwork above them; there is a high central dome, and a small one at each of the four corners.

The original building was nearly square, with an apse, but a large narthex was added two hundred years later, which somewhat spoils the appearance of the building, as it is inferior in style.

The interior is frescoed with saints, gaunt and Byzantine, on a ground which is now nearly black. The central dome is borne on four large square piers, on the right hand one of which is King Milutin, and on the left his Queen, sister of a Byzantine Emperor, stiff and gorgeous in their royal robes - the Queen with a huge jewelled gold crown and large round pendants (or ear-rings), recalling those of the Herzegovinian peasant women - the King long-faced, with a pointed beard. One of the piers is hollow, and a steep and narrow staircase inside it leads up to a small chapel in the roof, with a window giving into the church - said to have been made for the royal family to hear Mass from, though how they managed to climb on a stool and squeeze through that door and up the staircase in those royal robes I do not know.

The lower parts of all the frescoes are much damaged, as the Turks used the church as a stable, and until a hundred years ago it was several feet deep with mud and manure. The upper ones are fairly preserved and are said, probably with truth, to be contemporary with the building of the church - at any rate they are pre-Kosovo (1389), and have not suffered restoration.

The tall slits of windows admit little light. The interior is dim, with faded colour and embrowned gold - old-world, barbaric, decorative. Art to be decorative must be barbaric. When it becomes 'civilised' it becomes anaemic, and crawls feebly in pallid mauves and greens, with long spindle stalks that lack vitality to throw out more than one or two atrophied leaves. It has lost red blood and the joy of life.

In the more recent narthex are frescoes of St. Sava and his father St. Simeon, the first of the Nemanja line of Kings that led Servia to glory; it ended with Tsar Dushan. Servia rose with the Nemanjas - and fell with them.

St. Simeon is pictured not as king, but in a grey cloak as monk of Mount Athos, whither he retired. He is hooded, and wears a moustache and a beard in two points. St. Sava, first Bishop of Servia, is in his bishop's robes. Unlike the present Bishops of the Orthodox Church, his head is tonsured, the whole crown shaven, but the locks below left long and curling to the shoulders. He, too, wears moustache and beard. Both have long faces, and the long aquiline nose with the drooping tip so characteristic of the fair Albanian. This is a curious fact, as the paintings are undoubtedly very old, and though not contemporary portraits (St. Sava died in 1237), yet Byzantine art is so extraordinarily conservative that it is possible they are tradition likenesses. For the Nemanja stem sprang from the Zeta (Montenegro, the district where the mingling of Serb and Albanian blood seems most marked). Is it too fanciful to suggest that it was to a dash of Albanian blood that the victorious Nemanjas owed their success and the Montenegrins their independence? The now dwindled and poverty-stricken monastery formerly possessed a printing-press, and printed many church books, a few of which it still preserves.

The three ecclesiasts mourned the past and were hopeless of the future. They, and the young schoolmaster who had joined us, took me out to see the village that adjoins the monastery. It consists of about seventy stockaded 'houses', fifteen of which have recently been taken by Moslem Albanians, the rest all Orthodox Serbs. Many of these 'houses' are *zadrugas* (communal groups). I asked to see one. The Stareshina first shouted to an old woman feeding pigs from a petroleum can to call off the dogs. We entered and were heartily welcomed. The main house, recently built, was fairly smart, with a new tiled roof which projected far in front, and formed a verandah under which we sat. It, like most of the houses where stone is scarce, was a frame-house of mud and wattle. I take this to be one of the earliest types; that of *chepchis* (mud brick) seems a later development.

On the left a house just begun showed the method of construction. The house is merely a large frame of unshaped beams, resting on a base of three courses of unhewn stones. The uprights are roughly mortised into the horizontals. The cross-beams between the main uprights are quite childishly placed, with no science of how to support and strengthen the building. On to this frame are fastened the wattle walls, and the whole is thickly smeared with mud, and smoothly finished. In quite small sheds the uprights are driven straight into the ground, and the wattle wound round them. ...

The old lady wore her black hair in a very thick plait on either side of the face, doubled back so as to make a solid block, which, with a flat drapery on the top of the head, gave an odd, square, Egyptian effect. Her shirt-sleeves were most beautifully embroidered; she wore a little black kilted frill round her waist and a scarlet apron. The daughters-in-law appeared and her one unmarried daughter, who, we were proudly told, was betrothed. They all kissed me heartily, and insisted on making me coffee. Their interest in me was extreme. Never before had they seen a foreigner, and they had not the faintest idea whence I came, for the name of England and the British Empire were unknown to them. But the fact that it would take more than three weeks to ride to my vilayet on a horse was enough for them.

My unmarried condition bothered them horribly. They discussed it eagerly, to the great interests of the churchmen, who were equally curious but too polite to ask. We had arrived at questions which - even in Servian - were most embarrassingly personal and physiological, when luckily one of the pigs got its head jammed in the petroleum can, rushed thus bonneted shrieking through the yard, and diverted the conversation. A number of children came out of the three huts, all unusually clean and neat, well-grown and healthy. They were very markedly broad-headed at the temples, and some were almost blue-eyed. All were learning to read, write, and reckon, and were given very good characters by the schoolmaster.

The land was all worked on the *chiftlik* system, the workers getting three-quarters of the profits, the owner supplying the implements. This seemed to me liberal pay, and I astonished them by saying so. Even the priests were under the impression that it was only under the Turks that the people did not own the land they worked. Their amazement was great when I explained roughly how the agricultural labourer lived with us. The idea of paying rent amazed and shocked them. They regarded working for another as, under any circumstances, '*veliki zalum*' (great tyranny). I asked what was the objection supposing one was well paid. They replied, the master told them to go here and fetch straw, and to go there and sell hay when they did not want to do it - when to-morrow would do as well. Perhaps for a Christian master it might be all right, but it was always very hard to work for another. Their master forced them to work on Sunday.

About the Constitution they were hopeful. Since it had been started they had lived without fear. Previously they had always feared robbery and assault. If the beasts were not shut inside the stockade at night they would certainly be stolen. Only they feared lest Constitution meant that the land would always belong to the Turks. Many people had left the neighbourhood because of the great tyranny and had gone to America. Many others had been shot. There were much fewer Serbs here than formerly.

I very heartily wished good luck to this kindly hard-working family, and left their tidy homestead, when great herds of buffaloes, sheep, and goats were plodding into the village in a blinding cloud of dust which the setting sun turned to a golden glory. I was glad to turn in early that night, for it had been a long day crammed with new experiences. The jeromonah and the serving-man woke me at five next morning by hammering respectively on the slung wooden and iron bar, that served as bells, a rude rhythm.

The coachman had bargained to take us on to Prishtina, provided we left early. So about eight we said adieu. I wrote my name in Servian in the monastery book, and we drove off. It was bitterly cold. Up till yesterday the summer heat had been nearly intolerable. Even driving in the *strema* I had sweated through all my scanty attire. Now autumn had come at a blow, and a most bitter wind swept hill and plain. After barely an hour's drive over two low hills, we saw Prishtina below us, gay with red roofs, green trees, and white minarets. Within, it is frowsy, dirty, tumble-down - a shade better than Djakova, and that is all that can be said.

I marvelled that the Metropolitan should choose to reside here rather than at Prizren.

The population is mixed, and the statistics impossible to obtain, as every one gave different figures. There are about 2500 houses, of which about a quarter are Orthodox. Of these many are Vlahs, not Serbs. There are also a considerable number of Spanish Jews - some said as many as two hundred houses, and there are no Roman Catholics at all. The bulk of the population is Moslem, mostly Albanian; probably also some Moslem Serbs.

The bazar, partly roofed, but the roof all to pieces, was full of foreign rubbish of the cheapest description - one of the benefits brought by the railway. There was a sickening display of diseased meat in the butcher's quarter. The silver-workers here, as elsewhere, were all Christian. Of one - a Vlah from Monastir - I bought a charming little amulet, made of a mole's foot.

We lodged at an inn kept by a Vlah, who, as I was such a rare bird, most kindly invited me to visit his private house. And all his family in their best - the ladies dressed *alla Turka* - received me with great hospitality, and the very strongest *rakia* it has ever been my fate to sample. Marko was quite happy here. The Albanian and the Vlah meet as brothers. "Vlahs have sweet blood," said Marko; "not the Slavs." "Vlah are like us," said an Albanian to me once; "a man will marry his daughter to a Vlah; but a Slav is different - sour through and through."

The Vlah is believed by some to be the descendant of the Roman colonist and original inhabitant. It is possible that both Vlah and Albanian are unconsciously aware that "blood is thicker than water."

According to promise, I called on his Grace, the Servian Metropolitan. And the same night he sent two schoolmasters to invite and escort both Marko and myself to sup with him.

Off we went, and found a large party - the Metropolitan, his secretary the Archimandrite, and all the schoolmistresses who had been at Devich. The Metropolitan, in the highest spirits and most festive, received us with bottled beer, jam, and water. The whole party had only just recovered from the results of Devich. The schoolmistresses had all been violently sick, or had bad colds, and the Metropolitan completely knocked up. I was the only one who had got off scot-free. When the beer was done we adjourned to the supper-room. I was placed at the right of the Metropolitan. The Archimandrite, a most kindly man, took Marko under his wing. He spoke a little German, and, trying to be very friendly, said: "Ach, my dear Marko! You are an Albanian, and you have come to see our Old Servia. Ach, but that is very beautiful!"

Poor Marko was paralysed with horror. To the genuine Albanian the mere name Old Servia is as 'a red rag to a bull.'

We had a grand 'spread.' The Metropolitan insisted that, *alla franga*, it was correct to begin with a *hors d'oeuvre*. There ensued a great search in the dining-room cupboard, and the Metropolitan discussed which of many mysterious tins should be opened. His final selection turned out to be potted ham. We emptied the tin, and then started on a vast dinner of five courses, all good and extremely 'filling,' washed down with some good Servian white wine. And the Metropolitan enlivened the meal with humorous tales. It was late before I turned in at the *han*.

On the plain, just below Prishtina, on that fatal June day of 1389, fell Sultan Murad, slain by that best-beloved of Servian heroes, Milosh Obilich.

I drove down over the plain to Sultan Murad's tomb, passing, on the hill above, the turba of his standard-bearer, buried on the spot where he fell.

Murad's turba - or, rather, small mosque - stands in a walled-in ground, containing several graves, with a guardian's house at the entrance.

Rather to my surprise, I was at once admitted, and even invited to walk in with my boots on. Everything was changed now since 'Constitution'. If a female Giaour could come without escort to Kosovo Polje, God alone knew what would happen next. Nor did any one seem to mind.

As there were two Turks praying in the building, I refrained from desecrating it with Giaour boots ('Constitution' - if it is to mean anything - requiring, at any rate, respect for everybody's beliefs), and stood in the doorway.

In the centre, on a very fine Turkey carpet, stands the large coffin, covered with black cloth, and over it several coloured silk draperies - one, of crimson and silver, very handsome. At the head of the coffin is a great white turban of the old pattern, covered with a dark green and silver scarf. The decorations of the room are appalling. The walls are stencilled in crude colours to look like the cheapest wall-paper. Shiny *alla franga* wooden curtain-poles and red curtains of the lodging-house type adorn the windows; and over the coffin hangs a large glass chandelier.

The whole place had recently, said the guardian, been beautified. I stared at the hopeless incongruity of the adornment.

The nation that had done this had just dressed itself up in an imitation *alla franga* Constitution. Would it be any more suitable? I though of the Daw in borrowed plumes, the Wolf in sheep's clothing, and of the Old, old Man who "madly thrust a left-hand foot into a right-hand shoe."

It was bitterly cold; an icy wind swept the plain. I left the spot on which the Turk had established himself in Europe and wondered whether the fact that he proposed now to take a new lease of life and remain was one to rejoice over.

I myself was the first visible sign of 'Constitution' from the outer world, and, as such, of interest to the populace; so a Turkish officer travelling through Prishtina - an Ottoman Turk (not Moslem Slav or Albanian) - most kindly insisted on my visiting his family - temporarily established in a Moslem house - while Marko was entertained by officers below, in which company I too should have felt more at home. I was taken upstairs and shot into an apartment full of stout, pallid, collopy females, and a heap of children. There were nine women. I never discovered which belonged to whom. Door and windows were tightly shut; a *mangal* of hot charcoal burnt in the midst. The atmosphere was monkey-house.

Two of the women spoke Serb fluently, so I was thoroughly and effectively interviewed amid shrieks of laughter. The idea of an unmarried woman travelling with a man was new to them, and their conversation quite unprintable. They all sat on the floor smoking and eating oddments - roasted maize-cobs, bits of melon, sticky lumps of rahat-lakum, sugar-sticks. These people nibble all day. The floor was messy with seeds and bits. Heaps of soiled, crumpled garments were strewn around. Every one was touzled and dressed, half or wholly, *alla franga*, but wore their European clothes in Oriental manner - unbuttoned, crumpled, torn, and impossible. One, in European *dishabille*, had hitched up her white petticoats for greater convenience in squatting cross-legged. She was a handsome young woman, but her appearance with dangling pink stocking suspenders, of which she was very proud, and unbuttoned bodice, was unlovely.

The oldest lady had almost scarlet hair. Another, not so successful, had come out streaky, and, as the natural colour of her hair was black, the effect was comically tigerish. The eyebrows of all were painted black as broad as the finger, and joined in the middle, and their toe- as well as finger-nails were red with henna. All looked most unwholesome, and one had a row of burst glands oozing down the side of her neck. Only one was an effective colour arrangement. She was partly *alla Turka*, had scarlet hair with an orange handkerchief on it, and a striped white and yellow shirt. But she was as broad as she was long - and bulgy.

Being kept mainly for breeding purposes, their conversation was much like what that of a cow might be, could it talk. They were most friendly, plied me with coffee and pieces of all the eatables, and pressed me to stay the night - there was plenty of room for another - or come to-morrow. And I tore myself away with difficulty.

I give the above details because I invariably find that gentlemen of all nations are consumed with curiosity about the secrets of the harem. I thought of the bright, tidy Vlah women, of the civilised Serbs, of the poor Catholic women in Djakova, their clean rooms and intelligent questions; and I asked myself if they were not after all right when they said, "The Young Turk is the son of the Old Turk." Islam has, so far, done nothing but evil in Europe.

Having come so far, I decided to go on to Mitrovitza by rail to save time, and learnt the day, but not the hour, at which the one train ran - only that the station was a very long way off; that I must start early, and that if I went with some others who were going it would be all right. We got seats in a carriage with another man, a Moslem Slav. I was eating soup, not knowing when I should again see food, when the carriage arrived, and, urgently requested, left it, jumped into the carriage, and off we went over the hills at a hand-gallop in company with three other carriages - one filled with young men with tambourines and a fiddle, who played and sang loudly all the way; for a railway journey in these parts is a great event.

We arrived at 10.30 A. M. to learn that the train - which was generally late - was not even due till 12.30. "God be praised!" cried every one; "we are in time!" There were plenty of people already there - buffalo-carts - baggage - a regular hurly-burly, and a man had already lighted a fire on the platform and was cooking kebabs and vegetables for such as desired refreshment. Even Marko was surprised that I thought we were too early, and looked on a railway journey as "not by any to be enterprised nor taken in hand unadvisedly, lightly, or wantonly." The inspection, however, of *teskerehs* and the entering of the name (especially mine) and destination of each of us into the police book whiled away much time.

Moslem women, as fast as they arrived, were hastily driven into a separate waiting-room with opaque windows. I talked to our Moslem travelling companion, a native of Prishtina. There were very many more people than usual travelling, he said, because it was safe. Till now the railway had been of little use. It was three-quarters of an hour from the town, and the road was too dangerous - could never be ventured on unarmed; as for the plain, till now it had been most dangerous. "Look at me," he said, tapping his sash. "This is the first time in my life I have ever come out so far without a revolver. I have no weapon at all, and am not afraid."

I asked if it had been as dangerous for Moslems as Christians, and he replied that robbers did not mind what you were as long as you were worth robbing. He was so astonished at the present calm that he knew not what to make of it. It was "like a dream, and could not last." A female Giaour from abroad (myself) had crossed the plain without escort - after that, anything amazing might happen. He himself wanted peace and a good government.

The train was punctual. Its smooth motion after the jolting *strema* made Marko cry delightedly, "It is like swimming in oil!" I went third-class, and luckily travelled with a Spanish Jew and his wife, so sampled all the mixed races of Prishtina.

He, a splendid old man of seventy years with a patriarchal beard, was saying farewell for ever to Prishtina, for he meant to die in Jerusalem, whither he was now bound. His poor wife wept most bitterly at parting with her relations, who clung to the carriage door till the train started. He looked on stoically, moved only by the elemental passion - earth-hunger, the desire of a man for the land of his forebears. With all their worldly goods contained in a large basket and a sack, the aged couple were going to Sarajevo, where he would say good-bye to his old brother - and then to Jerusalem. I trust he has found peace in the Promised Land of his dreams.

The train ran through fertile land, cultivated fairly well, passing only one town, or rather village, of any size, Vuchitrn (wolf's thorn) - said to be largely Serb.

Mitrovitza, on rising ground at the very end of Kosovo plain, is small, but cleaner and less hopeless-looking than Prishtina. It is a new town made mainly since the railway; and, as it is on the junction of the Sitnitza and the Ibar, had a good and ample water supply, and fine vegetable gardens.

I strolled through the bazar, and was promptly hailed by a silversmith. "That foreign woman. Where does she come from?" "From London." "From London! Do you know my brother-in-law, X?" "I do." The world is very small. I had found a friend in a far country. We drank coffee, and I departed laden with messages for his people.

There are but ten Roman Catholic families in Mitrovitza, and one priest. The number of Orthodox I failed to learn; they are building a large new church. The large majority of the town are Moslems, who were not going to make census returns though ordered by 'Constitution' - the news having just come in that Ipek and Djakova had flatly refused; and that certain villages which had made a return had made a false one to dodge possible conscription.

We found quarters at the *han* of a friendly little Vlah, who said that he woke up every day surprised to still find peace. "We were living like snakes in holes, and now here we are out in the sun!" And we fed at a restaurant newly opened by some Italians from Fiume, who had hurried to be first on the spot when Baron Aehrenthal announced that the railway from Mitrovitza to Uvatz was about to be made - the railway which was to be the last link in the chain, and to convey Austrian troops to Saloniki. The plans for Austrian advance had for the time being been completely upset by that 'bolt from the blue,' Constitution. But Mitrovitza, though it looked so peaceful, is tinder waiting for a spark.

Here we come to the crucial race question.

Exact figures are unattainable, but of the general facts there can be no doubt. Kosovo plain is now, by a very large majority, Moslem Albanian. What proportion of Slav blood there may be (one should perhaps say, is) in these Albanians is of purely ethnographical interest and politically of no importance. Albanian predominance is proved by the fact that - so far as my experience goes, and I tried repeatedly - the Albanians are almost solely Albanophone, whereas the scattered Serbs usually speak both languages, and when addressed in Serb often replied at first in Albanian. Were it not for the support and instruction that has for long been supplied from without it is probable that the Serb element would have been almost, if not quite, absorbed or suppressed by this time. It has been an elemental struggle for existence and survival of the strongest, carried out in relentless obedience to Nature's law, which says, "There is not place for you both. You must kill - or be killed." Ineradicably fixed in the breast of the Albanian - of the primitive man of the mountain and of the plain - is the belief that the land has been his rightly for all time. The Serb conquered him, held him for a few passing centuries, was swept out and shall never return again. He has but done to the Serb as he was done by.

The celebrated Canon of Tsar Stefan Dushan throws light on the means employed to crush the conquered, when Great Servia was at its greatest. "Tsar Dushan, the Macedonian, Autocrat of Servia, Bulgaria, Hungary, Wallachia, and other countries... Laws established by the grace of God in the year 1349 at a meeting of the Patriarchs, etc.

Law 6. As to the Latin heresy, and those that draw true believers to its faith. The ecclesiastical authorities must strive to convert such to the true faith. If such a one will not be converted... he shall be punished by death. The Orthodox Tsar must eradicate all heresy from his state. The property of all such as refuse conversion shall be confiscated... Heretical priests of other communions who try to make proselytes will be sent to the mines or expelled from the country. Heretical churches will be consecrated and opened for priests of the Orthodox faith.

Law 8. If a Latin priest be found trying to convert a Christian to the Latin faith he shall be punished by death.

Law 10. If a heretic be found dwelling with Christians, he shall be marked on the face and expelled. Any sheltering him shall be treated the same way."

It appears also that certain pagan rites were still observed. Law 45 enacts that: "If there be heretics that burn the bodies of the dead, or dig them up for the purpose of burning them, the village where this takes place is to pay a fine, and the criminals be handed over to justice."

The fact that the whole 'village' is fined (just as the whole 'house' is excommunicated to-day, for the sin of concubinage with a sister-in-law), indicates that the whole village, if not wholly pagan, had pagan sympathies.

These laws imply no worse religious persecution than the whole of Europe has enjoyed at various times. On other subjects Dushan's laws are often good, and even in advance of their time.

But history shows that the Latins in the districts we are considering must have been mainly Albanians. Persecution was therefore not merely religious but racial. And that special legislation was needed against the Latins, and the express mention of what is to be done with their churches, tends to show that even in the strongest Servian days they were numerous enough to have to be reckoned with as a danger. The Serb strove to stamp out - or, shall we say, Slavise - the Albanian. The Albanian, circumstances being changed, has done as he was done by. He has employed mediaeval methods, for this is the land of the Living Past, and he has forced back the Serb tide. Kosovo Polje is Albanian.

Its borders, however, are still largely Serb. Roughly speaking, the territory between the railway and the Servian frontier is Serb. It at any rate has a large Servian majority, but there is a remarkable Catholic island in and around Janjitza, not far from the monastery of Grachanitza. In this district were silver mines worked, it is said, with much success, from the beginning of the thirteenth century. The present Catholic inhabitants are reported to be the descendants of the Italian colony settled there as miners. They now call themselves Albanian. I do not know enough of the district to offer an opinion on the subject. But it is an odd fact that, before hearing this tradition, I met a man whom I took, beyond doubt, to be an Italian, and he proved to be a Janjitza man.

From Mitrovitza to the Servian frontier is also mainly Servian, though the town and environs of Novi-bazar is largely Albanian. Beyond Novi-bazar the *sanjak* is practically solid Serb, Moslem, and Christian - no other race has any justifiable claim to it.

The Albanian has swept the centre of Kosovo vilayet. The Serbs are thick only along the Servian frontier and near the Montenegrin frontier, especially around Berana and Ipek. East of Prizren they begin to predominate. The land becomes more and more Slavonic. At which point Serbs turn into Bulgars is beyond the scope of this book. It is, I think, the fashion to draw the line too far westward.

Mitrovitza may be called a 'frontier' town. Albanians and Serbs alike claim it jealously. Austria (to gain her private ends) wins Albanian support by promising that never, never will she allow the *sanjak* to become Serb.

The town looked so peaceful that it was hard to believe that but six years ago it had been the scene of fierce fighting, in which Shtcherbina, the Russian Consul forced into the place in the teeth of Albanian opposition, was killed. Of his gallantry on behalf of the Slav interests that he was sent to protect there can be no question, nor of the indiscretion, alas! with which he set to work. Austria at once planted a consul to watch her own interests; and there the two most interested Powers watch to this day.

Just outside the town is a relic of the Serb empire - the fine ruins of the castle of Zvechana. Here, in 1336, was strangled King Stefan Dechanski, son of Milutin, the founder of Grachanitza. Stefan was Milutin's eldest son, but the young Byzantine Princess, his second wife, bore him another son and plotted to make him heir. In a fight that ensued Stefan was taken prisoner, and his stepmother prevailed upon his father to cast him into prison, where, to make matters sure, she ordered him to be blinded with red-hot irons. When freed after many years, behold he was not blind at all! The tale spread that he had been miraculously cured. He came to the throne with a great reputation for piety, and was the builder of many churches, notably the very beautiful white and pink marble church of Dechani - a thank-offering for the subjugation of the Bulgarians, whom he defeated in 1330.

His death is said by some to have been brought about by his son and heir, the great Stefan Dushan, but the patriotic Serb denies this. He was canonised as St. Stefan Dechanski, and his wonder-working shrine, pictured with his strangulation, draws many pious pilgrims still to the marble church of Dechani. Moslem and Catholic are in awe of it. Even the wild Catholic tribesmen of Nikaj tramp thither for the little round loaves of holy bread there distributed, and consider 'By the bread of Dechani' a binding oath.

Mitrovitza has little else to show. To leave it, I had to have my *teskereh* stamped. The official at the *konak*, in order to make a good job of it, licked the stamp three times and licked off all the gum. As it would not stick, he licked it four more times. As it still would not, he put it in his mouth and sucked it patiently. It then showed signs of melting altogether, so he called a colleague to advise. He suggested the gum-pot. They searched for it high and low, and called in a third official - luckily that day there was no press of business in that department. The gum was found and the stamp stuck. It took half-an-hour, but was thoroughly done in the end. And we left by rail for Ferizovich, where we arrived at 10.15 A. M. A Serb fellow-passenger pointed out, on the right of the line just before Prishtina, the hill to which Vuk Brankovich, Tsar Lazar's traitorous son-in-law, withdrew with his men and gave the victory to the Turk. "What askest thou of Vuk the accursed! Curséd be he, and curst be he that begat him. Curséd be his stem and his seed. He betrayed his Tsar at Kosovo. He deserted with twelve thousand men."

Ferizovich, till lately, had been of importance merely as a railway station. Now it is of historic interest as being the spot upon which the casting vote was thrown - the spot from which the voice came, "Let there be a Constitution." And there was a Constitution, and all Europe was shaken.

"Constantinople is the key of the Near East; Albania is the key of Constantinople," say the Albanians. European plans for tinkering and 'reforming' the Turkish empire have all ignored the Albanian, his rights, and his aspirations - and they have all failed. Outsiders might make this mistake. Those within the empire knew that, as far as Turkey in Europe is concerned, the side that could enlist the Albanians, solid, must "come out top."

The Young Turks' secret was well kept; but it would appear that certain Old Turks suspected something was brewing. One of these, Shemsi Pasha, sent mounted messengers through the Moslem tribes, summoning them at once to repel the attack of an expected enemy. One of the many men from whom I heard the tale persisted that the advance-guard of the Austrian army, forty battalions, ready on the frontier, had actually been seen, and that Austrian annexation had been imminent. The tribesmen flew to arms and hurried - some nine thousand strong - to the appointed spot, Ferizovich, where they were to receive orders. And there they fired on a train - reported to contain "enemies."

But Shemsi Pasha was "a day behind the fair." The Young Turks outwitted him. They shot him at Monastir; skilfully took advantage of the fact that the tribesmen were at Ferizovich; called on them to save the country, and explained that something called Constitution was the only way by which it could be done. The fierce, ignorant tribesmen, jealous only of their privileges and territorial rights, and absolutely unaware that this was not the job for which they had been originally summoned, loudly and unanimously demanded this unknown amulet, 'Constitution,' that was to keep their land intact, and save the Padishah.

The Sultan heard that the Moslem tribesmen - the men upon whom, above all others, he had always reckoned - were with the army. The game was up; he succumbed at once, and the Constitution was granted. That the main outline of this tale, which I found widely spread and believed, is correct, I believe is beyond all reasonable doubt. The tribes were tricked, and many folk had already found this out when I arrived in Djakova.

Such freedom as they had retained under the Old Turk, they did not mean to be swindled out of by the Young.

We arrived at Prizren to find it smiling sardonically. Four Frenchmen had come to report on 'the Constitution' - had come and gone.

"What did they see here?" I asked. "Nothing. They only dined, and left next morning for Djakova. One is in the Diplomatic Service, so of course they will not be allowed to see anything. The Young Turks have arranged it all. An escort of twenty-four suvarris, as a guard of honour, is with them, to prevent them talking to the wrong people, and a suvarri has been sent ahead to prepare a deputation of 'Christians rejoicing under the Constitution,' in case they wish to make inquiries. The escort will 'protect' them all the way. They will think they have done something very brave, and will report most favourably in the French newpapers." And they did.

[Taken from: Edith Durham, *High Albania* (London 1909, reprint Virago Press, London 1985), p. 232-300]

Albania's Golgotha

Indictment of the Exterminators of the Albanian People

(1913)

Leo Freundlich

On the eastern banks of the Adriatic, a mere three days journey from Vienna, live an autochthonous people who for centuries have been fighting for their freedom and independence against enemies and oppressors of all types. This nation has clung steadfast to its roots through countless wars and the cataclysms of history. Neither the great migrations nor wars with the Serbs, the Turks and other invaders have hindered the Albanians from maintaining their nationality, their language, and the purity and originality of their customs.

The history of this nation is an unbroken chain of bloody battles against violent oppressors, but not even the most unspeakable of atrocities have managed to annihilate this people. Intellectual life has flourished among the Albanians even though their oppressors endeavoured to cut off all cultural development at the root. This nation produced great generals and men of state for the Ottoman Empire. Albanians were among the best judges in Turkey and among the greatest authors of Turkish literature. Almost all the merchants of Montenegro were Albanian, as were many fine businessmen in the major cities of

Romania. The Albanians played an important role in Italy, too. Crispi was one of them. Greece's bravest soldiers were of Albanian blood.

In the wake of the cataclysms wrought by the Balkan War, the ancient dream of freedom and independence for this people is now becoming a reality. The Great Powers of Europe have decided to grant Albania its national autonomy.

But the Serbian thirst for conquest has now found a means of destroying the fair dream of this courageous and freedom-loving people before it can be realized. Serbian troops have invaded Albania with fire and sword. And if Albania cannot be conquered, then at least the Albanian people can be exterminated. This is the solution they propose.

* * *

On 18 October 1912, King Peter of Serbia issued a declaration 'To the Serbian People', proclaiming:

> "The Turkish governments showed no interest in their duties towards their citizens and turned a deaf ear to all complaints and suggestions. Things got so far out of hand that no one was satisfied with the situation in Turkey in Europe. It became unbearable for the Serbs, the Greeks and for the Albanians, too.
>
> By the grace of God, I have therefore ordered my brave army to join in the Holy War to free our brethren and to ensure a better future.
>
> In Old Serbia, my army will meet not only upon Christian Serbs, but also upon Moslem Serbs, who are equally dear to us, and in addition to them, upon Christian and Moslem Albanians with whom our people have shared joy and sorrow for thirteen centuries now. To all of them we bring freedom, brotherhood and equality."

How have the Serbs understood the declaration of their monarch, which is not even half a year old?

The thousand and thousands of men, women, children and old people who have been slain or tortured to death, the villages marauded and burnt to the ground, the women and young girls who have been raped, and the countryside plundered, ravaged and swimming in blood can give no answer to this question.

The Serbs came to Albania not as liberators but as exterminators of the Albanian people. The Ambassadors' Conference in London proposed drawing the borders of Albania according to ethnic and religious statistics to be gathered on site by a commission. The Serbs have hastened to prepare the statistics for them with machine guns, rifles and bayonettes. They have committed unspeakable atrocities. The shock and outrage produced by these crimes are outdone only by the sense of sorrow that such vile deeds could be committed in Europe, not far from the great centres of western culture, in this twentieth century. Our sorrow is made all the heavier by the fact that, despite the reports which have been cabled home for months now by the journalists of many nations, and despite the impassioned indictment launched to the world by Pierre Loti, nothing has been done to put an end to the killings.

A courageous people full of character is being crucified before the eyes of the world and Europe, civilized Christian Europe, remains silent!

Tens of thousands of defenceless people are being massacred, women are being raped, old people and children strangled, hundreds of villages burnt to the ground, priests slaughtered.

And Europe remains silent!

Serbia and Montenegro have set out to conquer a foreign country. But in that land live a freedom-loving, brave people who despite centuries of servitude have not yet become accustomed to bearing a foreign yoke. The solution is obvious. The Albanians must be exterminated!

A crazed and savage *soldateska* has turned this solution into a gruesome reality.

Countless villages have been razed to the ground, countless individuals have been butchered. Where once the humble cottages of poor Albanians stood, there is nothing left but smoke and ashes. A whole people is perishing on Calvary cross, and Europe remains silent!

* * *

The aim of this work is to rouse the conscience of European public opinion. The reports gathered here are but a small portion of the material available. More than what they contain is already known by the governments of Europe from official consular and press reports.

Up to now, however, the governments have chosen to remain silent. Now, any further silence means complicity.

The Great Powers must tell the crazed barbarians once and for all to keep their 'Hands off!' This wave of extermination must be ended with all possible rapidity. An international commission must be set up to investigate accusations made against the Serbian government.

Most important of all, Serbian and Montenegrin troops must withdraw from Albanian territory at once and the Greek blockade, which has cut the country off from all food supplies, must be lifted.

I call upon the governments of the Great Powers, I call upon European public opinion in the name of humanity, in the name of civilization, in the name of the wretched Albanian people.

I turn to the British public, to the nation which raised its voice so virtuously to protest against the Armenian massacres.

I direct my appeal to the French public which has shown so often that it will defend humanity and human rights.

A poor nation, suffering a horrible fate, appeals from the cross for help. Will Europe hear its call?

Leo Freundlich
Vienna, Easter Sunday 1913

The Albanians must be exterminated!

In connection with the news report that 300 unarmed Albanians of the Luma tribe were executed in Prizren without trial, the *Frankfurter Zeitung* writes: In the case in question, it seems to have been regular Serbian troops who committed the massacre. But there is no doubt whatsoever that even the heineous massacres committed by irregulars were carried out with the tacit approval and in full compliance with the will of the Serbian authorities." At the beginning of the war we ourselves were told quite openly by a Serbian official: "We are going to wipe out the Albanians." Despite European protests, this systematic policy of extermination is continuing unhindered. As a result, we regard it as our duty to expose the intentions of the Serbian rulers. The gentlemen in Belgrade will then indignantly deny everything, knowing full well that journalistic propriety prevents us from mentioning names.

It is evident that we would not make such a report if we were not fully convinced of its truth. In the case in question, the facts speak louder than any full confession could do. One massacre after another has been committed since Serbian troops crossed the border last autumn and occupied the land inhabited by the Albanians.

A war of extermination

Professor Schiemann published an article in *Kreuzzeitung*, writing: "Despite the rigorous censorship of Balkan allies and the pressure exerted upon war correspondents, private letters which have managed to reach us from the region in which the Serbs and Greeks are conducting their war offer an exceptionally sorry picture." The Serbs, as the article notes, are conducting a war of extermination against the Albanian nation which, if they could, they would eradicate completely.

The *Daily Chronicle* reported on 12 November 1912 that it was true that thousands of Arnauts (Albanians) had been massacred by the Serbs. 2,000 Moslem Arnauts were slaughtered near Skopje and a further 5,000 near Prizren. Many villages have been set on fire and their inhabitants slaughtered. Albanian householders were simply slain during house to house searches for arms, even when no weapons were found. The Serbs declared quite openly that the Moslem Albanians were to be exterminated because this was the only way of pacifying the country.

The war correspondent of the *Messaggero* of Rome reported heineous Serbian massacres of Albanians in the *vilayet* of Kosovo. After Albanian resistance, the towns of Ferizaj / Uroševac, Negotin / Negotino, Lipjan / Ljipljan, Babush / Babuš and others were completely destroyed and most of the inhabitants slaughtered. A Catholic priest reported that fierce fighting around Ferizaj / Uroševac had lasted for three days. After the town was taken, the Serbian commander ordered its fleeing inhabitants to return peacefully and lay down their arms. When they returned, three or four hundred people were massacred. There remained only half a dozen Moslem families in all of Ferizaj / Uroševac. Destitute Serbian families hastened to take possession of the homes of the wealthy families.

The *Humanité* of Paris published an official report submitted to a consulate in Salonika. The report described the activities of the Serbs in Albania: plundering, destruction, massacres. The number of Albanian villages totally or partially but systematically destroyed by the Serbs was estimated at thirty-one. The Kristos of Kumanova / Kumanovo, the Siro Diljovs of Skopje, the Alexandrovos of Štip and other leading guerrilla bands looted all the villages in the districts of Kratovo and Kočani, set them on fire and killed all the Moslem inhabitants. All the Moslems of Zhujova / Žujovo and Mešeli were slaughtered, as were a further two hundred people in Vetreni. In Bogdanc / Bogdanci, sixty Turks were locked in a mosque. They were then let out and slain, one by one. Thirty-four of the ninety-eight villages in the district of Kavadarci have been destroyed. The Turks, some of whom had made payoffs to one guerrilla band hoping to save their lives, were then butchered by another band of guerrillas. All the inhabitants of Drenova / Drenovo were put to death. Between this village and Palikura, a number of graves were found with the heads sticking out of the earth. These are the graves of wretched individuals who were buried alive!

Manhunts

Fritz Magnussen, war correspondent for the Danish newspaper *Riget*, who is generally known for his pro-Serbian sympathies, described the crimes committed by the Serbs against the Arnaut population in a telegramme that he had to send by special courier from Skopje to Zemun to avoid the rigorous censorship:

> Serbian military activities in Macedonia have taken on the character of an extermination of the Arnaut population. The army is conducting an unspeakable war of atrocities. According to officers and soldiers, 3,000 Arnauts were slaughtered in the region between Kumanova / Kumanovo and Skopje and 5,000 near Prishtina. The Arnaut villages were surrounded and set on fire. The inhabitants were then chased from their homes and shot like rats. The Serbian soldiers delighted in telling me of the manhunts they had conducted.

> The situation in Skopje is equally appalling. Rigorous searches of Arnaut homes are carried out and if anything vaguely resembling a weapon is discovered, the inhabitants are shot on the spot. It is very dangerous to travel the roads because of the constant shooting in and out of the houses.

> Yesterday, 36 Arnauts were sentenced to death by a military tribunal and shot on the spot. No day passes without Arnauts being put to death in the most barbarous manner. The river upstream is full of corpses. Hunting expeditions take place every day in the surrounding villages. Yesterday, a Serbian officer invited me to take part in such a hunt and boasted that he had put nine Arnauts to death the previous day with his own hands!

The *Reichspost* received a dossier about the massacres committed by Serbian guerrilla bands and regular troops in Albania from a person whose name and high rank is guarantee enough of the authenticity of the reports it contains. In the dossier we find the following information:

The city of Skopje and the surrounding district have been witness to inhuman crimes committed against the Albanians. For days on end, I saw manhunts conducted by armed Serbian bands and regular troops. For three days I could see the flames of burning villages in the sky. When the horrors were over, five villages in the direct vicinity of Skopje lay in ruins and their inhabitants were almost all slain, even though the Albanians offered no armed resistance to the invading Serbs. Behind the fortress of Skopje is a ravine which is still filled with the corpses of over one hundred victims of this campaign. Eighty Albanian bodies are also to be found in the ravine of Vodno / Vistala Voda near Skopje. Shortly after the invasion, a reliable informant of mine, whom I spoke to myself, visited the hospital in Skopje and encountered during this first visit 132 Albanians patients. The next day he could find only 80 and a few days later a mere 30 of them. The treatment meted out to these wounded Albanians is beyond imagination. They were refused food and drink, such that, according to witnesses, some of them died of starvation. Many of the patients, it is alleged, were still alive when they were thrown into the Vardar. The river flows through the town and is carrying with it twenty to thirty corpses a day. There were a number of Serbian volunteers quartered in my hotel in Skopje who boasted quite candidly of their marauding and manhunts, in particular when the wine got their tongues. One evening, they went out onto the street and shot a couple of unarmed Albanians who were simply passing by and minding their own business. The two murderers, who thereafter returned to the hotel and got drunk, were not bothered by the military authorities at all, even though everyone in town knew that they were guilty of the crime. A bloody scene also occurred in town at the Vardar bridge. Three Albanians who tried to cross into town to go to market were attacked by Serbian soldiers and simply murdered without trial. Digging graves seemed to be a problem for the soldiers, in particular since the earth is frozen over, so bodies have been thrown into wells. An informant counted 38 wells around Skopje which have been filled with Albanian corpses. Bandits play an important role in the pogroms, too. I myself was witness to a Serbian soldier who was showing off the two watches and 150 Turkish pounds he had taken as booty. When he saw a well-dressed Albanian pass by, he shouted in an almost genuine show of sympathy, "Pity there are so many of them. Otherwise, I would gladly spend a bullet on him." The Albanians are considered fair game and are protected by no law or court. Many of the excesses are, however, committed under the influence of drink. The most outrageous crimes were, indeed, committed by bands of drunken soldiers breaking into homes.

As I speak Serbian fluently, many Serbian officers and soldiers regarded me as one of theirs. And so it was that a Serbian soldier boasted to me of their attack on an Albanian village near Kumanova / Kumanovo. "Many of the villagers who were not able to flee, hid in their attics. We smoked them out, and when their houses were in flames, they came out of their hiding places like moles, screaming, cursing and begging for mercy. We shot them at the doorways, sparing our bullets only with the children on whom we used our bayonettes. We destroyed the whole village because shots had been fired out of one of the houses bearing a white flag." The military authorities did nothing to hinder these bloodbaths and many officers took part in the atrocities themselves. There was no Serb to be found who had not acted in the full conviction that, with these atrocities, he was doing his country a great service, and one which his superiors wanted of him.

* * *

Eighty-five Albanians were slain in their homes in Tetova / Tetovo and the town was looted without sign of an armed uprising beforehand. The heineous deeds committed against the women and girls, including twelve-year-old children, are indescribable. To top off such horrors, the fathers and husbands of the victims were forced by revolver to hold candles and be witness themselves to the outrages committed against their daughters and wives in their own homes. The town of Gostivar was only saved by paying off the Serbian commander with a sum of 200 Turkish pounds. Here only six Albanians were shot.

In Ferizaj / Uroševac, as opposed to the above-mentioned towns, the Albanians offered organized armed resistance. Fighting continued here for twenty-four hours, during which a woman whose husband had been slain seized a rifle and shot five Serbs before she was killed herself. Over 1,200 Albanians fell victim to the carnage in Ferizaj / Uroševac. The town is almost devoid of inhabitants now. There are only three Moslem Albanians over the age of fifteen left. In Gjilan / Gnjilane, too, where the Albanians put up no defence, almost all the inhabitants were killed by fire and sword. A very small number of fugitives survived the carnage. Now only ruins are left as witness to the destruction of Gjilan / Gnjilane.

The Serbian occupation of Prishtina was even bloodier. The Albanians estimate the number of their dead at 5,000. In all fairness, it must be noted that the flag on the parliament building was severely misused. After the white flag had been hoisted, Turkish officers suddenly opened fire on Serbian troops, apparently with the intention of thwarting the latters' ceasefire negotiations with the Albanians. Hundreds of Albanian families, even babies in their cradles, paid for this deed with their lives.

In Leskovac near Ferizaj / Uroševac, eight unarmed Albanians were stopped by Serbian soldiers and shot on the spot.

* * *

The town of Prizren offered no resistance to Serb forces, but this did not avert a bloodbath there. After Prishtina, Prizren was the hardest hit of the Albanian towns. The local population call it the 'Kingdom of Death'. Here the Serbian bands did their worst. They forced their way into homes and beat up anyone and everyone in their way, irrespective of age or sex. Corpses lined the streets for days while the Serbian victors were busy with other atrocities, and the native population which had survived did not dare to venture out of their homes. The attacks continued night after night throughout the town and region. Up to 400 people perished in the first few days of the Serbian occupation. Despite this, the commander, General Janković, with rifle in hand, forced notables and local tribal leaders to sign a declaration of gratitude to King Peter for their 'liberation by the Serbian army.' As Serbian troops were about to set off westwards, they could not find any horses to transport their equipment. They therefore requisitioned 200 Albanians, forcing them to carry goods weighing up to 50-60 kilos for seven hours during the night along bad roads in the direction of Luma. Seeing that the wretched group of bearers had managed to reach their goal, though most of them collapsed under the inhumane treatment they had suffered, the Serbian commander expressed his satisfaction and approval of the action.

A Fani woman called Dila took the road to Prizren with her sons, another relative and two men from the village of Gjugja in order to buy goods for her daughter's dowry. Before reaching Prizren, she applied for a laisser passer for herself and her companions from the command post of General Janković in order to proceed unimpeded. She was given the passes. When the group of five arrived in Suni, about four hours from Prizren, they were robbed of their possessions and the four men were tied up and thrown into a pit. Soldiers then shot the men from the edge of the pit. The mother, who had witnessed this scene, called out in desparation to her son. Seeing that he was no longer alive, she threw herself to the feet of the soldiers, begging them to kill her, too. They had tied her to a tree by the time some officers came by, having heard the shooting. The soldiers showed the officers a loaf of bread they had seized from the women, in which they had pressed two Mauser bullets as proof that the men had been trying to smuggle ammunition. The officers thereupon ordered the soldiers to go their way. The poor woman remained tied to the tree at the edge of the pit, in full view of her slain son, from Monday afternoon until Wednesday. On Wednesday, starving and exhausted by the chill of the late autumn nights, she was taken to Prizren. She was locked up that night and presented to the commander the next day. Although General Janković must have known that the poor woman standing before him was innocent, she was still not released. Instead, she was taken to the residence of the Serbian bishop where she remained in custody until the following day when she was given over to the Catholics, taken to a church and tended to.

In Prizren, there lived a baker named Gjoni i Prek Palit who supplied the Serbian troops with food. One day, a sergeant came by to order bread for the troops and happened to leave his rifle in the bakery. When soldiers later entered the bakery and saw the rifle, they arrested the baker for violating the weapons ban. He was taken to a military tribunal and executed. When Gini, the baker's brother, heard of the arrest, he ran to the sergeant and took him to the military police where the latter admitted the rifle was his and that he had only left it in the bakery for a short time. He knew the number of the rifle and recognized it immediately. Gini and his Serbian witness were then beaten up and chased away. Gini learned nothing of the fate of his arrested brother. Ten days later, the mother of the dead baker, who had been searching day and night for her son, came upon the body outside of town. She requested to be given the corpse so that she could give her son a Christian burial. This request was refused. A Catholic priest then hastened to the commander and in the name of religious freedom requested that the body be buried in the Catholic cemetery. He, too, was refused, and they were obliged to bury the body on the spot where they found it.

Officers also took part in the atrocities. It is said in Prizren that a soldier asked his officer for shoes or sandals. The officer replied he should confiscate the sandals from the next Albanian who happened to pass by. "Why else do you carry a rifle?" asked the officer, pointing to his own sandals.

* * *

Three Albanian villages in the vicinity of Prizren were totally destroyed and thirty local officials slain. They were accused of being pro-Austrian. In one of these villages, the soldiers forced the womenfolk out of their homes, tied them to one another and forced them to dance in a circle. They then opened fire and amused themselves by watching one victim after another fall to the ground in a pool of blood.

When it was reported to General Janković that the Luma tribe was preventing Serbian troops from advancing westwards towards the Adriatic, he ordered his men to proceed with extreme severity. All in all, twenty-seven villages on Luma territory were burnt to the ground and their inhabitants slain, even the children. It is here that one of the most appalling atrocities of the Serbian war of annihilation was committed against the Albanians. Women and children were tied to bundles of hay and set on fire before the eyes of their husbands and fathers. The women were then barbariously cut to pieces and the children bayonnetted. My informant, a respected and thoroughly reliable man, added in his report: "It is all so inconceivable, and yet it is true!" 400 men from Luma who gave themselves up voluntarily were taken to Prizren and executed day after day in groups of forty to sixty. Similar executions are still being carried out there. Hundreds of bodies still lie unburied in the Prizren region. Gjakova / Djakovica is also in ruins and its population decimated.

Sixty Albanians were slain in Tërstenik / Trstenik, thirty-two in Smira, twenty in Vërban / Vrban, nineteen in Ljubishta / Ljubište and all the males in Kamogllava / Kameno Glava, which is home to fifty families. In the latter village, the men were forced to appear for roll call and to salute. They were then tied up and executed without trial. Not very many survived in Presheva / Preševo either.

The total number of Albanians slain in the *vilayet* of Kosovo is estimated at 25,000, a figure which is by no means exaggerated.

* * *

On 20 March 1913, the *Albanische Korrespondenz* published this item: We have received the following report from reliable Albanian sources in Skopje. Serbian troops and volunteers are committing unspeakable atrocities in the vicinity of Skopje against the population of the territories they have occupied. European circles have been particularly outraged by the following events which were reliably recorded. The Serbian army took the village of Shashare at the end of February. Having removed all men and boys from the village, the soldiers then proceeded to rape the women and girls. Serbian soldiers committed the same heineous crimes in the village of Letnica. It must be stressed that both Shashare and Letnica have an exclusively Slavic and Catholic population. Serbian troops, thus, do not even stop at committing such degenerate acts against their own Christian people. Shashare is a settlement of over one hundred families.

These savage troops have committed even worse crimes in other areas. Two hundred eighty farms belonging to Albanian Moslems were set on fire in twenty-nine villages in the Karadag (Black) mountains and all the male inhabitants who had not flown fell under a hail of bullets and under the bayonettes of the soldiers. The Serbs marauded like the Huns from village to village. Other such pogroms have been carried out in the villages of Tërstenik / Trstenik, Senica, Vërban / Vrban, Ljubishta / Ljubište and Gjylekar / Djelekare. Two hundred thirty-eight men were pitilessly slaughtered here. In Sefer, an old women was burnt alive together with her Catholic servant. The suffering of the population knows no limits. In the village of Ljubishta / Ljubište, the atrocities have reached such a point that Moslem Albanian women have sold themselves to surviving Moslem men to serve them more or less as slaves. The Serbs took a man, an old woman and two children captive and burnt them alive in this village. In Gjylekar / Djelekare a pregnant women had her belly slit open with a bayonette and the offspring wrenched out of her body. In Prespa, an Albanian women whose husband had been taken away shot five Serbian soldiers. The Serbs then set the whole settlement aflame, ninety farms in all, and let it burn to the ground.

The Serbs are laying waste to whole regions and slaughtering their inhabitants. Their fury is directed against both the Moslems and the Catholics. The survivors remain behind in unspeakable misery and despair.

In a report published on 19 February 1913 by the *Deutsches Volksblatt*, we read: Few towns and villages (in the occupied areas) have escaped the attention of the Serbs completely and there are many Albanians who now press to take vengeance for the deaths of their wives and children. When the order was issued in the towns for the immediate surrender of all weapons, only very few people complied. Most of them hid their weapons at home or fled with them, for it is easier to separate an Albanian from his whole farm than from his rifle. In order to enforce the order, patrols were sent out to search homes. A gruesome fate awaited those caught with weapons. The military tribunal came to its findings within a matter of hours. One spectacular case took place in Tirana. Serbian soldiers went to the shop of a local merchant to buy goods. As they had no money with them, one of them left the merchant his rifle as security. Petrified at his own deed, the soldier subsequently went to his commander and brought charges against the merchant for stealing the rifle. A patrol was sent out in search of the Albanian and found him with the rifle in question. He was taken to a military tribunal and, despite his protestations that the rifle had only been left as security, was shot.

An Albanian from the village of Zalla, west of Kruja, shot a Serb who had broken into his home and was assaulting his wife, and took to flight.When the Serbs subsequently arrived at the scene of the crime and could not find the culprit, and - such is the sad truth - they slaughtered all the inhabitants, over one hundred persons including women and children, and set the village on fire.

* * *

The Serbian thirst for blood

The special correspondent of the *Daily Telegraph* reported the following: All the horrors of history have been outdone by the atrocious conduct of the troops of General Janković. On their march through Albania, the Serbs have treacherously slaughtered not only armed Albanians, but in their savagery even unarmed individuals - old people, women, children and babies at their mother's breasts.

Drunk with victory, Serbian officers have proclaimed that the only way of pacifying Albania is to exterminate the Albanians. They slaughtered 3,000 people in the region between Kumanova / Kumanovo and Skopje alone. 5,000 Albanians were murdered by the Serbs in the Prishtina area. These people did not die with honour on the battlefield, but were slain in a series of gruesome raids. The Serbian soldiers have found new methods of butchery to satisfy their thirst for blood. Houses were set on fire in several villages and the inhabitants slaughtered like rats when they tried to flee the flames. The men were slain before the eyes of their wives and children. The wretched women were then forced to look on as their children were literally hacked to pieces.

Executions were a daily entertainment for the Serbian soldiers. All inhabitants who had been found with weapons in their homes were executed. They were either shot or hanged. Up to thirty-six executions took place a day. How strange it is that the Serbian nationalists living in

Hungary should complain about massacres in Albania. Mr Tomić, the former secretary to the Serbian Prime Minister Pašić, reported on his trip from Prizren to Peja / Peć that on both sides of the road he saw nothing but the remnants of burnt-out villages which had been razed to the ground.

The roads were lined with gallows from which the bodies of Albanians were hanging. The road to Gjakova / Djakovica had become a Boulevard of Gibbets.

The Belgrade newspapers reported quite without shame on the heineous atrocities of the Serbs. When Colonel Osbić's regiment took Prizren, he commanded his compatriots, "Kill!" When his order was heard, so the Belgrade papers report, "the Serbian soldiers stormed into homes and slaughtered every human being they could lay their hands on."

The *Daily Telegraph* then gives the authentic statement of an Albanian notable: Anyone who denounces an Albanian to the Serbs can be sure that the Albanian will be executed. There were people who owed money to Moslem Albanians. They went and denounced them to the Serbs as traitors. The wretched Albanians were immediately hanged and the informers later found ways of acquiring the home and land of their victims for a ridiculously low price.

In Skopje, unarmed Albanians were simply shot and killed by Serbian officers. If even a hunting knife was found in a home, its owner was executed.

In Ferizaj / Uroševac, the Serbian commander invited Albanian fugitives to return to their home and surrender their weapons. When over four hundred of them did return, they were slaughtered. There were no more than a dozen Moslem families left alive in Ferizaj / Uroševac. The war correspondent of the *Messaggero* has confirmed this report.

In Pana, the Serbs killed their prisoners, in Varosh / Varoš and Prishtina the population was literally decimated. Serbian officers admitted themselves that they were on the 'hunt' for Albanians, and one of them boasted having killed nine Albanians in one day with his own hands.

A doctor working for the Red Cross reported, according to the same source: The Serbs have been massacring throughout Albania with no sign of mercy. Neither women nor children nor old people have been spared. I have seen villages burning in Old Serbia every day. Near Kratovo, General Stefanović had hundreds of prisoners lined up in two rows and machine gunned down. General Živković had 850 Albanian notables put to death in Senica because they had offered resistance.

The *Albanische Korrespondenz* reported from Trieste on 12 March: A letter from Kruja near Durrës (Durazzo) dated 27 February of this year was read out at the Albanian congress here. It read: All the buildings as well as the villas of Mashar Bey and Fuad Bey (n.b. who were taking part in the congress at the time) have been burnt to the ground. Ali Lam Osmani's brother was caught by the Serbs in Vinjoll near Kruja, buried to his thighs in the earth, and then shot. The letter concludes with the words: We shall never see one another again. Farewell until we meet in the other world!

The marauding Serbs!

Ahmed Djevad, secretary of the Comité de Publication D. A. C. B. reports, according to several witnesses: The most incredible amounts of valuables have been robbed and stolen by the Serbs in Strumica. Major Ivan Gribić, commander of the fourth batallion of the fourteenth Serbian line regiment alone had eighty wagons filled with furniture and carpets transported back to Serbia. All the young women and girls of Strumica have been raped and forcibly baptized. The rest of the wretched Moslem population is dying of starvation, destitution and disease...

The *Albanische Korrespondenz* reported from Trieste on 21 March 1913: The suffering in Albania has reached an unspeakable zenith. The Serbian troops who took Durrës (Durazzo) were immediately ordered to proceed into the countryside although no provision had been made for their food and drink. They were therefore forced to rely on food they confiscated from the population, which they did with exception cruelty. They took nine-tenths of all the stocks available, and refused to give written receipts for the goods they requisitioned.

The Serbian troops not only confiscated goods for their own usage. They seized or destroyed all the food that fell into their hands. Ancient olive trees which had been planted in the Venetian period and had provided sustenance to generations were cut down by the Serbs. Farm animals were slain. No sheep, no chickens, no corn which the Serbs could get their hands on remained untouched. They conducted extensive raids and looted wherever they could. In Durrës (Durazzo), the Serbs loaded ships with carpets and other stolen goods for transportation to Salonika whence the cargo was transferred back to Belgrade. Even antique benches from the government offices in Durrës were confiscated and loaded onto the booty ships.

Fazil Toptani Pasha, to whom we showed this report for confirmation, stated: Everything written in this report is true. These facts are but a small portion of the outrages committed in our country by these barbarians. They flooded into Albania slaughtering, looting and burning, and have caused more destruction than anyone could possibly imagine.

Dervish Hima told us: Tell the public that a good proportion of the Albanian people is on the verge of starvation. Spring has come, the time to sow the land, and the Serbs have stolen all the seed. Even if the Albanians had seed, they would not sow it, for they now have a saying: "Even if something manages to grow, the Serbs will destroy it." Such is the fear of the Serbs among our people!

Wholesale murder

A Romanian doctor, Dr Leonte, reported in the Bucharest newspaper *Adevărul* on 6 January 1913 that the horrors he saw committed by the Serbian army far outdid his worst fears. That hundreds of Moslem captives were forced to march a hundred kilometers was the least of what these wretches were to suffer. Whenever any of these poor individuals collapsed of hunger and exhaustion at the roadside, they were simply bayonetted by the first soldier passing, and the corpses were left to rot. The fields were still strewn with the bodies of slaughtered men and women, young and old, even children. When Serbian troops marched into Monastir / Bitola, all

Turkish patients being treated in the hospitals were slain in order to make room for wounded Serbs. The soldiers stole whatever they could get their hands on. Even banks were robbed. A Bulgarian professor who made himself unpopular by proposing a toast to King Ferdinand has disappeared without a trace since the evening of the toast. Dr Leonte gives other reports of atrocities similar to those committed in Kumanova / Kumanovo, Prizren etc.

* * *

The well-known war correspondent Hermenegild Wagner reported from Zemun on 20 November 1912: During my three-day stay in Nish, I heard shocking details of the inhumane acts committed by Serbian troops. I wish to note in this connection that I have respected witnesses for all details referred to.

In the fortress of Nish was a fifty-year-old Albanian woman being held on suspicion of having thrown bombs at Serbian troops marching into Ferizaj / Uroševac. Instead of bringing the accused before a military tribunal, she was given over to Serbian soldiers who literally shattered her skull with the butts of their rifles.

A Turkish lieutenant named Abdul Kadri Bey was beaten to death in the fortress of Nish. The autopsy showed a broken nose and a traumatized liver. The victim was kicked to death.

An Albanian who attempted to escape was bayonetted to death. The body was dreadfully battered about by the soldiers even while it was being taken to the morgue.

In the hospital of Nish, a number of Serbs entered a ward where Turkish patients were being treated. One of the Serbs called out, making a joke, "That's the one who wounded me!" Thererupon, a whole group of Serbs attacked the helpless patient and kicked him to death.

A Red Cross doctor told me with horror that the prisoners and injured patients one encountered in Nish and Belgrade were only there for show. "The Serbs," he added, "know no mercy. All Albanians caught, whether armed or not, are butchered on the spot. Women, children, old people. Dreadful things are happening down there (in Old Serbia). I don't know how many villages have been razed to the ground by Serbian troops. I saw them burning day after day... Near Kratovo, General Stefanović had hundreds of Albanian prisoners lined up in two rows and mowed down with machine guns. The general then declared: This brood must be exterminated so that Austria will never find her beloved Albanians again.

General Živković massacred 950 Albanian and Turkish notables near Senica when ten thousand Albanians slowed down the advance of Serbian troops.

The Serbs took very few of the wounded prisoner after the Battle of Kumanova / Kumanovo. King Peter himself visited the field hospital in Nish. One of the injured Serbs complained that the Albanians were firing upon the Serbs with rifles stolen from the Serbs themselves, and that he, too, had been wounded in this manner, to which King Peter replied: "The swine will pay for it!"

Serbian witnesses who were present at the battle told me with smiles on their faces how after the battle, all of the dead and injured Turks and Albanians were hurled into a shallow grave. The battlefield looked frightful after a heavy rainfall because the Turkish mass grave collapsed, leaving the hands, feet and skulls of distorted bodies sticking out of the mud.

Devastated villages

In Skopje, a returning Serbian officer explained quite seriously to me the justice of burning down eighty villages in Luma territory.

On 14 February, the *Deutsches Volksblatt* published a report from southern Hungary, warning: The Serbian government must come to realize that their official denials only serve to destroy Serbian credibility even further. We saw examples of such rallies following the murder of the king. At that time, the government solemnly and officially denied that King Alexander and Queen Draga had been murdered by the perjured officers, insisting instead that they had been quarrelling and had killed one another...

With regard to the Albanian massacres, it is extremely sad to note that the description of events which has filtered through to the public is indeed in full accord with the facts and has only one shortcoming, that it is incomplete. Many Serbs have confirmed the events themselves, often with great pride. Let it suffice for us to quote a statement made by someone who himself took part in the first stages of the war and who, though a Serb from the Kingdom, prefers to exercise his profession in southern Hungary for the moment, under Austrian 'oppression', in order to avoid as far as possible the 'cultural and religious liberality' reigning in his native land. This classic witness took obvious satisfaction in declaring that Serbian soldiers had ruthlessly mowed down whole groups of Albanian farmers, whose only 'crime' was that weapons had been found in their homes. When I expressed my astonishment at his statement, he replied placidly, "Should we have wasted our time escorting these people to some distant garrison town? It was much less work this way. We were then free and could go for a drink!" This pragmatic attitude seems to be extremely widespread among Serbian soldiers. An injured patient at a Belgrade hospital told a visitor, "We left the Turks alone but slaughtered the Albanian dogs wherever we could get our hands on them." Another indication is to be seen in the letter by a Serbian officer, published in the journal *Magyarorszag*, whose Balkan correspondent was Ivan Ivanović, Austrian deserter and former head of the Royal Serbian Press Office. In this letter, the officer declares that, after the occupation of Monastir / Bitola, he had with his own eyes seen his soldiers seize ten Turkish men, women and children each and burn them alive. Such statements can be heard from all the Serbs returning from the war. To their misfortune, they have not read the official Serbian denials published in the foreign press...

* * *

An Albanian from near Skopje reported: "When we saw the Serbian soldiers approaching our village, everyone ran back home. I myself was not afraid and, wanting to get a look at the strangers, came out in front of the house. There they were already. I offered one of the soldiers a small coin. He struck me on the head and I fell to the ground, where the soldiers left me. Storming into the house, they murdered my mother and father, set the house on fire, and proceeded to slaughter everyone else. When I finally got back up on my feet, everything was in flames."

In Sefer in the region of Gjilan / Gnjilane, the Serbs set fire to a cottage and hurled its two elderly owners, who had not had time to flee, alive into the conflagration. They tied the hands of one man together, told him to run away, and then shot him as he ran off.

Varying explanations were given this month for the burning down of the following towns and villages: Limbishte, Koliq / Kolić, Tërpeza / Trpeza and Gjylekar / Djelekare. In the last three villages, everyone was slaughtered, including women and children.

In the village of Bobaj in the district of Gjakova / Djakovica, four Serbian soldiers who had been caught trying to rape the women, were beaten up. This was enough for a punitive expedition to be sent in and Bobaj was put to the torch. All the inhabitants were slaughtered. When they had finished their work, the *soldateska* came upon seventy Catholic Albanians from Nikaj, who were going to market. Here, too, the soldiers carried out their bloody handwork.

In Peja / Peć, Serbian soldiers carried off three women. The Montenegrins also carried off three girls.

In Luma territory, thirty-two communities were burnt to the ground, and anyone who was captured there was slain.

In Dibër / Debar, too, Serbian soldiers committed dreadful atrocities. They stole whatever they could get their hands on. Then fresh troops arrived and set twenty-four villages on fire, killing all the inhabitants...

In Prizren, the Catholic priest was not allowed to administer communion to the dying. Whoever approached the parish priest was brought before a military tribunal.

* * *

The following report was received from Durrës (Durazzo) on
6 March: Serbian troops have burnt the following villages to the ground:
Zeza, Larushk, Monikla, Sheh and Gromni. In Zeza, twenty women and
girls were locked in their homes and burnt alive.

The inhabitants of the village of Kruja-Kurbin have taken to the
mountains, in order to save their lives, leaving behind all their
possessions.

* * *

On 12 March, the *Albanische Korrespondenz* reported from
Trieste: Letters from Tirana inform us that Serbian troops have recently
been committing atrocities in the vicinity. The inhabitants of Kaza
Tirana had offered accommodation to a unit of Albanian volunteers and
given them food and drink. When the Serbian military commander got
word of this, he had his troops encircle the village, whereupon all the
houses, including the estate belonging to Fuad Toptani Bey, were burnt
to the ground. Seventeen people died in the fire. Ten men and two
women were executed.

The Serbs are also murdering Christians

On 20 March, the *Reichspost* published a letter from Albania,
reading as follows:

> The parish priest of the sanctuary of Cernagora or Setnica, Don
> Tommaso, was robbed by Serbian soldiers of all the funds
> belonging to the church. The soldiers drew their bayonettes,
> forced him to open the safe and took out all the money
> belonging to the pilgrimage site.

The parish priest of Gjakova / Djakovica was threatened with death. He was told, "Either you give up your links with the Austrian protectorate or we will roast your brains!" The courageous reaction of the priest blew the wind out of their sails, however.

For three months now, the Serbs have been hindering the parish priest of Ferizaj / Uroševac in his freedom to exercise his office. They have been jailing anyone who talks to him or who goes to mass or confession. The same thing has happened to two priests from Prizren.

All imaginable pressure has been exerted against the Catholics of Janjeva / Janjevo (four hundred families, almost all of whom are ethnic Slavs) to convert to the schismatic church.

For hundreds of years now, about 8,000 Catholics, so-called Laramans or secret Catholics, have been living in this archdiocese. Because of Turkish persecution, they did not profess their faith openly. When the Serbs arrived, several hundred of these Laramans wanted to declare openly that they were Catholic. When a representative of the new government got word of this, they were ordered, "Either Moslem or Orthodox. Not Catholic!"

Near the sanctuary of Letnica is the village of Shashare (ninety families, all of them Catholic). Serbian soldiers took the village, assembled the men on a field and tied them up with ropes. They then looted the homes and brutally raped the women and girls.

Countless Albanian Catholics have been murdered. In Ponoshec / Ponoševac, for instance, thirty men were slaughtered one day while they were going about their business in the village. Their only crime was to admit that they were Albanian Catholics.

Near Zhur / Žur, entire families of innocent Catholic tribesmen who had come down to Prizren to purchase salt, oil, sugar etc. were treacherously murdered on their way. The same thing happened near Gjakova / Djakovica where a further seventy Catholics from the parish of Nikaj were slaughtered. The

Catholics are persecuted, whereas the native Orthodox are left alone.

In the vicinity of Dibër / Debar and Monastir / Bitola, as well as in Kosovo, many villages have now been burnt to the ground. The looting is unspeakable. It is sufficient to note that sheep are now being sold at a price of two francs each because nobody knows what to do with them all. So many have been stolen from the Albanians by the Serbs and Montenegrins.

They are now trying to stop us from speaking Albanian. A number of schools teaching Albanian have already been closed down.

The letter ends with the words, "May God have mercy upon us, and may Europe come and save us. Otherwise we are lost!"

* * *

In its issue of 21 March, the *Neue Freie Presse* reports: We have been told by informed sources that, according to recent reports, Catholics and Moslems are being persecuted both in the district of Gjakova / Djakovica and in the district of Dibër / Debar. Many deaths occur every day. The population has fled, leaving behind all their possessions. It is not only the Albanians who are the object of such persecution, but also Catholic and Moslem Slavs.

Slaughtered priests

On 20 March, the *Neue Freie Presse* reported: On 7 March, the *soldateska* joined fanatic Orthodox priests in and around Gjakova / Djakovica to forcefully convert the Catholic population to the Orthodox faith. About 300 persons, men, women and children, among whom Pater Angelus Palić, were bound with ropes and forced under threat of death to convert. An Orthodox priest pointed to the soldiers standing by with their rifles in hand and said, "Either you sign the declaration that you have converted to the one true faith or these soldiers of God will send your souls to hell."

All the prisoners then signed the forms prepared for them which contained a declaration of conversion to the Orthodox faith. Pater Angelus was the last. He was the only one of them who had the strength, in a calm and dignified manner, to refuse to give up his faith. Pater Angelus stood by his word, even when ordered three times to convert and even when entreated by the other forcefully converted Catholics. The result was one of the most appalling scenes imaginable in twentieth-century Europe.

After a sign from the Orthodox priest, the soldiers fell upon the Franciscan, ripped off his tunic and began beating him with the butts of their rifles. Pater Angelus collapsed after several of his bones and ribs had been fractured. At this moment, the Orthodox priest stopped the soldiers and asked him if he was now willing to convert. Again he shook his head and said placidly, "No, I will not abandon my faith and break my oath." Pater Angelus was beaten with the rifle butts again until one of the soldiers plunged a bayonette through the priest's lungs and put an end to his suffering.

A Serbian decree for more bloodshed

A decree was issued to the local authorities in the district of Kruja in western Albania, reading: "If anything occurs in the future or if but one Serbian soldier is killed in the town, in a village or in the vicinity, the town will be razed to the ground and all men over the age of fifteen will be bayonetted." The decree was signed: Kruja, 5 January 1913. Commanding officer: A. Petrović, Captain, first class.

Kruja is the birthplace of Scanderbeg, the national hero, whose castle still stands in the town. It is a place venerated by all Albanians!

Serbian voices

The *Deutsches Volksblatt* reported on 8 February: The Serbian Minister of Culture and Education, Ljuba Jovanović, has published a declaration in a Slav newspaper, stating: "The Moslems will of course be treated the same as everyone else with regard to their rights as citizens. As to their religious affairs, the *Vakuf* properties (belonging to religious foundations) will remain under Moslem jurisdiction and their monasteries will be held in the same respect as are the Christian ones. With the exception of the regular troops, the Moslems have not put up any resistance to Serbian occupation and, as a result, were not harmed by Serbian forces. The Albanians, for their part, have resisted the Serbian occupation and even shot at soldiers after having surrendered. Such shootings have taken place not only outdoors but also from within houses in occupied villages. This has led to what happens everywhere when non-combatants oppose a victorious army" (i.e. the massacre of the Albanians).

The Belgrade newspaper *Piemont*, which serves as the mouthpiece of radical circles within the army, dealt in its issue of 20 March with the problem of Shkodër (Scutari) and declared that Shkodër must fall to Montenegro. "If this does not happen," continued the newspaper, "the town must be razed to the ground."

Serbian officers boast of their vile deeds

The *Albanische Korrespondenz* reports from Durrës (Durazzo): The carnage perpetrated by the Serbs in Albania is outrageous. Serbian officers boast openly of their deeds. Serbian troops have acted infamously in Kosovo in particular. A Serbian officer reported here: "The womenfolk often hid their jewellery and were not willing to hand it over. In such cases, we shot one member of the family and, right away, were given all the valuables." Particularly shocking was the behaviour of the Serbs on Luma territory. The men were burnt alive. Old people, women and children were slaughtered. In Kruja, the birthplace of Scanderbeg, a good number of men and women were simply shot to death and many houses set on fire. The Serbian commander, Captain Petrović, published an *ukaz* officially announcing the evil deeds. In Tirana, several Albanians were sentenced to corporal punishment. The Serbs thrashed the wretched individuals until they died. In Kavaja and Elbasan, people were also officially beaten to death by the soldiers. A well-known, respected and wealthy gentleman, son of a Turkish officer, was shot in Durrës (Durazzo). The Serbian command later made his sentence known by wall posters on which they wrote that he had been accused of theft and sentenced to death. The Serbs have destroyed Catholic churches, saying that they are Austrian constructions and must disappear from the face of the earth. Serbian soldiers and officers harass the population day and night.

A Serbian soldier was recently found murdered. The Serbian commander ordered the immediate arrest of five Albanians who had nothing to do with the murder and had them shot.

A bloodbath in Shkodër (Scutari)

The *Albanische Korrespondenz* reports from Podgorica: After the battle of Brdica, which resulted in a sound defeat for the Serbs, Serbian forces entered the village of Barbullush on their retreat. The terrified inhabitants came out of their homes with crucifixes in their hands and begged for mercy, but to no avail. The crazed troops attacked the unarmed villagers and slaughtered men, women, old people and children. The maimed body of an eight-year-old child was found to contain no less than six bayonette wounds.

The Serbian denials

In recent times, the Serbian government has countered most reports of atrocities with official denials. Such disavowals have always been issued promptly, but all too often they lacked any semblance of credibility. Such grave and detailed accusations cannot be repudiated by a simple statement that the events in question did not occur.

The present and by no means complete selection of reports from various sources, not only Austrian, but also Italian, German, Danish, French and Russian, should have more weight in any court of human justice than all the formal denials issued by the Royal Serbian Press Office.

In an official denial dated 8 Febuary, the Serbian Press Office declared that, "Such atrocities alleged to have been perpetrated by the Serbian army are simply unthinkable today on the part of a people who are exceptionally religious and tolerant." We can only answer: An army whose officers assault their king and queen in the middle of the night, murder them, maim their corpses with fifty-eight sabre cuts and then throw them out the window is quite capable of such atrocities, in particular since the leader of the bloodbath which took place in the *konak* of Belgrade was none other than Colonel Popović, one of the leaders of the Serbian attack on Albania and currently commander of Serbian occupation forces in Durrës (Durazzo).

Vienna 1913

[Taken from *Albaniens Golgotha* (Vienna 1913). Translated from the German by Robert Elsie]

The Situation of the Albanian Minority in Yugoslavia

Memorandum
presented to the League of Nations
(1930)

Gjon Bisaku, Shtjefën Kurti and Luigj Gashi

TO HIS EXCELLENCY MR ERIC DRUMMOND,
Secretary General of the League of Nations,
Geneva

Excellency,

We, the under-signed,

Dom Gjon Bisaku of Prizren, until recently priest in the parish of Bec, District of Gjakova / Djakovica, Yugoslavia;

Dom Shtjefën Kurti of Prizren, until recently priest in the parish of Novosella / Novoselo, District of Gjakova / Djakovica, Yugoslavia;

Dom Luigj Gashi of Skopje, until recently priest in the parish of Smaç / Smač, District of Gjakova / Djakovica, Yugoslavia;

all three of us being missionaries of the Sacred Congregation of the Propaganda Fide, and Yugoslav citizens of Albanian nationality,

have the honour to submit to you, on behalf of the Albanian population of Yugoslavia, this petition on the state of this ethnic minority and beg Your Excellency to bring it to the attention of the Members of the League of Nations:

Mr Secretary General, we are not the first envoys of the Albanian population living in the Kingdom of Yugoslavia to have addressed the League of Nations concerning the lamentable state of this minority, created by Serb rule, and we will certainly not be the last to protest before this high institution of international law unless the political course taken by the rulers in Belgrade towards their Albanian subjects alters its bases and procedures.

This political course, which is already replete with excesses and misfortune, can be summed up in one phrase: To change the ethnic structure of the regions inhabited by Albanians at all costs. The strategies used to this end are as follows:

a)   various forms of persecution in order to force the population to emigrate;

b)   the use of violence to forcefully denationalize a defenceless population;

c)   forced exile or extermination of all people who refuse to leave the country or to submit peacefully to Serbification.

These three strategies correspond to three categories of oppression:

The victims of the first category are the over one hundred forty thousand Albanians who have been forced to leave their homes and belongings and to emigrate to Turkey, Albania and other neighbouring countries, anywhere they can find shelter, a bit of food and a little more human kindness.

The second category includes the population of 800,000 to 1,000,000 Albanians, Moslems for the most part, who live in compact settlements along the border to the Kingdom of Albania up to a line including Podgorica, Berana and Jenibazar in the north, the tributaries of the Morava river in the northwest and the course of the Vardar river in the south.

The last category includes the ever increasing number of Albanian figures in Yugoslavia who have been banned from the country because of their patriotic sentiments and the long list of obituaries of those who have paid with their lives for their opposition to denationalization, the most recent victim of which is our brother in Jesus Christ, the reverand Franciscan Father Shtjefën Gjeçovi, trapped by the gendarmes in an ambush and assassinated on 14 October last.

Excellency,

In order to be spared the fate of our esteemed advisor and friend Gjeçovi, we have been forced to abandon our homes and our sacred ministry on behalf of our grieving and wretched compatriots. Our main concern is to make known to the League of Nations and to the civilized world the suffering of our brethren living under Yugoslav oppression.

Condemned by misfortune to pass from one yoke to another, this part of the Albanian nation, no less important in numbers than that in the independent state of Albania, has not, for one single moment over the past centuries, known the benefits of liberty. The right to self-determination, proclaimed by the founder of the League of Nations, an apostle of international peace, remains our sacred aspiration. Indeed the League of Nations, which has set as its basic goal the elimination of the grounds of conflict between states, has also endeavoured, by means of Treaties on Minorities, to prevent the causes of misunderstanding between states and their subjects belonging to other races, language groups and religions.

The stipulations of these Treaties, solemnly agreed to by the Governments, have allayed many fears and, in particular, given rise to many expectations for peoples who are obliged to live under foreign rule. One of the most numerous of these peoples is, without a doubt, the Albanian minority in Yugoslavia. It finds itself in the sad situation of having to realize, more than many other similarly ruled populations, just how deceitful Governments can be, which, on the one hand collaborate in the work of the League of Nations, but on the other hand, do everything they can to avoid applying the conventions concerning them to which they have volontarily adhered. This is precisely the case of the stipulations concerning minorities contained in the Treaty of Saint Germain-en-Laye, signed by the Serb-Croat-Slovene (SHS) State on 10 September 1919. None of the benefits stipulated in the Treaty has been accorded to the Albanian minority in this country, from the protection of life and property to freedom of movement, as will be demonstrated in the appendices to follow. These stipulations have remained a dead letter, in particular those by which the Treaty, inspired by the loftiest of intentions for peace and humanity, has endeavoured to provide minorities with rights to resist forced denationalization. Eager to avail itself of the property deeds of the inhabitants of these ethnically Albanian regions, the Yugoslav Government makes nothing of the rights which the League of Nations has endeavoured to give our minority, and, what is more, shows no scruples whatsoever in its choice of means to attain its objective.

Excellency,

We come to protest, not out of animosity towards Yugoslav rule or towards any unjust treaties to which we have been forced to submit, but because of persecution deriving precisely from the violation of just treaties. Convinced that the League of Nations will not tolerate the systematic violation of the Treaty, the implementation of which it guarantees, the Albanian population of Yugoslavia, Moslems and Christians together, submit to the League their complaints in the profound conviction that they enjoy its protection.

Convinced that the esteemed League of Nations will willingly take our complaints into consideration, we also venture to draw its attention to measures conducive to alleviating the situation, which is becoming more and more intolerable every day and about which the Albanian minority raises its voice in protest. In our humble estimation, it would be very useful to send a commission of inquiry to check up from time to time on compliance with the Treaty on Minorities. Much more effective for ensuring its application, however, would be the setting up by the League of Nations of a Commission or the seconding of a Permanent Commissioner to reside in one of the towns in the minority region. An uninterrupted control would force the pledges taken to be respected, and would have a twofold advantage. Firstly, its vigilance would put an end to the ambiguous reports prepared by governments which refute the complaints made by the minorities and present a totally different situation to the League of Nations than that really existing. This is the case, for example, in the most recent Yugoslav document about the Albanian minority (No. C. 370 of 26 August 1929) in which it is stated that there are 'schools' in our region and that the Committee charged with investigating the matter is satisfied, believing these to be schools in which Albanian is taught. In reality, eight thousand Albanians do not have a single elementary school, just as they do not occupy a single post of importance in public administration. Secondly, the zeal with which the denationalization campaign is being waged would be moderated by the presence of the said Commissioner, and the various acts of violence and persecution could be eliminated to a large extent. In short, the watchful eye of the League of Nations would lead to an effective implementation of the treaties and to a normalization of relations between the rulers and the ruled.

Please be assured, Mr Secretary General, of our unshakable faith in the mission of the League of Nations and of the high esteem in which we hold Your Excellency.

Geneva, 5 May 1930

Signed:
Dom Jean Bisak
Dom Etienne Kurti
Dom Louis Gashi

List of Appendices
Documentation

In the following appendices, we have endeavoured to demonstrate with precise facts the truth of the claims we have had the honour to include in this memorandum. The events referred to are given as examples only and have been chosen at random from a multitude of similar cases. To be as clear as possible, we have made reference to the provisions of the Treaty on Minorities signed by the Kingdom of Yugoslavia and followed them by the facts which prove that these provisions have not been applied with regard to the Albanian minority.

The facts speak for themselves. Their authenticity cannot be denied, even in the knowledge that an official inquiry is impossible.

APPENDIX 1 - PROTECTION OF LIFE
I   The beginning of Serb rule
         Our calvary began in 1912. Inquiry of the Carnegie Endowment. References
II   Mass extermination
         1.   Localities of grief
         2.   The Dubnica massacre
         3.   A village wiped out for an offence of which it was innocent
III   Crimes attributed to the agents of the authorities
         Ten crimes in six months in one subprefecture alone
IV   The assassination of the Franciscan Father Gjeçovi
         A forerunner of Father Gjeçovi. The figure of Father Gjeçovi. A valued ethnographer. He was active in Yugoslavia as a missionary and as a scholar. Summoned to appear before the authorities, he was waylaid and murdered. Numerous witnesses but no testimony. A derailed inquiry

APPENDIX 2 - PROTECTION OF LIBERTY

I   The case of the authors of this memorandum
1.   Chauvinist absurdities. "There is no room for Albanians in Yugoslavia." Refugees for life
2.   Letter addressed to H.E. the Apostolic Nuncio in Belgrade. The assassination of Father Gjeçovi is "only the beginning". Reports on sermons. *Personae non gratae* in our own country. Why we were forced to abandon our country and our belongings

II   Forced emigration
1.   Emigration is due to persecution
2.   The means used to encourage emigration
3.   Emigration to Albania
4.   Emigration to Turkey
5.   Plundering of the emigrants
6.   Albanians are forced to emigrate in order that Montenegrins and Bosnians can settle their land

III   Various restrictions on personal freedom
1.   Imprisonment, searches, requisitions
2.   Censured clothing
3.   Freedom of movement
4.   Forced labour

APPENDIX 3 - RIGHT TO PROPERTY
1.   Forms of seizures
2.   Confiscations and expropriations
3.   Confiscation of public property
4.   The agrarian reform
5.   Compensation

APPENDIX 4 - CIVIL AND POLITICAL RIGHTS
1.   Being of Albanian origin is an impediment
2.   The Albanians have been excluded from municipal functions
3.   Justice is not impartial
4.   Arbitrary taxation
5.   Political rights are non-existent

APPENDIX 5 - USE OF THE NATIONAL LANGUAGE
1.   The Albanian language has been persecuted more than any other in the Balkans
2.   Restrictions continue for Albanians in Yugoslavia

APPENDIX 6 - SCHOOLS AND PRIVATE CHARITIES
1.   The Yugoslav Government has banned Albanian private schools
2.   Albanians are permitted no intellectual activity
3.   Even religion may not be taught in Albanian

APPENDIX 7 - PUBLIC EDUCATION
1.   The view of the committee set up by the League of Nations to examine the issue of minority education
2.   The Albanians are not oblivious to the benefits of schooling
3.   Teaching staff

APPENDIX 8 - PRIVATE PIOUS FOUNDATIONS
1.   The Yugoslav Government conficates the property of pious and charitable foundations
2.   The pious foundations of Albanian Christians have been plundered, too
3.   Not even cemeteries have been exempted
4.   Difficulties involving burials

APPENDIX 1
PROTECTION OF LIFE

> "The SHS State pledges to accord full and complete protection of life and liberty to all inhabitants irrespective of birth, nationality, language, race or religion."
>
> (Treaty on Minorities, Article 2)

I   The beginning of Serb rule

With regard to the protection of the life and liberty of the Albanian population living within the Kingdom of Yugoslavia, one could write volumes on end if one were to refer to all the instances in which this protection has been intentionally withheld.

The calvary of our people begins with the arrival of the 'liberating' Serb armies in 1912 in regions inhabited by an Albanian majority. The consequences of the conquest of this country were noted as follows in the appalling conclusions reached by the Commission of Inquiry set up by the Carnegie Endowment:

> "Houses and villages set on fire, mass murder of an unarmed, innocent population, unspeakable violence, plundering and all sorts of brutality - such are the means which have been and are being used by Serb and Montenegrin troops with the aim of altering the ethnic structure of regions inhabited exclusively by Albanians."

Nonetheless, it is not our intention to chronicle the events which took place before the signature of the Treaty on Minorities. Those wishing to know more about them may consult the press of the period in question as well as specialized publications in which they will find a record of many of the atrocities committed, including names, dates and places [18]

II   Mass Extermination

1.   Localities of grief

Prishtina, Mitrovica, Junik, Shtima / Shtimlje and Vrella / Vrela are names of localities calling to memory bloody events, mass murders committed for no purpose against an innocent population whose only crime was to be of Albanian nationality.

2.   The Dubnica massacre

On 10 February 1924, in Dubnica, District of Vuçitërna / Vučitrn, the village was encircled and then set on fire on the orders of the prefect Lukić and of the commander Petrović so that all the inhabitants would be burnt alive. Their crime had been the following: The gendarmes wanted to capture a bandit called Mehmet Konjuhi but had not succeeded. The bandit having escaped, the authorities laid the blame not only on the relatives of Mehmet Konjuhi, who were all massacred, but on the entire village. Twenty-five persons, including ten women, eight children under the age of eight, and six men over the age of fifty, died in the fire. No one was punished for this crime.

---

[18] See among others:

1. *Enquête dans les Balkans. Rapport de la Commission d'Enquête de la Dotation Carnegie pour la Paix Internationale*, Paris 1914;

2. *Albaniens Golgotha. Anklageakten gegen die Vernichter des Albanervolkes. Gesammelt und herausgegeben von Leo Freundlich*, Vienna 1913;

3. *Le droits de l'Albanie à ses frontières naturelles. Appel aux nations du monde civilisé*, Vlora 1921.

Here is the toll in this work summarizing Serb atrocities committed in Kosovo against the Albanian population: 12,371 killed, 22,110 imprisoned, 6,050 homes destroyed, 10,525 families looted.

3.   A village wiped out for an offence of which it was innocent

Bandits killed a gendarme in the region of Rugova. Colonel Radovan Radovanović was sent to investigate the case. Not being able to find the culprit, the colonel encircled the village closest to the place where the gendarme had been slain and set it on fire. We do not know how many people died.

III   Crimes and offences attributed to the agents of the authorities

The number of crimes committed sporadically by those supposed to protect and guarantee the lives of citizens is much higher than that resulting from the mass murders. In order to convey an idea of the numbers involved, we provide the following table for one subprefecture alone, that of Reka, District of Dibër / Debar, for a period of six months.

Name and locality of the victims	Name and office of the perpetrator	Date of the crime	Observations
1. Islam Zhuli of Zhuzhna	Corp. Čedomir of the Tanush / Tanuš police	November 1928	The victim was summoned on the pretext of a job and was slain on his way
2. Mexhid Bekiri of Bogda	Corp. Marković of the police in Jerodović	November 1928	
3. Veli Boga of Bogda	2nd police Lieut. Rada Terzić	November 1928	Slain on pretext of cowardice
4. Ismaili and Lazimi, both of Orguci	Popović and Marković of the Ternić police	10 Dec. 1928	Slain on their way to market in Gostivar
5. Musli Bajrami, mayor of Senca	Corp. Marković of the Ternić police	June 1929	Slain in front of his house
6. Jakup Ibrahimi of Nivishta	Officer Niko Milanović and a companion of the Tanush / Tanuš police	5 July 1929	Slain in the presence of his brother on his way back from Gostivar market
7. Zeqir Ismaili of Presenica	Serg. Kaprivić of the Reka	15 July 1929	One-time mayor
8. Zurap Fazlia of Ničpur	Serg. Lazović of the Mishrova / Mišrovo police	15 July 1929	Slain in front of his house
9. Rakip Muhtari of Grek	An agent of the subprefecture	18 July 1929	Released by the police after two days of arrest and slain near the church in Beka

IV   The assassination of the Franciscan Father Gjeçovi

The Franciscan Father Shtjefën Gjeçovi Kryeziu was assassinated on 14 October 1929 under circumstances which leave little doubt as to the motives of the crime.

Father Shtjefën Gjeçovi is unfortunately not the first Albanian Franciscan to have fallen as a martyr for his patriotic sentiments and his faith. The first was Father Luigj Palici who was summoned by soldiers under the command of a bandit dressed as an Orthodox priest and was ordered to renounce his Catholic faith publicly in favour of the Eastern Orthodox faith. He refused energetically and was maimed with the butt-ends of the soldiers' rifles and then stabbed to death with a bayonette. This took place in Gjakova / Djakovica on 7 March 1913.

Father Shtjefën Gjeçovi, for his part, was slain because of his stance as a good Christian and as a man devoted to justice and knowledge.

Born in 1874 in Janjeva / Janjevo in the District of Prishtina, now part of Yugoslavia, Father Shtjefën Gjeçovi opted for Albanian nationality despite the inconveniences this caused him during his stay on Yugoslav territory. After having finished his studies in philosophy and theology, he carried out his mission in Albania for many years and was held in high esteem by all those who came to know him. Devoted to the study of ethnography, he was the first person to bring to light a very important work on Albanian customary law, the *Kanun of Lekë Dukagjini*. He was much praised for this publication and received the title of doctor honoris causa from the University of Leipzig.

As a great admirer of the chivalrous customs of his people, he had long since begun an in-depth study on Albanian folklore, for which he had travelled widely throughout Albania. He had recently taken up duty, in continuation of his spiritual mission, in the village of Zym amongst the Albanians of Yugoslavia.

Zym, in the District of Prizren, Yugoslavia, is an Albanian village of one hundred twenty houses, of which one hundred houses are inhabited by Catholics and twenty by Moslems. In view of the nationality of the inhabitants, the Government only set up a school in this locality in 1926. One must not suppose, however, that teaching in Albanian, the mother tongue of the inhabitants, was permitted. The Government nominated to the post of teacher a Serb who, being Orthodox, trod on the religious sentiments of the pupils. Father Gjeçovi, of his own will, taught the children the catechism in Albanian and for this reason was not on good speaking terms with the Serb teacher who called him an 'Albanian nationalist'.

What is more, the Serb chauvinists regarded his research in the field of folklore as political propaganda. This was enough to bring about his downfall. Father Gjeçovi had on many occasions sensed the hostility of the Yugoslav authorities and of the members of the chauvinist association *Narodna Odbrana,* which terrorized the Albanian population throughout Yugoslavia quite openly. But he could not imagine that they would go so far as to take his life because of his views. Realizing that no favourable circumstances were at hand to do away with him without causing suspicion, their hired assassins resorted to the following infallible method.

Two gendarmes, probably attached to the police station near the village of Zym, approached Father Shtjefën Gjeçovi on 13 October last to notify him that he had been, summoned by the subprefect of Prizren and was to appear before him as soon as possible. Surprised by this order, Father Gjeçovi suspected something was afoot and was unwilling to depart alone. He therefore took with him a school employee and a guard from the municipal hall. On his arrival in Prizren, he first paid a visit to the Bishop, to inform the latter that he had been summoned by the subprefect. He then reported to the subprefect, who expressed his astonishment and declared that he had not issued any order to summon the priest. Father Gjeçovi's original suspicions had now become more concrete. He returned to the Bishop to inform the latter of what had taken place during his talk with the subprefect and set off for home, still accompanied by the two gentlemen. At a point along the road, not far from the village, they noticed two armed men approaching, who, after cursing the Reverand Father, fired on him. Gjeçovi was felled by the first shot. The bandits, to make sure of their deed, then advanced and riddled him with bullets.

It must be noted that on the road, in the immediate vicinity of the crime, there were numerous workers carrying out road-repairs. Also present were the two companions of the victim. The police station was not far off either. Despite all the witnesses, the assassins got away with their crime and departed in no hurry, like individuals who had finished their work and had nothing to fear. And they indeed had nothing to fear. The inquiry produced no results and never will produce any results, because this does not seem to be its purpose. On the contrary, attempts have been made to use the inquiry in order to stain the reputation of the victim and to step up the persecution of the Albanians. Despite all the evidence, they are endeavouring to camouflage the political character of the crime, which is nonetheless conclusive, given the history and circumstances of the crime and the satisfaction the assassination caused in Serbian nationalist circles. One of these people, a police officer, mocking the profound grief which the loss caused to the authors of this petition, alluded menacingly that Father Gjeçovi had received his just deserts and that the same fate awaited all of us with him.

APPENDIX 2
PROTECTION OF LIBERTY

(Concluded after the treaty on the protection of minorities had been signed)
(Treaty on Minorities, Article 2 et seq.)

I   The case of the authors of this memorandum
(The priests Gjon Bisaku, Shtjefën Kurti and Luigj Gashi)

1.   Chauvinist absurdities

We have been obliged to abandon our country because of ever-growing restrictions to our freedom of speech, of movement and of access to our parishioners, etc. All our movements and all our actions were suspect to the authorities simply because we refused to become Serb 'patriots' and serve the goals of the terrorist organization *Narodna Odbrana*, i. e. preaching to our compatriots the absurd idea of the Serb chauvinists that we should consider ourselves Albanized Serbs and consequently should not pray to God in Albanian or teach our children their mother tongue.

Our disobedience, considered a grave menace to the interests of the state, was not to be forgotten or pardoned. No longer able to tolerate the accusations and threats, we abandoned our parishes last December to seek the aid and protection of the central authorities in Belgrade. The Ministry of the Interior gave us the standard formal assurances, but did not regard our complaints as important. On the contrary, it would seem that our complaints, instead of calming relations, made the hostility of the authorities even more acute. As soon as we arrived in Skopje, we were informed that the police were looking for us and wanted to arrest us. We were reminded of the threat of one of the police officers who had told us, "There is no room for Albanians in Yugoslavia. The Gjeçovi affair is only the beginning - your turn will come." It was at this point that we decided to leave everything behind to save our lives and our honour.

As there was no question of us obtaining passports to get to Rome to the Sacred Congregation of the Propaganda Fide under whose orders we were working as missionaries, we were forced to leave for the Albanian border, confronting all the dangers inherent in such a crossing, in the hope of saving our lives in exchange for leaving behind everything: our country, our families and our possessions.

2.   Letter addressed to H.E. the Apostolic Nuncio in Belgrade before our departure

Most Illustrious and Reverend Excellency,

It is with profound grief that we have abandoned our families and friends and, most of all, our wretched people who enjoyed some small consolation from the fact that we had remained with them and shared their sufferings.

We would like to submit to Your Excellency a summary of the reasons for our departure. Our situation and our stay in the District of Gjakova / Djakovica has become futile and impossible over the last few years. The situation is becoming worse from year to year, and now the worst has happened - the assassination of Father Shtjefën Gjeçovi on 14 October 1929. Why? Who killed him? We leave it to others to judge, since Your Excellency is in possession of precise documents. What worries us most are the rumours and the statements made by police officers, such as the captain of the gendarmes in Prizren, who said, "This is only the beginning." The commander of the gendarmes in Peja

/ Peć, Popović said to one of us sneeringly, "Your turn will come!" Another officer, Zarko Andjelković boasted, "We killed Father Gjeçovi and now we are going to kill the priest in Peja / Peć." The Serbs we know warned us to be on our guard. Why? What had we done? They even ask us to submit summaries of our sermons at church, etc. One of us was told that he was a member of the Kosovo Committee of Shkodër, and another was accused of having built a church with foreign money, etc. In short, we have become 'personae non gratae' and are no longer welcome. The fact that we are 'personae non gratae' in the eyes of the government was confirmed Wednesday evening by our bishop at a meeting with the two deaneries of Peja / Peć and Gjakova / Djakovica when, talking to Father Ljubomir Galić, the latter told him it was true, adding that no priests could be found for these parishes.

Under such circumstances, what else could we do?

It would seem futile for us to remain there to be killed, not for our religion but because of base allegations such as those made against the late Father Gjeçovi, all the more so since we put no store in acts of blind heroism. Whether we remained or departed, our parishes would have been deprived of their priests in any case. We informed the bishop as much on several occasions. In order to save our lives, we now find ourselves compelled, against our will, to abandon our diocese, our parishes and our wretched but beloved people, not to mention our possessions.

We beg Your Most Illustrious and Reverend Excellency to contact the Sacred Congregation of the Propaganda Fide, whose servants we are, to request another mission in which we will be able to carry on with our sacrosanct ministries as priests, and to arrange that we be sent back to the Sacred Congregation to which we shall expose our trials and tribulations and our needs and to which we offer unconditional obedience. We would beg you to do this as quickly as possible since we have lost everything, are in the midst of our journey and are apprehensive that we may be followed and arrested.

In the hope that Your Excellency will have the kindness to take the above into consideration and to come to our assistance, we remain your very humble and devoted sons,

signed,
Dom Gjon Bisaku, Dom Luigj Gashi, Dom Shtjefën Kurti

Belgrade, 14 December 1929.

II   Forced emigration

1.   Emigration is due to persecution

Before the Serbian occupation, emigration was unknown among the Albanian population living in the regions now under Yugoslav rule. It is true that workers went abroad temporarily to neighbouring countries, but never with their families.

The mass emigration which has occurred since 1912 is due without a doubt to the various kinds of persecution which make life impossible for the poor people and force them to abandon their homes.

2.   The means used to encourage emigration

The means used by the Yugoslav authorities to force the Albanian population to leave the country are numerous. Death threats, restrictions on their freedoms in all areas of life, expropriation without compensation, house searches and frequent raids and arrests for no plausible reason, as well as a ban on teaching their national language and on expressing patriotic sentiments other than those desired by Serb nationalists. These means are utilized on a daily basis. These oppressive measures are carried out in good part by chauvinist associations such as the *Narodna Odbrana*.

3.   Emigration to Albania

At the present, there are about ten thousand refugees pretty well throughout Albania and they are in a miserable state. The Albanian Government seems to have made a laudable effort to shelter these refugees, but there can be no doubt that its good will alone will not be enough to receive and take care of all those still wishing to come. Consequently, it has been obliged to refuse entry visas for most of them. They have therefore taken refuge further afield, principally in Turkey.

4.   Emigration to Turkey

The number of emigrants in Turkey surpasses the figure of 130,000. The Turkish Government has taken advantage of these people to populate regions in Anatolia which are more or less deserted, but where a good number of them have perished because of the climate and deprivation. This exodus does not seem likely to end unless the persecution which has given rise to it is brought to an end. Two hundred Albanian families have recently left for Turkey. But the matter does not stop here. In its desire to get rid of the Albanians, the Government in Belgrade has initiated talks with the Government in Ankara on the transfer to Turkey of three to four hundred thousand Albanian Moslems from Kosovo. If nothing has yet come of the project, it is no doubt due to the influence of the League of Nations and to world public opinon which would have raised an outcry.

5.   Plundering of the emigrants

To encourage emigration to Turkey, the Yugoslav authorities provide certain favourable conditions such as the following. A young man of Albanian origin doing his military service is discharged early so as to be able to accompany his parents forced into emigration.

Emigration to Albania is not well looked upon. The Yugoslav Government has every interest in ensuring that these persecuted and dispossessed refugees settle farther away from its borders. As such, a thousand obstacles are put in the way of the wretched individuals wanting to be reunited with their families in Albania. A host of public employees and lawyers are only waiting for a chance to put the final touches on the misery of these poor people. To obtain passports, they are harassed and plagued until they agree to pay exorbitant sums, four or five thousand dinars, which often amount to their total savings.

The following are the most recent cases of inhuman exploitation we learned about before our departure:

a)   A Moslem Albanian peasant from the village of Leshan / Lešane in the District of Peja / Peć was forced to pay 6,000 dinars to the Serb lawyer Zonić in Peja / Peć as a passport tax.

b)   The Serb lawyer Ljuba Vuksanović of Peja / Peć demanded 8,000 dinars of another Albanian peasant to obtain a passport for him because the "procedure was extremely difficult."

c)   A Catholic Albanian from Skopje by the name of Geg Mata who had emigrated to Albania could only obtain a passport for his wife and son after five months of harassment and the payment of 2,000 dinars in bribes.

It must be noted in this connection that the normal passport tax is no more than fifty dinars.

6.   Albanians are forced to emigrate in order that Montenegrins and Bosnians can settle their land

Montenegrins and Bosnians from Srema and the Banat are invited to settle in the villages and live in the expropriated and confiscated homes of the Albanian refugees with the obvious purpose of changing the ethnic structure of the region. Such resettlements of people have occurred pretty well everywhere and the campaign is continuing with an ever-increasing intensity. We refer, as examples, to the following localities:

a)   In the District of Gjakova / Djakovica: the villages of Lugbunari, Piskota, Dubrava, Mali i Ereçit, Dashinoci, Mali i Vogël, Fusha Tyrbes, Beteshet e Marmullit, Neci etc., etc.

b)   In the District of Peja / Peć: Fusha e Isniqit / Istinić, Turjaka, Fusha e Krushecit, Malet e Leshanit, Krusheva, Vitomirica, etc., etc.

c)   In the District of Prizren: Fshaja, Gradisha, Xërxa / Zrze, Lapova / Lapovo etc., etc.

It has also happened that inhabitants of Albanian origin who left their homes temporarily returned to find Serbs living in them who had been granted absolute title to them by the authorities.

III   Various restrictions on personal freedom

1.   Imprisonment, searches, requisitions

Reference must be made first and foremost to the arrests and imprisonments which, in addition to house searches and various requisitions, constitute the most effective means utilized by the government authorities to harass the Albanian population. Any charge made against an Albanian leads to his immediate arrest, whether or not the accusation is true and the source is reliable. Charges usually arise from quarrels between individuals. They are often instigated by provocateurs and sometimes invented by government officials. An innocent allegation is often sufficient to turn the general climate of suspicion against the Albanian population into one of certainty that crimes have been committed, thus setting off a series of harsh measures against innocent individuals. There are numerous cases. They happen almost every day. Let us confine ourselves to a few recent examples:

a)   Hafëz Hilmi and Shukri Dogani, who until recently were mayors of localities in the Kaçanik / Kačanik area of the District of Skopje, were not on good speaking terms with the local authorities and were accused of collaboration in a 'Kosovo Committee' which exists only in the troubled imagination of Serb chauvinists. The above-mentioned men were imprisoned on the basis of this supposition.

b)   The merchant Mulla Rifati, born in the same region, was arrested on a similar charge.

c)   Sherif Gjinovci, a person well-known to the Albanian community in Yugoslavia, was arrested six months ago and accused of intervening in a feud between two feuding Albanian families.

2.   Clothing

In its violent actions aimed at the 'ethnic unification' of the state, the Belgrade Government also does its utmost to eliminate differences in clothing that give an indication of nationality in this part of the kingdom. In some places, such as Reka, where Orthodox Albanians live together with Slavs of the same religion and with Moslem Albanians, the differences are limited to various types of headgear. The Albanians wear the *kësula* whereas the Serbs wear the *čajkač*. To do away with this shocking distinction, Mr Sokolović, the subprefect, issued an order to all police stations in his region last May forbidding Albanian peasants from wearing the *kësula*. They are now forced to don the Serb cap. The police were only waiting for a pretext to tear up the Albanian caps.

3.   Freedom of movement

Another form of persecution is limiting freedom of movement. In many regions, the Albanians are not allowed to leave their villages without notifying the authorities beforehand. In order to visit a relative from another village, to go to a fair to sell produce or to travel to market to go shopping, i.e. any circumstances involving a departure from one's native village, one must notify the chief of police. This form of persecution increased substantially last year in the District of Dibër / Debar.

It goes without saying that the authorities do not provide any prompt or satisfactory services unless the peasant accompanies his request with a bribe.

4.   Forced labour

Serbs and Albanians of the region in question are employed in the construction and repair of national and local roads and in other public works. As to their treatment, a distinction is made. The Serbs are regularly paid as labourers whereas the Albanians are quite often not paid at all, or receive very little. In addition, they are obliged to provide their own tools and workhorses or oxen without recompense.

APPENDIX 3
THE RIGHT TO PROPERTY

"Persons having chosen another nationality will be at liberty to keep their immovables in the territory of the SHS State. They will be free to bring their goods and chattels of all kind with them"
(Treaty on Minorities, Article 3)

It is true that this article is more specifically aimed at those who choose Austrian, Hungarian or Bulgarian nationality, but in view of the general character of the treaty which is designed to protect all minorities, one can conclude that the regulations regarding the right to property, which conform by the way to common law existing in most countries, are also applicable to Albanians who have become nationals of the State of Albania, of another country or who have remained Yugoslav subjects.

1.   Forms of seizures

In reality, quite different measure are applied to the Albanians. Pure and simple expropriation without any compensation is one of the most common and efficient means of forcing the Albanians into exile. Confiscation of property is practised against our people on a vast scale. In addition to this is the agrarian reform, a package of government measures which was never passed by parliament, but which the authorities nonetheless utilize in their own fashion, depending on the persons in question.

2.   Confiscations and expropriations

The confiscation of property is carried out against persons who are absent and against all Albanians inhabitants whose Serbian patriotism is considered doubtful. As to formal charges, there is no need for them whatsoever. Any accusation by a Serb against an Albanian is tantamount to condemnation. Should there be need of further witnesses, members of the *Narodna Odbrana* and the *Bela Ruka* (White Hand) are always ready to serve the nation.

It would be impossible here to list all the cases of unjust confiscations we are aware of. We do wish, however, to cite a few examples in one specific region.

a)   The following persons from the District of Peja / Peć had their property confiscated without explanation: Jusuf Arifi of the village of Bec, Grosh Halili of the village of Turjaka, Tahir Bala of the village of Papiq, Bajram Sula of the village of Krestovec, and Memdu Bey, whose property was estimated at over 2,000 hectares.

b)   Most rich Albanian families have had their property confiscated to demoralize them, deprive them of political influence and oblige them to submit to the Yugoslav yoke without protesting. Here are a few examples from the District of Gjakova / Djakovica alone: Asllan and Kurt Bey Berisha, Ibrahim Bey, Ismet Bey Kryeziu, Ahmet Bey Berisha, Poloska, Halit Bakalli, Muhamet Pula, Prenk Gjoka, Mark Nikoll Biba of Brekoc, Muftar Dema of Zhub / Žub, Bek Hyseni of Zhub / Žub, Gjon Marku of Guska, Gjon Doda of Pllangçora.

3.   Confiscation of public property

Confiscations and expropriations have affected not only individuals but also collective groups. Albanian villages have been dispossessed of their farm and pasture land pretty well everywhere. Here are a few examples:

a)   In the District of Gjakova / Djakovica: Marmull, Rezina, Brodesana, Doblibarja, Meçeja, Cërmjan / Crmljan, Kryelan, Bardhaniq, Dashinoc, Lumëbardha, Lluga, Qerim, Lugbunar, Trakaniq, Novosella / Novoselo, Bec, Palabardh, Gergoc, Dobrigja, Firaja, Gramoçel, Fusha e Kronit të Plakës (Piskota), Babajt e Lloçit, Deçan / Dečani, Lloçan, Voksh, Kallavaja e Junikut, Batusha, Rracaj, Pacaj, Pllangçora, Dujaka, Hereç, Ponashec, Brovina, Nec, Babajt e Bokës, Koronica, Mejeja, Guska, Fusha e Tyrbes, Brekoc,

Vogova, Zhub / Žub, Firza, Moglica, Rraç, Pjetërshan, Kusar, Dol, Kushavec.

b)   Other examples from the District of Peja / Peć: Isniq / Istinić, Strellc / Streoc, Fusha, Pishtan, Baran / Barane, Leshan / Lešane and all the pasture land down to the Drin river and from there to Gjurakovc / Djurakovac, Rakosh / Rakoš, Ujmirë / Dobra Voda, and Rudnik.

The situation is similar in other regions inhabited by Albanians.

4.   The agrarian reform

Far more numerous are the victims of the so-called agrarian reform, which was applied with extreme rigour to the Albanian population. Under the reform, citizens having completed their military service are entitled to 5 hectares of arable land per person. Albanian families, which still maintain a patriarchal structure and include six to ten adult males, would accordingly have the right to thirty to fifty hectares of land. At the present moment, there is not a single farming family in all of Yugoslavia owning such a spread of land. Even properties of one hectare have been expropriated.

Here are a few examples which prove that the agrarian reform is nothing more than a pretext for plundering and inhumanity:

a)   Mark Vorfi, from the village of Fshaj in the District of Prizren, and his four brothers together owned ten hectares of land. The expropriation took everything away from them.

b)   Aleksandër Shaupi of the same village owned fifteen hectares of land. He has five brothers and, according to the law, would normally have a right to at least thirty hectares. At the present moment, they do not have a single hectare left.

c)   Jup Pozhegu of Gjakova / Djakovica owned eight hectares of land in the village of Bishtazhin (District of Prizren). All he has left at the moment is one square meter.

d)   In the autumn of 1929, twenty-six Albanian families from Rugova, District of Peja / Peć, were expelled from their homes and deprived of their possessions, and were forced to seek refuge with friends. They were forced to go begging in order to survive.

5.   Compensation

For two years, a compensation of 5% of the value of the property expropriated was offered in some regions to the dispossessed, but only to those persons well regarded by the authorities. Aside from this initial compensation, expropriated Albanian landowners have received nothing at all.

APPENDIX 4
CIVIL AND POLITICAL RIGHTS

"Complete equality (for all minorities) to enjoy civil and political rights, notably to accept public office, functions and honours".
(Treaty on Minorities, Article 7)

1.   Being of Albanian origin is an impediment

This stipulation in the Treaty has not been applied at all with regard to the Albanian population in Yugoslavia. Albanians, in particular those who have studied at universities abroad, no longer even try to obtain functions or jobs in the public service since they are aware from the start that the main condition for employment is not the qualification of the applicant, but rather nationality. This condition is of course not legally binding, but is strictly respected by those who are authorized to apply it. This explains the startling fact that a population of eight hundred thousand people is not represented in the public service by one single official of any importance, i. e. a prefect or subprefect. If some minor employees have been given jobs, they got them most certainly by being servile or sycophantic, whether because of their abject poverty or because they were lacking in morals.

2.   The Albanians have been excluded from municipal functions

The same condition exists for employment in the municipal administration, even though the local authorities were elected by the public. The Albanians are excluded from public office. Mayors who were formerly elected are now appointed directly by the Government. Municipal offices are organized in such a way as to keep representatives of the Albanian majority out of the administration. In more populated localities which have a municipal administration of their own and in which a Serb population also exists, albeit as a minority, municipal councils are still composed for the most part of Serbs. In grouping together small villages to form a municipality, great care is taken to include one Serb village with the four or five Albanian villages, with the sole purpose of keeping the Albanians out of the administration. Where such measures cannot be implemented, a Serb adviser is appointed to work with the mayor in question and, in actual fact, becomes head of the municipality himself.

Here are a few examples of the foregoing:

a)   In Peja / Peć, where the vast majority of the population is Albanian, the former mayor Nexhi Basha, an Albanian, was replaced by a Montenegrin called Maja who is hardly known at all to the population.

b)   The former mayor of Gjakova / Djakovica, Qazim Curri, who is of Albanian origin, found himself with a Serbian office administrator who took over all the decision-making.

c)   In Prizren, where there is also a large Albanian majority, there has not been one single Albanian mayor of a town or municipality since the Serb occupation of the country began.

d)   In Vogova, District of Gjakova / Djakovica, the mayor was an Albanian called Marc Ndou. He was replaced by a Montenegrin, Milan Popović, a bandit and thief who was subsequently convicted for his crimes. In subsequent elections, Ndre Bib Doda was voted in as major, but was nonetheless ousted and replaced by Radovan Popović, cousin of the above Milan Popović, who was no less notorious than his cousin as an implacable enemy of the Albanian population.

The same can be said of the municipalities of Ponashec, Deçan / Dečani, and Irziniq etc., all in the riding of Gjakova. The situation is no different in other regions.

3.   Justice is not impartial

As to justice, the Albanian population is poorly served since it has no legal recourse against a Serb.

Thousands of examples have proven to the Albanians that they have no chance whatsoever of winning a case in court. They can only repeat the popular wisdom that laws made and applied by a ruler are not to the advantage of his subjects. With this in mind, Albanians in Yugoslavia rarely go to court, not wishing to add more financial loss to the injustice they have incurred.

Here are a few examples:

a)   Myftar Dema, of the village of Vogova in the District of Gjakova / Djakovica, accused the mayor, Milan Popović, of embezzling 20,000 dinars belonging to the municipal authorities. The latter was indeed tried and imprisoned. But after one month in prison, he was released and given free rein to torment his accuser.

b)   A Serb called Krstić, together with his accomplices, killed sixty Moslem Albanians from Jabllanica / Jablanica (District of Gjakova / Djakovica) in one day, among whom was the influential Osman Aga Rashkovi. The family of the latter had the culprit brought to trial. In order to save him, despite the overwhelming evidence of his guilt, the authorities declared him to be deceased, even though Krstić is still alive and well and now living in Istog / Istok in the District of Peja / Peć.

c)   In the midst of an interrogation in the subprefecture of Gjakova / Djakovica, an Albanian, Lazër Dreni, was struck down with the butt of a fire arm by an employee of the subprefecture, Jovan Milić, in the presence of the secretary Djulaković. Milić was imprisoned for several hours for form's sake and then released.

4.   Arbitrary taxation

Arbitrary taxation measures are quite often applied to the Albanians. The taxpayer is not in a position to know exactly how much he will have to pay in taxes in a given year. He is normally at the mercy of tax officials who make him pay double or triple of what he is legally bound to pay.

Before the beginning of the dictatorship, over half the seats on the thirty-six-member tax commissions in Kosovo were occupied by Albanians. At present, their representation has been reduced to two. The other thirty-four members are Serbs.

5.   Political rights are non-existent

As is evident from the above, the political rights of citizens of Albanian origin simply do not exist. The Albanians hoped for one moment in 1925-1926 that they would be as free as the other citizens of Yugoslavia to occupy political positions in the country. They were soon disappointed, however. The political party formed under the leadership of Mr Ferhat Bey Draga was to take part in the elections with a list of fourteen candidates for the Chamber. But on the day of the elections, the candidates were prevented by various means from taking part in the elections. Some were placed under house arrest in their own homes. When they protested, the authorities replied that the measure had been taken in their own interests, since otherwise their lives would have been in danger.

The attempt was not without consequences for these courageous individuals. Most of them were sentenced to jail, under various pretexts. The party chairman Ferhat Bey Draga was sentenced to four years in prison. Nazim Gafuri was wounded and subsequently slain in front of a police station in Prishtina. Ramadan Fejzullahu was convicted and several candidates had their possessions confiscated. All of them suffered.

Under such conditions, it is evident that the Albanians could no longer even think of entering the political ring, even as a national minority.

APPENDIX 5
USE OF THE NATIONAL LANGUAGE

> "There shall be no restrictions on the use of the national language in the field of religion, in the press or in publications of any kind."
> (Treaty on Minorities, Article 7)

1.   The Albanian language has been persecuted more than any other in the Balkans

Rightfully considered the fundamental characteristic of nationality in the Balkans, language has always been the main object of contention between the conservative spirit of peoples and the efforts of governments to enforce national unity in the country by more or less forcible means.

In this respect, the Albanian people have suffered more than all the other Balkan peoples. Under Ottoman rule, the Albanians were not allowed to used their language freely. Education, press and publications in Albanian were luxuries enjoyed only by Albanians living in foreign countries. Even correspondence in Albanian addressed to friends or relatives abroad could result in the imprisonment of the author. The Turks used these methods to combat the national awakening of the Albanians, whereas Greek and Slav propaganda, acting as the due heir to the Ottoman Empire, did its utmost to denationalize the Albanian Orthodox population through church and schools.

2.   Restrictions continue for Albanians in Yugoslavia

This situation continues for the half of the Albanian people living under foreign rule.

A few examples will suffice to illustrate the truth of this assertion.

a)   In the Albanian regions of Yugoslavia, there are signs on the town halls saying that the usage of any language other than Serbian is forbidden.

b)   No newspaper, magazine or other publication in Albanian exists for the eight hundred thousand Albanians in Yugoslavia. The Belgrade Government may claim that intellectual activity is not prohibited under the law, but those who implement the law, the police and their officers, do their utmost to impede any such activity. If an Albanian were to venture to apply for authorization to publish a newspaper in Albanian, to hold an innocent public lecture in Albanian or to open a school to teach Albanian, he would not of course be punished for such an application, but would immediately be hounded by the police and the gendarmes on all sorts of charges, arrested and, in many cases, imprisoned or dispossessed.

c)   One of the undersigned, Dom Shtjefën Kurti, until recently priest in the parish of Novosella / Novoselo, District of Gjakova / Djakovica, was forbidden by the principal of the Serbian school, Radovan Milutinović, from using the Albanian language to teach village children the catechism.

d)   When Albanian children from the village of Skivjan, District of Gjakova / Djakovica, brought Albanian spellers to the Serbian school they attended, the Serb principal, Mr Zonić, confiscated the books immediately and punished the children for "daring to learn a language other than that of the state."

e)   Albanians are often reprimanded by telephone operators who order them to speak Serbian. If they do not comply, their calls are cut off.

APPENDIX 6
SCHOOLS AND PRIVATE CHARITIES

> "They (the minority) shall have, in addition, the
> right to found, manage and control at their own
> expense charitable, religious and social institutions,
> as well as schools and other educational facilities,
> with the right to make free use of their own
> language and to exercise their religion freely."
> (Treaty on Minorities, Article 8)

1.   The Yugoslav Government has banned Albanian
private schools

We have already seen what Albanian-language education was
like under Ottoman rule. It may be noted in this connection that at the
end of this rule, before the Balkan War, it was the Kosovo Albanians
who rose in revolt against the Turkish regime to obtain freedom for
national education. The policies of the Turkish administration in this
field were continued under the Serb occupation. As the ban was not
effectively enforced during the Great War, the Albanians in Yugoslavia
hastened to open private schools for the teaching of their mother tongue
(see below the list of such schools).

Once the Yugoslav Government was freed from the burdens of
the war in 1919, one of its first actions was to close down Albanian
schools. The school in Skopje was not closed until 1929, probably as a
consequence of an Albanian complaint to the League of Nations about
Yugoslav oppression.

2.   Albanians are permitted no intellectual activity

At the same time as private schools, the Yugoslav authorities
banned all social activity of an Albanian character. Intellectual, cultural
and musical societies have been dissolved in Gjakova / Djakovica, Peja
/ Peć, Prizren, Skopje and other important towns.

3.   Even religion may not be taught in Albanian

There can be no question of the free use of the Albanian language in the teaching of religion either. Orthodox Albanians from the Reka region, where they are in the majority, have been banned from using their language in church. Catholic Albanian priests from the regions of Gjakova / Djakovica, Prizren and Skopje etc. are considered agents of political propaganda if they so much as teach the catechism in Albanian. As to Moslem Albanians, they have no *medresa* where their religion can be taught in Albanian.

Schools have also been closed which had operated in the following towns: Plava with 50 pupils, Gucia / Gusinje with 60, Bec 45, Brodosana 50, Brovina 40, Lloçan 46, Irziniq 40, Novosella / Novoselo 48, Junik 40, Ponashec 45, Cërmjan / Crmljan 50, Zhub / Žub 48, Budisalk 70, Rakosh / Rakoš 80, Prizren 40, Skopje 73, etc.

The number of these schools and the number of pupils is not large. These are schools which were opened spontaneously in localities where an initial community organization already existed or in which the municipal administration, on top of its various obligations from the war, was able to maintain an Albanian-language school. If the regulations of the Treaty on Minorities were fully applied, the number of Albanian pupils in Yugoslavia would be no less that in Albania, given that half the Albanian population lives in Yugoslavia.

4. Table of Albanian private schools closed down by order of the Yugoslav Government

Locality	Instructors	No. of pupils
Ferizaj / Uroševac	Catholic priest	50
Zym	Pal Lumezi	40
Gjakova / Djakovica	Jusuf Puka, Sali Morina, Niman Ferizi, Ferid Imani, Ibrahim Kolçiu, Ibrahim Felmi, Lush Ndoca	840
Mitrovica	Catholic priest	160
Prishtina		90
Vuçitërna / Vučitrn	Haxhi Tafili	60
Peja / Peć	Murat Jakova, Hajdar Sheh Dula, Abdurrahman Çavolli, Mulla Resh Meta	256
Peja / Peć	Halit Kastrati, Shaqir Çavolli, Sadi Pejani	125
Peja / Peć	Shaban Kelmendi, Pal Lumezi etc.	232
Peja / Peć	Zef Maroviqi, Pal Lumezi etc.	257
Gjurakovc / Djurakovac	Mr Plakçori	221
Baran / Barane	Xhevet Kelmendi	176
Zlokuçan / Zlokučane	Ndue Vorfi	186
Strellc / Streoc	Adem Nexhipi	175
Istog / Istok	Osman Taraku	285
Prizren	Lazër Lumezi	76

APPENDIX 7
PUBLIC EDUCATION

"For localities in which considerable numbers of a minority population live, the Government shall accord appropriate facilities to ensure that in elementary schools, instruction is given to the children of the minority in their own language."
(Treaty on Minorities, Article 9)

1.   The view of the committee set up by the League of Nations to examine the issue of minority education

In pursuing its policies of denationalization, the Yugoslav Government, having closed down the Albanian schools, replaced them with Serbian schools. In its most recent document addressed to the League of Nations, the Government stated that there were 1,401 schools in the regions inhabited by Albanians, out of which 261 schools with 545 classes were attended especially by Albanian pupils. The committee set up under a council resolution dated 25 October 1920 to examine the issue, "believed it was in a position to interpret the phrasing in the Yugoslav document as meaning that the schools in question were schools for the minority per se, in which teaching was carried out in the Albanian language, or were schools having classes fulfilling this condition. Based on this interpretation, the Committee considered the information provided in the report by the Yugoslav Government to be satisfactory."

The Committee was either misled by an ambiguous phrase or had learnt the truth and preferred to issue a warning in this form. Whatever the case may be, we must insist that there is not a single school or a single class among the 545 referred to by the Yugoslav Government in which teaching is conducted in Albanian, just as not one of the 7,565 Albanian pupils attending school is being taught in his own language.

2.   The Albanians are not oblivious to the benefits of schooling

The number of these pupils, notes the Yugoslav Government, is very low due to the particular living conditions of the Albanians who inhabit small settlements in isolated mountain regions and show no understanding of the benefits of schooling. We have no intention of arguing with the Yugoslav Government, but cannot pass over such an accusation without demonstrating how baseless it is. Not even one third of the Albanians in Yugoslavia live in 'isolated' mountain regions. This might be stated more reasonably of the Albanians in the Kingdom of Albania. Despite communications difficulties and the smaller amount of funds earmarked for public education in Albania, the percentage of pupils is not less there than it is in the Kingdom of Yugoslavia. This goes to show that the Albanians are by no means oblivious to the benefits of schooling, but only, of course, in places where schools provide real educational benefits and do not simply promulgate hatred towards the nationality and the mother tongue of the pupils. The schools in question are more like workshops for denationalization. This is why the Albanians are leery of sending their children to attend them.

3.   Teaching staff

As to the teaching staff, it must be mentioned that teachers of Albanian nationality are extremely rare. Those who do exist are not employed to teach Albanian or to teach in Albanian. Even hodjas teaching religion to Moslem pupils are obliged to teach in Serbian.

APPENDIX 8
PRIVATE PIOUS FOUNDATIONS

"The Yugoslav State pledges to provide full protection to Moslem mosques. All assistance and authorizations will be accorded to pious foundations (*vakufs*) and to existing Moslem religious and charitable institutions, and the SHS Government shall accord all necessary assistance for the creation of new religious or charitable institutions such as is guaranteed to other private institutions of this nature."
(Treaty on Minorities, Article 10)

1.   The Yugoslav Government conficates property of pious and charitable foundations

Not only has the Yugoslav Government not assisted in the creation of new Moslem pious institutions, it has even confiscated the property of many existing charitable institutions (*vakufs*). Let us refer to a number of cases:

a)   The Grand Mosque of Burmalli in the city of Skopje was expropriated without the consent of the community and without compensation. An officers' club was built on the site. It is possible that consent was obtained subsequently by threats from General Terzić who had already made his opinion known: either a million dinar or two bombs to blow up the mosque.

b)   The Mosque of Gazi Mustafa Pasha in the city of Skopje maintained a first-rate charitable institution. It held full title to thirteen villages, among them Kreshova, Bullaçana, Rashtak and Novosella / Novoselo. The executor of this property, Shevket Bey, son of Haxhi Mustafa Bey, had all this property confiscated by the Government. This foundation used to distribute 200 loaves of bread to the poor of the city every day.

c)   The Fevri Mosque in the town of Tetova / Tetovo was set on fire in broad daylight and surrounded by the police so that people who had arrived on the scene could not put the fire out. It was the fifth time it had been set on fire. The mosque had been saved four times by the swift reaction of the population.

d)   In Tetova / Tetovo again, the foundation or *vakuf* of the Harabati *teke* (Moslem order), had its property, consisting of about one thousand hectares of farmland, confiscated. Montenegrins were then settled on this land. Deprived of its revenues, the monastery was itself dissolved.

2.   The pious foundations of Albanian Christians have been plundered, too

Such torment is not confined to the religious institutions of Moslem Albanians. It also affects the foundations of Christian Albanians. For example:

a)   In Gjakova / Djakovica the property of the Catholic church was confiscated and, despite protests from priests and followers, Orthodox Montenegrins were brought in to settle the land.

b)   In the village of Novosella / Novoselo, inhabited exclusively by Catholic Albanians, the church was in possession of a *çiflik* (property) called 'Mali i Vogël'. It was dispossessed of this property which was settled by Montenegrins brought in expressly for this purpose.

3.   Not even cemeteries have been exempted

Such unjust measures have also been taken against Christian and Moslem Albanian cemeteries. Here are a few examples:

a)   The old Catholic cemetery of Peja / Peć was confiscated and the land was given to a Montenegrin who turned it into a vineyard. The Albanian priest won his case, but the new owner was not expelled, probably for 'political reasons', and continues to grow grapes on the land.

b)   The Moslem cemetery in Tetova / Tetovo, which also belonged to a *vakuf*, suffered the same fate. Part of the land was given to the authorities to serve as a nursery. The rest was distributed free of charge to Orthodox Serbs from the region, and not to the Moslem community (it being Albanian). The tombstones, many of which were of great value due to their artistry, were not handed over to the Moslem community, but were used as construction material for the railway station. Even today, one can seen inscriptions from tombstones on the façade of the said building.

4.   Difficulties involving burials

The saddest thing of all in this matter is that the authorities, simply to create a nuisance, have long been postponing the decision as to a new site for a cemetery. In the meantime, the poor people do not know where to bury their dead because the authorities send them from one place to another. Their intentions are obvious: to make the population so desperate, finding justice nowhere, that they will be willing to emigrate. This is but one element.

The same has occurred in many other localities, for example in Peja / Peć, Gjakova / Djakovica and Skopje where the *vakufs* were deprived of their cemeteries without any compensaton.

* * *

In conclusion, we have the honour to stress that these are but a few examples among thousands of others.

[Taken from *La Situation de la minorité albanaise en Yougoslavie* (Geneva 1930). Translated from the French original by Robert Elsie]

The Expulsion of the Albanians

Memorandum presented in Belgrade on 7 March 1937

Vaso Čubrilović

The expulsion of the Albanians

The problem of the Albanians in the life of our country and people did not arise yesterday. It played a major role in our life in the Middle Ages, but its importance only became decisive towards the end of the seventeenth century, at a time when the masses of the Serbian people were displaced northwards out of their former ancestral territory of Rashka / Raška, supplanted by Albanian highlanders. Gradually, the latter came down from their mountains to the fertile plains of Metohija and Kosovo. Spreading northwards, they continued in the direction of southern and western Morava and, crossing the Shar mountains, descended into Polog and, from there, towards the Vardar. Thus, by the nineteenth century was formed the Albanian triangle, a wedge which, with its Debar-Rogozna axis in the rear, penetrated as far into our territories as Nish / Niš and separated our ancient land of Rashka from Macedonia and the Vardar Valley.

In the nineteenth century, this wedge, inhabited by wild Albanian elements, prevented the maintenance of any strong cultural, educational and economic links between our northern and southern territories. This was also the main reason why, until 1878, Serbia was unable to establish and maintain continuous links with Macedonia through Vranja and the Black Mountain of Skopje and thus to exercise its cultural and political influence on the Vardar Valley, to the extent that one would have expected in view of conducive geographical factors and historical traditions in these regions. Although the Bulgarians began their life as a nation later than the Serbs, they had greater success initially. This explains why there are permanent settlements of southern Slavs from Vidin in the north to Ohrid in the south. Serbia began to slice off pieces of this Albanian wedge as early as the first uprising, by expelling the northernmost Albanian settlers from Jagodina.

Thanks to the wide-ranging national plans of Jovan Ristić, Serbia sliced off another piece of this wedge with the annexation of Toplica and Kosanica. At that time, the regions between Jastrebac and southern Morava were radically cleared of Albanians.

From 1918 onwards, it was the task of our present state to suppress what remained of the Albanian triangle, but it did not succeed. Though there are a number of reasons for this, we shall examine only the most important of them.

1.   The fundamental mistake made by the authorities in charge at that time was that, forgetting where they were, they wanted to solve all the major ethnic problems of the troubled and bloody Balkans by Western methods. Turkey brought to the Balkans the customs of the Sheriat, according to which victory in war and the occupation of a country conferred the right on the victor to dispose of the lives and property of the subjected inhabitants. Even the Balkan Christians learned from the Turks that not only state power and domination, but also home and property could be won and lost by the sword. This concept of land ownership in the Balkans was to be softened somewhat by laws, ordinances and international agreements brought about under pressure from Europe, but it has, to a good extent, remained a primary instrument of leverage for Turkey and the Balkan states up to this very day. We need not evoke the distant past. It is sufficient to refer to a few cases which have taken place in recent times: the transfer of Greeks from Asia Minor to Greece and of Turks from Greece to Asia Minor, or the recent

expulsion of Turks from Bulgaria and Romania to Turkey. While all the Balkan states, since 1912, have solved or are on the point of solving their problems with national minorities through mass population transfers, we have stuck to the slow and cumbersome strategy of gradual colonization. The result has been negative, as evident from the statistics of the eighteen districts which make up the Albanian triangle. These figures show that the natural growth of the Albanian population in these regions is still greater than the total increase in our population from both natural growth and new settlers (from 1921 to 1931, the Albanian population increased by 68,060, while the Serbs showed an increase of 58,745, i.e. a difference of 9,315 in favour of the Albanians). Taking into account the intractable character of the Albanians, the pronounced increase in their numbers and the ever-increasing difficulties of colonization will eventually put in question even those few successes we have achieved in our colonization from 1918 onwards.

2.   Even the strategy of gradual colonization was not properly applied. Worse still in a matter of such importance, there was no specific state plan for every government and regime to adhere to and implement. Work was intermittent, in fits and starts, with each new minister undoing what his predecsssor had done and himself creating nothing solid. Laws and regulations were amended but, weak as they were, were never implemented. Some individuals, especially deputies from other regions, who could not manage to secure a mandate at home, would go down south and butter up the non-national elements to gain a mandate there, thus sacrificing major national and state interests. The colonization apparatus was extremely costly, inflated and loaded with people who were not only incompetent, but were also frequently without scruples. Their activities are indeed a topic in itself. Finally, one need only total up the huge sums this state has invested in colonization and divide them by the number of families settled to prove how costly every new household established since the war has been, regardless of whether or not this expenditure was met by the settlers themselves or by the state. Likewise, it would be interesting to compare the amounts paid out for personal expenditures and those for materials needed for colonization. In

the past, Serbia went about this matter quite differently. Karageorge, during the first uprising, as well as Miloš, Mihajlo and Jovan Ristić had no special ministry of land reform, no general land inspectors, or costly apparatus, and still, they managed to purge Serbia of foreign elements and populate it with our own people who felled the endless forests of Shumadia (Šumadija), tranforming them from the wild state they were once in to the fertile Shumadia we know today.

3.   Even those few thousand families who were settled after the war did not remain where they were originally located. There was more success in Kosovo, especially in the Lab / Llap valley, where the Toplicans penetrated of their own accord from north to south. Our oldest and most stable settlements there were established with elements from various Serbian regions. In Drenica and Metohija we had no success at all. Colonization should never be carried out with Montenegrins alone. We do not think that they are suitable as colonists because of their pastoral indolence. This applies to the first generation only. The second generation is quite different, more active and more practical. The village of Petrovo in Miroć north of the Danube, the most advanced village in Krajina, is inhabited exclusively by Montenegrins. In Serbia today, there are thousands of other flourishing towns, especially in Toplica and Kosanica, which were established by Montenegrins of the first generation who mixed with more advanced elements. The foregoing consideration, nonetheless, still applies in Metohija where, since the settlers are on their own ancestral lands, old customs still abound. A visit to any coffee-house in Peja / Peć is sufficient proof. This is why our colonization has had so little success throughout Metohija. It must be admitted, on the other hand, that these colonies were poorly situated on barren, scrub-covered land, and were almost totally lacking in basic agricultural equipment. These people should have been given more assistance than other colonists because they were among the poorest Montenegrin elements.

4.   Without doubt, the main cause for the lack of success in our colonization of these regions was that the best land remained in the hands of the Albanians. The only possible means for our mass colonization of these regions to succeed is for us to take

the land away from them. This could have been achieved easily during the rebellion after the war, when the insurgents were active, by expelling part of the Albanian population to Albania, by refusing to legalize their usurpations and by buying up their pasture land. Here, we must refer once again to the gross error committed in our post-war strategy, that of the right to own land. Instead of taking advantage of the strategy used by the Albanians themselves for ownership of the land they usurped (scarcely any of them had deeds issued by the Turks, and those who did, got them only for land purchased), we not only legalized all these usurpations to the detriment of our state and nation, but worse still, we accustomed the Albanians to western European attitudes to private property. Prior to that, they could never have understood such concepts. In this way, we ourselves handed them a weapon with which to defend themselves, keeping the best land for themselves and rendering impossible the nationalization of a region of supreme importance to us.

It is apparent from the above that our colonization strategy in the south has not yielded the results which ought to have been achieved and which now impose themselves upon us as a major necessity of state. We are not criticizing this strategy merely for the sake of criticism, but so that, on the basis of our past experience, we can find the right way to solve this problem.

The problem of colonization of the southern regions

Reading the first part of this paper and comprehending the problem of colonization of the south, one realizes immediately that the primary issue at stake are the regions north and south of the Shar mountains. This is no coincidence. The wedge of Albanians on both sides of the Shar range is of great national and strategic significance to our state. We have already mentioned the way the population structure came into existence there and the importance of these regions for links to the lands of the Vardar Valley, which are firmly within the limits of our ancient territories. The strength of Serbian expansion ever since the foundation of the first Serbian state in the ninth century has lain in the continuity both of this expansion and of the expansion of ancient

Rashka / Raška in all directions, including southwards. But this continuity has been interrupted by the Albanians, and until the ancient link between Serbia and Montenegro on the one hand, and Macedonia on the other, is re-established along the whole line from the River Drin to southern Morava, we will not be secure in the possession of our territories. From an ethnic point of view, the Macedonians will only unite with us, if they receive true ethnic support from their Serbian motherland, something which they have lacked to this day. This can only be achieved through the destruction of the Albanian wedge.

From a military and strategic point of view, the Albanian wedge occupies one of the most vital points in our country, the starting point from which major Balkan rivers flow to the Adriatic Sea, to the Black Sea and to the Aegean. Possession of this strategic point determines, to a large degree, the fate of the central Balkans, and in particular, the fate of the main line of Balkan communications from the Morava to the Vardar. It is no coincidence that many battles of decisive importance to the destiny of the Balkans were fought here (Nemanja against the Greeks, the Serbs against the Turks in 1389, Hunyadi against the Turks in 1446). In the twentieth century, only a country inhabited by its own people can be confident of its security. It is therefore imperative that we not allow such points of strategic importance to be held by hostile and alien elements. This is all the more true in this case in that the element in question has the support of a nation state of the same race. Today this state is powerless, but even as such, it has become a base for Italian imperialism which aims to use the country as a means of penetrating into the heart of our nation. Our people, who are willing and able to defend their land and country, are the most reliable element in the fight against such penetration.

With the exception of this block of eighteen districts, the Albanians and other national minorities in other parts of the south are scattered and, therefore, constitute less of a threat to the life of our nation and state. Nationalizing the regions around the Shar mountains would mean that we can stifle irredentism once and for all, and ensure our control over these territories forever.

Colonization from the north should be kept to a minimum in the regions inhabited by the Macedonians. Here land is scarce and for this reason, the Macedonians would resist an influx of settlers from the north, all the more so because they would regard this influx as a sign of mistrust on our part. As such, even such a minimal colonization would do us more harm than good. If we do send people down there, to the region south of the Black Mountain of Skopje, they should be people from Vranje and Leskovac, who are closer in mentality and culture to the Macedonians. By no means should we send people from the Dinaric region because their irritable and uncontrolled temperaments would only arouse the hostility of the local population. We repeat that this problem will only be solved when our colonies advancing from the north through Kosovo and Metohija in the direction of the Shar mountains and Polog have reached Macedonian settlements.

The problem of the Sandjak of Novi Pazar is solving itself and no longer plays the role it did in the life of our country before 1912. Let it suffice to mention that with the elimination of the Albanians, the last link between our Moslems in Bosnia and Novi Pazar and the rest of the Moslem world will have been cut. They are becoming a religious minority, the only Moslem minority in the Balkans, and this fact will accelerate their assimilation.

Montenegro has become a serious problem recently. This barren land cannot sustain the population which, despite resettlement, increased by 16% from 1912 to 1931. This impulsive, pastoral people has contributed many essential characteristics to our race over the centuries. Channelled in the right direction, their energy will not be destructive, and could, if directed towards the southeast, be employed for the common good of the country.

Summing up:

The Albanians cannot be dispelled by means of gradual colonization alone. They are the only people who, over the last millenium, managed not only to resist the nucleus of our state, Rashka and Zeta, but also to harm us by pushing our ethnic borders northwards and eastwards. When in the last millenium our ethnic borders were shifted up to Subotica in the north and to the Kupa River in the northwest, the Albanians drove us out of the Shkodër (Scutari) region, out of the former capital of Bodin, and out of Metohija and Kosovo. The only way and only means to cope with them is through the brute force of an organized state, in which we have always been superior to them. If since 1912 we have had no success in the struggle against them, we have only ourselves to blame since we have not used this force as we should have. There is no possibility for us to assimilate the Albanians. On the contrary, because their roots are in Albania, their national awareness has been awakened, and if we do not settle the score with them once and for all, within 20-30 years we shall have to cope with a terrible irredentism, the signs of which are already apparent and will inevitably put all our southern territories in jeopardy.

The international problems of colonization

If we proceed on the assumption that the gradual displacement of the Albanians by means of gradual colonization is ineffective, we are then left with only one course - that of mass resettlement. In this connection, we must consider two countries: Albania and Turkey.

With its sparse population, its many undrained swamps and uncultivated valleys, Albania would have no difficulty admitting some hundred thousand Albanians from our country. With its vast and uninhabited frontiers in Asia Minor and Kurdistan, modern Turkey, for its part, offers seemingly unlimited opportunities for internal colonization. Despite efforts on the part of Kemal Atatürk, the Turks have not yet been able to fill the vacuum created by the evacuation of the Greeks from Asia Minor to Greece and of some of the Kurds to Persia. Hence, the greatest possibilities lie in sending the bulk of our displaced Albanians there.

Firstly, I stress that we must not limit ourselves to diplomatic *démarches* with the Ankara government, but must employ all means available to convince Tirana to accept some of our displaced people, too. I believe that we will come up against difficulties in Tirana because Italy will try to hinder the process. Be this as it may, money plays an important role in Tirana. In negotiations on the issue, the Albanian government should be informed that we will stop at nothing to achieve the final solution to this question. At the same time, we should tell them about colonization subsidies available, stressing that no controls will be exercised over them. Eventually, notables in Tirana will see the material gains involved and be persuaded through secret channels not to raise any objections to the whole business.

We have heard that Turkey has agreed, initially, to accept about 200,000 of our displaced persons on condition that they are Albanians, something which is most advantageous to us. We must comply with Turkey's wish immediately and sign a convention for the resettlement of the Albanian population as soon as possible. Concerning the resettlement of this Albanian population, we must study conventions which Turkey signed recently with Greece, Romania and Bulgaria, paying particular attention to two aspects: Turkey should accept the largest possible contingent and should be given maximum assistance from a financial point of view, in particular for the swift organization of transportation facilities. As is inevitable in such cases, this problem will no doubt give rise to some international concern. Over the last hundred years, whenever such actions have been carried out in the Balkans, there has always been some power which has protested because the action did not conform to its interests. In the present case, Albania and Italy may make some protest. We have already pointed out that attempts should be made to conclude an agreement with Albania on this matter and, failing this, we should at least secure its silence on the evacuation of the Albanians to Turkey. We repeat that skilful action and money properly used in Tirana may be decisive in this matter. World opinion, especially that financed by Italy, will be upset a little. Nevertheless, the world today has grown used to things much worse than this and is so preoccupied with its day-to-day problems that this issue should not be a cause for concern. At a time when Germany can expel tens of thousands of Jews and Russia can shift millions of people from one part of the continent to another, the evacuation of a few hundred thousand Albanians will not set off a world war. Be this as it may, decision-makers should know ahead of time what they want and unfalteringly pursue those goals, regardless of possible international repercussions.

Italy, no doubt, will raise more difficulties, but at present the country is extremely preoccupied by problems of its own in Abyssinia. Austria, for its part, will not dare to go very far in its opposition. To tell the truth, the greatest danger lies in the possibility that our great allies, France and Britain, may interfere. These two countries must be given the calm and resolute reply that the security of the Morava-Vardar line is in their interests. That this is so was confirmed during the last great war and that line can only be made more secure, for them and for us, if in ethnic terms, we completely dominate the region around the Shar mountains and Kosovo.

The mode of evacuation

As we have already stressed, the mass evacuation of the Albanians from their triangle is the only effective course we can take. In order to relocate a whole people, the first prerequisite is the creation of a suitable psychosis. This can be done in various ways.

It is well known that the Moslem masses are generally readily influenced by religion and are prone to superstition and fanaticism. Therefore, we must first of all win over the clergy and men of influence through money and threats in order for them to give their support to the evacuation of the Albanians. Agitators, especially from Turkey, must be found as quickly as possible to promote the evacuation, if Turkey will provide them for us. They must laud the beauties of the new territories in Turkey and the easy and pleasant life to be had there, and must kindle religious fanaticism among the masses and awaken pride in the Turkish state. Our press can be of colossal assistance by describing how gently the evacuation of the Turks from Dobruja took place and how easily they settled in their new regions. Such information would create the requisite predisposition for the masses of Albanians to be willing to leave.

Another means would be coercion by the state apparatus. The law must be enforced to the letter so as to make staying intolerable for the Albanians: fines, imprisonment, the ruthless application of all police regulations, such as the prohibition of smuggling, cutting forests, damaging agriculture, leaving dogs unchained, compulsory labour and any other measure that an experienced police force can contrive. From the economic aspect, this should include the refusal to recognize old land deeds. The work of the land registry should be accompanied from the start by the ruthless collection of taxes and the payment of all private and public debts, the requisitioning of all public and municipal pasture land, the cancellation of concessions, the withdrawal of permits to exercise an occupation, dismissal from government, private and municipal offices etc., all of which will speed up the process of evacuation. Health measures should include the harsh application of all regulations, even within homes, the pulling down of encircling walls and high hedges around private houses, and the rigorous implementation of veterinary measures which will result in a ban on selling livestock on the market, etc. All these measures can be applied in a practical and effective way. The Albanians are very touchy when it comes to religion. They must therefore be harassed on this score, too. This can be achieved through the ill-treatment of their clergy, the demolition of their cemeteries, the prohibition of polygamy, and especially the inflexible application of the regulation compelling girls to attend elementary school, wherever they are.

Private initiative, too, can assist greatly in this direction. We should distribute weapons to our colonists, as need be. The old form of Chetnik action should be organized and secretly assisted. In particular, a mass migration of Montenegrins should be launched from the mountain pastures in order to create a large-scale conflict with the Albanians in Metohija. This conflict should be prepared and encouraged by people we can trust. This can be easily achieved since the Albanians have, indeed, revolted. The whole affair can be presented as a conflict between clans and, if need be, can be ascribed to economic reasons. Finally, local riots can be incited. These will be bloodily suppressed by the most effective means, though by colonists from the Montenegrin clans and the Chetniks, rather than by means of the army.

There remains one more method Serbia employed with great practical effect after 1878, that is, secretly razing Albanian villages and urban settlements to the ground.

The organization of the evacuation

From the attached map[19], it is apparent what regions must be cleared. They are: Upper Dibër / Debar, Lower Polog, Upper Polog, the Shar mountains, Drenica, Peja / Peć, Istog / Istok, Vuçitërna / Vučitrn, Stavica, Llap / Lab, Graçanica / Gračanica, Nerodimja / Nerodimje, Gjakova / Djakovica, Podgor, Gora (Dragash), Lugu i Drinit / Podrimje, Gjilan / Gnjilane and Kaçanik / Kačanik. Of these regions, which together form the Albanian wedge, the most important for us at the

---

[19] The author of the memorandum attaches to the document a detailed map of the region to be cleared [editor's note].

moment are: Peja / Peć, Gjakova / Djakovica, Lugu i Drinit / Podrimje, Gora (Dragash), Podgor, Shar, Istog / Istok and Drenica, all to the north of the Shar mountains, Upper Dibër / Debar and the two Pologs to the south, and the Shar mountains themselves. These are border regions that must be cleared of Albanians at any cost. The internal regions such as Kaçanik / Kačanik, Gjilan / Gnjilane, Nerodimja / Nerodimje, Graçanica / Gračanica, Llap / Lab, and Vuçitërna / Vučitrn etc. must be weakened if possible, particularly Kaçanik / Kačanik and Llap / Lab, while the others should be gradually and systematically colonized over a period of decades.

The above-mentioned methods should be used primarily in the border regions, if we wish to clear them of Albanians.

During resettlement, the following must be kept in mind:

In the first place, resettlement should begin in the villages and then move to the towns. The villages are the more dangerous, being more compact. Then, the mistake of removing only the poor should be avoided. The middle and wealthy classes make up the backbone of every nation. They, too, must therefore be persecuted and driven out. Lacking the support which their economically independent compatriots have, the poor will then submit more quickly. This question is of great importance, and I emphasize this, because one of the main causes for the failure of our colonization in the south has been that the poor were expelled while the rich remained. We were, thus, no better off because we gained very little land for the settlement of our colonists. To create a proper psychosis for resettlement, everything possible must be done to evacuate whole villages, or at least whole families. It must be prevented at all costs that part of a family is transferred while other members remain behind. Our state is willing to spend millions not to make life easier for the Albanians, but to get rid of as many of them as possible. For this reason, those who remain behind must be barred absolutely from purchasing property from those evacuated. This should be taken into consideration in the evacuation of individuals and of whole villages if we want to make things as easy as possible for them during the process of relocation.

Once they agree to move, they should be given all the assistance they require. Administrative formalities should be simplified, their property paid for on the spot, travel documents issued without the least formality, and they should be assisted in getting to the nearest railway station. Trains should be made available for them as far as Salonika, and from there, they should be transported immediately by ship to Asia. It is very important that the journey be easy, comfortable and cheap. Train travel should perhaps be made free of charge and displaced persons should be assisted with food because, whether or not large masses of people can be evacuated or not depends largely on conditions of transport. Fear of difficulties en route is a major factor in keeping people from departing. This fear must be overcome by solving all the problems connected with the journey quickly and energetically. Particular care must therefore be taken to ensure that these people have the fewest possible difficulties en route. Simple people often have trouble finding their way, so it would be advisable to have major travel enterprises study transportation systems and adapt them accordingly. The displaced person must pass from hand to hand without feeling that his movement is a burden. Only in this way will it be possible to create a proper flow of Albanian evacuees and empty the south of them.

Depopulating and repopulating regions

The problem of the establishment of colonies in the depopulated regions is no less important than the expulsion of the Albanians.

The first question to arise is: Who is to be settled here? The most natural thing would be to populate these regions with elements of our people from destitute areas: Montenegrins in the first place, but also Hercegovinians, Ličanas and Krajšniks. The Montenegrins are the most appropriate for several reasons, and Metohija, Drenica and Kosovo are the most natural places for them to descend into from their impoverished mountain homelands. The increase of population in Montenegro has caused much poverty there which, in recent times, has given rise to continual social and political unrest. This is unfavourable for our control of the country and is very dangerous for the maintenance of law and order in the future. Giving them maize and pensions is useless. The only solution is to send them down into the fertile regions of Metohija, Drenica and Kosovo. The Montenegrins will prove to be excellent instruments to overcome the Albanians since they are akin to them in mentality and temperament. They must be settled initially in the regions north of the Shar mountains. Along with them, however, people from Ličan, Krajšnica, Serbia, Čačak, Užice and Toplica should be brought in as colonists as well. This is necessary in order to create improved working habits and organization among the Montenegrins, and to break down the nomadic group mentality, the spirit of collectivity which characterizes the highlanders, by mixing and by intermarriage with people from various Dinaric regions. In this way, a new type of Montenegrin can be created with a less local and more broad-minded, Serbian outlook.

Suitable conditions should be created for southern Serbian emigrants living in the regions south of the Shar mountains so that they can take possession of the fertile lands. They are honest, hardworking people who would be grateful to the state all their lives if better living conditions could be created for them in rural areas. The rural southern Serbs have a right to expect more care and attention than we are giving them today. Settling these poor people in Polog (Upper and Lower) and Dibër / Debar and allocating pasture land to them instead of to the Albanians will give them a sense of belonging to the state and they will be more willing, accordingly, to defend its borders.

Colonization south of the Shar mountains and the Black Mountain of Skopje can also be achieved with Serbs from Vranje, Leskovac, Pirot and Vlasenica, especially those from destitute mountain villages. We repeat that the Dinarics should not be allowed to expand south of the line formed by the Black Mountain of Skopje and the Shar mountain range.

It is essential to avoid bureaucracy and petty formalities in the settlement of villages cleared of Albanians. The first and immediate step is to give the colonists deeds to the land they are settling. One of the main reasons for the failure of our colonization so far has been that settlers did not feel secure on their land because they did not receive a title to it and were thus left to the mercy of unscrupulous petty officials and local politicians. The peasant only feels secure if he knows that no one can take his land away from him. Such a guarantee should therefore be provided from the start. On the other hand, it is dangerous to give colonists the full and unrestricted ownership to land. In principle, homesteaders are carrying out a mission on behalf of the state and the nation, and must carry through with their mission if they are to keep their homesteads. They should not, therefore, have full and unrestricted ownership of the property in question. Because there are so many different types of people among them, from village workers who have lost their inner attachment to land to herdsmen who will have to adapt themselves to agriculture, their attachment to the land must have force of law. This will ensure that they begin to love their new home and region, and if they do not succeed in this, their children at least will. For this reason, colonists should be prevented by law from obtaining full ownership of the land for any period of less than thirty years, even though the deeds are handed out at the start. According to the laws of our country, women do not enjoy the right to inherit property. In order to avoid fragmentation of property into tiny parcels, women must be excluded from inheriting such homesteads except in cases where the colonist has no male descendant and plans to bring a bridegroom into the household. The properties which have been given to the colonists up to now have been small. Bearing in mind intensive farming methods here, the fall in prices for farm products, and the large size of families among the colonists, 5-10 hectares of land is insufficient to ensure the economic survival of the settlers.

It is better to settle a region with a smaller number of colonists, giving them better conditions for development, than with a large number of rural semi-proletarians. This is another cause of failure in our colonization of the south and of the north up to now.

Individuals suitable for settling land under very difficult conditions are rare among other nations. Those few successes we have achieved in our colonization strategy have been the result of the aptitude of our race for colonization. It is only our peasants who are able to survive when shifted from one environment to another and put up against scrubland which has never been used for agriculture. Think of how they would flourish if the state were to carry out its duties and provide them with everything they needed.

On 10 February 1865, the government of Prince Mihajlo passed a law on the 'Settlement of Foreigners in Serbia'. Under this law, the Serbian government granted poor colonists from neighbouring regions 1.8 hectares of arable land, 1.8 hectares of non-arable land, a house, a yoke of oxen, a cart, two goats or sheep, a sow, necessary tools and 120 grosh in cash. In addition to this, they were of course given maize for food to last them until the first harvest. One plough was provided for every two families. These fixed and movable assets were granted to the settlers for a term of fifteen years, without the right to sell them. At the end of this period, the assets became their property. For the first five years, the settlers were exempt from all kinds of government taxes. For ten years they were also exempt from universal compulsory service in the regular army and for five years from service in the people's militia. The response from all sides was such that within a few months all homesteads were taken and we were immediately able to colonize more land than we have been able to do for several years since the war. Had the government granted such favourable conditions for settlers after 1918, our situation in the Vojvodina and in southern Serbia would be much different. This is how we must act in the future, if we want to achieve success.

There are also lessons to be learned from the colonization of Toplica and Kosanica after 1878 when the Albanians were expelled from this region. The method of colonization here was laid down in the law of 3 January 1880. On 3 February of the same year, the People's Council approved an amendment to the law on agrarian relations under the motto "land for the peasants." Without hesitation, Serbia applied for its first foreign loan in order to pay Turkey for the lands taken. It did not set up any ministry of agrarian reform or costly apparatus to deal with the problem of colonization. Everything was managed in a simple and practical manner. The police distributed land to all those who were willing to work it. People came from Montenegro, Sjenica, Vranje, Kosovo, Peja / Peć etc. and, in a matter of thirty years, Toplica and Kosanica, once Albanian regions of ill-repute, gave Serbia the finest regiment of the 1912-1918 wars, the Second Iron Regiment. During that period, Toplica and Kosanica paid and repaid, with the blood of their sons, for the millions of dinars which Serbia had spent to settle these regions.

It is only by following this example and understanding what is required, sparing neither money nor blood, that our nation can create a new Toplica out of Kosovo and Metohija.

Hence, if we want the colonists to remain where they are, we must assure them of all necessary means of livelihood within the first few years and severely prohibit any speculation with the houses and property of the displaced Albanians. The government must reserve itself the unlimited right to dispose of the fixed and movable assets of the

Albanians and must settle its own colonists there as soon as the Albanians have departed. This is important because it rarely happens that a whole village departs at once. The first to be settled in these villages should be the Montenegrins who, with their arrogant, irrascible and merciless behaviour, will drive the remaining Albanians away. Then colonists from other regions can be brought in.

This paper deals with the colonization of southern Serbia only. The problem of the Vojvodina, in particular with the Hungarian triangle in Bačka, i.e. Senta - Kula - Bačka Topola, is however no less important to us. Destroying this triangle in the Vojvodina is indeed just as essential as eradicating the Albanian wedge around the Shar mountains. Tens of thousands of Hungarian farmhands have been left behind since the break-up of the big estates in the Vojvodina and constitute a great burden for the Serbian and German farm owners in the region. Some of these Hungarian and even German farm labourers and small proprietors could be sent to the south because in Bačka, on the border with Hungary, they constitute a real threat, all the more so since the Serbs in Bačka represent only 25% of the population. In southern Serbia, they would become good citizens by defending their property against Albania and would integrate well into our people. What is more important, since they are more progressive and of a higher cultural level than our peasants, they would provide a good example of advanced farming methods. We stress, however, that Serbs from the Vojvodina should not be sent to the south for colonization. There is still much land to be colonized in the Vojvodina so that they should be given homesteads there instead. It must be noted that in the 1928-1929 period, there was a widespread movement among Hungarians and Germans from the Vojvodina to move to southern Serbia. Not understanding the problem, our authorities were against such a movement and nipped it in the bud. Any such reaction on the part of the government today must be countered, and the public must be instructed to encourage the movement of Hungarians and Germans from the Vojvodina, especially those from Bačka, to the south.

The colonization apparatus

Of particular importance for the solution of the question under discussion is the existence of a proper apparatus to direct the whole business. The poor work done by the apparatus implementing our colonization strategy in the past was in good part responsible for its failures. To avoid the same mistakes in the future, we must carry out a reorganization.

No other question demands such continuity of implementation as our colonization strategy. We have pointed out that one of the main reasons for the failure of our colonies both in the north and in the south has been the inconsistent work and the vacillations on policy implemented after each change of government. If this is to be avoided in the future, our colonization strategy must be entrusted to the General Staff of the army. Why? Simply for reasons of defence. Our army is intent on settling our people along the borders, especially in the most delicate sectors. To this end, it will do its utmost to secure these borders with the firmest possible settlements. The General Staff, as the prime institution for the defence of our national interests, can contribute a great deal to our colonization strategy as a whole. It will know very well how to protect the colonization strategy from the private interference of those who want to use it for their own personal interests, and from external influence. Another important fact is that it would be easier for the General Staff to convince the responsible bodies of the importance of the issue and to force them to take effective action. The People's Council would have more faith in it and would grant the necessary credits to it more readily than to others.

The General Staff would guide all the work via a government Commission for Colonization. This Commission would be quite independent, though under the direct supervision of the Chief of General Staff, and would have under its control all bodies involved in our colonization strategy. Representatives of various interested ministries, national associations, technical organizations and scholarly institutions would also be made to take part in this Commission.

The greatest mistake of our colonization strategy in the past lay in the fact that the untrained and incompetent bureaucrats had the main say, and dealt with problems only superficially and in a piecemeal manner. We need only recall the settlement campaign carried out by volunteers from Hungary in Ovce Polje and Kadrifikovo, or the emigrants from Istria and Gorica who settled around Demir Kapija. The matter requires close collaboration between the government, private initiative and scholarly institutions. Private initiative can operate in many directions. The People's Defence, the Sokolašas, the Chetnik Associations etc. could take action against the Albanians which would be inappropriate for the state. Associations of agronomists, doctors, engineers and cooperatives etc. could provide valuable assistance with their technical advisors in solving the many problems which will arise during the colonization campaign. Cultural associations, such as Prosveta in Sarajevo, Matica Srbska in Novi Sad, the St. Sava Associations in Belgrade etc. have their role to play, too.

Undoubtedly, our institutions of higher learning have begun to lose the prestige they once had. The main reason for this is that the university and the Academy of Sciences are becoming increasingly estranged from real life and are neglecting their main duty in a relatively backward country such as ours: i. e. paving the way for the application of the scientific achievements of the twentieth century. Many billions would have been saved in this country, many mistakes would have been avoided in our government policy, including our colonization policy, had the problems been studied seriously and objectively in advance by competent scholars before they were taken up for solution. Our policy of colonization, likewise, would have acquired a more serious approach, greater continuity and effective application, had the opinions of experts and scholars been sought in advance. To start with, the Royal Serbian Academy of Sciences and the University of Belgrade ought to take the initiative to organize scientific studies of the whole problem of colonization in our country. This would be feasible for many reasons. At the university we have experts on every aspect of colonization. Teachers and academicians at the university are independent scholars, less subject to external political influence. They already have good experience in such fields and their scholarly work is a guarantee of objectivity. They should, therefore, take the initiative of setting up a colonization institute, the task of which would be to pursue colonization studies. The government, for its part, should detach from the ministries all the institutions which have been engaged with this problem so far, and create a special institution, "The Colonization Inspection Office"

The Colonization Inspection Office would be headed by an Inspector General, appointed by decree on the recommendation of the Minister of War, the Chief of General Staff and the Prime Minister. All the work in the colonization institute and in the Colonization Inspection Office would be carried out on orders from and under the supervision of the government Commission for Colonization, while the Inspector General would be answerable to the Chief of General Staff.

The colonization institute would be divided into the following sections: 1) organization, 2) education and culture, 3) finance, 4) agriculture, 5) construction, 6) hygiene, etc. In agreement with scientific, cultural and educational associations and institutions, and with national associations, the various sections would study problems of colonization and prepare directives, thus supplying our colonization policy with solid, scientifically elaborated material on the basis of which decisions could be taken. Managing this institute would be people from the Commission for Colonization, including representatives of the above-mentioned ministries, the university, the Academy of Sciences and private, national, education and cultural organizations who would be elected or appointed to this body. In this case, care must be taken not to bring in people just for honour's sake, but only men who love and are dedicated to this great work.

The heads and employees of the institute should be selected by competition. The institute would then supply the Colonization Inspection Office with scientifically elaborated material for the implementation of our colonization strategy. Should differences of opinion arise between the Colonization Inspection Office and the institute over some fundamental question, the Chief of General Staff would have the final say.

The Colonization Inspection Office must have its executive headquarters in the territory and be made up of people selected for their enthusiasm and readiness for this work, whether or not they are employed by the government. They should, if possible, be selected by means of competition and should be appointed upon the proposal of the Chief of General Staff. Compromised or incompetent cadres must be dismissed. During its work, the Colonization Inspection Office and its organs must avoid bureaucracy as much as possible, while keeping in mind one thing only - the expulsion of the Albanians as quickly as possible and resettlement by our colonists.

The police apparatus will play a very important role in this action. It is, therefore, essential to select and second the most energetic and honest officers. Their transfer should be made with the approval of the Chief of General Staff, and for such a difficult job they should be paid from secret loans. Stern measures must be taken against anyone who commits the slightest infraction. A special commissar, who would execute the orders of the state colonization inspector, must be appointed for the whole of the eighteen districts mentioned. The prefects of the districts must be given special, wide-ranging powers for their work, as well as appropriate instructions. Our political parties should be told curtly that rivalry among them during elections in these districts is strictly prohibited, and that any interference by deputies in favour of the Albanians is categorically forbidden.

The government institute and the Colonization Inspection Office would elaborate the technical details for organizing the evacuation of the Albanians and the relocation of our settlers. It would not be bad, perhaps, if another private organization were to be created, in addition to these two official institutions. This private organization would be created out of existing associations and have the task of assisting in the implementation of our colonization strategy through private initiative. It would be best if the federation of our cultural and education associations could take over this job. Its main task would be to coordinate and assist in the promotion of links between them and the colonization institute.

Funding

Whenever our colonization strategy has been criticized for its lack of success, its defenders have always excused themselves with the inadequacy of funds the government has allocated to this work. We do not deny that this has been the case up to a point. It must be said, however, that more has been spent in our country on the maintenance of this apparatus and its irrational activities than on the work of colonization itself. Nevertheless, even though the government has not provided as much as it should have, it must be understood that every country has its own primary and secondary interests to look after. Among a country's primary interests, without doubt, is the maintenance of its rule in regions of national insecurity by colonizing such regions with its own people. All other commitments are of an importance secondary to this. Funds can and must be found to deal with this problem. We have already mentioned the colonization of Toplica and Kosanica and the benefits derived from this. Given that the small Kingdom of Serbia did not hesitate to make great financial sacrifices, indeed did not even hesitate as a free and independent kingdom to seek its first loan for colonization, is it possible that our present-day Yugoslavia would be unable to do the same? It can and must. That it lacks the means to do so, is simply not true.

Let us calculate approximately how much it would cost our country to expel 200,000 Albanians and settle the region with as great a number of our people.

The resettlement of 40,000 Albanian families, taking an average family as having five members and an average of 15,000 dinars for each family, would cost a total of 600 million dinars. The colonization apparatus for the settling of 40,000 Serbian families might reach a total of 200 million dinars. In any case, the whole operation would not cost more than 800 million dinars. This is because:

1.   The evacuated Albanians would leave behind not only land, but also their houses and implements. Thus, not only would the overwhelming majority of our colonists be settled in the homes of the Albanians but, with a little assistance in food and livestock, they would soon recover economically and become independent. We stress in this connection that absolutely no private speculation with the possessions left behind by the Albanians would be tolerated. The government must be the one to take control of these possessions and distribute them to the settlers.

2.   Military forces should be employed, where required, during the setting up of new colonies, as was the case with the construction of Sremska Rača and the reconstruction of the villages destroyed by the 1931 earthquake. To this end, the army should be given the right and possibility to set up a kind of compulsory labour service for public projects, just as Stambolisky created the *Trudova pronist* in Bulgaria and Hitler the *Arbeitsdienst* in Germany, that is, by calling up reservists or

extending the term of military service. It would be an especially good idea for our young people, after finishing their training and after graduating from university, to be entrusted with such work. Were this to be the case, many of them, by taking part in constructive activities in the public interest, would become more conscious and look at things from a more realistic perspective. Such a scheme could be carried out easily by giving priority in public service employment to those young people who have spent a specific period of time working on behalf of our colonization strategy. This would also help reduce unemployment among our young intelligentsia, which is an increasingly acute social problem in our country.

3.   In collaboration with specialized organizations and associations, we must find the cheapest means of clearing the land of scrub, of irrigating farms, of draining swamps, etc. as well as of constructing homes. Private companies should be informed that, since the government assists them with reduced customs and railway tariffs, loans and other means for the procurement of supplies and material necessary for their work, it also has the right, considering the importance of this action, to insist that such supplies and material be made available at the lowest possible price. Supplies and material should be procured by means of cartels, in agreement with which, the government would specify the quantity, quality and price of the material in question without fictitious deals being involved. Government enterprises, the railways and, in particular, forestry enterprises such as Šipad etc. should be placed at the unrestricted disposal of the government Commission for Colonization.

4.   During colonization, the government may grant settlers property on credit or for cash. Many of the settlers will purchase land in the new regions by selling their original property in their place of birth. This will enable the government to recuperate a good portion of the money it has laid out. However, we stress that land must only be sold to persons who give proof that they will settle on it permanently and work it. Land given on credit must not be too expensive. The interest rate must be minimal and repayment should be deferred for several years to give the settlers time to get established, i. e.

repayment should only begin when the settlers have sufficient economic strength.

Taking this as a basis, the government, which must cover all administrative expenses for these activities from its normal revenues, can procure funds from two sources. One would be the pruning of unnecessary expenditures and expenditures earmarked for other less urgent sectors. The other possible source of funds would be loans, which would be provided by state banks, alone or with private capital on the basis of a compulsory domestic credit line. This would be backed up by securities issued by the government as well as by contributions from the settlers themselves when they become independent.

It might not be a bad idea if the financing and purchasing of land were to be arranged by agricultural banks working in collaboration with co-operatives under the direct supervision and direction of the government Commission for Colonization. However, it is still too early to make any definitive pronouncement on this matter because the conditions under which Turkey will accept the population displaced from our territories are not yet known.

Taken altogether, the sum of a few hundred million dinars is no great expense for the government when compared to the real benefits gained from such an action. By securing the most sensitive regions in the south of our country for our own people, we could save the lives of several divisions in case of war. Giving land to several tens of thousands of families from economically weaker regions, Montenegro in particular, would, on the one hand, help ease the appalling economic suffering of such regions and, on the other hand, create many new jobs during the process of colonization. It would be possible to find employment for 10,000 workers, thus giving a boost to our sluggish economy.

In view of the supreme national, military, strategic and economic significance of this action, it is clearly the duty of the government to sacrifice a few hundred million dinars. At a time when the government can spend one billion dinars on the construction of an international highway from Subotica to Čaribrod, the possible benefits of which we shall only enjoy at some time in the distant future, it can and must be in a position to come up with a few hundred million dinars to give us back possession of the cradle of our nation.

Conclusions

In view of all that has been said, it is no coincidence that in our examination of colonization in the south, we hold the view that the only effective means of solving this problem is the mass expulsion of the Albanians. Gradual colonization has had no success in our country, nor in other countries for that matter. If the state wishes to intervene in favour of its own people in the struggle for land, it can only be successful by acting brutally. Otherwise, the native, who has his roots in his place of birth and is at home there, will always be stronger than the colonist. In our case, we must keep this fact very much in mind, because we have to do with a hardy, resistant and prolific race which the late Cvijić described as being the most expansive in the Balkans. From 1870 to 1914, Germany spent billions of marks on the gradual colonization of its eastern territories by purchasing land from the Poles, but the fecundity of Polish women defeated German organization and money. Thus, Poland regained its Poznań in 1918. Our above-mentioned statistics of the 1921-1931 period show that it was the fecundity of Albanian women which defeated our colonization policy, too. We must draw our conclusions from this, and we must do so quickly while there is still time to correct matters.

All of Europe is in a state of turmoil. We do not know what each new day and night will bring. Albanian nationalism is on the rise in our territories, too. Should a global conflict or social revolution occur, both of which are possible in the near future, leaving the situation as it is would jeopardize all our territories in the south. The purpose of this paper is to avert such an occurrence.

Dr Vaso Čubrilović
(signed)

[Taken from *Iseljavanje Arnauta*. Retranslated from the Serbo-Croatian by Robert Elsie, on the basis of an existing English version]

Convention

Regulating the Emigration of the Turkish Population from the Region of Southern Serbia in Yugoslavia (1938)

The Government of the Turkish Republic and the Government of His Majesty, the King of Yugoslavia,

noting the tendency shown by certain elements of the Turkish Moslem population to emigrate from the region of southern Serbia, and

noting that the said population, which has not failed to appreciate the liberal and generous treatment it has always enjoyed in Yugoslavia, is solemnly resolved to leave the territory of the Kingdom out of its legitimate desire for reunification with its natural ethnic motherland,

have decided to conclude a Convention in order to regulate, in a spirit of profound friendship, the conditions for the said emigration and have to this effect designated their respective plenipotentiaries, i. e.

for His Majesty, the King of Yugoslavia: Mr

for His Excellency, the President of the Turkish Republic: Mr who, having communicated to one another proof of their full power and authority, accepted as being in proper form, reached agreement on the following provisions:

Article 1

Subject to the benefits of the present Convention shall be Yugoslav Moslem subjects of Turkish origin and language and of Turkish culture.

Not subject to the benefits of the present Convention shall be persons banned from entering Turkey under Turkish laws and regulations presently in force, nomads and Gypsies.

Article 2

The regions designated for emigration under the present Convention shall be the following:

1)   the districts of the Banovina of Vardar, i.e.:
The Shar mountains (Prizren), Gora (Dragash / Dragaš), Podgora (Suhareka / Suva Reka), Nerodimja / Nerodimlje (Ferijaz / Uroševac) Lower Polog (Tetova / Tetovo), Upper Polog (Gostivar), Galic (Rostusa), Dibër / Debar (Dibër / Debar), Struga (Struga), Graçanica / Gračanica (Prishtina), Kaçanik / Kačanik (Kaçanik / Kačanik), Gjilan / Gnjilane (Gjilan / Gnjilane), Presheva / Preševo (Presheva / Preševo), Prespa (Resen), Ohrid (Ohrid), Kërçova / Kičevo (Kërçova / Kičevo), Kruševo (Kruševo), Poreč (Južni Brod), Prilep (Prilep), Marihovo (Marihovo), Bitola, Kavadare, Negotino na Vardaru (Negotino na Vardaru), Skopje (Skopje), Kumanova / Kumanovo (Kumanova / Kumanovo), Veles (Veles), Ovče Pole (Sveti Nikole), Štip (Štip), Kočani (Kočani), Radoviš (Radoviš), Strumica (Strumica), Dojran (Valandovo), Gevgelija (Gevgelija), Kriva Palanka (Kriva Palanka), Kratovo (Kratovo), Carevo Selo (Carevo Selo), Maleš (Berovo);

2)   the districts of the Banovina of Zeta, i.e.:
Peja / Peć (Peja / Peć), Istog / Istok (Istog / Istok), Mitrovica e
Kosovës / Kosovska Mitrovica (Mitrovica e Kosovës /
Kosovska Mitrovica), Gjakova / Djakovica (Gjakova /
Djakovica), Lugu i Drinit / Podrima (Rahovec / Orahovac);

3)   the districts of the Banovina of Morava, i.e.:
Llap / Lab (Podujeva / Podujevo), Vuçitërna / Vučitrn
(Vuçitërna / Vučitrn), Drenica (Sërbica / Srbica).

The Yugoslav Government shall decide in which regions
emigration will begin.

Article 3

The number of families which the Turkish Government will
accept from the regions specified under Article 2 and in accordance
with the conditions of the present Convention shall be 40,000.

The term 'family' shall be understood to mean persons of the
same lineage and their children who, at the time of signature of this
Convention, were living on an undivided common rural estate and under
one roof.

Article 4

The return of these 40,000 families to their motherland shall be
completed within six years, in the following quotas:

1)   in 1939: 4,000 families
2)   in 1940: 6,000 families
3)   in 1941: 7,000 families
4)   in 1942: 7,000 families
5)   in 1943: 8,000 families
6)   in 1944: 8,000 families

If these annual quotas cannot be realized as a result of
circumstances, the two parties shall agree, through their respective
legations, on the number of emigrants to be deported by the one side

and to be accepted by the other, three months before the start of the period of emigration. It is understood, however, that any alterations in the annual number of emigrants shall not extend the six-year period of emigration for more than one year.

The periods of annual emigration shall last from the beginning of the month of May until the 15th of October, with the exception of the contingent of emigrants for the first year, who shall only start to be evacuated by the beginning of the month of July 1939.

Article 5

This Convention on emigration applies only to the rural population of the above-mentioned regions.

As to Turkish Moslems of the urban population of the above-mentioned regions, their persons and belongings shall not be subject to the provisions of the present Convention.

Should they wish to emigrate to Turkey, they may do so as free emigrants in accordance with the emigration law in Turkey. In such cases, they shall be free to liquidate their rural and urban assets. They shall be accorded all requisite assistance from the Yugoslav Government for the transfer to Turkey of monies deriving from the liquidation of their assets and from the Turkish Government for their definitive entry permits into Turkey.

Article 6

Under the present Convention, the ownership of all rural immovables belonging to prospective emigrants shall be transferred to the Yugoslav state at the moment the Yugoslav Government presents the annual list of emigrants to the representatives of Turkey in Yugoslavia.

As to urban immovables, they shall remain at the free disposal of their owners.

It is understood that the Yugoslav Government shall only take possession of the above-mentioned rural immovables when the emigrants already specified on the list have left their domiciles for the port of embarkation. The Yugoslav Government gives its assurance under the present Convention that the present owners shall enjoy the full possession of their property until transfer of ownership to the Yugoslav Government.

Once the above-mention property has transferred ownership, the Yugoslav Government shall dispose of it freely in accordance with the provisions of the law currently in force on the colonization of the regions of southern Serbia.

Article 7

Under this agreement, the Yugoslav Government shall pay to the Turkish Government the sum of 500 Turkish pounds per family, equivalent to a total sum of 20,000,000 Turkish pounds for all 40,000 families, irrespective of the number of members in each family.

With the payment of this total sum, ownership of all the rural immovables of the emigrants shall be transferred, pursuant to Article 6, to the Yugoslav Government.

With regard to rural movables and immovables belonging to the Moslem Community or *vakufs*, it is understood that this Convention shall have no bearing on the provisions of existing laws which regulate such assets.

Article 8

On the first of April and the first of October of each year, the Yugoslav Government shall pay a semi-annual instalment proportionate to the number of emigrating families to have been deported that year, a sum which may be decreased or increased according to their numbers. The payment of the amount indicated in the previous article shall thus be made in twelve instalments over a period of six years.

Article 9

The Yugoslav Government shall pay each instalment in the following manner:

30% in foreign currency which shall be put at the disposal of the Government of the Turkish Republic via the National Bank of Yugoslavia;

70% in dinars deposited at the National Bank of Yugoslavia in a current account credited to the Government of the Turkish Republic.

The National Bank of Yugoslavia shall notify the Turkish Legation in Belgrade of each deposit as soon as it has been made and transferred to the said current account.

Article 10

The National Bank of Yugoslavia and the Central Bank of the Turkish Republic shall, in joint accord, stipulate the exchange rate from dinars to Turkish pounds for each day of payment.

Article 11

Funds deposited in the National Bank of Yugoslavia shall be utilized by the Government of the Turkish Republic for all types of expenditures and payments made in Yugoslavia for the purchase of all kinds of Yugoslav merchandise aside from goods presently unauthorized for export except by payment of foreign currency, i.e. copper, wool, hides, walnut wood, oil-seed fruits, olives, wheat and maize.

The purchase of all these goods shall be made for export to Turkey.

These goods shall be exempt from all taxes, duties and other export charges.

It is also understood that such exports shall not be subject to regulations of any trade agreements signed or to be signed, but rather wholly to the provisions of the present Convention.

Article 12

Persons to be deported within the emigration period and who form part of the current annual quota shall be obliged to sign a written declaration in the presence of the Yugoslav authorities, pursuant to Article 55 of the current Yugoslav Citizenship Law, renouncing their Yugoslav citizenship. Such persons shall have the right to be considered immigrants under Turkish law from the moment the appointed representatives of Turkey have added their names to the annual list for emigration to Turkey.

Article 13

Emigrants shall be free to liquidate and to take with them all of the movable property belonging to them, such as personal effects, livestock or farm animals, equipment, machinery etc. for agricultural or industrial use or for the exercise of any profession.

The Yugoslav Government shall, however, only cover transportation costs to the port of embarkation in Salonika for the emigrants, their movables, their used agricultural equipment and, for each family, four head of large livestock and ten head of small livestock, excluding their recently born young.

For the transportation of additional livestock, the emigrants shall benefit from reduced tariffs in force. It is to be understood, however, that additional livestock will not surpass six head of large livestock and twenty head of small livestock, excluding their recently born young.

The export of livestock, shall be carried out in line with the provisions of existing veterinary conventions, and veterinary certificates shall be issued to the emigrants free of charge.

The emigrants shall also be free to import their personal jewellery, including necklaces of brazen gold and silver pieces worn by the womenfolk, each female emigrant being able to take one such necklace with her.

In addition, each head of family shall be free to take with him, on his departure from Yugoslavia, a sum of 2,000 dinars in cash as well as foreign currency to an exchange-rate value of 4,000 dinars.

Article 14

With the dinars left over from the sale of their urban movables and immovables, emigrants shall be permitted to buy, on the domestic market, such merchandise as need not be purchased for export with foreign currency, such merchandise as is not prohibited in Yugoslavia and such merchandise as is not banned from import to Turkey.

All such merchandise shall be exempt from taxes, duties and other export charges.

Article 15

The National Bank of Yugoslavia shall open a special current account at the Central Bank of the Turkish Republic in the name of the Government of the Turkish Republic in which all emigrants shall be free to deposit all or part of the monies in their possession in order to ensure their transfer by the purchase of merchandise in Yugoslavia. The National Bank of Yugoslavia shall give notice to the Legation of Turkey in Belgrade of each deposit, together with details about the depositor.

The monies transferred to Turkey by the purchase of merchandise in Yugoslavia, shall be reimbursed to the persons in question by the Central Bank of the Turkish Republic.

Article 16

Funds, real estate and all other valuables belonging to minors or other persons under the care of a guardian or of a competent Yugoslav court shall be transferred and given over to the Government of the Turkish Republic which from that moment shall assume the responsibility for and the protection of such persons until they reach the age of majority or the end of guardianship in accordance with Turkish legislation.

Article 17

All Turkish Moslem youths whose families are registered in the annual lists for emigration and who are serving in the Yugoslav army, shall be released from military service immediately and shall be evacuated at the same time as their families.

Similarly, Turkish Moslem youths living in a region in which the population has been designated for emigration within the current year shall not be conscripted.

Article 18

A special Commission shall be set up by the Yugoslav Government to prepare the detailed annual lists of emigrants with all necessary information on climate and on the trades and professions of the emigrants.

These lists shall be submitted to the representatives of the Turkish Government and, once approved by them, shall serve as a basis for the issuing of Turkish passports and for calculating the number of emigrating families.

This Yugoslav Commission shall be in constant contact with the Turkish delegates and, on their request, shall provide them with all the information they should require.

Article 19

The departure and embarkation of the emigrants shall be realized on the basis of collective Turkish passports which shall be issued to them by the consular authorities of the Government of the

Turkish Republic in Yugoslavia. These collective Turkish passports, all necessary documents issued in advance by the Yugoslav authorities for the preparation of the lists, and the exit visas for the passports shall be absolutely free of charge.

Article 20

A Turkish-Yugoslav joint Commission shall be set up in the Yugoslav free zone in Salonika, composed of representatives appointed by the two Governments, who, in joint accord, shall take all measures necessitated by circumstance for the arrival, assistance and embarkation of the emigrants.

Article 21

This Convention shall enter into force on the date of its ratification by the two Governments.

In testimony whereof, the respective plenipotentiaries have signed the present Convention and affixed to it their seals.

Done in French in two original copies in the year nineteen thirty-eight.

M.R. V.M.   H. S. Dr C. A.

[Taken from *Convention réglementant l'émigration de la population turque de la région de la Serbie du Sud en Yougoslavie.* Translated from the French by Robert Elsie]

Draft on Albania
(1939)

Ivo Andrić

I.   The Balkan war and Albania

Access to the Adriatic for the Serbian army

According to a secret appendix to the treaty of alliance between Bulgaria and Serbia, dated 29 February 1912, Serbia was granted a right to the territories to the north and west of the Shar mountains previously held by Turkey. In connection with this provision, Serbian troops, in order to provide their country with an access to the sea, advanced on Lezha on 15 November 1912 and gradually took possession of the whole of northern Albania right down to Tirana and Durrës. On 25 November 1912, Pašić published a statement in the London Times indicating that Serbia claimed Durrës with a considerable hinterland.

The establishment of an autonomous Albania

On 20 December 1912, however, the Conference of Ambassadors in London resolved to set up an autonomous Albania, giving Serbia only the right to a trading outlet on the Adriatic Sea. On 20 March 1913, the same conference resolved to cede Shkodër to Albania. Montenegro refused to accept the decision of the Great Powers and was supported in this regard by Serbia, which sent troops to reinforce the siege of Shkodër. The Great Powers countered (on 21 March) with a naval demonstration, only Russia abstaining. Austro-Hungarian, English, French, German and Italian destroyers gathered in the vicinity of Bari and forced Serbian troops to retreat from their positions in the Shkodër region.

The blockade of the Montenegrin coast

On 12 April, the Great Powers announced a blockade of the Montenegrin coastline. The Montenegrin government, however, persisted in its siege of Shkodër, which finally capitulated on 20 April. King Nikolla of Montenegro was, nonetheless, force to yield, and on 4 May, in a telegramme sent to Sir Edward Grey, he ceded Shkodër to the Great Powers. The international occupation of Shkodër was to last from 5 May 1913 to the beginning of the World War.

II.   Serbia and Greece divide their spheres of influence in Albania

Though under pressure from the Great Powers, primarily from Austria, Serbia did not give up hope, despite the fact that it had been forced to retreat from the Adriatic and northern Albania.

The spheres of influence of Greece and Serbia in the newly established autonomous Albania were laid down in a declaration which formed a secret appendix to the treaty of alliance, dated 19 May 1913, between Greece and Serbia. The territory north of the Seman river from the sea up to the mouth of the Devoll river, and north of the Devoll river up to Mount Komjan was to be within the Serbian sphere of influence.

The regions of Albania south of this line were to belong to the Greek sphere of influence. In case of riots in Albania, the two countries were to reach an agreement on the position they would adopt. These are the maximum demands which we presented to Albania in a written document.

III.   The London Agreement and Albania

The London Agreement, signed on 26 April 1915 between France, Great Britain, Russia and Italy, contained the following provisions with regard to Albania:

1.   The note to Article 5 states: "The following Adriatic territory shall be assigned by the four Allied Powers to Croatia, Serbia and Montenegro:... And, in the Lower Adriatic (in the region interesting Serbia and Montenegro) the whole coast from Cape Planka as far as the River Drin, with the important harbours of Spalato, Ragusa, Cattaro, Antivari, Dulcigno and St. Jean de Medua... The port of Durazzo to be assigned to the independent Moslem State of Albania."

2.   Article 6 reads as follows: "Italy shall receive full sovereignty over Valona, the island of Saseno and surrounding territory of sufficient extent to assure defence of these points (from the Voïussa to the north and east, approximately to the northern boundary of the district of Chimara on the south)."

3.   Article 7 reads as follows:... "and if the central portion of Albania is reserved for the establishment of a small autonomous neutralised State, Italy shall not oppose the division of Northern and Southern Albania between Montenegro, Serbia and Greece, should France, Great Britain and Russia so desire... Italy shall be charged with the representation of the State of Albania in its relations with foreign Powers."

As early as 1915, therefore, the Great Powers had adopted the principle of a partition of Albania and conceded that Italy, Serbia and Greece had vested interests in Albania. The two Balkan countries were granted the right to revise borders, whereas Italy was granted Vlora as well as a protectorate over rump Albania.

IV.   Albania at the peace conference

The standpoint of the Great Powers

At the peace conference, allied forces (France, Great Britain and the United States of America) initially proposed for Albania the southern and eastern borders which had been established at the London Conference of 1913. The allied forces recognized Italy's full sovereignty over Vlora and the requisite hinterland, giving Italy, in addition, a mandate to administer the independent state of Albania under the control of the League of Nations (Memorandum of 9 December 1919).

Our standpoint

(Against the mandate of Italy. In favour of an independent Albania. Arguments for the revision of borders and for our acquisition of Shkodër and northern Albania).

In our reply of 8 January 1920, we rejected the proposal for giving Italy a mandate over Albania, pointing out that this would be a repeat of the Bosnia-Hercegovina issue. "This resolution," we said in our reply, "would create an offensive border in Italy's favour against our country which, for its part, would be deprived of protection. This would mean an offensive advantage to one side and a strategic disadvantage to the other."

For economic and strategic reasons, we asked for a revision of the border in our favour (the middle of the Drin and Buna rivers, as well as Kelmendi and Kastrati), as foreseen at the London Conference of 1913. In addition to this revision, our delegation declared that the best solution for Albania would be the establishment of an independent state within the borders of 1913 and of an autonomous administration.

If this solution were not to be adopted, or if the southern part of Albania were to belong to other countries, our delegation would asked for the northern part of Albania down to the Drin river. "Our country has ancient claims on these areas, as our memorandum states. Shkodër is the one-time capital of Serbian rulers. Our nation has shed much blood for Shkodër, in particular during the 1913 war which cost Serbia the lives of several thousand soldiers and cost Montenegro one-third of its army. In order to comply with the wish of the Great Powers, Serbian and Montenegrin troops withdrew from Shkodër and the northern part of Albania in 1913. Austria had mobilized its forces and threatened war. Shkodër could have belonged to Montenegro, had Montenegro agreed to cede Lovcen to Austria or have it neutralized. But, Montenegro refused to cede this position of strategic importance to Austria."

"The Drin valley, together with Shkodër, forms a geographical and economic entity with Montenegro and borderland areas of Serbia. For central Serbia and for Montenegro, the Drin valley is the only direct and indeed the shortest natural outlet to the Adriatic. The vital Danube-Adriatic railway should pass through the Drin valley. The Conference of Ambassadors, held in London in 1913, recognized Serbia's right of access to the sea."

"Shkodër is also intimately linked to the Buna river which provides Montenegrin trade with a natural outlet to the sea. From as early as the Treaty of Berlin, Montenegro has enjoyed the right of free navigation down the Buna river. Most of Lake Shkodër belongs to Montenegro. Due to Turkish negligence, the best Montenegrin lands are still flooded by the waters of Lake Shkodër. Our country is, therefore, most interested in regulating the Buna and Drin rivers, not only for navigation down the Buna, but also because 12,000 to 20,000 hectares of very fertile land could thereby be drained and an equal area could be ameliorated. Two-thirds of this land belongs to Montenegro."

The Italian standpoint

(According to the memorandum of 10 January 1920)

1.	Italy requests of the League of Nations a mandate to administer the independent state of Albania.

2.   The northern and eastern borders of Albania will be those
         drawn at the Conference of London. The southern border will
         be a matter of further examination.

3.   Italy will be granted sovereignty over the city of Vlora, with
         enough hinterland for its protection and economic
         development.

The Allies agree that Shkodër and northern Albania be annexed by Yugoslavia

Proposing a comprehensive solution to the Adriatic question, Clemenceau, who was chairing the Peace Conference, said to Pašić and Trumbić on 13 January 1920, with regard to the cession of Rijeka to Italy: "The SHS state (i. e. the Kingdom of the Serbs, Croats and Slovenes) will thus ascend to the zenith of its power, even without the acquisition of Shkodër, the Drin and San Giovanni di Medua (Shëngjin)."

We did not agree to this, in view of the fact that Italy retained Vlora and got its mandate over Albania.

Our final reply at the Peace Conference

In our final reply at the Peace Conference, on 14 January 1920, we stated that we still held the view that the best solution would be that the administration of Albania, within the borders drawn in 1913, be conferred to a local, autonomous government with no authority being held over it by any foreign power. If this solution, however, was not accepted and parts of Albanian territory were to be ceded to other countries, our delegation would then lay claim to part of northern Albania (a map with delineated borders was submitted), for which it promised an autonomous regime.

The standpoint of the late Pašić

When it seemed certain that the Allies would allow Italy to consolidate its hold over central Albania, the chairman of our delegation, Pašić, informed the government in Belgrade at the end of 1919 that the moment had come for us, "compelled by circumstance, to change our policy towards Albania." This letter reads as follows:

"Given that, because of Italian encroachment and of the support which Italy receives from the Powers, we cannot return to the situation which existed in Albania prior to the evacuation of our army and prior to the regime of Esad Pasha, and given that the Albania we favour will not come to be because the Allies have agreed to cede Vlora and its hinterland to Italy and to give Italy a protectorate over certain parts of Albania, we must, under such circumstances, stake our claims to different and better borders with the part of Albanian territory to come under the Italian protectorate."

"The 'minimum' we will accept from the Allies is: the border along the Black Drin river down to the confluence of the White Drin river and from there along the Great Drin river down to the sea."

"We should also claim a 'maximum', so that Italy receives as little territory as possible. The maximum of our claims should be: the Mat river to its source, and hence directly eastwards to the Black Drin river. The Mat and Drin rivers would thus constitute our borders with the Italian protectorate."

V. The Italian occupation of Albania in the aftermath of war and its definitive withdrawal after failure in Vlora

Once the war was over, Italian troops, on the basis of an Allied military resolution, occupied the entire territory of Albania including the northern part which had been accorded to us under the London Agreement. Shkodër alone was under the joint occupation of French and Italian troops.

In view of the hostile attitude taken by Italy towards the SHS state (the Kingdom of the Serbs, Croats and Slovenes) at the time, we considered Italy's military occupation of Albania a grave threat to our existence. A bitter struggle was waged between the Italians and us on Albanian territory. The Italians hence raised the issues of Montenegro and Macedonia, as well as the idea of a Greater Albania extending right to Kaçaniku / Kačaniku. We took action against them, at times secretly and at times overtly, by bribing Albanian leaders and by countering with the idea of an 'independent Albania' and of the 'Balkans for the Balkan peoples'.

The dissatisfaction of the Albanian population, which we supported, compelled the Italians to pull their troops out of inland Albania at the beginning of 1920 and to concentrate them in the vicinity of Valona (Vlora), from which region they were forced to withdraw in June of that year after an accord had been reached with the Tirana government for the evacuation of all Albanian territory, including the island of Sazan.

The evacuation of Albania was accomplished as a result of organized resistance on the part of the Albanians, though one should not forget the fact that Italy was politically and militarily very weak at the time. Even at the present day, there are Albanians who think they could drive the Italians out of Albania whenever they liked. This self-confidence will prove fatal to them because they do not realize that the fascist regime in Italy is not the same as the Italy of 1920 under the parliamentary governments of Nitti, Giolitti and Facto.

VI.   Albania before the Conference of Ambassadors

As the evacuation of Italian troops from Albania clarified the situation on the ground, the Conference of Ambassadors was in a position by November 1921 to take a decision on the recognition of Albania as an independent and sovereign state. In contrast to earlier promises, i. e. for Vlora and for a mandate over Albania, the Great Powers recognized only Italy's special interest in the maintenance of

Albanian independence. Albania became a member of the League of Nations, hoping that this would help ensure and sustain its independence.

Before the Conference of Ambassadors met, we endeavoured once again, though in vain, to have the borders revised and moved down towards Shkodër and the Drin river, citing historical reasons for Shkodër and economic and communications reasons for the Drin. The French expert at the Conference, Larochue, consoled us with these words: "The royal government made a mistake by not adopting the French proposal at the time for the partition of Albania. Pašić had agreed to the idea, but the government in Belgrade rejected it." In order to get the Italians out of Vlora, we had to abandon Shkodër and the border extending down to the Drin river.

Since we had permanently endorsed the indivisibility of Albanian territory, as set forth in 1913, and Albanian independence, it could be assumed that the solution proposed by the Conference of Ambassadors was satisfactory to us. This has not been the case, however. We have been running into difficulties in our relations with Albania and in our relations with Italy over Albania, even though Albania has been proclaimed an independent country and has been granted membership in the League of Nations.

The Republic of Mirdita

Since the Conference of Ambassadors had taken a decision on the borders of Albania and on the conditions for its independence, we signed a co-operation agreement with the leaders of Mirdita in the middle of 1921. This agreement envisaged the setting up of an independent Mirdita republic which would be protected by the armed forces of the SHS state (the Kingdom of the Serbs, Croats and Slovenes) and whose interests abroad would be represented by the Belgrade government. The Tirana government suppressed this movement and we were subsequently accused and condemned before the League of Nations.

VII. The Rome pact, Pašić, Mussolini and Albania

In spirit, the Rome pact of January 1924 stipulated that both Rome and Belgrade respect the independence of Albania and the principle of non-interference in the country's internal affairs, and that they exhange information about developments in Albania. This did not, however, hinder the Italian government from backing Fan Noli in June 1924 in his rebellion against Ahmet Zogu, nor did it hinder our government from making it possible for Ahmet Zogu to launch an attack on Albania in December of the same year from our territory, and to seize power. Neither Rome nor Belgrade could resist intrigues and appeals from their Albanian 'friends' who requested support to exercise or assume power, promising loyalty and co-operation in return, and who then changed their minds at the first opportunity.

VIII. The Tirana pact and its implications

Giving instructions to our representatives in Albania, the late Pašić used to say to them: "We want an independent, but a weak and unstable Albania." Time has shown that such a wish was impossible. A weak and unstable Albania had to ask for support and protection wherever it could find it. A regime which was threatened by Italy would turn to us, whereas a regime which we wanted to overthrow would turn to Italy for protection.

In 1926, a weak and unstable Albania requested the protection and support of Italy. Having received initial guarantees for his regime, Ahmet Zogu later, in 1927, consented to the conclusion of a twenty-year military alliance and received hundreds of millions of lire for public works. Both economically and financially, he thoroughly subordinated Albania to Italy and took on many Italian advisors. A situation was thus created which much resembled the kind of protectorate we had opposed at the Peace Conference.

The greatest threat to us from Albania in recent years has been the military buildup, as well as fortifications and irredentist activities. We saw a threat in all Italian activities and in the 'offensive border' which we had opposed in Paris when the Allies proposed that Italy be granted a mandate over Albania.

It is of interest to note here that we protested and opposed the Italian penetration of Albania and the Balkans, but none of the other Balkan countries supported us on this issue. The two Mediterranean naval powers, France and England, did not oppose the blockade of the Adriatic Sea. Indeed, Sir Austen Chamberlain consented to the Tirana pact at his meeting with Mussolini in Leghorn (Livorno) in 1926. French representatives in Tirana constantly advised King Zogu to avoid conflict with the Italians.

IX.   The Italian-Yugoslav friendship pact of 25 March 1937

As long as they maintain friendly relations towards one another, Italy and Yugoslavia can agree on Albania, based on the following: Italy has a vested interest in Vlora and we should not threaten this part of the Albanian coast. We should acknowledge and respect Italy's interest. It is in Yugoslavia's vital interest that we not be threatened on our own borders in southern Serbia, both in Kosovo (inhabited by Albanians) and in the Shkodër / Montenegro region. This was no doubt taken into consideration in the secret protocol supplementing the friendship pact, which also envisaged a stop to further fortifications in the Librazhd and Milot regions. As far as financial and economic interests in Albania are concerned, we do not have, nor do we intend to invest any considerable funds there. Our side thus offers no competition or objections to the Italians, provided of course that they comply with the second secret obligation towards us which they undertook two years ago, i. e. that they seek no special privileges in their political, economic and financial activities which would directly or indirectly compromise the independence of the Albanian state.

The friendship pact of 25 March 1937 has thus created a tolerable 'modus vivendi' for us and for Italy on Albanian soil, where in the past we have so often been involved in conflicts and mutual suspicions.

A quite different question is whether this truce in Albania will pass the test of time in view of the much more tense and complex situation in the Mediterrean and in the Balkans.

X.   Maintaining or changing the status quo

The independence of Albania has been weakened but not destroyed

The independence of a country is a concept which constantly changes in meaning for its neighbours. This independence can be either complete or reduced, depending on circumstances. As to present-day Albania, one cannot say that its domestic and foreign policies are independent of Italy. Yet, Albania is considered an independent state by the international community. According to international law, the Albanian coastline in not Italian, but rather under the sovereignty of that Balkan country. Italy has not yet encroached upon the Balkans. Italy possesses sovereign territory in Zadar, but this does not offer any possibility for further expansion. Italy also exerts influence in Albania, but it has no freedom of action there compared to that in its own country. The Albanians are still showing opposition to Italian penetration by putting obstacles in its way and slowing it down.

'The Balkans for the Balkan peoples'

The traditional policy of Serbia has been 'The Balkans for the Balkan peoples'. This principle was applied earlier in the struggle against the Ottoman Empire and against the Austro-Hungarian monarchy. Yugoslavia made efficient use of it in its struggle against the provisions of the London Agreement which allowed Italy to advance into Dalmatia and Albania. This principle, in our view, has always constituted the best guarantee for peace in the Balkans, for co-operation between the Balkan nations and for their unimpeded development. The presence of any of the Great Powers in the Balkans means opening the floodgates to intrigue and invasion.

Italian expansion

Is it conceivable that Italy, having made itself lord of southern and central Albania, will confine itself to that narrow strip of coastline? We did not believe this would be the case twenty years ago when the Great Powers offered Vlora and its hinterland to Italy. It is even harder to believe it now that Italy is showing much more swagger and bravado in its foreign policy.

A dangerous precedent

When a non-Balkan Great Power seizes a part of Balkan territory on which it has no ethnic claims whatsoever, this constitutes a dangerous precedent for us and for all the peoples of the Balkans. Other Great Powers could come up with similar claims from other directions. The case of Italy in Albania is a particular threat to us because the London Agreement first recognized not only Italy's claims to southern Albania, but also to Dalmatia. The revival of the provisions of the London Agreement in one part of the Balkans creates a dangerous precedent for the revival of other provisions, too.

The partition of Albania

In dealing with this issue in a comprehensive manner, it should be stressed that we must avoid an open or covert conflict with Italy at all costs. We must also avoid allowing Italy to occupy all of Albania, which would pose a threat to us in sensitive areas such as the Bay of Kotor and Kosovo.

Taking the above into consideration, we regard the partition of Albania as a necessary and inevitable evil and as a great disadvantage to us, but one from which we must nonetheless endeavour to derive as much benefit as possible, i. e. we must take advantage of the lesser of two evils.

Our compensations

These compensations are registered in documents which were prepared twenty years ago when the question of a partition of Albania was being discussed.

The maximum we set and asked for at that time was the border along the Mat and Black Drin rivers to ensure the strategic security of Montenegro and Kosovo. We would also have to ensure the basins of Lakes Ohrid and Prespa by annexing Pogradec as well as the Slav villages of Mali i Thatë / Golo Brdo and those between Prespa and Korça.

Taking possession of Shkodër could, in this case, be of great moral and economic significance. It would enable us to carry out major waterworks activities and to recuperate fertile land needed to feed Montenegro. The presence of northern Albania within the framework of Yugoslavia would facilitate the existence of new communications links between northern and southern Serbia and the Adriatic.

After the partition of Albania, Kosovo would lose its attraction as a centre for the Albanian minority which, under the new situation, could be more easily assimilated. We would eventually gain 200,000 to 300,000 Albanians, but these are mostly Catholics whose relations with the Moslem Albanians have never been good. The deportation of Moslem Albanians to Turkey could then be carried out since, under the new circumstances, there would be no major impediment to such a move.

[Taken from *Elaborat dra Ive Andrića o Albaniji iz 1939. godine.* ed. Bogdan Krizman. in: Časopis za suvremenu povijest, Zagreb, 9 (1977), 2, p. 77-89. Retranslated from the Serbo-Croatian by Robert Elsie, on the basis of an existing English version]

The minority problem in the new Yugoslavia

Memorandum of 3 November 1944

Vaso Čubrilović

Reasons why the minority problem in Yugoslavia must be solved

Quite aside from the disloyalty of hte minorities, there are other important interests of state which compel us to take advantage of the current war to solve the problem of minorities by expelling them. Our minorities, as we have previously stressed, do not constitute a danger to us because of their numbers but rather because of their geopolitical position and the ties which they maintain with the neighbouring peoples to whom they are related. It is because of such ties that the neighbouring peoples have been able to use them to wage war against us. At present, the minorities are nothing more than stumbling-blocks in our relations with these neighbouring states. The democratic federation of Yugoslavia will only achieve peace and ensure its development if it can be made ethnically pure and if, by solving its minority problems, it can remove the causes of friction with neighbouring states once and for all.

Taking a look at the relevant charts and maps, it can been seen that our minorities occupy very important positions in our country, both from an economic and from a strategical point of view. The Vojvodina on the banks of the Danube, for instance, is Central Europe's gateway to the Balkans. In geopolitical terms, it is the strategic key to the peninsula. Without it, the nations of Yugoslavia, i. e. Serbia and Croatia, would lose their control over the Drava, Sava, Danube and Morava rivers and would once again become the backwater of a new Austria or of a new Turkey. The Vojvodina is the breadbasket of all of Yugoslavia and, even if not a single Serb or Croat lived there, we would still have to fight to keep it in order to feed millions of our citizens in the poorer regions to the south of the Sava and Danube. Devising a plan for the economic future of Yugoslavia would be senseless without the Vojvodina and its grain reserves. The regions to the south of the Sava and Danube with their mineral resources, forest reserves and hydroelectric potential provide all the prerequisites for modern industry, but this industry can only be set up if the plains of the Vojvodina provide the working masses in these new industries with food. We Serbs and Croats, however, make up only a relative majority of the population in the Vojvodina. It could happen, as a result of the war, that the Hungarians take over Bačka and the Germans, with their people in the Banat, set up a miniature Reich there.

The situation is similar in the area around the Shar mountains, inhabited now by an overwhelming majority of Albanians. This region is the watershed of major Balkan rivers which flow into three seas. Because of this, Kosovo and Metohija have always been considered a strategic area in the Balkans. By occupying the central part of the Balkans, Kosovo and Metohija separate Serbia from Montenegro and these two, in turn, from Macedonia. The countries of the Yugoslav federation will never be strongly attached to one another so long as they have no direct ethnic border with one another. This matter is of particular concern for Macedonia. The upper reaches of the Vardar river are held by the Albanians whereas the lower reaches of the river are in the hands of the Greeks. We southern Slavs hold only the middle portion. Our position is too weak not to be challenged, as Italy did when it ceded to Albania not only Kosovo and Metohija but also Dibër / Debar, Kërçova / Kičevo, Gostivar and Tetova / Tetovo. We must have no illusions about what the future of Europe may bring. This horrendous war will certainly not be the last. We will find ourselves at the crossroads again and will once more be exposed to attack in some new war. It is therefore the duty of those who hold the destiny of this country in their hands to be prepared for all eventualities and to ensure that events we have lived through in this war never occur again. The statesmen of the old Yugoslavia never considered this in 1918 when they agreed to incorporate the national minorities within the borders of the newly-created state. For political reasons, they even gave their support to the minorities, and we are the ones who have had to pay the price, sacrificing tens of thousands of lives. Such a calamity must never be repeated. The fertile valleys of Polog, Kosovo and Metohija are important in economic terms. Surrounding them are our wretched lands: Montenegro, the Sandjak of Novi Pazar, the areas to the north of the Shar mountains and the destitute Macedonian settlements to the south of the Shar. These people rightfully demand that the lands from which they have been driven by the Albanians over the last 150 years be returned to them.

I have given deliberate priority to the Vojvodina and to Old Serbia (Kosovo), considering that these two regions represent the crux of our minority problem. In endeavouring to solve this problem, we must not, however, be guided by a desire to avenge the violence perpetrated against our peoples. Our policy on this issue must be guided simply by reasons of state. There are minorities scattered in other regions of the country, too. In view of the atrocious crimes committed by the German Reich on Slavic lands with the help of local ethnic Germans, we have every right to demand that these regions be cleansed of this group. The new political border between our country and Austria must also constitute the ethnic border between Slavs and Germans. The problem of these tens of thousands of Germans does remain, but it can be dealt with by the Slavs themselves without major complications. The German and Hungarian minorities in Croatia, Slavonia, Bosnia and Hercegovina are but scattered islands in an ethnic sea of southern Slavic peoples and can either be expelled or assimilated without great resistance. The biggest problem we are facing is how to break up the blocks of minorities inhabiting strategic geopolitical positions. The federal government must bring all the power of the state to bear in solving this problem.

After examining why the cleansing of minorities is necessary, let us now see what options are available for carrying out the task. In actual fact, conditions for implementation are quite favourable. In 1918, Europe held the view that the minority problem could be solved by giving privileges to such groups. The experience of this war has proven to all of Europe that this approach was wrong. The unscrupulous exploitation of German minorities by the Third Reich has made it obvious that the only just solution to the problem is the deportation of the minorities. The Third Reich itself has carried out a brutal policy of colonization, transferring millions of people from one corner of Europe to the other. At the same time, it had plans for the expulsion of entire nations, endeavouring to maintain its rule in eastern and southeastern Europe by means of an elaborate settlement policy. Had it won the war, we southern Slavs, the Serbs in particular, would have been wiped off the face of the earth. Germany's allies, Italy and Hungary, took the same approach to solving the minority problem. It is therefore understandable that our Allies have taken the stand during this war that the minority problem ought be solved through evacuation and resettlement. The fraternal Soviet Union took advantage of this method even before the war. It long ago resettled the Karelians from the Finnish border. Koreans and Chinese were transferred from coastal regions in the Far East to as far as Turkistan. When the Soviet Union occupied Bessarabia in 1940, it expelled 150,000 Bessarabian Germans from the region. An entire camp of barracks was constructed that year by the Germans on the plain of Zemun, at the point where the Sava flows into the Danube. We, the inhabitants of Belgrade, had an opportunity to watch the Germans at the time being transported to the camp, before they were transferred back to the Reich. Even at the present time, the Soviet Union has resumed the population transfers it initiated before the war, resettling Poles from the Ukraine and Byelorussia to the other side of the Polish-Soviet border, and at the same time, bringing Ukrainians and Byelorussians back to the Soviet Union. With these examples in mind, we, too, have a right to demand of our Allies that our problem with minorities be solved in the same manner, i. e. by expulsion.

We should have more right than any other country in Europe to demand of our Allies that they approve the evacuation of our minorities. No country on this continent has suffered so much as we have at the hands of nations ethnically related to our minorities. Over one million people, including women and children, have perished here in this appalling war, three times as many as were slain on the front with rifle in hand. Much responsibility for these killings can be laid at the door of the minorities in our country. This we have told to our Allies and have proven it to them. I am deeply convinced that they will appreciate the problem and support our intentions. I have faith in the fraternal Soviet

Union, in particular. We were the only nation overrun by the Germans to rise in arms from behind the lines in the summer of 1941 when Hitler was leading his Nazi hordes onwards to Leningrad, Moscow and Stalingrad. For three years, we fought against all odds in our national liberation movements. We have a right to hope, therefore, that the fraternal Soviet Union will help us solve our minority problem here, as they have solved theirs there.

It is easiest to resolve the minority question through expulsions in times of war such as this. The countries concerned have been our adversaries in the present war. They attacked us, we did not attack them. They laid waste to our land and selfishly exploited their minorities here to wage war against us. We have no territorial claims against them, with the exception of our claims against Italy to Istria, Gorica (Gorizia) and Gradiska (Gradisca). Therefore, with all the more right as victors, we are justified in asking them to take their minorities back.

With its mass displacement of persons, this war has created a climate for resettlement. Our minorities are aware of their deeds and will therefore not put up much resistance when expelled. All in all, considering the above-mentioned factors, there has never been a more favourable moment than the present for the solution of the minority question. A just resolution of the problem, however, depends on the attitude, level of awareness and energy of the people to decide on the fate of the ethnic groups in this country. I am deeply convinced that the people appreciate the importance of the issue and will know how to proceed. It is for this reason that I am writing these lines.

How to solve the minority problem in the new Yugoslavia

If we take the stand, as we do, that the only just solution to the minority problem is expulsion, we are faced with a number of issues which have to be dealt with. Should all minorities be expelled or only certain ethnic groups? From which regions should ethnic minorities be expelled first? And what is more important, how are we to resettle the deserted towns and villages? I have a few suggestions to make in this connection.

As to priorities for expulsion, I hold the opinion that we should consider the following order: the Germans, the Hungarians, the Albanians, the Italians and the Romanians. We have already referred to the actions of the Germans, Hungarians and Albanians during the war here. In principle, they all deserve to lose their right of citizenship in this country. In view of the atrocities committed by the Germans, both in our country and throughout Europe, they have lost all rights and must be persecuted ruthlessly. The Hungarians here and in Hungary still deserve some consideration, despite the Bačka massacre and their service under the Germans as militiamen in Russia. Not all the measures to be carried out against the Germans should be applied to them. The same goes for the Albanians in Old Serbia (Kosovo) and Macedonia. Nonetheless, if we wish to solve the minority problem, we will have to take over Bačka, Kosovo and Metohija in ethnic terms and drive out hundreds of thousands of Hungarians and Albanians. The fascist regime in Italy treated our people in Istria, Gorica (Gorizia) and Gradiska (Gradisca) dreadfully. When we regain these territories, we will have to reoccupy them ethnically by moving out all the Italians who settled there after 1 December 1918. Only with the Romanians will matters be easier. Several hundred thousand Romanians live on our side of the Banat, while a smaller number of our people live on the Romanian side. We should have no difficulty in bringing about an exchange of population on the basis of a political agreement with the government in Bucharest.

The second important question to be answered is which regions should be cleansed of minorities first. I have already stressed that our main consideration is not how many people we expel, but which regions to expel them from. Minorities scattered about as individual families and small communities pose no danger to us. The greatest threat is from large blocks of minorities in border regions of strategic and economic importance. These ethnic groups pose a particular danger if living on the border across from a country of the same nationality. Accordingly, it is essential for us to cleanse the Germans and Hungarians from the Vojvodina and the Albanians from Old Serbia (Kosovo) and Macedonia. Germans should also be expelled from Kočevje, Maribor and other border regions in Slovenia. We shall return to this problem later.

Let us begin with the Vojvodina. If we take a look at the ethnic map of this country of ours, we see a colourful mosaic, much like a beautiful carpet from Pirot. The careful observer will soon be able to distinguish certain ethnic blocks that make up the major patches on the carpet. He will notice, for instance, the mass of Hungarian settlements situated in northeastern and central Bačka. Here is the main block of ethnic Hungarians in our country, from Horgoš in the north, through to Senta, Bačka Topola, Kula and Odžaci. Of the approximately half a million Hungarians living in Yugoslavia in 1941, almost 300,000 lived in Bačka. The remaining 200,000 are scattered about in the Banat, in Syrmia (Srem), Croatia and Slavonia where significant groups are to be found. Driving 200,000 Hungarians out of Bačka would bring about a solution to the Hungarian problem in our country.

The German problem is not so simple. Germans are spread around the entire country, though most of them live on the fertile plains of Bačka, in the Banat and in Syrmia (Srem). They are present not only in central and northeastern Bačka, but also in the southwest, in the regions of Apatin, Novi Vrbas, Odžaci, Stara Palanka, and, to a considerable extent, in Novi Sad and Sombor. If we want to create an absolute majority for our people in Bačka, we must clean out the Germans. Bačka is also the key to our hold over the Vojvodina. The half a million or so Hungarians and Germans there compare to a little over 300,000 Slavs (Serbs, Croats and Slovenes taken together). Therefore, particular attention must be focussed on this region in solving the minority problem.

The situation in the Banat is much better. This region was not depopulated in the war to the extent Bačka was. Here we have an absolute majority and the only minority of any great significance are the Germans. They are settled in the following areas: Pančevo, Bela Crkva, Vršac and Beckerek, and should be expelled from this region. In Syrmia (Srem), the Germans are settled in: Zemun, Stara Pazova, Ruma and Šid. Here they possess the best land and must be evacuated, too. In Slovenia, the areas around Kočevje and Maribor must be freed of Germans. If possible, we should destroy and eradicate German and Hungarian settlements in the rest of the provinces, too, in order to ensure their complete disappearance from the region. If we were successful in expelling five to six hundred thousand Germans and Hungarians from Bačka, the Banat and Syrmia and in settling our people there instead, the Vojvodina would be ours forever.

We must be more straightforward and practical in dealing with the Albanians in Old Serbia (Kosovo) and Macedonia in order to conquer Kosovo and Metohija ethnically and, at the same time, avoid a conflict with the neighbouring people in Albania. We must also take great care in considering the areas from which Albanians should be expelled and resettled so as not to affect a single Albanian village, indeed a single Albanian home more than necessary. If we are to reach our goal of linking Montenegro, Serbia and Macedonia, we must bring about a complete change in the ethnic structure of Kosovo and Metohija. Most important of all, we must cleanse Metohija. As the border region to neighbouring Montenegro, it will be most suitable for Montenegrin colonization. After all, the Metohija and Drenica Albanians are at present the most loyal servants of the Germans, as they were a few years ago of the Italians. Dreadful atrocities were committed by the Albanians in the Macedonian villages of the upper Vardar valley. The Macedonians, therefore, rightfully demand their expulsion. A detailed plan must be elaborated to specify with accuracy which villages and areas of Old Serbia (Kosovo) and Macedonia are to be cleansed, and the plan must be implemented accordingly.

In principle, we would have nothing against the evacuation of all minorities from our country. This is something we can still consider. The above-mentioned points in the Vojvodina, Slovenia, Old Serbia (Kosovo) and Macedonia constitute simply a minimum if we want to ensure future possession of these regions.

If we agree in principle that the minority problem can only be solved through expulsion, and that expulsions should be carried out as proposed above, we are then faced with the problem of how this is to be accomplished.

The first thing I would like to mention in this connection is that wars are most suitable for solving such problems. Like storms, they blow through countries, uprooting and blotting out peoples. What takes decades and centuries to accomplish in peaceful times, can be accomplished within a matter of months and years in a war. Let us not delude ourselves. If we wish to solve this problem, we will only be able to do so during the war. The leaders of old Yugoslavia thought after 1918 that they could break down the major ethnic blocks in the country by colonization. We have wasted billions of dinars on settling volunteers and other colonists throughout the Vojvodina, Kosovo and

Metohija. In the Vojvodina over a twenty year period, we managed to change the ethnic balance in our favour by a few percentage points, but the German and Hungarian minorities still remain in Bačka. From 1918 to 1938, the Albanians increased their numbers in Kosovo and Metohija more by natural growth than we were able to do by bringing in settlers. Driving our colonists out of Bačka, Kosovo and Metohija, the Hungarians and Albanians were thus able to cancel out the few results we obtained. In order to prevent this from happening again, the army must be brought in, even during the war, to cleanse the regions we wish to settle with our own people, doing so in a well-planned but ruthless manner. I do not yet wish to discuss details as to how this should be accomplished but, should this project be approved in principle, I would be more than willing to make my knowledge and experience available to the Supreme Command, to the National Liberation Army and to the partisan units in order to work out a more detailed plan. For the moment, I wish only to stress that the Germans and Hungarians must be expelled unconditionally from their lands in the Vojvodina, and the Albanians must be driven out of Metohija, Kosovo and Polog.

Aside from ethnic cleansing during military operations, other methods must be applied to force the national minorities out. In view of their behaviour during the war, they must be stripped of all minority rights. All members of national minorities who were in any way of service to the occupants should be brought before military tribunals and shown no mercy. Concentration camps should be set up for them, their property confiscated, their families placed likewise in concentrations camps and, at the first opportunity, they should be expelled to their national states. The fraternal Soviet Army could be of enormous assistance in this question in dealing with the Hungarians and Germans. In expelling minorities, particular attention should be devoted to the intelligentsia and to the wealthiest strata of society. These are the people who behaved the worst towards us, serving the occupants loyally, and these are the elements who will be the most dangerous if they are allowed to remain in their native regions. The poor workers and peasants were not particularly sympathetic to German and Hungarian fascism and should not be persecuted. The same applies to Albanian beys and the Albanian bourgeoisie. Those same people who served the regimes loyally in old Yugoslavia and made money by doing the dirty work are the ones who committed the most murders after 1941.

If the expulsion of minorities is agreed upon, there are other questions which will have to be dealt with, but we will come to them later.

Colonizing abandoned lands

Resettling abandoned towns and villages with our people is of paramount importance for the following reason. Interests of state require that lands abandoned by minorities be settled as quickly as possible so that the minorities and all of Europe can be confronted with a *fait accompli*. Economic interests dictate that this populaton transfer be accomplished with the least possible damage to the economic life of the country. Abandoned land must therefore not be left uncultivated, factories must go on working and the workshops of craftsmen must not be closed down. This is not as easy to accomplish as one might think. No matter how much thought and preparation go into the organization and implementation of expelling minorities, we cannot avoid temporary setbacks in the economy. We must not let this discourage us from our main objective and must ensure that such setbacks are kept to an absolute minimum. The matter is all the more pressing because the national minorities are presently settled on the most fertile land in the Vojvodina, Slavonia, Old Serbia (Kosovo) and Macedonia. The Germans are in control of crops used for manufacturing. If we want to hold on to our sugar and linen industries, we will have to find quick replacements for the expelled German farmers. The same goes for craftsmen and manufacturers. Over 80% of all craftsmen in the Vojvodina are Germans, as are a substantial, though lower percentage in Croatia and Slovenia. Germans run the mills, the breweries and the linen industry in the Vojvodina and the Hungarians control the sugar industry. These facts must be taken into consideration and a strategy must be worked out accordingly so that all these sectors can be taken over and can continue to function after the departure of the Germans and Hungarians.

We must settle our people at once on the land vacated by the minorities. After 1918, volunteers and native settlers were at the forefront of the colonization campaign. They were given five hectares of land each, some tools, and houses on occasion. The colonies progressed slowly though, because the plots were too small, the tools insufficient and the cattle lacking. Problems were also compounded by the fact that, in many cases, highlanders from Montenegro, the Krajina and Lika were the ones settled on the plains of the Vojvodina, and they had great difficulty adapting to the new climate and way of life there. Many of them therefore began selling their property and, up to 1941, the government was forced to intervene and purchase much land to stop it from falling back into the hands of the ethnic minorities. This time, colonization activities must be carried out with much more foresight and seriousness of purpose, and must be run along more scientific lines.

The national liberation movement will have the same duty in colonization which the government of old Yugoslavia did after 1918. The best fighters in the movement have been recruited from the destitute regions south of the Sava and Danube, as well as from poor families north of these rivers. Thousands of peasant families will be demanding compensation for their destroyed property in villages razed to the ground in Bosnia and Hercegovina, Montenegro, Dalmatia, Lika, Banja, Croatia and Serbia and they will have to be compensated. The best possible reward for them would be land abandoned by the Germans, Hungarians and Albanians. But the mistakes which were made after 1918 must not be allowed to occur again. Property left behind by ethnic minorities must, first and foremost, be given to partisan fighters and to members of the national liberation movement in general. In this connection, we should adhere to the maxim that land be given only to those willing to work it. Land is, after all, a commodity and should not be speculated with. There is no room in the new Yugoslavia for *spahi*-type landowners. In old Yugoslavia, it often happened that volunteers would rent out their land instead of working it themselves.

In settling the Vojvodina, Kosovo and Metohija, we must adhere to a certain premise. The problem of the rural proletariat in Yugoslavia cannot be solved by giving everyone tiny plots of land. What we need more is rapid industrialization. The plains of the Vojvodina must not serve simply at the settling grounds for hundreds of thousands of hungry Montenegrin, Hercegovinian and Krajšnik peasants, but rather as an agricultural base for feeding the entire nation and for its industrialization. With this in mind, there are two approaches we could take in order to create a food surplus for the rest of the country: 1) We could set up larger entities in colonized villages, comprising 5 hectares. A good portion of their production could then be brought to market. 2) The government could retain for itself a considerable part of the land abandoned by the minorities and use it according to its own needs. The best would be a combination of these two approaches. I cannot underscore the importance of this issue enough. Lack of space prevents me from going into further detail.

Manufacturing and trades are just as important as agriculture, but they are problems which are much easier to solve. Manufacturing in the agricultural sector in the Vojvodina must be nationalized, as must all large companies which are hostile to the state. With trades, the situation is somewhat more difficult, but they must be nationalized too. Support can be given to native craftsmen and apprentices by allowing them to take over abandoned workshops.

Of paramount importance is that the colonization of land abandoned by national minorities be carried out in conformity with all international regulations and practices. We should therefore seek the approval of our Allies and endeavour right away to obtain a legal right to confiscate the property of hostile minorities. The government Commission on War Criminals should publicize material showing to the outside world and to our Allies what crimes the national minorities committed throughout our country. I made this proposal previously, but omitted it, and am introducing it again.

Organization of activities

We have already stressed the importance of the ethnic cleansing of minorities in times of war. Accordingly, the role of the army takes on major significance in such activities. It is the armed forces who have the duty to expel minorities from our country. It is therefore essential that military commanders in the regions inhabited by the Hungarians receive precise instructions as to what is to be done and how it is to be done. It would be desirable for the Supreme Command of the National Liberation Army and partisan units to create a special department within their ranks whose duty it would be to carry out ethnic cleansing during wartime. This department should assemble a small number of experts and specialists in minority affairs from various regions. These people would provide the Supreme Command with requisite know-how and would prepare detailed proposals for dealing with the various minorities in our country during the war. After expelling the minorities, the armed forces would then have to guard abandoned facilities before the installment of a civilian authority. They could also ensure that the land be cultivated. This can only be accomplished if a special department is created, through which the work can be implemented. This department should remain within the purview of the armed forces even when the duties are later transferred to a ministry or given into trusteeship.

The complexity of activities involved in the expulsion of several million people and the resettlement of hundreds of thousands of our people in abandoned towns and villages requires the setting up of one further institution to supervise the whole campaign, and such an institution, ministry or commission, should be set up as soon as possible. After 1918, we had a ministry of agrarian reform whose duty it was to carry out reforms and thereby quench the thirst of our peasants for land. All in all, the ministry was not too badly organized. That it did not manage to fulfil its duties was due to the fact that too much bureaucracy was involved and that our nationally-minded political leaders were incompetent. I have had the opportunity since 1919 to follow up on the work accomplished by the staff of that ministry. They soon became corrupt and bureaucratic. The ministry continued to exist for years, but not to assist the colonists. It was simply there to sustain its employees. Experts have estimated that of the one billion dinars which old Yugoslavia earmarked for agrarian reform, only two hundred million were ever spent on the colonists. Eight hundred million dinars were swallowed up by government salaries. This waste must be avoided if we set up a new ministry for colonization. The job must not be entrusted to the current officials of the department for agrarian reform in the ministry of agriculture. New people must be hired who understand what is at stake and who will be ready and willing to devote all their time and energy to this enormous task. Once the ministry has been set up, and it will be a temporary institution by the way, officials from public offices and private companies should be appointed by means of special order. They should be given good salaries and promoted accordingly. No mercy should be shown to anyone involved in corruption. The risk of corruption has always been present and will continue to be present in affairs of this nature, especially where property belonging to millions of people is involved.

A thorough presentation of the organization of this ministry would take us beyond the scope of this report. For the time being, I only wish to stress that public emloyees should be selected with great care and national liberation committees should supervise the ministry's work closely. These committees could be of great assistance in determining how the national minorities can best be expelled and how colonists can best be brought in. In any case, the federal government will have to transfer a great part of its work in certain regions to the national liberation committees. We should take this fact into consideration now, at a time when we are just beginning to elaborate our colonization policy. The scope of each institution's activities must be fixed in advance. Continuation of this work is easily hindered by infighting over jurisdiction. For the moment, the most important institution on site, aside from the army, will be the national liberation committees. The enormous bitterness felt towards the national minorities by our people because of the atrocities they committed against us is being expressed throughout the country by an uncontrollable rage towards them. This hostility and the irrevocable wish of the masses of our people for the minorities to disappear must be utilized in a constructive manner. We must not let ourselves slip into anarchy and plundering. This rage must serve the goals of our nation, as presented above. Precise instructions must therefore be transmitted to all national liberation committees as soon as possible to tell them what to do and how they should go about it. These committees will be responsible for organizing the expulsions, but they must also take care that farm land continue to be cultivated and that abandoned properties, workshops and factories not be left unguarded. It would perhaps be a good idea for specialized units, from the village to the national level, to be created within such committees. Our people should be taught from the start to know their rights and their duties. So important is this issue, that it would be advisable for Marshal Tito, as Supreme Commander of the National Liberation Army, to issue instructions of his own to the army and to the national liberation committees in this respect. The matter is urgent, and the setting up of appropriate institutions takes time.

The national liberation committees could be just as useful in settling colonists in the abandoned villages as they are in cleansing the countryside of minorities. I have already stressed that one of the reasons for the failure of our colonization strategy from 1918 to 1941 was that land was given to people who had no interest in working it themselves. Such a mistake must not be repeated. We must come up with ways and means of finding the right peasants and homesteaders for colonization. Such people are not particularly mobile, but when they do move to a new locality, they become rooted there very quickly. The national liberation committees in the areas where potential colonists come from must find the right type of settlers for the new colonies. They must also take care to replace the shortages in skilled workers and craftsmen left in the Vojvodina by the expulsion of the Germans. They should be assisted in their work by experts, social groups, professional groups, cooperatives and trade unions. With the help of the latter, the job of expelling the whole population of a town becomes much easier.

I have set down here only the broad outlines of a strategy for the expulsion of national minorities and for the resettlement of the regions in question. There are a good number of other aspects which must be considered, too, but this would involve too much detail for the time being and can be left to a later date. For the moment, I would like to restrict myself to a number of immediate issues. War is still raging over our country as we discuss whether or not to expel the minorities and how to resettle the land. Reports are coming in from those parts of the country where military operations are still underway that our people are ruthlessly advancing upon the national minorities who were against us during the war. The rage of our people must be channeled without delay. What is most urgent for the moment are: 1) sending instructions to the army and to national liberation committees on what to do, 2) taking measures, with the assistance of the fraternal Soviet Army, to get support for the cleansing of the Germans and Hungarians, 3) taking measures to ensure that abandoned land be cultivated as autumn approaches and that factories and workshops be guarded, and 4) beginning at once with the resettlement of the abandoned towns and villages by our people. All plundering and manipulation of the property of such minorities must be subject to the threat of capital punishment.

These are measures which must be taken immediately. The rest of the work should begin as quickly as possible, too. I omitted to mention that it is essential for the property earmarked for colonists in towns and villages to be transferred into their names. Dirty tricks were played on the poor colonists under the old agrarian reform by unscrupulous officials and political opportunists. First, the land was distributed to the colonists and then it was taken away from them. Such things must be avoided at all costs. Property given to the peasants should be transferred into their names, as should houses and workshops.

Whether or not the peasants join together and form co-operatives for collective farming is an entirely different matter. In my opinion, this would indeed be the best way to work the land with the help of modern farm machinery. Because of its importance, this issue merits further discussion. I wish only to stress that collective farming is easier to introduce in regions to be colonized.

Conclusion

This memorandum on the minority problem may have turned out a bit long, but the issue is of such importance to the future of our country that I was, more than anything, concerned about having omitted something. We may never again have such an opportunity to make our country ethnically pure. All other problems our country is currently facing, be they of a national, political, social or economic nature, fade in comparison. If we do not solve the minority problem now, we will never solve it. It is my hope that the leaders of the national liberation movement will assess this issue as I have, and will approach the problem with the same energy and self-sacrifice they exhibited when, in 1941, they plunged into the terrible war of liberation for the creation of a new, democratic and federal Yugoslavia. If this report can contribute even modestly to this lofty objective, its aim will have been fulfilled.

Belgrade   Vaso Čubrilović
3 November 1944   [signed]
                                        University Professor

[Taken from *Manjinski problem u novoj Jugoslaviji*. Retranslated from the Serbo-Croatian by Robert Elsie, on the basis of an existing English version.]

4.　Conversations with contemporaries

Interview with Bujar Bukoshi

[Robert Elsie]: Mr. Bukoshi, you are the Prime Minister of the Republic of Kosovo. As such, you are in the rather absurd situation of being head of a government which does not really exist and of a country which does not really exist either. Who elected you, and does the international community take you seriously?

[Bujar Bukoshi]: I am confident that I head a government which exists and am therefore not, as you suggest, in an absurd situation. To determine whether a government exists or not, you have to ascertain whether it has the overwhelming support of the organ that mandated it. In my case, it was the Co-ordinating Council of Albanian Political Parties and the President of the Republic, who extended the government's interim mandate after the democratic elections of May 1992. When Parliament is not able to convene for a plenary session, the President has the power under the constitution to give a government legitimacy. Furthermore, if you do not accept reality at face value, look at the way states have been created and have come to function in the past. In all cases, the number one condition for self-government has been and still is a representative government holding real power over people in a given territory. This must not be confused with the fact that a government, for a certain period of time, may not be recognized internationally. International recognition is not what determines whether a government exists or not. Recognition only sanctions its place in the international arena and allows it to take part, on equal footing, in the international community and in resulting exchanges. So much for my government. Whether it is taken seriously or not, on this point I do not really have much to say. The many diplomatic activities which the

President and I are involved in, and which you can read about in the press, show that this government is taking an active part in all talks and negotiations on Kosovo and Kosovo-related issues. And not without good reasons, either. Why is Kosovo invited to take part in various international conferences and activities? Simply because it is a recognized entity and a state in the process of formation.

The same argument can be given for your suggestion that Kosovo does not really exist. Again you must not confuse two separate phenomena: existence in time and space, and international recognition, which can come at any point, but does not change the heart of the matter. Kosovo exists, has existed and will continue to exist. Kosovo has been under occupation for far too long and has decided to go on its own. It is within this context that it has created the essential features of a modern democratic state. True, this state does not yet function as a normal state would. Being in a virtual war situation, the state must act in line with its own priorities. But it exists and will be recognized, there is no doubt about that.

[RE]: How much of a government do you have? Do you have a cabinet with ministers who meet regularly? And can you actually govern?

[BB]:   My government resembles any government in a parliamentary democracy. It was created in October 1991 by the Co-ordinating Council of the Albanian Political Parties, as the executive arm of the movement that proclaimed independence. I was appointed its chairman and was initially conferred the task of leading the country up to the general elections of 24 May 1992. Hence, it is an interim government, whose mandate has been extended owing to the impossibility of convening the Parliament that emerged from these elections.

There are six ministers in my government, covering such vital fields of public life as education, health, information, finance, foreign affairs and justice. True, we do not have a Ministry of Defence or a Ministry of the Interior because, at the moment, we do not have control over our territory. But we will have them in due course, too. Besides ministers, there are a number of special appointees to various posts such as migration, civil affairs and solidarity. The government meets regularly to discuss routine business and to respond to new situations and developments.

Can we actually govern? You'd better ask the people that support us. But let me make one thing absolutely clear. There are two basic prerequisites for a government to exercise its mandate: one is control over territory, which we do not have under the present conditions of occupation; and two, more importantly, overwhelming support from the people and their representatives. My government enjoys the support of the Co-ordinating Council and of the people which that forum represents.

It is true that, in exile, we cannot fulfil the functions of a government fully. But neither can life go on normally under occupation. We have had to resort to alternative ways and means, as one would in any such situation. Despite the present conditions, we have managed to keep public life going, we have managed to channel funds to the most needy and vulnerable members of society in Kosovo. We have also managed to organize an efficient system of education in Albanian and to provide basic medical services to our people. In Kosovo itself, we have succeeded in setting up the basics of local government, with councils that communicate with their voters and report to us. In sum, one could say that the Government of the Republic of Kosovo is present and is at work.

Let us not forget that the people of Kosovo feel the presence of their government through another means, too, and that is through the exchanges and support the world gives us. Our diplomatic activities are part and parcel of our mandate, part and parcel of the process of governing.

[RE]: The seat of the Government of the Republic of Kosovo is not in Prishtina or in Prizren, but Bonn in Germany. Why are you in exile when President Rugova manages to live and work in downtown Prishtina, despite military occupation?

[BB]: I will answer that part of the question that concerns the government. In the first place, having resorted to peaceful means to attain our goal of independence, we have resolved not to get involved in a conflict which was not of our making. Therefore, soon after my election to the post, and aware of the hostile attitude of the Serbian regime, the Co-ordinating Council decided to take the government out of Kosovo, a choice that was deemed better than going into hiding and functioning underground. I still think this was the best option. There is a simple fact not to be forgotten: a totalitarian regime, be it a military one or not, may tolerate political parties with a dissenting voice, but it will *not* tolerate an alternative government that claims sovereignty over what it considers to be its lands and subjects. Secondly, the existence of a government, and an efficient one, too, is strong evidence of the self-governing capabilities of a people. Thirdly, a government, even in exile, is a government, meaning a focal point of contacts and communication with the international community, which *de facto*, if not *de jure*, recognizes its existence and legitimacy.

There have been calls in Kosovo by some party leaders to move the government back to Kosovo. That remains an option which would be ideal, but only under ideal circumstances. We are all willing to go back to Prishtina provided the situation warrants it and circumstances permit it. So far, neither the Co-ordinating Council, nor the Parliament, nor the President have seen any reason to call the government back to Kosovo, which I believe, at least for the moment, would mean calling it back to extinction.

[RE]: May I ask you who finances your Government and what you do with your revenue?

[B]: Who finances my government? When I say that the Government of the Republic of Kosovo functions as such, I mean it can afford to function. Like any other government, we have a budget that is tailored to the needs of public expenses, and to the survival of the most essential sectors of public life in Kosovo. All citizens of the Republic of Kosovo working and living abroad at present are duty-bound to pay three percent of their income to the state budget, money that goes to financing many good causes. When I say duty-bound, I mean a morally binding obligation to finance the activities of their representative government. The three percent scheme can in no way be legally binding, for it cannot be enforced under the existing conditions of life in Kosovo and elsewhere. There exist special committees, all tied to and chaired by our Finance Minister. Some people meet their obligations, others don't, and that is why I say it is morally binding. The funds thus collected are paid into a bank account and used, with utmost caution I might add, to keep public life running in Kosovo and to keep its institutions functioning. Other sources of income, like elsewhere again, are donations from private businesses and individuals, which, like everything else, are paid into the same account. So, in sum, the Government of the Republic of Kosovo is financed by its own people, and the money goes back to them, in a redistributed form, to serve those who need it most.

The Fund of the Republic of Kosovo is neither a secret nor an illegal activity. Since it is a powerful instrument for the survival of Kosovo as an institutional entity, it has been and remains a target of attacks and criticism from a whole spectrum of people, who are motivated by various reasons. The first category of critics are those who meet their obligations and want to know rightly where their money is going. In this context, we have instituted a system whereby every contributor, however insignificant the sum remitted, is acknowledged with a receipt for his or her share in a special letter of receipt and gratitude. Virtually every transaction through the bank goes into our computerized ledger system, and is open for inspection and scrutiny. In addition, with a view to curbing speculation and illegal activities with money, the Government of the Republic of Kosovo has instructed its citizens to refuse to pay cash to people who pretend to be our mandated representatives, but who are in fact simply swindlers. The 'Three Percent Commissions' of the Republic of Kosovo neither request nor accept cash. Whoever does so, even in the name of political parties, has no connection whatsoever with the activities of the Government in this field. Others making a lot of noise (and most of them affiliated to political parties) already see Kosovo as a fertile land of democracy and concentrate sinply on enhancing their own status within the system. I do not care much for people like this and am not going to bother giving any further views on them.

Where does the money go?

Firstly, it finances the activities of the President and his team, and of the government and its various organs in Kosovo and elsewhere. Here, this money supports and sustains a considerable diplomatic activity by the representatives of the Republic of Kosovo abroad. This is a very important and even vital aspect, without which Kosovo would have remained an unknown entity and would have been reduced simply

to a question of human and minority rights abuses, a land without
representation and without a leadership capable of fulfilling the mandate
of its people.

Secondly, and equally important, is the earmarking of
considerable funds to support Kosovo's parallel system of education, its
social welfare and support system, medicare, academic, educational and
cultural activities, and other sectors of public life in the Republic. Had
it not been for these funds, virtually nothing could have been
accomplished to substantiate independent public life in Kosovo. This
has become a reality now. The scheme works perfectly and is yielding
first results, not only in the form of a challenge to the occupant, but also
in the form of concerted and committed action to build on achievements
and to construct the edifice of an independent and sovereign Kosovo.

*[RE]: It has been several years now since the enactment of the
Constitution of Kaçanik and still the Parliament of Kosovo has not met.
Why not, or is my question too naive?*

[BB]: Your question is not naive. On the contrary, it is the
reflection of a legitimate concern felt right across the spectrum of public
life in Kosovo and wherever Kosovo is an issue. Many are the reasons
why the Parliament that emerged from the May 1992 elections has not
convened so far. One is the situation in Kosovo itself. Repression, not
only in words but also in deeds, is on the increase day in day out. Since
May 1992 there has hardly been a day in the life of the people of
Kosovo without someone being 'processed' in the outrageous Apartheid
system which has been institutionalized there. The Constitution of
Kaçanik remains the fundamental law of the state while it is in the
process of formation, and I stress this again, while it is in the process of
formation. Secondly, and connected to the above, is the situation
outside the borders of Kosovo, i.e. in Bosnia and elsewhere. The
leadership of Kosovo does not want to be instrumentalized and become
a scapegoat to fulfil the goals of ultranationalists in former Yugoslavia,
mainly in Serbia. The matter is, we do not deem it timely and
appropriate to convene our Parliament for fear that it could offer a
pretext for escalating the Yugoslav conflict in the south of the Balkans.
Maybe we have been wrong. I have the feeling that we may have
overreacted in our passivity. And here comes the third reason: our slack
decision-making process, our belated response to events and probably

our exaggerated perception of things. From here in Germany, I feel I ought not to blame those in Prishtina, but, on the other hand, I am not here of my own will. Caution taken to the extreme can easily be translated into cowardice, and the Balkans are no place for timid souls. We claim that we have excellent organizational structures, and this is true, but I wish they were more operational and not simply underground. Gandhiism is not my philosophy, neither is it my attribute nor is it the motivation of my actions. The Krajina region in Croatia was not liberated through inactivity. This is simply one example of why I stand for a more active policy. To come back to the question of Parliament, in a final analysis I think there were favourable moments when it could have been convened. There is a fourth reason, too, again related to us and our performance, and this is accommodation with what we have already attained. One cannot deny the fact that there are people amongst us who, as employees, have settled into their little niches in our edifice at a time when everybody else in Kosovo is unemployed. These individuals, who can easily become groups that dictate policy, are afraid of losing their semblance of power, and are therefore reluctant, if not to say averse to dealing with change and initiative. They are afraid of living life to the full and prefer a semi-existence, a crippled life.

I have outlined four reasons, two of which we must attribute to ourselves and our inactivity. So, is the situation that bad? I would not dramatize it, but it is no grounds for revelry either. Kosovo's Parliament functions in its relevant groups. It legislates and the government implements accordingly. The President of the Republic, in accordance with the Constitution, has assumed some of the powers of the legislative, and in this context, Dr Rugova and his team have a lot of extra work to do. In sum, the situation is not alarming, but it is not satisfactory either. We need our institutions and we must be prepared to die for them. Without institutions, there can be no self-government. Whoever's devious activities aim at destroying them, can hardly be a supporter of Kosovo's independence, but belongs to the same class of people as those who would like to perpetuate the do-nothing attitude and passivity.

[RE]: Are you encouraged or disappointed by the attitude of the international community towards Kosovo? Does the West understand the urgency of the situation? Is there more interest in Kosovo than five years ago, or less, as a result of the war in Bosnia-Herzegovina?

[BB]: Let me start with the end of your question. You may think that as long as Bosnia is burning, it will continue to be in the limelight and in the focus of international attention, if for no other reason than to placate public opinion in the Western countries. And there is some logic in this 'first come first served' approach. The international community, however, has failed to deliver in Bosnia, and for a very long time now, it has been seeking to save face, only exacerbating the crises of the international forums it is organized into. I am pretty well certain that, had there been resolve to face up to what the Yugoslav crisis is all about, namely the creation of 'Greater Serbia' by all possible means, the situation would have progressed and perhaps been solved by now. It is very easy to say that in Bosnia we have to do with a civil war, but this line of reasoning is far from the truth. You may want to distance yourself from the situation by labelling it civil war, an internal matter of one country, a simple question of the abuse of individual human rights, etc. This can buy you some time, but will still destroy your future. When the war started in Bosnia in 1992, it was the Yugoslav Army that was held to be the culprit, and when, soon after, the culprit forced the world to its knees, the language used began to be modified 'slightly' in order to come up with the vaguer wording we have today. In conclusion, if today you interpret the Bosnian situation simply in terms of a civil war, you fall victim to distorted thinking and reinforce an attitude which is counterproductive to solving the crisis.

The same is true of Kosovo. Kosovo now is a well-known issue everywhere. Four years ago we almost always had to inform our counterparts about the history, geography, politics, economics, ethnography and whatnot of the region, whereas today we only need to present our options and negotiate on ways and means of realizing them. This has been enormous progress and development, and, to come back to your question, we remain encouraged by the attitude of the international community. Disappointment does arise, however, at the resolve of this community not to question the status quo, however fragile it may be. As with Bosnia, Kosovo is seen in many diplomatic circles as the case of a majority that must be given autonomy, at least for a certain period of time, on probation so to speak. When confronted with the option of outright independence, their resistance to our appeals for support becomes almost insurmountable. Why? Simple because desk-officers in the various ministries and even the ministers themselves, to make things easier, see the start of the Yugoslav crisis in 1991, at the time when Slovenia and Croatia first drifted off, i. e. when Slobodan Milošević had already accomplished his political goal of unifying the Serbs to the detriment of other peoples. The London Conference on former Yugoslavia held in 1992 and the decisions of the Badinter Commission serving as its appendix misled hard-line thinkers and turned international resolve into ineffectiveness. You cannot attempt to provide just solutions if your comprehension of the situation is inaccurate from the start. The Socialist Federal Republic of Yugoslavia began breaking up in 1989-1990 when Kosovo and the Vojvodina, two constituent units of the Yugoslav federation, were forcefully stripped of their semi-independent status. The 1974 Yugoslav Constitution should have served as the basis for determining how this multinational state was going to break up into independent states, rather than the forcefully imposed 1992 Constitution of the so-called Federal Republic of Yugoslavia. This is a great source of concern for us.

But Kosovo is, nonetheless, present wherever the Yugoslav crisis is discussed. Suffice it to mention our participation on an equal footing in government and non-government institutions. Why are we present? There are two reasons. Firstly, because we have to make our case clear to the world, and secondly, because the region remains explosive. The dangers of a spillover of the conflict persist. The West is well aware of the urgency of the crisis in Kosovo and appreciates our efforts to contain the situation. What we have to do under these circumstances is not only to express our gratitude for the support extended to us, but also to discern where appreciation for our efforts has become simply grotesque mimicry and despicable ridicule. It is an urgent situation which requires careful handling. If not, the region can easily be plunged into a conflagration of unpredictable consequences. We are continuing on this path because the signals coming from relevant sections of the international community are encouraging. But to keep this encouragement coming, we will have to work hard to show the world that we are determined to realize our aspirations even if we have to pay a high price for them.

[RE]: And what of the Republic of Albania? Are you satisfied or disappointed with Tirana's handling of the Kosovo issue? What more could Albania do?

[BB]: Let me take this opportunity to thank the President of Albania and his government for their outstanding appreciation of the unresolved national question, of which Kosovo is a major component. It is no coincidence that before 1992, Kosovo was only randomly referred to, in vague, sometimes euphoric terms. Today the Republic of Albania makes Kosovo a focal point in its diplomatic activity. Tirana has given the world an example of genuine brotherhood. It is so far the only country which has recognized us and is working to get the world to do the same.

Let me make one thing quite clear. The Kosovo representatives on their own can do much in the field of information diplomacy and can thus affect changes in attitudes among world diplomats, but without the representatives of the Republic of Albania, who are the people who work out the drafts and defend them, our results would leave much to be desired. The Republic of Albania has offered us its co-operation and has provided us with facilities to this end. Albanian diplomatic activity rests on two pillars, one of which is the national question. We co-operate on a bilateral basis and in this regard make frequent visits to Tirana. We have quite a few joint projects, our satellite television service for instance, and other projects in the works. We also work with Albania in multilateral diplomacy, having, to this end, co-ordinating teams that provide one another with a constant flow of information. In short, Kosovo would not have been the Kosovo it is today, i.e. a well-known Kosovo, without Albania and the latter's open-minded policy of defending its national interests, and probably its own survival. On the other side of the coin, Albanian foreign policy would not have been successful, had it not been for the contributions we have made towards the solution of our national question.

Nonetheless, there has been much visible and vocal 'dissatisfaction' with Albania and the level of its assistance to Kosovo, though wrongly so in my opinion. It takes little effort to appreciate the enormous difficulties Albania has been facing and the gigantic steps it has taken on the road to democracy and to a market economy. One must keep in mind that Kosovo would never even have existed as a political stalemate, had Albania shown more resolve from the start. Let me respond to all those who are unduly critical of Albania. I assert that the country has done much more than its domestic circumstances would normally have permitted it to do. Can it do even more? The answer is unequivocally: yes, it can and it will. In addition to the onerous legacy of the past, Albania has had to deal with the problems of the present, including a resurgence of anti-Kosovar sentiment in the country. Given its situation, could Albania have been more efficient? Undoubtedly yes! When I praise Albania's role in our cause, I refer to the country's readiness and commitment, but not necessarily its concrete performance, for we know here that we still have a long way to go. Albania's commitment as a state to our cause does exist and is of immeasurable assistance. There are, nonetheless, individuals within the Albanian administration who hold other views and among these people are some who bear direct responsibility for transforming this commitment into concrete action and results. In this respect, I feel Albania can do more than it has in the past to advance the cause of Albanians living outside the country's borders. That Bosnia has been in the way, so to speak, should be a cause for reflection but not a deterrent for further action.

[RE]: Do you have any contacts with the Serbian government or with the Serbian opposition which you consider positive?

[BB]: No, we do not have any direct contacts with the Serbs. This is not because we refuse to meet them, it is simply because at this point in time they refuse to face up to the realities of the situation. We continue observing one another from a distance, but there have been no concrete initiatives. We do not have any official contacts with the Serbian opposition, either. The reason for this is that, with all of Serbia in the grips of war fever, the Serbian opposition is trying to cash in on the widespread nationalism there, striving, as it were, to cut the ground from under Milošević's feet. Furthermore, their views on Kosovo do not differ much from those of the government at the moment, and, frankly, we do not expect them to change, unless there is a quick end to the war and the Serbs are defeated. Some inofficial contacts do exist, not on the part of the Government of the Republic of Kosovo, but by various individuals, be they party representatives or not. Seminars organized by government and non-government organizations are held from time to time and bring together representatives of a wide range of groups. It is at such venues that Albanians may happen to meet Serb representatives inofficially. So far, the feedback from such meetings has left much to be desired, for I cannot remember any positive result.

[RE]: If you alone could choose, what sort of status and future would you give to Kosovo?

[BB]: I have made my choice. Kosovo must be independent and must strive to preserve its self-government with or without the current leadership. For me there is no turning back so long as the people of Kosovo, in their overwhelming majority, support independence. When some of us speak of international protection, or even of a protectorate, this should not be interpreted as meaning that we would be willing to discard independence for a lesser status. What it does mean is that Albanians and Serbs should no longer live a life of subordination to one another. Albanians are prepared to live with the Serbs of Kosovo in a democratic Kosovo. The Belgrade regime has given the Serbs in Kosovo enormous privileges over the rest of the population in recent years. If the Serbs are resolved not to live with us on an equal basis, one can only interpret this as meaning that they misunderstand their loss of privileges as inequality and as a loss of freedom. Let me reiterate. The status that Kosovo presently has and the status it intends to realize to the full is that of complete independence. Problems of interpretation arise primarily because we have not yet managed to receive international recognition. We must present our case in the broadest possible terms, the most important element of which is our resolve to use peaceful means to attain our goal. This will undoubtedly delay the process, but it is essential that no more lives be lost.

Some might say that independence by peaceful means is an illusion, a ruse for the gullible. My answer to this is that, at the moment, I feel we have no other viable option. But this I will explain to the people of Kosovo and let them decide for themselves. In case of a decision that falls short of independence, I would seriously consider resignation. I am Prime Minister because I believe I can accomplish something along the lines I have presented. Will it take time? Yes, a lot. Will it be painful? Yes, it will. It will demand the sacrifice of perhaps more than just one generation? Will it ever come true? Yes, there is no doubt about it.

[RE]: Irrespective of your desires and plans for the future of Kosovo, how do you think the political situation will continue to evolve in the years to come?

[BB]: In view of what is happening in former Yugoslavia, predictions can easily be proven wrong, for we see aggression having its way. We see international law being twisted and turned into unrecognizable forms and shapes, almost to inexistence. We count the fatalities, the missing and displaced persons. Everything in the Balkans has become chaotic and Kosovo finds itself in the very eye of the storm. Here it must hold out and survive.

Predictions? Milošević will be in power for some time to come and 'Greater Serbia' will continue to be on the agenda, but will perhaps begin to use more democratic means to assert itself. In simple terms this translates as follows - the Serbian Parliament will continue to bully itself into passing discriminatory laws against the other ethnic groups, thus keeping tension high. This means that some peoples will continue to live in a virtual Apartheid situation, which will only serve to encourage extremism. The Serbs will continue to put up with the federation for a while until they resolve once again that they would be better off in a single state and find a 'democratic' way of making this dream a reality (although their leaders will certainly be reluctant to lose their 'posts').

I am afraid to say anything about the Bosnians. In the best case scenario, they will have their own diminished state. But Kosovo will one day be free, on the understanding that this is the best solution for everyone involved.

Interview with Adem Demaçi

[Robert Elsie]: Adem, the first time I tried to visit you after your release from prison, none of my friends and acquaintances in Prishtina would take me there. They were all afraid of being seen in your street by the Serbian militia. Tell me about your early political activities, your arrest and why you believe you were held in prison for twenty-eight years. Were you really such a dangerous person?

[Adem Demaçi]: It is true that when I got out of prison there was still a good deal of fear of the police, but not as much as it may have seemed at the time. My release from prison was one indication of a major change of policy in the post-Titoist leadership of Yugoslavia.

As to my early political activities, there is a good deal I could tell you because I unwittingly began my 'political career' at a very early age. It was in the first year of secondary school in 1946 that I ventured to ask our Serbian teacher Ms Zora Pečenović a 'political' question: "Teacher, why do we Albanian students have to learn Serbian when the Serbian students don't have to learn Albanian?" This question caused quite a scandal for the school administration, but thanks to the principal, Jani Gjino, I was not expelled from school. This, you could say, was the beginning of my political career. The totalitarian regime in Yugoslavia had committed many crimes against my people which could not go unnoticed by the Albanians and even by me as a child.

Every year, 'hostile organizations' were uncovered at our secondary school in Prishtina and such activities were not devoid of impact on the students. When I finished high school, I went to study in Belgrade, where, again, it was not hard to see that the Albanians were being discriminated against.

In the winter of 1955, a group headed by Rexhep Latifi-Abdullahu and Burhan Pasholli was imprisoned in Skopje. At that time, the security forces in Belgrade invited a good number of Albanian students there for 'informative talks' at one of their centres (*Zeleni Venac*, No. 5). I didn't know it at the time, but, as I subsequently learned, one of the prisoners from the group headed by Rexhep Latifi had mentioned my name during interrogation as a person who posed a potential threat to the regime. It is true that I had spoken to that person openly and had expressed my dissatisfaction. As a result, the Belgrade regime kept me under surveillance from that time on.

When I returned to Prishtina, I joined the staff of the newspaper Rilindja as a journalist. One of the men I worked with, a stooge of the Serbian authorities, proposed that I join the Communist League of Yugoslavia. I pretended not to understand, but when he insisted, I replied: "You would do better to look after your own affairs and not get involved in mine because, otherwise, the day may come, when they kick me out of the party, that they will start asking who invited Adem Demaçi to join the party in the first place."

The ranks of Albanian intellectuals were growing, though slowly and with difficulty. With its network of informants, the UDBA realized that something was going on among these Albanian intellectuals and, with its long and fruitful experience in such matters, decided to select a sacrificial lamb. By getting rid of me, they hoped to sow panic among Albanian intellectuals. It was not that I myself was dangerous for the regime, but rather that the regime felt an urgent need to nip the formation of all opposition in the bud. I had spoken openly with many people on various occasions about Serbia's domineering, discriminatory and destructive policies towards the Albanians, but I had not really achieved anything. My only great deed at the time was to be my own defence at my trial. People in the courtroom broke into tears. The Serbs were nonetheless ruthless and I was given a draconic sentence.

Since that time, when I took up the challenge put forward by the Yugoslav regime, I have continued my 'struggle' to free my people.

[RE]: The Ranković years up to 1966 were ones of open terror for the Albanians in Yugoslavia, at a time when the rest of the country seemed to be liberalizing and opening up. In the broader context, your arrest and imprisonment would seem to have been related to the ideological split between Tito's communist party in Yugoslavia and Enver Hoxha's communist party in Albania. The Albanian nationalist movement in Kosovo was still to a good extent a matter of Marxist revolutionary cells struggling against the 'Titoist revisionists', and many Kosovo nationalists had a naive confidence in 'Comrade Enver'. Do you regard your confrontation with Belgrade has having been part of a political struggle of divergent views within the communist world or simply as a quest for obtaining ethnic equality and freedom within the Yugoslav system? What was important to you at the time?

[AD]: Open terror for the Albanians did not begin with the Ranković years. The terror began in October of 1912 when the Serbian army occupied over half of Albanian territory and committed an appalling bloodbath in the process. Since that time, there has not been one day up to the present that the prisons of Serbia and subsequently of Yugoslavia have not been overflowing with Albanian patriots. The leadership in Serbia and Yugoslavia has changed. Governments and regimes of various ideologies have come and gone, but their anti-Albanian policies have remained unchanged. The era we call the 'Ranković years' was terrible indeed, but it was not the only age of terror, nor was it even the zenith of the terror. In old Yugoslavia, for instance, in the winter of 1921, the Serbian army and police committed atrocities in the villages of Prapashtica, Kecekolla and Dabishevci which rank among the worst in history. They burnt women and children alive in their homes and committed countless other crimes which cannot be forgotten.

But since we began our conversation with the Ranković years, let us continue with them. Ranković was the author of much terror, including the bloodbath of Bar in 1945 when 4,000 young Albanian soldiers were slaughtered in the most barbaric fashion. Ranković, with Tito's knowledge, was also the one behind the unspeakable prison camps, such as Goli Otok and Stara Gradiška, and the mass expulsion of Albanians to Turkey. When the Tito regime was forced by the Stalinists to look for support from the West, after quashing Milovan Djilas and his attempts to make a few basic changes to the totalitarian system, it was also compelled to make some cosmetic modifications, but never gave up its monopoly on power. After all, there were people in key positions throughout Yugoslavia whose job it was to collaborate and keep Ranković and Tito in power. Indeed, it was the tactical modifications, alterations and concessions which enabled the police state to survive in Yugoslavia. The West, sorely in need of a collaborator and an agent in the Eastern bloc, was more than willing to sanction these modifications and approved of them much more heartily than they warranted. A belief reigned in the West for quite some time that Tito had managed to solve the problem of co-existence in a multi-national state such as Yugoslavia. In actual fact, all of Yugoslavia had been thrown into the cold of a brutal police state and none of the ethnic groups in the country was satisfied out in the cold. Most unsatisfied were the Albanians who were the most oppressed of all. The Albanians were the only non-Slavic ethnic group (aside from the Hungarians) to be kept forcibly, against their will, within a community of southern Slavic nations.

As far as I was concerned, my only political interest was the preservation, defence and salvation of the Albanians from ultimate annihilation. Contacts and relations between the political parties of Tito and Enver Hoxha were never the cause or reason for the incarceration of large number of Albanian patriots. In fact, I know of only one organization which bore an ideological name, an anti-revisionist committee. Aside from this one, all the other organizations were of a more irredentist character, i.e. they strove for the unification of territory stolen by the Serb occupants with the Albanian motherland.

As to me personally, I had an opportunity at high school in Prishtina to meet a number of refugees who had fled the Hoxha regime and I began to realize that something had gone wrong there. But on the other hand, I cannot say that I did not entertain a 'naive confidence in Comrade Enver', as you say. After all, he was at least doing something for the liberation of subjugated Albanians. We regarded every deterioration of relations between these two totalitarian parties, the Titoists and the Hoxhists, as a possible sign that the Hoxha regime would do more for the liberation of the Albanians in Yugoslavia. Enver Hoxha was a crafty politician and, in his speeches and actions, he nourished many a hope and illusion among us. It is obvious that we considered Albania as our natural ally for the liberation of the subjugated part of our people. We believed that the backing of a country with its own armed forces, its own police and diplomats, could mean real and objective support for our aspirations. When Zogu was in power, the Kosovo Albanians collaborated with him in their own interests, without asking questions about who he was and how he had come to power. We made the same mistake with respect to the Hoxha regime. We never asked how he rose to power within the party, how he took over the government and what methods he used to keep power. We were young at the time and did not know how to analyse situations properly. For this reason, there were indeed many people who had a blind faith in Enver Hoxha and his words, but not because they were communists. We knew what communism was because we were living ourselves in a communist regime.

My efforts were directed towards saving my people from annihilation, and nothing else. We were simply trying to extract ourselves from the Yugoslav system.

[RE]: All right, as a Yugoslav citizen of Albanian nationality, I can see it is understandable that you looked towards the Albanian motherland for salvation from 'Slav oppression', as did many intellectuals in Kosovo at the time. But what exactly did you know about the political realities of Enver Hoxha's Albania? And what did you not know at the time? Were there things you preferred not to know?

[AD]: It is understandable that we looked upon Albania as a mother, and it is therefore normal that we hoped she would support us. All that we knew of reality in Albania was what the centralist and monopolistic propaganda of the Hoxha regime told us. An important role was also played by anti-Albanian propaganda from Belgrade. Because we hated the Belgrade regime and believed nothing it said, we interpreted all its insults of and attacks against the Hoxha regime as exactly the opposite, as compliments. We found ourselves caught between two lies: a positive lie from Tirana and negative propaganda from Belgrade. We refused to believe that the Hoxha regime was no better than ours and that the same form of totalitarianism and bureaucracy reigned in Tirana. We refused to believe this because it would have destroyed our illusions and sapped our strength to fight for our freedom. How could we struggle for independence from an evil Yugoslavia if it were only to join an equally evil Albania? From the start, therefore, we never attempted to study or analyze what was actually going on in Albania. We were quite happy to live with the outrageous lies spread by Enver Hoxha. And, as you know, he was an unequalled master in telling lies.

[RE]: Some people tell me you are still a communist at heart. Is that true? Do you have any nostalgia for the past? And do you regret the collapse of the country we called Yugoslavia?

[AD]: It is no surprise to me that people have told you and will continue to tell you that I am a communist. The truth of the matter is that I have never been a communist or a member of any communist party. I did realize one thing, though. Had we spread anti-communist propaganda, we would have lost the modicum of support we had hoped the Hoxha regime would give us. I read books in Albanian and Serbian on communism as an ideology, as well as the major works of Marx, Engels and Lenin. Of Enver Hoxha I read only the speech he gave in 1961 at the conference of eighty-one communist and workers' parties in Moscow. Of Stalin I never read a thing. I have, of course, also read a variety of anti-communist, neutral and philosophical works, as would any individual in search of the truth. During my third prison sentence, I had access to the complete works of Hegel in a Serbian translation. It was then that I discovered to what extent Marx and Engels had deformed Hegel's philosophy and what incredible tricks Lenin had played with this philosophy to attain his own objectives.

It is absurd to call me a communist because I have never believed in communism. There are certain forces interested in eliminating me from political and public life. Many of these individuals were themselves in the service of Tito's party and helped the Serbian bureaucrats in their subjugation of the Albanian people, receiving in recompense a few scraps from the table of the rulers in Belgrade. They were in the service of the regime right until it collapsed. The moment it fell, they turned into fanatic democrats and began attacking their former bosses and the Serbs in general, and became more nationalist than any ultra-nationalist could possibly imagine. They are trying to cover up their own collaboration by attacking a whole generation of young people who did not abandon their patriotic stance even though they rotted in Serbian prisons. They attack the latter as being Hoxhists and Marxist-Leninists though this ideology was only a cover used by true patriots to further the goal of national liberation.

As to nostalgia for the past, I have none, nor is there any reason I should have, because I spent over half of my life, during what we called Yugoslavia, in its prison system. I am one of the many individuals who did his utmost to destroy what we called Yugoslavia, which was nothing more than a prison of nations. I do not regret the destruction of that country. All I regret is the fact that my people are still living under the Serbian and Montenegrin yoke. If they are to survive and preserve their ethnic identity, they will have to come to terms with dramatic changes in the future. I also regret that most of my people still do not understand the seriousness of this historic moment and do not deal with reality. They do not know how to judge individuals and parties on the basis of what the latter have accomplished over the past five years and still cherish the illusion that someone else will come and do the work for them.

[RE]:   When I finally managed to meet you, on 18 August 1990, I was quite surprised by the conciliatory tone and attitude you expressed towards the Serbs, who had, after all, abused and imprisoned you for almost three decades. I remember you reciting to me the dedication from your novel 'Gjarpijt e gjakut' (The snakes of blood), published in Prishtina in 1958:

> *"Not to the valiant*
> *Who raise their hand in crime,*
> *But to the men*
> *Who extend their hands in reconciliation."*

Since your release, you and your people have lived through five years of heavy-handed and unwanted military occupation, and of daily human rights violations in Kosovo, which are at least tolerated by Belgrade. Are you personally still willing to extend your hand in reconciliation? And what of your people? Will the hatred ever subside on the dusty Plain of the Blackbirds?

[AD]: I remember the day you came to visit me. I seem to remember it was my sister who found one of the remaining original copies of my novel *Gjarpijt e gjakut* for you. I noticed your delight when I talked about the Serbs. I spoke not with hatred in my voice, but with compassion because, by destroying us, they have destroyed themselves just as thoroughly. I never imagined at the time that such sinister forces, mediaeval in terms of their ideology but very modern in terms of military equipment, would rise to the surface in Serbia. You have seen what has happened in the five years since our first meeting. The subjugated peoples of former Yugoslavia, including my own, have lived through untold horrors precipitated by ultra-nationalist forces in Belgrade. Despite all that has happened, I still have the ability to distinguish between the forces which were and are in power and the simple people of Serbia, who are the most manipulated people on earth nowadays. One way or another, they have been convinced not only to put up with the regime in Belgrade, but to support it in its endeavours to occupy foreign land and to enslave other peoples, in particular my people who have suffered so much.

Despite everything, I still believe that it is wrong to accuse the whole of the Serbian people of these crimes because they are living under a totalitarian regime which will do anything to remain in power. This regime exercises not only a military and police dictatorship over other peoples and its own people, but also a cultural and information dictatorship.

With regard to what my people have gone through over the past five years, you must remember that these have only been the most recent years in a long history of subjugation beginning in 1912, or to put it another way, these are the most recent of the evils my people have lived through since the creation of the first Serbian state in 1878. As an Albanologist, you will certainly have heard of the barbaric wave of ethnic cleansing which that Serbian state carried out against 600 villages with an Albanian majority in the districts of Kurshumli / Kuršumlija, Prokuple / Prokuplje, Nish / Niš and Leskovc / Leskovac. The Serbian regime at the time chased the Albanians from their homes, burning women and children alive. Its actions were in flagrant violation of its internationally undertaken obligations to respect the rights of those Albanians who found themselves within the borders of that new state.

In your question, you use the wording "at least tolerated by Belgrade". The sad fact of the matter is that all these evils have been encouraged, inspired, supported and carried out by Belgrade. The Serbs of Kosovo are merely being used as instruments for the ethnic cleansing of Albanian land.

The Albanian people well full know that all the tragic events which have taken place and continue to take place to their detriment, have their origins in Belgrade. For this very reason, the Albanians are able to co-exist with the Serbs living in Kosovo and are willing to understand that these Serbs have been turned into tools of blind anti-Albanian hatred. This conviction constitutes a healthy foundation - provided that no greater tragedy occurs in the future - for a resumption of normal relations and co-operation between the Albanians and Serbs who live on Albanian land. By 'normal relations and co-operation' I mean a situation in which the Albanians are in a position of equality with the others and not in the position of servitude that the police regime in Belgrade has reserved for us.

As far as my people are concerned, I am confident that they are willing to put an end to ethnic hatred 'on the dusty Plain of the Blackbirds', as you put it.

[RE]: There was a spontaneous wave of enthusiasm among your compatriots when you were released from prison in April 1990. Some interpreted your release as an attempt by Belgrade to show a sign of good will. Why do you think you were released?

[AD]: There was indeed a wave of enthusiasm among my people at the time. But that I was released was simply a concession on the part of the Yugoslav leadership to gain time and counter the pressure of public opinion after the international community discovered that I had been languishing in Yugoslav prisons for almost thirty years and that the regime in Belgrade had done its utmost to cover this fact up.

I was released from prison because my sentence would have been up in five and a half months anyway and because an early release could be used to deceive world opinion. Another element involved in my release was rivalry among the various leaders of Yugoslavia who, after the death of Tito, were planning to divide up the country.

[RE]: I was told after your release that people from all over Kosovo and western Macedonia - construction workers, carpenters, masons, electricians etc. - travelled to Prishtina, sacrificing their free time and energy, and built you a new home, free of charge. Is that true?

[AD]: Yes, the story is true indeed. Even when I happen to meet these people nowadays, they still refuse to tell me their names. They simply greet me with a smile and go their way.

[RE]: While in prison, you were recognized by Amnesty International as a prisoner of conscience and became known to many as the Nelson Mandela of Europa. Since your release, you have also received much international acclaim, including the 1991 Sakharov Prize. As head of the Council for the Protection of Human Rights and Freedoms, you travel widely and have spoken openly about the political situation in Kosovo and about the continuing human rights violations there. Do you consider yourself a free man now?

[AD]: While I was in prison, some time in the late eighties, I received a Christmas card from Amnesty International signed by one Ms Annette White and by a fourteen-year-old girl named Jane Debny. I subsequently learned that Amnesty International had been informed by Mr Mihail Mihailov, who was in America at the time, of my fate and my imprisonment and had recognized me as a prisoner of conscience. I had met Mr Mihailov in prison, in the fortress of Požarevac where we were both doing time.

The multiparty system is a façade, a spotlight held over countless parties who have their functions to fulfil. In the present system in Serbia, the Albanian parties and other humanitarian organizations exist formally, but they are powerless to act against wanton police violence and against the discriminatory and destructive policies of the Belgrade regime. The 'activities' of all these parties, institutions and various individuals within the country and abroad simply serve as an alibi for the Belgrade regime, proof that democracy exists in this country. The regime can point out that the Albanians, after all, have their own parties, institutions and politicians that speak freely on issues and are not hindered by anyone. Do not be deceived into believing that this tactic works does not work in the outside world, which is not well informed about our situation. It does much to justify Serbian policies against the Albanians. It is true that we Albanians speak openly, we travel and protest, we lament our fate but, despite all the noise we make, the Belgrade regime continues to act as it wishes without any hindrance, and its actions are aimed at the destruction of all the vital arteries of Albanian existence, to make life for the Albanians on their own land impossible and thus to bring about an ethnic cleansing of the Albanians or, as they say in their own words, the 'Serbification' of Kosovo.

I am free to speak and to write, but no more than this. I have no power to hinder any of the actions of the Belgrade regime to annihilate the Albanians in Kosovo. My so-called freedom is therefore very much a theoretical freedom.

[RE]: Optimally, the protection of human rights should not be linked to ethnic concerns, i.e. to the interests of one ethnic group over another. Do you have any contacts or collaboration with Serbian human rights activists or groups? What is the attitude of the Serbian opposition towards human rights violations in Kosovo? Do you have any positive contacts with them?

[AD]: With regard to the protection of human rights, we can do no more than speak out. Our organization, which is called the Council for the Protection of Human Rights and Freedoms, is no more than a 'council of condolences'. We have no power to protect anyone's human rights, not even the human rights of our members who are brutally beaten by the Serbian police and sentenced to long terms in prison. All we can do is record, as far as possible, the infringements and violations of human rights, irrespective of nationality. We check this information and distribute it within the country and abroad. Many reports prepared by foreign governments have used our information as a basis for presenting the real situation in Kosovo.

Our council co-operates with individuals and similar organizations in Belgrade, such as the Fund for Humanitarian Rights, and more recently with the Council for the Defence of Human Rights. With the exception of a few very small parties of minimal influence, the attitude of the Serbian opposition to human rights violations in Kosovo does not differ substantially from that of the government. Indeed, in certain respects they are more extreme in their declarations than Milošević himself. In February 1993, I was invited by Belgrade television (a broadcasting station with a radius of about 200 km) for a talkshow on Studio B lasting 100 minutes. There, I was given an opportunity to speak directly to TV audiences and answer many of their very aggressive questions.

There is a sort of semi-opposition in Belgrade called the Circle of Belgrade Intellectuals. I was invited by this circle to Belgrade on 26-28 November 1993 to meet these intellectuals. I was also invited to the studios of Radio B 92 for a five minute interview, to an independent TV station in Belgrade, and to a meeting of a large group of intellectuals in a Belgrade auditorium. This is, more or less, the extent of our contacts with the opposition in Belgrade.

We are waiting for a concrete sign from the Belgrade opposition that they are willing to accept other possibilities for solving the Kosovo question, taking into account the political will of the Albanians and offering immediate and open contacts between us. But such contacts remain impossible, and this is not our fault, as long as they insist on demanding that we take part in elections to overthrow the Belgrade regime without having anything more to offer to us than what the present regime has to offer, i.e. subjugation and Serbian colonization.

[RE]: You were born and raised in Kosovo, in an ethnically mixed region of Albanians and Serbs. Did you have any good Serbian friends when you were growing up? And do you have any Serbian friends now? If not, why not?

[AD]: It is true that I was born and raised in servitude in an ethnically mixed region of Albanians, Serbs, Montenegrins, and Roma etc. Our direct neighbours on the other side of the street and to the left of our house were Serbs. When we were little, we played football together without any problems. One of these neighbours became a police inspector when he grew up and took part in the action leading to my imprisonment in 1964. I did not hold this against him and when I got out of prison, I spoke to him without rancour. His mother is still alive. I never pass her on the street without greeting her, although I notice she is a bit uneasy that some of the Serbs might see her talking to me.

I have Serbian friends in Belgrade whom I have known since the time we were in prison together, for instance the well-known film maker Lazar Stojanović, the sociologist Milan Nikolić and others. I also have friends I got to know after I got out of prison, such as the noted Belgrade architect Bogdan Bogdanović, the lawyer Srdja Popović, and many others.

I do my best to maintain old friendships with Serbs and Montenegrins in Kosovo, but the Belgrade regime is vigilant and uses all the means at its disposal to inhibit contacts between Albanians and Serbs. I used to have a Montenegrin girlfriend, Cvija Roksandić, who did not abandon me while I was in prison, nor indeed when I got out of prison. She told me what she had gone through because people had seen us together. Unfortunately, she died and, as I received the news of her death a day late, I was unable to pay her my last respects.

[RE]: If you alone could choose, what sort of status and future would you give to Kosovo?

[AD]: If I alone could choose the future of Kosovo, and if my people would listen to me and if the Serbian people would accept my decision, I would propose a type of federation for the peoples of this part of former Yugoslavia such as the Swiss Confederation. I regard this as the best and only feasible solution, in which the interests of all sides could be taken into account. Such a state could also serve as an embryo for a Swiss-type confederation of all the peoples of the Balkans. But I am very much afraid that this proposal is more akin to fantasy than to reality.

[RE]: Irrespective of your desires and plans for the future of Kosovo, how do you think the political situation will continue to evolve in the years to come?

[AD]: Although it is extremely difficult to rid oneself of hope, I will attempt for once to judge the situation devoid of all hope and expectation, though I cannot guarantee I will succeed. After all, no human being can live without hope.

To tell you the truth, I do not regard the perspectives of my people as very bright at the moment. They are faced with an enormous historic challenge and, in their present situation, are not yet ready to play the historic role attributed to them. I am not at all easy when I ponder on the future of my people because they are able to do very little for themselves, particularly since the historic challenge we are being faced with is colossal indeed. My people were confronted with democracy in a very turbulent age without having had time to grow up and gain any useful political experience. They came out of the cold of the totalitarian dictatorships of Tito and Enver Hoxha and entered the blazing heat of multiparty parliamentary democracy at virtually the same time. But multiparty democracy in Kosovo took a different form, that of an ultranationalist Serbian dictatorship based on totally new criteria. It has been exceedingly difficult for my people to adapt to these new circumstances. Too much is being demanded of us at once: a totally new way of thinking, new approaches and new methods. What else can I say? If you rob me of my hope and expectations, I don't know what will become of me.

Interview with Rexhep Qosja

[Robert Elsie]: Professor Qosja, you have long been known as a scholar, writer and literary historian, but in recent years you seem to have become a father figure of the Albanian nation. How does it feel to have six or seven million children?

[Rexhep Qosja]: Perhaps they call me a father figure because of my comprehensive approach to the Albanian question. There can be no doubt that some people use the term 'father of the Albanian nation' to do me respect whereas others use it as a term of reproach. I myself do not particularly like the term. The Albanian nation, one of the oldest in the Balkans, is historically mature enough to have no need for a father. What the Albanian people do need, however, is liberation in the as yet unliberated parts of the country. In the other part of the country, which is now an independent state, what they need is democratic institutions and a state of law, in short a truely democratic government.

[RE]: Like many of your compatriots, you are striving to find an adequate solution to the Albanian question, i.e. the Kosovo dilemma. If I understand it properly, you are the proponant of a more radical political course than that taken by the Democratic League of Kosova (LDK). What is the difference between your stance and that of the LDK?

[RQ]: The Albanian question cannot be reduced to the question of Kosovo, even though Kosovo is its most important element. I regard the Albanian question as one embracing all unliberated Albanians living on Albanian territory bordering on Albania, i.e. in regions which are ethnically and geographically continuous with Albania and in which the Albanians constitute either the only inhabitants or the vast majority of the inhabitants. These regions include not only Kosovo, but also Western Macedonia and Albanian land, inhabited by Albanians, in Montenegro. Any comprehensive solution to the Albanian question must take the problem of all these Albanians into account. Another aspect of the Albanian question is the consolidation of democracy, and the material and cultural development of the Albanians in general. As such, the Albanian question for me today is both a national question and a question of national development.

There is no doubt that great differences exist between my views on the solution of the Albanian question and the policies of the LDK. The LDK is a political party which, when it addresses the Albanian question, thinks only of the Kosovo question. I have already stated how I define the Albanian question. The LDK is a party which is involved in party politics, i.e. in the struggle for power, and thus acts as if it were in power, even though under occupation. I, for my part, am an individual and have no ambitions to take power, but simply wish to see the unfree Albanians freed.

The LDK has set up a 'co-ordinating council' with other Albanian political parties in Kosovo but this council does not unite them into a national movement because it is not an organ which can make decisions binding for the parties involved. I personally believe that we must maintain the party system as the basic element of our democratic future, but that we must unite them rather into a national liberation movement led by a 'national council' which would make decisions binding for all those participating in the movement. We must unite them into a movement which would move forward and not be pent up in offices where all political activity is reduced to making speeches and resolutions, and holding press conferences!

The LDK is a party which has looked on for four years now and said nothing about the mass migration of young Albanians to other European countries. For my part, in my writings and in my speeches, I have always appealed to these young people to remain in Kosovo, knowing full well that their departure means the strength we need for liberation is being sapped.

The LDK is a party which has reduced all its co-operation with Albania to co-operation with one party, i.e. with the party in power, and with one person, i.e. Sali Berisha. I, for my part, believe that we must co-operate with all political forces in Albania, we must co-operate with Albania as a whole, as well as with Albanians abroad, and as a result, create a pan-Albanian organization which would set national policy for a solution to the Albanian question.

The LDK is a party which has opposed the idea of national reconciliation and unity. Several intellectuals and I joined together in an attempt, initiated in Tirana, but unfortunately unsuccessful, to realize this ideal and to prepare for a national programme which would serve as a binding platform of national policy for a solution to the Albanian question.

The LDK is a party which has pursued a disreputable and submissive political course towards Serbia, a course of nothing more than words. I, for my part, have endeavoured to promote concrete resistance, involving all types of civil disobedience - strikes, protests, demonstrations and the refusal to fulfil any civil duties towards the Serbian occupation regime.

The LDK is a party which, with its submissive and servile policies, has negated the historic role of its own people. I, for my part, have striven for our objectives to be realized relying primarily on our own strength, our own activities, capacities and sacrifice, but also of course on the Great Powers, or at least on those of the Powers who best appreciate our situation. I am aware that no small nation can solve its major problems without support from the Great Powers and that small peoples are of necessity dependent upon the Great Powers. I nonetheless believe, and have always stressed, that support from the Great Powers, in the first instance from the United States and Germany, will only be proportionate to our own involvement, to our resistance and sacrifice. If we do what the LDK and the other small parties have done up to the present, that is, if we do nothing at all, neither the United States, which has shown goodwill towards us, nor the other Great Powers will be able to do anything more for us than they have done in the past. They can do no more than grant us the old autonomy status, which is in fact nothing at all.

The LDK is a party which has been propagating lies not only with regard to its activities, but also with regard to the policies of the Albanian Government and to the attitude of the international community on the Albanian question. For my part, I have always stressed that we cannot continue spreading communist lies and propaganda. We must tell the people the whole truth: the good where there is good to be told, and the bad where setbacks occur.

In conclusion, the LDK is a party which for almost five years now has been dragging the Albanian people of Kosovo down and down, such that we can do nothing but lament the years we have lost and the humiliation we have suffered. Our current misery in Kosovo and the back burner role the Kosovo question plays in international politics show that the LDK has been pursuing a course of action which, as has become more than evident, is to the benefit of Serbia. The LDK, in my opinion, has taken upon itself great national and moral responsibility and, as a matter of course, will have to pay coming generations for everything wrong it has done, for everything it has neglected and for everything it has hindered others from doing. In short, with its wishy-washy policies made to seem resolute by the propaganda drums of present politicians in Tirana, the LDK has divested the right of the Kosovo Albanians for ethnic self-determination of the moral fibre which sacrifice would convey upon it. Such policies, which merit nothing but universal pity, have robbed us of our historical dignity and of our legitimate right to decide sovereignly on our own destiny. I believe that the course pursued by the LDK up to now represents not the wishes of the majority of its members, but only the line of the leadership itself. The discord seething within the party nowadays is eminent proof that the LDK will remain stuck in the same hole it has been in for years now.

[RE]: Many Albanians, particularly those in Kosovo, regard the reunification of Kosovo and Albania proper as inevitable in the long term. Some openly advocate the creation of a Greater Albania. You yourself have used the term 'ethnic Albania' and 'ethnic borders'. What do you mean by this and where would these concrete borders be?

[RQ]:   The notion of a Greater Albania was created by supporters of Serbian nationalism who, in pursuing their ideal of a Greater Serbia, turned their attention to and subsequently took over

Kosovo, in which the Albanians have always been in the vast majority, and Macedonia in which there were hardly any Serbs up to after the Balkan Wars. Albania, including Kosovo with its 90% Albanian majority within its borders, should not be called Greater Albania, but simply a real or normal Albania. Ethnic Albania is the national state of the Albanian people which would be composed of present-day Albania and ethnic and historical Albanian lands geographically continuous with Albania in which the Albanians constitute either the only inhabitants or the vast majority of the inhabitants. Ethnic Albania is the union of Western Albania (the present-day Albanian state) and Eastern Albania (Albanian territory as yet unliberated).

[RE]: Do you think you could sit down at a table with Serbian intellectuals and agree upon an ethnic division of the region? If not, is your 'ethnic Albania' anything more than a dream?

[RQ]: There are Serbian intellectuals who think, and indeed, who say that Serbia must not keep the Albanians within its sphere against their will, because it has no right to do so. I am profoundly convinced that if we had put up more active resistance in Kosovo over the past four or five years and not confined ourselves to press conferences of the LDK and of other parties, and if, by making use of the whole spectrum of civil disobedience, we had shown our resolve to realize our legitimate right to ethnic self-determination, the number of these Serbian intellectuals would be much larger than it is. But as a result of the political course pursued by the LDK leadership, the number of these Serbian intellectuals has now decreased substantially.

It is wrong to speak of a division of Kosovo or, as you say, of the region. It is better to speak of altering the border between Albania and Yugoslavia (Serbia and Montenegro). The Kosovo Albanians, for instance, have the right to as much territory as their proportion of the population warrents, and the Serbs the right to as much territory as the proportion of their population warrents. This principle must also hold for the Albanians and Serbs in Presheva / Preševo, Bujanovc / Bujanovac, and Medvegja / Medvedja. Yugoslavia (Serbia and Montenegro) cannot keep the Albanians within its sphere by force. It will simply be worn down by us. It will be worn down by our resolve to be free and independent and to live as a united people with our brothers and sisters in Albania. It will be worn down by our high birth-rates. It will be worn down by its own violence. History is on our side. History is working against the Serbian occupation of Kosovo.

[RE]: Ideals and political reality are quite different matters, especially in the Balkans. The people of Kosovo, in their vast majority, support the existence of the Republic of Kosovo, its government and its constitution, even though no country on earth, not even the Republic of Albania, has recognized Kosovo officially. As a geopolitical reality, Kosovo is nothing more than a part of Greater Serbia. Do you recognize the Republic of Kosovo as it exists today, and do you think that this republic will ever become a political reality, a country like all the others?

[RQ]: Recognizing a country means recognizing its sovereignty, freedom and independence, the token of which is a government with all inherent attributes: an administration, policies, a police force, an army, foreign relations, and an economy. How can I recognize a national 'government' which calls itself a government while under Serbian occupation? What guarantee can it offer for the sovereignty of Kosovo? Absolutely none. How can I recognize a President, a Member of Parliament or a Minister who travels through the country carrying Serbian I. D., who crosses the border of Kosovo using a Serbian passport, and who fulfils all his duties as a citizen towards the Serbian state? How can I recognize a President or Member of Parliament whom any Serbian policeman can seize by the ear and drag off wherever he wants, whenever he wants. No, that is not a government. It is a tragicomedy staged in order to smother active resistance. This pseudo-government, which Serbia tolerates and which has unwittingly become Serbia's rearguard while it is busy with the war in Bosnia and Croatia, has helped put us in the position we are in now, i. e. in the worst political, social and moral situation we have been in for eighty-three years. Up to now, this pseudo-government has done nothing but serve the interests of those who believe they are governing. It has driven every thinking Albanian to desperation. The Albanian people of Kosovo do not merit such a humiliation.

I am not sure that solving the Albanian question by creating a second Albanian state in the Balkans is a good idea, primarily because the other Balkan states would oppose the move. I am in favour of solving the Kosovo question, and thus the Albanian question, by uniting the Albanians, i.e. by uniting the territory geographically continuous with Albania, on which they constitute either the only inhabitants or the vast majority of the inhabitants, into one state - into a united Albania.

[RE]: You have been involved in controversial exchanges with political leaders in the Republic of Albania and rumour has it that you are not always well received in Tirana. What is the essence of your dissatisfaction with politicians in Tirana, if any? What is the Albanian government doing right and what is it doing wrong on the Kosovo issue?

[RQ]: You can only say that I am not well received in Tirana if you identify the people, society and the country as a whole with the regime, or indeed if you identify the people, society and the country as a whole with some of the leading politicians there. The regime in Albania is not the same as the Albanian people. It is not Albania. I have criticised it because of my love for Albania. You cannot conclude, since the regime has not treated me well, that I am not well received in Tirana because, in the Albanian-speaking world, it still holds true that the people are one thing and their regime quite another. Albanian regimes are not yet democratic. Both intellectuals and the simple people in the street have treated me very well and I can assure you that I have been treated better there than by any Albanians from Albanian territory in former Yugoslavia. It is true that some government officials have not received me well, but I have no particular desire to be received by them anyway. I am not and do not intend to be an intellectual who kowtows to those in power.

You have asked me what the Albanian government is doing right on the Kosovo issue. Albanian diplomats, though farther afield than they were before, are dealing with the Kosovo issue. Albanian embassies do their best to arrange meetings between Albanian figures from Kosovo and Macedonia and representatives of the various governments around the world and of international institutions and forums. And this is a good thing.

You have asked me what the Albanian government is doing wrong on the Kosovo issue. The Albanian government still has no clear and fixed policy on the Albanian question. Plans for solving the Kosovo problem used to change almost every week; now they change almost every month.

The Albanian government has cut back its co-operation with political forces in Kosovo to co-operation with one political party, indeed with two or three individuals from that party. By doing so, it has divided our movement and scattered it to the winds. By reducing co-operation with Kosovo Albanians to co-operation with a few well-known persons, it has deprived our movement of the moral fibre which unity would give it, and has weakened and diminished our ability to act politically or otherwise.

The Albanian government maintains political and economic relations with Montenegro, behind which stand relations with Serbia, and these relations cannot but have a negative impact on options for solving the Kosovo problem in a just manner.

The Albanian government, which has joined the blockade against Yugoslavia (Serbia and Montenegro), is breaking this blockade in Montenegro and is furnishing Serbia with Albanian oil. It is no longer a secret that an agreement was reached to this end between Sali Berisha and the Montenegrin President, Bulatović, during the latter's visit to Tirana three years ago. If there is only one Albanian people - and there is only one -, and if we assume that it is not possible to carry out policies in the name of the half of the Albanian people living in Albania without taking into consideration the interests of the other half living across the border, just as it is not possible for the half living across the border to carry out policies without taking into consideration the interests of those living in Albania, we arrive at the conclusion that, by selling oil to Serbia and Montenegro, the regime of Sali Berisha is promoting the Serbian occupation of Kosovo. I am convinced that this regime will be condemned by history for this, and perhaps not just by history.

[RE]: What expectations do the people of Kosovo have of Albania? Do they feel supported or betrayed by Albania?

[RQ]: The Albanian people of Kosovo have never been, nor will they ever be betrayed by Albania. No, Kosovo is a large and open wound on the body of Albania, a source of constant pain. Ever since the

Balkan Wars, the Albanians have proven themselves to be patriots in their attitude towards Kosovo and its fate. The people of Albania have always given exemplary proof of such patriotism. This cannot be said, however, of Albanian regimes, with the exception of those of Ismail Qemali and Fan Noli, and this can certainly not be said of the leaders of the present-day regime. The current servile leaders do their best to conform to international opinion of the day, which promises them a long rule if they do not demand any more than we are demanding at present: a *modus vivendi*, basic freedom of action, human rights and autonomy for Kosovo.

[RE]: You will no doubt have heard that there is a good deal of anti-Kosovo sentiment in the population of the Republic of Albania, in particular in Tirana and in the south. How do you account for this?

[RQ]: Anti-Kosovo sentiment may exist on the part of some individuals, interest groups or political groupings, but by no means on the part of the people of Albania. Some short-sighted individuals fear competition on the job market arising from unification and others may fear competition for power. But these individuals, who in fact represent no one at all, are few and far between on both sides of the border. Anti-Kosovo sentiment in Albania or anti-Albanian sentiment in Kosovo is like the armchair trivia of 'true patriots' who confuse the Nation with their own town, village or native region.

Such sentiment, anti-patriotic in its essence, is unnatural for the people because they have an innate and infinite desire for unification. In other words, we must not generalize about such individual cases.

[RE]: Intellectuals are of considerable significance in developing countries such as Albania, but it would seem at the moment that many intellectuals, both in Kosovo and in Albania, are not taking an active part in the political life of the country. Why is this?

[RQ]: Albanian intellectuals have suffered from extremely bitter experience with politics. Most of them, though not all of them, were forced to submit to their regimes. They were oppressed, persecuted, and abused by politics. For this reason, many of them do not like politics at all. There is, however, another reason why Albanian intellectuals do not like to get mixed up in politics nowadays. This is the image they have of Balkan politicians: untrustworthy, two-faced individuals who are subservient to foreigners, deceptive, uneducated, despotic and in the final analysis despised by their people.

[RE]: To what extent does the international community, the European Union and the United States for instance, understand the situation in Kosovo? Are you satisfied or disappointed by the attitude of the outside world?

[RQ]: The international community, the European Union and the United States, still think they can solve the question of Kosovo by ensuring human rights and autonomy within Serbia. This shows that they do not understand the issue involved and approach the problem of Kosovo in a superficial manner. If they understood the essence of the issue, they would realize that public order, peace and justice can never be established in Kosovo until it is united with Albania. The attitude of the international community towards the Kosovo problem has been disappointing, but history has taught us that we can expect little from it. Just as disappointing, however, has been our own attitude towards ourselves.

[RE]: You were born and raised in an ethnically mixed region of Albanians and Serbs. Did you have any good Serbian friends when you were growing up? And do you have any Serbian friends now? If not, why not? What future do you see for the Serbian minority living within a future ethnic Albania?

[RQ]: I was born in the region of Plava / Plav and Gucia / Gusinje which since the Balkan Wars has remained under Montenegrin and then Yugoslav control. In the early days, under Turkish rule, this region was part of the Vilayet of Kosovo. In my home town, there was only one Montenegrin family which had been brought in as colonists. They had a son who was one year younger than I was. The two of us never had any problems getting along, although we were never really friends. I was raised and educated in Prishtina where I work and have a family, and where I will be buried when I die. We were members of an association with Serbian intellectuals, mostly writers, - the Writers' Union of Kosovo. We also worked with Serbian intellectuals at the university. I had quite normal, proper relations with them. Today, I have no relations with them at all.

In an ethnic Albania, I would support and stand up for all rights for the Serbian minority: human rights, political rights, civil rights and even the right to self-determination. What surprises me is why they do not accept these same rights for us.

[RE]: If you alone could choose, what sort of status and future would you give to Kosovo?

[RQ]: I would unite Kosovo with Albania. As a democrat, I would organize a referendum throughout united Albanian territory and I am convinced that 99.99% of the Albanian people would declare themselves in favour of unification. I would then organize elections to a Constitutional Assembly and, after the promulgation of a Constitution, presidential elections would be held to elect the President of Albania.

[RE]: Irrespective of your desires and plans for the future of Kosovo, how do you think the political situation will continue to evolve in the years to come?

[RQ]: In my book *Strategjia e Bashkimit Kombëtar* (The Strategy of National Unity), published in 1992, I wrote that solving the Albanian question will be a long process. Our policies over the past four to five years have only led to further delay in this long process. Delay in decisive moments is a historical deficiency of our people, and we are losing time again as a result of present policies. Much effort will be needed to compensate for time lost. It will be very difficult to reconstruct what has been scattered to the winds in our national movement as a result of political short-sightedness on the part of the present regime in Tirana and on the part of the LDK in Kosovo with its sectarian policies. It will be difficult, but not impossible. Life for Albanians in Kosovo will continue to be tedious. Serbian terror will continue in waves of varying intensity and there is nothing much we can do about it. There may be a great rise in tension between the Albanians on the one hand and the Serbs and Montenegrins on the other. One thing is sure, however. The day will come when Kosovo will leave Serbia and be united with Albania. In making this assertion, I rely on historical experience which has shown that when a people is resolute in its will to be free and independent, it will become free and independent. Occupation terror cannot overcome the desire of a people for freedom. Nor will political stagnation and the ethics of its own political caste cause the people to despair.

Interview with Agim Vinca

[Robert Elsie]: Professor Vinca, as a longtime teacher at the University of Prishtina, you have been observing events in Kosovo for many years now. Did you ever think ten or fifteen years ago that things would turn out the way they did? Have developments over the last decade and a half surprised you or did you see them coming and as inevitable?

[Agim Vinca]: It is very difficult for an individual, irrespective of his profession or abilities, to predict the future. This is particularly true in the Balkans where unforeseen and unexpected events occur often. There is one thing I can say for certain, though. I knew that the unsolved Kosovo question and the unsolved Albanian question in former Yugoslavia on the one hand, and Serbian hegemonist policies in the Balkans on the other, were sooner or later bound to produce a dramatic situation. More such events may take place in the future and they may be even more dramatic, for the same reasons.

[RE]: In the seventies, Albanians and Serbs managed to live in relative harmony with one another. At present, the two peoples are engaged in a bitter struggle with one another. What do you see as the key factors which brought about such a deterioration of the situation?

[AV]: Relations between the Albanians and Serbs have never been peaceful and have certainly never been harmonious. In the seventies, when you first visited Kosovo, they may have seemed peaceful and harmonious on the surface, but under the surface things were boiling. It was like a volcano ready to explode at any moment. And that is precisely what happened. In the spring of 1981, when young Albanians, in peaceful demonstrations in Prishtina and elsewhere, sought to improve the political status of Kosovo from that of an autonomous region to that of a republic, the Serbs, who even in Tito's Yugoslavia had more than their 'share of the pie' in the ruling party, in the police and in the army, could hardly wait for the chance to 'dissuade' the 'revolting and ungrateful' Albanians. Serbian politicians in Belgrade never came to accept even the level of civil rights and development accorded to the Albanians under the Constitution of 1974. The Serbs and Montenegrins in Kosovo itself, for their part, who were to serve as instruments in the hands of their leaders, had lost their privileges and misunderstood this loss as 'inequality' and as 'discrimination' on the part of the Albanians. To change the situation in their favour, they initiated an extensive and savage propaganda campaign against Kosovo and the Albanians, using all means and mechanisms at their disposal: the League of Communists and other political and social organizations, the media, the courts, the prison system, tanks, the police force and the army, etc.

This is a more or less true description of Albanian-Serbian relations in the seventies and eighties, but it is also valid for earlier and later periods, i. e. for the past and the present. If we wanted to use a figurative term for these relations, we could make use of a quotation by the well-known American poet Carl Sandburg, author of the collection 'The People, Yes', who wrote: "The sheep and the wolf are not agreed upon a definition of the word liberty." Anyone who knows anything about the history of these two Balkan peoples and their relations will be aware who the 'wolf' is and who the 'sheep' is.

[RE]: After so much intense rivalry and hatred, do you think Albanians and Serbs in Kosovo will be able to live in peace and harmony with one another again, or must they separate and go their own ways?

[AV]: In order for the Albanians and Serbs to put an end to their rivalry and hatred once and for all, they must, as the internationally known Serbian intellectual Bogdan Bogdanović has reiterated, separate as friends and live side by side as good neighbours (cf. *Zëri*, Prishtina, 6 April 1991, p. 6-7). Such a separation, which of necessity implies the independence of Kosovo, i.e. its separation from Serbia and Yugoslavia, is a *conditio sine qua non* for the normal material and intellectual advancement of these two peoples in the Balkans as well as for peace and security in the region. Not only the Serbs, still caught up in their own mediaeval mythomania, but also the international community must come to understand the historical necessity of such a separation. And the sooner, the better.

[RE]: For the Serbs, the Kosovo Albanians remain a very foreign people. For the Albanians, however, the Serbs cannot be that foreign. After all, every educated Albanian in Kosovo speaks Serbian fluently and has been raised in close contact with Serbian culture. Do you personally understand what goes on in the Serbian mind?

[AV]: Realistically speaking, the Serbs are (and must be) every bit as foreign to the Albanians as the Albanians are to the Serbs. Why? Because the Albanian language and culture are well known to be the language and culture of a separate people who do not form part of the major groupings of European peoples. They have nothing in common with the languages and cultures of the southern Slavs, the Serbs for instance. That Albanian intellectuals and even, to a large extent, uneducated Albanians speak Serbian, and that the Albanians in Macedonia also speak Macedonian, whereas their fellow Serbian and Macedonian citizens show absolutely no interest in learning Albanian proves, firstly, that the Albanians have a subordinate, colonial status and, secondly, that they have no aversion for the languages and cultures of other peoples. Be this as it may, we Albanian intellectuals do not hold the Serbian people as a whole responsible for what is happening in Kosovo today, for the day-to-day violence and systematic terror exercised against the Albanians, against their language, their schools, their culture, their institutions of higher learning, etc., in short, against their existence and identity as a people, but rather the present policies of the chauvinist regime in Belgrade, which is manipulating the emotions of its people to its own hegemonist and careerist ends.

[RE]: Compared to the situation in Kosovo, relations between the Albanians and Macedonians in the Former Yugoslav Republic of Macedonia where you come from would seem quite peaceful, almost harmonious. And yet, the Albanians in western Macedonia are openly

and systematically discriminated against by their Macedonian neighbours. What is a difference in the relationship of the Serbs and Albanians and that of the Macedonians and Albanians?

[AV]: Relations between the Albanians and Macedonians in the Former Yugoslav Republic of Macedonia appear peaceful and harmonious, but they are not so in reality. Why? The answer lies in the second part of your question. The Albanians in the FYR of Macedonia, who are living on their own lands, are *openly and systematically discriminated against* in all spheres of life. This discrimination, which during the savage anti-Albanian campaign of the eighties took on grotesque forms (the Albanians were, for instance, forbidden from giving their children the Albanian names they wanted to give them, such as Ilir or Teuta, and were forced to use the Slav names for the towns and cities they had lived in for centuries, even when speaking and writing in their own language: Skopje instead of the Albanian form Shkup, Debar instead of the Albanian form Dibër, etc.) has continued to this very day, five years after the introduction of the multi-party, but not democratic system. Experts say that in some respects, this discrimination has even increased! Nonetheless, there is an essential difference between Albanian-Serbian relations (in Kosovo) and Albanian-Macedonian relations (in Macedonia). The difference actually has more to do with the political position of the 'conflicting parties' than with the relations between them. The Albanians in the FYR of Macedonia are within the system (they take part in elections, in parliament and even in government). Up to now, however, they have had absolutely no benefit from such 'co-operation' because the demands of the Albanian members in the Macedonian Parliament are always ignored and outvoted. The people of Kosovo, on the other hand, have declared their own independent state, the Republic of Kosova, and are endeavouring peacefully to make this independence a reality.

[RE]: Are you optimistic about the future of relations between the Albanians and Macedonians? Do you want Macedonia to survive as an independent republic, or would you recommend a partition of the country? What do you see as the best practical solution for the inhabitants of the Former Yugoslav Republic of Macedonia?

[AV]: A person can have many wishes and desires, but in politics, they must give way to political realities. Sometimes I think that

Macedonia as a state is an artificial creation, an experiment being conducted by the Americans, etc., but for the moment, this state is a political reality. I believe that Macedonia, equipped with a *constitution*, must take on the form of a binational state, i. e. that of its two major peoples, the Macedonians and Albanians, and of the other ethnic groups who live there. Only as such can it survive and prosper as a country, in particular if it wishes, as it claims, to be a democratic country. Otherwise, it will fade into history as did its 'mother' called Yugoslavia.

Am I optimistic about the future of relations between the Albanians and the Macedonians? I don't know. For the moment I am disappointed and frustrated about the course of events which has been to the detriment of the Albanians.

[RE]: What expectations do the Albanians of Kosovo and Macedonia have of Albania? Do they feel supported or betrayed by Albania?

[AV]: The Albanians of Kosovo, Macedonia and other Albanian territory unjustly cut off from Albania (the Albanians of Montenegro, of so-called 'eastern Kosovo' i.e. Presheva / Preševo, Bujanovc / Bujanovac, and Medvegja / Medvedja, and of Chameria) consider Albania the defender of their aspirations for freedom, independence and national unity, and as the principal defender of their national and human rights. In short, the Albanians living on ethnic Albanian territory in the Balkans consider Albania as a bulwark of Albanian national interests. This is how they see Albania and how they will always see it until they realize their long-term aspiration, i. e. national unity, a legitimate and natural demand of any divided people.

Whether Albania is in a position to fulfil this function at the present moment and whether it will be able to fulfil this function in the long run is another question. Albania has inherited many serious problems from the past and, on top of this, its present political course is more determined by the interests of the Albanian state than by the interests of the nation as a whole.

[RE]:   To what extent does the international community, the European Union and the United States for instance, understand the situation in Kosovo? Are you satisfied or disappointed by the attitude of the outside world?

[AV]: The international community (the European Union, the United States, the North Atlantic Treaty Organization, etc.), preoccupied primarily by the Bosnian question and by other problems which have arisen since the desintegration of Yugoslavia, etc., seems to have forgotten Kosovo and the Albanians. To a great extent, the Albanians have contributed to this 'oblivion' themselves, or at least their political representatives have (I refer here principally to the two largest Albanian political parties in Kosovo and Macedonia: the Democratic League of Kosovo and the Party for Democratic Prosperity) who, with their 'wait and see' tactics and never-ending patience and in particular with their political lethargy, put the Albanian political movement of the eighties to sleep and, in doing so, have subverted world interest in Kosovo and the Albanians. The foreign delegations which visit Prishtina from time to time and make declarations about a solution to the Kosovo question within the framework of Serbia or of rump Yugoslavia, now known (at least to the Serbs) as the Federal Republic of Yugoslavia, are sufficient proof of a false approach taken to the Kosovo question, an issue which is not (and cannot be) an 'internal Serbian affair', as the other side insists, but which is a crucial problem for the region as a whole. Such views would almost make you think that concessions have been made to Serbia and its aggressive course, perhaps out of a lack of goodwill and perhaps out of a lack of understanding and respect for the Gandhian pacifism pursued by the Democratic League of Kosovo and its leader, Ibrahim Rugova. Serbian violence and police repression continue unabated in Kosovo, as do the mass show trials. The colonization of Kosovo is being carried out with the help of Serbian settlers from the Krajina region, etc., and all this time, the international community remains virtually silent or at least contents itself to an occasional verbal denunciation. The FYR of Macedonia, for its part, also systematically violates the national and human rights of the Albanians, who make up at least one-third of its population, and yet Macedonia has been accepted unconditionally as a member of international organizations such as the Council of Europe and the Organization for Security and Co-operation in Europe. As such, I am disappointed by the attitude of the international community towards Kosovo and the Albanians. For the moment at least.

[RE]: You were born and raised in the Struga in Macedonia and have lived for quite a long time in Kosovo. Did you have any good Macedonian or Serbian friends when you were growing up? And do you have any Macedonian or Serbian friends now? If not, why not?

[AV]: It takes two to be friends, just as it takes two to fight. For my part, I spent my early years and my childhood in a purely Albanian environment. In later years I rarely encountered willingness on the part of Serbian or Macedonian colleagues I happened to be with for closer relations or for a real friendship. This is primarily because of their prejudice against the Albanians. When in 1991, following the introduction of the so-called 'emergency measures' at the University of Prishtina, Albanian teachers were being expelled from the education system, not one of their Serbian or Montenegrin colleagues raised his or her voice to come to the defence of their Albanian 'friends'.

[RE]: If you alone could choose, what sort of status and future would you give to Kosovo?

[AV]: I am convinced, and have been convinced since the early days of my youth, that the only just and permanent solution to the Albanian question in the Balkans is the unification of Kosovo and other territories, where the Albanians constitute the only or majority inhabitants with Albania. These territories were unjustly separated from Albania by military occupation from neighbouring states and as a result of the subsequent sanctioning of these occupations by the Great Powers at the Congress of Berlin in 1878 and at the Conference of London in 1912-1913. How can unification be brought about? By the free and unhindered expression of the will of the people in an internationally-supervised plebiscite, and not by force.

[RE]: Irrespective of your desires and plans for the future of Kosovo and Macedonia, how do you think the political situation will continue to evolve in the years to come?

[AV]: I foresee a long political, diplomatic and propaganda struggle both between the Albanians and the Serbs and between the Albanians and the Macedonians (ending, sooner or later, in favour of the Albanians because they have truth and justice on their side). I only hope that this struggle will never turn into an armed conflict, which would be to the detriment of everyone.

5.   Bibliography

Works in Western languages

A propos des événements de Kosove.
(8 Nëntori, Tirana 1981) 190 pp.

About the events in Kosova.
(8 Nëntori, Tirana 1981) 184 pp.

ALLAIN, Marie-Françoise
Guerre ou terreur au Kosovo? Deux façons de mourir.
in: Esprit, Paris, 1993, 3-4, p. 76-85.

Kosovo. Le crime annoncé. Entretien avec Ismaïl Kadaré.
in: Esprit, Paris, 1993, 6, p. 81-93.

ALLAIN, Marie-Françoise & GALMICHE, Xavier
Ibrahim Rugova. La question du Kosovo. Entretiens avec Marie-Françoise Allain et Xavier Galmiche. Préfacé de Ismail Kadaré. ISBN 2-213-59247-0.
(Fayard, Paris 1994) 263 pp.

ALVAREZ CABAL, Rosa & ROMERO BLASCO, Jesús M.
La balcanització dels Balcans. El cas de Kosovo.
in. Documents d'anàlisi geogràfica, Universitat Autonoma de Barcelona, Barcelona, 17 (1990), p. 107-120.

AMADORI-VIRGILJ, Giovanni
La questione rumeliota (Macedonia, Vecchia Serbia, Albania, Epiro) e la politica italiana.
(Tip. N. Garofalo, Bitonto 1908)

Amnesty International (ed.)
Yougoslavie: les prisonniers pour délit d'opinion.
(Amnesty International, Paris 1982) 94 pp.

Yougoslavie: l'opposition muselée.
(Amnesty International, Paris 1985) 116 pp.

Yugoslavia. Prisoners of conscience. ISBN 0-86210-084-4.
(Amnesty International, New York 1985) 95 pp.

Jugoslawien. Gewaltlose politische Gefangene.
(Amnesty International, Sektion der Bundesrepublik Deutschland,
Bonn 1987) 85 pp.

Yugoslavia. Ethnic Albanians. Victims of torture and ill-treatment by
police in Kosovo province.
(Amnesty International, New York 1992) 27 pp.

Yugoslavia. Ethnic Albanians. Trial by truncheon. AI Index: EUR
70/01/94.
(Amnesty International, London 1994) 15 pp.

Yugoslavia. Police violence against ethnic Albanians in Kosovo
province. AI Index: EUR 70/06/94.
(Amnesty International, London 1994) 16 pp.

Yugoslavia. Police violence in Kosovo province. The victims. AI
Index: EUR 70/16/94.
(Amnesty International, London 1994) 27 pp.

ANDERSON, Kenneth
Yugoslavia. The crisis in Kosovo. A report from Helsinki Watch and
the International Helsinki Federation for Human Rights. ISBN 0-
929692-56-X.
(Helsinki Watch, New York 1990) ii + 45 pp.

ARTISIEN, Patrick
Albanian-Yugoslav relations in the post-war period.
(University of Bradford, Bradford 1978)

Yugoslavia and Albania in the 1970s.
in: Coexistence, Glasgow, 15 (1978), p. 219-227.

Albanian nationalism and Yugoslav socialism. The case of Kosovo.
in: Coexistence, Glasgow, 16.2 (1979), p. 173-189.

Friends or foes? Yugoslav-Albanian relations over the last 40 years.
Postgraduate School of Yugoslav Studies. Bradford Studies on
Yugoslavia, No. 2.
(University of Bradford. Bradford 1980) 36 pp.

A note on Kosovo and the future of Yugoslav-Albanian relations. A
Balkan perspective.
in: Soviet studies, Glasgow, 36.2 (1984), p. 267-276.

518 Bibliography

ARTISIEN, Patrick F. R. & HOWELLS, R.A.
The disturbances in Kosovo and the Yugoslavian-Albanian relationship.
in: Europa Archiv, Bonn, 36, 21 (1981), p. 639-648.

Yugoslavia, Albania and the Kosovo riots.
in: The World Today, Royal Institute of International Affairs, London, 37, 11 (1981), p. 419-427.

Association des amitiés franco-albanaises (ed.)
Les relations albano-yougoslaves 1912-1982. Dossier établi par l'Institut d'études sur l'Albanie socialiste. ISBN 2-904741-00-3.
(Association des amitiés franco-albanaises, Paris 1983) 175 pp.

BAJRAMI, Hakif
L'Oppression et la résistance des Albanais à Kosove.
in: Studia albanica, Tirana, 18, 2 (1981), p. 73-99.

BALKANICUS (= PROTIĆ, Stojan)
Das albanische Problem und die Beziehungen zwischen Serbien und Österreich-Ungarn, von Balkanicus (pseud.). Ins Deutsche übertragen von Dr. jur. L. Markowitsch.
(O. Wigand, Leipzig 1913) 104 pp.

Le problème albanais, la Serbie et l'Autriche-Hongrie.
(A. Challamel, Paris 1913) 84 pp.

BANAC, Ivo
The national question in Yugoslavia. Origins, history, politics. ISBN 0-8014-1675-2.
(Cornell University Press, Ithaca NY 1984) 452 pp.

BARTL, Peter
Die albanischen Muslime zur Zeit des nationalen Unabhängigkeitsbewegung 1878-1912. Albanische Forschungen 8.
(Harrassowitz, Wiesbaden 1968) 207 pp.

Grundzüge der jugoslawischen Geschichte.
(Wissenschaftliche Buchgesellschaft, Darmstadt 1985) ix + 190 pp.

Albanien. Vom Mittelalter bis zur Gegenwart. ISBN 3-7917-1451-1.
(Friedrich Pustet, Regensburg 1995) 304 pp.

BASKIN, Mark
Crisis in Kosovo.
in: Problems of communism, Washington, 32. 2 (1983), p. 61-74.

BATAKOVIĆ, Dušan T.
The Kosovo chronicles. Prevod na engleski. ISBN 8644700065.
(Plato, Belgrade 1992) 218 pp.

Kosovo. La spirale de la haine. Les faits, les acteurs, l'histoire. Traduit
du serbo-croate par Slobodan Despot. ISBN 2-8251-0389-6.
(L'Age d'Homme, Lausanne 1993) 96 pp.

Yougoslavie. Nations, religions, idéologies. Traduit du serbo-croate
par Bruno Guillard et Slobodan Despot.
(L'Age d'Homme, Lausanne, 1994) 334 pp.

BAXHAKU, Fatos
Die Bevölkerungsstruktur der ethnischen Grenzzone von Albanern,
Serben und makedonischen Slawen (zweite Hälfte des 19. bis Anfang
des 20. Jahrhunderts).
in: Österreichische Osthefte, Vienna, 36.2 (1994), p. 245-264.

BECKMANN-PETEY, Monika
Der jugoslawische Föderalismus. Untersuchungen zur
Gegenwartskunde Südosteuropas, 29. ISBN 3-486-55867-6.
(Oldenbourg, Munich 1990) 376 pp.

BENDER, R. J.
Die Krisenprovinz Kosovo. Ein jugoslawischer Peripherraum im
Umbruch.
in: Zeitschrift für Balkanologie, Berlin, 20 (1984), p. 4-24.

BENNETT, Christopher
Yugoslavia's bloody collapse. Causes, course and consequences. ISBN
0-8147-1234-7.
(New York State Press, New York 1995) 272 pp.

BERISHA, Ibrahim et al.
Serbian colonization and ethnic cleansing in Kosova. Documents and
evidence. A publication of the Kosova Information Center.
(Kosova Information Center, Prishtina 1993) 102 pp.

Ɣ

BIBERAJ, Elez Hysen
Albanian-Yugoslav relations and the question of Kosovë.
in: East European quarterly, Washington, 16.4 (winter 1982), p. 485-501.

The conflict in Kosovo.
in: Survey, London, 28. 3 (1984), p. 39-47.

Albania and China. A study of an unequal alliance.
(Westview, Boulder CO. 1986) 163 pp.

Albania, a socialist maverick. Westview Profiles. Nations of Contemporary Eastern Europe. ISBN 0-8133-0513-6.
(Westview, Boulder CO. 1990) 157 pp.

Yugoslavia, the continuing crisis.
(Research Institute for the Study of Conflict and Terrorism, London 1989) 24 pp.

Kosovo. The Balkan powder keg.
in: Conflict studies, London, 258 (Feb. 1993), 26 pp.

BISAK, Jean, KURTI, Etienne, & GASHI, Louis (= BISAKU, Gjon, KURTI, Shtjefën, & GASHI, Luigj)
La situation de la minorité albanaise en Yugoslavie. Mémoire présenté à la Société des Nations.
(Geneva 1930) 43 pp.

Mémoire présenté à la Société des Nations. La situation des Albanais en Yougoslavie. Promemorie e paraqitur në Lidhjen e Kombeve (1930). Gjendja e shqiptarëve në Jugosllavi.
(Koha, Tirana 1995) 91 pp.

BLAKU, Rifat
Actions menées par l'Etat serbe en vue du nettoyage ethnique de la Kosove et des autres territoires albanais occupés.
(Centre d'Information de la République de Kosove, Geneva 1995) 33 pp.

BLAND, William B.
Albania. World Bibliographical Series, Vol. 94. ISBN 1-85109-037-1.
(Clio Press, Oxford 1988) 291 pp.

BOGDANOVIĆ, Dimitrije
Kosovo alla luce della storia delle relazioni tra Albanesi e Slavi del Sud.
in: Balcanica, Belgrade, 13 (1982), p. 20-40.

La question du Kosovo hier et aujourd'hui.
in: Revue des études slaves, Paris, 56, 3 (1984), p. 387-400.

BRAILSFORD, Henry N.
Macedonia. Its races and their future.
(Methuen, London 1906; reprint Arno, New York 1970) 340 pp.

BREMER, Alida (ed.)
Jugoslawische (Sch)erben. Probleme und Perspektiven. ISBN 3-929759-00-4.
(Fibre, Osnabrück & Münster 1993) 207 pp.

BREY, Thomas
Alte nationale Gegensätze in Jugoslawien neu belebt.
in: Osteuropa, Stuttgart, 35,3 (1985), p. 198-203.

BUDA, Aleks et al (ed.)
The Albanians and their territories. Academy of Sciences of the PSR of Albania.
(8 Nëntori, Tirana 1985) 494 pp.

Die Albaner und ihre Gebiete. Herausgegeben von der Akademie der Wissenschaften der SVRA.
(8 Nëntori, Tirana 1986) 559 pp.

BUGAJSKI, Janusz
Ethnic politics in Eastern Europe. A guide to nationality policies, organizations, and parties. With a new postscript. ISBN 1-56324-282-6.
(M.E. Sharpe, Armonk NY & London 1994, 1995) 493 pp.

BÜSCHENFELD, Herbert
Kosovo. Gefahrenherd für den Bestand Jugoslawiens.
in: Geographische Rundschau, Brunswick, 34.4 (1982), p. 180-186.

Kosovo. Nationalitätenkonflikt im Armenhaus Jugoslawiens. Problemräume Europas, Bd. 11. ISBN 3-7614-1360-2.
(Aulis / Deubner, Cologne 1991) 38 pp.

CANA, Zekeria
La politique du gouvernement serbe à l'égard du mouvement national albanais, 1908-1912.
in: Studia albanica, Tirana, 20, 2 (1983), p. 57-80.

Carnegie Endowment for International Peace (ed.)
The other Balkan wars. A 1913 Carnegie Endowment inquiry in retrospect with a new introduction and reflections on the present conflict by George F. Kennan. International Commission to Enquire into the Causes and Conduct of the Balkan Wars. ISBN 0-87003-032-9.
(Carnegie Endowment Book, Washington 1993) 413 pp.

CASTELLAN, Georges
Histoire des Balkans. XIVe-XXe siècle. ISBN 2-213-8572-05/6.
(Fayard, Paris 1991) 532 pp.

Le monde des Balkans. Poudrière ou zone de paix? ISBN 2-7117-8460-6.
(Vuibert, Paris 1994) 213 pp.

CHAMPY, Philippe
La question du Kosovo de 1912 à nos jours.
in: Cahiers de l'INEAS, Paris, 2 (1984), p. 107-126.

COHEN, Lenard J.
Broken bonds. The disintegration of Yugoslavia. ISBN 0-8133-8030-8.
(Westview, Boulder CO 1993) 299 pp.

Broken bonds. Yugoslavia's disintegration and Balkan politics in transition. Second edition. ISBN 0-8133-2477-7.
(Westview Press, Boulder 1995) 386 pp.

CONFORTI, Gerardo
L'Albania e gli stati balcanici. Scritti varii.
(Scipione Ammirato, Lecce 1901) 247 pp.

Conseil pour la Défense des Droits et des Libertés de l'Homme
Violations des droits nationaux, des droits de l'homme et des libertés fondamentales des Albanais en Kosove. Rapport 1994.
(Centre d'Information de la République de Kosove, Geneva 1995) 16 pp.

ÇOPANI, Adem
Die Krise in Kosova. Der Konflikt in Jugoslawien. Albaniens
Perspektive.
in: Dardania. Zeitschrift für Geschichte, Kultur und Information,
Vienna, 1995, 4, p. 213-223.

COSTA, Nicholas J.
Kosovo. A tragedy in the making.
in: East European quarterly, Boulder CO, 21. 2 (1987), p. 87-97.

Albania. A European enigma. East European Monographs CDXIII.
ISBN 0-88033-307-3.
(East European Monographs, Boulder CO, Distributed by Columbia
UP, New York 1995) 188 pp.

CRNOBRNJA, Mihailo
The Yugoslav drama. ISBN 0-7735-1203-9.
(University of Toronto, Toronto 1994) 264 pp.

ČUBRILOVIĆ, Vasa
The expulsion of the Albanians.
Memorandum presented on March 7, 1937 in Belgrade.
Typescript.

CUKIC, Dragan (ed.)
Kosovo. Curiosités et beautés.
(Turistički zavez, Prishtina 1971) 226 pp.

CVIIC, Christopher
Remaking the Balkans. Royal Institute of International Affairs,
Chatham House Papers. ISBN 0-86187-086-7.
(Pinter, London 1991) viii + 113 pp.

CVIJIĆ, Jovan
La péninsule balkanique. Géographie humaine. Avec cartes.
(Armand Colin, Paris 1918) viii + 528 pp.

DANIEL, Odile
Albanie. Une bibliographie historique. Centre régional de publications
de Meudon-Bellevue. R.C.P. Identités culturelles dans les sociétés
paysannes d'Europe centrale et balkanique. ISBN 2-222-03236-9.
(Editions du CNRS, Paris 1985) 616 pp.

524 Bibliography

DANYLOW, Peter
Die außenpolitischen Beziehungen Albaniens zu Jugoslawien und zur UdSSR, 1944-1961. Studien zur modernen Geschichte 26. ISBN 3-486-50851-2.
(Oldenbourg, Munich & Vienna 1982) 232 pp.

DE VRIES, Franklin (ed.)
Het Albanees-Servisch conflict om Kosovo.
(IPIS, Antwerp 1994) 52 pp.

Kosovo. The conflict between the Serbs and the Albanians and the role of the international community.
(1995) 64 pp.

DEDIJER, Vladimir
Il sangre tradito. Relazioni jugoslavo-albanesi 1938-49. Documenti ufficiali, lettere, fotografie...
(Editoriale periodici italiani, Milan 1949) 221 pp.

Democratic League of Kosova (ed.)
The frozen smiles. Violence against Albanian children in Kosova. Democratic League of Kosova. Commission for Children's Rights of Women's Forum.
(Democratic League of Kosova, Prishtina 1992) 47 pp.

DESSANTOLO, Vitomir
Die Montenegriner als Werkzeug der Serben zur Verdrängung der Albaner?
in: Gärung in Mittel- und Osteuropa, Brugg 1989, p. 141-150.

DJILAS, Milovan
Conversations with Stalin. Translated from the Serbo-Croat by Michael B. Petrovich.
(Harcourt, Brace and World, New York 1962) 214 pp.

DJUREVIĆ, Dragoljub
Die Politik, die Maßnahmen und die erreichten Resultate in der Nachkriegsentwicklung der unzureichend entwickelten Republiken und des Autonomen Gebiets Kosovo. Informationssekretariat des Parlaments der SFR Jugoslawien...
(Dopisna delavska univ., Ljubljana 1977) 127 pp.

DOGO, Marco
Kosovo. Albanesi e Serbi: le radici del conflitto. ISBN 88-85350-13-5.
(Marco, Lungro di Cosenza 1992) v + 375 pp.

DORICH, William
Kosovo. Compiled and produced by William Dorich. ISBN 1-882383-00-1.
(Kosovo Charity Fund, Serbian Orthodox Diocese of Western America, Alhambra CA 1992) 176 pp.

DRAGNICH, Alex N.
Serbia's historical heritage. East European Monographs 347. ISBN 0-88033-244-1.
(East European Monographs, Boulder CO, Distributed by Columbia UP, New York 1994) 121 pp.

DRAGNICH, Alex N. & TODOROVICH, Slavko
The Saga of Kosovo. Focus on Serbian-Albanian relations. East European Monographs, 170. ISBN 0-88033-062-7.
(East European Monographs, Boulder CO, Distributed by Columbia UP, New York 1984) 203 pp.

DUDA, Helge
Nationalismus, Nationalität, Nation. Der Fall Albaniens unter besonderer Berücksichtigung des Kosovo. Junge Wissenschaft. Schriften der Hochschule für Politik München, Band 2. ISBN 3-925355-64-2.
(Ernst Vögel, Munich 1991) 140 pp.

DURHAM, Mary Edith
Through the lands of the Serb.
(Edward Arnold, London 1904) 345 pp.

The Burden of the Balkans.
(Edward Arnold, London 1905) 331 pp.
(Thoman Nelson & Sons, London 1905) 384 pp.

High Albania
(Edward Arnold, London 1909; reprint New York 1970, Virago, London 1985) 352 pp.

The Struggle for Scutari. Turk, Slav and Albanian.
(Edward Arnold, London 1914) 320 pp.

Twenty years of Balkan tangle.
(George Allen & Unwin, London 1920) 295 pp.

Die slawische Gefahr. Zwanzig Jahre Balkan-Erinnerungen von M. Edith Durham. Deutsch herausgegeben von Hermann Lutz. (Robert Lutz, Stuttgart s.a. [post 1923]) 356 pp.

Venti anni di groviglio balcanico. Tradotto da Stefania Pelli-Bossi. (F. Le Monnier, Florence 1923; reprint Argo, Lecce 1994?) 341 pp.

EDWARDS, Lovett Fielding
Profane pilgrimage. Wanderings through Yugoslavia. (Duckworth, London 1938) 292 pp.

ELSIE, Robert
Dictionary of Albanian literature. ISBN 0-313-25186-X. (Greenwood, Westport CT, New York & London 1986) 171 pp.

Albanische Literatur und Kultur nach sechsundvierzig Jahren Sozialismus. Ein Zustandsbericht. in: Südosteuropa, Zeitschrift für Gegenwartsforschung, Munich, 40 (1991), p. 600-613.

Evolution and revolution in modern Albanian literature. in: World literature today, Norman OK., 65.2 (Spring) 1991, p. 256-263.

The last Albanian waiter. in: Index on censorship, London, 21.9 (1992), p. 12-13.

Anthology of modern Albanian poetry. An elusive eagle soars. Edited and translated with an introduction by Robert Elsie. UNESCO collection of representative works. ISBN 1-85610-017-0. (Forest Books, London & Boston 1993) 213 pp.

The Albanian media in Kosovo and the spectre of ethnic cleansing. in: Südosteuropa, Zeitschrift für Gegenwartsforschung, Munich, 44 (1995), p. 614-619.

History of Albanian literature. East European Monographs 379. ISBN 0-88033-276-X. 2 volumes. (Social Science Monographs, Boulder. Distributed by Columbia University Press, New York 1995) xv + 1,054 pp.

EMMERT, Thomas Allan
Serbian Golgotha. Kosovo 1389. East European Monographs, 277. (East European Monographs, Distributed by Columbia UP, New York 1990) 240 pp.

ERCOLE, Francesco et al.
Le terre albanesi redente (1942).
(Reale Accademia d'Italia, 1942) 280 pp.

Events in the SAP of Kosovo. The causes and consequences of irredentist and counterrevolutionary subversion.
in: Review of international affairs, Belgrade, 1981

FAENSEN, Johannes
Die Albaner von Kosova und die Einheit der albanischen Literatursprache.
in: Ethnogenese und Staatsbildung in Südosteuropa. Beiträge des Südosteuropa-Arbeitskreises der Deutschen Forschungsgemeinschaft zum III. Internationalen Südosteuropa-Kongreß des Association Internationale d'Etudes du Sud-Est Européen, Bukarest, 4.-10.9.1974 (Vandenhoeck & Ruprecht, Göttingen 1974), p. 158-166.

Die albanische Nationalbewegung. Osteuropa-Institut an der Freien Universität Berlin. Balkanologische Veröffentlichungen 4. ISBN 3-447-02120-9.
(in Komm. Harrassowitz, Wiesbaden 1980) 195 pp.

FALASCHI, Renzo
Kosovo. Patria dei Dardani.
in: Rivista di studi politici internazionali, Florence, 60. 3 (1993), p. 331-340.

FELDER, David W.
Conflict over Kosovo. ISBN 0-910959-89-7.
(Felder Games & Books, 1995) 44 pp.

FÉRON, Bernard
Yougoslavie. Origines d'un conflit. ISBN 2-501-01990-3.
(Le Monde / Marabout, Paris 1993) 178 pp.

FITZPATRICK, Catherine A.
Yugoslavia. The freedom to conform.
(Helsinki Watch Committee, New York 1982) 30 pp.

FRASHËRI, Sami (= FRASCHERY, Chemseddine Samy bey)
Was war Albanien, was ist es, was wird es werden? Gedanken und Betrachtungen über die unser geheiligtes Vaterland Albanien bedrohenden Gefahren und deren Abwendung. Aus dem Türkischen übersetzt von A. Traxler.
(Alfred Holder, Vienna & Leipzig 1913) 69 pp.

528 Bibliography

FREUNDLICH, Leo
Albaniens Golgotha. Anklageakten wider die Vernichter des Albanervolkes.
(Roller, Vienna 1913) 32 pp.

Albania's Golgotha. Indictment against the exterminators of the Albanian people. Collected and edited by Leo Freundlich in Vienna 1913, translated from German and commented by S. S: Juka, New York, 1991. Reprinted, edited and commented by Hans Peter Rullmann, Hamburg 1992. ISBN 3-925652-41-8.
in: That was Yugoslavia, Information and facts, Hamburg, 10-12 (1992), 54 pp.

GARDE, Paul
Vie et mort de la Yougoslavie. ISBN 2-213-59260-8.
(Fayard, Paris 1992, 2nd edition 1994) 444 pp.

Gärung in Mittel- und Osteuropa. Knjižnica sloboda.
(Adria, Brugg 1989) 118 pp.

GASHI, Alush (ed.)
The denial of human and national rights of Albanians in Kosova.
(Illyria, New York 1992) 313 pp.

GASHI, Dardan
Ghandismus oder Machiavellismus? Kosova: ein Krieg, der wartet.
in: Dardania. Zeitschrift für Geschichte, Kultur und Information, Vienna, 1995, 4, p. 199-206.

GASHI, Dardan & STEINER, Ingrid
Albanien. Archaisch, orientalisch, europäisch. Brennpunkt Osteuropa. ISBN 3-900478-76-7.
(ProMedia, Vienna 1994) 278 pp.

GEORGEVITCH, Vladan (= DJORDJEVIĆ, Vladan)
Die Albanesen und die Großmächte.
(Hirsel, Leipzig 1913) 172 pp.

GERSIN, K. (= ŽUPANIĆ, Niko)
Altserbien und die albanesische Frage.
(Anzengruber, Vienna 1912) 55 pp.

Gesellschaft für Bedrohte Völker (ed.)
   Die Albaner im Kosovo. Menschenrechte für Bedrohte Völker. Report
   Nr. 1.
   (Gesellschaft für Bedrohte Völker, Göttingen 1991) 112 pp.

GLENNY, Misha
   The fall of Yugoslavia. The third Balkan war. ISBN 0-14-017288-2.
   (Penguin, London 1992) 208 pp.

GOPCEVIC, Spiridion (= GOPČEVIĆ, Spiridion)
   Oberalbanien und seine Liga. Ethnographisch-politisch-historisch
   geschildert.
   (Pierersche Hofbuchdruckerei, Leipzig 1881) 586 pp.

   Makedonien und Alt-Serbien. Mit 67 Original-Illustrationen und einer
   ethnographischen Karte.
   (L. W. Seidel, Vienna 1889) 512 pp.

   Das Fürstentum Albanien. Seine Vergangenheit, ethnographischen
   Verhältnisse, politische Lage und Aussichten für die Zukunft.
   Veröffentlichungen des Allgemeinen Vereins für Deutsche Literatur,
   38, 4.
   (Hermann Paetel, Berlin 1914) 357 pp.

GRAVIER, Gaston
   La Vieille-Serbie et les Albanais.
   in: Revue de Paris, Paris 1.11.1911, 23 pp.

GRIFFIN, M., & WARD, S.
   Albanians and Serbs. The conflict continues.
   in: Geographical magazine, London, 61.5 (1989), p. 21-24.

GRIFFITH, William E.
   Albania and the Sino-Soviet rift.
   (MIT, Cambridge MA 1963) xv + 423 pp.

GRMEK, Mirko, GJIDARA, Marc & ŠIMAC, Neven
   Le nettoyage ethnique. Documents historiques sur une idéologie serbe.
   ISBN 2-213-03098-7.
   (Fayard, Paris 1993) 340 pp.

GROTHE, Hugo
   Das albanische Problem. Politisches und Wirtschaftliches.
   (Gebauer-Schwetschke, Halle/Saale 1914) vi + 30 pp.

530 Bibliography

GROTZKY, Johannes
Balkankrieg. Der Zerfall Jugoslawiens und die Folgen. ISBN 3-492-11894-1.
(Piper, Munich 1993) 201 pp.

GRUENWALD, Oskar & ROSENBLUM-CALE, Karen
Human rights in Yugoslavia. ISBN 0-8290-1054-8.
(Irvington Publ., New York 1986) xiv + 673 pp.

GYURKOVICS, Georg von (= DJURKOVIĆ, Djordje)
Albanien. Schilderung von Land und Leuten.
(Alfred Hölder, Vienna 1881) 160 pp.

HALL, Derek R.
Albania and the Albanians. ISBN 1-85567-010-0.
(Pinter, London 1994) 304 pp.

HALLIDAY, Jon
The Artful Albanian. The memoirs of Enver Hoxha.
(Chatto & Windus, London 1986) 394 pp.

HASANI, Sinan
Kosovo. Zustand und Perspektiven.
(Aktuelna pitanja socijalizma, Belgrade s.a. [1987]) 56 pp.

Helsinki Watch Committee / Human Rights Watch (ed.)
Report on Yugoslavia.
(Helsinki Watch Committee, New York 1984) 24 pp.

HEMMER, Hans O.
Ein vergessenes Volk. Albaner in Kosovo.
in: Gewerkschaftliche Monatshefte, Cologne, 43, 2 (1992), p. 118-123.

HETZER, Armin & ROMAN, Viorel S.
Albanien. Ein bibliographischer Forschungsbericht mit Titelübersetzungen und Standortnachweisen. Albania. A bibliographic research surey with location codes. ISBN 3-598-21133-3.
(K. G. Saur, Munich & New York 1983) 653 pp.

HIBBERT, Reginald
Albania's national liberation struggle. The bitter victory.
(Pinter, London / St. Martin's Press, New York 1991) 269 pp.

History of the Party of Labor of Albania.
(Naim Frashëri, Tirana 1971)

HOESCH, Edgar (= HÖSCH, Edgar)
  The Balkans. A short history from Greek times to the present day.
  (Faber and Faber, London 1972) 213 pp.

  Geschichte der Balkanländer. Von der Frühzeit bis zur Gegenwart. 2.
  durchges. und erw. Aufl.
  (Beck, Munich 1993) 375 pp.

HOXHA, Enver
  Yugoslav 'self-administration'. A capitalist theory and practice. Against
  E. Kardelj's anti-socialist views expressed in a book...
  (8 Nëntori, Tirana 1978) 101 pp.

  With Stalin. Memoirs.
  (8 Nëntori, Tirana 1979) 223 pp.

  Les Titistes. Notes historiques.
  (8 Nëntori, Tirana 1982) 667 pp.

  The Titoites.
  (8 Nëntori, Tirana 1982)

HUDELIST, Darko
  Deux mondes séparés par le Vardar.
  in: Les Temps modernes, Paris, 519 (1989), p. 23-83.

International Helsinki Federation for Human Rights (ed.)
  The health care situation in Kosovo.
  (IHF, Vienna 1991)

  From autonomy to colonisation. Human rights in Kosovo 1989-1993.
  (IHF, Vienna 1993)

Internationale Gesellschaft für Menschenrechte (ed.)
  Amnestie für alle politischen Gefangenen in Jugoslawien. Die Petition.
  ISBN 3-89248-002-8.
  (IGFM, Frankfurt am Main 1986) 98 pp.

  Ethnische Säuberung in Kosova. Keine Menschenrechte für die
  Kosova-Albaner in ihrer Heimat. Eine Dokumentation der IGFM,
  Bestandsaufnahme.
  (IGFM, Frankfurt am Main 1993) 17 pp.

IPPEN, Theodor Anton
Novibazar und Kossovo (Das alte Raszien). Eine Studie.
(A. Hölder, Vienna 1892) 158 pp.

ISLAMI, Hivzi
Demographic reality in Kosova.
(Kosova Information Center, Prishtina s.a.[ca.1994?]) 53 pp.

ISMAJLI, Rexhep
Die Albaner im ehemaligen Jugoslawien.
in: Jugoslawische (Sch)erben. Probleme und Perspektiven. Bremer,
Alida (ed.).
(Fibre Verlag, Osnabrück & Münster 1993) p. 69-74.

Die Albaner im ehemaligen Jugoslawien haben das Recht auf
Selbstbestimmung.
(LDK, Prishtina / Stuttgart 1993) 15 pp.

Kosova and the Albanians in former Yugoslavia.
(Kosova Information Center, Prishtina 1993) 83 pp.

Die Albaner und Südosteuropa.
in: Dardania. Zeitschrift für Geschichte, Kultur und Information,
Vienna, 1995, 4, p. 151-159.

ITALIAANDER, Rolf (ed.)
Albanien. Vorposten Chinas.
(Delp, Munich 1970) 282 pp.

JACQUES, Edwin E.
The Albanians. An ethnic history from prehistoric times to the present.
ISBN 0-89950-932-0.
(McFarland & Co., Jefferson NC 1994) 768 pp.

JANDOT, Gabriel
L'Albanie d'Enver Hoxha (1944-1985). ISBN 3-7384-2603-4.
(L'Harmattan, Paris 1994) 383 pp.

JELAVICH, Barbara
History of the Balkans. 2 vol. ISBN 0-521-25249-1, 0-521-25448-5.
(Cambridge University Press, Cambridge 1983) 416 & 476 pp.

JELAVICH, Charles
Garašanins Načertanije und das großserbische Programm.
in: Südosteuropa-Studien, Munich, 34 (1985), p. 131-147.

JELAVICH, Charles & Barbara
The Balkans in transition. Essays on the development of Balkan life and politics since the eighteenth century.
(University of California Press, Berkeley 1963; reprint Archon, Hamden CT 1974) 451 pp.

The establishment of the Balkan national states, 1804-1920. ISBN 0-295-95449-2.
(University of Washington Press, Seattle 1977; reprint 1986) 358 pp.

JEVTITCH, Athanase, Archimandrite (= JEVTIĆ, Atanasije)
Dossier Kosovo. Traduit du serbe par Mira Traïkovitch & Jean-Louis Palierne. Préfacé par Père Patric Ranson. ISBN 2-8251-0138-9.
(L'Age d'Homme, Lausanne 1991) 215 pp.

JUKA, Safete Sophie
Kosova. The Albanians in Yugoslavia in light of historical documents. An essay. ISBN 0-9613601-0-0.
(Waldon Press, New York 1984) 72 pp.

KADARE, Ismail
L'année noire. Le cortège de la noce s'est figé dans la glace. Traduit de l'albanais par Jusuf Vrioni et Alexandre Zotos. ISBN 2-213-01942-8.
(Fayard, Paris 1987) 239 pp.

KALESHI, Hasan
Das türkische Vordringen auf dem Balkan und die Islamisierung. Faktoren für die Erhaltung der ethnischen und nationalen Existenz des albanischen Volkes.
in: Südeuropa unter dem Halbmond. Prof. Georg Stadtmüller zum 65. Geburtstag gewidmet. BARTL, Peter & GLASSL, Horst (ed.) (Munich 1975), p. 125-138.

Die Albaner in Kosovo im 15. Jahrhundert.
in: Akten des Internationalen Albanologischen Kolloquiums. Zum Gedächtnis an Univ.-Prof. Dr. Norbert Jokl. Innsbruck, 28.IX.-3.X.1972. Hermann Maria Ölberg (ed.). (Innsbruck 1977) p. 513-524

KALESHI, Hasan & KORNRUMPF, Hans-Jürgen
Das Vilajet Prizren im 19. Jahrhundert.
in: Südost-Forschungen, Munich, 26 (1967). p. 176-238.

KAPLAN, Robert D.
Balkan Ghosts. A journey through history. ISBN 0-679-74981-0.
(Vintage Books, New York 1993) 307 pp.

KASER, Karl
Hirten, Kämpfer, Stammeshelden. Ursprünge und Gegenwart des balkanischen Patriarchats. ISBN 3-205-05545-4.
(Böhlau, Vienna, Cologne & Weimar 1992) 462 pp.

KEKEZI, Haralliq & HIDA, Rexhep (ed.)
What the Kosovars say and demand. Collection of studies, articles, interviews and commentaries. 3 vol.
(8 Nëntori, Tirana 1990, 1990, 1991) 373, 403, 494 pp.

KING, Robert R.
Minorities under communism. Nationalities as a source of tension among Balkan communist states.
(Harvard UP, Cambridge MA 1973) 326 pp.

KOHL, Christine von & LIBAL, Wolfgang
Kosovo. Gordischer Knoten des Balkan. ISBN 3-203-51161-4.
(Europaverlag, Vienna & Zürich 1992) 178 pp.

KOKALARI, Hamit
Kossovo. Berceau du peuple albanais et foyer de la renaissance nationale.
(Tirana 1943) 285 pp.

Kosova Information Center (ed.)
Albanian democratic movement in former Yugoslavia. Documents 1990-1993. Kosova, Macedonia, southern Serbia, Montenegro.
(Kosova Information Center, Prishtina 1993) 57 pp.

KRULIC, Joseph
La crise du Kosovo et l'identité serbe.
in: L'autre Europe, Paris, 23 (1990), p. 63-72.

Histoire de la Yougoslavie de 1945 à nos jours. ISBN 2-87027-481-5.
(Complexe, Brussels 1993) 256 pp.

KUPCHAN, Charles A.
Nationalism and nationalities in the new Europe. A Council on Foreign Relations book.
(Cornell University Press, Ithaca NY 1995) 224 pp.

LABRY, Raoul
Avec l'armée serbe en retraite à travers l'Albanie et le Monténégro. Journal de route d'un officier d'administration de la mission médicale militaire française en Serbie.
(Perrin, Paris 1916) xxv + 212 pp.

LARRABEE, F. Stephen
The volatile powder keg. Balkan security after the cold war. A Rand study. ISBN 1-879383-22-5.
(American University Press, Washington 1994) 346 pp.

LEE, Michele
Kosovo between Yugoslavia and Albania.
in: New left review, London,140 (July/Aug. 1983), p. 62-91.

LENDVAI, Paul
Eagles in cobwebs. Nationalism and communism in the Balkans.
(Doubleday, Garden City NJ; MacDonald, London 1969) xii + 396 pp.

LHOMEL, Edith
Le Kosovo. Foyer de dissensions entre l'Albanie et la Yougoslavie.
in: L'URSS et l'Europe de l'Est en 1982-1983, Paris 1983. La documentation française. Notes et études documentaires. No. 4737-4738. p. 49-62.

LIBAL, Wolfgang
Das Ende Jugoslawiens. Selbstzerstörung, Krieg und Ohnmacht der Welt. ISBN 3-203-51204-1.
(Europaverlag, Vienna & Zürich 1993) 215 pp.

Mazedonien zwischen der Fronten. Jünger Staat mit alten Konflikten. ISBN 3-203-51201-7.
(Europaverlag, Vienna & Zürich 1993) 147 pp.

Livre blanc. L'Ancienneté albanaise et la nationalité de Kosovo comme une réalité historique et politique.
(Unikomb, Prishtina 1992) 136 pp.

Livre noir. Purification ethnique et crimes de guerre dans l'ex-Yougoslavie. Préface de Paul Fouchet. ISBN 2-86959-164-0.
(Arléa, Paris 1993) 508 pp.

536   Bibliography

LOGORECI, Anton
    Albania and Yugoslavia.
    in: Contemporary review, London, 177 (1950), p. 360-364.

    The Albanians. Europe's forgotten survivors.
    (Victor Gollancz, London 1977) 230 pp.

LÖHR, Hanns C.
    Die albanische Frage. Konferenzdiplomatie und Nationalstaatbildung
    im Vorfeld des Ersten Weltkrieges unter besonderer Berücksichtigung
    der deutschen Außenpolitik. Dissertation.
    (Universität Bochum, Bochum 1992) 364 pp.

LUTOVAC, Milisav V.
    La Metohija. Etude de géographie humaine. Travaux publiés par
    l'Institut d'études slaves, 14.
    (Institut d'études slaves, Paris 1935) 96 pp.

MACKENZIE, Georgena Muir & IRBY, A. P.
    Travels in the Slavonic provinces of Turkey in Europe. Pref. Right
    Hon. W. E. Gladstone. 2 vol. ISBN 0-405-02758-3.
    (Daldy, Isbister & Co., London 1877; reprint Arno, New York 1971)
    313 + 342 pp.

MACLEAN, Fitzroy
    Eastern approaches.
    (Jonathan Cape, London 1949) 543 pp.

MAGAŠ, Branka
    Yugoslavia. The spectre of Balkanization.
    in: New left review, London, 174 (March/April 1989), p. 3-31.

    The destruction of Yugoslavia. Tracking the break-up 1980-1992.
    ISBN 0-86091-593-X.
    (Verso, London 1993) 366 pp.

MAGNUSSON, Kjell
    The Serbian reaction. Kosovo and ethnic mobilization among the
    Serbs.
    in: Nordic journal of Soviet and East European studies, Uppsala, 4, 3
    (1987), p. 3-30.

MARKO, Joseph
Perspektiven des zukünftigen politischen und rechtlichen Status
Kosovos.
in: Journal für Rechtspolitik, Vienna, 1, 1 (1993), p. 20-41.

MARMULLAKU, Ramadan
Albania and the Albanians. Translated from the Serbo-Croatian by
Margot and Boško Milosavljević. ISBN 0-903983-13-3.
(Archon, Hamden CT / Hurst, London 1975) 178 pp.

MEDLICOTT, William Norton
Bismark, Gladstone and the Concert of Europe.
(Athlone, London 1956) 353 pp.

The Congress of Berlin and after. A diplomatic history of the near
eastern settlement, 1878-1880.
(Methuen, London 1938; reprint Cass, London 1963) 442 pp.

MEIER, Iren
Verzweiflung und Widerstand im Kosovo.
in: Reformatio. Zeitschrift für Kultur, Poltik und Kirche. Berne, 43. 3
(1994), p. 179-181.

MEIER, Victor
Yugoslavia's national question.
in: Problems of communism, Washington, 32, 2 (1983), p. 47-60.

Wie Jugoslawien verspielt wurde. ISBN 3-406-39241-5.
(Beck, Munich 1995) 464 pp.

MELVILLE, Ralph & SCHRÖDER, Hans-Jürgen (ed.)
Der Berliner Kongress von 1878. Die Politik der Großmächte und die
Probleme der Modernisierung in Südosteuropa in der zweiten Hälfte
des 19. Jahrhunderts. Veröffentlichungen des Instituts für Europäische
Geschichte Mainz. Abteilung Universalgeschichte, Beiheft 7. ISBN 3-
515-02939-1.
(Franz Steiner, Wiesbaden 1982) 539 pp.

MERTUS, Julie
Open wounds. Human rights abuses in Kosovo. ISBN 1-56432-131-2.
(Human Rights Watch, New York 1993) xvii + 148 pp.

METULI, Met Haxhi
The bloodthirsty vampires of Serbia.
(Toena, Tirana 1994) 184 pp.

538　　　　　　　Bibliography

MIHAČEVIĆ, Lovro
　　Durch Albanien. Reiseeindrücke. Aus dem Kroatischen übersetzt
　　durch Otto Szlavnik.
　　(Bonifatius, Prague 1913) 208 pp.

MIHALJČIĆ, Rade
　　The Battle of Kosovo in history and in popular tradition. ISBN
　　8613003664.
　　(Beogradski izdavačko-grafički zavod, Belgrade 1989) 247 pp.

MILO, Paskal
　　Les relations albano-yugoslaves de 1922 à 1924.
　　in: Studia albanica, Tirana, 1990, 2, p. 53-77.

Ministère de l'Information de la Republique de Kosove
　　Memorandum sur la situation des médias en Kosove.
　　(Centre d'Information de la République de Kosove, Geneva 1995)
　　23 pp.

MLADENOV, Stefan
　　Bemerkungen über die Albaner und das Albanische in
　　Nordmakedonien und Altserbien.
　　in: Balkan-Archiv, Leipzig, 1 (1925), p. 43-70.

MONNESLAND, Svein
　　Kosovo-myten.
　　in: Nordisk Østforum, Oslo, 3 (1989), p. 28-34.

MURZAKU, Thoma
　　The Albanians as a formed ethnic-political entity confronted with the
　　Slav states of the Balkans in the 10th-11th centuries.
　　in: Problems of the formation of the Albanian people, their language
　　and culture, Tirana 1984, p. 212-224.

NEUBACHER, Hermann
　　Sonderauftrag Südost 1940-1945. Bericht eines fliegenden
　　Diplomaten.
　　(Musterschmidt, Göttingen 1956) 215 pp.

NIKOLIĆ, Miodrag
　　Autonomous province of Kosovo and Metohija.
　　(Medjunarodna politika, Belgrade 1965) 42 pp.

　　La région autonome de Kosovo et Metohija.
　　(Medjunarodna politika, Belgrade 1965) 47 pp.

NIZICH, Ivana
Yugoslavia. Human rights abuses in Kosovo, 1990-1992. ISBN 1-56432-086-3.
(IHF / Helsinki Watch, New York 1992) 59 pp.

OESTREICH, Karl
Reiseeindrücke aus dem Vilayet Kossovo von Dr Karl Oestrich in Frankfurt a. M.
in: Abhandlungen der k.k. Geographischen Gesellschaft in Wien, Vienna 2 (1900), 46 pp.

Makedonien und die Albanesen. Eine politisch-ethnographische Skizze, zumeist auf Grund eigener Reiseeindrücke.
in: Jahresbericht des Frankfurter Vereins für Geographie und Statistik, Frankfurt, 66/67 (1901/1902, 1902/1903), p. 5-28.

ORLOVITCH, Paul (= ORLOVIĆ, P.)
La question de la Vieille-Serbie.
(Hachette, Paris 1903) 49 pp.

PANO, Nicholas Christopher
People's Republic of Albania.
(John Hopkins Press, Baltimore 1968) 183 pp.

PAVLOWITSCH, Stevan K.
The improbable survivor. Yugoslavia and its problems, 1918-1988. ISBN 1-85065-039-X.
(Hurst, London 1988) 167 pp.

PAVLOWITSCH, Stevan K. & BIBERAJ, Elez
The Albanian problem in Yugoslavia. Two views. Conflict studies. No. 137/138.
(Institute for the Study of Conflicts, London 1982) 43 pp.

PEINSIPP, Walter
Das Volk der Shkypetaren. Geschichte, Gesellschaft- und Verhaltensordnung. Ein Beitrag zur Rechtsarchäologie und zur soziologische Anthropologie des Balkan. ISBN 3-205-07262-6.
(Böhlau, Vienna, Cologne & Graz 1985) 303 pp.

PEŠAKOVIĆ, Milentije
Autonomous provinces in Yugoslavia.
(Medjunarodna politika, Belgrade 1964) 49 pp.

PETROVIĆ, Ranko & FILIPOVIĆ, Gordana (ed.)
    Kosovo. Past and present. Translated by Margot and Boško
    Milosavljević.
    (Review of International Affairs, Belgrade 1989) 384 pp.

PETROVICH, Michael B.
    A history of modern Serbia. 2 vol. ISBN 0-15-140950-1.
    (Harcourt, Brace Jovanovich, New York 1976) 731 pp.

PETTIFER, James
    Kosovo. Round one to Serbia.
    in: The World Today. Royal Institute of International Affairs, London,
    49, 3 (1993), p. 43-44.

PIPA, Arshi
    The political situation of the Albanians in Yugoslavia, with particular
    attention to the Kosovo problem. A critical approach.
    in: East European quarterly, Boulder CO, 23.2 (June 1989), p. 159-
    181.

    Albanian Stalinism. Ideo-political aspects. East European Monographs
    287. ISBN 0 88033 184 4.
    (East European Monographs, Distributed by Columbia UP, New York
    1990) 291 pp.

    The interplay with Serbian, Albanian and Kosovar Stalinism in the
    Kosova tragedy.
    in: Albanica, Washington, 1 (winter 1990), p. 9-41.

    Serbian apologetics. Markovic on Kosova.
    in: Albanica, Washington, 1 (winter 1990), p. 52-62.

PIPA, Arshi & REPISHTI, Sami (ed.)
    Studies on Kosova. East European Monographs 155.
    (East European Monographs, Boulder CO, Distributed by Columbia
    UP, New York 1984) 279 pp.

PLLANA, Emin
    Les raisons et la manière de l'exode des refugiés albanais du territoire
    du Sandjak de Nish à Kosovë, 1877-1878.
    in: Studia albanica, Tirana, 22,1 (1985), p. 179-200.

POLLO, Stefanaq & PUTO, Arben (ed.)
    Histoire de l'Albanie des origines à nos jours.
    (Horvath, Roanne 1974) 372 pp.

The history of Albania from its origins to present day. With the collaboration of Kristo Frashëri and Skënder Anamali. Translated from the French by Carol Wiseman, Ginnie Hole.
(Routledge & Kegan Paul, London & Boston 1981) 322 pp.

POPOVIC, Alexandre
Les musulmans du sud-est européen dans la période post-ottomane. Problèmes d'approche.
in: Journal asiatique, Paris, 263 (1975), p. 317-360.

Problèmes d'approche de l'Islam albanais 1912-1967.
in: Actes du Deuxième Congrès international d'études des cultures de la Méditerrannée occidentale (Malte, juin 1976), Algiers 1978, p. 446-450.

La communauté musulmane d'Albanie dans la période post-ottomane.
in: Zeitschrift für Balkanologie, Berlin, 19 (1983), p. 151-216.

L'Islam balkanique. Les musulmans du sud-est européen dans la période post-ottomane. Balkanologische Veröffentlichungen No. 11.
(Harrassowitz, Berlin, Wiesbaden 1986) 478 pp.

Les musulmans yougoslaves (1845-1989). Médiateurs et métaphores.
(L'Age d'Homme, Lausanne 1990) 69 pp.

POULTON, Hugh
The Balkans. Minorities and states in conflict. Foreword by Milovan Djilas. ISBN 1-873194-40-4.
(Minority Rights Publications, London 1991) 262 pp.

PRIFTI, Kristaq
Le mouvement national albanais de 1896 à 1900. La ligue de Peje.
(Académie des Sciences, Tirana 1989) 296 pp.

PRIFTI, Kristaq, NASI, Lefter, OMARI, Luan, XHUFI, Pëllumb, PULAHA, Selami, POLLO, Stefanaq, & SHTYLLA, Zamir (ed.)
The Truth on Kosova. Academy of Sciences of the Republic of Albania. Institute of History.
(Encyclopedia Publishing House, Tirana 1993) 351 pp.

PRIFTI, Peter R.
Kosovo in ferment. Project on communism, revisionism and revolution.
(MIT, Cambridge MA 1969) 37 pp.

Socialist Albania since 1944. Domestic and foreign developments. Studies in communism, revisionism and revolution. No. 23. William E. Griffith, general editor.
(MIT, Cambridge MA 1978) xv + 312 pp.

PRNJAT, Branko
Kosovo. Zustand und Perspektiven.
(Aktuelna pitanja socijalizma, Belgrade ca. 1987) 56 pp.

PULAHA, Selami
L'autochtonéité des Albanais en Kosovë et le prétendu exode des Serbes à la fin du XVIIe siècle.
(8 Nëntori, Tirana 1985) 81 pp.

Die Autochthonie der Albaner in Kosova und die sogenannte Aussiedlungen der Serben gegen Ende des 17. Jahrhunderts.
(8 Nëntori, Tirana 1986) 86 pp.

PULAHA, Selami & PRIFTI, Kristaq (ed.)
La ligue albanaise de Prizren 1878-1881. Documents 1.
(Académie des Sciences, Tirana 1988) 474 pp.

PUTO, Arben
L'indépendance albanaise et la diplomatie des grandes puissances, 1912-1914.
(8 Nëntori, Tirana 1982) 526 pp.

La question albanaise dans les actes internationaux de l'époque impérialiste. Recueil de documents. 2 vol.
(8 Nëntori, Tirana 1985, 1988) 403 & 697 pp.

QIRA, Zijadin
Cell number 31.
(Vantage, New York 1970) 269 pp.

QOSJA, Rexhep
La mort me vient de ces yeux-là. Treize contes qui peuvent faire un roman. Traduit de l'albanais par Christian Gut. Préface de Ismaïl Kadaré. ISBN 2-07-073073-5.
(Gallimard, Paris 1994) 321 pp.

La question albanaise. Traduit de l'albanais par Christian Gut. ISBN 2-57-9411-01/6.
(Fayard, Paris 1995) 326 pp.

RAIFI, Mensur (ed.)
The angry cloud. An anthology of Albanian stories from Yugoslavia.
Translated from the Albanian by John Hodgson.
(Kosova Assoc. of Literary Translators, Prishtina 1990) 112 pp.

RAMET, Sabrina Pedro
The problem of Albanian nationalism in Yugoslavia.
in: Orbis, Quarterly journal of world affairs, Greenwich CT, 25, 2
(summer 1981), p. 369-388.

Nationalism and federalism in Yugoslavia.
(Indiana UP, Bloomington 1984) 299 pp.

Kosovo and the limits of Yugoslav socialist patriotism.
in: Canadian review of studies in nationalism. Revue canadienne des
études sur le nationalisme, Charlottetown, 16, 1-2 (1989), p. 227-250.

The breakup of Yugoslavia.
in: Global affairs, Washington, VI.2 (spring 1991) p. 93-110.

Social Currents in Eastern Europe.
(Duke UP, London 1991) 435 pp.

Why Albanian irredentism in Kosovo will not go away.
in: Social Currents in Eastern Europe (Duke UP, London 1991),
p. 173-194.

Nationalism and federalism in Yugoslavia, 1962-1991. 2nd edition.
(Indiana UP, Bloomington and Indianapolis 1992) xviii + 346 pp.

REKA, Hazir
Walking through the darkness. Ecja nëpër terr. Hodanje po mraku.
Kosova 1988-1990.
(Dodona International, s.l. [Oslo?] 1991) 162 pp.

REUTER, Jens
Die Albaner in Jugoslawien. Untersuchungen zur Gegenwartskunde
Südosteuropas. Band 20. ISBN 3-486-51281-1.
(Oldenbourg, Munich 1982) 140 pp.

Bildungspolitik in Kosovo.
in: Südosteuropa, Zeitschrift für Gegenwartsforschung, Munich, 32
(1983), p. 8-16.

Politik und Wirtschaft in Kosovo.
in: Südosteuropa, Zeitschrift für Gegenwartsforschung, Munich, 34 (1985), p. 10-23.

Unruheherd Kosovo. Resultat einer gescheiterten Politik.
in: Südosteuropa, Zeitschrift für Gegenwartsforschung, Munich, 35 (1986), p. 631-644.

Die albanische Minderheit in Makedonien.
in: Südosteuropa, Zeitschrift für Gegenwartsforschung, Munich, 36 (1987), p. 587-597.

Das Kosovo-Problem im Kontext der jugoslawischen-albanischen Beziehungen.
in: Sonderheft Albanien. Südosteuropa, Zeitschrift für Gegenwartsforschung, Munich 36 (1987), p. 718-727.
also in: Albanien in Umbruch. Eine Bestandsaufnahme. Untersuchungen zur Gegenswartskunde Südosteuropas. Herausgegeben vom Südost-Institut. Schriftleitung Franz-Lothar Altmann. Band 28 (Munich 1990), p. 81-96.

Politische Gefangene in Jugoslawien.
in: Südosteuropa, Zeitschrift für Gegenwartsforschung, Munich, 36 (1987), p. 298-308.

Das Albanerproblem in Jugoslawien. Kosovo und Mazedonien als Brennpunkte.
in: Europäische Rundschau, Vienna, 17 (1989), p. 61-68.

Die jüngste Entwicklung in Kosovo.
in: Südosteuropa, Zeitschrift für Gegenwartsforschung, Munich, 38 (1989), p. 333-343.

Konfligierende politische Ordnungsvorstellungen als Hintergrund der Krise in Jugoslawien.
in: Südosteuropa, Zeitschrift für Gegenwartsforschung, Munich, 38 (1989), p. 1-16.

Die jugoslawisch-albanischen Beziehungen seit dem Amtsantritt von Ramiz Alia.
in: Albanien und Vergangenheit und Gegenwart. Internationales Symposium der Südosteuropa-Gesellschaft in Zusammenarbeit mit der Albanischen Akademie der Wissenschaften. Winterscheider Mühle bei Bonn, 12.-15. September 1989. Südosteuropa Studien, 48. Klaus-Detlev Grothusen (ed.). (Südosteuropa-Gesellschaft, Munich 1991) p. 99-105.

Die Kosovo-Albaner im ehemaligen Jugoslawien.
in: Volksgruppen in Ostmittel- und Südosteuropa.. Hrsg. von Georg Brunner und Hans Lemberg. Südosteuropa-Studien, Bd. 52 (Nomos, Baden-Baden 1994)

Die politische Entwicklung in Kosovo 1992/93.
in: Südosteuropa, Zeitschrift für Gegenwartsforschung, Munich, 43, 1-2 (1994), p. 18-30.

RIDGEWAY, James & UDOVICKI, Jasminka (ed.)
Yugoslavia's ethnic nightmare. The inside story of Europe's unfolding ordeal. ISBN 1-55652-215-0.
(Lawrence Hill Books / Chicago Review, New York 1994) 280 pp.

ROUX, Michel
Langue et pouvoir en Yougoslavie. Le cas des Albanais.
in: Pluriel, Paris, (1980), 22, p. 93-108.

Le Kosovo. Développement régional et intégration nationale en Yougoslavie.
in: Hérodote, Paris (1982), 25, p. 10-48.
reprint in: Studia albanica, Tirana, 1982, 1, p. 103-136.

Minorité nationale, territoire et développement: les Albanais de Yougoslavie. Thèse d'Etat.
(Université de Toulouse, Toulouse 1990)

Minorité nationale, territoire et développement: les Albanais de Yougoslavie.
in: Albanica, Washington, 1 (winter 1990), p. 42-51.

Les Albanais de Yougoslavie. Minorité nationale territoire et développement. Publié avec le concours de Centre National de la Recherche Scientifique.
(Maison des Sciences de l'Homme, Paris 1992) 546 pp.

RUGOVA, Ibrahim
Independence and democracy, interviews and articles. Pavarësia dhe demokracia, intervista dhe artikuj.
(Fjala, Prishtina 1991) 237 pp.

RULLMANN, Hans Peter
Serbian tanks bring 'peace and justice'. The Albanians in Yugoslavia. ISBN 3-925652-22-1.
(Ostdienst, Hamburg 1989) 72 pp.

Die Albaner. Jugoslawiens drittgrößtes Volk. Referendum über die Zukunft Jugoslawiens. ISBN 3-925652-31-0.
(Ostdienst, Hamburg 1991) 48 pp.

Kosovo-Report. Das Pulverfaß, das Jugoslawien sprengt. ISBN 3-925652-27-2.
(Ostdienst, Hamburg 1991) 60 pp.

Die Albaner in den Trümmern Jugoslawiens. ISBN 3-925652-42-6.
(Ostdienst, Hamburg 1992) 20 pp.

RUPNIK, Jacques
La crise de Kosovo et l'après titisme.
in: L'Alternative, Paris, 18 (1982), p. 53-56.

La 'deuxième bataille' du Kosovo.
in: L'autre Europe, Paris, 10 (1986), p. 41-46.

RUSINOW, Dennison Ivan
The Yugoslav experiment, 1948-1974. Royal Institute of International Affairs. ISBN 0-903983-65-6.
(C. Hurst, London 1977) xxi + 410 pp.

The other Albania. Kosovo 1979.
in: American universities field staff reports, Hanover NH, 5 (1980), 11 + 17 pp.

Events in the SAP of Kosovo. Documentation.
in: Review of international affairs, Belgrade, 1981.

Unfinished business. The Yugoslav national question.
in: American universities field staff reports, Hanover NH, 35 (1981), 13 pp.

RUSINOW, Dennison Ivan (ed.)
Yugoslavia. A fractured federalism. ISBN 0-943875-08-0.
(Wilson Center Press, Washington DC 1988) 182 pp.

SAMARDŽIĆ, Radovan (ed.)
Le Kosovo-Metohija dans l'histoire serbe. ISBN 2-8251-0139-7.
(L'Age de l'Homme, Lausanne 1990) 351 pp.

SAMARY, Catherine
Le marché contre l'autogestion. L'expérience yougoslave. ISBN 2-86600-379-9.
(Publisud, Malakoff 1988) 331 pp.

Krieg in Jugoslawien. Vom titoistischen Sonderweg zum nationalistischen Exzeß. ISBN 3-929008-53-X.
(ISP Verlag, Cologne 1992) 160 pp.

Yugoslavia dismembered. Translated by Peter Drucker. ISBN 0-85345-922-3.
(Monthly Review Press, New York 1995) 185 pp.

SAVOLDI, Valentino & GJERGJI, Lush
Resistenza nonviolenta nella ex-Jugoslavia. Dal Kossovo la testimonianza dei protagonisti. ISBN 88-307-0481-4.
(EMI, Bologna 1993) 96 pp.

SCHIRÒ, Giuseppe
Gli Albanesi e la questione balcanica.
(Ferd. Bideri, Naples 1904) 603 pp.

SCOTTI, Giacomo
Albanesi in Jugoslavia.
in: L'osservatore, politico, letterario, i fumetti il tempo lo spazio. Rivista mesile da Giuseppe Longo. An. XV, Milan 1969, Nr. 4, p. 63-75

SEEWAN, Gerhard (ed.)
Minderheitenfragen in Südosteuropa. Beiträge der internationalen Konferenz: The Minority question in historical perspective 1900-1990. Inter University Center, Dubrovnik, 8.-14. April 1991. Untersuchungen zur Gegenwartskunde Südosteuropas, 27. ISBN 3-486-52881-5.

(Oldenbourg, Munich 1992) 434 pp.
Minderheiten als Konfliktpotential in Ostmittel- und Südosteuropa.
Südosteuropa Schriften, 16.
(Südosteuropa-Gesellschaft, Munich 1995) 390 pp.

SENKEVIČ, Irina Grigor'evna
Osvoboditel'noe dviženie albanskogo naroda v 1905-1912 gg.
(Izd. Akademii Nauk, Moscow 1959) 263 pp.

Albanija v period vostočnogo krizisa 1875-1881 gg.
(Nauka, Moscow 1965) 230 pp.

SESTINI, Aldo
La Metochia.
in: Bollettino della Società Geográfica Italiana, Rome, Ser. VII, Vol. 7
(1942), p. 29-35.

SHOUP, Paul
Communism and the Yugoslav national question.
(Columbia UP, New York 1968) 308 pp.

SINGLETON, Frederick
Albania and her neighbours. The end of isolation. Royal Institute of
International Affairs.
in: World Today, Royal Institute of International Affairs, London, 31.9
(1975) p. 383-390.

Twentieth-century Yugoslavia.
(MacMillan, London 1976) 346 pp.

A short history of the Yugoslav peoples.
(Cambridge UP, Cambridge 1985) 309 pp.

SKENDI, Stavro
Albanian political thought and revolutionary activity, 1881-1912.
in: Südost-Forschungen, Munich, 13 (1954), p. 159-199.

Albania. Mid-European Studies Center Series.
(Praeger, New York; Stevens & Sons, London 1956) 389 pp.

Albanian national awakening, 1878-1912.
(Princeton UP, Princeton 1967) 498 pp.

SKENDO, Lumo (= FRASHËRI, Mid'hat)
Albanais et Slaves.

(Librairie centrale des nationalités, Lausanne 1916) 45 pp.

STADTMÜLLER, Georg
Forschungen zur albanischen Frühgeschichte.
(Budapest 1942, 2nd edition Harrassowitz, Wiesbaden 1966) 221 pp.

Geschichte Südosteuropas.
(Oldenbourg, Munich 1950; reprint 1976) 528 pp.

STAVILECI, Esat
Kosova and the Albanians. Its past, present and future.
(Independent Association of Lawyers of Kosova, Prishtina 1992) 64 pp.

Kosova and Albanians. Between negation (foreign rule) and independence.
(Independent Association of Lawyers of Kosova, Prishtina 1995) 93 pp.

STAVRIANOS, Leften S.
The Balkans since 1453.
(Rinehart & Co., New York 1958) 970 pp.

STIPČEVIĆ, Aleksandar
The Illyrians. History and culture. Translated from Serbo-Croatian.
(Noyes Press, Park Bridge NJ 1977) 291 pp.

Die Frage der illyrisch-albanischen Kontinuität und ihre politische Aktualität heute.
in: Dardania. Zeitschrift für Geschichte, Kultur und Information, Vienna, 1995, 4, p. 11-25.

STOIANOVICH, Traian
Balkan worlds. The first and last Europe. ISBN 1-56324-033-5.
(M. E. Sharpe, Armonk NY 1994) 433 pp.

STOJANOVIĆ, Mihailo D.
The Great Powers and the Balkans, 1875-1878.
(Cambridge UP, Cambridge 1939) 296 pp.

STOKES, Gale
Nationalism in the Balkans. Annotated bibliography. ISBN 0-8240-9161-2.
(Garland, New York 1986) xvii + 243 pp.

550   Bibliography

STURESJÖ, Örjan
    Kosovo - ett jugoslaviskt dilemma.
    in: Världspolitikens dagsfrågor, Stockholm, 4 (1990), 32 pp.

SUGAR, Peter F.
    Southeastern Europe under Ottoman rule, 1354-1804. History of East
    Central Europe 5. ISBN 0-295-95443-4.
    (Univ. of Washington Press, Seattle and London 1977) 384 pp.

SUNDHAUSSEN, Holm
    Geschichte Jugoslawiens, 1918-1980. ISBN 3-17-007289-7.
    (W. Kohlhammer, Stuttgart 1982) 224 pp.

TCHOSSITCH, Dobritsa (= ČOSIĆ, Dobrica)
    Un homme dans son époque. Entretiens avec Slavoljub Djoukitch.
    Traduit du serbo-croate par Dejan M. Babić.
    (L'Age d'Homme, Lausanne 1991) 286 pp.

    L'Effondrement de la Yougoslavie. Positions d'un résistant. Traduit du
    serbe par Slobodan Despot. ISBN 2-8251-0357-8.
    (L'Age d'homme, Lausanne 1994) 175 pp.

TITO, Josip Broz
    The national question.
    (STP, Belgrade 1983) 220 pp.

TOMAŠEVIĆ, Nebojša (ed.)
    Facts about Kosovo. Facts about the Socialist Autonomous Province of
    Kosovo.
    (Provincial Committee for Information, Prishtina 1983) 60 pp.

TOMASHEVICH, George
    The problem of Kosovo through the centuries. A historical and
    anthropological overview.
    in: Australian Slavonic and East European studies, Parksville, 4 (1990),
    p. 213-228.

TOMITCH, Yovan (= TOMIĆ, Jovan N.)
    Les Albanais en Vieille-Serbie et dans le Sandjak de Novi Bazar.
    (Hachette, Paris 1913) 86 pp.

TORCHE, Denis
    Les liens entre l'identité nationale et le fait migratoire. Le cas des
    Albanais de Yougoslavie.
    in: Revue suisse de sociologie, Geneva, 15, 1 (1989), p. 115.138.

TROTSKY, Leon
   The Balkan wars. ISBN 0-913460-67-2.
   (Monad, New York 1980)

TRUMAN, Ivan
   The Serbian Orthodox Church in Kosovo.
   in: Sobornost, London 7, 1 (1985), p. 44-48.

Über die Ereignisse in Kosova. Artikel aus *Zëri i Popullit* und anderen Organen.
(8 Nëntori, Tirana 1981) 198 pp.

UMILTA, Carlo
   Jugoslavia e Albania. Memorie di un diplomatico.
   (Garzanti, Milan 1947) vii + 201 pp.

VERLI, Marenglen
   A propos d'un accord conclu en 1924.
   in: Studia albanica, Tirana, 25, 1 (1988), p. 105-117.

   A propos de la législation agraire de colonisation appliquée en Kosovë
   de 1919 à 1941.
   in. Studia albanica, Tirana, 26, 2 (1989), p. 103-122.

VICKERS, Miranda
   Albania. A modern history. ISBN 1-85043-749-1
   (I. B. Tauris, London / St. Martin's, New York 1994) 288 pp.

   The status of Kosovo in Socialist Yugoslavia. ISSN 0413-5043, no. 1.
   (Research Unit in South European Studies, University of Bradford
   1994) 64 pp.

VOJE, Ignacij
   Die Entwicklung des Kosovo im Lichte der ethnischen Prozesse bis
   zur Mitte des 18. Jahrhunderts.
   in: Österreichische Osthefte, Vienna, 33, 2 (1991), p. 358-383.

VUCINICH, Wayne S. (ed.)
   Contemporary Yugoslavia. Twenty years of socialist experiment.
   (University of California Press, Berkeley & Los Angeles 1969) 441 pp.

VUKMANOVIĆ-TEMPO, Svetozar
   Mein Weg mit Tito. Ein Revolutionär erinnert sich.
   (Droemer Knaur, Munich 1972) 408 pp.

   Struggle for the Balkans. ISBN 0-85036-347-0.

(Merlin, London 1990) 355 pp.

WASSA, Effendi (= VASA, Pashko)
Albanien und die Albanesen. Eine historisch-kritische Studie von Wassa Effendi, Beamter der Kaiserlich Türkischen Regierung, Christlich-Albanischer Nationalität.
(Julius Springer, Berlin 1879) 68 pp.

Etudes sur l'Albanie et les Albanais par Wassa Effendi.
(La Turquie, Constantinople 1879) 113 pp.

The truth on Albania and the Albanians. Historical and critical. By Wassa Effendi, an Albanian Christian functionary. Translated by Edward St. John Fairman.
(National Press Agency, London 1879) 48 pp.

La vérité sur l'Albanie et les Albanais. Etude historique et critique par Wassa Effendi, fonctionnnaire chrétien albanais.
(Société Anon. de Publ. Périodiques, Paris 1879) 103 pp.

WEST, Rebecca
Black lamb and grey falcon. A journey through Yugoslavia.
(Viking Press, New York 1942; reprint: Penguin, London 1986) 1,181 pp.

WILKINSON, H. R.
Jugoslav Kosmet. The evolution of a frontier province and its landscape.
in: Institute of British Geographers, Transactions and Papers, London, 21 (1955), p. 171-193.

WOLF, Jean
La Macédoine déchirée et la renaissance yougoslave.
(Cujas, Paris 1985) 324 pp.

WOODWARD, Susan L.
Balkan tragedy. Chaos and dissolution after the Cold War. ISBN 0-8157-9513-0.
(The Brookings Institution, Washington 1995) 536 pp.

YELEN, Anne
Kossovo 1389-1989. Bataille pour les droits de l'âme.
(L'Age de l'Homme, Lausanne 1989) 163 pp.

YOVITCHITCH, Lena A. (= JOVICHIĆ, Lenka A.)
 Pages from here and there in Serbia. By Lena A. Yovitchitch, with a
 preface by Professor Bogdan Popovitch.
 (Cvijanovich, Belgrade 1926) iii + 169 pp.

Yugoslav-Albanian relations.
 (Review of International Affairs, Belgrade 1984) 304 pp.

ZAJMI, Gazmend
 Dimensions of the question of Kosova in the Balkans. Individuality
 and the question of Kosova as a question of self-determination.
 (Academy of Sciences and Arts of Kosova / Kosova Information
 Center, Prishtina 1994) 190 pp.

ZANGA, Louis
 Jugoslawische Nationalitätenpolitik im Fall Kosovo.
 in: Osteuropa, Stuttgart, 25.7 (1975), p. 506-516.

ZÜLCH, Tilman (ed.)
 Ethnische Säuberung. Völkermord für Großserbien. Eine
 Dokumentation der Gesellschaft für bedrohte Völker. ISBN 3-630-
 71084-0-12.
 (Luchterhand, Hamburg & Zürich 1993) 170 pp.

ŽUPANIĆ, Niko
 Altserbien und die albanesische Frage.
 (Anzengruber, Vienna 1912) 55 pp.

Works in Balkan languages

ABDYLI, Ramiz
Gjendja dhe pozita e klasës punëtore në Kosovë, 1918-1941.
(Prishtina 1986) 222 pp.

ACIN-KOSTA, Miloš
Branioci Kosova, 1389-1989. 2. dop. i pros. izd. ISBN 0-931931304.
(Ravnogorski venac, Washington 1989) xxxii + 470 pp.

AGANI, Fehmi
Demokracia, kombi, vetëvendosja.
(Dukagjini, Peja 1994) 233 pp.

ALEN, Mari-Fransoaz & GALMISH, Ksavie (= ALLAIN, Marie-Françoise &
GALMICHE, Xavier)
Ibrahim Rugova. Çështja e Kosovës. Parathënia Ismail Kadare.
Përktheu Rexhep Ismajli, Eqrem Basha.
(Dukagjini, Peja 1994) 200 pp.

ALTIMARI, Francesco et al.
Albanci. Avtorji besedila Francesco Altimari.
(Cankarjeva založba, Ljubljana 1984) 276 pp.

AVDIC VLLASI, Nadira
Za odbranu Azema Vllasija. Izbor članaka.
(Republiska Konferenca ZSMS, Ljubljana 1989) 176 pp.

AVDIU Kamber, GASHI-LUCAJ, Marije, & NIKAJ, Mark (ed.)
Kosova. Fakte dhe shifra.
(Komiteti krahinor i informatave i KSA të Kosovës, Ljubljana 1987)
80 pp.

BAJRAMI, Hakif
Rrethanat shoqërore dhe politike në Kosovë më 1918-1941.
(Instituti i Historisë së Kosovës, Prishtina 1981) 363 pp.

Partia komuniste e Jugosllavisë në Kosovë, 1919-1941.
(Prishtina 1982)

Konventa jugosllavo-turke e vitit 1938 për shpërnguljen e shqiptarëve.
in: Gjurmime albanologjike, Seria e shkencave historike, Prishtina, 12
(1983), p. 243-271.

Shtypja dhe rezistenca e shqiptarëve në Kosovë, 1929-1941.
in: Studime historike, Tirana, 35, 2 (1986), p. 115-149.

Tragjedia e Tivarit. Çka i parapriu tragjedisë, qëllimet dhe pasojat.
(Grafotext, Prishtina 1993) 226 pp.

BAKIĆ, Radovan
Promjene u razmještaju stanovništva SAP Kosova.
(Jedinstvo, Prishtina 1978) 163 pp.

BALETA, Abdi
Shqiptarët përballë shovinizmit serbo-grek.
(Kohë, Tirana 1995) 352 pp.

BALEVSKI, Milčo (= BALEVSKI, Millço)
Albanija po Enver Hodža.
(Maked. kn., Skopje 1987) 299 pp.

Shqipëria pas Enver Hoxhës.
(Flaka e vëllazërimit, Skopje 1988) 399 pp.

BALKANICUS (= PROTIĆ, Stojan)
Albanski problem i Srbija i Austro-Ugarska.
(Izdav. knjižarnica Gece Kona, Belgrade 1913) 111 pp.

BANAC, Ivo
Nacionalno pitanje u Jugoslaviji. Porijeklo, povijest, politika. Preveo
s engleskoj. ISBN 86-3430-237-7.
(Globus, Zagreb 1988) 420 pp.

BARJAKTAREVIĆ, Radojica
Besanje noći. Istina o srpskom pokretu. ISBN 86-7019-156-3.
(Pergament, Prishtina 1995) 360 pp.

BATAKOVIĆ, Dušan T.
Savremenici o Kosovu i Metohiji, 1852-1912.
(Srpska književna zadruga, Belgrade 1988) xxxvii + 464 pp.

Dečansko pitanje. Posebna izdanja. Istorijski Institut, Knj. 26.
(Prosveta, Belgrade 1989) 231 pp.

556   Bibliography

Kosovo i Metohija u srpsko-arbanaškim odnosima. Studije i Članci.
ISBN 86-7019-071-0.
(Jedinstvo, Prishtina / Decje Novine, Gornji Milanovac 1991) 283 pp.

Bela knjiga o neprijatelskoj politici vlade Narodne Republike Albanije prema
Federativnoj Narodnoj Republici Jugoslaviji.
(Državni Sekretariat za Inostrane Poslove FNRJ, Belgrade 1961)
142 pp.

BELEGU, Xhafer
    Lidhja e Prizrenit e veprimet e sajë, 1878-1881.
    (Kristo Luarasi, Tirana 1939) 199 pp.

BEQIRI, Shaip
    Sfida e gjeniut. Kadare, Ekzili, Kosova.
    (Buzuku, Prishtina 1991) 491 pp.

BERISHA, Emin
    Privredni i društveni razvoj SAP Kosova 1947-1972.
    (Pokrajinski zavod za statistiku SAP Kosova, Prishtina 1974) 237 pp.

BERISHA, Emin & STOLIQI, Mlladen (ed.)
    Zhvillimi i Kosovës, 1966-1977. Konferenca XII e LK të Kosovës.
    (Enti i Statistikës i KSA të Kosovës, Prishtina 1978) 437 pp.

BERISHA, Kolë M.
    Ditari i një izolanti.
    (Zëri, Prishtina 1991) 167 pp.

BIBERAJ, Elez Hysen
    Kosova, Fuçi baroti e Ballkanit.
    (Dardania, Tirana 1994) 72 pp.

BILANDŽIĆ, Dušan
    Jugoslavija poslije Tita, 1980-1985. ISBN 86-3430-041-2.
    (Globus, Zagreb 1986) 253 pp.

BISAKU, Gjon, KURTI, Shtjefën, & GASHI, Luigj (= BISAK, Jean, KURTI,
Etienne, & GASHI, Louis)
    Promemorie e paraqitur në Lidhjen e Kombeve (1930). Gjendja e
    shqiptarëve në Jugosllavi. Mémoire présenté à la Société des Nations.
    La situation des Albanais en Yougoslavie.
    (Koha, Tirana 1995) 91 pp.

BJELETIĆ, Dobrosav (ed.)
Šta i kako dalje na Kosovu. Dalja društveno-politička aktivnost SSRNJ u realizaciji političke platforme za akciju SKJ u razvoju socijalističkog samoupravljanja, bratstva i jedinstva i zajedništva na Kosovu.
(Narodna knjiga, Belgrade 1985) 249 pp.

BOBI, Gani
Konteksti i vetëkulturës.
(Dukagjini, Peja 1994) 152 pp.

BOGDANOVIĆ, Dimitrije
Knjiga o Kosovu. Posebna izdanja. Knj. 566.
(Srpska Akademija Nauka i Umetnosti, Belgrade 1985) 299 pp.

Razgovori o Kosovu.
(Srpska Akademija Nauka i Umetnosti, Belgrade 1986) 116 pp.

Knjiga o Kosovu, Razgovori o Kosovu. ISBN 86-391-0194-9.
(Književne novine, Belgrade / Jedinstvo, Prishtina 1990) 470 pp.

BOJOVIĆ, Petar
Odbrana Kosovoga Polja 1915 g. i zaštita odstupanija srpske vojske preko Albanije i Crne Gore.
(Hipnos, Belgrade 1990) 105 pp.

BOVAN, Vladimir
Narodna književnost Srba na Kosovu i Metohiji. 2 vol. ISBN 86-7019-034-6.
(Jedinstvo, Prishtina 1989) 408 & 440 pp.

BRAHA, Shaban
Gjenocidi serbomadh dhe qëndresa shqiptare, 1844-1990.
(Lumi-T, Gjakova 1991) 584 pp.

BRAJOVIQI, Petar, ISLAMI, Nehat, KURTESHI, Ilaz, RISTIQI, Dushan, STAVILECI, Esat, & SHESHLIA, Millan (ed.)
Kosova. Krahina Socialiste Autonome e Kosovës.
(OPGBG Borba, Prishtina 1982) 172 pp.

BRESTOVCI, Sadulla
Qëndrimi i Serbisë ndaj shqiptarëve dhe lëvizjes së tyre kombëtare të viteve 1862-1868.
in: Gjurmime albanologjike, Seria e shkencave historike, Prishtina, 6 (1977), p. 7-48.

Qëndrimi i Serbisë ndaj shqiptarëve dhe lëvizjes së tyre kombëtare të viteve 1868-1875.
in: Gjurmime albanologjike, Seria e shkencave historike, Prishtina, 7 (1978), p. 125-149.

Marrëdhëniet shqiptare-serbo-malazeze (1830-1878).
(Instituti Albanologjik, Prishtina 1983) 291 pp.

BUZA, Kujtim
Nëpër vende historike të Kosovës. Vizatime nga piktori Kujtim Buza.
(8 Nëntori, Tirana 1980) 94 pp.

ÇAMI, Muin
Shqipëria në marrëdhëniet ndërkombëtare (1914-1918).
(Akademia e Shkencave, Tirana 1987) 367 pp.

CANA, Zekeria
Politika e qeverisë serbe ndaj lëvizjes kombëtare shqiptare 1908-1912.
in: Gjurmime albanologjike, Seria e shkencave historike, Prishtina, 6 (1977), p. 71-116.

Lëvizja kombëtare shqiptare në Kosovë 1908-1912.
(Rilindja, Prishtina 1979; reprint 8 Nëntori, Tirana 1982) 318 pp.

Dimitrije Tucoviqi. Koha dhe vepra.
(Rilindja, Prishtina 1983) 334 pp.

Shpalime historike.
(Rilindja, Prishtina 1983)

Socialdemokracia serbe dhe çështje shqiptare 1903-1914.
(Instituti Albanologjik, Prishtina 1986) 376 pp.

Populli shqiptar në kapërcyell të shekullit XX.
(Instituti Albanologjik, Prishtina 1990) 342 pp.

CEROVIĆ, Vuksan
Kosovo. Kontrarevolucija koja teče. ISBN 86-7335-073-5.
(Nova Knjiga, Belgrade / Jedinstvo, Prishtina, 1989) 444 pp.

ČOSIĆ, Dobrica (= TCHOSSITCH, Dobritsa)
Stvarno i moguće. Članci i ogledi. Drugo dopunjeno izdanje. ISBN 8636105552.
(Cankarjeva založba, Ljubljana 1988) 227 pp.

Srpsko pitanje. Demokratsko pitanje. ISBN 8676070709.
(Politika, Belgrade 1992) 241 pp.

ČUBRILOVIĆ, Vasa
Iseljavanje Arnauta.
Manuscript in the Institute of Military History of the Yugoslav
People's Army (Vojno Istorijski Institut JNA). Archives of the former
Yugoslav Army (Arhiv Bivše Jugoslovenske Vojske), Belgrade,
7 March 1937. No. 2, Fasc. 4, Box 69. 19 pp.

Manjinski problem u novoj Jugoslaviji.
Typescript. Belgrade, 3 November 1944. 22 pp.

Istorija političke misle u Srbiji XIX veka.
(Prosveta, Belgrade 1958) 578 pp.

Odabrani istorijski radovi.
(Narodna knjiga, Belgrade 1983) 666 pp.

ČUPIĆ, Mirko
Nasilje iza paravana vlasti. Osvrti, komentari, članci. ISBN 86-7019-
050-8.
(Jedinstvo, Prishtina 1989) 279 pp.

CVIJIĆ, Jovan
Balkansko poluostrov i južnoslovenske zemlje. Osnove
antropogeografije. 2 vol.
(Državna Štamparija Kraljevine SHS, Belgrade 1922; reprint Belgrade
1966) 582 pp.

DEDIJER, Vladimir
Jugoslovansko-albanski odnosi (1939-1948). Na podlagi uradnih
dokumentov, pisem in drugega gradiva publikacijo ured. i obdel.
(Borba, Ljubljana 1949) 145 pp.

Jugoslovensko-albanski odnosi (1939-1948). Na osnovu službenih
dokumenta, pisama i drugog materijala.
(Borba, Zagreb 1949) 225 pp.

Marrëdhanjet jugosllavo-shqiptare 1939-1948.
(Prosveta, Belgrade 1949) 240 pp.

DIZDAREVIĆ, Nijaz
Albanski dnevnik. ISBN 86-3430-474-4.
(Globus, Zagreb / Oslobodenje, Sarajevo 1988) 217 pp.

560 Bibliography

DJAKOVIĆ, Spasoje
Sukobi na Kosovu. Drugo dopunjeno izdanije.
(Narodna knjiga, Belgrade 1986) 455 pp.

DJOKOVIĆ, Milorad
Kosmetski dosije. Ispovesti i sudbine prognanih Kosovaca. ISBN 86-81563-04-1.
(AIZ Dosije, Belgrade 1990) 235 pp.

DJORDJEVIĆ, Dimitrije
Izlazak Srbije na Jadransko More i konferencija ambasadoru u Londonu 1912.
(s. e., Belgrade 1956) 160 pp.

DJORDJEVIĆ, Vladan (= GEORGEVITCH, Vladan)
Arnauti i velike sili.
(Jevta M. Pavlović, Belgrade 1913) 188 pp.

DJUKIĆ, Miodrag et al.
Enver Hodžina Albanija.
(Tanjug, Belgrade 1981) 269 pp.

DJUKIĆ, Slavoljub
Izmedju slave i anateme. Politička biografija Slobodana Miloševića.
(Filip Visnić, Belgrade 1995?) 286 pp.

DJURETIĆ, Veselin
Razaranje srpstva u XX veku. Ideološka upotreba istorije. 2. izd.
Balkanološki Institut. ISBN 8671790142.
(Srpska Akademija Nauka i Umetnosti, Belgrade 1992) 392 pp.

DJURKOVIĆ, Djordje (= GYURKOVICS, Georg von)
Albanija. Crte o zemlji i narodu.
(Zemaljska Štamparija, Sarajevo 1884) 207 pp.

DOÇI, Rexhep
Iliro-shqiptarët dhe serbët në Kosovë.
(Instituti Albanologjik, Prishtina 199?) 345 pp.

DODEROVIĆ, Milorad
Kako se dogodio Solević. ISBN 8671290697.
(Gradina, Niš 1990) 140 pp.

DRAGOJAVAC, D.
Aspekte aktuale të çështjes kombëtare në Jugosllavi.
(Rilindja, Prishtina 1985) 355 pp.

DRINI, Skënder
Bajram Curri.
(8 Nëntori, Tirana 1983) 376 pp.

DURHAM, Mary Edith
Njëzet vjet ngatëresa ballkanike. Shqipëruar nga inglishtia prej S.
Toto.
(Mesagjeritë shqiptare, Tirana 1944) 289 pp.

Brenga e Ballkanit dhe vepra të tjera për Shqipërinë dhe Shqiptarët.
(8 Nëntori, Tirana 1990) 586 pp.

ELEZI, Mehmet
Shansi i tretë. Esse.
(Adam & Peck, New York 1993) 145 pp.

Ankth ballkanik. Esse.
(Dardania, Tirana 1993) 79 pp.

ELSIE, Robert
Një fund dhe një fillim. Vëzhgime mbi letërsinë dhe kulturën shqiptare
bashkëkohore. Përktheu nga anglishtja Abdyrrahim Myftiu. ISBN 86-
7785-024-4.
(Buzuku, Prishtina 1995) 190 pp.

Një fund dhe një fillim. Vëzhgime mbi letërsinë dhe kulturën shqiptare
bashkëkohore. Përktheu nga anglishtja Abdyrrahim Myftiu.
(Globus R, Tirana 1995) 187 pp.

FAZLIJA, Asllan
Autonomija e Kosovës e Metohisë në Jugosllavinë Socialiste.
(Rilindja, Prishtina 1966) 133 pp.

FOLIĆ, Milutin (= FOLIQ, Milutin)
Komunistička Partija Jugoslavije na Kosovu, 1919-1941. ISBN 86-
7019-015-X.
(Jedinstvo, Prishtina 1987) xi + 441 pp.

Partia komuniste e Jugosllavisë në Kosovë, 1919-1941.
(Rilindja, Prishtina 1987) 466 pp.

FOLIQ, Milutin
    cf. FOLIĆ, Milutin

Forum i Intelektualëve të Shqipërisë (ed.)
    Zëri i inteligjencës për çështjen kombëtare.
    (Eurorilindja, Tirana 1995) 191 pp.

FRASHËRI, Kristo
    Lidhja shqiptare e Prizrenit, 1878-1881.
    (8 Nëntori, Tirana 1979) 248 pp.

    Lidhja shqiptare e Prizrenit, 1878-1881. Në 2 vëllime.
    (Akademia e Shkencave, Tirana 1989)

FRASHËRI, Sami (= FRASCHERY, Chemseddine Samy bey)
    Shqipëria - Ç'ka qënë, ç'është e ç'do të bëhetë? Mendime për shpëtimt
    të mëmëdheut nga reziket që e kanë rethuarë.
    (Bucharest 1899; reprint Mbrothësia, Sofia 1907) 96 pp.

FREUNDLICH, Leo
    Golgota shqiptare. Akuza kundër shfarosësve të popullit shqiptar.
    (Lilo, Tirana 1995) 91 pp.

GABER, Slavko & KUZMANIĆ, Tonči (ed.)
    Kosovo Srbija Jugoslavija. ISBN 86-7347-023-4.
    (Univerzitetna Konferenca ZSMA, Ljubljana 1989) 342 pp.

GARAŠANIN, Ilija
    Načertanija.
    in: Delo, 1906, vol. 38.

GARAŠANIN, Milutin (ed.)
    Iliri i Albanci. Serija predavanja održanih od 21. maja do 4. juna 1986.
    godine. ISBN 86-7025-040-3.
    (Srpska Akademija Nauka i Umetnosti, Belgrade 1988) 375 pp.

GASHI, Gjergj Gj.
    Albanski mučenici u razdoblju 1846-1848.
    (OOUR Tiskara, Zagreb 1988)

    Martirët shqiptarë gjatë viteve 1846-1948.
    (Drita, Ferizaj 1994) 302 pp.

GASHI, Skënder
  Antroponomia e shqiptarëve në Kosovë në shekullin XV në dritën e
  burimeve onomastike turko-osmane.
  in: Gjurmime albanologjike, Seria e shkencave historike, Prishtina, 7
  (1978), p. 47-68.

GJINI, Gaspër
  Skopsko-prizrenska biskupija kroz stoleća.
  (Kršćanska Sadašnjost, Zagreb 1986) 240 pp,

GOPČEVIĆ, Spiridion (= GOPCEVIC, Spiridion)
  Stara Srbija i Makedonija.
  (Dimitrijevič, Belgrade 1890)

GORANI, Hajrullah
  Punëtoria kosovare. Forcë reale për liri kombëtare dhe demokraci.
  Intervista, fjalime dhe biseda.
  (Pjetër Bogdani, Tirana 1991) 160 pp.

GRUDA, Prenk
  Ditari i nji zemrës së lëndueme 1937-1975.
  (s.e., Detroit 1985, reprint Tirana 1995) 766 pp.

HADRI, Ali
  Kosovo i Metohija u Kraljevini Jugoslavije.
  in: Istorijski glasnik, Belgrade, 1967, 1-2, p. 51-84.

  Pozita dhe gjendja e Kosovës në Mbretërinë e Jugosllavisë (1918-
  1941)
  in: Gjurmime albanologjike, Seria e shkencave historike, Prishtina,
  1968, 2, p. 163-194.

  Historia e popullit shqiptar. Për shkollat e mesme.
  (Enti i teksteve, Prishtina 1971) 245 pp.

  Lëvizja nacionalçlirimtare në Kosovë (1941-1945).
  (Rilindja, Prishtina 1971) 483 pp.

  Istorija albanskog naroda.
  (Zavod za učbenike i nastavna sredstva, Prishtina 1972) 190 pp.

  Këshillat nacionalçlirimtare në Kosovë (1941-1945).
  (Enti i historisë së Kosovës, Prishtina 1974) 207 pp.

Narodno-oslobodilački odbori na Kosovu, 1941-1945.
(Zavod za istoriju Kosova, Prishtina 1975) 154 pp.

HADRI, Ali (ed.)
Konferenca shkencore e 100-vjetorit të Lidhjes Shqiptare të Prizrenit.
Referate dhe kumtesa të mbajtura në seksionin e historisë. Prishtinë 6-9 qershor 1978. 2 vol.
(Akademia e Shkencave dhe e Arteve e Kosovës, Prishtina 1981)

HADRI, Ali & PEJANOVIĆ, Dušan
Autonomna Pokrajina Kosovo i Metohija.
(Narodna Armija, Belgrade 1968) 125 pp.

HADŽI-VASILJEVIĆ, Jovan
Pitanje o Staroj Srbiji i skopaljsko vladičansko pitanje.
(Jocković, Belgrade 1902) 111 pp.

Arnautski pokreti u XIX veku.
(Davidović, Belgrade 1905) 66 pp.

Stara Srbija i Maćedonija.
(Dimitrijević, Belgrade 1906) iv + 96 pp.

Arbanaška Liga. Arnautska kongra i sprski narod u turskom carstvu (1878-1882).
(Srbija, Belgrade 1909) iv + 127 pp.

Južna Stara Srbija. Istorijska, etnografska i politička istraživanja.
(Davidović, Belgrade 1909, 1913) 558, 460 pp.

Četnička akcija u Staroj Srbiji i Maćedoniji.
(Sv. Sava, Belgrade 1928) 24 pp.

Kroz Albaniju 1915 godine s moravskom divizijom II poziva.
(Sv. Sava, Belgrade 1929) 44 pp.

Arnauti naše krvi. Arnautaši.
(Drag: Popović, Belgrade 1939) 39 pp.

HASANI, Sinan
Kosovo. Istine e zabludi. ISBN 86-7125-001-6.
(Centar za Informacije i Publicitet, Zagreb 1986) 358 pp.

Kosova. Të vërtetat e mashtrimet.
(Rilindja, Prishtina 1987) 398 pp.

HAXHIU, Ajet
Hasan Prishtina dhe lëvizja patriotike e Kosovës.
(Naim Frashëri, Tirana 1964) 231 pp.

Shota dhe Azem Galica.
(8 Nëntori, Tirana 1976) 282 pp.

HIBBERT, Reginald
Fitorja e hidhur. Lufta nacionalçlirimtare e Shqipërisë.
(Lidhja e Shkrimtarëve, Tirana 1993) 422 pp.

HORVAT, Branko
Kosovsko pitanje. 2. dop. izd. ISBN 86-3430-310-1.
(Globus, Zagreb 1989) 329 pp.

HOTI, Izber
Lëvizja ilegale antifashiste në Kosovën lindore, 1941-1944.
(Rilindja, Prishtina 1990) 210 pp.

HOTI, Ukshin
Filozofia politike e çështjes shqiptare.
(Rozafa, Tirana 1995) 240 pp.

HOXHA, Enver
'Vetadministrimi' jugosllav. Teori dhe praktikë kapitaliste. Kundër
pikëpamjeve antisocialiste të E. Kardelit...
(8 Nëntori, Tirana 1978) 115 pp.

HOXHA, Fadil
Jemi në shtëpinë tonë. 3 vol.
(Rilindja, Prishtina 1986) 343, 320, 336 pp.

HOXHA, Hajredin (= HODŽA, Hajredin)
Elemente të presionit ekonomik ndaj shqiptarëve në Jugosllavinë e
vjetër.
in: Përparimi, Prishtina, 16, 4 (1970), p. 309-334.

Politika e eliminimit të shqiptarëve nga trualli i Jugosllavisë së vjetër.
in: Përparimi, Prishtina, 16, 5 (1970), p. 430-446.

Politika e terrorit dhe gjenocidit ndaj shqiptarëve.
in: Përparimi, Prishtina, 17, 5 (1971), p. 351-371.

Afirmimi i kombësisë shqiptare në Jugosllavi. Nacionalizmi dhe irredentizmi stalinian në Shqipëri.
(Rilindja, Prishtina 1983) 243 pp.

Afirmacija albanske nacionalnosti u Jugoslaviji.
(Rilindja, Prishtina 1984) 220 pp.

HOXHA, Sherafedin
Shtypi i kombeve dhe i kombësive të Kosovës (1871-1983).
(Rilindja, Prishtina 1987) 239 pp.

HRABAK, Bogumil
Arbanaški upadi i pobune na Kosovu i u Makedoniji od kraja 1912. do kraja 1915. godine. Nacionalno nerazvijeni i nejedinstveni Arbanasi kao orude u rukama zainteresovanih država.
(Narodni muzej u Vranju, Vranje 1988) 237 pp.

HUDELIST, Darko
Kosovo. Bitka bez iluzija. ISBN 86-7125-029-6.
(Centar za informacije i publicitet, Zagreb 1989) 383 pp.

IGIĆ, Živorad
Kosovo i Metohija (1981-1991). Uvod u Jugoslovensku krizu. Dnevnik. Knjiga 1. ISBN 86-7019-108-3.
(Jedinstvo, Prishtina / Oktoih, Podgorica 1992) 366 pp.

ISLAMI, Hivzi
Popullsia e Kosovës. Studim demografik.
(Enti i teksteve, Prishtina 1980) 375 pp.

Fshati i Kosovës. Kontribut për studimin sociologjiko-demografik të evolucionit rural.
(Rilindja, Prishtina 1985) 277 pp.

Kosova dhe shqiptarët. Çështje demografike.
(Pena, Prishtina 1991) 244 pp.

Rrjedha demografike shqiptare.
(Dukagjini, Peja 1994) 269 pp.

ISMAJLI, Rexhep
Gjuhë dhe etni. Artikuj dhe ese.
(Rilindja, Prishtina 1991) 450 pp.

Etni e modernitet.
(Dukagjini, Peja 1994) 218 pp.

IVANIĆ, Ivan
Na Kosovu. Sa Šara po Kosovu na Zvečan.
(Milan Arsenijović, Belgrade 1903) 181 pp.

IVANOV, Pavle Dželetović
21. SS Divizija Skenderbeg.
(Nova knjiga, Belgrade 1987) 277 pp.

Jevreji Kosova i Metohije. ISBN 86-7431-024-9.
(Panpublik, Belgrade 1988) 208 pp.

IVIĆ, Pavle (ed.)
Zbornik okruglog stola o naučnom istraživanju Kosova. Održanog 26.
i 27. februara 1985. godine. ISBN 86-7025-089-6.
(Srpska Akademija Nauka i Umetnosti, Belgrade 1988) viii + 228 pp.

JASTREBOV, Ivan Stepanović
Stara Serbija i Albanija. Putevyja zapiski. Srpska Kraljevska
Akademija, Spomenik 41.
(Srpska Kraljevska Akademija, Belgrade 1904) xi + 267 pp.

JEVRIĆ, Milorad
Srpsko Kosovo.
(Novi Svet, Prishtina 1993) 175 pp.

JEVTIĆ, Atanasije (= JEVTITCH, Athanase)
Zadužbine Kosova. Spomenici i znamenja srpskog naroda. ISBN 86-
7405-001-8.
(Eparhija Raško-Prizren, Prizren 1987) 875 pp.

Stradanja Srba na Kosovu i Metohiju od 1941. do 1990. ISBN
86-7019-065-6.
(Jedinstvo, Prishtina 1990) 469 pp.

JOVANOVIĆ, Batrić
Kosovo. Inflacija socijalne razlike.
(Partizanska knj. Belgrade 1985) 331 pp.

JOVANOVIĆ, Jovan
Južna Srbija od kraja XVIII veka do oslobodjenja.
(Kon, Belgrade 1938) 186 pp.

JOVIČIĆ, Vladimir, PETROVIĆ, Milorad & JOVIČIĆ, Olja
Kosovo u svesti i nadahnuću srpskoga naroda. ISBN 86-7355-007-6.
(Glas Podrinja, Šabac / Nova knjiga, Belgrade 1988) 642 pp.

KADARE, Ismail
Koha e shkrimeve. Tregime, novela, përshkrime.
(Naim Frashëri, Tirana 1986) 405 pp.

KARAPANDŽIĆ, Bor. M.
Srpsko Kosovo i Metohija. Zločini Arnauta nad srpskim narodom.
(Cleveland OH 1986) 340 pp.

KASUMI, Haki
Bashkësitë fetare në Kosovë, 1945-1980.
(Instituti i Historisë, Prishtina 1988) 198 pp.

KEKEZI, Haralliq & HIDA, Rexhep (ed.)
Ç'thonë dhe ç'kërkojnë Kosovarët. Përmbledhje studimesh, artikujsh,
intervistesh dhe komentesh. 3 vol.
(8 Nëntori, Tirana 1988, 1990, 1990) 373, 389, 491 pp.

KELMENDI, Fehmi
Kush janë shqiptarët.
(Biel/Bienne 1990) 83 pp.

KERČOV, Sava, RADOŠ, Jovo & RAIČ, Aleksandar
Mitinzi u Vojvodini 1988. godine. Radjenje političkog pluralizma.
(Dnevnik, Novi Sad 1990) 299 pp.

KEŠETOVIČ, Muhamed
Kontrarevolucija na Kosovu. Pokušaj i sprečavanje. Politički esej.
(Zadruga, Belgrade 1984) 197 pp.

Drama na Kosovu. 2. izd. ISBN 86-23-06011-3.
(Naučna knjiga, Belgrade 1988) 380 pp.

KOKALARI, Hamit
Kosova - djepi i shqiptarizmit. Me parathanie të Prof. Abas Ermenjit.
(Mesagjerit Shqiptare, Tirana 1943; reprint Lidhja Kosovare, Rome
1962) 128 pp.

KORSIKA, Bojan et al (ed.)
Srbija i Albanci. Pregled politike Srbije prema Albancima. 3 vol.
(Univerzitetni konferenci Zveze Socialistične Mladine Slovenije
Maribor in Ljubljana, Časopis za kritiko znanosti, Ljubljana 1989)
153, 93, 131 pp.

KRAJA, Mehmet
Vite të humbura. Publicistikë.
(Lidhja e Shkrimtarëve, Tirana 1995) 276 pp.

KRASNIQI, Mark (= KRASNIĆI, Mark)
Savremene društveno-geografske promene na Kosovu i Metohiji.
(Muzej Kosova i Metohije, Prishtina 1963) 343 pp.

Disa burime pak të njohura mbi popullsinë e Kosovës.
in: Studime historike, Tirana, 33, 2 (1979), p. 97-104.

Gjurmë e gjurmime.
(Instituti Albanologjik, Prishtina 1979; reprint 8 Nëntori, Tirana 1982)
492 pp.

Kosova sot. Referat i paraqitur në senatin belg.
(Prishtina 1992) 45 pp.

Qëndrime e reagime. Vol. 1-4.
(Partia Shqiptare Demokristiane e Kosovës, Prishtina 1995) 239, 276,
321, 319 pp.

KRESTIĆ, Vasilije & LEKIĆ, Djordje
Kosovo i Metohija. Tokom vekova. Zublja. ISBN 86-7019-130-4.
(Grigorije Božovic, Prishtina 1995) 401 pp.

KRIZMAN, Bogdan
Elaborat dra Ive Andrića o Albaniji iz 1939. godine.
in: Časopis za suvremenu povijest, Zagreb, 9 (1977), 2, p. 77-89.

KRSTIĆ, Branislav
Kosovo imedju istorijskog i etničkog prava. ISBN 86-82225-02-6.
(Kuća Vid, Belgrade 1994) 319 pp.

KRSTIĆ, Djordjo (= KËRSTIQ, Gjorgje)
Kolonizacija u južnoj Srbiji.
(Bosanka Pošta, Sarajevo 1928)

Kolonizimi i Serbisë jugore. Gjendja e shqiptarëve në Jugosllavi.
(Koha, Tirana 1994) 96 pp.

Kushtetuta e Krahinës Socialiste Autonome të Kosovës. Me Ligjin Kushtetues
për zbatimin e Kushtetutës së Krahinës Socialiste Autonome të Kosovës.
(Rilindja, Prishtina 1974) 215 pp.

Libri i bardhë. Lashtësia shqiptare dhe shtetësia e Kosovës si realitet historik
dhe politik.
(Unikomb, Prishtina 1992) 110 pp.

LLESHI, Qazim
    Qytetet e Kosovës. Studim urbanologjik.
    (Universitet, Prishtina 1977) 400 pp.

LUČIĆ, Dejan V.
    Tajne albanske mafije. ISBN 86-81397-01-X.
    (Kosmos, Belgrade 1988) 228 pp.

MACKENZIE, G. Muir & IRBY, A. P.
    Pătuvanja iz slavjanskite provincii na evropeiska Turcija. Prev. ot angl.
    V. Dimitrova.
    (Otečestvenija Front, Sofia 1983) 147 pp.

MALETIĆ, Mihajlo (ed.)
    Kosovo nekad i danas. Kosova dikur e sot.
    (NIP Borba i Ekonomska politika, Belgrade 1973) 1024 pp.

    Socijalistička Republika Srbija. Socijalistička Autonomna Pokrajina
    Kosovo. V Tom. Republika e Sërbisë. Krahina Socialiste Autonome e
    Kosovës. Vëllimi V.
    (Književne novine, Belgrade 1986) 436 pp.

MALIQI, Shkëlzen
    Nyja e Kosovës, as Vllasi as Millosheviqi.
    (Knjižna zbirka KRT, Ljubljana 1990) 304 pp.

    Shqiptarët dhe Evropa.
    (Dukagjini, Peja 1994) 210 pp.

MALIQI, Shkëlzen & JANJIQ, Dushko (ed.)
    Konflikt apo dialog. Marrëdhëniet shqiptaro-serbe dhe integrimi i
    Ballkanit. Përmbledhje punimesh.
    (Dukagjini, Peja 1995) 330 pp.

MALOKU, Sherif
Kosova. Tërësi e lashtë gjeografike e politike.
(Enti i teksteve, Prishtina 1994)

MARENIN, N.
Albanija i Albancite.
(Voennija žurnal, Sofia 1902) 96 pp.

Severna Albanija i Stara Srbija.
(Sofia 1903)

MARKOVIĆ, Svetozar
Socijalistička Autonomna Pokrajina Kosovo danas. Krahina Socialiste
Autonome Kosova sot.
(Izdavačka radna organizacija, Belgrade 1984) 187 pp.

MEKULI, Esad & ĆUKIĆ, Dragan (ed.)
Priština.
(Izdanje Skupštine Opštine Priština, Prishtina 1965)

MIHAČEVIĆ, Lovro
Po Albaniji. Dojmovi s puta.
(Matica Hrvatska, Zagreb 1911) 144 pp.

MIHAILOVIĆ-ŠILJA, Živorad
Podzemni rat na Kosovu i Metohiji 1389-1989. ISBN 86-7465-002-3.
(RO Jugoslovenska Estrada, Belgrade 1989) 252 pp.

MIHALJČIĆ, Rade
Boj na Kosovu. Starija i novije saznanja.
(Izdavačka kuća književne novine, Belgrade 1992) 618 pp.

MIJAĆ, Božidar
Kosovo kao crkveno-teološki problem.
(s.l. s.a. [ca. 1990]) 375 pp.

MIKIĆ, Djordje
Društvene i ekonomske prilike kosovskih Srba u XIX i početkom XX
veka. ISBN 86-7025-077-2.
(Srpska Akademija Nauka i Umetnosti, Belgrade 1988) viii + 343 pp.

MILANOVIĆ, Vujadin
Univerzitet u Prištini i mreži velikoalbanske strategije. ISBN
86-391-0077-2.
(Književne novine, Belgrade / Jedinstvo, Prishtina 1990) 361 pp.

MILATOVIĆ, Arso
Kosmet 1935-1945. Moje svedočenje. ISBN 8623700856.
(Naučna knjiga, Belgrade 1990) 503 pp.

MILO, Paskal
Marrëdhëniet shqiptare-jugosllave në vitet 1922-1924.
in: Studime historike, Tirana, 44, 1 (1990), p. 107-126.

Shqipëria dhe Jugosllavia (1918-1927).
(Enciklopedike, Tirana 1992) 496 pp.

MILOŠEVIĆ, Slobodan
Godine raspleta. 3. izd. ISBN 8613003516.
(Beogradski izdavačko-grafički zavod, Belgrade 1989) 348 pp.

MIŠOVIĆ, Miloš
Ko je tražio republiku. Kosovo 1945-1985. 2. izd. ISBN 86-331-0121-
1.
(Narodna knjiga, Belgrade 1987) 461 pp.

MITROVIĆ, Andrej
Srbi i Albanci u XX veku. Ciklus predavanja 7-10. maj 1990. ISBN
86-7025-141-8.
(Srpska Akademija Nauka i Umetnosti, Belgrade 1991) viii + 457 pp.

MLADENOVIĆ, Marko
Budjenje srpskog naroda. ISBN 86-81277-20-0.
(Sfairos, Belgrade 1989) 312 pp.

MORAČIĆ, Dragoljub (ed.)
Naučni skup kosovska kriza. Uzroci i putevi izlaska (1989. Priština,
Srbija). ISBN 86-7019-032-X.
(Jedinstvo, Prishtina 1989) 395 pp.

MORINA, Tafil
Vitet e dhembjes dhe të krenarisë.
(s.e., Prishtina 1995) 71 pp.

MUGOŠA, Dušan
Kad sam bio u Albaniji.
(Nin, Belgrade 1971-1972)

Na zadatku.
(Četvrti jul, Belgrade 1973) 197 pp.

MURZAKU, Thoma
Politika e Serbisë kundrejt Shqipërisë gjatë luftës ballkanike 1912-1913.
(Akademia e Shkencave, Tirana 1987) 416 pp.

MYZYRI, Hysni (ed.)
Historia e popullit shqiptar për shkollat e mesme.
(Libri shkollor, Tirana 1994) 263 pp.

NASI, Lefter
Lëvizja kaçake në Kosovë, 1918-1928.
in: Studime historike, Tirana, 37, 1 (1983), p. 209-216.

Masat për rikolonizimin e Kosovës në vitet 1945-1947.
in: Studime historike, Tirana, 44, 2 (1990), p. 55-72.

Ripushtimi i Kosovës. Shtator 1944 - Korrik 1945.
(Akademia e Shkencave, Tirana 1994) 236 pp.

Aspekte të shtypjes kombëtare e politike të shqiptarëve në Kosovë (1981-1986).
(Dardania, Tirana 1995) 147 pp.

NEJAŠMIĆ, Ivica
Bibliografija radova o unutrašnjoj migraciji stanovništva Jugoslavije u poslijeratnom razdoblju, 1945-1986.
(IMN, Zagreb 1989) 158 pp.

NIKOLAJEVIĆ, Milivoj J.
Severna Stara Srbija. Vojno-geografska i istorijska studija.
(Kraljevsko-srpska državna štamparija, Belgrade 1892) iv + 120 pp.

NIKOLIĆ, Miodrag
Revolucionarni radički pokret na Kosovu i Metohiji, 1895-1922.
(Izd. Istorijske Komisije Oblasnog Komiteta Saveza Komunista Srbije za Kosovo i Metohiju, Prishtina 1962) 204 pp.

Kosovo i Metohija. Pregled društveno-ekonomskog razvitka.
(Sedma sila, Belgrade 1963) 63 pp.

NUŠIĆ, Branislav F.
Kosovo. Opis zemlje i naroda. 2 vol.
(Matica srpska, Novi Sad 1902, 1903; reprint Prosveta, Belgrade 1986) 180, 116 pp.

574 Bibliography

S Kosova na sinje more. Beleške s puta kroz Arbanase 1894 godine.
(Mite Stajić, Belgrade 1902) 112 pp.

OBRADOVIĆ, Milovan
Agrarna reforma i kolonizacija na Kosovu (1918-1941).
(Institut za istoriju Kosova, Prishtina 1981) 357 pp.

OCIĆ, Djordje
I Srbi su Crnogorci. Kosovo i srpsko pitanje.
(Narodna knjiga, Belgrade 1989) 211 pp.

ORAOVAĆ, Tomo P.
Arbanaško pitanje i srpsko pravo.
(Rajković i Ćuković, Belgrade 1913) 128 pp.

ORLOVIĆ, P. (= ORLOVITCH, Paul)
Pitanie o Staroj Srbiji.
(Jocković, Belgrade 1901) 37 pp.

Stara Srbija i Arbanasi.
(Belgrade 1904)

PAPOVIĆ, Radivoje
Kosovo i na nebu i na zemlju. ISBN 86-7115-045-3.
(Udruženje uzdavača i knjižara Jugoslavije, Belgrade 1994) 242 pp.

PAVIĆ, Radovan
Srbija, Makedonija i Kosmet prema Albaniji i Albancima.
in: Politička misao, Časopis za politička znanosti, Zagreb, 28, 1 (1991).

PAVLE, Bishop of Raška and Prizren
Zadužbine Kosova. Spomenici i znamenja srpskog naroda. ISBN
8674050018.
(Eparhija raško-prizrenska, Prizren / Bogoslovski Fakultet, Belgrade
1987) 875 pp.

PEROVIĆ, Marko
Ekonomski odnosi Jugoslavije i Albanije 1947-1948.
(Savez novinara Jugoslavije, Belgrade 1951) 191 pp.

PERUNIČIĆ, Branko
Svedočanstvo o Kosovu, 1901-1913. ISBN 86-23-02006-6f.
(Naučna knjiga, Belgrade 1988) 537 pp.

Zulumi aga i begova u kosovskom vilajetu, 1878-1913. ISBN 86-7335-059-X.
(Nova knjiga, Belgrade 1989) 670 pp.

PETKOVIĆ, Ranko & FILIPOVIĆ, Gordana (ed.)
Kosovo. Prošlost i sadašnjost.
(Medjunarodna politika, Belgrade 1989) 364 pp.

PETRANOVIĆ, Branko
Istorija Jugoslavije, 1918-1978.
(Nolit, Belgrade 1981) 648 pp.

PETROVIĆ, Ruza & BLAGOJEVIĆ, Marina
Seobe Srba i Crnogoraca sa Kosova i iz Metohije. Rezultati ankete sprovedene 1985-1986 godine. ISBN 86-7025-127-2.
(Srpska Akademija Nauka i Umetnosti, Belgrade 1989) vii + 339 pp.

PIRRAKU, Muhamet
Kultura kombëtare shqiptare deri në Lidhjen e Prizrenit.
(Instituti Albanologjik, Prishtina 1989) 604 pp.

Kalvari i shqiptarësisë së Kosovës. Tivari 1945.
(Instituti Albanologjik, Prishtina 1993) 75 pp.

PLLANA, Emin
Kosova dhe reformat në Turqi, 1839-1912.
(Enti i historisë së Kosovës, Prishtina 1978) 300 pp.

Reformat osmane dhe qëndresa e shqiptarëve ndaj tyre (1856-1878). in: Gjurmime albanologjike, Seria e shkencave historike, Prishtina, 7 (1978), p. 101-124.

Shkaqet dhe mënyra e shpërnguljes së muhaxhirëve shqiptare nga territori i Sanxhakut të Nishit në Kosovë (1877-1878). in: Studime historike, Tirana, 38, 2 (1984), p. 105-130.

POLLO, Stefanaq & BUDA, Aleks
Historia e popullit shqiptar. 2 vol.
(Universiteti Shtetëror i Tiranës, Tirana 1965 & 1967; reprint Enti i botimeve shkollare, Prishtina 1968) 498 & 879 pp.

POLLO, Stefanaq & PULAHA, Selami
Akte të Rilindjes kombëtare shqiptare, 1878-1912. Memorandume, vendime, protesta, thirrje.
(Akademia e Shkencave, Tirana 1978) 286 pp.

576 Bibliography

POPOVIĆ, Janićije
Život Srba na Kosovu 1812-1912.
(Književne novine, Belgrade 1987) 400 pp.

POPOVIĆ, Srdja
Kosovski čvor. Drešiti ili seći?
(Chronos, Belgrade 1990) 159 pp.

PRIFTI, Kristaq
Lidhja shqiptare e Prizrenit në dokumentet osmane 1878-1881.
(Akademia e Shkencave, Tirana 1978) 523 pp.

Lidhja shqiptare e Pejës. Lëvizja kombëtare, 1896-1900.
(Akademia e Shkencave, Tirana 1984) 448 pp.

PRIFTI, Kristaq, NASI, Lefter, OMARI, Luan, XHUFI, Pëllumb, PULAHA,
Selami, POLLO, Stefanaq, & SHTYLLA, Zamir (ed.)
E vërteta mbi Kosovën dhe shqiptarët në Jugosllavi.
(Akademia e Shkencave e RPS të Shqipërisë, Tirana 1990) 643 pp.

PULAHA, Selami
Autoktonia e shqiptarëve në Kosovë dhe e ashtuquajtura shpërngulje e
Serbëve në fund të shek. XVII.
in: Studime historike, Tirana, 36, 1 (1982), p. 139-167.

Popullsia shqiptare e Kosovës gjatë shek. XV-XVI. Studime dhe
dokumente.
(8 Nëntori, Tirana 1984) 721 pp.

PULAHA, Selami, MANSAKU, Seit & GJERGJI, Andromaqi (ed.)
Shqiptarët dhe trojet e tyre.
(8 Nëntori, Tirana 1982) 527 pp.

PUTO, Arben
Pavarësia shqiptare dhe diplomacia e fuqive të mëdha, 1912-1914.
(8 Nëntori, Tirana 1978) 652 pp.

Çështja shqiptare në aktet ndërkombëtare të periudhës së
imperializmit. Përmbledhje dokumentesh me një vështrim historik. 2
vol.
(8 Nëntori, Tirana 1984, 1987) 403, 686 pp.

QORRI, Besim
Shqipnia e vërtetë. Studim historik dhe ethnografik.
(Atdheu, Tirana 1944) 233 pp.

QOSJA, Rexhep
Vdekja më vjen prej syvë të tillë. Trembëdhjetë tregime që mund të bënin një roman.
(Rilindja, Prishtina 1974) 295 pp.

Nazaštićena sudbina. O Albancima u Jugoslaviji danas. ISBN 86-7595-001-2.
(HSLS, Zagreb 1990) 297 pp.

Populli i ndaluar.
(Mega Medium, Prishtina 1990; reprint Enciklopedike, Tirana 1990) 493 pp.

Strategjia e bashkimit shqiptar.
(Instituti Albanologjik, Prishtina 1992)

Çështja shqiptare. Historia dhe politika.
(Instituti Albanologjik, Prishtina 1994) 363 pp.

RADONČIĆ, Fahrudin
Adem Demaçi. Ispovijest. Deset tisuća dana robije.
(Danas, Zagreb 1990) 96 pp.

RAHIMI, Shukri
Vilajeti i Kosovës më 1878-1912.
(Enti i teksteve, Prishtina 1969) 209 pp.

Lufta e shqiptarëve për autonomi (1897-1912).
(Enti i teksteve, Prishtina 1980) 242 pp.

Gjurmime historike të Rilindjes kombëtare.
(Instituti Albanologjik, Prishtina 1986) 396 pp.

RAJOVIĆ, Radošin (= RAJOVIQ, R.)
Autonomija Kosova. Istorijsko-pravna studija.
(Ekonomika, Belgrade 1985) 583 pp.

Autonomia e Kosovës. Studim historiko-juridik.
(Rilindja, Prishtina 1987) 498 pp.

RAKIĆ, Milan
Konzulska pisma, 1905-1991.
(Prosveta, Belgrade 1985) 409 pp.

578   Bibliography

RAMADANI, Hasan
        Maqedonia. E përkëdhelura e Evropës.
        (s.e., Oslo 1995) 48 pp.

RANDELS, Djordje
        Od Kosova do Kosova. Posebna izdanja.
        (Dnevnik, Novi Sad 1990) 138 pp.

REXHEPAGIQ, Jashar (= REDŽEPAGIĆ, Jašar)
        Razvoj prosvete i školstva albanske narodnosti na teritoriji današnje
        Jugoslavije do 1918. godine. Zajednica naučnih ustanova Kosova i
        Metohije. Knjiga 7.
        (Zajednica naučnih ustanova Kosova i Metohije, Prishtina 1968)
        367 pp

        Zhvillimi i arësimit dhe i sistemit shkollor të kombësisë shqiptare në
        territorin e Jugosllavisë së sotme deri në vitin 1918.
        (ETM, Prishtina 1970) 351 pp.

RIZAJ, Skënder
        Memorandumi i shqiptarëve drejtuar kundër Paqës së Shën Stefanit
        (1878).
        in: Gjurmime albanologjike, Seria e shkencave historike, Prishtina, 6
        (1977), p. 195-203.

        Mbi të ashtuquajturën dyndje e madhe serbe nga Kosova në krye me
        patrikun Arsenije Çarnojeviq (1690).
        in: Gjurmime albanologjike, Seria e shkencave historike, Prishtina, 12
        (1983), p. 81-103.

        Kosova gjatë shekujve XV, XVI dhe XVII. Administrimi, ekonomia,
        shoqëria dhe lëvizja popullore.
        (Rilindja, Prishtina 1982; reprint 8 Nëntori, Tirana 1987) 610 pp.

        Shqiptarët dhe Serbët në Kosovë.
        (Zëri i Rinisë, Prishtina 1991) 167 pp.

        Kosova dhe shqiptarët dje, sot dhe nesër.
        (Akademia e Intelektualëve Shqiptarë e Shkencave dhe e Arteve,
        Prishtina 1992) 157 pp.

RRAPI, Gjergj
        Kosova e viteve të ndrydhura. Diskutime të autorizuara.
        (Prishtina 1993) 170 pp.

RUGOVA, Ibrahim
Vepra e Bogdanit 1675-1685.
(Rilindja, Prishtina 1982) 313 pp.

Kahe dhe premisa të kritikës letrare shqiptare 1504-1983.
(Instituti Albanologjik, Prishtina 1986) 441 pp.

Refuzimi estetik.
(Rilindja, Prishtina 1987) 318 pp.

Pavarësia dhe demokracia, intervista dhe artikuj. Independence and
democracy, interviews and articles.
(Fjala, Prishtina 1991) 237 pp.

RUGOVA, Ibrahim & HAMITI, Sabri
Kritika letrare. Tekste, shënime, komente.
(Rilindja, Prishtina 1979) 487 pp.

RUSHITI, Liman
Lëvizja kaçake në Kosovë, 1918-1928.
(Instituti i Historisë së Kosovës, Prishtina 1981) 278 pp.

Rrethanat politiko-shoqërore në Kosovë, 1912-1918.
(Rilindja, Prishtina 1986) 214 pp.

SALIHU, Ismet
Vrasjet në Krahinën Socialiste Autonome të Kosovës.
(Rilindja, Prishtina 1985) 356 pp.

SALIU, Kurtesh
Lindja, zhvillimi, pozita dhe aspektet e autonomitetit të Krahinës
Socialiste Autonome të Kosovës në Jugosllavinë socialiste.
(Enti i teksteve, Prishtina 1984) 214 pp.

SAMARDŽIĆ, Radovan
Kosovo i Metohija u srpskoj istoriji. ISBN 86-379-0104-2.
(Srpska književna zadruga, Belgrade 1989) 436 pp.

Kosovsko opredeljenje. Istorijski ogledi.
(Srpska književna zadruga, Belgrade 1990) 247 pp.

SAMIM VISOKA, Vasfi (= SAMIMI, Vasfi; VISOKU, Vasfi Samim)
Shqipërija e vërtetë. Nëna Kosovë. Ndjenja dhe mendime. (Përshtypje
udhtimi nga Tokat e Liruara). Tiranë-Kosovë 1938- 1943.
(Shtyp. e Shtetit, Tirana 1943) 144 pp.

SAVIĆ, Radmila
    Arbanasi na srpskom tlu. ISBN 86-81277-29-4.
    (Sfairos, Belgrade 1989) 225 pp.

SHALA, Blerim
    Kosovo. Krv i suze.
    (Založba alternativnega tiska, Ljubljana 1990) 134 pp.

SHALA, Hasan & KONJUSHA, Selman
    Historia e fshehur.
    (Fjala, Prishtina 1995)

SHALA, Xheladin
    Marrëdhëniet shqiptaro-serbe 1912-1918.
    (Instituti Albanologjik, Prishtina 1990) 367 pp.

SHARANOVIQ, Mihaillo (= ŠARANOVIĆ, M.) (ed.)
    Shqipëria e Enver Hoxhës.
    (Tanjug, Belgrade 1981) 277 pp.

SHATRI, Xh.
    Vështrim i përgjithshëm mbi politikën serbomadhe në Kosovë.
    (Geneva, s.a.) 190 pp.

SHKRELI, Azem
    Muri përfundi shqipeve.
    (Bota shqiptare, Zürich 1993) 87 pp.

Shtypi botëror rreth ngjarjeve në Kosovë.
    (8 Nëntori, Tirana 1981) 96 pp.

SLIJEPČEVIĆ, Djoko M.
    Srpsko-arbanaški odnosi kroz vekove sa posebnim osvrtom na novije
    vreme.
    (Selbstverlag, Munich 1974; reprint 1983?) 439 pp.

Šta se dogadjalo na Kosovu.
    (Mala biblioteka politike, Belgrade 1981) 169 pp.

STANKOVIĆ, Todor P.
    Beleške o Staroj Srbiji i Maćedoniji.
    (Štamp. Kralj. Srbije, Niš 1915) 194 pp.

STANOJECIĆ, Stanoje
Istorija srpskoga naroda. ISBN 86-81459-06-6.
(Prosveta, Belgrade 1993) 431 pp.

STAVILECI, Esat
Kosova dhe shqiptarët ndërmjet kërcënimeve të brëndshme dhe
premtimeve të jashtme. Kosovo i Albanci izmedju unutarnjih prijetnji
i vanjskih obecanja.
(Shoqata e Pavarur e Juristëve të Kosovës, Prishtina 1991) 159 pp.

STIPČEVIĆ, Aleksandar
Iliri. Povijest, život, kultura.
(Zagreb 1974; reprint Školska knjiga, Zagreb 1991) 203 pp.

STOJANČEVIĆ, Vladimir
Srbija i Albanci u XIX i početkom XX veka. Ciklus predavanja 10-25.
novembar 1987. ISBN 86-7025-094-2.
(Srpska Akademija Nauka i Umetnosti, Belgrade 1990) 311 pp.

STOJANOVIĆ, Radosav
Ziveti s genocidom. Hronika kosovskog beščašća, 1981-1989. ISBN
86-81277-35-9.
(Sfairos, Belgrade 1990) 274 pp.

ŠUFFLAY, Milan von (= SHYFFLAY, Milan)
Srbi i Arbanasi. Njihova simbioza u sredjem vjeku. Biblioteka Arhiva
za Arbanasku Starinu, Jezik i Etnologiju. 1.
(Izdanje Seminaria za Arbanasku Filologiju, Belgrade 1925; reprint
Azur, Zagreb 1991) 142 pp.

Serbët dhe shqiptarët. Përkthyer prej sllavishtes nga Zef Fekeçi e Karl
Gurakuqi.
(Tirana 1926, retransl. Prishtina 1968) 238 pp.

SYLA, Fazli, BERANI, Shaqir, BERISHA, Anton, KRASNIQI, Bajram &
RUGOVA, Ibrahim (ed.)
Njëzet vjet të Institutit Albanologjik (1967-1987). Botim jubilar. Vingt
ans de l'Institut Albanologique (1967-1987). Edition jubilaire.
(Instituti Albanologjik, Prishtina 1987) 301 pp.

TËRNAVA, Muhamet
Shqiptarët në qytetet e Kosovës në shekujt XV-XVI.
in: Studime historike, Tirana, 33 (1972), 2, p. 105-145.

Popullsia e Kosovës gjatë shekujve XIV-XVI.
(Instituti Albanologjik, Prishtina 1995) 491 pp.

TITO, Josip Broz
Çështja kombëtare dhe vetëqeverisja.
(Rilindja, Prishtina 1976) 223 pp.

TITO, Josip Broz, KARDELJ, Edvard, & ATLAGIĆ, David
Poslednja istupanja Josipa Broza Tita i Edvarda Kardelja pred
političkim aktivom SAP Kosova.
(Komunist, Belgrade 1981) 36 pp.

TODOROVIĆ, Desanka
Jugoslavija i balkanske države, 1918-1923.
(Narodna knjiga, Belgrade 1979) 271 pp.

TOMIĆ, Jaša
Rat na Kosovu i Staroj Srbiji 1912 godine. ISBN 86-7455-005-3.
(Električna štamparija dra Svetozara Miletića, Novi Sad 1913; reprint
Prosveta, Niš 1988) 199 pp.

Rat u Albaniji i pod Skadrom 1912 i 1913 godine.
(Električna štamparija dra Svetozara Miletića, Novi Sad 1913) 175 pp.

TOMIĆ, Jovan N. (= TOMITCH, Yovan)
O Arnautima u Staroj Srbiji i Sandžaku.
(Knjižara Gece Kona, Belgrade 1913) 93 pp.

O Arnautima u Staroj Srbiji i Sandžaku. ISBN 86-7019-164-4.
(Grigorije Božović, Prishtina / Prosveta, Belgrade 1995) 82 pp.

TORY, Iztok
Ptice na Kosovu. Tragična zgodba v petih dejanjih s prologom i
epilogom - a bez konca.
(Lumi, Ljubljana 1990) 234 pp.

TRIFUNOSKI, Jovan F.
Albansko stanovništvo u Socialističkoj Republici Makedoniji. ISBN
86-391-0134-5.
(Belgrade 1988) 182 pp.

Bibliography 583

TUCOVIĆ, Dimitrije (= TUCOVIQ, Dimitrije)
Srbija e Arbanija. Jedan prilog kritici zavojevačke politike srpske buržoazije.
(Sava Radenković i brata, Belgrade 1914; reprint Kultura, Belgrade 1946, 1974) 118 pp.

Sërbia e Shqipëria, Një kontribut për kritikën e politikës pushtuese të borgjezisë sërbe.
(Rilindja, Prishtina 1975) 118 pp.

UKA, Sabit
Vendbanimet e Sanxhakut të Nishit të banuara me popullatë shqiptare dhe të përzier deri në vitet 1877-1878.
in: Gjurmime albanologjike, Seria e shkencave historike, Prishtina, 12 (1983), p. 105-124.

Shpërngulja e shqiptarëve nga Serbia jugore më 1877-1878 dhe vendosja e tyre në rrafshin e Kosovës.
(Zëri, Prishtina 1991)

Dëbimi i shqiptarëve nga Sanxhaku i Nishit dhe vendosja e tyre ne Kosovë, 1878-1912. 2 vol.
(Valton, Prishtina 1994) 300 & 339 pp.

UROŠEVIĆ, Atanansije
Kosovo. Srpska Akademija Nauka i Umetnosti. Srpski Etnografski Zbornik, Knj 78.
(Naučno delo, Belgrade 1965) 387 pp.

Etnički procesi na Kosovu tokom turske vladavine. ISBN 86-7025-015-2.
(Srpska Akademija Nauka i Umetnosti, Belgrade 1987) viii + 112 pp.

VASIĆ, Dragiša
Dva meseca u jugoslovenskom Sibiru.
(Gece Kona, Belgrade 1921) 66 pp.

VASILJEVIĆ, Jovan Hadži
Muslimani naše krvi u južnoj Srbiji. ISBN 86-7019-165-2.
(Grigorije Božović, Prishtina / Prosveta, Belgrade 1995) 81 pp.

VERLI, Marenglen
Përpjekjet serbo-malazeze për kolonizimin e Kosovës dhe të viseve të tjera shqiptare në vitet 1913-1915.
in: Studime historike, Tirana, (1983), 4, p. 127-146.

Pikëpamjet i përfaqësuesve të borgjezisë serbe rreth reformës agrare kolonizuese në trevat shqiptare, 1918-1941.
in: Studime historike, Tirana, 43, 3 (1989), p. 65-76.

Reforma agrare kolonizuese në Kosovë. Akademia e Shkencave të Republikës së Shqipërisë.
(Iliria, Bonn & Tirana 1991) 215 pp.

Shfrytëzimi ekonomik i Kosovës 1970-1990.
(Dituria, Tirana 1994) 125 pp.

VINCA, Agim
Populli i pandalur.
(Zëri, Prishtina 1992) 327 pp.

VLLASI, Azem
Majstori mraka. Zatvorski zapisi. ISBN 86-3430-621-6.
(Globus, Zagreb 1990) 237 pp.

VOKRRI, Abdulla
Shkollat dhe arsimi në Kosovë ndërmjet dy luftërave botërore (1918-1941).
(Enti i teksteve, Prishtina 1990) 389 pp.

VUČETIĆ, Milenko
Vllasi. ISBN 86-7125-054-7.
(Centar za Informacije i Publicitet, Zagreb 1989) 371 pp.

VUJINOVIĆ, Janko
Kosovo je grdno sudilište. ISBN 8639101728.
(NIRO, Belgrade 1989) 374 pp.

VUKANOVIĆ, Tatomir
Bibliografija Kosovsko-Metohijske oblasti.
in: Glasnik Muzeja Kosova i Metohije, Prishtina, 1 (1956), p. 412-437; 2 (1957); 3 (1958), p. 287-301; 4/5 (1959/1960), p. 383-393.

Srbi na Kosovu. 3 vol.
(Nova Jugoslavija, Vranje 1986)

VUKMANOVIĆ-TEMPO, Svetozar
Revolucija koja teče. Memoari. 2 vol.
(Komunist, Belgrade 1971)

VUKOVIĆ, Ilija
Autonomaštvo i separatizam na Kosovu.
(Nova knjiga, Belgrade 1985) 238 pp.

Stramputice Hajredina Hodže.
(Nova knjiga, Belgrade 1985) 184 pp.

VULLKANI, H.
Beharet e mëngjesit të përgjakshëm.
(Prizren 1981) 148 pp.

XOXI, Koli
Lidhja shqiptare e Prizrenit (1878-1881).
(8 Nëntori, Tirana 1978) 190 pp.

ZAJMI, Gazmend
Pozita e gjuhëve në Krahinën Autonome të Kosovës në periudhën 1945-1970.
in: Përparimi, Prishtina 7 (1971).

ZAJMI, Tahir
Lidhja e Prizrenit dhe lufta heroike e popullit për mbrojtjen e Kosovës.
(Brussels 1964) 126 pp.

ZEJNELI, Zejnel
Ko je izdao revoluciju.
(Jedinstvo, Prishtina 1988) 268 pp.

ZEQO, Moikom
Rexhep Qosja dhe çështja kombëtare shqiptare.
(s.e., Tirana 1994) 280 pp.

ŽIVANČEVIĆ, Predrag
Emigranti. Naseljavanje Kosova i Metohije iz Albanije. ISBN 8671450953.
(Eksportpres, Belgrade 1989) 137 pp.

ZLATAR, Pero
Albanija u eri Enveru Hoxhe. 2 vol.
(Grafički zavod Hrvatske, Zagreb 1984)

Gospodar zemlje orlova. Politički životopis.
(Grafički zavod Hrvatske, Zagreb 1984) 331 pp.

Enver Hodža. Politička biografija.
(Rad, Belgrade 1986) 392 pp.

ZOGAJ, Agim & SHALA, Blerim
Dëshmi për Kosovën, 1989-1991.
(Zëri, Prishtina 1995)

6. List of Contributors

Ivo Andrić

Bosnian Serb short-story writer and novelist. Born in Travnik (Bosnia) in 1892, Ivo Andrić was educated in Zagreb, Graz and Vienna. After World War I, he joined the diplomatic service and served as Yugoslav ambassador to Berlin in 1940. The best known of his many prose works is: *The Bridge on the Drina*, London 1959. In 1961, he was awarded the Nobel Prize for Literature. He died in 1975.

Gjon Bisaku, Shtjefën Kurti, Luigj Gashi

Catholic priests working as missionaries in Kosovo in the 1920s on behalf of the Sacred Congregation of the Propaganda Gide.

Bujar Bukoshi

Kosovo Albanian political figure. Born in Suhareka / Suva Reka (Kosovo) in 1947, Bujar Bukoshi studied medicine in Belgrade and Berlin. As a specialist in urology, he served for a number of years as Associate Professor of Surgery at the Faculty of Medicine of the University of Prishtina, and in October 1991 was elected to the post of Prime Minister of the Republic of Kosovo. He leads his government from exile in Germany.

Vaso Čubrilović

Bosnian Serb scholar and political figure. Čubrilović was born in Bosanska Gradiška in 1897. As a student, he participated in the assassination in Sarajevo of Archduke Ferdinand of Austria-Hungary in 1914, the event which precipitated the First World War. Between the two wars, he was professor at the Faculty of Arts in Belgrade. A leading member of the Serbian Academy of Sciences and Art, Čubrilović also held several ministerial portfolios after World War II. Among his writings is the monograph *Istorija političke misle u Srbiji XIX veka*, Belgrade 1958 (History of political thought in Serbia in the 19th century). He died in 1990.

Adem Demaçi

Kosovo Albanian prose writer, former political prisoner and human rights activist. Born in 1936, Demaçi is author of the controversial novel *Gjarpijt e gjakut*, Prishtina 1958 (The snakes of blood), on the theme of vendetta. He was held for twenty-eight years, between 1958 and 1990, as a political prisoner of the Belgrade regime and was considered at the time one of Yugoslavia's more prominent political dissidents. Since his release from prison on 28 April 1990, he has been active in the field of human rights and is currently head of the *Council for the Protection of Human Rights and Freedoms* in Prishtina. In 1991, Adem Demaçi was awarded the Sakharov Prize in Strasbourg.

Edith Durham

British traveller, writer and expert on the Balkans. Mary Edith Durham was born in London in 1863. She travelled widely through Albania, Montenegro and Serbia in the first two decades of the twentieth century, both as a traveller and on relief work. Among her monographs are: *Through the lands of the Serb*, London 1904; *The Burden of the Balkans*, London 1905; *High Albania*, London 1909; *The Struggle for Scutari*, London 1914; *Twenty years of Balkan tangle* London 1920; and *Some tribal origins, laws and customs of the Balkans*, London 1928. She died in 1944.

Robert Elsie

Canadian writer, translator, critic and specialist on Albanian affairs. Robert Elsie was born in Vancouver, Canada, in 1950. He studied at the University of British Columbia, the Free University of Berlin, the *Ecole Pratique des Hautes Etudes* in Paris and the Dublin Institute for Advanced Studies, finishing his doctorate in comparative linguistics at the University of Bonn in 1978. In addition to numerous translations, he is the author of *Dictionary of Albanian literature*, New York 1986; *An Elusive eagle soars, Anthology of modern Albanian poetry*, London 1993; *Albanian folktales and legends*, Tirana 1994; and *History of Albanian literature*, New York 1995.

Leo Freundlich

Austrian Jewish writer and parliamentarian. Freundlich represented the Social-Democratic party in Vienna around the time of the First World War.

Rexhep Ismajli

Kosovo Albanian scholar and critic. Rexhep Ismajli was born in 1947 in Presheva / Preševo, a predominantly Albanian town in southern Serbia, not far from Kosovo itself. He studied in Prishtina and Paris and taught Albanian language and literature at the University of Prishtina. Among his major publications are: *Shumësia e tekstit*, Prishtina 1977 (Text plurality); *Gramatika e parë e gjuhës shqipe*, Prishtina 1983 (The first grammar of the Albanian language); *Artikuj mbi gjuhën shqipe*, Prishtina 1987 (Articles on the Albanian language); *Gjuhë dhe etni, Artikuj dhe ese*, Prishtina 1991 (Language and ethnos, Articles and essays); *Kosova and the Albanians in former Yugoslavia*, Prishtina 1993; and *Etni e modernitet*, Peja / Peć 1994 (Ethnos and modernity). He has also been a leading figure in the LDK (Democratic League of Kosovo).

Ismail Kadare

Albanian prose writer and poet. Born in Gjirokastër in southern Albania in 1936, Ismail Kadare studied in Tirana and at the Gorky Institute of World Literature in Moscow. He is the only Albanian writer to have gained a broad international reputation, which began with the French-language publication of his novel *The General of the Dead Army* in 1970 (English translation: London 1971). Of his other major prose works in English, mention can be made of: *Chronicle in stone*, London & New York 1987; *Doruntine*, London & New York 1988; *Broken April*, New York 1990; *The Palace of dreams*, New York 1993; *Albanian spring: the anatomy of tyranny*, London 1994; *The Concert*, London & New York 1994; and *The Three-Arched Bridge*, London 1994. He lives presently in Paris.

Christine von Kohl

Human rights activist and writer. Based in Vienna as head of the International Helsinki Federation, Christine von Kohl has work actively in international circles to promote human rights and to endeavour to solve the Balkan puzzle.

Wolfgang Libal

Writer, journalist and leading member of the International Helsinki Federation. Wolfgang Libal is also author of *Das Ende Jugoslawiens, Selbstzerstörung, Krieg und Ohnmacht der Welt*, Vienna & Zürich 1993 (The End of Yugoslavia, self-destruction, war and the world's impotency); and *Mazedonien zwischen den Fronten, jünger Staat mit alten Konflikten*, Vienna & Zürich 1993 (Macedonia between the fronts, a young state with ancient conflicts).

Rexhep Qosja

Kosovo Albanian scholar, writer and literary critic. Born in 1936, Qosja studied Albanian language and literature in Prishtina and Belgrade and is now a member of the Kosovo Academy of Sciences and Art, as well as a leading political figure in Kosovo. He is the author of many works on Albanian literature and on the present political situation, among which are: *Dialogje me shkrimtarët*, Prishtina 1968 (Dialogues with writers); *Panteoni i rralluar*, Prishtina 1973 (A rarified Pantheon); *Morfologjia e një fushate*, Prishtina 1980 (The morphology of a campaign); a three-volume *Historia e letërsisë shqipe, Romantizmi*, Prishtina 1984, 1984, 1986 (History of Albanian literature, Romanticism); *Populli i ndaluar*, Prishtina 1990 (The banned people); *Strategjia e bashkimit shqiptar*, Prishtina 1992 (The strategy of Albanian unification); and *Çështja shqiptare, Historia dhe politika*, Prishtina 1994 (The Albanian question, History and politics), which has been translated into French as *La question albanaise* (Paris 1995). His novel *Vdekja më vjen prej syve të tillë*, Prishtina 1974 (Death comes with such eyes), has also been translated into French as *La mort me vient de ces yeux-là*, Paris 1994.

Agim Vinca

Kosovo Albanian scholar, literary critic, poet and political commentator. Agim Vinca was born in Veleshta near Struga in Macedonia in 1947. He studied Albanian language and literature at the University of Prishtina where he taught contemporary literature until he was expelled in September 1991 by the Serbian military. In addition to his verse collections, he is author of works of criticism such as: *Struktura e zhvillimit të poezisë së sotme shqipe 1945-1980*, Prishtina

1985 (The structure of the development of modern Albanian poetry 1945-1980), *Orët e poezisë,* Prishtina 1990 (Poetry hours), and *Alternativa letrare shqiptare,* Skopje 1995 (The Albanian literary alternative), as well as of the extensive political monograph: *Populli i pandalur,* Prishtina 1992 (The unstopped people). Agim Vinca is a leading member of the Forum of Albanian Intellectuals in Prishtina and of the Albanian Writers' Union of Macedonia.